Vol. 19 No. 1
February 1977

JOURNAL OF INTERAMERICAN STUDIES

and WORLD AFFAIRS

A Publication of the Center for Advanced International Studies,

The University of Miami

SAGE PUBLICATIONS

Journal of INTERAMERICAN STUDIES and WORLD AFFAIRS

The editors and publisher wish to acknowledge with gratitude the assistance and encouragement of the Center for Advanced International Studies, University of Miami, in providing ancillary services and support for this journal.

Journal of
INTERAMERICAN
STUDIES
and WORLD AFFAIRS

Vol. 19
No. 1
February
1977

CONTENTS

Through Glasses Darkly: An Assessment of Various Theoretical Approaches to Interamerican Relations
YALE H. FERGUSON 3

Social Security Policy and the Working Class in Twentieth-Century Brazil
JAMES M. MALLOY 35

Economic, Social, and Cultural Rights and the Interamerican System
LAWRENCE J. LeBLANC 61

The Antipositivist Movement in Prerevolutionary Mexico, 1892-1911
WILLIAM DIRK RAAT 83

Housing and the Urban Poor: The Case of Bogota, Colombia
TIMOTHY O'DEA GAUHAN 99

COMMENT
The Mexican Presidential Succession
EVELYN P. STEVENS 125

BOOKS RECEIVED 127

SAGE PUBLICATIONS / *Beverly Hills* *London*

POLICY: THE JOURNAL OF INTERAMERICAN STUDIES AND WORLD AFFAIRS reflects the interests of the scholarly community and interested public concerned with the social, economic, political, and cultural aspects of life in Latin America (including the Caribbean); particularly in those instances where the subject is of concern to more than one of the traditional disciplines. As these concerns change, so will the content of the journal.

ARTICLES which have special relevance for interrelationships between American nations and of those nations with the rest of the world will be given special consideration. An effort will be made to include occasional articles that state an unusual or even discordant position on a subject of broad interest to be supplemented by critical comments of authorities representing differing positions on the topic. The editors continue to welcome articles by scholars from all parts of the world.

MANUSCRIPTS should be submitted in duplicate to: Editor, JOURNAL OF INTERAMERICAN STUDIES AND WORLD AFFAIRS, Box 24-8134, University of Miami, Coral Gables, Florida 33124. Manuscripts should be typewritten, double-spaced, with footnotes, references, tables, and charts on separate pages, and should follow the current journal style. A brief biographical paragraph describing each author's current affiliation, research interests, and recent publications should accompany the manuscript.

CORRESPONDENCE regarding book reviews should be sent directly to: Book Review Editor, JOURNAL OF INTERAMERICAN STUDIES AND WORLD AFFAIRS, Box 24-8134, University of Miami, Coral Gables, Florida 33124.

JOURNAL OF INTERAMERICAN STUDIES AND WORLD AFFAIRS is published four times annually—in February, May, August, and November.

Subscriptions: Regular institutional rate $22.50. Individuals may subscribe at a one-year rate of $13.50. Add $1.00 per year for subscriptions outside the United States. Orders from U.K., Europe, the Middle East, and Africa should be sent to the London office (address below). Noninstitutional orders **must** be paid by personal check.

Second-class postage paid at Beverly Hills, California.

Inquiries: Address all correspondence and permissions requests to SAGE PUBLICATIONS, INC., 275 South Beverly Drive, Beverly Hills, California 90212. Inquiries and subscriptions from U.K., Europe, the Middle East, and Africa should be sent to SAGE PUBLICATIONS LTD, St George's House, 44 Hatton Garden, London EC1N 8ER. Other orders should be sent to the Beverly Hills office.

Advertising: Current rates and specifications may be obtained by writing to the Advertising Manager at the Beverly Hills office (address above).

This journal is abstracted in **Historical Abstracts, Human Resources Abstracts, Sage Urban Studies Abstracts,** and **International Political Science Abstracts.** It is indexed in **Public Affairs Information Service, Current Contents, Social Sciences Citation Index, Social Sciences Index,** and **ABC POL SCI.**

Back Issues: Information about availability and prices of back issues may be obtained from the publisher's order department (address above). Write to London office for sterling prices.

Claims for undelivered copies must be made no later than three months following month of publication. The publisher will supply missing copies when losses have been sustained in transit and where the reserve stock will permit.

Change of Address: Six weeks' advance notice must be given when notifying of change of address. Please send old address label along with the new address to insure proper identification. Please specify name of journal.

YALE H. FERGUSON
Department of Political Science
Hill Hall, 7th Floor
Rutgers University
Newark, NJ 07102

THROUGH GLASSES DARKLY

An Assessment of Various Theoretical Approaches to Interamerican Relations

In the past decade or so the international relations of Latin America–for many years the subject of legalistic, institutional, polemical, or purely descriptive analyses–has been investigated on a much more sophisticated basis.[1] *Dependencia* has emerged as a major organizing concept in much of the literature, and "bureaucratic politics" has provided a focus for some of the work emanating from North American scholars on U.S. Latin American policies. There are a number of other frameworks as well. Welcome as the wealth of new studies is, they nevertheless present us for the first time with a problem of assessing the utility of various theoretical approaches or at least with the challenge of relating them to one another in a meaningful fashion.

As Julio Cotler and Richard R. Fagen (1974: 9-11) suggest in their thought-provoking introduction to a recent collection of diverse essays, different analysts often appear to be speaking past each other, and perhaps inevitably so, for their theoretical perspectives seem to be in important respects incompatible or even mutually exclusive. Cotler and Fagen maintain that the situation is not merely a lack of communication between

Journal of Interamerican Studies and World Affairs, Vol. 19 No. 1, February 1977

proponents of separate viewpoints, but outright "paradigmatic competition" which is at root an epistemological controversy that "involves conflicting perspectives on the meaning of knowledge, understanding, and explanation in the social sciences." The controversy, according to Cotler and Fagen, not only "leads organically to different evaluations of the meaning of change in concrete policies" but is also reflected in "the multitude of purposes to which a single case [the Alliance for Progress in their example] can be lent." In their view, there is little or no convergence between the complexity of the Alliance as seen from the perspective of bureaucratic politics and the *dependencia* unity found in the Alliance by other writers, despite a superficial "consensus" to the effect that "both the detailed study of the parts of the system and the continuing analysis of the system as a whole are needed." "Even were the elements under investigation held constant," Cotler and Fagen argue, "investigators approaching the Alliance from different theoretical perspectives will *necessarily* use it in different ways to discover different 'truths'." That is: "The meanings of the Alliance, which is to say its reality as reconstructed, are not and cannot be independent of the theoretical perspectives brought to bear on it, . . . More research–further information about the Alliance, no matter how detailed or exhaustive–will not adjudicate or reconcile all the differences."

Cotler and Fagen indicate that they "have not chosen to explore the epistemological assumptions undergirding this statement," confining themselves to the observations that "(1) research is always a reconstruction of reality, and (2) theory is a principal arbitrator of the validity of the reconstruction." However, these observations make the epistemological assumptions involved fairly clear, and they are entirely sound as far as they go. James N. Rosenau (1973: 111), for example, has remarked that "we can never know politics objectively and must settle for intersubjective truths about it." The very process of building concepts, theories, and models is one of abstracting from reality, which by definition means that the resulting reconstruction of reality is less than complete. As Rosenau (1973: 109) puts it:

> unable to perceive and depict the universe of interest to him in its entirety, the observer must select some dimensions as important, while dismissing others as trivial. In mapping a country, the geographer is likely to select mountains and rivers as important and treat hills and brooks as less important, thus yielding a map that is comprehensible and storable even as it is also a distortion of "reality." More importantly, while the map grossly distorts the objective truth, it is likely to be adequate and fully usable with respect to the task for which it was designed.

Two comments can and should be made about this line of reasoning. First, it is incumbent upon those who are confronted with a variety of concepts, theories, and so forth to assess what each purports to do, how well it does it, and especially what each fails to do well (the nature, extent, and significance of the distortion introduced). Some may confuse more than they clarify. Second, we must constantly be attempting to build better theory, to fashion more effective glasses through which we can view the real universe. The central danger in the truth-as-an-intersubjective-consensus notion is that we will accept greater distortion than we have to, merely because we expect too little in terms of a reconstruction of reality. Different frameworks may not be as mutually exclusive as they first appear and may, in fact, be to some extent regarded as complementary in helping us achieve a more satisfying (if always inevitably incomplete) view.

It is to these two ends, then, that the present essay is directed.

Actors

On each intellectual map, which are the mountains and rivers, as distinct from hills and brooks; through particular glasses, what is in sharp focus, and what is a blur? One way of categorizing various theoretical approaches is by the actor(s) that each regards as most significant in explaining international behavior. This is closely related to the traditional "levels of analysis" problem in international politics, which we will use as a springboard for discussion. However, we will be stressing that the three traditional levels–individual, state, and international system–*at least as traditionally conceived* do not entirely capture the more subtle distinctions introduced by contemporary paradigms.

The Individual

The most fundamental level is that of the human individual as actor. As Kenneth Waltz (1959) and some others have discussed it, this level amounts to little more than generalizations about "human nature" which–aside from varying widely (e.g., Locke and Hobbes)–actually tell us less about individuals than about mankind in general. It is not especially helpful to know that most humans have a capacity for aggression, cooperation, and so forth.

Another, more useful conception of the individual-as-actor (see, for example, de Rivera, 1968) emphasizes the personality factors involved in individual behavior and influence ("idiosyncratic behavior" and its consequences). One senses, for example, that the unique personalities of John F. Kennedy and Fidel Castro had much to do with their actions and special impact on the interamerican scene. Nevertheless, there are several major difficulties with this approach. One is rather obvious, the task of constructing a meaningful personality "profile" of the individual in question. A more basic difficulty is that few individuals, in fact, act autonomously in international affairs. Lee Harvey Oswald did (unless he was indeed part of a conspiracy) and so apparently did "Ché" Guevara when he embarked on his final Bolivian adventure, but the personalities of JFK and Fidel presumably were both constrained and given unusual prominence because of their respective roles as chief of state. How do we separate personality from role and establish the relative significance of each?

As a further illustration, consider two individuals whose personalities have often been regarded as important in accounting for U.S. Latin American politics in the mid-1960s, President Lyndon B. Johnson and Assistant Secretary of State for Latin American Affairs (later Undersecretary) Thomas A. Mann. Johnson was fond of generalizing from his experience with "Mexicans" back home in Texas, to wit:

> if you didn't watch they'll come right into your yard and take it over if you let them. And the next day they'll be right there on your porch, barefoot and weighing one hundred and thirty pounds, and they'll take that too. But if you say to 'em at the start, "Hold on, just wait a minute," they'll know they're dealing with someone who'll stand up. And after that you can get along fine. [quoted in Halberstam, 1972: 531]

One is tempted to argue that this quotation sheds considerable light on the president's vigorous response to the supposed threat of communist takeovers in Brazil and the Dominican Republic. However, recall that Kennedy acted no less vigorously against missiles in Cuba, and Nixon-Kissinger against the Allende government. Query: was Johnson acting out his personal predispositions or merely responding as "any" U.S. president would have responded under comparable circumstances?

Mann was widely known as a Texas conservative, and there is no doubt that his personal biases found expression in such policies as U.S. identification with hard-line anticommunist regimes and active support for U.S. business interests in Latin America. On the other hand, Mann represented precisely that sector of governmental opinion, including the "old Latin American hands" in the State Department and the Pentagon, which Kennedy decision makers had regularly overruled (Schlesinger, 1965: 202).[2] In this sense, Mann was not so much an individual actor as he was the spokesman for a powerful intragovernmental faction that had emerged triumphant (after a partial and brief eclipse) in the Washington game of "bureaucratic politics." Yet Mann's additional role as Special Assistant to the President, his personal friendship with President Johnson, and the fact that he was "Lyndon Johnson's kind of man" (Geyelin, 1966: 99) suggest that what was involved was less a "bureaucratic" victory than the establishment (or restablishment) of a broad consensus as to values and policies that was shared at this time, for all practical purposes, by the U.S. government as a whole. As Johnson said he intended, the United States spoke with "one voice" in Latin American affairs, and Mann was that voice.

The State

It is customary to point out that the state is the primary unit into which the world is divided and as such must be regarded as the main actor in international relations. This often leads to broad generalizations about state behavior, such as all states are to some degree nationalistic, all states are concerned about national security, and (Hans Morgenthau's dubious proposition) all states pursue their "national interest" defined as power. As late as the post-World War II era, harking back to Wilson, there were also shaky assumptions in some quarters about the peace-loving nature of democracies contrasting with the aggressive inclinations of dictatorships. A modern counterpart is the work of Rudolph Rummel (1968), Barbara and Stephen Salmore (forthcoming), and others on national attributes and foreign policy (for a survey of this literature see Sullivan, 1976: ch. 4).

Today, most discussions from the state-as-actor perspective center on the foreign-policy-making process and especially, at least as far as hemisphere relations are concerned, on the origins and nature of U.S. policies. Within this context the principal choice is between what Graham Allison (1971) and others have labeled the "rational" model, that of a unified national foreign-policy decision-making system pursuing well-defined goals, and other models that stress diversity in the foreign-policy decision-making system and policy outcomes. Critics of the rational model maintain that it is normally inaccurate to regard the state as a "black box" or a "billiard ball"—that what often passes as "state" behavior is, in fact, the behavior of specific domestic bureaucracies or interest groups who exercise unusual influence over the decision-making process.

The rational model gains some support from the ideological dimension in foreign policy (see Blachman and Hellman, forthcoming; includes Ferguson, forthcoming). Abraham F. Lowenthal, whose essay on the Alliance points to the utility of the bureaucratic approach, nevertheless acknowledges (1974: 234): "Generally accepted values, images, and premises set some of the parameters for United States foreign policy, and explication of all these should be central for foreign policy analysis." He indeed sees this as "perhaps the most fruitful area for research" (1974: 234n.).

Promising though an emphasis on ideology may be in analyzing foreign policy, it, too, has some serious limitations. First, there is the hard task of identifying relevant values and distinguishing these from less basic goals and policies. Second, even if we are able to identify values, their precise relationship to policy goals and means—and hence their significance—is far from clear. The dictates of specific values in terms of policy goals and means leave a great deal of room for subjective interpretation by decision makers. One might even go so far as to argue that ideology has little meaning except as it is interpreted and reinterpreted by decision makers in the "language" of policies. In any event, the "parameters" Lowenthal mentions do appear to be fairly flexible ones. What, for example, does fidelity to the value of free enterprise capitalism "require" of the decision maker in terms of concrete policies? All U.S. administrations as a rule have gone to bat for U.S. corporations threatened with expropriation without prospect of "prompt, adequate, and effective" compensation in Latin America, but some administrations have done so with much more vigor and enthusiasm than others.[3] There has also been a dramatic shift in official attitudes over the years on the issue of the propriety of extending U.S. aid for government enterprises in Latin America.

Decision-makers' leeway has been increased by the fact that basic values have themselves been to some extent competing or inconsistent. A major conflict, for instance, has existed between the values of national security and democracy, which most administrations have resolved by downgrading democracy as a goal and supporting conservative Latin American dictatorships. The Kennedy Administration regarded support for democracy as in the interest of U.S. national security but backed away from this position in cases where it was deemed that an unyielding pro-democracy posture might result in a political vacuum with uncertain consequences, a possible communist takeover, or a government that would not further the economic and social development goals of the Alliance (economic and social development values intervening here; see Ferguson, 1972: 348-371).

Another reason why it is difficult to be precise about the relationship between ideology and policy goals and means is that policy makers obviously have much more to consider than simple ideological rectitude. They have to be concerned, as well, about how successful their policies will be in the "real world." There thus has operated a sort of ongoing "feedback effect," whereby practical experience–sometimes in a crisis context–has clarified and called into question the ideological dimension in prevailing U.S. goals and policies. Decision makers have responded to this feedback in one or both of two ways, either of them usually resulting in some change in ends and/or means. They have shifted the priority assigned to one or more tenet of U.S. ideology in relation to others and/or reinterpreted the demands of the same ideological tenet to accommodate policy change. The Cuban Revolution (coming on the heels of Vice-President Nixon's disastrous goodwill tour) is a classic example: it spurred the United States not only to attach a new priority to socioeconomic development and democracy (temporarily) in Latin America but also to abandon its ideological opposition to economic planning and commodity agreements which previously had been seen as undue interference with free market forces. (This period is discussed in detail in Wagner, 1970.)

U.S. decision makers themselves have clouded the relationship between ideology and policy by their attachment to the ideological tenet of "pragmatism." Pragmatism is a perfect example of what might be termed "the attitude of ideology toward itself," advancing as it does the proposition that "practical" responses to the "real world" *should take precedence* over the dictates of ideology. As we have indicated, pragmatism is itself an ideological tenet; but decision makers have not so regarded it, and it has therefore regularly allowed them to conceal from themselves the ideological premises behind their policies. The concealing function of pragmatism has been enhanced by its links to the concept of the "national interest," which purports to provide a similarly "objective" guide for national policy. In fact, this vague concept has normally been interpreted by U.S. decision makers as virtually synonymous with the "struggle for power" and the necessary exclusion of "morality" from diplomatic intercourse. It is no accident that Robert A. Packenham found (1973b: 245) that Morgenthau, the grand old man of the "realist" school, was the sole political theorist whose ideas were familiar to many of the U.S. officials he interviewed. Bernard Brodie writes (1973: 368) of a "strong and rigid" "professional tradition" among U.S. foreign policy makers holding that the intrusion of moral considerations is "inherently mischievous, that is, . . . likely to cause the warping of what would otherwise be trimly correct thinking about foreign affairs." Pragmatism and the national interest concept have also been closely associated with a self-consciously "tough," "hard-nosed" brand of decision-making and a profound distrust of policies favored by "soft-headed" "liberal" "intellectuals." Richard J. Barnet (1972: 109ff.) observes: "One of the first lessons a national security manager learns after a day in the bureaucratic climate of the Pentagon, State Department, White House, or CIA is that toughness is the most highly prized virtue." This Barnet terms "bureaucratic *machismo.*"

A second "rational" approach to the analysis of foreign policy searches for a hypothetical "foreign policy consensus."

This approach does not deny the relevance of ideology but sidesteps the problems inherent in identifying values and establishing their precise relationship to particular goals and policies, by focusing solely on goals and policies. However, like ideology, foreign policy consensus is a rather amorphous concept. At any given time, some policy makers may not accept all of the supposed consensus, that is, the consensus may not be as broad as many would interpret it to be. Moreover, U.S. policies have rarely, if ever, evidenced the degree of order and unity that the consensus concept would seem to imply. As Christopher Mitchell (1974: 198-199) has noted, there has often been poor coordination between specific goals and the means adopted to pursue them, and confusion has been multiplied by the existence of plural goals that have been to some extent incompatible. The result is that at times the primary characteristic of U.S. policies has appeared to many observers to be an "incoherence" which is far from "rational." One is reminded of the frequent complaint that "the United States has no Latin American policy."

This view of U.S. policy as essentially fragmented gains further credence from the "liberal" critique of the Alliance for Progress, one of three "perspectives" on the Alliance that Lowenthal outlines. It is ironic that the liberal critique should sustain a fragmented view, because liberals start from the proposition that the Alliance as originally conceived was a rational policy, which derived from a widely perceived convergence of U.S. and Latin American interests in the development of the hemisphere. Yet liberal explanations for the shortcomings of the Alliance do point to fragmentation. In Lowenthal's words (in Cotler and Fagen, 1974: 218):

> All have in common . . . the assertion of a dichotomy between benevolent U.S. intentions and unfortunate actions; the latter are attributed to particular causes, even sometimes to accidental or contingent forces. The Alliance's disappointing record tends to be chalked up to "halfhearted execution" or to "lack of implementation." . . . It is argued that the Alliance's original aims were attenuated, and some even dropped, because of a series of intense

short-term pressures to which responsible U.S. officials understandably but "erroneously" succumbed: pressures to score immediate political impact, to gain Congressional support for foreign aid by serving local or special interests, and to help alleviate the U.S. balance of payments difficulties. Objectives apparently assumed to be consistent at first–economic growth, social equity, political stability, constitutional democracy, the promotion of U.S. private economic interests, and the protection of U.S. national security–turned out to be in conflict, and some were necessarily subordinated to others; liberal writers usually argue that the "wrong" aims were given preference.

Packenham's analysis of the ideology implicit in the U.S. foreign aid program from World War II to 1968 offers us such a good illustration of the limitations (as well as strengths) of a "rational" model that it is worth examining in some detail. He discusses (1973b: 4-5) three "doctrines" regarding the relationship between aid and political development that U.S. policy makers from time to time have adopted. The "economic" doctrine held that economic and technical assistance contributed to economic development, and economic development to political development. The "security" doctrine assumed that "aid should not be used so much to achieve economic development and with it a host of congenial political results, but more . . . as a Cold War tool . . . to promote political stability, win alliances for the United States, and impede the emergence of radical or Communist regimes." The "explicit democratic" doctrine sought "to maximize the likelihood that aid might contribute to the growth and strengthening of liberal democratic political systems in the Third World."

According to Packenham (1973b: 163)–and this is his most provocative argument–although the three doctrines are "ostensibly separate and conflicting," they are "actually integrated and consistent components of a coherent liberal tradition, which grew out of a unique historical experience." Packenham finds his inspiration in Louis Hartz's notion of the "Liberal tradition in America" or "American exceptionalism." He contends (1973b: see especially ch. 3) that all three doctrines rest on "the four main liberal assumptions": (1) "change and development are easy"; (2) "all good things [desirable forms of development] go together"; (3) "radicalism and revolution are bad"; and (4) "distributing power is more important than accumulating power."

Packenham does not maintain (1973b: xxi) "that the liberal tradition explains all U.S. policies and activities toward Asia, Africa, and Latin America." He states: "Obviously, other political, social, economic, military, and cultural factors are also relevant and necessary as explanations of American attitudes and policies. Security needs and perceptions (often grossly distorted and exaggerated) were particularly potent variables in producing an anti-Communism that at times seemed almost obsessive." However, Packenham insists (1973b: 7) that he is seeking "the *prevailing* similarities and continuities, not only within and between [officials and academicians], but also over time, across party lines, and among various administrations and political leaders." He continues:

> In this sense most American politicians and academicians are liberals (or "Liberals"): Richard Nixon as well as Hubert Humphrey, John Foster Dulles as well as Dean Acheson or Dean Rusk or Harry Truman, Lyndon Johnson as well as John Kennedy. Such, at any rate, is the perspective from which this book is written. This does not deny, of course, the existence of differences in policies, personalities, and attitudes among these men, or among administrations, or over time. From other perspectives these differences might be very interesting or important. Nor, of course, does it deny that these differences can produce policies and actions with very significant contrasts in their consequences. It does say that for a variety of reasons . . . the similarities prevail.

Packenham is impressed by the ideological unity in U.S. policies; other analysts, with considerable justification (as he himself acknowledges), may be inclined to stress the diversity. Even accepting his list of prominent articles of faith under which U.S. policy makers have operated allows us to perceive glaring internal inconsistencies in the assumptions themselves, and between policies that flowed from one assumption, and one or more of the other assumptions in the package. For instance, if "all good things go together" in development, why have policy makers felt it necessary to worry about "radicalism and revolution" that they regarded as "bad"? Another example: "radicalism and revolution are bad" may help explain Johnson's and Nixon's affinity for military governments, but does not such a policy run counter to the dictates of "distributing power is more important than accumulating power"?

Packenham comments (1973b: 164), with regard to U.S. past support for both democratic and conservative dictatorial regimes, that both "responses are perfectly consistent with the liberal tradition, although obviously not each response is consistent with each component of it." He says: "Indeed, there is no single assumption in American political thought which explains all the variety in the American responses. Nor should this be surprising. As a whole, however, the four assumptions of the liberal tradition account for much of the variety."

The four assumptions may indeed "account for much of the variety," as Packenham suggests. But it is at least debatable whether other lists of assumptions and values might account for more, whether any single label like "Liberal" should be attached to such a list, and whether the "Liberal" label is not a poor choice in any event since U.S. goals and policies have so often been anything but liberal in the plain-meaning sense of the word! And the nagging problem remains: how to explain the policy diversity that is *not* accounted for by whatever ideological framework we ultimately choose to regard as relevant?

From another standpoint, Packenham's classification of the three "doctrines," which point to some of the goals that specific U.S. programs have been designed to serve, would seem to shed light on the U.S. foreign policy consensus. One might, in fact, argue that U.S. policies toward Latin America over the years have involved three basic goals: (1) to protect the United States from external threats to its security; (2) to promote the growth of American capitalism through the expansion of markets and investment opportunities in Latin America; and (3) to bring the presumed blessings of democracy and development to "benighted" lands south of the border. However, it is obvious that the meaning and priority that U.S. decision makers have attached to each of these goals have shifted over time, as have the policies that decision makers have deemed appropriate to the pursuit of each goal. We are back again to the problem of accounting for diversity.

Alternatives to the rational model help us account for *more* of the diversity and, in this sense, are perhaps less "alternatives" than "complements." In this category are two additional models advanced by Allison.

The first of these, "organizational process," views policy as the outcome of the habitual behavior of various subunits of the national government, each of which has its own area of responsibility, its own characteristic outlook, and its own customary mode of operation.

The second model, "bureaucratic politics," suggests that policy is best conceived as the outcome of bargaining between certain individuals occupying key bureaucratic roles in the government. Some writers, including Lowenthal, consolidate both of Allison's models into one under the single heading of "bureaucratic politics." The implication here is that the habitual organizational behavior of bureaucracies rarely "counts" in the decision-making system except insofar as their leaders engage and prove effective in the bureaucratic politics "game."

Still another model is implicit in the "radical" view of the Alliance, the third "perspective" that Lowenthal outlines. Although some of the conclusions drawn from this model are not very convincing, it is significant in that it transcends both the rational and bureaucratic politics models and points beyond them to a neglected dimension of the foreign policy-making process—the role of nongovernmental domestic political actors. "Radicals" see the U.S. government as acting in a rational (that is, unified) fashion to promote capitalist expansion and to suppress—if necessary, by covert operations or by military force—threats to that expansion. Moreover, they regard this pattern of behavior as a near-inevitable consequence of U.S.

government bureaucratic links with the private sector (the military-industrial complex and the like).

Drawing on the consolidated bureaucratic politics model, we may conceive of the U.S. government actor as a large network of individuals occupying roles in bureaucratic structures that are to some extent—but by no means entirely—autonomous and competing entities in the decision-making process. A major cleavage is built into the constitutional division between Congress and the executive branch. Congress is itself a collection of individuals clustered in various committees, and the president who occupies the central role in the executive branch may be seen as both an individual and a bureaucratic institution (the White House Office). Each bureaucratic structure develops a "stake" in specific goals and policies in particular issue-areas, and relatively stable ties with certain elites in the private sector. The public at large sets general constraints on foreign policy and normally reacts, as Gabriel A. Almond describes it (1960: 53-65), in terms of "mood" ("withdrawal-intervention," "idealism-cynicism," and so on). What Almond (1960: 138) calls "policy and opinion elites," including those heading formal interest groups, on matters of special interest to them "give structure to the public" and provide "the effective means of access" to decision makers in the executive branch and Congress.

This perspective allows us to perceive the often-contingent nature of the decision-making process and policy outcomes that is obscured by the rational model. We can appreciate, for example, the extended debate between State and Treasury over the issue of an appropriate response to the Allende nationalizations, which was eventually resolved by the White House in favor of a hard line; the clandestine strategy of the CIA that was undertaken with the approval of the White House and apparently without the knowledge of State; the lobbying efforts of ITT and other affected companies in the executive branch and Congress; and the secret negotiations between ITT and the CIA. Likewise: the struggle of the White House and State to get the Pentagon and congressional conservatives to accept a compromise on the Panama Canal; the Pentagon's long-standing resistance to changes in rules governing territorial waters, an issue that has been further complicated by the offshore and inshore fishing industries and their congressional allies; the log-rolling between liberals and conservatives in Congress on military and economic aid; the partially successful efforts of businessmen and labor in affected industries, as well as congressmen bent on punishing cartels, to defeat the executive branch's initiative to extend generalized trade preferences to the developing countries; and so forth.

What is often said about the president's general role in policy-making applies as well to Latin American policies. Presidential leadership certainly does not guarantee unified, rational policies. Policies nominally accepted by the bureaucracies may be frustrated in implementation (*obedezco pero no cumplo*),[4] and there is always Congress to consider. However, the president regularly resolves disputes between the bureaucracies, and when he has sufficient skill and especially the will to do so, he can go far toward imposing goals and policies on his administration. Normally the president can have his way if he cares enough to issue firm directives and then to see that a close watch is kept on those who carry them out. The priority attached to Latin American affairs is obviously significant here: at times when the attention of the president and his immediate advisers is focused elsewhere, there is more room for bureaucracies and special interests to maneuver and to establish their own spheres of influence over policies.

The degree of crisis perceived by decision makers is a potent variable in this connection. It is useful to think of crisis as having both scope (general or confined to particular issues) and intensity (extreme to low-level). Generalized concern of a moderate to high intensity for Latin America as a region in crisis pervaded official Washington in the late 1950s and early 1960s. Those were exceptional times. Since the 1965 Dominican episode, Latin American affairs have slid far down the list of U.S. foreign policy priorities, and attention has largely been confined to specific issues as they have arisen: Allende's election in Chile, the availability of hemisphere supplies of petroleum, Castro's intervention in the Angolan conflict, and so forth. Kissinger, at the outset of the Nixon Administration, took pains to curtail one traditional source of low-level crises by letting it be known that the United States henceforth would not feel obliged to produce a major policy initiative for each important interamerican conference. However, some such conferences have continued to serve as occasions for policy reviews. In any event, we may hypothesize that perception of crisis, whether general or confined to certain issues, tends to decentralize decision-making and encourage policy innovation. Conversely, an absence of crisis perception tends to decentralize decision-making and contributes to policy stability (see Wagner, 1970; Hermann, 1969).

Our discussion has been limited to foreign policy-making in the United States. We have little hard information about the process in Latin America, although we know a great deal about decision-making regarding domestic policies in some countries. Clearly, this is a prime area for future research. One senses that the rational model holds more promise for analysis of authoritarian political systems with strong executives, but this observation must be tempered with the recognition that authoritarian regimes, too, have bureaucracies and political factions. In some democratic systems, the military constitutes a "veto" group that makes the Pentagon seem pale by comparison! Foreign policy-making in the more complex Latin American democracies more closely resembles the process in the United States. Recall, for example, the success of the powerful Association of Chambers of Commerce and Industry in blocking Venezuelan entrance into the Andean Common Market prior to the Caldera administration (see Clark, 1972).

The International System

There are parallels at the "international" level to the bureaucratic and interest-group actors that inhabit the "black box" of the state. One of these types of actors, the international governmental organization actor (IGO), has been the object of scholarly attention for many years. Examples from the Latin American subsystem include the Economic Commission for Latin America (ECLA), the Inter-American Development Bank (IDB), the Andean Common Market (ANCOM), and the new Latin American Economic System (SELA, a successor to CECLA). Analysts have not customarily regarded IGOs as presenting a serious challenge to the traditional state-centric view of international relations, since the constituent unit of IGOs is, after all, governments. However, the behavior of IGOs has always been something more than the mere sum of their parts.

A state-centric view is even more difficult to reconcile with recent work on "transnationalism" (see, for example, Keohane and Nye, 1971; Mansbach et al., 1976), which centers on international nongovernmental actors (INGOs) like multinational corporations, foundations, international organizations of political parties (e.g., the Christian Democratic Organization of America or ODCA) or labor unions (e.g., the Inter-American Regional Workers' Organization or ORIT), ADELA (an investment group of over 200 of the largest banks and industrial enterprises in the United States, Europe, Japan, and Latin America), and the Council of the Americas (a representative of more than 200 U.S.-based multinational corporations operating in Latin America). When the annual revenues of a multinational corporation are several times the gross national product of a host country, which was the case for instance in the 1968 dispute involving Standard Oil of New Jersey and the government of Peru, the state-centric model obviously needs at least some modification. States may still be the most important actor in international relations, but they are definitely neither the only "autonomous" nor the only significant actor.

Most system-level analyses focus not on actors per se, but rather on pattern(s) arising from the *interaction* of a variety of actors. Studies of "linkages," of which Douglas A. Chalmers' (1969) is an excellent example, fall into this category. Chalmers observes that Latin America from the beginning developed "on the periphery" of a succession of predominant external powers and that external influence can perhaps best be understood by ignoring national boundaries and concentrating on the "linkages" between an ever-more-complex set of discrete "linkage groups" located within and without "domestic" societies. Such domestic groups as the military, intellectuals, commercial elites, political parties, labor unions, and guerrilla bands have developed their own special ties with the outside world; and a prominent feature of Latin American linkage patterns is that some major "external" groups are often physically present on the nation's home ground. The concept of "penetrated" societies thus seems eminently applicable to Latin America. Chalmers demonstrates that these patterns have had a profound impact on the paternalistic "infrastructure," lack of "institutionalization," and issues of Latin American political systems, as well as on the Latin American "style of problem-solving."

Dependency theory, which has gained increasing currency in recent years, might be seen as linkage theory with a more definite economic emphasis. Theorists of dependency (see, for example, various essays in Cotler and Fagen, 1974; Chilcote, 1974; Latin American Perspectives, 1974; Kahl, 1976) have stressed the alleged influence of the expanding role of foreign-based multinational corporations on past, present, and future development in Latin America. It is difficult to pinpoint a single "theory," although there are some common themes (Francis, 1975 pulls together some of these themes). Marxist writers like André Gunder Frank tend to view dependency in the framework of Lenin's theory of imperialism as a "natural" stage in the evolution of world capitalism (see, for example, Frank, 1967; Bodenheimer, 1971; Cockcroft et al., 1972). Moreover, from a policy standpoint, they are less sanguine about the possibilities of reaching an accommodation with foreign firms and indeed are inclined to argue that the only hope for a marked reduction in dependency lies in socialist revolutions. On the other hand, the thinking of less doctrinaire writers like Osvaldo Sunkel (1973a, 1973b) is a logical extension of the economic theories propounded by ECLA and its former Executive Secretary, Raúl Prebisch, in the 1950s and 1960s.

Dependency theory has met with some skepticism not only from the foreign business community, but also from a number of scholars (see, for example, Ray, 1973; Nove, 1974) who have criticized especially the Marxist perspective linking dependency with imperialism and blaming virtually all the ills of Latin American societies on foreign domination. It might be argued that the former critics have difficulty being objective and that the latter have in a sense set up a straw man by not giving more attention to the works of better writers like Sunkel.

Nevertheless, several lines of criticism do appear to be well founded. First, dependency as a concept needs considerable refinement (see Packenham, 1973a). There are different degrees and forms of dependency. At a minimum, dependency would seem to have economic, political, social, and cultural aspects which—though doubtless interrelated—are nonetheless distinct. Second, as Robert R. Kaufman et al. (1975: 329-330) have maintained:

> substantially more systematic attention needs to be paid to a host of political, social, and cultural variables which may intervene between economic dependency and its alleged effects. . . . Some dependency theorists, most notably Cardoso and Faletto, have written quite suggestively about the way in which the political order mediates the impact of foreign economic penetration, about imperatives of particular types of domestic production and class relations and about subcultural or historical factors particular to specific segments or countries of Latin America.

Like most single-factor explanations, dependency theory tells only part of the story. One gathers that writers on dependency who contributed to the Cotler and Fagen collection would at least partially agree. According to Cotler and Fagen (1974: 17-18):

> Even those most committed to classical Marxist models would admit that they offer only the most general guidance to the study of specific foreign policies or the emergence and changing behavior of

> transnational actors. At the same time, those most experienced in the detailed investigation of specific instances of the interplay of economics and politics are quick to confess that their findings to date usually have limited transfer value. The revealed "truths" about Guatemala are not necessarily the "truths" about Argentina, and yesterday's relationships are not necessarily today's or tomorrow's. . . . In all of this, politics is seen as critical to determining specific outcomes, however fundamental economic factors may be in setting limits on what is possible or probable.

However, Cotler and Fagen also observe: "But when the moment arrives to reach beyond confessions and generalizations of this sort, agreements fragment, disciplinary chauvinisms erupt, sacred texts are quoted, and ideological, professional, and national differences become paramount."

Third, turning to policy, it may be that most writers on dependency present too extreme an indictment of the multinational corporation. This is not to suggest that many of their arguments about the dangers inherent in the present pattern of multinational expansion are not valid; however, it may be that the reality of interdependence indicates that some sort of an accommodation with the multinationals is both possible and desirable. For their part, concerned Latin American governments appear to be making increasing use of a variety of means at their disposal (including stringent investment codes) to curb the multinationals without excluding them entirely (see Mansbach et al., 1976: ch. 8).

Fourth, dependency theory diverts attention from what might be described as the "leading edge" of hemisphere relations, the steady emergence of a Pan-Latin-American subsystem and links between Latin American and extrahemispheric developing countries that are in interesting ways independent of the United States. We seem to be on the brink of a new era to which dependency theory itself helped give impetus but which is now moving beyond the bounds of the dependency model. Again quoting Cotler and Fagen (1974: 18-20):

> The central intellectual problem in the study of inter-American relations is to understand the structure and functioning of the system of North American domination—imperfect, halting, and

> contradictory though that system might be. . . . But despite the heuristic value of this model, the questions that it poses do not exhaust the subject matter of hemispheric relations, and at times they actually distort, by making it difficult to recognize that Latin America is important for reasons not directly related to its subordinate status. . . . If scholarship on inter-American relations is not to be cast into the dustbin of history—along with outmoded forms of social and economic organization—then it must face squarely the challenge of a Latin America that can no longer be understood as merely the shadow cast by the Colossus of the North.

Another system-level approach to theory-building centers around the concept of "integration" (for detailed assessment of integration theory and its applicability to the EEC, see Mansbach et al., 1976). While most of the work in this field has focused on Europe and the EEC, some of it has dealt with Latin America; and, in any event, integration theory offers us a useful perspective on regional subsystems and institutions like ANCOM, the Latin American Free Trade Association (LAFTA), the Central American Common Market (CACM), SELA, and developing-country cartels.

Like dependency theory, integration theory has suffered from the lack of a precise definition of the central concept. There has long been considerable uncertainty as to whether integration should be regarded as a "process" or an "outcome" (Haas, 1970). It is now generally agreed that a variety of outcomes (forms of integration) are possible and that it is the task of the theorist to determine what process(es) may be involved in shaping each one of them. Two obvious basic outcomes, for example, are economic integration and political integration, and there may be numerous subtypes worth distinguishing. The theorist is interested in such questions as what institutions emerge in each case and the extent to which the parties act as a group in making decisions with or without common institutions (Nye, 1971: 27-28, throughout).

There is also a consensus that the integration process is much less automatic than was originally assumed. Some of the early work on the conditions prevailing within and among particular groups of countries that supposedly favored or militated against integration and studies of transaction flows now seem largely irrelevant (for example, see Reinton, 1972). Although it appears probable that some degree of "objective" interdependence is necessary for successful integration, it is not clear whether a certain level of transactions is a *precondition* for the process of integration, whether it is the *result* of such a process, or whether it is no more than an *indicator* or "symptom" of the process.

Moreover, the initial assumption of "neofunctionalist" writers (see, for example, Haas, 1964; Haas and Schmitter, 1966), that once governments became involved in the joint performance of one or more tasks there would be an almost inevitable "spillover" to other tasks, has been abandoned. Stanley Hoffman (1968) pointed out that this thesis failed to distinguish between sectors of "high politics" and those of "low politics." According to Hoffman, spillover and further integration were much more likely to occur in the latter, mainly economic sectors that could be handled on a technical basis, than in other more inherently controversial sectors. Joseph S. Nye (1968b) added that economic issues, too, tend to be high politics in the developing world. Karl Kaiser (1967) went still further to argue that the distinction between high and low politics exists solely in the minds of actors and may shift on occasion even within particular policy sectors.

Current thinking, as outlined by Philippe C. Schmitter (1970: 846; one of the original neofunctionalists), is that there are several "strategic options" available to actors engaged in integration experiments in specific sectors. The options include "spillover," "spill-around," "build-up," "retrench," "muddle-about," "spill-back," and "encapsulate." We shall not pause to define each of these options, but it is notable that several of them involve an actual *decrease* in the "scope" of existing joint tasks and community institutions ("disintegration"). Schmitter maintains (1970: 867) that "encapsulation"—the "marginal modification" of a single sector without significant advance or spillover—will be the one likely to prevail most frequently. Contemporary theory (see Lindberg and Scheingold, 1970: ch. 4) also indicates that integration will be attended by shifting coalitions among actors of various kinds, with regular use being made of mechanisms usually associated with coalitions like "side payments" and "log-rolling."

In addition, neofunctionalists have explored some of the external factors influencing integration. Nye (1968a) criticized early theories for paying insufficient attention to the role of outside powers like the United States acting as "catalysts" for integration schemes. Schmitter (1969: 165) hypothesized (his "externalization" thesis) that regional integration would be enhanced by the need for participants to adopt common policies vis-à-vis nonparticipants. Nevertheless, other scholars (see Hansen, 1973) warn, the likelihood remains that participants will continue to have somewhat different "images of the world" and opinions about the future of the region of that world, as well as varying bilateral ties to the external universe—with the result that yet another set of controversial issues may be injected to impede the integration process.

An interesting article by Jorge I. Domínguez (1971), while not explicitly a study of integration, in essence represents an attempt to gain an overview of integrative (and disintegrative) processes at work in the international system as a whole—with particular emphasis on the changing role of the "world's peripheries." Domínguez discusses the political and economic "fragmentation" of the international system in the post-World War II era, the subsequent building of new "selective international linkages" among the countries of the periphery ("the growth of continental subsystems") and between the peripheries and "center" countries, and the resulting new "international hierarchy." This new hierarchy is extremely complex, Domínguez maintains, since center-periphery superordinate-subordinate relationships are "replicated" on regional and subregional levels. He states (1971: 207): "More countries are center powers than ever before, though they are largely centers of local subsystems. The international hierarchy has not withered. It has added new layers in the peripheries." Dominguez does not draw these conclusions, but his analysis reaffirms what we said earlier about dependency theory's neglect of emerging relationships that are to some extent independent of the traditional center and suggests, as well, that the concept of dependency should be extended to include the subordination of client states to local centers in the peripheries. In Latin America today, Brazil, Mexico, and possibly Venezuela give evidence of becoming just such local centers.

The last system-level perspective we will review is the "complex conglomerate" model that provided a framework for a recent research project (NOSTAC I) in which the author was engaged (Mansbach et al., 1976). The model makes few assumptions, except that the international system can best be understood as the patterns arising from the interaction of a variety of actors and that actor behavior will tend to cluster in particular issue-areas. Of special, though not exclusive, interest to the researchers was the role of nonstate actors (actors other than governments) in the international system.

Our approach was essentially inductive. First, we coded "event" data for three regional systems—the Middle East, Western Europe, and Latin America—over a period of 25 years. No distinction was made between domestic and international events. Without regard for nation-state boundaries, we wanted to know who (what actor or actors) did what (types of behavior) to whom (what actor or actors) in each of the regional systems over time. For each event we coded an initiator, the behavior of the initiator, a target of the behavior, and an indirect target (if any). With these data in hand, we were able to determine—for each time slice in each region and across the three regions—which actors were the most active initiators and targets of behavior and which actors were the principal sources of cooperation, conflict, and violence. By means of factor analysis, we discerned the major issues or "superissues" that dominated the politics of each region. Further examination of the data revealed the rank order of superissues; the alignment (coalition behavior) of actors with respect to particular superissues; the specific issues involved in each superissue; and the degree to which each regional system was characterized by cooperative, conflictful, and violent behavior.

Some of the conclusions emanating from the study may be of interest. Of all the dyadic interactions in the three regions for 25 years, under half involved states simultaneously as actors and targets, and over 11 percent involved nonstate actors exclusively. In Latin America 83.5 percent of interactions involved some kind of nonstate actor. With the exception of IGOs and multinational corporations, the behavior of nonstate actors was markedly more conflictful than state (government) behavior. Over the 25 years in three regions, state-state interactions accounted for 52.5 percent of verbal cooperation and 59.6 percent of cooperative deeds, but only 39.5 percent of verbal conflict, 19.9 percent of conflict deeds, and a mere 18 percent of violence. Hence, we observed: the more conflictful the behavior, the less the state-centric model can explain; the more cooperative the behavior, the more the state-centric model can explain.

In one researcher's opinion, it is unfortunate that the data collected for the project were inadequate treat governments as anything other than unified actors.[5] Other biases, as well, may have been built into the particular data base, the *New York Times*, chosen as the best (least deficient) for our purposes (on this point see Mansbach et al., 1976: 303-305). However, aside from illuminating the role of nonstate actors, perhaps the most important contribution of the study was its determined blurring of the domestic-international distinction. This distinction has always been especially misleading in the Latin American context.

Conclusions: The Inelegant Utility Of the Issue-Area Approach

At the outset we commented that different theoretical frameworks may not be as mutually exclusive as they first appear. To be sure, different frameworks have evolved in response to theorists' desires to answer different sets of questions, and it will continue to be difficult to decide which is *the most* illuminating of several possible approaches when one is investigating almost *any* aspect of the interamerican terrain. As Cotler and Fagen suggest, for instance, it *may* ultimately be impossible to resolve whether the dependency or bureaucratic perspective tells us more about the Alliance.

However, perhaps the choice need not always be made. Where theorists in their messianic zeal have so often erred is in failing to perceive and/or acknowledge the limitations of their own particular pairs of analytical glasses and the utility of those worn by others. Each approach may be appreciated for the insights it offers. To return to the cartographic analogy, it would be ideal if particular maps with individual emphases on certain features of the terrain (at the expense of others) could somehow be overlaid to achieve a composite view. If the composite view in some cases is murky or even opaque, that is, if it falls short of the neat "explanation" for phenomena for which social scientists yearn, this may only indicate that the real universe is in *significant* respects more complicated than prevailing intellectual reconstructions—and may point the way to more sophisticated theory.

The issue-area unit of analysis is unusually appealing, in part because it is sufficiently broad to accommodate a variety of approaches while providing, at the same time, a meaningful structure for inquiry. In this conception "interamerican relations" is a major international subsystem within the global complex conglomerate, and this subsystem is itself a cluster of "minisystem" issue-areas. The boundaries of these minisystems are defined by specific policy issues and evidence characteristic patterns of actor involvement and behavior.

It would be presumptuous to argue that issue-area analysis promises an eventual "synthesis" of competing frameworks, but it is noteworthy that a number of those we have outlined do appear to point in the issue-area direction. Specific issues like military aid, the Panama Canal, territorial waters, or trade preferences involve certain national decision makers, values, goals and policies, bureaucracies, interest groups, IGOs, and INGOS–and not others. The linkages that Chalmers highlights are between discrete groups; dependency assumes several forms; integration processes and outcomes vary by sector; and Domínguez describes the new international hierarchy as the product of *selective* international linkages "for specific purposes."

Analysts adopting the issue-area approach may proceed within its bounds to answer whatever questions may be of special interest to them, impressionistically or systematically as the data and methodological tools at their disposal allow. The following list of questions–except for the first two items which are fundamental to the issue-area unit of analysis–is advanced solely for the purpose of illustration:

(1) What are the boundaries of the issue-area to be investigated?

(2) What actors of all types are involved in the issue-area?

(3) How do these actors behave in the issue-area, and why do they behave as they do? This question directs us to weigh the relative importance as explanatory factors of the role that actors occupy in particular decision-making systems, idiosyncratic behavior, ideology and established goals and policies, bureaucratic politics, and actors' perceptions of the constraints imposed by the larger system that is the issue-area and by developments in other issue-areas (feedback, crises, and so on).

(4) What are the patterns of interaction among actors that characterize the issue-area as a whole? How are values allocated within the system? Are there discernible systemwide decision-making institutions? Is there a trend toward or away from joint decision-making? What outcomes result from decision-making? What actors or groups of actors appear to be the most influential in producing these outcomes? What resources do actors command that make them influential? How do different actors align and ally? Are there discernible relationships of dependency between actors? Is behavior in the system essentially cooperative or prone to conflict and violence?

Answering these questions and additional ones that other analysts may consider relevant will by no means be easy. There will still be debate as to the weight that ought to be assigned, for example, to bureaucratic politics or rational perspectives as explanations for "government" behavior within an issue-area. In its very comprehensiveness, the issue-area framework lacks what Rosenau terms "the elegance of the parasimonious model." However, the concept of issue-area is not so complex as to be utterly unmanageable. And, given our present state of ignorance, it is perhaps advisable to strive less for elegance and parsimony than to keep our theoretical options open.

NOTES

1. This essay is a revised version of a paper originally presented at the International Studies Association meeting in Toronto, Canada, February 28, 1976.
2. Schlesinger (1965: 202) recalls that Mann "had an old Latin American hand's skepticism about the grandoise schemes of the New Frontiersmen and, on occasion, even responded a little to the crochets of Admiral Burke."
3. The Kennedy Administration was the least receptive to business influence of any in recent history. As Lowenthal (1974: 231-232) points out, business was not a key part of JFK's domestic constituency, and neither the president nor his Latin American advisers were particularly attuned to opinions from that sector. Among Kennedy's first 200 appointments, there were three times as many individuals from universities and foundations as from business (18 versus 6 percent), compared with seven businessmen for every university-foundation appointee under Eisenhower (42 versus 6 percent).
4. "I obey but do not enforce"–the response often made by Spanish colonial administrators to the King's commands.
5. NOSTAC II at Rutgers is currently investigating bureaucratic politics and related phenomena in an issue-area context.

REFERENCES

ALLISON, G. T. (1971) The Essence of Decision: Conceptual Models and the Cuban Missile Crisis. Cambridge, Mass.: Harvard Univ. Press.

ALMOND, G. A. (1960) The American People and Foreign Policy. New York: Praeger.

BARNET, R. J. (1972) The Roots of War. New York: Atheneum.

BLACHMAN, M. and R. HELLMAN [eds.] (forthcoming) Terms of Conflict: Ideology in Latin American Politics. Philadelphia: ISHI Publications.

BODENHEIMER, S. (1971) "Dependency and imperialism: the roots of Latin American underdevelopment." Politics and Society 1 (May): 327-357.

BRODIE, B. (1973) War and Politics. New York: Macmillan.

CHALMERS, D. A. (1969) "Developing on the periphery: external factors in Latin American politics," pp. 67-93 in J. Rosenau (ed.) Linkage Politics. New York: Free Press.

CHILCOTE, R. [ed.] (1974) Latin America: The Struggle with Dependency and Beyond. New York: Halsted.

CLARK, R. P. (1972) "Economic integration and the political process: linkage politics in Venezuela," pp. 522-543 in Y. H. Ferguson (ed.) Contemporary Inter-American Relations: A Reader in Theory and Issues. Englewood Cliffs, N.J.: Prentice-Hall.

COCKCROFT, J. D., A. G. FRANK, and D. L. JOHNSON (1972) Dependence and Underdevelopment: Latin America's Political Economy. Garden City, N.Y.: Doubleday.

COTLER, J. and R. R. FAGEN [eds.] (1974) Latin America and the United States: The Changing Political Realities. Stanford, Ca.: Stanford Univ. Press.

DE RIVERA, J. H. (1968) The Psychological Dimension of Foreign Policy. Columbus, Ohio: Merrill.

DOMINGUEZ, J. I. (1971) "Mice that do not roar: some aspects of international politics in the world's peripheries." International Organization 27 (Spring): 175-208.

FERGUSON, Y. H. (forthcoming) "The ideological dimension in United States Latin American policies," in M. Blachman and R. Hellman (eds.) Terms of Conflict: Ideology in Latin American Politics. Philadelphia: ISHI Publications.

--- (1972) "The United States and political development in Latin America," pp. 348-391 in Y. H. Ferguson (ed.) Contemporary Inter-American Relations: A Reader in Theory and Issues. Englewood Cliffs, N.J.: Prentice-Hall.

FRANCIS, M. (1975) "Dependency as a theory of international relations." Paper delivered at the International Studies Association meeting in Washington, D.C., March 19.

FRANK, A. G. (1967) Capitalism and Underdevelopment in Latin America. New York: Monthly Review Press.

GEYELIN, P. (1966) Lyndon B. Johnson and the World. New York: Praeger.

HAAS, E. (1970) "The study of regional integration: reflections on the joy and anguish of pretheorizing," pp. 607-646 in L. N. Lindberg and S. A. Scheingold (eds.) Regional Integration: Theory and Research. Special issue of International Organization 24 (Autumn).

--- (1964) Beyond the Nation-State. Stanford, Ca.: Stanford Univ. Press.

--- and P. C. SCHMITTER (1966) "Economics and differential patterns of political integration: projections about unity in Latin America," pp. 259-299 in International Political Communities: An Anthology. Garden City, N.Y.: Doubleday.

HALBERSTAM, D. (1972) The Best and the Brightest. New York: Random House.

HANSEN, R. D. (1973) "Regional integration: forward march, parade rest, or dismissed?" International Organization 27 (Spring): 225-254.

HERMANN, C. F. (1969) "International crisis as a situational variable," pp. 409-421 in J. Rosenau (ed.) International Politics and Foreign Policy. New York: Free Press.

HOFFMANN, S. (1968) "Obstinate or obsolete? The fate of the nation-state and the case of Europe," pp. 177-230 in J. S. Nye, Jr. (ed.) International Regionalism: Readings. Boston: Little, Brown.

KAHL, J. A. (1976) Modernization, Exploitation and Dependency in Latin America: Germani, González Casanova, and Cardoso. New Brunswick, N.J.: Transaction Books.

KAISER, K. (1967) "The U.S. and the EEC in the Atlantic System: the problem of theory." J. of Common Market Studies 5 (June): 388-425.

KAUFMAN, R., D. S. GELLER, and H. I. CHERNOTSKY (1975) "A preliminary test of the theory of dependency." Comparative Politics 7 (April): 303-330.

KEOHANE, R. O. and J. S. NYE, Jr. [eds.] (1971) Transnational Relations and World Politics. Special issue of International Organization 25 (Summer).

Latin American Perspectives (1974) "Dependency theory: a reassessment." Vol. 1 (Spring).

LINDBERG, L. N. and S. A. SCHEINGOLD [eds.] (1970) Regional Integration: Theory and Research. Special issue of International Organization 24 (Autumn).

LOWENTHAL, A. F. (1974) " 'Liberal,' 'radical,' and 'bureaucratic' perspectives on U.S. Latin American policy: the alliance for progress in retrospect," pp. 212-235 in J. Cotler and R. R. Fagen (eds.) Latin America and the United States: The Changing Political Realities. Stanford, Ca.: Stanford Univ. Press.

MANSBACH, R. W., Y. H. FERGUSON, and D. E. LAMPERT (1976) The Web of World Politics: Nonstate Actors in the Global System. Englewood Cliffs, N.J.: Prentice-Hall.

MITCHELL, C. (1974) "Dominance and fragmentation in U.S. Latin American policy," pp. 176-204 in J. Cotler and R. R. Fagen (eds.) Latin America and the United States: The Changing Political Realities. Stanford, Ca.: Stanford Univ. Press.

NOVE, A. (1974) "On reading André Gunder Frank." J. of Development Studies 10 (April/July): 445-455.

NYE, J. S., Jr. (1971) Peace in Parts. Boston: Little, Brown.

--- (1968a) "Central American regional integration," p. 377-429 in J. S. Nye, Jr. (ed.) International Regionalism: Readings. Boston: Little, Brown.

--- (1968b) "Patterns and catalysts in regional integration," pp. 333-349 in J. S. Nye, Jr. (ed.) International Regionalism: Readings. Boston: Little, Brown.

PACKENHAM, R. A. (1973a) "Latin American dependency theories: strengths and weaknesses." Paper delivered at American Political Science Association meeting in New Orleans, September 4-8.

--- (1973b) Liberal America and the Third World: Political Development Ideas in Foreign Aid and Social Science. Princeton, N.J.: Princeton Univ. Press.

RAY, D. (1973) "The dependency model of Latin American underdevelopment: three basic fallacies." J. of Interamerican Studies and World Affairs 15 (February): 4-20.

REINTON, P. O. (1972) "International structure and international integration: the case of Latin America," pp. 124-150 in Y. H. Ferguson (ed.) Contemporary Inter-American Relations: A Reader in Theory and Issues. Englewood Cliffs, N.J.: Prentice-Hall.

ROSENAU, J. N. (1973) The Dramas of Politics. Boston: Little, Brown.

RUMMEL, R. J. (1968) "The relationship between national attributes and foreign conflict behavior," pp. 187-214 in J. D. Singer (ed.) Quantitative International Politics: Insights and Evidence. Beverly Hills, Ca.: Sage.

SALMORE, S. A. and B. G. SALMORE (forthcoming) "Regime structure and foreign policy," in M. A. East (ed.) Theoretical Bases for Comparative Foreign Policy Studies. Beverly Hills, Ca.: Sage.

SCHLESINGER, A. M., Jr. (1965) A Thousand Days: John F. Kennedy in the White House. Boston: Houghton Mifflin.

SCHMITTER, P. C. (1970) "A revised theory of regional integration," pp. 836-868 in L. N. Lindberg and S. A. Scheingold (eds.) Regional Integration: Theory and Research. Special issue of International Organization 24 (Autumn).

--- (1969) "Three neo-functional hypotheses about international integration." International Organization 23 (Winter): 161-166.

SULLIVAN, M. P. (1976) International Relations: Theories and Evidence. Englewood Cliffs, N.J.: Prentice-Hall.

SUNKEL, O. (1973a) "The crisis of the nation-state in Latin America: challenge and response," pp. 352-369 in Y. H. Ferguson and W. F. Weiker (eds.) Continuing Issues in International Politics. Pacific Palisades, Ca.: Goodyear.

--- (1973b) "Transnational capitalism and national disintegration in Latin America." Social and Economic Studies (University of the West Indies, Jamaica) 22 (March): 132-176.

WAGNER, R. H. (1970) United States Policy Toward Latin America: A Study in Domestic and International Politics. Stanford, Ca.: Stanford Univ. Press.

WALTZ, K. (1959) Man, the State, and War. New York: Columbia Univ. Press.

Yale H. Ferguson is Associate Professor of Political Science at Rutgers University–Newark, an Associate in the Graduate Program at Rutgers–New Brunswick and a member of the University-wide Latin American Institute. He is editor of Contemporary Inter-American Relations: A Reader in Theory and Issues *and coeditor of* Continuing Issues in International Politics *and* The Web of World Politics: Nonstate Actors in the Global System.

JAMES M. MALLOY
Department of Political Science
261 Mervis Hall
University of Pittsburgh
Pittsburgh, PA 15260

SOCIAL SECURITY POLICY AND THE WORKING CLASS IN TWENTIETH-CENTURY BRAZIL

A crucial feature of political life in twentieth-century Brazil has been the growing role of the state as the central regulator of social, economic, and political life. One aspect of the expansion of the public sector in Brazil, as elsewhere, has been the accumulation by the state of a number of important social and economic functions previously exercised outside the public domain. One important function adopted by the state in Brazil is that of social protection, in the form of an elaborate and complex social insurance system. Presently some form of social protection reaches almost the entire rural population and some 78 percent of the urban population. The main social protection organization—Instituto Nacional da Previdência Social (INPS)—boasts the second largest budget in the nation (in 1975 CR $43 billion in contrast to the federal budget of Cr $113 billion) and a bureaucracy of over 102,700 employees.

The purpose of this article is to analyze the evolution of Brazilian public policy around the question of social protection. Focus will be on the political and administrative development of the social insurance system as played out by the interactions between the state and groups seeking to represent the interests of the clients of the social insurance system.

Journal of Interamerican Studies and World Affairs, Vol. 19 No. 1, February 1977

Until recently there has been a tendency to view social policies in Brazil as radical innovations introduced after 1930 by the Vargas regime in reaction to the socially uncreative governments of the old republic (1889-1930). This paper will show that in the early 1920s sectors of the established elite adopted social insurance programs as a paternalistic means of coping with an emergent working class, and that the Vargas regime in fact built on these earlier experiments. During the first Vargas regime (1930-1945) a large and complex social insurance system was elaborated as part of a general attempt to strengthen the central state structure. Following the precedents of the 1920s, Vargas built a system that fragmented the working class and undercut the ability of workers to mount a coherent class-based challenge to the existing patterns of domination and control. Despite the successful strengthening of the state, the social insurance administrative structure designed by the Vargas regime allowed particularistic groups to entrench themselves in the administrative structure and to use it as a base to bloc innovations and reforms advocated from the 1940s on by an influential cadre of social security technocrats. The issue of social insurance reform became acute during the postwar populist phase of Brazilian politics and reflected the general political crisis that led to the coup of 1964. Since 1964, under the guidance of technocrats, the social insurance system has been reorganized in such a way as to contribute to the overall weakening of the political power of organized labor and to increase significantly the power and control of the central state. Indeed, this policy area clearly reflects the much discussed military-technocratic alliance said to be a defining characteristic of Brazil's present authoritarian regime.

Origins of Social Insurance Policy

Government sponsored social protection programs in Brazil are traceable back to the colonial period. However, prior to the twentieth century such programs were restricted to civil servants and members of the armed forces. It was not until the second decade of this century that government sponsored social protection was extended to employees in the private sector. Moreover, when such protection was extended into the private sector it was based on legal and administrative criteria quite different from those applying to civil servants and the military. Hence, social protection policies in the private and public sectors have evolved along separate paths and today remain quite different from each other. In this paper we will be concerned mainly with protection policies and programs toward employees in the private sector (Sussekind, 1955; Rosa Borges, 1948).

The question of extending social insurance protection into the private sector was only part of the larger issue of coping with the increasing demands of an emerging working class at the end of the nineteenth and the beginning of the twentieth centuries. The "social question" was an increasingly intense focal point of political and social struggle throughout the Old Republic (1889-1930; Simão, 1966; Rodrigues, 1968). The drama was played out in a context that reflected both internal and external factors.

Internally, an important factor was a growing level of labor unrest spurred on by the proliferation of increasingly vocal and militant worker organizations. The early history of the Brazilian labor movement is still a subject of debate, and much further research needs to be done. Most observers tend to agree, however, that while the degree of organization increased steadily in the first two decades of the twentieth century, local organizations tended to be fragile. Moreover, the labor movement was ideologically diverse and unable to mount and sustain either a national labor organization or an effective class-based political party. Nonetheless, strikes and protests increased in both number and effectiveness and became a matter of increasing concern to the guardians of the status quo. Agitation reached its peak in 1917 when a relatively successful general strike was launched. Parallel to labor agitation was growing disaffection among the middle class toward the status quo, and the appearance within the army of a nationalist movement oriented toward a basic overhaul of the system. The possibility of these forces joining together into a serious revolutionary movement constituted a real threat to the old order (Carone, 1972).

The internal struggles in Brazil were also affected by stimuli from the international sphere in an early version of the demonstration effect. Increasingly, Brazilian intellectuals concerned with the social question began to examine European (especially French and German) programs and legislation as well as social security schemes adopted in neighboring countries such as Argentina, Chile, and Uruguay. These external influences were heightened considerably by the World War I and the Versailles peace treaty in which the signatories, including Brazil, committed themselves to a comprehensive effort to cope with the problems of the working class. From these external stimuli, activist intellectuals (mainly from the middle classes) developed three lines of argument: (a) that Brazil was demonstrating its backwardness by not confronting the social problem as the more advanced nations had; (b) as a signatory of the treaty and a member of the International Labor Organization, Brazil had assumed before the world a moral and legal duty to resolve the social question; and (c) a more subtle argument that the problems in Brazil were not yet as serious as those in the more industrial countries and, therefore, through prudent and timely reform Brazil could achieve a more harmonious process of development. The latter concept was to become central to the ideology of the Vargas regime. Brazil, in effect, could take advantage of its backwardness to achieve a new, more felicitous form of progress. There developed in this period a core of middle class intellectual activists aware of, and to some extent identified with, a growing international cadre of "labor relations experts" dedicated to reformist solutions of the social question. The first fruit of this group's efforts was a 1919 law providing compulsory insurance for work-related accidents (Moraes Filho, 1950; Lacerda, 1960).

It seems fairly certain that most labor agitation in this period had minimal ideological content and was oriented mainly to demands for better wages and working conditions. In any event, by 1920 some status quo politicians sought to diffuse the pressure from below and build support for themselves by promising to meet specific worker demands. Most notable was Artur Bernardes, who, in a successful presidential campaign in 1922, actively sought labor support by promising, among other things, the institution of social security protection (Carone, 1972; Fausto, 1976).

Once in office, Bernardes followed a dual policy toward the labor movement. On one hand he instituted a policy of brutal repression aimed mainly at radical organizers; on the other he sought to neutralize the thrust of certain key worker groups by granting concessions. In April 1923 he established a national labor council to advise on matters pertinent to the working class. More concretely on January 24, 1923 the legislature passed the famed "Lei de Eloy Chaves," proposed originally by representative Eloy Chaves of São Paulo. The law provided for the obligatory creation in each railway company of a fund for retirement and survivor's pensions (Caixa de Aposentadoria e Pensões—hereafter referred to as CAP). In 1926 the system of CAPs was extended to dock and ship workers. It is most interesting to note that the Lei de Eloy Chaves was openly based on Argentine legislation and that the owners of the São Paulo Railway Company specifically approached Chaves to present the bill (Ministério do Trabalho Previdência Social, 1973: 18).

Based on an analysis of the secondary literature available for the period, it seems reasonable to argue that by the 1920s organized labor had sufficient power to call attention to its problems—expressed in the concept of the social question—and to create a climate of threat to the status quo such that established political leaders felt compelled to develop programs to cope with labor problems. However, it seems apparent that organized labor did not have sufficient power to define the central issues of the social question in its own terms, nor to initiate and define specific programs like that embodied in the Lei Eloy Chaves.

At this point it would be useful to analyze the Lei Eloy Chaves and the speech Representative Chaves made when he introduced the draft law. The law provided for the creation of a specific CAP for each railroad company in the nation. From the beginning, then, social protection was oriented to specific work based groups, not to broad class-based categories. The administrative structure began by dividing workers horizontally, in a class sense, even while it united them vertically across class lines–all employees regardless of income or job status were included in each CAP. This administrative device of dividing employees horizontally within classes while uniting them vertically across classes remained basic to the social protection system until the creation of INPS in 1966.

The CAPs were designed to give four basic benefits which again remained central to all subsequent schemes: first, medical aid in the form of curative care and the provision of medicines; second, retirement benefits (aposentadoria) for time of service, old age, and invalidity; third, survivor benefits for the dependents of employees (Pensão); and fourth, a cash payment to cover the funeral expenses of employees. Thus, the law was geared to provide basic protection to a family against four basic risks that might interfere with the head of the family's ability to work and earn an income. In addition, the law was the first to establish the principle (central to the Vargas labor legislation) that after ten years an employee could be fired only for grave cause, with the burden of proof on the employer.

Each CAP was to be funded from three sources: each employee would contribute 3 percent of his monthly income, each company would contribute 1 percent of its gross income, and the federal government would contribute a sum collected from the public through taxes on railroad services. This concept was the base of what later would be enshrined in the national constitution as the triple contribution to the social protection system. The funding scheme related directly to the benefit scheme. Each member of the CAP received benefits proportional to his monthly contributions. Thus, there was an internal differentiation in the CAPs based on income, with higher paid employees contributing more and getting more back in benefits from the CAP. This differentiation based on income continues in effect in INPS today.

While these juridical and legal concepts were clearly imported from Europe and other countries, especially Argentina, it is also clear that they built rather directly on the organizing principles of the long existent private mutual aid societies. The major difference from the private mutual societies was the fact that the membership was obligatory and the government contributed to the fund. More important is that from the beginning social protection in Brazil was not based on a concept of a right to social security inherent in one's status as a citizen, but a concept of social insurance in which protection was a contractually achieved right based on contributions over time. Implicit in this concept is the idea that not only did a worker in a CAP have a contractually acquired right to protection from certain risks, but that he also had a duty to help protect and insure his future by giving up part of current earnings. In short, the Lei de Eloy Chaves became the basis of a compulsory state-imposed social insurance system.

Administratively, the CAPs were established as autonomous public entities under the general supervision of the state, but self-regulating in internal affairs. These first CAPs were governed by a Conselho de Administração made up of representatives of the owners of the company and the employees of the company. Hence, they embodied a concept of internal government based on the direct representation of employers and employees as the key interested parties of the CAP. This principle of administrative representation, somewhat modified over the years, remained in effect again until the creation of INPS (Ministério do Trabalho e Previdência Social, 1965).

In presenting the law to the Câmara de Deputados, Representative Chaves made a speech in which he described how and why he came to propose the legislation. In the first instance he presented himself as representing the aspirations of an important groups of servants of the nation, e.g., railroad workers. Specifically he argued that to have sufficient motivation to work effectively a worker must feel secure in his old age and know that his family will be cared for if he dies or is incapacitated.

> Through his efforts and labor he should also be able to see at the end of the hard road a secure and calm retirement. The thorns and anguish of a working life can only be endured if there is hope for a final prize. [Ministério do Trabalho e Previdência Social, 1965: 13]

Although he presented himself as a representative of the aspirations of a group of workers, it is interesting to note that in describing how he drafted the bill he makes no reference to any consultations with workers, union leaders, or any organization of workers. Rather, he pointed first to the influence of Argentine legislation and then identifies three Brazilians who advised and helped him to draft the law. The first two were businessmen connected with the Companhia Paulista de Estradas de Ferro–Sr. Francisco de Monlevade, inspector general of the company, and Sr. Adolpho Pinto, chief of the central office of the company. The third advisor was a close friend and noted jurist, Dr. Prudente de Morais Filho.

It is of more than passing interest to note that Eloy Chaves was secretary of justice in São Paulo during the general strike of 1917. Thus, he had firsthand experience in observing the disruptive power of labor as well as the dangers inherent in the situation if left to continue as it was. It is probably not at all coincidental that the law pertained to one of the best organized groups of workers of the time which controlled a public service critical to the general economic health of the nation, not to mention the coffee economy of the state of São Paulo.

In his speech, Chaves made clear his concern for conflict in the present situation and the need of responsible leaders to develop alternative programs to those who advocated radical change. Indeed, he presented the law as a way to avoid class conflict and promote social harmony in a climate of law and order.

> To the class struggle, which is advised by radicals and by other minds which are disturbed by strange and complicated passions, I confidently oppose the peaceful, orderly and intimate collaboration of all for the common good of the nation. [Ministério do Trabalho e Previdência Social, 1965: 16]

Chaves obviously saw this law as an attempt to dampen social conflict by dealing with one dimension of the social question. However, it also seems clear that while he was responding to the challenge presented by organized labor, at least one group, labor itself, played little or no role in drafting the law. Indeed, the entire tone of the speech conveys the impression of a concerned member of the elite counseling cautious elite sponsored reforms lest the situation get out of control.

> It is our responsibility as witnesses of these extraordinary times to create solutions and heal the wounds and chaos originating from them. We're in new times: the under-privileged classes justly hope for a greater share from life and its comfort. It behooves us to attend to them with a friendly and liberal spirit. [Ministério do Trabalho e Previdência Social, 1965: 16]

In his formal presentation Chaves presented the law as a wise and judicious response to labor agitation and as an act of noblesse oblige. Perhaps his most revealing comments came at the end of his speech, when he told a story. One Saturday after working into the afternoon at one of his factories, he began to drive to his country home. On his way he encountered a young employee and his sister who asked for a ride to their house.

> I immediately said yes, and tranquilly drove across the city as the "chauffeur" of my two humble workers. [Ministério do Trabalho e Previdência Social, 1965: 17]

The imagery of the story is rather clear and reflects a paternalistic and elitist view of social legislation. The workers are young (children), humble, and respectful. He helps them by providing a ride, but they occupy the back seat while he drives the machine. The duty and self-interest of the elite is to direct the social machine to its goal and thereby create tranquility.

It is my view that this elitist and paternalistic attitude toward social reform was reflective not only of Chaves, but also expressed attitudes deeply held by formulators of social protection policies from his time to the present. Moreover, I would argue that, on its inception, social policy was primarily initiated at the elite level and designed to diffuse labor agitation and protect the status quo.

By 1929 the bare outline of a social insurance system had been established. It was a relatively small program which covered only about 140,435 employees in the private sector. Yet it is important to note that by 1929 most of the juridical and administrative concepts relevant to a social insurance system, as well as a paternalistic and elitist attitude toward workers, had been established. Social insurance as a means to deal with the social question had become common coin, and Getúlio Vargas incorporated the concept as defined by Chaves into his campaign platform in 1930.

The Revolution of 1930

The "revolution of 1930," which brought Getúlio Vargas to the presidency of Brazil for a 15 year period, led to a fundamental reorganization of the relationships between state and society in Brazil. Social insurance policy was an important component of this process. As I argued above, however, Vargas and his team did not really define concepts and principles in the area of social security; rather, they systematically implemented a previous set of policy concepts within a broader scheme of reorganizing the relationships between state and society.

The question of Getúlio Vargas' ideology, and whether he had one at all, is and will remain a subject of acrid debate among scholars. In retrospect, however, whatever his ideological orientations or lack thereof, Vargas, the master of state-craft, followed a rather consistent pattern of policies with regard to the role of the state. Again in retrospect, three goals appear to stand out: Vargas struggled mightily to make the state the pivot and regulator of national socioeconomic relations; as part of that strategy he sought to liberate the state from both internal and external pressures and to endow the state with as much autonomy as possible; finally, he instituted a process of modernization of social relationships which, at least after 1937, was based on a policy of industrialization. In a sense, the state became, under Vargas, both a means and an end; he sought to use the state to create a more coherent, modern, and powerful nation which would express its power to the world in the form of a relatively autonomous and powerful state. One can argue that it was a process of adapting the form of the traditional patrimonial state to the substance of the modern era (Faoro, 1975; Schwartzman, 1976).

Central to Vargas' efforts was the adoption of a systematic approach to the organization of economic relations, with the state defining and regulating both the form and content of labor-management relations. The organ charged with bringing about this revolution was the new Ministry of Labor created in 1930 (Carone, 1974; Skidmore, 1970). Many of the intellectuals concerned with the social question in previous years were integrated into the ministry as advisors by the first labor minister, Lindolfo Collor. Whether Vargas did or did not have an ideology, it is clear that over the years functionaries in the labor ministry, as well as others around Vargas, developed a clear corporatist approach to the organization of economic relations in Brazil—a fact more or less ratified by the constitution of the Estado Nôvo (Aguiar Walker, 1968; Schmitter, 1971; Erickson, 1977).

Most students of the period agree that Vargas and his team sought to increase the autonomous regulatory power of the state by co-opting potential pressure groups into a system of officially sanctioned groups divided from each other horizontally, but integrated vertically across class lines in a structure where control flowed from the top down. This system of co-optation and control was aimed particularly at the labor movement in an attempt to (a) neutralize labor as a source of support for opposition groups and (b) depoliticize labor organizations as a source of autonomous articulation of group demands, while (c) enlisting labor as a major prop (albeit passive) of the regime. To these ends there was developed in the Vargas period an elaborate body of legislation regulating labor organizations, labor-management relations, and the general conditions of working life. One component of this elaborate approach was the expansion and development of the social security system. Thus, while social security previously had been a relatively isolated and ad hoc approach to labor agitation, under Vargas it was an integral part of a self-conscious global approach to statecraft and state-society relations.

The modern state has increased its power relative to society through a process of accumulating "functions" previously exercised outside the public domain. One such function has been that of social protection. Under Vargas, the state systematically expanded its role—and hence power and authority in the field of social protection—as well as many other functional areas. Since the 1930s, this functional power and authority has been steadily expanded to the point where social protection policy is a critical area in which the state directly impinges on the daily lives of a vast number of Brazil's citizens. It is important to note that while social security policy was linked to an attempt to control and co-opt labor, it was also a policy emerging out of modern statecraft.

During the 1930s, social insurance protection was expanded on a step-by-step, group-by-group basis until by 1938 almost all of the actively employed and organized urban working class was covered. Extension of coverage was restricted to the organized urban working class and there was no attempt to expand the concept to the unorganized self-employed or to the vast number of rural workers. At first, expansion of coverage was based on creating new CAPs. In 1933, however, a relatively new concept was introduced. Rather than create CAPs in each enterprise, the idea was conceived of organizing protection around national functional categories of workers—i.e., all dock workers, bank workers, commercial workers, industrial workers, and so on. This idea was tied to a general organizational principle, introduced at the time, of forming all labor organizations around a limited number of "professional" categories defined by economic sector. This conception of labor as not being a class, as such, but a series of separate professional groups defined by specific occupations persists until today.

In 1933 a new type of social security institution appeared (most of the old CAPs remained)—called the Instituto de Aposentadoria e Pensões (hereafter IAP)—which organized as its insured population all workers in a specific occupational category. The IAP was obviously an important conceptual and organizational innovation. However, the concept of IAP followed logically from that of the CAP and involved mainly a movement from the more concrete notion of company-based groups to the more abstract notion of "professional" functional category. As the general thrust of the process of modernization involves a movement from more concrete to more abstract modes of social organization, the creation of IAPs can be seen as a part of the general project of modernization initiated by Vargas. But it is important to keep in mind that the social security system remained a highly particularistic system that continued to divide the urban working population into discrete functional units.

Social security protection was granted on a group-by-group basis. The first groups to achieve coverage were those in public services, followed by broad categories such as bank and commercial workers, and finally, in 1938, the broadest and most amorphous category—industrial workers.[1] During the same period, coverage of civil servants was consolidated and reorganized, culminating in the formation in 1938 of an institute for assistance to civil servants, IPASE. The military, in turn, had its own separate system. The pattern of expansion in the private sphere reflected two basic realities. First, it reflected the economic development pattern Brazil had followed in the first part of the twentieth century, i.e., a primary product export-oriented economy. Social protection, then, moved from those in infrastructure activities servicing the export sector, to banking and commerce, and finally to the weakest economic sector industry. The sequence also reflected the power of specific groups arising from their strategic location in the economy and their level of organizational sophistication, with the more dispersed and poorly organized industrial workers receiving protection last.[2]

However, while the sequence of the extension of social security protection reflected the power of specific groups, these groups did not initiate the basic concepts of social protection or define the basic norms of the system. The basic ideas were defined in the 1920s, seized by Vargas as a campaign banner in 1930, and then enshrined in the constitution in 1934. After 1930, the formulation and implementation of specific programs were in the hands of the Ministry of Labor. The concepts, norms, and rules of the game were defined from above. Groups used their power to demand what had already been defined as a right (in the limited contractual sense defined earlier). The state, through the Ministry of Labor, decided when and how to grant the recognized right. The ministry responded to pressure (on occasion rather strong), but again in the form of conceding to specific groups a generally recognized formal obligation. The sequence of protection emerged from direct bargaining between the Ministry of Labor and specific groups, and, when protection was conceded, each group received not only its own institute but also its own specific social security law. Groups, therefore, used their power not only to demand protection, but also to bargain for a better scheme of protection than other groups. The result was a bewildering array of laws and operating norms, and a variety of different patterns of protection (Valerius, 1949). The highly particularistic approach of the government encouraged a group-specific orientation among working groups which divided them, fostered intergroup competition, and undermined any basis of class solidarity.

By the end of the 1930s, Brazil had a complex social security system based on a series of CAPs and IAPs functioning according to a variety of laws and operating procedures. In 1938 there existed 99 CAPs and five IAPs, with an insured population of close to three million persons. Organizationally, these institutions were autonomous public entities operating under the general supervision of the Ministry of Labor. In all cases, the president of the institution was nominated by the president of the Republic. Aside from a president, each institute had some type of colleagial administrative organ formed around equal representation of employer and employee organizations. Thus, in all cases, the syndical structure was directly tied into the social security institutions. This linkage was to prove extremely important. One of the unanticipated consequences of the particular type of social security system adopted by the Vargas regime was the creation of a critical political resource that would grow in importance in the years to come. The CAPS and IAPs constituted a political resource in at least three ways: (1) they controlled large sums of investment funds, the disposition of which could be subjected to political influence; (2) the very ability to control the allocation of a wide range of benefits to a large number of people had great political potentiality; and (3) the institutes and Caixas generated a growing number of jobs which could be doled out on political grounds.

Another important development during this period was the appearance within the social security system of a group of social security specialists. By the early 1940s, these specialists made up an identifiable group of social security technocrats who over the next three decades were to play prominent roles in the evolution of Brazil's social security system both as analysts of the system and as social security administrators and activists. It is no exaggeration to say that this group of technocrats has played a pivotal role in every important change in social security policy in Brazil from the 1940s until the present.

This cadre of social security technocrats was formed mainly among functionaries employed by two of the chief social security institutions of the period. The first group was formed in the Ministry of Labor and was made up of lawyers working on social security matters and actuarial specialists employed by the ministry to oversee the CAPs and the IAPs.

Another, and perhaps more important, group of specialists was formed around administrative employees of the Instituto de Aposentadoria e Pensões dos Industriários (IAPR) established in 1938. The IAPI was the last major institute to be organized and was set up to serve what at that point was the most amorphous and least well organized group of workers. As a result, the organizers of the IAPI did not confront the same type of organized group power as the originators of the other institutes and CAPs. Hence, they were able to plan and staff the IAPI with a minimum of pressure and, in fact, took two years—1936-1938—to plan out the operations of the institute.

The head of the commission which set up IAPI, engineer João Carlos Vital, was determined to establish the institute on firm technical, administrative, and actuarial criteria. To this end numerous studies, including an industrial census and elaborate actuarial projections, were made. Finally, the staff of the institute was chosen by a strictly enforced nationwide test designed to recruit a highly qualified elite of young administrators (Vital, 1939). From the beginning, IAPI was staffed by a cohesive young group of professionals with a highly developed sense of group identity as being more professional and technical than the staffs of the other institutes.[3] Aside from their technical approach to the administration of IAPI, the group produced a large number of "scholar" specialists who wrote extensively on general problems of social insurance in Brazil. In addition, they kept up with the major international trends in social security and became an important means by which international thought and practice were transmitted to the Brazilian context; and, by publishing in international journals, they made the international community aware of developments in Brazil. In short, they formed a cadre of scholar-administrators who projected themselves into an international arena of status and prestige formed by groups of specialists in other nations, all of whom communicated with each other through international journals and organizations such as the ILO. Given their technical orientation, it is not surprising that this group used international programs and criteria to analyze critically social insurance policy in Brazil and developed plans and programs to make Brazil a source of internationally recognized innovation in social insurance policy.

The Question of Reform

The period 1940-1945 was a period of turmoil internationally and one of internal challenge and conflict in Brazil. As in 1914-1918, a world war again produced a major drive for reformist social policies in general and change in social security policy in particular. In social security policy, major events were the publication in 1941 of the Beveridge plan for social security reform in Great Britain and the Chapultepec conference in 1945 on social problems in the postwar world. Both had significant impact in Latin America, including Brazil. Throughout the continent, social security specialists began to propose extensive programs of reform based on the Beveridge report and the Chaultepec conference. In Brazil, as elsewhere, these programs, while varying considerably, began to focus on three central reformist goals: universalization of coverage, uniformization of benefits, and administrative unification of social insurance systems (Rosenberg and Malloy, 1976).

In Brazil, important internal processes were also at work. In 1941 the Vargas regime moved to systematize and coordinate the system of labor relations built during the previous decade. The major product of this consolidating process was the consolidação dos leis do trabalho, CLT, in 1943. At the same time Vargas sought to consolidate a critical pillar of his labor policies, the social insurance system, by empowering a commission of the Labor Ministry, headed by João Carlos Vital, to come up with appropriate plans for reorganization of the system. Vital incorporated into his commission a number of social security technocrats, particularly from the Ministry of Labor. The commission came up with a plan for a total overhaul of the system based on the principles of universalization, uniformization, and administrative unification. The plan which provided for the creation of a single institution (Instituto Brasileiro de Servico Social, ISSB) was actually decried into law in 1945 (Comissão Organizadora, 1945).

The promulgation of the plan ISSB set off an internal struggle over social insurance in Brazil which was not really resolved effectively until 1966. The first attempts at reform of Previdência Social appear to reflect an important pattern of public policy formulation in contemporary Brazil. ISSB represented a technically formulated program in which the technocratic goals and values of a cadre of specialists converged with and reinforced the political goals of centralization and control of Vargas. As such, the plan flowed out of the tendency embodied in the first Vargas period (but traceable back to the empire) toward centralization of power and the administrative dominance of the state over organized social groups.

Yet Vargas and the technocrats were unable to enforce the program. This fact reflected structural aspects of the system created by Vargas and the political context of the 1944-1945 period. The structure of state-labor relations, built by the Vargas regime, carried within it fundamental contradictions which came to the fore in the new political context of the postwar world. These contradictions–most important in the area of social insurance policy–were an underlying feature of the political crisis of the 1960s which culminated in the "Revolution" of 1964.

Prior to 1945 Vargas did not follow a politics of mobilization but rather a policy of the selective incorporation of groups into a centrally controlled structure of vertical organizations flowing like pillars from the state center down to the working class. In the area of social insurance policy (one of the key dimensions of the overall system), the result was a series of theoretically autonomous public agencies administering a multiplicity of different social insurance schemes (CAPs and IAPs) providing different benefits and services to their members, with some groups receiving protection superior to that of others (Malloy, 1977). Hence, the system built within it a number of groups with a vested interest in blocking any reforms that challenged their superior schemes (Fundação Getúlio Vargas, 1950).

In addition, the administrative structure of all the institutes provided for the direct participation of officially sanctioned unions (both employer and employee) in administering the insurance funds. Through this mechanism labor leaders were able to penetrate the funds and convert them into an important source of political power within the Vargas framework. Not surprisingly, the CAPs and IAPs became an important political resource and, therefore, a focal point of competition for control. Thus, union leaders and politicians created by the Vargas system itself also developed a vested interest in maintaining a multiple fund system in which they had guaranteed access to such an important means to build clientele groups and thereby increase their power and influence.

Resistance to the reform Previdência Social came from three main sources: first, specific worker groups (especially bank workers, railway workers, and public service workers) who had superior benefits and services; second, the growing number of employees of the funds (by the 1960s the institutes employed over 95,000 civil servants) who feared for their jobs; and third, labor leaders and politicians who sought to protect their base of power. As is well known, the political context began to change dramatically in 1944-1945 (Skidmore, 1970). Feeling himself threatened by forces outside his coalition, Vargas began to shift to a politics of mobilization and to adopt a more populist political style (Weffort, 1973). He thus became more dependent on organized labor as well as the ability of worker groups and labor leaders to resist unwanted policy initiatives such as social insurance reform. While still a part of the original Vargas coalition, key segments of organized labor were beginning to develop the ability to act as a more autonomous political force. As a result, there began to develop within the Vargas "political family" itself a conflict between groups such as the social security technocrats, who represented the original centralizing technical-administrative model of the regime, and certain union groups who began to represent a more decentralized and at least potentially participationist model. This conflict was to become increasingly acute in subsequent years, particularly in the intensely "populist" period of the late 1950s and early 1960s (Erickson, 1977).

After the fall of Vargas, the battle over social security reform shifted for the first time to the legislative arena. The first salvo in the new battle was fired in 1947 when federal deputy Aluizio Alves, with the aid of a cadre of social security technocrats, introduced a projecto de lei Orgânica da Previdência Social (draft social insurance bill; Alves, 1953). The first phase of the struggle centered around the projecto and lasted for almost 13 years.

The struggle during this period reflected the original divisions that developed over the plan ISSB. The major group pushing for the lei orgânica were the now even more cohesive social security technocrats who sought to mobilize support among some of the political leaders of the Brazilian labor party (Partido Trabalhista Brasileiro, PTB) as well as among the leaders of those unions which represented workers, such as industrial workers, who had less attractive schemes of benefits and services. An important power base of the technocrats during this period was the newly founded Fundação Getúlio Vargas, led by such old line Vargas technocrats as João Carlos Vital, originator of the IAPI and author of plan ISSB, and Alim Pedro, a former president of IAPI. It is interesting to note that the social security technocrats acted as advisors to every one of the five versions of the original draft law and published a number of detailed studies, large parts of which were incorporated into subsequent projects.[4] Arrayed against reform were the privileged groups, social security bureaucrats, and those union leaders and politicians identified with these groups.

More fundamentally, the struggle for social security reform can be seen as part of the general struggle between the more antipolitical administrative technocratic wing of the original Vargas coalition and the politicized and increasingly autonomous populist labor wing of the coalition. Thus, whatever groups were arrayed against Varguismo, as such, the period was also dominated by a profound split between two different and increasingly antagonistic dimensions of Varguismo itself. Ironically, reforms which apparently would have led to a more equitable system of social insurance were being blocked primarily by those groups who, in principle at least, spoke in the name of the working class. One reason, of course, was the fact that many of the old line union leaders (pelegos) were primarily interested in protecting their personal power bases. However, it seems fair to argue that many resisted because they saw reform as a threat to their control over the institutes and, thereby, their ability to act as a more autonomous political force in the general political struggle of the period. The institute, as an important source of political power, was a central issue in the struggle over social insurance reform.

By 1960 a compromise on the issue of reform had been reached within the disparate elements of the Vargas coalition, and, finally, a new lei Orgânica da Previdência Social was passed. Again, the social security technocrats played a large role in writing the law and in advising the senators and deputies who guided the bill through the legislature. However, the new law and the compromise behind it reflected clearly the real nature of the political stakes at issue. Of the original goals of universalization, uniformization, and unification, only one was achieved. In principle the new law provided for uniform benefits for all the insured (Cardoso de Oliveira, 1961). Although coverage was expanded to the urban self-employed, domestics and the entire rural sector continued to be excluded from any coverage. Most importantly, the law did not provide for administrative unification (the real issue as far as political power was concerned), and the system remained based on a multiplicity of autonomous institutes.[5] In fact, the law provided some administrative changes that actually increased in power and control of the union leaders over the institutes (Erickson, 1977).

Between 1960 and 1964 the Previdência Social system became an even more intense focal point of political struggle, and the institutes even more highly politicized than before. Beyond this there was another and perhaps more critical development. Previously, the institutes had been controlled mainly by old line pelegos. In the 1960s, under the leadership of Minister of Labor Almino Afonso, the institutes began to come under the control of more radical nationalist labor leaders and became a base of power for those in the populist coalition of Goulart, who were pushing for radical reforms of the entire national system (Erickson, 1977). Thus, aside from the conflict between the supporters of the centralizing administrative model and those of the decentralizing autonomous model, the Previdência Social system had become a point of struggle between those who proposed major political and economic reforms and those who resisted such radical transformations of the overall socioeconomic system.

The Dominance of the Administrative Technocratic Model

From the point of view of the relations between the state and the working class, the Revolution of 1964 was clearly a return to the early Vargas tradition of the dominance of the state. Moreover, reacting to the intense mobilization of the populist period, the new military regime clearly sought to depoliticize social policy questions, demobilize labor, and, in effect, eliminate organized labor as a significant political force in the formulation of public policy. If Vargas in the early period followed a politics of the "controlled inclusion" of labor into a state dominant coalition, the new regime has followed a politics of the "controlled exclusion" of labor from a new state dominant coalition. Again, social insurance policy has been an integral part of a generalized attempt to restructure the relations between the state and the working class so as to assure the dominance of the principle of "antipolitical" administrative-technocratic control.

Immediately after the revolution, an "apolitical" social security technocrat, Arnaldo Sussekind, was appointed labor minister, and under his leadership all of the institutes were intervened and social security technocrats replaced the existing "political" offices of the institutes. Shortly thereafter a number of commissions were formed to propose fundamental reform of social insurance. All of these commissions were staffed and dominated by members of the cadre of social security technocrats formed in the 1930s and 1940s. Most prominent among these, and in terms of numbers preponderant, were members of the original team of scholar-technocrats developed in IAPI.

The most politically important reform was the administrative unification in 1966 of the former institutes into a single national Instituto de Previdência Social (INPS). The new instituto was organized so as to eliminate effectively any real influence of labor leaders or representatives of other interest groups on its affairs and to assure the dominance of an administrative technocratic elite appointed by the executive. The planning of social insurance policy increasingly has been integrated into the regime's general process of socioeconomic planning. Thus, in a sense, social insurance has been "depoliticized" and converted into a question of administration. More importantly, the new system has eliminated an important source of organized labor's political power and contributed to the general weakening of organized labor as an autonomous political force.

Since 1966 the social insurance system has been dominated administratively by the original cadre of social security technocrats, most particularly by technocrats drawn from IAPI.[6] Under the tutelage of these technocrats, numerous other reforms have been implemented. Coverage has been extended to rural workers,[7] domestics, and other groups, so that by the 1980s some form of coverage will reach virtually all of the population. In addition, insurance of work accidents, formerly in private hands, is now controlled by INPS. In 1974 a new ministry of Previdência e Assistência Social was formed to oversee the entire system and to develop new programs, benefits, and services. Thus, most of the original reformist goals defined in the 1940s have been achieved.

Since 1964 the battle which first developed in the 1940s around the question of social insurance reform between the centralizing technical administrative model and the decentralizing political participationist model has clearly been resolved in favor of the former. Again, this model–in the area of social insurance policy at least–emerged from a situation in which a technically formulated program, reflecting the goals and values of a cadre of specialists, converged with and reinforced the political goals of centralization and control of the military regime established in 1964.

NOTES

1. The chronological order was: railways, 1923; maritime and docks, 1926; public service, 1931; mines, 1932; banks, 1934; commerce, 1934; industrial, 1938.

2. This pattern in Brazil followed closely the general pattern of expansion in other Latin American countries that adopted programs prior to the 1940s (Mesa-Lago, 1977).

3. This interpretation is based on interviews conducted in Brazil during 1974-1975 with João Carlos Vital, ex-members of the IAPI staff, and other social security experts.

4. The most important study was entitled *Previdência Social no Brasil e no Estrangeiro,* published by the Fundação Getúilo Vargas (1950).

5. By this point there had been some consolidation of the smaller CAPs, and the system was organized around six major autonomous institutes.

6. Among the many ex-IAPI administrators who have played an important role since 1964 are Francisco Luiz Torres de Oliveira, José Dias Correa Sobrinho, and Celso Barroso Leite.

7. Rural workers have a different benefit scheme, which is administered by a separate Fund for the Assistance of Rural Workers (FUNRURAL).

REFERENCES

AGUIAR WALKER, N. (1968) "Corporativismo y clase Trabajadora." Desarrollo Económico 8 (1968): 313-348.

ALVES, A. (1953) Lei Orgânica Da Previdência Social. Rio de Janeiro: Camâra Dos Deputados.

CARDOSO DE OLIVEIRA, M. (1961) Previdência Social Brasileira e a sua Nova Lei Orgânica. Rio de Janeiro: Record.

CARONE, E. (1974) A República Nova: 1930-1937. São Paulo: Difusão Européia do Livro.

--- (1972) A República Velha. São Paulo: Difusão Européia do Livro.

Comissao Organizadora (1945) Relatória Final da Comissão Organizadora do ISSB. Rio de Janeiro.

ERICKSON, K. P. (1977) The Brazilian Corporative State and Working Class Politics. Berkeley: Univ. of California Press.

FAORO, R. (1975) Os Donos Do Poder. São Paulo: Universidade de São Paulo.

FAUSTO, B. (1976) Trabalho Urbano e Conflito Social. São Paulo: DIFEL.

Fundação Getúlio Vargas (1950) Previdência Social no Brasil e no Estrangeiro. Rio de Janeiro: Fundação Getúlio Vargas.

LACERDA, M. (1960) Evolução Legislativa do Direito Social Brasileiro. Rio de Janeiro: Ministério do Trabalho.

MALLOY, J. (1977) "Social insurance policy in Brazil: a study in the politics of inequality." Inter-American Economic Affairs (Winter).

MESA-LAGO, C. (1977) Social Security in Latin America: Pressure Groups, Stratification and Inequality. Pittsburgh: Univ. of Pittsburgh Press.

Ministério do Trabalho e Previdência Social (1973) Assistência Médica na Previdência Social. Rio de Janeiro.

--- (1965) Eloy Chaves: Precursor da Previdência Social no Brasil. Rio de Janeiro.

MORAES FILHO, E. (1950) O Problema do Sindicato Unico no Brasil. Rio de Janeiro.

RODRIGUES, J. A. (1968) Sindicato e Desenvolvimento no Brasil. São Paulo: Difusão Européia do Livro.

ROSA BORGES, D. (1948) Seguro Social no Brasil. Rio de Janeiro: José Olympio.

ROSENBERG, M. and J. MALLOY (1976) "Politics, participation, and social security in Latin America." Paper presented to The Seminar on Faces of Participation in Latin America, University of Texas at San Antonio, November 12-13, 1976.

SCHMITTER, P. (1971) Interest Conflict and Political Change in Brazil. Stanford, Calif.: Stanford Univ. Press.

SCHWARTZMAN, S. (1976) São Paulo e O Estado Nacional. São Paulo: DIFEL.

SIMAO, A. (1966) Sindicato e Estado. São Paulo: Universidade de São Paulo.

SKIDMORE, T. (1970) Politics in Brazil, 1930-1964: An Experiment in Democracy. New York: Oxford Univ. Press.

SUSSEKIND, A. (1955) Previdência Social Brasileira. Rio de Janeiro: Freitas Bastos.

VALERIUS, V. (1949) Legislação Brasileira de Previdência Social. Rio de Janeiro: Aurora.

VITAL, J. (1939) A Creação e a Organização do Instituto de Aposentadoria e Pensões dos Industriários. Rio de Janeiro.

WEFFORT, F. (1973) "Origens Do Sindicalismo Populista no Brasil." ESTUDOS CEBRAP 4 (1973): 65-107.

James M. Malloy is Professor of Political Science at the University of Pittsburgh, author of Bolivia: The Uncompleted Revolution, *and editor of and contributor to* Authoritarianism and Corporatism in Latin America. *His extensive past research has focused on Bolivia and Peru and more recently has shifted to Brazil, with an emphasis on social security within public policy.*

LAWRENCE J. LeBLANC
Department of Political Science
Marquette University
526 North 14th Street
Milwaukee, WI 53233

ECONOMIC, SOCIAL, AND CULTURAL RIGHTS AND THE INTERAMERICAN SYSTEM

The human rights proclaimed and affirmed in the various international declarations, conventions, and covenants adopted since World War II fall into two broad categories: civil and political; and economic, social, and cultural. The former includes the traditional rights of man, such as the rights to life and liberty; the latter includes such rights as the right to work, to social security, and to the preservation of one's health and well-being.

International agreement in principle on most civil and political rights as human rights has been relatively easy to achieve; disagreement has occurred—and is likely to continue to occur—primarily over their precise meaning. Virtually everyone endorses, for example, a right to life; not everyone agrees, however, that capital punishment or abortion must therefore be prohibited by law. In the case of economic, social, and cultural rights, on the other hand, there has been—and will likely continue to be—substantial disagreement in principle. Here,

AUTHOR'S NOTE: The author wishes to thank the Committee on Research of Marquette University for research support.

Journal of Interamerican Studies and World Affairs, Vol. 19 No. 1, February 1977

questions are raised concerning the status, or authenticity, of the rights themselves. Are such rights as the right to work or to the preservation of one's health and well-being human rights at all? Or are they standards which governments should strive to meet for the benefit of their citizens? Is governmental action toward the realization of the rights or standards imperative or merely desirable?

Diverse points of view have been expressed on these issues whenever economic, social, and cultural rights have been the subject of discussion in the United Nations, the Council of Europe, and the Organization of American States (OAS). Their resolution, or partial resolution, in the United Nations and the Council of Europe has been well explored in the literature (Robertson, 1963, 1972; Eide and Schou, 1968; Van Dyke, 1970). The purpose of this essay is to explore their resolution in the OAS.

The OAS is not an organization known for modesty when it comes to adopting statements on economic and social matters: some deal directly with human rights *as such*, examples being the American Declaration of the Rights and Duties of Man (1948) and the American Convention on Human Rights (1969); others proclaim objectives of governmental policy which, if pursued vigorously, would lead to the creation of conditions making possible the realization of the rights. Examples here include the Charter of Punta del Este–the Alliance for Progress–(1961); the Protocol of Buenos Aires–revisions of the OAS Charter–(1967); and the Declaration of the Presidents of America (1967). We are concerned almost exclusively with the instruments which deal with human rights as such–the declaration and the convention; it was in drafting these instruments that the issues identified above were raised and extensively debated. Specifically, we are to examine the rationale for the adoption of provisions on economic, social, and cultural rights in these instruments, the bases for agreement and disagreement, the various formulas put forth to resolve them, and the probable or possible implications of the compromises reached.

The American Declaration of The Rights and Duties of Man

The American Declaration of the Rights and Duties of Man went through various drafting stages before it was adopted in its present form at the Ninth International Conference of American States in 1948. The first two drafts of the declaration were prepared by the Inter-American Juridical Committee (IAJC), which had been charged with the task by resolution of the Inter-American Conference on Problems of War and Peace held in Mexico in 1945. The final product, however, scarcely resembles what the IAJC had proposed, either in the field of civil and political rights or in the field of economic, social, and cultural rights.

In drafting the declaration, the IAJC advanced the view that detailed articles on economic, social, and cultural rights should be included in it. The committee (IAJC, 1945: 20) cited documents of various public and private international organizations as reflecting a trend toward proclaiming "not only the traditional political rights already recognized in the national constitutions of the great majority of states, but the newer economic and social rights of a positive character which [had] come to be recognized . . . as a necessary inference from the conception of the democratic state as a cooperative commonwealth seeking the general welfare of all its members." According to the IAJC (1945: 21), the "theory underlying the newer body of economic and social rights" was the "broad principle of distributive justice." The committee noted:

> A generation or more ago states had but a limited understanding of the obligation of the community to promote the welfare of its individual citizens. The rights of the individual were rights against the interference of the state, not rights to the active assistance of the state. But within more recent years, it has come to be understood that the individual can not always by his own efforts attain the standards of living adequate to the development of his human personality, [and the] relation between spiritual development and

> standards of material welfare has come to be more generally recognized. . . . Thus the fundamental rights of the individual may be regarded as growing with the growth of civilization, taking on new forms with the new ideals of social justice. [IAJC, 1945: 21-22]

The committee recognized a difference between the "newer body" of rights and the more traditional civil and political rights. It could see no "substantial obstacles" to putting into effect civil political rights, since they were generally recognized in constitutions and need not "call for any effort on the part of the state which is not already within its reach" (IAJC, 1945: 57). Respect for civil and political rights could be achieved largely by noninterference of a state in the normal activities of its people, except where interference might be necessary to protect the rights of one individual against another. In contrast, respect for economic and social rights would call for the active assistance "of the state bringing its material resources to the aid of those . . . unable to enjoy their rights by their own unaided efforts" (IAJC, 1945: 57). Consequently, the IAJC did not expect that the "objectives proclaimed by a declaration of rights and duties [could] be attained by the mere passage of social legislation of the most advanced character" (IAJC, 1945: 57). Time would be required in all cases before the "ideal of social justice" would be reached. International assistance for those states unable to "raise the social conditions of their people up to the level contemplated" was to be expected (IAJC, 1945: 57).

Despite the difference between the two kinds of rights, and the difficulties involved in implementing the economic, social, and cultural rights in particular, the IAJC was contending that all individuals should be able to make claims against the state with regard to such matters as work and social security. The conception of the democratic state as a cooperative commonwealth seeking the general welfare of all its members implied the elevation of matters which traditionally had not been considered rights to the status of human rights. This attitude was reflected in a number of articles which the IAJC proposed for adoption. Consider, for example, a portion of the first draft of the article on the Right of Life: "Every person has the right to life. . . . It includes the right to sustenance and support in the case of those unable to support themselves by their own efforts; and it implies a duty of the state to see to it that such support is made available" (IAJC, 1945, Article I: 8). Consider, further, a portion of the article on the Right to Work: "Every person has the right to work as a means of supporting himself and contributing to the support of his family. . . . The state has a duty to assist the individual in the exercise of his right to work when his own efforts are not adequate to secure employment; it must make every effort to promote stability of employment and to insure proper conditions of labor, and it must fix minimum standards of just compensation" (IAJC, 1945, Article XIV: 9).

The IAJC's views were not, as we shall see, wholeheartedly shared by the delegates who attended the Ninth International Conference of American States in 1948. In more recent years, however, similar stands have been taken by prominent international and national leaders. One of the most liberal positions on the issue was taken by Pope John XXIII. In his encyclical *Pacem in Terris* he stated:

> Man has the right to life. He has the right to bodily integrity and to the means necessary for the proper development of life, particularly food, clothing, shelter, medical care, rest, and, finally, the necessary social services. In consequence, he has the right to be looked after in the event of ill-health; disability stemming from his work; widowhood; old-age; enforced unemployment; or whenever through no fault of his own he is deprived of the means of livelihood.

Statesmen, particularly those from socialist and some third world states, take similar stands. In fact, some are inclined to place more emphasis on the economic, social, and cultural rights than on the historic civil and political rights. Numerous politicians in individual states also frequently endorse one or another of the controversial rights. On the American scene, for example, Senator Edward Kennedy speaks of a right of all Americans to an adequate standard of health care in proposing health insurance legislation in the United States Congress.

In brief, then, the Juridical Committee's rationale for the inclusion of provisions on economic, social, and cultural rights in the declaration was in a sense prophetic. The rationale has come to enjoy considerable support among international and national leaders. Still, there is opposition. Many deplore any effort to treat the newer body of rights and the historic natural rights as "equally authentic," arguing in many cases that a human right *"is by definition a universal moral right,* something which no one may be deprived without a grave affront to justice; something which is owing to every human being simply because he is human" (Cranston, 1962, 1973). Consequently, the alleged economic, social, and cultural rights cannot be considered human rights in the same sense in which the historic natural rights—such as the rights to life and liberty—are rights, mainly because the differences in economic development among states precludes securing them through legislative action everywhere for everyone.

The different points of view are not without practical consequence domestically or internationally. In the United Nations, for example, they led to the adoption of two separate international covenants on human rights by the General Assembly in 1966, one of which deals exclusively with the economic, social, and cultural rights; the Council of Europe, where the disagreements were less intense, also adopted a separate instrument, the European Social Charter; the American states, as we shall see, have yet to take a clear stand. Moreover, the disagreement is likely to continue for a long time to come. What criterion or criteria are to be used in determining what is a human right? Are human rights only those which are the historic natural rights? If so, the economic, social, and cultural rights should properly be regarded as standards which governments should strive to meet but are not necessarily obligated to do so. Are human rights determined by international consensus—those which "come to be understood" as rights—to use the language of the Inter-American Juridical Committee? Or is some other criterion to be employed (see Bilder, 1969)? Whatever is ultimately adopted, it is clear that for the economic, social, and cultural rights to be considered human rights there must be a corresponding duty or obligation on the part of the state to see to it that they are respected. Those who champion these rights, as the IAJC did when it drafted the American Declaration, assert a duty of the state with regard to them.

When the Declaration came up for adoption at the Ninth International Conference of American States in 1948, however, the delegates were substantially less enthusiastic, and their reserve was reflected in the ways in which they altered various articles proposed by the Juridical Committee. The alterations revealed in fact the different points of view which jurists, as opposed to statesmen, could bring to bear on the same subject matter. The jurists were influenced by the principle of social justice; the statesmen were influenced by political considerations. Several examples should illustrate the point.

Article 14 of the declaration (the Right to Work) proclaims in part that "Every person has the right to work . . . insofar as existing conditions of employment permit." There is no indication that governmental action aimed at the creation of conditions making possible full employment is desirable, let alone imperative. In fact, to the contrary, another article of the declaration, Article 37, provides in part that "It is the duty of every person to work, as far as his capacity and possibilities permit, in order to obtain the means of livelihood or to benefit his community."

The IAJC had not proposed for inclusion in the declaration an article which dealt expressly with a right to the preservation of one's health and well-being. Instead it had dealt indirectly with this matter in its article on the Right to Social Security (IAJC, 1945, Article XVI: 10). The statesmen who adopted the declaration, in contrast, inserted an article which deals exclusively with the right to an adequate standard of health care, but they failed to take an unequivocal stand. Article 11 of the declaration reads:

> Every person has the right to the preservation of his health through sanitary and social measures relating to food, clothing, housing and medical care, to the extent permitted by public and community resources.

The last clause seriously qualifies the alleged right. Nonetheless, the United States inserted for the record a statement to the effect that Article 11 should "not be interpreted as implying any preference as between private and public control over health and sanitation facilities" (U.S. Department of State, 1948: 81). This interpretation raises the question whether a person can claim a right to the preservation of his health and well-being if the health and sanitation facilities are in private hands. The statement typifies the United States' pronouncements on such matters.

An additional, and very fundamental, alteration of the IAJC's draft made by the statesmen who adopted the declaration deserves mention: they adopted a separate chapter which contains ten articles on the Duties of Man, and at the same time they deleted every reference to the duties of states which were given more emphasis by the Juridical Committee. The committee had made references to the duties of man in some of its articles in order to emphasize that rights and duties are correlative. Nonetheless, both drafts of the declaration prepared by the IAJC were much more liberal in the proclamation of the duties of states (IAJC, 1945: 1-11; 1948: 2-10). However, these proclamations were deleted before the declaration was adopted: ten articles on the duties of man were adopted instead—e.g., the "duty of every person to aid, support, educate and protect his minor children" (Article XXX); the "duty of every person to acquire at least an elementary education" (Article XXXI); the "duty of every person to cooperate with the state and the community with respect to social security and welfare" (Article XXXV); and the "duty of every person to work" (Article XXVII). In short, the statesmen who adopted the declaration placed the burden of the enjoyment of the economic, social, and cultural rights proclaimed in it on the *individual*; precisely the reverse of what the Juridical Committee proposed.

Nor can we look to two other related instruments, also adopted in 1948, for relief–the OAS Charter and the Inter-American Charter of Social Guarantees. The original charter contained three separate chapters on economic, social, and cultural standards. Article 29 (a), for example, provided in part that "All human beings . . . have the right to attain material well-being and spiritual growth under circumstances of liberty, dignity, equality of opportunity, and economic security." This provision, however, was "understood as being 'without prejudice to the provisions of the laws of each country relative to the exercise of specific professions or activities or any other type of work' " (U.S. Department of State, 1948: 39). With regard to the alleged right to work in Article 29 (b), it was "likewise agreed for insertion in the record" that the provision did "not imply that the state is obligated 'to provide work to all but rather that it should attempt to promote adequate economic conditions in order that all persons may have work' " (U.S. Department of State, 1948: 39). The relevant chapters of the original charter were vastly expanded by the Protocol of Buenos Aires which is now in effect. In most cases, however, the member states have "pledged themselves" to cooperate to achieve certain basic *objectives*–"so far as their resources may permit and their laws may provide" (Ball, 1969: 538).

Nor can we look for unequivocal statements on the matter in the Inter-American Charter of Social Guarantees. This charter on the rights of workers is staggering in its detail (it contains 39 substantive articles), but it fails to take a clear stand on what is expected of the state in the realization of the rights it purports to proclaim. Moreover, its adoption was not supported unanimously by the American states. Predictably, the United States opposed the project on the charter; it then voted against its adoption in part because it considered that "detailed questions regarding such matters as working conditions, social insurance, vacations for workers, etc.," should be dealt with through "collective bargaining between employers and employees" (U.S. Department of State, 1948: 72).

However desirable the adoption of legislation aimed at the realization of the rights proclaimed in the Charter of Social Guarantees might be, it has not come to enjoy the prestige which the American Declaration now enjoys. The declaration, though lacking contractually binding force, has come to be the "working agreement" of the OAS in the field of human rights (Schreiber, 1970). Particularly since the creation of the Inter-American Commission on Human Rights (IACHR) in 1959, the declaration has almost acquired the status of a "sacred" document–in the field of civil and political rights. In fact, it would be no exaggeration to say that it is because of the painstaking, yet prudent, efforts of this commission (with the support of a small number of American states) to promote and protect the rights proclaimed in the declaration that it has come to enjoy its present status. The commission rarely refers to the duties proclaimed in the declaration, though it recognizes legitimate expectations of states, and the declaration has for all practical purposes developed into the "American Declaration of Human Rights."

There appear to be two main reasons why the Juridical Committee's draft of the declaration was drastically altered at the Ninth International Conference of American States in 1948. The first is that the attitude of the American states on human rights was different at the Ninth International Conference in 1948 from what it had been at the Conference on the Problems of War and Peace in 1945. Due principally to the nature of the times when they met in 1945, the American states adopted sweeping resolutions on what was to be done about human rights in the future. The resolution which directed the IAJC to draft the declaration, for example, stipulated that it was ultimately to be considered for adoption as a convention. However, while some consideration was given to adopting the declaration as a treaty or as an annex to the OAS Charter at the Ninth International Conference of American States in 1948, it was decided to adopt it as a simple resolution of the conference instead (1948: 4-6). The principle of nonintervention in the internal affairs of states was the overriding consideration.

The second reason why the Juridical Committee's draft of the declaration was altered—and this one relates specifically to the articles on economic, social, and cultural rights—was essentially ideological. As we have seen, there was no clear agreement among the American states on whether the economic, social, and cultural rights were human rights at all—whether the civil and political and the economic, social, and cultural rights should be considered equally authentic, as the IAJC had reasoned. It is clear that the U.S. delegation did not share this view. The stripping of the declaration of all references to the duties of states, which the enjoyment of the economic, social, and cultural rights necessarily entails, suggests that the United States was not alone. As noted earlier, the declaration placed the burden of the enjoyment of the economic, social, and cultural rights proclaimed in it on the *individual,* not on the state.

The American Convention on Human Rights

The American Convention on Human Rights was hammered into shape and adopted by the delegates who attended the

Inter-American Specialized Conference on Human Rights in San José, Costa Rica, in November 1969. Known as the Pact of San José, the convention has since been ratified by the governments of Costa Rica and Columbia. Prospects for its entry into force in the near future are not good, since ratification by 11 member states of the OAS is required. Nevertheless, the convention might well be used by the present Inter-American Commission on Human Rights as a basis upon which to build a *customary* interamerican human rights law. In fact, there are signs that the commission has this in mind. In the report it prepared on its recent mission to Chile to investigate alleged violations of human rights by the junta which overthrew the Allende regime, the commission cited Article 27 of the convention (Suspension of Guarantees) in reaching its judgment. The Allende government had not ratified the convention; the junta was therefore not legally bound by its provisions. Nevertheless, the commission disputed the junta's claim that the situation in Chile resembled a "state of war," therefore justifying its suspension of Chilean constitutional guarantees. Moreover, in view of statements made by the junta to the effect that it intended to suspend constitutional guarantees indefinitely, the commission pointed out that Article 27 of the convention expressly states that such guarantees may be suspended only for such time as required by the exigencies of the situation, and that, even if the convention is not in force, Article 27 in particular nevertheless represents the "most accepted doctrine" of the American states on the suspension of constitutional guarantees (IACHR, 1974). The commission could, of course, cite numerous other articles of the convention in the future for the same reason.

The adoption of the convention in 1969 fulfilled the dream of many American statesman who had since World War II advocated the adoption of a convention which would hopefully be ratified by the great majority of OAS member states. It is not necessary here to trace in detail the history of the convention. Suffice it to say that between 1945 and 1969 resolutions were adopted at various interamerican conferences and meetings expressing an interest in the conclusion of a convention, but progress toward this end was difficult for various reasons. The most important reason was a reluctance on the part of several OAS member states to accept international obligations in a field which they considered to be a matter primarily of domestic concern. Still, through the years three draft conventions were prepared, one by the Inter-American Council of Jurists (IACJ) and two others by the governments of Chile and Uruguay. By resolution of the Second Special Inter-American Conference in 1965, the Inter-American Commission on Human Rights was charged with studying the various drafts and preparing a preliminary draft convention for an interamerican specialized conference. The OAS Council adopted the commission's draft in 1968 as the working draft convention for the Inter-American Specialized Conference on Human Rights, held in 1969.

The three draft conventions prepared by the IACJ and the governments of Chile and Uruguay contained detailed articles on civil and political as well as on economic, social, and cultural rights, though in the case of the latter different measures for their implementation were proposed. When the IACHR prepared the working draft of the convention, however, it took a different position, and justified its action on several grounds. In the first place, the commission felt that, "initially, the Convention should contemplate only those rights and freedoms in regard to which the American states are now in a position to extend international protection." Second, it felt that the then proposed amendments to the OAS Charter (the Protocol of Buenos Aires) emphasized the importance of economic, social, and cultural rights, and that it would be sufficient for the convention to contain a provision in which the parties would "acknowledge the need to incorporate gradually into their domestic legislation such measures as are required to fully implement those rights." And third, the commission felt that in light of the experience of the Council of Europe and the United Nations, the economic, social, and cultural rights should be covered by a special system of international protection; it offered to "begin examining this system of protection if the governments of the member states agree that it do so" (IACHR, 1967: 19-20).

In place of the many detailed articles which appeared in the three drafts, the commission recommended only two relatively brief ones. The first called for the "progressive development" of economic, social, and cultural rights, reflecting the commission's concern that those proclaimed in the American Declaration, or in the Protocol of Buenos Aires, be respected. Specifically, it provided in the first paragraph that the parties to the convention "recognize the need to dedicate their utmost efforts to adopting and, as appropriate, guaranteeing, in their domestic laws, the other rights set forth in the American Declaration" *not* affirmed in the convention; and in the second paragraph that they also "declare their intention of including and, as appropriate, maintaining and perfecting, in their domestic legislation," provisions most conducive to economic growth, equitable distribution of income, and other economic and social measures to benefit everyone—all standards affirmed in the Protocol of Buenos Aires (IACHR, 1969: Article 25).

Various objections were raised to this article by several American states even before the Inter-American Specialized Conference on Human Rights convened. A few states, most notably Chile (before Allende came to power), favored reintroducing the detailed list of articles contained in previous drafts. Chile argued that the commission's article warranted "raising considerable objections as to form and substance," for it provided only "indirect" and "insufficient" recognition of the economic, social, and cultural rights. Furthermore, Chile contended that if the American states "desired to adhere to the rule that a single convention should be prepared," the procedure that should be followed was to list the rights and establish "in detail the means for their promotion and supervision" (IASCHR, 1969, Doc. 7: 5-6).

Mexico took a different stand, opposing the reintroduction of the detailed articles and expressing serious doubts whether even the commission's relatively harmless article should be adopted. The Mexican position struck at the heart of the controversy over economic, social, and cultural rights:

> unlike all the other rights referred to in the draft–which are rights that the individual enjoys as a person or as a member of a given social group–it is difficult to establish precisely at a given moment who would be the person directly affected in the event that the rights contained in [the commission's article] were violated. A similar objection could be made as regards the degree of difficulty of determining, in such event, what would be the authority responsible for such a violation. [IASCHR, 1969, Doc. 11: 3]

Various other objections to the commission's article were raised, mostly as to form, not substance. There was some discussion of all points of view at the Inter-American Specialized Conference on Human Rights, since the article, as well as the second one proposed by the commission, were "considered by the delegations from the beginning to be a matter of great controversy" (IASCHR, 1969, Doc. 60: 12). It seems clear from the proceedings, however, that only a handful of delegations was in favor of reintroducing the detailed list of rights. The Uruguayan position on the question might well have reflected the views of most delegations–namely, that the commission's article "incorporated a purely declarative set of conclusions" reached at Buenos Aires, which did not seem "appropriate" for inclusion in the convention, but which nevertheless would be "unwise politically" to oppose (IASCHR, 1969, Doc. 6: 3). The compromise was to delete the first paragraph of the commission's article, the one which referred to the *other* rights proclaimed in the declaration and *not* affirmed in the convention (these could be incorporated at a later date in accordance with Article 31 of the convention), and to revise the second paragraph and adopt it as Article 26.

> The States Parties undertake to adopt measures, both internally and through international cooperation, especially those of an economic and technical nature, with a view to achieving progressively, by legislation or other appropriate means, the full realization of the rights implicit in the economic, social, educational, scientific, and cultural standards set forth in the Charter of the Organization of American States as amended by the Protocol of Buenos Aires.

The second article recommended by the commission called for the submission of periodic reports by parties to the convention on the measures they had taken toward the realization of the economic, social, and cultural rights, and it read as follows (IACHR, 1969: Article 26):

> The States Parties shall report periodically to the Commission on Human Rights on the measures they have taken to achieve the purposes set forth in the preceding article [the commission's draft of Article 26]. The Commission shall make appropriate recommendations, and, when such measures have been widely accepted, shall promote the conclusion of a Special convention, or additional protocols to this Convention, in order to include them in this Convention or in such other instrument as is considered appropriate.

This article reflected the importance which the commission attached to economic, social, and cultural rights, although, as noted above, it did not feel that the American states were ready to accept extensive obligations to promote them at the present time. Had the article been adopted, the commission might have proceeded to promote the conclusion of a special agreement similar to the European Social Charter or the International Covenant on Economic, Social and Cultural Rights. But again various objections were raised.

The United States advocated the deletion of the article on the ground that the reports "would largely duplicate the reports already being prepared by all Members of the OAS for the

Inter-American Economic and Social Council," and that since the IACHR had ready access to those reports, "no real purpose" would be served in duplicating them (IASCHR, 1969, Doc. 10: 25). Argentina's objection to the article was more pointed; it objected on the ground that the article would give the IACHR "the right to make appropriate recommendations to the states," and this "was very evidently something above and beyond its competence and capabilities" (IASCHR, 1969, Doc. 8: 3). Even Chile, the champion of detailed articles on economic, social, and cultural rights in the convention, wondered whether it would not be best to limit the competence of the IACHR to civil and political rights, and have reports on economic, social, and cultural rights submitted to the Inter-American Economic and Social Council (IASCHR, 1969, Doc. 7: 5-6). Apparently the same political reasons which led to the adoption of Article 26 also led to the adoption of Article 42.

> The States Parties shall transmit to the Commission a copy of each of the reports and studies that they submit annually to the Executive Committees of the Inter-American Economic and Social Council and the Inter-American Council for Education, Science and Culture, in their respective fields, so that the Commission may *watch over* the promotion of the rights implicit in the economic, social, educational, scientific, and cultural standards set forth in the Charter of the Organization of American States as amended by the Protocol of Buenos Aires. [emphasis added]

This article does not specifically authorize the commission to make "appropriate recommendations," or to "promote the conclusion" of a special convention or additional protocols to the American Convention, on economic, social, and cultural rights. Those provisions were deliberately deleted from the commission's draft, and suggest that the delegates who attended the Inter-American Specialized Conference on Human Rights wanted to deny the commission any significant role in this field in the future.

It is also noteworthy that both articles of the convention examined here–Article 26 and Article 42–refer to the "rights implicit" in the revised "standards set forth" in the OAS Charter. Choosing this language was at best unfortunate, for it makes the provisions of the revised charter less compelling than they already are, and it opens the way for debate on what are or are not implicit in the standards. In short, ratification of the American Convention on Human Rights would not entail the assumption of any new meaningful obligations in the field of economic, social, and cultural rights. The only obligation would be to transmit copies of reports submitted to other inter-american bodies to the Commission on Human Rights. It is unlikely that the commission could, or would, interpret Article 41 (b) of the convention–which would authorize it to "make recommendations to the governments of the member states"–as authorizing it to make very specific recommendations in this field. A party to the convention could in such an event cite the language of Article 42, which authorizes the commission only to *watch over* the promotion of these rights, which the parties to the convention would *undertake* to promote (Article 26).

Conclusion

International action on human rights is a relatively recent development in international relations. Such action as did occur prior to World War II occurred sporadically and generally in response to specific needs such as the elimination of slavery. The atrocities committed during World War II, however, led many to see a need for providing comprehensive protection to all persons in all nations against all forms of injustice. The task of providing this protection was to be spearheaded by the major international organizations created in the postwar period. Progress in this direction has been slow and uneven. Among the most important reasons why this has been so is the fact that many states have been, and continue to be, reluctant to hold themselves internationally accountable for their human rights policies—policies which they have traditionally considered almost exclusively of domestic concern. Nevertheless, some progress has been made. The large number of resolutions, declarations, covenants, and conventions adopted in the field of human rights have defined in some detail a host of rights and have led to the creation of a number of international agencies, such as commissions and courts, to promote and protect them. A number of governments have been pressured by other governments, by international organizations, and by private groups to bring their human rights policies in line with the internationally proclaimed standards. All indications are that this trend is not likely to be reversed; to the contrary, international efforts to promote and protect human rights are likely to become more important in the future. Thus, the human rights movement has potentially far-reaching implications for human welfare, and its development, problems, and prospects deserve attention.

We have been concerned here with only one aspect of the problem, the economic, social, and cultural rights, and specifically with how the OAS has dealt with them. These rights have provoked considerable controversy in recent years, and, as we have seen, the American states have thus far failed to adopt an unequivocal stand on them so that effective international measures could be taken toward their implementation. Two considerations have made progress in this direction virtually impossible. In the first place, economic, social, and cultural rights have not yet come to be as widely endorsed in principle as rights as have the traditional civil and political rights. To be sure, there are increasing demands for "social justice," and the constitutions and domestic legislation of a large number of American states are quite liberal in affirming rights to work, social security, and so on. How seriously these rights are taken is debatable—more often than not they fall within the realm of so-called "ideal" rights, i.e., rights which *ought* to be respected and would be respected in an ideal system. Progress has been complicated by a second consideration, namely, that in the last analysis the enjoyment of the economic and social rights will depend on the assumption of a duty or obligation on the part of the state to take measures toward their realization. In short, there is a fundamental difference between the two categories of rights. Respect for civil and political rights can be achieved largely by noninterference of a government in the activities of its people. Obviously, they might be violated with impunity, and often are in many American states, but this is a problem which could exist in advanced industrial societies as well as in those which are relatively underdeveloped economically. Respect for economic and social rights, on the other hand, depends on active assistance of the state, on the assumption of a duty or obligation on the part of the state to provide, for example, medical treatment to persons whose lives could be prolonged but who are unable to pay for such treatment.

The two principal interamerican human rights instruments, the American Declaration of the Rights and Duties of Man and the American Convention on Human Rights, fail to establish duties of states in the field of economic and social rights. The declaration as adopted differs substantially from what had been proposed by the Juridical Committee when it drafted it. The jurists were inclined to perceive the democratic state as a cooperative commonwealth, and from this it followed that states were obliged to take measures aimed at social justice. The statesmen who adopted the declaration, however, were not persuaded. Reflecting the more widely held view at the time, they opted for the more conservative formula of emphasizing the duties of individuals in the economic and social field. There was some disagreement over what to do about the controversial rights when the American Convention on Human Rights was drafted (the fact that they attracted some support suggests that attitudes of some states have changed), but they lacked the broad support essential to include them in the convention. Many Latin American states have been unwilling and even unable to commit themselves internationally to observe economic and social rights; the United States, though able in many cases, has also been unwilling.

Whatever progress is made in this field, then, at least for the foreseeable future, is likely to be made on the domestic level. To the extent that the vast body of existing and proposed domestic legislation in the various American states is vigorously applied, the enjoyment of the rights shall eventually obtain. In turn, this may open the way for assuming duties in this field on the international level.

REFERENCES

BALL, M. (1969) The OAS in Transition. Durham, N.C.: Duke Univ. Press.

BILDER, R. (1969) "Rethinking international human rights: some basic questions." Wisconsin Law Rev.: 171-217.

CRANSTON, M. (1973) What are Human Rights? London: The Bodley Head.

--- (1962) Human Rights To-Day. London: Ampersand.

EIDE, A. and A. SCHOU [eds] (1968) International Protection of Human Rights. New York: Wiley Interscience.

Inter-American Commission on Human Rights [IACHR] (1974) Report on the Status of Human Rights in Chile. OEA/Ser. L/VII. 34, Doc. 21.

--- (1969) Annotations on the Draft Inter-American Convention on Protection of Human Rights. OEA/ Ser. L/V/II.19, Doc. 53.

--- (1967) Report on the Work Accomplished During its Fifteenth Session (Special). OEA/ Ser. L/V/II.16, Doc. 20.

Inter-American Juridical Committee ½IAJC] (1948) Project of Declaration of the International Rights and Duties of Man. Washington, D.C.: Pan American Union.

--- (1945) Draft Declaration of the International Rights and Duties of Man and Accompanying Report. Washington, D.C.: Pan American Union.

Inter-American Juridical Committee [IAJC] (1948) Project of Declaration of the tions of the Governments of the Member States Regarding the Draft American Convention on Human Rights: Uruguay. OEA/ Ser. K/XVI/1.1, Doc.6.

--- (1969) Observations of the Governments of the Member States Regarding the Draft American Convention on Human Rights: Chile. Doc. 7

--- (1969) Observations of the Governments of the Member States Regarding the Draft American Convention on Human Rights: Argentina. Doc. 8.

--- (1969) Observations of the Governments of the Member States Regarding the Draft American Convention on Human Rights: United States. Doc. 10.

--- (1969) Observations of the Governments of the Member States Regarding the Draft American Convention on Human Rights: Mexico. Doc. 11.

--- (1969) Report of the Rapporteur of Committee I "Protection." Doc. 60.

Ninth International Conference of American States (1948) Acta. (Comision VI, 3ª Sesion) Doc. CB-287-C, C. VI-13.

ROBERTSON, A. H. (1972) Human Rights in the World. Manchester, Eng.: Manchester Univ. Press.

--- (1963) Human Rights in Europe. Dobbs Ferry: Oceana.

SCHREIBER, A. (1970) The Inter-American Commission on Human Rights. Leyden: A. W. Sijthoff.

U.S. Department of State (1948) Ninth International Conference of American States: Report of the Delegation of the United States of America with Related Documents. Washington, D.C.: Government Printing Office.

VAN DYKE, V. (1970) Human Rights, the United States, and World Community. New York: Oxford Univ. Press.

Lawrence J. LeBlanc is Assistant Professor of Political Science at Marquette University, whose book The OAS and the Promotion and Protection of Human Rights *is forthcoming from Martinus Nijhoff.*

WILLIAM DIRK RAAT
Department of History
State University of New York
Fredonia, NY 14063

THE ANTIPOSITIVIST MOVEMENT IN PREREVOLUTIONARY MEXICO, 1892-1911

The activities of the Liberal Union group in the election year of 1892, along with the subsequent appointment that next year of José Ives Limantour as Secretary of Treasury, marked the beginning of the rise of an influential clique of technocrats within the bureaucracy of Don Porfirio Díaz. In addition to Limantour, this group included, among others, Francisco Bulnes, Justo Sierra, Rosendo Pineda, Pablo Macedo, and Miguel Macedo. The name the critics used to describe this clique was that of the "scientists" or the *Científicos.* This name was selected, among other reasons, to express the belief of the opposition that the members of the Científico group were imbued with the scientific and positivistic doctrines of the French philosopher and architect of positivism, Auguste Comte. With the coming of the Científicos to power the course of antipositivism was redirected, given an additional emphasis, and expanded to meet the needs of liberal and clerical critics of the regime. It is likely that for the intellectual history of the Porfiriato the issue of antipositivism was more important politically and socially than that of positivism, the actual diffusion of the latter being quite narrow and restricted to academic circles (Raat, 1969).

After 1900, with urban and agrarian labor unrest increasing, liberal critics and their worker allies became more vocal and

Journal of Interamerican Studies and World Affairs, Vol. 19 No. 1, February 1977

daring in their attacks on the Porfiristas and Científicos in government. Daniel Cabrera's publication, *El Hijo del Ahuizote,* is of special importance since its stinging voice and anti-Díaz diatribes served as an ideological, and therefore political, link between the traditional liberal, i.e., anticlerical, concerns of Camilio Arriaga and the men of San Luis Potosí, and the radical anarchist and mutualist interests of the revolutionaries of the North. Not only did Cabrera champion Arriaga's call for the formation of liberal clubs throughout Mexico in 1901 and 1902, but he also opposed the imprisonment of the Flores Magón brothers and the suppression of the liberal organization of San Luis Potosí known as the club "Ponciano Arriaga" (De Vore, 1966: 15-42; Cockcroft, 1968). As will be demonstrated, Cabrera did not hesitate to equate Científico rule with positivist ideology, and positivism with antiliberalism.

Prior to the election of 1904, Cabrera was also influential in promoting the antireelectionist movement which was both anti-Díaz and against the vice-presidential ambitions of the governor of Nuevo León, Bernardo Reyes. The *antireeleccionista* movement of 1903 gained new strength between 1908 and 1909 when the liberals developed a party organization, known as the Democratic Party, and took as their candidate General Bernardo Reyes. Prior to 1910, the left wing of the Democratic Party reorganized themselves into the National Democratic Party and abandoned the Reyistas to support Francisco Madero's antireelectionist movement (De Vore, 1966: 57-58; Niemeyer, 1966). Like the liberals and radicals, the Reyista "Democrats," and in particular the apologist Juan Pedro Didapp, exploited the issue of antipositivism in their struggle with Científico rule.

It was ironic that the enemies of the liberals—that is, individual clerics as well as official spokesmen for the church—joined their voices with the former in the swelling chorus of antipositivism. As is well known, the Catholic Church maintained a low profile through many of the years of the Porfiriato. Díaz's conciliation policy alleviated the church's major grievance, i.e., the anticlerical legislation of the Reform. Unlike

Cabrera, the voice of the Catholic press—*La Voz de México*—did not usually attack the personality of Don Porfirio, and unlike the liberals, did not usually equate Científico rule with despotic positivism.[1] Rather, most of the Catholic arguments dealt only with the issue of the philosophical and moral implications of positivism to theology. But when the clerical spokesmen did leave the safety of the cloister, positivism was abstractly blamed for an entire spectrum of social and political evils, from prostitution to Masonry. It is the concern of this essay to illustrate some of these liberal and clerical expressions of antipositivism in prerevolutionary Mexico.

After 1900 the liberal camp was almost unanimous in its opposition to the Científicos. Most liberal newspapers refused to consider the Científico group of the Liberal Union a legitimate heir of liberalism. They, along with their labor counterparts, wanted to rid the government of personalistic rule and return to the institutional restraints of constitutional government. Down with militarism, up with the constitution, away with the dictator, and liberty for the people were the rallying cries. To most liberal and labor publications, the Científicos were as responsible as Don Porfirio for their wretched conditions.

El Diablito Bromista (1903a), which described itself as an organ of the working class, decried a political situation in which the "Científico Party" ruled the country with an iron hand and would not present to the people either a program or a candidate for their approval. The most notorious of the Científicos in their eyes were Limantour and Bulnes. Limantour, according to the labor position, was responsible for making Mexico the real estate of foreign capitalists at the expense of the native poor. And Bulnes, the author of *El Verdadero Juárez,* by ridiculing Juárez and his tradition was an enemy to the constitution and the Mexican nation (El Diablito Bromista, 1903b, 1904). Other labor journals like *La Guacamaya* (1904) and *La Palanca* (1904) echoed these phrases concerning the Científicos in general and Bulnes in particular.

At least one liberal, pro-worker newspaper did not hesitate to equate positivism with Científico rule. This was the organ called *El Diablito Rojo* ("The Little Red Devil"). For this newspaper it mattered not what school of thought was founded by Barreda at the Preparatory School–the only "true positivism" was that which was practiced by the Científicos. And this type of positivism was nothing more than money-grubbing. The Científicos were literally robbing the poor to feed the rich. Love in the positivist value system meant only love of money. The editors of *El Diablito Rojo* even coined a new term to describe the Científico philosophy. Making a play on the word *peseta* they equated the philosophy of *Positivismo* with that of *Pesetivismo* (1908, 1901).

One of the more vocal of radical publications was Daniel Cabrera's *El Hijo del Ahuizote.* It was published from 1885 to 1903. After 1903, with its closing, Cabrera started another newspaper called *El Ahuizote Jacobino,* which continued to publish articles of an anticlerical, anti-Díaz, and anti-imperialistic nature throughout 1904 and 1905.[2] *El Hijo del Ahuizote* was the legitimate heir of a famous predecessor entitled *El Ahuizote. El Ahuizote* had been a strong enemy of Lerdo de Tejada during his presidential administration and had been closed at his insistence. This is why *El Hijo del Ahuizote* ("The Son of Ahuizote") often ran the subtitle, "This Child has no Mother." Cabrera's newspaper was a liberal weekly of "bloodthirsty" caricatures. It was dedicated to fighting the supporters of the Díaz regime. Cabrera, who was the uncle of Luis Cabrera (an active *antireeleccionista* and later minister of the treasury under Carranza), often suffered persecution and imprisonment at the hand of Díaz (Lepidus, 1928: 59).

In attacking Díaz, Cabrera had as a major political concern the development of a Confederation of Liberal Clubs. This would give a unified voice to the several liberal factions throughout the country. Some of the principles of the confederation as outlined by Cabrera were as follows: first, an exact and respectful observance of the laws; second, the promotion of liberal, civic education along with improved public schools for both children and adults; third, the abolition of all personalistic tendencies in government and a return to the principles of the constitution and the reform; fourth, the creation of free public libraries; fifth, to introduce reform in the legislature with emphasis on a reduction of the economic power of the clergy (El Hijo de Ahuizote, 1902c). In addition to this specific program, the Cabrera newspaper repeated the themes of nationalism ("Mexico para los mexicanos"), *gachupinismo* (a slogan filled with antiforeigner hatred), antimilitarism, anti-*caciquismo* (being against one man rule) and *política Tuxte-pecana* (a reference to Díaz's Plan of Tuxtepec in which he promised no reelection in 1876).

The enemies of Cabrera were many and varied. His association of Liberal Clubs, which he called collectively the Liberal Party, was considered to be the only legitimate heir of liberalism. This, according to Cabrera, was the party of Juárez, of the *Reforma,* of Ayutla, and the constitution of 1857. In addition to being anti-Díaz, Cabrera opposed all those individuals around Díaz who he thought were responsible for enthroning the "military dictator." He called this group the party of *porfirismo.* As a liberal he also fought against the *Partido Conservador,* i.e., the "reactionaries" of the Catholic Church. In addition to these groups he feared the activities of the Reyists and the Científicos. Reyes, who had closed the Liberal Clubs of Lampazos and San Luis Potosí, was considered to be only another potential military dictator who was even more dangerous than Díaz. As for the Científicos, the party of Sierra, Pineda, Bulnes, Limantour, and the Macedo brothers, Cabrera taught that they were nothing other than decadent poets, ambitious politicans, and sick philosophers (El Hijo del Ahuizote, 1902b).

In 1894 both an article and a caricature appeared in Cabrera's organ with the title of "Girondinos y Jacobinos." The terms were obviously taken from those revolutionary groups which were active during the French Revolution. But in the Mexican context the "Girondinos" were the Científicos while the "Jacobinos" referred to old guard liberals, both of which were active in the Liberal Union Convention of 1892. This was one of the first caricatures to equate positivism and evolutionism with the Científicos. The setting was one in which the Científicos and the liberals were fighting in congress over the nature of the supreme court (a reform which was advocated by the Liberal Union manifesto). A table set with food represented the national congress. The Científicos were separated from the liberals with the table between them. On the table were set such delicacies as Científico beans ("frijoles científicos") and Evolutionary bread ("pan grande evolucionista"). The two forces were throwing their plates at each other. On a plate held by Sierra was the word "positivismo," while the other Científico plates were labeled finance and evolution. The liberals were holding plates which symbolized their nineteenth-century concern with traditional liberalism. The caption read as follows: "Without leaving a bone to chew upon, they arrive to have an unpleasant time. Never understanding that what is not the same dinner cannot be thrown with what is not the same plates." The message was simple. Agreement was impossible because the Científicos were speaking the language of positivism, a language foreign to traditional liberalism (El Hijo del Ahuizote, 1894).

In listing the "reelectionists" several individual Científicos were identified by Cabrera's newspaper as positivists. And even though positivism was never strictly defined, it was assumed that the reader would associate materialism and corruption with the term. Pancho Bulnes (Francisco Bulnes) was described as a positivist poet who wanted to return to the government of Manuel González. Pancho Bulnes was a man of great talent, for he had been able to keep the great Caesar content with his "scientific humility." As for Ramón Prida, he may have been a bad journalist but he was certainly a good positivist. The description of these men, along with Pablo Macedo and others, was one in which positivism was a derogatory condition which affected the heads of state. The antiintellectual content of Cabrera's type of positivism would certainly have startled Comte (El Hijo del Ahuizote, 1889, 1896a, 1896b, 1896c, 1899).

It was ironic that the anti-Científico Cabrera would be labeled in turn by other opponents with the hate word "Cienfífico." By the end of 1902 Bernardo Reyes' presidential ambitions were being promoted by his son through a newspaper called *La Protesta.* Both *La Protesta* and the army reserves which Reyes was developing came to the attention of Cabrera. His newspaper immediately started to attack the Reyists as a group which was promoting military dictatorship (El Hijo del Ahuizote, 1902a). Because of his unfriendly attitude toward Reyes, the newspaper *La Nación* started to assert that Cabrera's newspaper was in the pay of the Científicos. Cabrera felt obligated to print a denial publicly disassociating himself from the hated Científicos (El Hijo del Ahuizote, 1903). Yet the incident was illustrative in that it showed how meaningless the label of "Científico" could be when used and overused in the politics of opposition.

The activities of *La Protesta* not only led Cabrera to increase his hostility toward Reyes, but also brought the dismissal of Reyes from the Díaz cabinet. At first Díaz was unaware that *La Protesta*'s anti-Limantour and anti-Científico editorial policy was being directed by Reyes through his son Rodolfo. But Díaz soon found out, due to the enterprising activity of Limantour himself. Reyes was guilty of undermining his fellow cabinet members, and, more importantly, the means he chose–i.e., a public organ–was intolerable and bad for the image of government. Not only was Reyes forced to leave Mexico City for Nuevo León, he also was supposed to give up the paper. On his departure Reyes appointed a new director of *La Protesta.* This man was also an apologist for the Reyista cause and, as such, no friend of the Científicos. His name was Juan Pedro Didapp (Velasco Valdés, 1955: 159).[3]

Very little is known concerning Didapp's life. From his own writings and the bibliography by Iguíniz (1926) some generalizations can be made. He was born in the state of Durango in 1874 and died, possibly in Europe, in 1914. In 1906 he was a Mexican consul in Argentina, and in 1910 he was the Mexican consul in Norfolk, Virginia. Between 1912 and 1913 he appeared before the Smith Committee of the U.S. Senate bearing witness to alleged ties of interest between the Madero family of northern Mexico and Standard Oil (Calvert, 1968: 74-76).

In Mexican history he was of most importance from 1903 to 1904, when he served as an apologist for the Reyista forces. Not only did he support Reyes against the Científicos, but he seemed to favor any group which was hostile to the Científicos. During these years Didapp (1903, 1904a, 1904b) published several works in which Reyes was defended and the Limantour clique and positivism were damned.

In these works Didapp argued that the origin of positivism was due to its introduction by Horacio Barreda at the National Preparatory School in the late 1860s. He held that the disciples of Barreda eventually obtained important positions in government, especially in the cabinet of Díaz. Didapp implied that French Positivism reinforced Spencer's doctrine of evolution in the public life of the nation. It was from 1890 to 1895 that Didapp noted the rise of the Limantour clique. He identified their origin with the National Liberal Convention of 1892, which he asserted was neither liberal nor national. This group of men he negatively called the Científicos (evidently the term was well current by the time of Didapp's writing). They were considered to be men of money who did not represent the will of the people. For Didapp, the words *positivista* and *científico* shared identical meanings, both of which indicated something evil for Mexico (Didapp, 1903: 183-197).

Didapp's study of the Liberal Union manifesto indicated to him that the Científicos, with Limantour as their leader, were representatives of foreign interests. This was why, so Didapp reasoned, the Científicos were imbued with the foreign ideologies of Comte and Spencer. He also considered the Científico-backed National Liberal Convention to be a farce. Obviously their concern was not one of nominating Díaz, in spite of the nominal moves in that direction. The *Convención Nacional Porfirista,* which had the backing of Reyes, had already met for that purpose. The "secret" meaning behind the National Liberal

Convention was that of promoting Limantour for the presidency. And who was Limantour? Nothing other than a foreigner who undermined the traditional military glory of Mexico (Didapp, 1903: 199-216).

Unlike Cabrera, Didapp was in favor of both Díaz and the military dictatorship which both Díaz and Reyes represented. As such, the major change which he laid at the feet of the Científicos was that they, through the writings of the scientific orator of the Liberal Union manifesto (Justo Sierra), were enemies of both the army and the military dictatorship of Díaz. The Científico manifesto, at least in Didapp's reading, had declared personalistic rule and militarism odious to the climate of Mexico. This meant for Didapp that the Científicos were enemies of both the government and the people. Why? Because, first, the Díaz government was a form of military rule. Without this type of rule the government would return to its prior state of anarchy and be subject to the caprice of foreigners (something Didapp implied the Científicos preferred). And, second, the Medican people were by history and nature a military people. The positivists (Didapp used the terms interchangeably), he concluded, were nothing other than representatives of a foreign interest who were imbued with a foreign philosophy (Didapp, 1903: 199-216).

One factor is worth noting in Didapp's list of Científico characteristics. Didapp (1903: 254) did not hesitate to assert that all of the Científicos, or at least a major part of them, professed the ideas of positivism ("Son científicos todos, ó la mayor parte, de los que profesan las ideas positivistas"). And he also went further to allege that the economic policies of Limantour and his group were destructive of the nation's interests because, as the intellectual children of Barreda and as disciples of Comte, their thinking was based on false premises (not defined by Didapp; 1903: 224f.).

In his writing of the next year, Didapp singled out Francisco Bulnes and Ramón Corral as the two individuals who best symbolized the "atheism" and "tyranny" of the Científicos: Bulnes because of his writings against the national hero Juárez, and Corral because of the intrigue which was used by the Científicos to prevent Reyes from rightfully receiving the vice-presidential position. Coining a phrase which others would later use, Didapp (1904: 669-671) stated that the "political positivists," as represented by Bulnes and Corral, followed only one maxim of government in obtaining personal wealth: "*El fin justifica los medios*" (italics Didapp's).

He finally concluded his long harangue with a tribute to Juárez, the symbol of the Republic and the column which supported the most powerful Mexican party—the party of Reyes, the party of liberty. In this tribute he cried that "the enemies of Juárez were the same who were the enemies of Christ, i.e., the Jews, who in Mexico were the 'Científicos' " ("Los enemigos de Juárez son los mismos que fueron de Cristo: los judíos, que aquíen México son los 'científicos' "; 1904b: 685). Thus, Didapp, like liberal and labor spokesmen before him, ushered positivism into the political arena so as to bolster his claims of tyranny, corruption, materialism, and atheism on the part of the "positivist thinking" Científicos. In this latter charge of irreligion his views were complemented by the position of the church and individual clerics.

Both contemporary and later writers have testified to the fact that under Díaz there occurred a church-state compromise in which the anticlerical legislation of the Reform was allowed to fall into disuse (Zayas Enriquez, 1899: 44; Mecham, 1934: 456-458). Díaz's conciliation policy was a major grievance for liberals like Cabrera, especially that part of the agreement which allowed science to be taught in the public schools while religious instruction was to remain with the church and the church-operated schools. It was the conciliation policy more than anything else which prevented the Catholics from becoming too political in the public arena.

Yet the church as an organization, as well as individual clerics, did have grievances. One factor which annoyed the Catholics was Díaz's juggling act in which he attempted to balance off the Protestants, the Masons, and the Catholics against one another. Protestant missionaries were given the protection of law. And Díaz, as Grand Master of the *Rito Nacional,* used this group of Masons (which was sometimes allied with certain Protestant groups) to not only counter the power of the church, but to oppose Masons of the Scottish Rite group. In this type of power structure, no group, including the church, could develop a total sense of political security (Murray, 1965: 296-314).

In expressing the grievances which the Catholic Church held against positivism the clerical press, especially *La Voz de México,* was of prime importance. Throughout the 1890s the clerics, through their press, constantly blamed the problem of prostitution upon positivism and atheism (González Navarro, 1957: 413). And as early as 1892, the same year of the Liberal Union manifesto, *La Voz de México* featured a three-part series by the cleric Rafael Cárlos, which was designed to refute the modern errors of materialism–i.e., positivism of the Littré variety. The central position of Cárlos's article was that Littré's positivism was identical in content with the dangerous philosophy of socialism. In conclusion, the article prayed to God that France would disentangle herself from the road of decadence and ruin and would return once again to her ancient and grand providential mission. The message was a simple one. Positivism, whether in France or Mexico, could only lead away from God and toward godless socialism (a brand of economy which the Catholic Church with its many private holdings was not about to sanction; Cárlos, 1892).

Although some Catholics modified their position against socialism after 1900 with the development of the social justice argument, the First Ecumenical Congress, meeting in 1906, still declared positivism to be equivalent to atheism. Positivism was not only the cause of prostitution, but of many other private and social problems as well. To prostitution the Catholics added the following conditions to their list of problems which were the result, at least in part, of the teachings of positivism in Mexico: depopulation, divorce, illegitimate births, infanticides, adolescent crimes, abandonment of infants, suicides of minors, pornography, scandal, drunkenness, pauperism, strikes, financial panics, speculation with public funds, and so on. The panacea was obvious–rid the country of atheistic positivism (Callcott, 1965: 178).

Several clerics, writing independently from the church, also added their writings to the voice of antipositivism. Valverde Téllez's bibliography of positivist and antipositivist materials entitled *Bibliografía filosófica mexicana* was especially designed to make available those writings which were considered refutations of positivism. Another cleric, Ignacio Gamboa of Yucatan, waged war not only on Comte and Littré, but Haeckel and Maudsley as well. They were all grouped together under the collective title of positivist thinkers. The material evolutionary theory of Haeckel and Maudsley's organic psychology were treated as positivist doctrines which equated positivism with materialism. The sole purpose of positivism, for Gamboa (1899: 17-68), was one of separating man from God, thereby leading him into anarchism, nihilism, and modern communism.[4] The Catholic Church was the only salvation of mankind.

Writing at a later date, the Catholic thinker Francisco Zavala (1907: iii-vii) of Guadalajara argued that positivism, socialism, and Masonry all committed the same error, i.e., asserting that the state could replace God in the lives of men. When the positivism of Comte (who he said should have dwelled in a madhouse) was extended to the political realm, Zavala asserted that it was expressed externally by imperialism and internally by either socialism (absolute oligarchy) or anarchism (absolute dissolution). Rule by positivists would be destructive of Mexico in that the positivist oligarchy would confiscate ecclesiastical property, increase the foreign debt, and lead to a loss of national independence for Mexico. Thus, the dangers of positivism, which Zavala sometimes called *negativismo,* were the same which Catholicism faced with socialism and anarchism (Zavala, 1909: 3-5, 36-38). In feeling the impending chaos and apparent dislocations of Mexican society in 1909, Zavala was like many other observers in that he sought some rationale which would explain his sense of insecurity. In Zavala's case that rationale was positivism.

Unlike other clerical writers, the role of positivism in education and politics was important to Zavala. In education, positivism—according to Zavala—was the enemy of those who cultivated the development of the spirit. He believed that the National Preparatory School was the center of positivistic sectarianism and had been active in propagandizing the youth of Mexico with the atheistic logic of Comte, Mill, Spencer, Bain, and Parra. In an article for *La Voz de México,* Zavala (1908) asserted that positivist history was no more truthful than the myths of paganism. Thus, as late as 1908 and 1909 the issue of positivist logic and education at the Preparatory School was still an important issue for this cleric (Zavala, 1908: 436).

Zavala (1908: 87-89) also feared the effect of positivism on Mexican politics. He believed that Jacobin liberalism, Masonry, and positivism were all a part of the same tradition of materialism. In fact, the materialistic notions of the Jacobins, who invented the cult of the god of Reason, acted as a causal agent in giving rise to the atheistic notions of positivism. Both Jacobins and positivists, as well as Masons, had been guilty of secularizing religion in the political life of Mexico. Only God could save Mexico from her wayward Mexicans.

Over this issue of secular religion, Zavala (1908: 29-31) displayed an unusual concern. Zavala asserted that Gabino Barreda, Porfirio Parra, Manuel Flores, and Justo Sierra were responsible for instituting the Religion of Humanity in Mexico. Barreda was the founder, Parra the logician, Flores the educator, and Sierra was the minister of this church. The morality of this religion was a type of "altruism" in which the people were infected with a positivist materialism which eventually caused criminality, socialism, anarchism, and nihilism. Mexico's only salvation could be found in God's morality.

When the Catholic reaction to positivism after 1892 is compared to that prior to the 1890s, certain differences become apparent. Whereas earlier clerics such as Jose de Jésus Cuevas (1885: 24-42) had identified positivism with official governmental policy, the clerics of the 1890s and 1900s not only did not attack Díaz, but they usually failed even to make the liberal's identification of positivism with Científico rule. In this sense the later Catholics were an exception to the major trends of antipositivism since Cuevas.

It can also be noted that the nature and scope of the problem had changed. The two major issues for earlier liberals and clerics were the dangers of materialistic positivism for Catholic theology and the role of positivist logic at the Preparatory School in undermining the morality of the youth. After 1900 these problems were still present. But the issues had been greatly expanded. Society was obviously changing. Economic dislocation was at hand and the revolution was on the horizon. Problems created by urbanization and industrialization were now existent. The city not only gave rise to new social problems such as drunkenness and prostitution, but also became the meeting place of labor groups with new radical ideas. In dealing with this problem, i.e., in attempting to create some kind of orderly understanding, the issue of positivism was expanded to meet new needs. Positivism was now the cause of the new materialism. For churchmen the foreign ideologies of socialism and anarchism, as well as imperialism, were due in the main to the influence of positivism in Mexico.

Thus, antipositivism, in both liberal and clerical camps, was a cause which tended to exaggerate the destructive importance of positivism on the life of the nation. Liberal critics evoked the specter of positivism in their campaign against the church and the government. Labor spokesmen did likewise. And, on the other end of the political spectrum, conservatives within the church also joined the antipositivist crusade. Antipositivism now evoked an emotional response which it had not known at an earlier date.

NOTES

1. This is not to say that the Catholic press was not critical of the Científicos (e.g., see La Voz de México, 1908).

2. These ideas are reflected in various issues of *El Ahuizote Jacobino* (1905): for anticlericalism see January 1, 1905; for antiimperialism see January 8 and February 19; and for anti-Díaz and anti-Científico caricatures see August 13 and August 19.

3. Jorge Vera Estañol also associates Rodolfo Reyes with *La Protesta* and refers to it as an anti-Limantourista publication (see Vera Estañol, 1957: 86-87).

4. The relationship between Marxism and positivism is a complicated one. Suffice it to say that the orthodox positivist Aragón, or the Chilean scholar Luis Lagarrigue, did make theoretical distinctions concerning the two systems of thought. While positivism accepted the communist idea that social problems had their origin in material conditions, they rejected the political solutions of the communists. While positivism accepted the participation of the people in public life, it transformed this political cooperation from the state, where the communists had assigned it, to a material cooperation of public opinion. Instead of making the state the sole owner of capital, positivism taught that ownership would be divided between capitalists and laborers inside of an industrial state. Again positivism held that moral education of the proletariat was prior to the workers' organization into a union (see Lagarrigue, n.d.: 431-440).

REFERENCES

El Ahuizote Jacobino [Mexico] (1905).

CALLCOTT, W. H. (1965) Liberalism in Mexico. Hamden, Conn.: Archon.

CALVERT, P. (1968) The Mexican Revolution, 1910-1914. The Diplomacy of Anglo-American Conflict. Cambridge: Univ. Press.

CARLOS, R. (1892) "Refutación de los errores dominantes." La Voz de México (5 February, 27 April).

COCKCROFT, J. D. (1968) Intellectual Precursors of the Mexican Revolution, 1900-1913. Austin: Univ. of Texas Press.

CUEVAS, J. de J. (1885) El positivismo en México. Zacatecas: Tip. de Comercio.

DE VORE, B. B. (1966) Land and Liberty: A History of the Mexican Revolution. New York: Pageant.

El Diablito Bromista [México] (1904) "Los Científicos. . . . " (27 November).

--- (1903a) "Mercaran Científicos." (25 October).

--- (1903b) "La vuelta de Limantour." (27 November).

El Diablito Rojo [México] (1908) "Positivismo y Pesetivismo." (6 April).

--- (1901) "Amor y positivismo." (11 March).

DIDAPP, J. P. (1904a) Gobiernos militares de México. Los ataques al ejército y las maquinaciones políticas del Partido Clienífico para regir los destinos nacionales. México.

--- (1904b) Explotadores políticos de México. Bulnes y el Partido Científico ante el derecho ajeno. México: Tip. de los Sucs. de Francisco Díaz de León.

--- (1903) Partídos políticos de México. La política del dinero y la política del patriotismo. México: Editor, Jacionto Gil, "Libreria Española."

GAMBOA, I. (1899) El positivismo filosófico y su influencia en el estado actual de la sociedad humana. Yucatan: Imprenta "Lorede Mola."

GONZALEZ NAVARRO, M. (1957) La vida social, vol. 4 of D. Cosío Villegas (ed.) Historia Moderna de México. México: Editorial Hermes.
La Guacamaya [México] (1904) "Quienes Bulnes?" (20 October).
El Hijo de Ahuizote [México] (1903) 4 January.
——— (1902a) 14 December.
——— (1902b) "Los Partidos Nuevos." (6 July).
——— (1902c) "Objecto de los Clubs Liberals." (23 February).
——— (1899) 15 January.
——— (1896a) 30 August; (1896b) 16 August; (1896c) 9 August.
——— (1894) "Girondinos y Jacobinos." (28 January).
——— (1889) 3 March.
IGUINIZ, J. B. (1926) Bibliografía de novelistas mexicanos. México.
LAGARRIGUE, L. (n.d.) "Positivismo y Comunismo," in vol. 2 of A. Aragón, Porfirio Díaz: Estudio historicofilosófico. México: Editora Intercontinental.
LEPIDUS, H. (1928) The History of Mexican Journalism: University of Missouri Bulletin, Series 49, 29, 4. Columbia: Univ. of Missouri.
MECHAM, J. L. (1934) Church and State in Latin America. Chapel Hill: Univ. of North Carolina Press.
MURRAY, P. V. (1965) The Catholic Church in Mexico. Vol. 1. México: Ediciones de Libros con Fines Culturales.
NIEMEYER, E. V., Jr. (1966) El General Bernardo Reyes. Monterrey: Univ. de Nuevo León.
La Palanca [México] (1904) "Soleme protesta." (11 September).
RAAT, W. D. (1969) "Agustín Aragón and Mexico's religion of humanity." J. of Interamer. Studies 11 (July): 441-457.
VELASCO VALDES, M. (1955) Historia del periodismo mexicano. México: Porrua.
VERA ESTANOL, J. (1957) La revolucion mexicana. Origines y resultados. México: Porrua.
La Voz de México [México] (1908) "Los viajeros científicos." (9 December).
ZAVALA, F. J. (1909) El positivismo. Guadalajara: Tip. de "El Regional."
——— (1908) "Criticismo." La Voz de México (29 December).
——— (1907) El socialismo y la iglesia. Guadalajara: Imp. de "El Regional."
ZAYAS ENRIQUEZ, R. de (1899) Los Estados Unidos Mexicanos, sus progresos en veinte años de paz, 1877-1897. New York: H. A. Rost.

William Dirk Raat is Associate Professor of Latin American History at the State University of New York, Fredonia. He is author of several articles and essays on Mexican social and intellectual history and in 1968 received the James L. Robertson Award from the Conference on Latin American History for his article on "Leopoldo Zea and Mexican Positivism." His most recent book was published by SepSetentas and is entitled El Positivismo Durante El Porfiriato. *Professor Raat is currently finishing a book on the suppression of alien Mexican radicals in the United States prior to the Mexican Revolution.*

TIMOTHY O'DEA GAUHAN
Political Science Department
San Jose State University
San Jose, CA 95192

HOUSING AND THE URBAN POOR

The Case of Bogotá, Colombia

In a setting as complex as the modern city we can expect that a number of diverse factors wil combine to influence the urban environment and the quality of life and well being of those who reside in it. In the major cities of the developing world, where change is typically rapid, economic and social relationships are diverse, and the patterns of development are often different and in some ways more complex than those of the cities of industrialized nations, and the forces which shape the character of urban life are particularly numerous and often confusing.

The present paper examines a single component of the total environment of the Latin American city of Bogotá, Colombia: the low-income housing market. We begin by looking at some of the more important environmental, socioeconomic, and political factors that have shaped the character of the low-income housing market of the city, with an emphasis on the impact of public policy. Second, we describe some of the basic character-

AUTHOR'S NOTE: James Spillane S.J., Richard Butler, George Antunes, Robert Dix, and John Ambler all read early drafts of this paper. None is responsible for the content of the paper and each contributed toward its improvement. Research for the present article was completed while the author was an associate of the Program of Development Studies at Rice University and a Social Science Research Council Collaborative Research Fellow in Bogotá.

Journal of Interamerican Studies and World Affairs, Vol. 19 No. 1, February 1977

istics of this housing market and focus primarily on its economic aspects. Finally, the implications of a number of public policy alternatives and their effects on the city and its residents are discussed.

Major Factors Affecting Low-Income Housing in Bogotá

Nearly 50 percent of the population of the city of Bogotá falls in the "lower socioresidential stratum" of the city's population (Simmons and Cardona, 1972: 169). In quantitative terms this means that "in Bogotá, 33% of the population suffers from a lack of the most elemental services. . . . Fifty percent of the housing is below the hygienic standard, that is, at the level of slums. Thirteen percent don't have running water. Around 1962, 211,000 families housed themselves in 155,000 housing units, of which only 81,000 were classified as 'acceptable'. Around the same date it was estimated that the construction of 75,000 housing units was necessary to house, with a minimum of comfort, the whole population of Bogotá" (Avila Bernal, 1973: 184). While poverty is nothing new to Colombia, such widespread *urban* poverty affecting such great numbers of people is a relatively new phenomenon. During this century, however, and especially in the past 25 years, a number of forces have combined to make low-income housing one of the major problems facing Bogotá. Four categories of factors have contributed most substantially toward shaping the character of low-income housing in the city: population growth and transfer, patterns of economic development in the city and nation, topographical and environmental factors, and government policy response to the housing problem of the city. In order to understand the dimensions of the problems of low-income housing in Bogotá let us briefly examine each of these categories.

POPULATION GROWTH AND TRANSFER

As in most Latin American countries, Colombia's population has grown and moved cityward at a very rapid rate in the last several decades. Of Colombia's 8.75 million people in 1938, only 30 percent lived in urban areas. Today the population of the country has grown to around 25 million, and the number of people living in urban areas is estimated to be near 60 percent. There are now three urban centers in Colombia with population levels near or over one million, whereas at midcentury there were none. In the capital city of Bogotá the process of population growth and immigration have been spectacular. Since the turn of the century the city has grown from roughly 145,000 to over two million. It is estimated that, since 1950, well over 50 percent of this growth is attributable to migrants and their children (Cardona and Simmons, 1973a: 10). Not only was Bogotá the largest city in Colombia during this period, it was also growing relatively faster than Colombia's other major cities in terms of net population increase and—with the exception of the Caribbean port city of Barranquilla—in terms of net increase due to population transfer.

This phenomenal growth is not expected to abate in the near future. According to projections by the Inter-American Development Bank, Bogotá will reach a population of 5.2 million by 1980 and will have experienced a growth rate of 67.9 percent between 1960 and 1980, higher than any of the other nine largest cities in Latin America (cited in Avila Bernal, 1973: 185).

When it is noted that approximately 54 percent of the migrants to the city and 43 percent of those born in the city are of the low socioresidential strata, the implications of this population growth pattern begin to emerge. In the period 1951-1961, when the population growth of the city was over 150 percent, the housing deficit in Bogotá grew from 37,000 units to 73,000 units (Consultécnicos, 1972: 7). More recent data, collected in 1972 (Zorro Sanchez, 1974: 103), indicate continued rapid expansion of the city's housing deficit owing to the growing number of poor in the city.

PATTERNS OF ECONOMIC DEVELOPMENT

Despite a rather impressive annual economic growth rate of around 5 to 7 percent in recent years, a large majority of the Colombian population still lives in a state of poverty. Also, even though current rural-to-urban migration flows are stimulated by the wage differentials that exist between the rural and urban sectors (Fierro, 1973), and though some occupational mobility exists in the lower levels of the urban sectors (Cardona and Simmons, 1973b), poverty continues to plague the urban centers of Colombia as well as the rural areas. The causes and dimensions of urban poverty are far too numerous and complex to be treated here. Suffice it to say that long-established patterns of land and income distribution, the reliance on a few primary products for competition in the world economy, late (and often capital-intensive) industrialization, the relative weakness of the trade unions, and the aforementioned population growth have all contributed to the persistence of poverty in Colombia.

Of particular importance to the case of Bogotá are the rapid population growth of the city and the inability of the industrial sector to provide the necessary employment for the city's working class. This pattern of economic development has resulted in high unemployment in Bogotá, high underemployment, and employment skewed toward those occupations where salaries have traditionally been the lowest (i.e., the unskilled services). As one author has noted, the housing problem is simply one of the manifestations of a more profound problem: "the low income of the majority of the population" (Zorro Sanchez, 1974: 12).

TOPOGRAPHICAL AND ENVIRONMENTAL CHARACTERISTICS OF THE CITY OF BOGOTA AND ITS REGION

Arriving by air, one can gain an immediate appreciation of some of the environmental factors that have influenced the development of low-income housing in Bogotá. Sprawling along the base of a small mountain range, the city may be divided topographically into three principal zones: a high zone beginning at the lower flanks of the mountains, an intermediate zone, and a lower zone extending to the savanna of Bogotá (Amato, 1970: 169). The lower zone is characterized by a very flat terrain. It has less rain than the intermediate and high zones and better drainage than the intermediate zone. The lower zone is also subject to intensive and mechanized cultivation, again unlike the other two zones. At the other extreme, we find in the upper reaches of the high zone steep terrain and rocky soil not well suited for agricultural use, heavy rain most of the year, and erosion. The intermediate zone is flat like the lower zone but has more rain, poorer drainage, and is less desirable for agricultural purposes than the lower zone.

These physical characteristics of Bogotá, along with other factors (such as the legal ones discussed below), have had the result of severely limiting the supply of land available for low-income housing in Bogotá and in limiting it spatially to the high and intermediate zones of the city. The steep terrain and erosion that characterize the upper reaches of the high zone make it undesirable for housing developments. Moreover, the visibility of the high zone from other parts of the city makes the development of clandestine squatter settlements difficult. The desirability of the land in the lower zone has served to remove this land from the low-income housing market. Being highly suited to cattle raising and having been cultivated for centuries, the value of this land is, in most cases, prohibitively high for low-income housing. Added to this are a number of favorable climatic and topographic characteristics of this area which have drawn high-income groups to it, making it unavailable for those with low incomes. As a consequence, we find that, with few exceptions, low-income housing in Bogotá is located in the lower reaches of the high zone and in the intermediate zone, squeezed between the mountains of the high zone and the high-income *barrios* in the low zone. Thus, with the exception of some land to the west of the city that is as yet undeveloped (and is mostly zoned for industrial use), the supply of land for low-income housing has little potential for expansion.

GOVERNMENT POLICY RESPONSES TO THE PROBLEMS OF LOW-INCOME HOUSING

A final set of factors to be considered here includes a strange potpourri of de jure and de facto political decisions (and nondecisions) that have influenced the development of the city over the years. Among the most important of these policy outputs is the National Development Plan of 1972 which calls for programs to stimulate personal savings and investment in construction, especially in urban areas. To implement these elements of the plan, the government has created a system of value-constant (i.e., the return on investment is adjusted for the rate of inflation) savings and loans and has sought through a number of means to channel the savings stimulated by this system into investment in urban construction, primarily in the form of commercial buildings and upper-income housing. In terms of low-income housing in Bogotá, these programs have had two important results, both negative (at least in the short run). First, by encouraging construction and employment in the urban areas and to a large degree discouraging them in the rural areas (see Colombia National Planning Office, 1974: 2-20), the policies being implemented in the name of the plan have stimulated the migration of low-income groups to the cities, thereby increasing the demand for housing. Second, while the system of constant value savings and loans has served as a stimulus to personal savings, it has also resulted in the virtual exclusion of low-income groups from the home-loan market. While the plan may have served to stimulate construction in general, in cities like Bogotá it has done little to expand the supply of low-income housing.

A correlative influence on the rate of migration (and thus indirectly on the demand for low-income housing) in the realm of national governmental policy has been the rapid and marked decline in recent years in efforts by the national government to implement agrarian reform. While attempts at agrarian reform were much lauded in the early years of INCORA (the Colombian National Institute for Agrarian Reform), efforts at redistributing agricultural land have been drastically reduced in recent years. There is little doubt that the failure of the agrarian reform program in Colombia has stimulated migration to cities like Bogotá.

One final influence of note from the national level has come in the form of a series of "nondecisions" in the area of urban reform. Since 1960, no fewer than 11 pieces of major legislation dealing with urban reform have been introduced in the Colombian National Legislature. These bills have dealt with a wide variety of issues directly related to problems of low-income housing, including rent controls, expropriation of urban land to be used for housing construction, provisions for transforming tenants into property owners, value limits on future housing construction (to reduce the low-income housing deficit), taxes on unimproved land, the nationalization of savings and loan associations, and many more (Solaun et al., 1973). Despite support from a number of governmental and nongovernmental groups, including planners, legislators, and pressure groups, and despite the need for such legislation to help resolve some of the problems that rapid urbanization has brought, not one of these attempts at urban reform has passed the legislature (in fact, only one of these bills has even cleared committee). Thus, the inability of the Colombian Congress to act has had an important influence on low-income housing.

Government policies at the local level have also had an important impact on the low-income housing market in Bogotá. Let us look at the areas where this impact has been the greatest.

Zoning. Over the past 30 years, local zoning laws have served to reinforce the physical and environmental factors mentioned above in limiting the supply of land available for low-income housing in Bogotá. The development of zoning regulations in the city has primarily been in response to the increase in the city's population and the housing problems this increase has created.

> Prior to 1944, Bogotá did not have any official zoning regulations. New urbanizations were springing up all about the city, particularly during the period after 1938. The elites became alarmed that their new residential areas might be undermined by the encroachment of undesirable use. They were particularly concerned that the mushrooming *obrero* (worker) barrios should be confined to specified areas within the city. The elites found support for their position in German Zea, the Mayor of Bogotá for 1938-41. Zea called for regulations which would divide the city into sectors which would be zoned according to the class of inhabitants living in various areas or according to its activities. [Amato, 1970: 222]

From the first zoning ordinance of 1944 to the *Plano Oficial de Zonificación General de la Ciudad* of 1968 which is currently in effect, zoning ordinances in Bogotá have effectively served to segregate and limit the land available for low-class housing and "the early zoning of the city permanently fixed the spatial distribution of socio-economic groups and bears testimony of the desire and ability of the elites to structure the city in conformity to their own interest" (Amato, 1970: 222).

Housing standards. The controversy over housing standards for Latin American cities is a long-standing and complex one (for contrasting views see Turner, 1971 and Colombian National Planning Office, 1974: 69-80). For our purposes it is sufficient to note that statutory housing norms have had an important impact on housing in Bogotá. The laws of the city stipulate two types of requirements for new subdivisions. First, developers must provide streets, parks, water, sewers, electricity, and other services *before* their land can be sold for housing. A second and related requirement is that before registered legal title can be awarded to those building homes on previously undeveloped land, the aforementioned services must be present.

These housing standards, combined with the character of the credit market and widespread poverty noted earlier, have added to the housing problem of the city. Fully developed land and dwelling are simply out of reach for many low-income families. Although many of these families have resorted to illegal "pirate" housing, as is discussed below, this phenomenon has brought with it its own set of problems—as shall be noted.

De facto acquiescence in the development of illegal settlements. The subject of statutory housing standards has another important aspect. That is that while statutory housing standards exist in Bogotá, and indeed serve to limit the supply of legal low-income housing in the city to some extent, they are only selectively implemented. This has given rise to the famous illegal settlements of Bogotá known as *barrios piratas* (pirate neighborhoods), whose impact on the low-income housing market cannot be overemphasized. Barrios pirates usually develop in the following way. An individual owning a large tract of land in or near the city will sell small plots to poor families *without* providing the legally required services. These families then construct and occupy housing units, despite the lack of basic services. Thus, while these barrios differ from squatter settlements in that they do not result from land invasions, like squatter settlements they are illegal. In 1972 an estimated 59 percent of the population of Bogotá resided in these pirate barrios, which accounted for 38.4 percent of the total area of the city developed for housing. A 22.4 percent growth rate has occurred for this type of housing in the five years preceding 1972 (Consultécnicos, 1972: 10-23).

Their sheer numbers (209 barrios in 1971) and the number of people involved indicate that the barrios piratas have the de facto approval, or at least acquiescence, of local government. Thus, we find a public policy which de jure has established a fairly rigorous set of housing standards (unattainable for the majority of low-income individuals), and which de facto sanctions a low-income housing market that is essentially normless and is accompanied by a brutally usurious credit system and acute service deficiencies.

Another important feature of this de facto system of illegal housing is that a large number of barrios piratas eventually become "regularized." This means that through "spontaneous" development (i.e., the gradual improvement of individual dwellings and the eventual acquisition of public services) these barrios eventually come to meet the statutory housing standards, thereby enabling residents to acquire registered title to their homes. In 1971, 99 (or 47 percent) of the barrios piratas had been regularized (Consultécnicos, 1972: 265-274).

The three factors just discussed—de jure standards, de facto normlessness, and the gradual regularization of illegal barrios—have combined to provide a highly important "safety valve" for a city which has experienced a high and increasing demand for low-income housing during a period in which the supply of such housing has remained limited. The dynamics of the process involved and the degree to which it is officially recognized by policy makers in Colombia are revealed in the following statement:

> A simple, largely unplanned solution served for a time in Colombia of providing a site (or acquiescence in the illegal acquisition of a site unlicensed for building) and permitting the owner to build as, how and when he could, and providing services later in one way or another. In the course of time many such neighborhoods which started out as ramshackle and unsanitary slums became acceptable barrios and the original occupants built up a patrimony, and an additional income by renting rooms or setting up small shops. A sense of neighborhood was preserved and services gradually improved . . . most such building has occurred in barrios piratas. [Colombian National Planning Office, 1974: 69]

Government response to invasion barrios. Unlike many of the principal urban centers of Latin America, Bogotá has not experienced the emergence of a large number of squatter settlements, or *barrios de invasión* as they are known in Bogotá itself. While the officially recognized number of seven such barrios may be too low, there is no question that the phenomenon is relatively rare in Bogotá. A government study published in 1972 suggests that less than 1 percent of the housing stock of the city is composed of invasion barrios (Colombian National Planning Office, 1972: 30).

Two factors already discussed explain in part why invasion barrios have failed to develop in Bogotá, where migration rates and income levels are comparable to such invasion-plagued cities as Lima, Mexico City, and even the Colombian city of Cartagena. The first of these is the physical environment of the city. Surrounded on one side by highly valued land and on the other by steep, eroding mountains (where any clandestine settlement activity is highly visible), squatter settlements have had very little room to develop. In fact, those that have developed have usually risen at the base of the mountains (barrios Juan XXIII and El Consuelo), in the industrial zone on the western fringe of the city (barrio Nuevo Chile), or on long-unused public land (barrio Policarpa Salvarrienta). A second factor which has no doubt served to limit the number of invasion barrios in Bogotá is the "safety valve" effect of the barrios piratas. While the price of land in such barrios is often quite high (especially relative to family income), the greater security of tenure, the lower risk of open confrontation with the authorities and the prospect of eventual legalization offered by barrios piratas probably have diverted many potential squatters.

Beyond these factors we must also take note of the government's responses to past invasion attempts. Almost all land invasions in Bogotá have met with firm police action. Of those that have succeeded, several invasion attempts were usually needed before the settlement was established. Finally, it should be noted that of the seven invasion barrios officially identified, only one has been regularized. This is a far lower regularization rate than that attained by the much more favored pirate barrios. Because of this combination of government responses to invasion barrios in Bogotá, pirate barrios have clearly become the illegal housing solution of choice in the city.

Supply and Demand Characteristics of the Low-Income Housing Market in Bogotá

Having discussed a number of factors related to the development of low-income housing in Bogotá, we now turn to the related questions of (1) how these factors have influenced this housing market and (2) the nature of their influence.

Before proceeding with this analysis it is necessary to point out that while the term "housing" implies a domicile (physical dwelling) and the space (land) that it occupies, this is not an exhaustive definition of the term. Housing includes these two basic elements and a whole list or "bundle" of related goods and services. For example, Colombian planners have noted that "housing is not merely a building frame. It is that plus accessibility, plus services, plus amenities and opportunity for diversion, nearness to schools, shops and jobs" (Colombian National Planning Office, 1974: 72). Depending on the analytical question at hand, the "bundle" of goods and services may be subdivided in a number of ways and examined from a number of perspectives. For the purposes of the present analysis, an important distinction to be made is that between the "basic" goods and services of housing and the other "nonbasic" goods and services found in the bundle known as housing. We define as the basic goods of housing the minimal space (prepared land) and domicile (physical dwelling) required by an individual or family. Basic services are those required for subsistence. Nonbasic goods and services of housing, on the other hand, are those discussed by the authors cited above: many public services, easy accessibility, private sanitation services, cooking and eating facilities, and the like.

Having made the distinction between these components of the housing bundle, we need to note the difference in the income elasticity of demand between the two. Shelter is such a primary human need that the demand for basic housing is highly inelastic. That is to say that if the cost of basic housing is relatively high, low-income families will still spend a large portion of their income on it. On the other hand, the demand for nonbasic housing is more elastic, and, therefore, low-income consumers will tend to spend the remainder of their disposable income on other inelastic goods such as food and clothing.

One other important point concerning the supply and demand of the low-income housing market in Bogotá needs to be pointed out. The supply of low-income housing is low and, under present circumstances at least, relatively fixed because of the topographical and environmental characteristics and government policy responses discussed earlier. When combined with the increase of demand for such land resulting from population increases, this fixed level of supply is manifested in the housing deficit noted earlier. One method of expanding the supply of land (or, more accurately, space) required for low-income housing would be the construction of high-rise, multifamily units. But, with current financial constraints, such an approach would most certainly require some subsidization which the government has been unwilling to provide to date.

Understanding these basic aspects of the supply and demand for low-income housing in Bogotá, we may now examine their impact on the low-income housing market of the city. The following are some of the more important characteristics of the low-income housing market resulting from this structure of supply and demand.

Cost. As is noted by the National Planning Department of Colombia, "the rise in land values is a reflection of a rise in demand and of ability to pay a higher price" (Colombian National Planning Office, 1974: 59). Thus, with the increase in demand for low-income housing brought on by the growth in the number of low-income families in the city and the fixed supply of land available, low-income housing is relatively expensive in Bogotá. Because of a lack of accurate data, the expense of housing relative to family income is difficult to calculate. For example, the *Encuesta de Hogares* of 1971 showed that of the 45 percent of the families of Bogotá whose incomes are less than $2,500 pesos per month (roughly U.S. $120), between 22 percent and 28 percent of the family income is spent on housing (Zorro Sanchez, 1974: 72). However, this figure only refers to rent and does not include families who own or are acquiring their housing. In *Mercado de Tierras en Barrios Clandestinos de Bogotá,* the District Planning Office cites four somewhat representative surveys of low-income barrios that report the cost of housing for families both renting and buying (Planning Department of the District of Bogotá, 1973: 49). The amount of family income spent on housing reported in these studies varies from 17 percent to 25 percent. But these figures do not include initial down payments or monthly expenditures for services. We must also remember that when we speak of housing in this context it often means housing of the more "basic" variety (less many of the "nonbasic" goods and services). When we consider that low-income families must spend upward of 50 percent of their income on food and, therefore, may spend one-half or more of what remains on housing, the relatively high cost of housing for low-income families is seen.

Density. The density of housing may be discussed in terms of the concentration of either families or individuals in housing units. As Table 1 indicates, the high cost of housing has resulted in *high density* in the low-income housing market of Bogotá. The number of families per housing unit for families earning $3,000 pesos per month and below is 1.38, compared with 1.03 for those families earning above that figure. While low-income families spend a relatively large amount for housing, they

TABLE 1
Housing, Households and Population in Bogota (1972)

Monthly Income (in Pesos)	Housing Units	Households	Households by Housing Units	Population	Persons per Household
50- 500	10,871	17,648	1.64	74,612	4.28
500- 1,000	60,047	89,962	1.50	445,571	4.98
1,000- 1,500	64,165	87,587	1.36	479,694	5.48
1,500- 2,000	57,865	71,799	1.24	421,187	5.87
2,000- 3,000	59,808	70,248	1.17	416,419	5.92
5,000- 15,000	56,421	61,283	1.09	355,388	5.98
15,000- 30,000	56,303	58,399	1.04	358,260	6.13
30,000 and more	8,369	8,506	1.02	60,433	7.10
No information	1,990	1,990	1.00	12,210	6.14
	31,667	35,767	1.13	214,666	6.00
TOTAL	407,416	503,089	1.23	2,850,170	5.67

SOURCE: (Carlos Zorro Sanchez, 1974: 103)

consume a relatively small amount of housing in terms of space and services. Thus, we note the prevalence of shared housing or *inquilinatos* in Bogotá. The *Encuesta de Hogares* of 1970 of the National Department of Statistics noted that 35.7 percent of the families of Bogotá live in "rooms." In the usual case this means a room (of these families, 65 percent live in *one* room) or rooms in a larger housing unit where such services as water, sanitary services, and cooking facilities either are shared with a number of other families or are nonexistent.

Services. If housing is relatively expensive for low-income families, and if the demand for nonbasic housing is elastic, we should expect to find low-income families consuming relatively little in the way of nonbasic goods and services, preferring instead to spend what remains of their incomes on goods and services with a greater inelasticity of demand, such as food and clothing. As the figures quoted by Avila Bernal (1973) and cited at the beginning of this paper suggest, numbers of families in Bogotá are apparently foregoing many of these housing-related services that in other contexts would be considered essential. The following official government figures, aggregated at the barrio level, illustrate the dimensions of the problem of services in the low-income housing market of Bogotá:

- 74 barrios with water from shared community fountains only
- 40 barrios with no water service
- 139 barrios with no sewage
- 38 barrios without electricity
- 63 barrios without telephones
- 69 barrios without trash collection
- 200 barrios without paved access roads [Consultécnicos, 1972: 265-274]

Legality. The legality of the property deed may be considered as one of the housing-related services for which there is a relatively elastic demand among low-income families in

TABLE 2

Estimated Self-Construction Submarket 1964 and 1970

	1964				1970			
	Persons	Families	Housing	Buildings	Persons	Families	Housing	Buildings
Invasion Barrios	13,751	2,210	1,842	1,763	31,020	9,955	4,129	3,951
Pirata Barrios	596,687	98,472	72,030	65,841	758,371	125,107	9,158	83,650
TOTAL	610,438	100,682	73,872	67,604	789,391	135,062	9,568	87,601
Percent Increase	- - -	- - -	- - -	- - -	29.32	34.15	29.47	29.58

SOURCE: Data from Colombian National Planning Department (1971a).

TABLE 3

Types of Housing Solutions in Bogota (in thousands of housing units)

	Non-Public Commercial	Self-Construction	Public Housing
All Families (all types of tenancy)	240 (54%)	163 (34%)	42 (12%)
All Families (owning or acquiring)	49 (24%)	114 (56%)	40 (20%)
Families under $3,500 Pesos per Month (owning or acquiring)	8 (06%)	98 (71%)	32 (23%)

SOURCE: Data from Colombian National Planning Department (1971b).

Bogotá. Legality as a service provides not only security of tenure but also mobility by facilitating the sale and transfer of title and the acquisition of mortgage loans. Large numbers of families in Bogotá are willing to invest in "basic housing" while foregoing this service in favor of other necessities. According to figures prepared for the Planning Department of the District of Bogotá, 1,682,202 people lived in 202 clandestine barrios in the special district of Bogotá in 1972, and this number was growing at an annual rate of 16.2 percent (Consultécnicos, 1972: 49). However, because the demand for legality is elastic, it will be noted that in 1972 100 clandestine barrios had solicited regularization and were in the process of becoming regularized. In the same year, according to the Planning Department of the District of Bogotá, 50 barrios were legalized in the special district (Consultécnicos, 1972: 49). Thus, through a long-term investment process many families living in illegal barrios eventually acquire the service of legality.

Self-construction. A matter related to both legality and the other housing-related services discussed above is the prevalence of the phenomenon of self-construction in the low-income housing market of Bogotá. Because low-income housing is relatively costly—to the point of prohibiting the own-account construction of both basic and nonbasic housing in the majority of cases—and because the demand for nonbasic housing and related services is relatively elastic, we find that much of the construction of low-income housing in Bogotá is "spontaneous" and "progressive." Tables 2 and 3 provide some idea of the growth and size of the self-construction submarket in Bogotá. Especially striking in Table 3 is the importance of self-construction in providing basic and nonbasic housing for homeowners, and especially low-income homeowners, in Bogotá. It is clear from these data that the "legal" commercial housing market as presently constituted is simply inadequate to provide low-income housing for the city.

Public Policy and the Urban Poor: A Critical View

Having surveyed these important economic characteristics of the low-income housing market in Bogotá, let us take a closer look at the role of public policy in the area of housing—with emphasis on its present and future impact on the poor of the city.

During the years when the housing problems of Bogotá were reaching their current critical levels, public policy at all levels was generally characterized by ineffective response or outright neglect. The government policies which probably have had the greatest impact on urban housing have been designed for purposes other than solving housing-related problems. For example, the decision to deemphasize the agrarian reform program in Colombia (which has resulted in increased migration to Bogotá and other cities) was most certainly made to develop large scale agriculture, encourage urbanization for economic reasons, and to placate influential landowning groups. Similarly, the National Development Plan—which encourages urbanization (and thus migration), stimulates construction in urban areas (but not of low-cost housing), and seeks to alleviate urban unemployment—was likewise designed with little or no consideration made for the major problems in the area of low-income urban housing.

Nor have public policies on the local level been directed toward a frontal attack on the housing problems of the city. Neither the zoning regulations of the city nor the regulations dealing with construction and other standards were designed to solve the housing problems we have discussed here. But, as we have seen, all of these government policies have had a dramatic impact—a negative impact in each instance—on the low-income housing market of the city.

The government policies explicitly directed toward solving the housing problems have not been very effective in doing so. Public housing accounts for only about 12 percent of the housing in a city where 72 percent of the households have an income of $3,000 pesos per month, where the are 1.23

households per housing unit, and where 71 percent of the low-income home owners have resorted to self-construction in the building of their homes. Many of the public housing projects of the *Instituto de Crédito Territorial* (ICT) and the *Caja de Vivienda* (the national and local agencies charged with administering the majority of public housing policy in Bogotá) have been of the "showcase" variety, usually affecting few people. Also, ICT projects are generally populated by families from the upper strata of the poor and lower-middle class families. Those with very low incomes, recent migrants, and the unemployed–the very groups most in need of housing–almost never qualify for these government projects. There also appears to be a disproportionately large number of public employees (police, minor bureaucrats, and the like) who *do* manage to qualify for these projects, suggesting that public housing may often be little more than a variation of the old patron-client game–a familiar phenomenon in a variety of contexts in Colombia. In Bogotá we find that, except for some relatively weak programs of federal government agencies such as the ICT and some local government agencies, public policy in the field of housing has been at worst neglectful and at best ineffective in resolving the tremendous problems faced by the vast majority of the poor of the city.

While long-range comprehensive planning has gained increasing acceptance by decision makers in Colombia, government planning as yet has not addressed itself frontally to the problems of popular housing. This neglect on the part of government planners and decision makers, combined with the structure of supply and demand in the low-income housing market, has led to a rather curious situation as regards the distribution of wealth in Bogotá. Mindful of certain criticisms of the National Development Plan, especially those dealing with the impact of the plan on the distribution of wealth and income in Colombia, the Department of National Planning in 1974 published a document suggesting policy alternatives for the future. This document merits some close attention here, especially in regard to its analysis of urban land values, urban housing, and the role of government.

As the document notes, the rise in urban land values resulting from the supply and demand patterns mentioned here earlier has important implications for national development because, unlike the case of agricultural land where the rise in value is usually not so significant and is often due to permanent improvements made for agricultural purposes, "the rise in value (of urban land sites) is almost exclusively attributable to the growing scarcity in relation to the growth of the community. It is the community itself that creates the rise in land values" (Colombian National Planning Office, 1974: 61-62). The impact of the relationship between the supply and demand of urban land on the distribution of wealth is profound, as is noted by the Department of National Planning. The document further states that the rise in urban land values is rapidly becoming one of the chief sources of inequality of wealth, income, and opportunity in the country.

The solution proposed by the Department of National Planning is, in principle, a simple one. They suggest policy measures that would

> define certain areas and certain sized lots in metropolitan areas where a rise in land values after a certain date would be subject to capture by public authorities for specific uses. If annual assessments were carried out accurately to correspond to commercial values it would be relatively simple to calculate the rises attributable to works on which a valorization tax had been paid, and then to the capture, say of 75% of the remainder. This could either be paid over a two or three year term, or be carried over at a value constant basis at 8% until the ownership of the land was transferred. [Colombian National Planning Office, 1974: 65]

Such a policy designed to "capture" the rising land values for public use would, according to the Department of National Planning, serve the dual purpose of providing funds needed for urban planning and of stemming the forces leading to badly skewed income distributions.

This document recommends a rather radical departure from current policy in suggesting that the government capture surplus land values which are then to be used for providing public services, the financing of housing, and other such purposes. The extent to which such a recommendation will actually be implemented in the future is a matter of speculation. As we noted previously, several earlier attempts to radically alter urban policy have met with little success in the Colombian Congress. Whether such a plan to redistribute wealth in the urban centers can be implemented at this point in the political history of the country is, to say the least, questionable.

Whether or not this new plan is ever implemented, we have already pointed out at least three ways in which the government is *already* redistributing wealth in favor of some of the poor through its housing policy. The three are (1) acquiescence in the establishment of invasion barrios; (2) acquiescence in the temporary illegal status of private barrios, and (3) the establishment of subsidized government housing. We will now examine briefly the redistributive aspects of these three government policies.

INVASION BARRIOS

When urban land is invaded for the purpose of establishing a housing settlement, the government has the choice of applying the amount of force required to expell the invaders or not doing so. When the latter alternative is chosen the resulting housing settlement is established with the de facto acquiescence of the government, for whatever reason. As we have noted, this rarely has occurred in Bogotá—but, where it has, it has had the following effects. In the first place, it has in almost every case brought urban land into the low-income housing market that otherwise probably would not have been used for that purpose. Thus, by expanding the supply of urban land to be used for low-income housing, the invaders have decreased the demand for all other units of low-income housing, thereby decreasing their cost. More important, however, once the land developed by the invaders has become a part of the housing market, the rising value of the land and the increased value added through investment in construction become profit for the invader. As invaders tend to come from the very lowest income groups, the redistribution of wealth that takes place through this process is liable to have a significant economic impact on this group.

PIRATE BARRIOS

The realities of the mortgage market combined with statutory housing standards make the purchase of a home out of reach for a great many urban dwellers in Colombia. High interest rates for loans combined with the need for a high original investment (for land plus the requisite services) preclude many low-income families from investing in housing. Consequently, profits from the rising value of urban land are captured by high-income groups in the form of rent. By acquiescing in the establishment of illegal pirate barrios, however, the government enables many low-income families to invest in housing. While the original investment is usually quite low (involving only land and "basic" housing), over a number of years the investment usually expands to include those goods and services for which the demand is more elastic. If, after a number of years, a pirate barrio becomes legalized and residents acquire registered title to their land, the transferability and, hence, the value of the land are increased. In any event, the establishment of pirate barrios has the effect of expanding the supply of low-income housing (for it is assumed that much of this housing would not come into existence otherwise) and of enabling low-income groups to profit from the rise in urban land values by allowing them to invest in housing where they otherwise would not be able to do so.

GOVERNMENT HOUSING PROJECTS

The redistributive effects of government housing are more direct and obvious than in the other cases cited. In such housing projects the requisite services are generally subsidized by the government. Likewise, loans usually are provided at below the market value. The redistributive effect is, as in the case of invasion and pirate barrios, that low-income families are able to invest in housing and to profit from the increase in the value of urban land where they otherwise would be excluded from doing so.

Conclusion: Public Housing Policy and the Future of Bogotá

As we have just noted, government policies and, in some cases, the lack of coherent policies have combined to have the net effect of the distribution of wealth to certain groups. The overall desirability of this situation is somewhat mitigated, however, by the fact that recent migrants and low-income families who rent are the ones who must still pay for the high cost of urban land. Furthermore, since the pirate housing market is essentially an extralegal one, the poor remain unprotected from unscrupulous urbanizers. Discussions with officials at the District Planning Office, the local government agency in charge of legalizing pirate barrios in Bogotá, have lead this author to conclude that most individuals who buy land in pirate barrios have almost no understanding of the legal issues involved in acquiring legal title to their land or the services required to legalize their barrio. It appears, therefore, that a great deal more governmental action is needed in this area if the tremendous problems that exist today are to be confronted effectively. Public revenues acquired through "captured land values" or through more traditional means might well be used for some form of government housing, rent subsidies, and other means to assist recent migrants and those in the lower strata of the poor. Attempts should also be made toward more efficient use of land for government housing. The traditional approach of providing single-unit housing for numbers of low and lower-middle income families has proved to have a very limited success.

Another area where government action seems desirable is the legal codes relating to housing. As we noted, the government has seen fit to impose some relatively tight requirements for housing construction and minimum services while continuing to allow illegal barrios to form. Government action to eliminate the legal bottlenecks that exist in the area of barrio legalization would have a number of beneficial effects. First, the tremendous uncertainty and potential for exploitation would be removed from the urban poor who are seeking to acquire land for housing. Also, by facilitating the transfer of land title the process of filtration in the housing market would be facilitated and some distortions in the supply and demand for housing would be eliminated by increasing mobility within the housing market.

As concerns the question of standards, there is also a need for new directions in public policy. The standards presently in effect are probably unrealistic given the extent and degree of the poverty in the city. There is much to be said, however, for realistic standards, universally and rigidly enforced, providing that they are combined with an active government program of assistance to low-income property owners in complying with these norms. The establishment of "urban extension programs" (along the lines of rural extension programs that provide technical aid to farmers) to aid low-income barrio dwellers with construction and service problems and the provision of financing for services and property loans are public policies worthy of consideration. In any event, it is suggested that future government housing policies for Bogotá must be comprehensive enough to include innovative solutions to the problems of the low-income housing market if the housing needs of the city are to be met.

REFERENCES

AMATO, P. (1970) "An analysis of the changing patterns of elite residential areas in Bogotá, Colombia." Ph.D. dissertation, Cornell University.

AVILA BERNAL, A. (1973) "La Población y el problema de La Vivienda en Colombia." Bogotá: Revista de La Cámara de Comercio de Bogotá 15: 182-193.

CARDONA, R. and A. SIMMONS (1973a) "Apuntes Sobre La Llamada 'Crisis' en Las Grandes Ciudades." Bogotá: Monografías de la Corporación Centro Regional de Población.

--- (1973b) "Hacia un Modelo Sobre Las Migraciones Internas en América Latina." Unpublished paper presented at the Primera Reunión Latino-Americana Sobre Políticos de Migración, Urbanización y Distribución de La Población, Bogotá.

Colombian National Planning Office (1974) "Colombian urban policy in the plan of development." Bogotá: Colombian National Planning Office Document.

--- (1972) Política de Vivienda. Bogotá: Resumen de La Unidad de Desarrollo Regional y Urbano.

--- (1971a) Informe No. 5, "Stock de Vivienda del Sector Popular en Bogotá (Auto-construcción no Institucional)." Bogotá.

--- (1971b) "Algunas Características del Sector de Auto-construcción de Vivienda; Proyecciónes de su Importancia Relativa en el Futuro." Bogotá.

Consultécnicos (1972) Estudio de Normas Mínimas de Urbanización, Servicios Públicos y Servicios Comunitarios. Bogotá: Instituto de Crédito Territorial.

FIERRO, M. G. (1973) "Algunos Problemas Relacionados con la Migración Interna en Colombia." Documento CEDE No. 003. Bogotá: Centro de Estudios Sobre Desarrollo Económico.

Planning Department of the District of Bogotá (1973) Mercado de Tierras en Barrios Clandestinos de Bogotá. Bogotá: Departamento Administrativo de Planificación Distrital.

SIMMONS, A. B. and R. CARDONA (1972) "Rural-urban migration: who comes, who stays, who returns? The case of Bogotá, Colombia." International Migration Rev. 6: 166-181.

SOLAUN, M., F. CEPEDA, and B. BAGLEY (1973) "Urban reform in Colombia. The impact of the 'politics of games' on public policy," in F. R. Rabinovitz and F. M. Trueblood (eds.) Latin American Urban Research, Vol. III. Beverly Hills, Calif.: Sage.

TURNER, J.F.C. (1971) Housing and People. Cambridge: MIT Press.

ZORRO SANCHEZ, C. (1974) "Primera Etapa del Estudio Sobre Desarrollo Inquilinatos." Documento CEDE No. 010. Bogotá: Centro de Estudios Sobre Desarrollo Econónico.

Timothy O'Dea Gauhan is a Visiting Assistant Professor of Political Science at Arizona State University. His publications and professional conference papers include works on low-income housing, political attitudes in low-income barrios *of Bogotá, Colombia, and politics of primitive societies.*

COMMENT

THE MEXICAN PRESIDENTIAL SUCCESSION

Martin Needler's review essay ("Daniel Cosío Villegas and the Interpretation of Mexico's Political System") in a recent issue of this journal raises some provocative questions about the ability of a Mexican president to pick his successor. Like most students of Mexican politics, I have made some notes on the subject with the intention of enlarging on them at a future date. The remarks below, taken from those notes, indicate how I think attention might be focused in order to progress toward clarification of the problem.

It seems to me that the president's designation of his successor, instead of manifesting the power of his office, reveals an important structural weakness in the Mexican political system. The president is saddled with the job because there is no legitimate mechanism for resolving the muted but intense conflicts that always arise within the PRI over the final choice. The incumbent president is almost the *only* Mexican (with the exception of any living ex-president) who has no political future to risk by indicating his preference; other party members have everything to lose. To support a possible "also ran" is to invite a six-year exile in political limbo.[1] Like assistant professors in a tight academic marketplace, party members behave very circumspectly. Thus, naming the candidate is the last important service to the party performed by the president in office.

It was this structural deficiency that Carlos Madrazo sought to correct in 1966 by advocating "democratization" of the candidate selection process. His rather modest plan, proposed for local-level elective posts,

Journal of Interamerican Studies and World Affairs, Vol. 19 No. 1, February 1977

threatened prematurely to bring existing conflicts into the open, where they could only have been resolved at the cost of too many political aspirations. In 1976 the surprise switch from Moya Palencia to López Portillo as the candidate-designate may have occurred because Moya had "burned" himself by too openly assuming that he had the nomination (and therefore the election) in the bag, and because President Echeverría found that premature revelation of his initial preference had increased the already high level of conflict in the party.[2] PRI watchers inside and outside of Mexico had been surprised by the early apparent choice of Moya. By his last-minute change to López Portillo, President Echeverría reintroduced the principle of uncertainty so necessary to the functioning of the party machine. How long this principle will continue to work before the whole apparatus needs a complete overhaul is a problem that becomes more urgent with the passing of each *sexenio.*

–*Evelyn P. Stevens*
Case Western Reserve University
Cleveland, Ohio 44106

NOTES

1. See Frank Brandenburg's *The Making of Modern Mexico* (Englewood Cliffs, N.J.: Prentice-Hall, 1964), p. 147. This is still a valid description of the perils of openly choosing sides too soon in the pre-*tapado* process.

2. On the significance of the term *quemado,* see my *Protest and Response in Mexico* (Cambridge, Mass.: MIT Press, 1974), pp. 26, 269, and 280.

BOOKS RECEIVED

GENERAL AND REGIONAL LATIN AMERICA

Blasier, Cole. THE HOVERING GIANT: U.S. RESPONSES TO REVOLUTIONARY CHANGE IN LATIN AMERICA. Pittsburgh: University of Pittsburgh Press, 1976. Illustrations, tables, notes, index. xix, 315 pp. $15.95 cloth, $4.95 paper.

Bryant, Shasta M. A SELECTIVE BIBLIOGRAPHY OF BIBLIOGRAPHIES OF HISPANIC AMERICAN LITERATURE. Austin: Institute of Latin American Studies, University of Texas, 1976. Index. 100 pp. Paper.

Carvajal, M. J. and David T. Geithman. FAMILY PLANNING AND FAMILY SIZE DETERMINATION: THE EVIDENCE FROM SEVEN LATIN AMERICAN CITIES. (Latin American Monographs No. 18, Center for Latin American Studies.) Gainesville: University of Florida Press, 1976. Appendices, bibliography. 96 pp. $5.00.

Duncan, W. Raymond. LATIN AMERICAN POLITICS: A DEVELOPMENTAL APPROACH. New York: Praeger Publishers, 1976. Tables, maps, appendices, index. 277 pp. $10.00 paper.

Eckstein, Susan. THE IMPACT OF REVOLUTION: A COMPARATIVE ANALYSIS OF MEXICO AND BOLIVIA. (Sage Professional Papers in Contemporary Political Sociology Series.) Beverly Hills and London: Sage Publications, 1976. Notes, references. 53 pp. $3.00 paper.

Grieb, Kenneth J. THE LATIN AMERICAN POLICY OF WARREN G. HARDING. Fort Worth: Texas Christian University Press, 1976. Bibliography, index. viii, 223 pp. $5.00 paper.

Halperin, Ernst. TERRORISM IN LATIN AMERICA. (Sage Policy Papers/The Washington Papers 33.) Beverly Hills and London: Sage Publications, 1976. Notes, references, map. 92 pp. $3.00 paper.

Kautsky, John H. PATTERNS OF MODERNIZING REVOLUTIONS: MEXICO AND THE SOVIET UNION. (Sage Professional Papers in Comparative Politics Series.) Beverly Hills and London: Sage Publications, 1975. Notes, references. 59 pp. $3.00 paper.

Liebman, Seymour B. EXPLORING THE LATIN AMERICAN MIND. Chicago: Nelson-Hall, 1976. Bibliography, index. xi, 192 pp.

Loehr, William, David Price, and Satish Raichur. A COMPARISON OF U.S. AND MULTILATERAL AID RECIPIENTS IN LATIN AMERICA, 1957-1971. (Sage

Professional Papers in International Studies Series.) Beverly Hills and London: Sage Publications, 1976. Notes, references, appendices. 48 pp. $3.00 paper.

Malloy, James M., editor. ESTUDIOS ANDINOS 10. NACION Y ESTADO EN AMERICA LATINA: NUEVAS PERSPECTIVAS. Pittsburgh: Center for Latin American Studies, University of Pittsburgh, 1975. Notas, referencias. 308 pp. Paper.

Parkinson, F. LATIN AMERICA, THE COLD WAR AND THE WORLD POWERS, 1945-1973. (Sage Library of Social Research.) Beverly Hills and London: Sage Publications, 1974. Bibliography, index. 288 pp. $12.00 cloth, $7.00 paper.

Paz, Octavio. THE SIREN AND THE SEASHELL: AND OTHER ESSAYS ON POETS AND POETRY. (Translated by Lysander Kemp and Margaret Sayers Peden; illustrated by Barry Moser.) Austin and London: University of Texas Press, 1976. Illustrations, editor's note, index. viii, 188 pp. $9.95.

Rangel, Carlos. DEL BUEN SALVAJE AL BUEN REVOLUCIONARIO. Caracas: Monte Avila Editores, C.A., 1976. 257 pp. Paper.

Ross, Waldo. PROBLEMATICA DE LA LITERATURA HISPANOAMERICANA. Berlin: Colloquium Verlag, 1976. Index. 64 pp. Paper.

Sánchez-Marco, Francisco. ACERCAMIENTO HISTORICO A LA SOCIO-LINGUISTICA. Hidalgo y Matamoros, Tlalpan, Mexico: Centro de Investigaciones Superiores, Instituto Nacional de Antropología e Historia, Ediciónes La Casa Chata, 1976. Bibliography, index. 236 pp. Paper.

Schenkel, Peter and Marco Ordonez, editores. COMUNICACION Y CAMBIO SOCIAL. Quito: El Instituto Latinoamericano de Investigaciones Sociales ILDIS, and El Centro Internacional de Estudios Superiores de Comunicación para América Latina, CIESPAL, 1975. 333 pp. Paper.

Silverman, Milton. THE DRUGGING OF THE AMERICAS: HOW MULTI-NATIONAL DRUG COMPANIES SAY ONE THING. . . . Berkeley: University of California Press, 1976. Tables, explanation of tables, references, index. xiv, 147 pp. $8.50.

Solari, Aldo E., Rolando Franco, and Joel Jutkowitz. TEORIA, ACCION, SOCIAL Y DESARROLLO EN AMERICA LATINA. México: Siglo XXI Editores, S.A., 1976. Tables, 636 pp.

Tambs, Lewis A., editor. UNITED STATES POLICY TOWARDS LATIN AMERICA: ANTECEDENTS AND ALTERNATIVES. Tempe: Center for Latin American Studies, Arizona State University, 1976. Footnotes, contributors. 219 pp. Paper.

Wachter, Susan M. LATIN AMERICAN INFLATION: THE STRUCTURALIST - MONETARIST DEBATE. Lexington, Mass.: D. C. Heath & Co., 1976. List of figures, tables, notes, bibliography, index. xiv, 165 pp. $13.50.

COUNTRIES OF LATIN AMERICA

BOLIVIA

Andrade, Victor. MY MISSIONS FOR REVOLUTIONARY BOLIVIA, 1944-1962. (Edited and with an introduction by Cole Blasier.) Pittsburgh: University of Pittsburgh Press, 1976. Index of personal names. xv, 200 pp.

BRAZIL

Keith, Henry H. and Robert A. Hayes. PERSPECTIVES ON ARMED POLITICS IN BRAZIL. Tempe: Center for Latin American Studies, Arizona State University, 1976. Glossary of terms. xxix, 258 pp. Paper.

Perlman, Janice E. THE MYTH OF MARGINALITY: URBAN POVERTY AND POLITICS IN RIO DE JANEIRO. Berkeley, Los Angeles and London: University of California Press, 1976. Foreward by Fernando Henrique Cardoso. Tables and figures, appendix, notes, bibliography, index. xxi, 341 pp.

Perry, William. CONTEMPORARY BRAZILIAN FOREIGN POLICY: THE INTERNATIONAL STRATEGY OF AN EMERGING POWER. (Foreign Policy Papers 6.) Beverly Hills and London: Sage Publications, 1976. Notes and references. 90 pp. $3.00 paper.

Rodrigues, José Honório. INDEPENDENCIA: REVOLUCAO E CONTRA-REVOLUCAO. 5v. v. 1. A evolucao política; v. 2. Economica e sociedade; v. 3. As Forcas Armadas; v. 4. A liderança nacional; em co-edicao com a Ed. de Universidade de São Paulo; v. 5. A política internacional. Rio de Janeiro: Livraria Francisco Alves Editora S.A., 1976. v.1, 389 pp.; v.2, 207 pp.; v.3, 315 pp.; v. 4, 210 pp.; v.5, 343 pp. Paper.

Stepan, Nancy. BEGINNINGS OF BRAZILIAN SCIENCE. New York: Neale Watson Academic Publications, Inc., 1976. Bibliography, plates, index. 186 pp. $12.95.

CARIBBEAN REGION

Farber, Samuel. REVOLUTION AND REACTION IN CUBA 1933-1960: A POLITICAL SOCIOLOGY FROM MACHADO TO CASTRO. Middletown, Conn.: Wesleyan University Press, 1976. Major events in Cuban history, 1868-1960, notes, bibliography, index. xix, 283 pp. $15.95.

Figueredo Díaz, Felix. LA GUERRA DE CUBA EN 1878, LA PROTESTA DE BARAGUA. (Cuadernos de Historia de la Salud Pública.) La Habana: Ministerio de Salud Pública, 1973. 338 pp.

Moreno Fraginals, Manuel. THE SUGARMILL: THE SOCIOECONOMIC COMPLEX OF SUGAR IN CUBA, 1760-1860. (Translated by Cedric Belfrage.) New York: Monthly Review Press, 1976. Notes, index. 182 pp. $23.50.

Perez Jr., Louis A. ARMY POLITICS IN CUBA, 1898-1958. Pittsburgh: University of Pittsburgh Press, 1976. Notes, bibliography, index. xvi, 240 pp. $9.95.

Roca, Sergio. CUBAN ECONOMIC POLICY AND IDEOLOGY: THE TEN MILLION TON SUGAR HARVEST. (Sage Professional Papers in International Studies Series.) Beverly Hills and London: Sage Publications, 1976. Notes, references. 72 pp. $3.00 paper.

Rodríguez Expósitio, César and Félix Figueredo y Díaz. UN HOMBRE DEL 68 Y DE LA PROTESTA DE BARAGUA. (Cuadernos de la Historia de la Sanidad Pública, No. 55.) La Habana: Ministerio de Salud Pública, 1973. 417 pp.

CENTRAL AMERICA

Karnes, Thomas L. THE FAILURE OF UNION: CENTRAL AMERICA, 1824-1975. (Revised edition.) Tempe: Center for Latin American Studies, Arizona State University, 1976. Bibliography, index. x, 283 pp.

Kelley, David Humiston. DECIPHERING THE MAYA SCRIPT. Austin and London: University of Texas Press, 1976. Illustrations, glossary, bibliography, index. xvii, 334 pp.

Latin America Bibliography Series No. 2. CENTRAL AMERICA, A BIBLIOGRAPHY. Los Angeles: Latin American Studies Center, California State University, 1976. 52 pp. Paper.

Mayo, John K., Robert C. Hornik, and Emile G. McAnany. EDUCATIONAL REFORM WITH TELEVISION: THE EL SALVADOR EXPERIENCE. Palo Alto: Stanford University Press, 1976. Appendices, tables and illustrations, figures, index. 216 pp. $11.50.

Meyer, Harvey K. HISTORICAL DICTIONARY OF HONDURAS. (Latin American Historical Dictionaries 13.) Metuchen, N.J.: Scarecrow Press, 1976. Bibliography, list of maps. xiv, 399 pp.

Vogt, Evan Z. TORTILLAS FOR THE GODS: A SYMBOLIC ANALYSIS OF ZINACANTECO RITUALS. Cambridge and London: Harvard University Press, 1976. Figures and tables, appendices, glossary, bibliography, index. xv, 224 pp.

CHILE

ALGUNOS FUNDAMENTOS DE LA INTERVENCION MILITAR EN CHILE, SEPTIEMBRE 1973. (Segunda Edición Ampliada.) Santiago: Editora Nacional Gabriela Mistral, 1974. Pictures. 133 pp. Paper.

Business School of Valparaíso, Adolfo Ibañez Foundation. THE CHILEAN ECONOMY UNDER THE POPULAR UNITY GOVERNMENT: THE CHILEAN WAY TO MARXIST SOCIALISM. Santiago: Editora Nacional Gabriela Mistral, 1974. Tables. 80 pp. Paper.

Casanova, Manuel. UNA INTEGRACION EQUITATIVA: ROL DE DERECHO EN EL ACUERDO DE CARTAGENA. Santiago: Corporación de Promoción Universitaria, No. 33, 1976. Bibliography, index. 300 pp. Paper.

CHILE, AYER, HOY. (Published by Military Junta.) Santiago: Editorial Nacional Gabriela Mistral, 1974. Pictures. 99 pp. Paper.

CHILE LIGHTS THE FREEDOM TORCH. (Published by Military Junta.) Santiago: Editorial Gabriela Mistral, 1974. Pictures. 68 pp. Paper.

Domic, Juraj. DESTRUCCION DE LAS FUERZAS ARMADAS POR EL PARTIDO COMMUNISTA. (Colección Ciencia Política No. 2.) Santiago: Editorial Vaitea, 1975. 38 pp. Paper.

Domic, Juraj. LA VIA NO CAPITALISTA DE DESARROLLO. (Colección Ciencia Política No. 1.) Santiago: Editorial Vaitea, 1975. 32 pp. Paper.

Donoso Loero, Teresa. HISTORIA DE LOS CRISTIANOS POR EL SOCIALISMO EN CHILE. Santiago: Editorial Vaitea, 1976. 209 pp. Paper.

Fontaine, Arturo, et al. NUESTRO CAMINO. (Centro de Legislación y Jurisprudencia, Inscription No. 45, 315.) Santiago: Ediciones Encina Ltda., 1976. Prologue. 260 pp. Paper.

Frei, Eduardo. EL MANDATO DE LA HISTORIA Y LAS EXIGENCIAS DEL PORVENIR. Santiago: Editorial del Pacífico, 1975. 112 pp.

Ibañez S.M., Gonzalo. EL SENTIDO DE LA LIBERTAD EN EL CONCILIO VATICANO II. (Colección Ciencia Política No. 6.) Santiago: Editorial Vaitea, 1976. 35 pp.

Kaufman, Robert R. TRANSITIONS TO STABLE AUTHORITARIAN-CORPORATE REGIMES: THE CHILEAN CASE? (Sage Professional Papers in Comparative Politics Series.) Beverly Hills and London: Sage Publications, 1976. Notes, references. 68 pp. $3.00 paper.

Klosson, Boris. TECNICA SOVIETICA PARA LA CONQUISTA DEL PODER TOTAL: LA EXPERIENCIA COMUNISTA EN CHILE. (Based on conference dictated by Klosson.) Santiago: Editora Nacional Gabriela Mistral, 1976. 125 pp.

Nunn, Frederick M. THE MILITARY IN CHILEAN HISTORY: ESSAYS ON CIVIL-MILITARY RELATIONS, 1810-1973. Albuquerque: University of New Mexico Press, 1976. Bibliographical notes, index. xiv, 343 pp. $15.00.

Ortega, Hugo, Fernando Nuñez, and Rolando Klagges. EDUCACION SUPERIOR EN CHILE EN EL CAMPO DE LAS CIENCIAS AGROPECUARIAS Y FORESTALES. Santiago: Corporación de Promoción Universitaria, No. 32, 1976. Bibliography. 267 pp. Paper.

Scherz García, Luís. LA UNIVERSIDAD LATINOAMERICANA EN LA DECADA DEL 80. Santiago: Corporación de Promoción Universitaria, No. 34, 1976. 250 pp. Paper.

Schiefelbein, Ernesto and Noel McGinn. EL SISTEMA ESCOLAR Y EL PROBLEMA DEL INGRESO A LA UNIVERSIDAD. Santiago: Corporación de Promoción Universitaria, No. 35, 1976. Tables. 532 pp. Paper.

SIETE ESTUDIOS. HOMENAJE DE LA FACULTAD DE CIENCIAS HUMANAS A EUGENIO PEREIRA SALAS. Pedro Cunill G., Guillermo Feliu C., Christian Guerrero Y., Alvaro Jara H., Richard Krebs W., Rolando Mellafe R., Mario Orellana R. Santiago: Universidad de Chile, Sede Santiago Oriente, Facultad de Ciencias Humanas, 1975. 190 pp. Paper.

Silva, Lautaro. ALLENDE: EL FIN DE UNA AVENTURA. Santiago: Ediciónes Patria Nueva, 1976. Pictures. 386 pp. Paper.

Villa Lopez de Paez, Mireya. LA REPUBLICA SOCIALISTA DE CHILE DE 1932 Y SUS PROYECCIONES. Serie materiales de Trabajo No. 2. Tesis de grado de la autora para su licenciatura. Caracas: Instituto Latinoamericano de Investigaciones Sociales (ILDIS) Fundación Friedrich Ebert, 1975. 52 pp. Paper.

ECUADOR

Moncada, Jose. INTEGRACION ANDINA Y DESARROLLO ECONOMICO: EL CASO ECUATORIANO. Serie materiales de Trabajo No. 3. Caracas: ILDIS, Fundación Friedrich Ebert, 1975. 84 pp. Paper.

MEXICO

Anderson, Arthur J.O., Frances Berdan, and James Lockhart, editors. BEYOND THE CODICES: THE NAHUA VIEW OF COLONIAL MEXICO. (With a linguistic essay by Ronald W. Langacker.) Berkeley: UCLA Latin American Studies Series, University of California Press, 1976. Appendices, bibliography, illustrations. ix, 235 pp. $12.00.

Anderson, Rodney D. OUTCASTS IN THEIR OWN LAND: MEXICAN INDUSTRIAL WORKERS, 1906-1911. DeKalb: Northern Illinois University Press, 1976. Illustrations, appendices, bibliographical comments, bibliography, index. xxiii, 407 pp. $15.00.

Bailey, David C. and William H. Beezley. A GUIDE TO HISTORICAL SOURCES IN SALTILLO, COAHUILA. (Monograph Series No. 13.) East Lansing: Latin American Studies Center, Michigan State University, 1975. Foreward by John M. Hunter. Bibliography. 101 pp. $3.00 paper.

Centro de Estudios Lingüísticos y Literarios de El Colegio de Mexico. COPLAS DEL FELIZ AMOR. (Cancionero Folkórico de México, Tomo I, Margit Frenk Alatorre, directora.) Guanajuato: Empresa El Colegio de México, 1975. Bibliography, index. 426 pp. Paper.

Cosío Villegas, Daniel. LA SUCESION: DESENLACE Y PERSPECTIVAS. Tabasco: Editorial Joaquin Mortiz, S. A., 1976. 118 pp. Paper.

Davis, Thomas B. ASPECTS OF FREEMASONRY IN MODERN MEXICO: AN EXAMPLE OF SOCIAL CLEAVAGE. New York: Vantage Press, 1976. Index. xxiv, 421 pp. $10.00.

Geijerstam, Claes af. POPULAR MUSIC IN MEXICO. Albuquerque: The University of New Mexico Press, 1976. Notes, bibliography, comments on recordings, index, illustrations. xiv, 187 pp. $10.00.

Knowlton, Robert J. CHURCH PROPERTY AND THE MEXICAN REFORM, 1856-1910. DeKalb: Northern Illinois University Press, 1976. Appendices, bibliography, index. xii, 265 pp. $12.50.

Krauze, Enrique. CAUDILLOS CULTURALES EN LA REVOLUCION MEXICANA. México: Siglo XXI Editores, S.A., 1976. Pictures. 329 pp. Paper.

Ladd, Doris M. THE MEXICAN MOBILITY AT INDEPENDENCE 1780-1826. (Latin American Monographs, No. 40. Institute of Latin American Studies, The University of Texas at Austin.) Austin: University of Texas Press, 1976. Appendices, notes, glossary, bibliography, index. 316 pp. $15.95 cloth, $5.95 paper.

Lafaye, Jacques. QUETZALCOATL AND GUADALUPE: THE FORMATION OF MEXICAN NATIONAL CONSCIOUSNESS 1531-1813. (Foreward by Octavio Paz.) Translated by Benjamin Keen. Chicago: University of Chicago Press, 1976. Chronology, notes, index. xxx, 336 pp. $22.00.

Malagón Barceló, Javier. HISTORIA MENOR. (Historical essays first published in 1944-45.) México: Sepsetentas, 1976. 164 pp. Paper.

Meyer, Jean A. THE CRISTERO REBELLION: THE MEXICAN PEOPLE BETWEEN CHURCH AND STATE 1926-1929. (Translated by Richard Southern.) New York and London: Cambridge University Press, Cambridge Latin American Studies No. 24, 1976. 260 pp. $19.50.

Osborn, Thomas Noel II. HIGHER EDUCATION IN MEXICO. El Paso: Texas Western Press, University of Texas at El Paso, 1976. List of tables, bibliography, appendix, index. xv, 150 pp. $8.00.

Palmer, Colin A. SLAVES OF THE WHITE GOD: BLACKS IN MEXICO, 1570-1650. Cambridge and London: Harvard University Press, 1976. Tables, glossary, bibliography, notes, index. viii, 234 pp.

Perissinotto, Giorgio Sabino Antonio. FONOLOGIA DEL ESPANOL HABLADO EN LA CIUDAD DE MEXICO: ENSAYO DE UN METODO SOCIOLINGUISTICO. (Translated by Raúl Avila.) Guanajuato: El Colegio de México, 1975. Bibliography, appendix, tables. 134 pp. Paper.

Sepúlveda Amor, Bernardo, Olga Pellicer de Brody, and Lorenzo Meyer. LAS EMPRESAS TRANSNACIONALES EN MEXICO. Guanajuato: El Colegio de México, 1974. Tables. 167 pp. Paper.

Unikel, Louis. EL DESARROLLO URBANO DE MEXICO. Guanajuato: El Colegio de México, 1976. Bibliography. 466 pp. Paper.

Warman, Arturo. . . . Y VENIMOS A CONTRADECIR, LOS CAMPESINOS DE MORELOS Y EL ESTADO NACIONAL. Hidalgo y Matamoros, Tlalpan, México: Centro de Investigaciones Superiores del INAH, Ediciones de la Casa Chata. Maps, bibliography. 351 pp. Paper.

Wilkie, James W., Michael C. Meyer, and Edna Monzon de Wilkie. CONTEMPORARY MEXICO: PAPERS OF THE IV INTERNATIONAL CONGRESS OF MEXICAN HISTORY. Berkeley: Latin American Studies Series Vol. 29, UCLA Latin American Center, 1976. Appendix, program of the Congress, index. 858 pp.

PERU

Bernales B., Enrique. MOVIMIENTOS SOCIALES Y MOVIMIENTOS UNIVERSITARIOS EN EL PERU. Lima: Pontificia Universidad Católica del Peru, 1975. Tables, bibliography. 57 pp.

Bolton, Ralph and Sylvia Forman, editors. ESTUDIOS ANDINOS 11: CONFLICTO E INTEGRACION EN LOS ANDES. Pittsburgh: University of Pittsburgh, Centro de Estudios Latinoamericanos, 1976. 257 pp. Paper.

Calderón Cockburn, Julio, Alfredo Filomeno, and Henry García Pease. PERU: 1968-1974, CRONOLOGIA POLITICA, TOMO III. Lima: Desco, Centro de Estudios y Promoción del Desarrollo, Area de Estudios Política, 1975. Sources and methodology, index. 1135 pp.

Chaplin, David, editor. PERUVIAN NATIONALISM: A CORPORATIST REVOLUTION. Edison, N.J.: Transaction Books, 1976. Index. 494 pp.

Collier, David. SQUATTERS AND OLIGARCHS: AUTHORITARIAN RULE AND POLICY CHANGE IN PERU. Baltimore: The Johns Hopkins University Press, 1976. Tables, figures, appendices, notes, selected bibliography, index. xi, 187 pp. $10.95.

Fitzgerald, E.V.K. THE STATE AND ECONOMIC DEVELOPMENT: PERU SINCE 1968. Cambridge: Cambridge University Press, 1976. Tables, appendices, bibliography. ix, 127 pp.

Middlebrook, Kevin J. and David Scott Palmer. MILITARY GOVERNMENT AND CORPORATIVIST POLITICAL DEVELOPMENT, LESSONS FROM PERU. (Sage Professional Papers in Comparative Politics Series.) Beverly Hills and London: Sage Publications, 1975. Bibliography, diagrams. 60 pp.

Neale-Silva, Eduardo. CESAR VALLEJO EN SU FACE TRILCICA. Madison: University of Wisconsin Press, 1976. Epílogo, apéndice, registro de poemas, índice de nombres propios, lexico poético. 663 pp. $20.00 paper.

VENEZUELA

Grases, Pedro. LA OBRA DE PEDRO GRASES. Caracas: Las Prensas Venezolanas de Editorial Arte, 1976. Libros y folletos, ediciónes, compilaciónes y prólogos, nota personal, índice. 300 pp. Paper.

Kamen-Kaye, Dorothy. VENEZUELAN FOLKWAYS: TWENTIETH-CENTURY SURVIVALS OF FOLK BELIEFS, CUSTOMS, AND TRADITIONS OF CARACAS AND THE VENEZUELAN COUNTRYSIDE. (Originally, CARACAS EVERYDAY.) Detroit: Blaine Ethridge, reprint of *The Caracas Journal,* 1947. New foreward by Raquel Cisternas. xix, 256 pp. $14.50.

Nazoa, Aquiles. LEONCIO MARTINEZ. Genial y Ingenioso–La Obra Literaria y Gráfica del Gran Artista Caraqueno Leoncio Martínez en una selección de Aquiles Nazoa. Ordenada por el doctor Rafeal Dominguez Sisco, presidente del Concejo Municipal del Distrito Federal. Caracas: Litografía Técnocolor, 1976. 159 pp.

Nazoa, Aquiles. RAUL SANTANA: CON UN PUEBLO EN EL BOLSILLO. (Concejo Municipal del Distrito Federal.) Caracus: Litografía Técnocolor S. A., 1976. 159 pp.

Nectario María, Brother. INDICE DE DOCUMENTOS REFERENTES A LOS OBISPOS DE VENEZUELA, 1532/1816, EXISTENTES EN LOS ARCHIVO GENERAL DE INDIAS DE SEVILLA. (Universidad Católica Andrés Bello, Instituto de Investigaciónes Históricas.) Caracas: Las Prensas Venezolanas de Editorial Arte, 1975. Presentación, índice. 298 pp. Paper.

Nuñez, Enrique Bernardo. JUICIOS SO RE LA HISTORIA DE VENEZUELA: CUBAGUA, ORINOCO, TRES MOMENTOS EN LA CONTROVERSIA DE LIMITES DE GUAYANA. (Concejo Municipal del Distrito Federal.) Caracas: Cromoprint C.A., 1976. Prólogo de Pedro Beroes, appendix. v, 202 pp.

MISCELLANEOUS

Baaklini, Abdo I. and James J. Heaphey. LEGISLATIVE INSTITUTION BUILDING IN BRAZIL, COSTA RICA, AND LEBANON. (Sage Professional Papers in Administrative and Policy Studies Series.) Beverly Hills and London: Sage Publications, 1976. Notes, references. 60 pp. $3.00 paper.

Bingham de Urquidi, Mary. MISERICORDIA EN MADRID. México: B. Costa-Amic, 1975. Introduction. 497 pp. Paper.

Butterworth, Robert Lyle, with Margaret E. Scranton. MANAGING INTERSTATE CONFLICT, 1947-1974: DATA WITH SYNOPSES. (Thirty-nine of 310 conflicts summarized involve nations of Latin America and the Caribbean.) Pittsburgh: University Center for International Studies, University of Pittsburgh, 1976. Appendix, index. vii, 535 pp. $16.95 cloth, $6.95 paper.

Casanova Albarez, Francisco. NEW HORIZONS FOR THE THIRD WORLD. (Foreward by Sol M. Linowitz.) Washington, D.C.: Public Affairs Press, 1976. Appendices. 136 pp. $6.00 paper.

Correa, Marcial Rubio. PORTUGAL: DEL GOLPE A LAS ELECCIONES. Lima: DESCO, Centro de Estudios y Promoción del Desarrollo, 1976. 150 pp. Paper.

d'A Jones, Peter. SINCE COLUMBUS: PLURALISM AND POVERTY IN THE HISTORY OF THE AMERICAS. Totowa, N.J.: Rowman and Littlefield, 1976. Maps and illustrations, index. xvi, 282 pp. $12.50.

Dozer, Donald Marquand, ed. THE MONROE DOCTRINE: ITS MODERN SIGNIFICANCE. (Revised edition.) Tempe: Center for Latin American Studies, Arizona State University, 1976. Chronological highlights of the Monroe Doctrine, notes on sources. xii, 262 pp. Paper.

Kilson, Martin L. and Robert I. Rotberg, editors. THE AFRICAN DIASPORA: INTERPRETIVE ESSAYS. (Essays on Brazil and the French and British Caribbean are included.) Cambridge and London: Harvard University Press, 1976. Appendix, authors, index. 510 pp. $18.50.

Latin America Bibliography Series No. 1. LATIN AMERICA AND JAPAN, A BIBLIOGRAPHY. (Latin American Studies Center.) Los Angeles: California State University, 1975. 19 pp. Paper.

Loewenberg, J. Joseph, Walter J. Gershenfeld, H. J. Glasbeek, B. A. Hepple, and Kenneth F. Walker. COMPULSORY ARBITRATION: AN INTERNATIONAL COMPARISON. (One of five country surveys concerns Jamaica.) Lexington: Lexington Books, D. C. Heath & Co., 1976. List of tables. xv, 213 pp. $17.00.

McCall, Louis A. REGIONAL INTEGRATION: A COMPARISON OF EUROPEAN AND CENTRAL AMERICAN DYNAMICS. (Sage Professional Papers in International Studies Series.) Beverly Hills and London: Sage Publications, 1976. Notes, bibliography. 80 pp. $3.00 paper.

Ogelsby, J.C.M. GRINGOS FROM THE FAR NORTH: ESSAYS IN THE HISTORY OF CANADIAN-LATIN AMERICAN RELATIONS 1866-1968. Toronto: Macmillan of Canada. Appendix, bibliography, index. xiv, 346 pp. $17.95.

Onushkin, Victor G., editors. PLANNING THE DEVELOPMENT OF UNIVERSITIES–III. (Includes case studies on the Federal University of Bahia, Brazil; National Autonomous University of Nicaragua; University of the South, Bahia Blanca, Argentina; and University of Cuyo–Mendoza–Argintina.) Paris: International Institute for Educational Planning, the UNESCO Press, 1974. 454 pp. Paper.

Organisation for Economic Cooperation and Development (OECD). GEOGRAPHICAL DISTRIBUTION OF FINANCIAL FLOWS TO DEVELOPING COUNTRIES: DATA ON DISBURSEMENTS AND COMMITMENTS IN 1974. (In French and English.) Paris: OECD, 1976, xvii, 112 pp. Paper.

Sorkin, Alan L. HEALTH ECONOMICS IN DEVELOPING COUNTRIES. Lexington: D. C. Heath and Company, 1976. List of tables, notes, index. xiv, 200 pp. $16.00.

Tapia Valdes, Jorge. NEO-AUTORITARISMO O NEO-FASCISMO? ENSAYO DE INTERPRETACION JURIDICO-INSTITUCIONAL. Serie materiales de trabajo No. 4. (Three of the five chapters deal with Brazil, Argentina, and Chile.) Caracas: Instituto Latinoamericano de Investigaciones Sociales (ILDIS) Fundación Friedrich Ebert, 1976. 80 pp. Paper.

Young, Crawford. THE POLITICS OF CULTURAL PLURALISM. (Chapter on Latin American Indians: Fugitive Ethnicity.) Madison: University of Wisconsin Press, 1976. Maps, tables, index. xii, 560 pp. $20.00.

Publisher's Note: The following information is printed in accordance with U.S. postal regulations: Statement of Ownership, Management and Circulation (required by 39 U.S.C. 3685). 1. Title of Publication: JOURNAL OF INTERAMERICAN STUDIES AND WORLD AFFAIRS. 2. Date of Filing: October 15, 1976. 3. Frequency of Issue: Quarterly. 3A. No. of Issues Published Annually: 4 (four). 3B. Annual Subscription Price: institutions, $22.50; individuals, $13.50. 4. Location of Known Office of Publication: 275 South Beverly Drive, Beverly Hills (Los Angeles), California 90212. 5. Location of the Headquarters or General Business Offices of the Publishers: 275 South Beverly Drive, Beverly Hills (Los Angeles), California 90212. 6. Names and Complete Addresses of Publisher, Editor, and Managing Editor: Publisher: Sara Miller McCune, 1102 South Oakhurst Street, Los Angeles, California 90035; Editor: John P. Harrison, Box 248134, Univ. of Miami, Coral Gables, FL 33124; Managing Editor: None. 7. Owner (If owned by a corporation, its name and address must be stated and also immediately thereunder the names and addresses of stockholders owning or holding 1% or more of total amount of stock. If not owned by a corporation, the names and addresses of the individual owners must be given. If owned by a partnership or other unincorporated firm, its name and address, as well as that of each individual must be given.): Sage Publications, Inc., 275 South Beverly Drive, Beverly Hills, California 90212; Sara Miller McCune, 1102 South Oakhurst Street, Los Angeles, California 90035; Marvin Sirot, Mohawk Lane, Greenwich, Connecticut 06830; Gustave Sirot, Wingate Road, Guilford, Connecticut 06340; John B. Hurford, 220 East 63rd Street, New York, New York 10021; Albert L. Zesiger, 1125 Fifth Avenue, New York, New York 10028; Judith C. Zesiger, 1125 Fifth Avenue, New York, New York 10028. 8. Known Bondholders, Mortgagees, and Other Security Holders Owning or Holding 1% or More of Total Amount of Bonds, Mortgages or Other Securities: None. 9. For Completion by Nonprofit Organizations Authorized to Mail at Special Rates (Section 132.122, PSM): Not Applicable.

	Av. No. Copies Each Issue During Preceding 12 Months	Actual No. of Copies of Single Issue Published Nearest to Filing Date
10. Extent and Nature of Circulation		
A. Total no. copies printed (net press run) . . .	1638	1600
B. Paid circulation:		
1. Sales through dealers and carriers, street vendors and counter sales	33	25
2. Mail subscriptions	1224	1155
C. Total paid circulation (sum of 10B1 and 10B2)	1257	1180
D. Free distribution by mail, carrier or other means: samples, complimentary, and other free copies	103	90
E. Total distribution (sum of C & D)	1360	1270
F. Copies not distributed:		
1. Office use, left-over, unaccounted, spoiled after printing	278	330
2. Returns from news agents	—	—
G. Total (sum of E, F1 and 2—should equal net press run shown in A)	1638	1600

11. I certify that the statements made by me above are correct and complete. (Signed) Sara Miller McCune, Publisher and President. 12. 39 U.S.C. 3626 provides in pertinent part: "No person who would have been entitled to mail matter under former section 4359 of this title shall mail such matter at the rates provided under this subsection unless he files annually with the Postal Service a written request for permission to mail matter at such rates." In accordance with the provisions of this statute, I hereby request permission to mail the publication named in Item 1 at the reduced postage rates presently authorized by 39 U.S.C. 3626. (Signed) Sara Miller McCune, Publisher and President.

Advertising Supplement:

Journal of Interamerican Studies and World Affairs

This supplement has been prepared especially for our readers to bring them information and announcements of professional interest. By placing advertisements in the pages of this journal, our advertisers have indicated a desire to communicate with our readers. We hope our readers will acknowledge their indirect support of the journal and its purposes by mentioning the journal in correspondence with advertisers.

Vol. 19 No. 2
May 1977

JOURNAL OF INTERAMERICAN STUDIES

and WORLD AFFAIRS

A Publication of the Center for Advanced International Studies,
The University of Miami

SAGE PUBLICATIONS

Journal of INTERAMERICAN STUDIES and WORLD AFFAIRS

The editors and publisher wish to acknowledge with gratitude the assistance and encouragement of the Center for Advanced International Studies, University of Miami, in providing ancillary services and support for this journal.

Journal of
INTERAMERICAN
STUDIES
and WORLD AFFAIRS

Vol. 19
No. 2
May
1977

CONTENTS

Patronage, Politics, and the Articulation of Local Community and National Society in Pre-1968 Brazil
SIDNEY M. GREENFIELD 139

Barros Arana, Vicuña Mackenna, Amunátegui: The Historian as National Educator
GERTRUDE MATYOKA YEAGER 173

Agrarian Policies in Dependent Societies: Costa Rica
MITCHELL A. SELIGSON 201

Foreign Técnicos and the Modernization of Paraguay, 1840-1870
JOHN HOYT WILLIAMS 233

REVIEW ESSAYS

Pantaleon and the Visitors
GABRIEL ESCOBAR M. 259

Autobiography and Decision-Making in Mexican Politics
RODERIC A. CAMP 275

BOOKS RECEIVED 285

SAGE PUBLICATIONS / *Beverly Hills* *London*

POLICY: THE JOURNAL OF INTERAMERICAN STUDIES AND WORLD AFFAIRS reflects the interests of the scholarly community and interested public concerned with the social, economic, political, and cultural aspects of life in Latin America (including the Caribbean); particularly in those instances where the subject is of concern to more than one of the traditional disciplines. As these concerns change, so will the content of the journal.

ARTICLES which have special relevance for interrelationships between American nations and of those nations with the rest of the world will be given special consideration. An effort will be made to include occasional articles that state an unusual or even discordant position on a subject of broad interest to be supplemented by critical comments of authorities representing differing positions on the topic. The editors continue to welcome articles by scholars from all parts of the world.

MANUSCRIPTS should be submitted in duplicate to: Editor, JOURNAL OF INTERAMERICAN STUDIES AND WORLD AFFAIRS, Box 24-8134, University of Miami, Coral Gables, Florida 33124. Manuscripts should be typewritten, double-spaced, with footnotes, references, tables, and charts on separate pages, and should follow the current journal style. A brief biographical paragraph describing each author's current affiliation, research interests, and recent publications should accompany the manuscript.

CORRESPONDENCE regarding book reviews should be sent directly to: Book Review Editor, JOURNAL OF INTERAMERICAN STUDIES AND WORLD AFFAIRS, Box 24-8134, University of Miami, Coral Gables, Florida 33124.

JOURNAL OF INTERAMERICAN STUDIES AND WORLD AFFAIRS is published four times annually—in February, May, August, and November.

Subscriptions: Regular institutional rate $22.50. Individuals may subscribe at a one-year rate of $13.50. Add $1.00 per year for subscriptions outside the United States. Orders from U.K., Europe, the Middle East, and Africa should be sent to the London office (address below). Noninstitutional orders **must** be paid by personal check.

Second-class postage paid at Beverly Hills, California.

Inquiries: Address all correspondence and permissions requests to SAGE PUBLICATIONS, INC., 275 South Beverly Drive, Beverly Hills, California 90212. Inquiries and subscriptions from U.K., Europe, the Middle East, and Africa should be sent to SAGE PUBLICATIONS LTD, St George's House, 44 Hatton Garden, London EC1N 8ER. Other orders should be sent to the Beverly Hills office.

Advertising: Current rates and specifications may be obtained by writing to the Advertising Manager at the Beverly Hills office (address above).

This journal is abstracted in **Historical Abstracts, Human Resources Abstracts, Sage Urban Studies Abstracts,** and **International Political Science Abstracts.** It is indexed in **Public Affairs Information Service, Current Contents, Social Sciences Citation Index, Social Sciences Index,** and **ABC POL SCI.**

Back Issues: Information about availability and prices of back issues may be obtained from the publisher's order department (address above). Write to London office for sterling prices.

Claims for undelivered copies must be made no later than three months following month of publication. The publisher will supply missing copies when losses have been sustained in transit and where the reserve stock will permit.

Change of Address: Six weeks' advance notice must be given when notifying of change of address. Please send old address label along with the new address to insure proper identification. Please specify name of journal.

SIDNEY M. GREENFIELD
Departments of Anthropology and Sociology
University of Wisconsin–Milwaukee
Milwaukee, WI 53201

PATRONAGE, POLITICS, AND THE ARTICULATION OF LOCAL COMMUNITY AND NATIONAL SOCIETY IN PRE-1968 BRAZIL

The following pages examine the relationship between the transactions that constitute systems of patronage and clientage and politics as it operated in the Brazilian state of Minas Gerais in the mid-1960s. The objective will be to show how the asymmetrical exchanges of patronage and the political-electoral system served to articulate local communities with the institutional systems of the larger society.

The data and analysis will be presented through an examination of the activities of individuals in two small *município* communities in the Zona da Mata of the State of Minas Gerais during the critical election campaign for governor in the year 1965. By examining some of the activities of a local doctor and a lawyer involved in politics, we shall be able to make explicit the transactional process by means of which segments of local

---

AUTHOR'S NOTE: Gratitude is expressed to the Social Science Research Council, the Graduate School of the University of Wisconsin, and the Agency for International Development for the financial support that made the fieldwork in Minas Gerais possible. All views, interpretations, and conclusions herein contained, however, are those of the author and not necessarily those of the supporting organizations.

Journal of Interamerican Studies and World Affairs, Vol. 19 No. 2, May 1977

communities in the region were articulated, through the political-electoral process, to the state and national level institutions of Brazilian society.

The Zona da Mata of Minas Gerais is a rugged and hilly region of old mountains similar in its physical features to the Paraíba Valley to the south and southwest of which it is a geographical extension (see Stein, 1957 for the lower Paraíba Valley). The topography of the region is mountainous, dominated by old, eroded hillsides that, although not especially high, are quite steep. The landscape, for example, generally rises to a peak rapidly only to drop sharply some 50 to 100 meters to a shallow trough. Then, after forming a narrow valley cut by a stream, the land rises precipitously to another peak, only to drop again forming another trough in what gives the feeling of being an endless sea of hills and valleys.

The land was first settled in the nineteenth century when the cultivation of coffee spread northwestward from Rio de Janeiro. The region in which the study was conducted, which is the extreme north of the zone, was settled in the late nineteenth and early twentieth centuries as the lands to the south became exhausted and their ability to produce coffee declined.

By the mid-twentieth century, the combination of soil erosion and exhaustion and market decline had reduced drastically the importance of coffee in the local economy. Food crops, primarily corn, beans, and rice, with some sugar cane, are grown at present both for the local inhabitants and for sale in the market.

The decline of agriculture as a source of wealth and income has stimulated a shift to cattle raising, to supply the growing market of Rio de Janeiro and its suburbs with meat and milk. But the roads in the northern municípios of the Zona da Mata are poor and do not connect with the major highways built by the state and federal governments. Therefore, they are too far away from the market for beef and dairy products to partake in the profits that are rapidly transforming the southern part of the region. In the north, agriculture still dominates the economy, and since the land is poor, for the most part, so are the people. The area we are discussing, then, is a poor one in which but limited resources are produced locally. The result, when compounded by the *latifundia* tradition and the concentration of land in the hands of the few, is poverty and hardship for most, conditions that must be understood as background for the analysis that follows.

The following events took place in the fall of the year 1965 at a time of singular importance to the Brazilian body politic. A campaign was being waged, amongst other offices, for governor of the State of Minas Gerais. In April of 1964, a military coup had deposed the then President of Brazil, João Goulart, and replaced him with Marshall Castello Branco, the first of what were to be a series of military officers to occupy the presidential palace. The governor of the state of Minas Gerais, Magalhães Pinto, has been one of the more influential and prestigious civilian political leaders to participate in the coup on the side of the military.

According to the constitution then current, executive officers at the level of the president and governors of states were not permitted to serve more than one consecutive term in office. Although they could contest for other offices, and seek the same office at a later point in time, they could not succeed themselves as chief executive officer of a state or of the nation. In response to this provision of the constitution, Magalhães Pinto had to step down from the governorship at the end of 1965.

In an effort to test its ability to stand on the principle that government should rest on the consent of the governed, as determined in open elections, and to test its popularity, the military regime had authorized the holding of elections for all offices that fell vacant at the end of 1965—with the exception, of course, of the presidency then held by Marshall Castello Branco. Those elections were held in October of 1965.

The gubernatorial contest in the state of Minas Gerais was of special interest. Although Magalhães Pinto was unable to seek reelection himself, he did, as was the custom, hand-pick the candidate to run on his party ticket and on his record. The most important issue on that record, the popular support for which might be judged from the vote received by his designated successor, was his participation in and support for the 1964 coup.

The man selected by the government forces in Minas Gerais, undoubtedly in consultation with the military both in the state and in Rio de Janeiro (or Brasília since the federal government was then in the process of being transferred to the new capital), was a kinsman of the incumbent governor named Roberto Resende. Resende, a doctor by training, had been a loyal supporter of Pinto and also of the military during the coup.

Of importance for our story is the fact that the eyes of the nation, and of political forces throughout the Western world, were focused on Minas Gerais, where popular support of the military regime was to be tested. Resende, the candidate of Magalhães Pinto, his UDN party,[1] and the military government, was carrying the standard of those who had conducted the coup into the popular electoral arena in a campaign for a major office in one of the most important states for the first time since the coup had occurred. His success was vital. If he won, his election could be interpreted by the military as a vote of confidence for their action against Goulart. If he lost, however, popular rejection could lead the regime to seek support and moral justification for its actions and continuing control somewhere other than in the principle of the assent of the governed.

As the election campaign unfolded, a rather unique series of events took place in the small município of Capela Nova in the Zona da Mata. One afternoon in late September, an attorney and member of the state legislature named Antonio Vieira da Sousa, who lived in the município that was the original base of operations for my research, went, with me at his side, to the neighboring município of Capela Nova in response to word that one of the leaders of his political party, the *Partido Republicano* (PR), which was supporting Resende as part of the new realignment of political parties, had been imprisoned. After some investigation, we learned that he had been incarcerated when he attempted to defend his son and a group of friends who had been arrested at a dance the previous day for disturbing the peace.

It is not uncommon for young Brazilian males from elite families in the interior to get drunk, cut up, and cause some general commotion at dances and parties. In fact, it might be considered standard occurrence. As a rule, they were encouraged in this behavior, most often by their fathers and other male kinsmen. The behavior, then, was reinforced by the rest of the community as, for example, in the esteem and often hero worship accorded them by the younger boys and males of the lower classes whose approval and envy of these actions often was the subject of discussions in the local bars for months on end. Also, however, such exploits contribute to the reputations that the young men have with the girls of the community. At best, a young elite male might be urged to exercise some restraint by his proud father. For formal sanctions to be invoked is almost unheard of. These, instead, are used against the members of the lower classes, who are punished and jailed regularly for demonstrating openly such acts of "aggression and violence." However, the sons of the elite are scarcely to be restrained, and certainly not jailed. And, furthermore, to jail the father, a man of prominence and respect, a political leader, landowner, and merchant, for defending his son for the demonstration of his manhood is unheard of. Why, then, did this happen?

There are special times and circumstances when arrests of prominent people take place in the municípios of the interior of states like Minas Gerais. One of these is during election campaigns. It is not unheard of, for example, for those who control the local government and its police to have their opponents arrested as part of the harassment to which competing factions try to subject each other. When this happens, those being oppressed often gain help and relief from relatives, friends, and associates at the state and federal level who exert pressure to have them released and the charges dropped.

In the case of Capela Nova, the elites arrested were part of the faction out of power at the local level. However, as indicated, they belonged to one of the political parties, the PR, that was part of the coalition supporting the candidacy of Roberto Resende for state governor and, hence, the incumbent military government.

It is obvious, therefore, that although on the outs with the local government, the PR faction in Capela Nova had good connections at the state and national level, whose power and influence could have been assumed to have been sufficient to spare them the humiliation of being first arrested and then put in jail. After all, they were supporting the candidate on whose shoulders the revolutionary forces were pinning their hopes for popular endorsement. However, in spite of this, they continued to be harassed by their opponents and jailed for the performance of acts that were not only normal, but also expected from people in the community in their circumstances.

To understand the plight of the leaders of the PR faction in Capela Nova, some background must be given on their opponents, a faction led by Dr. Nestor Santos. Dr. Santos, a practicing physician, had once been a member of the PR and was a kinsman of the man who had been jailed for defending his son against the police. Furthermore, Dr. Santos once had served as vice-mayor during the term his now jailed relative had served as major of Capela Nova. Both at the time had been elected on the PR ticket.

His present opponents now argued that Dr. Santos was an ambitious man, not satisfied with the rewards given him by the state level administration of which his party was a member in a delicate coalition. This ambition, they claim, led him to accept an offer made to him by the representatives of the *Partido Trabalhista Brasíleira* (PTB) who came to the município shortly after João Goulart had assumed the presidency of the nation. Goulart, it must be remembered, was the standard-bearer and major figure in the PTB nationally.

When offered campaign funds, and a series of promises to be fulfilled later, Santos had agreed to oppose his former associates (and kinsmen) and run for mayor in Capela Nova on the PTB ticket. He was elected by an overwhelming majority in 1962 and remained in office after the coup.

Of the many rewards obtained from the Goulart administration prior to its being deposed, the one most talked about locally was Dr. Santos' appointment as a director and staff doctor at a new hospital built with federal funds in a regional center some 60 kilometers north of Capela Nova. The doctor traveled there once a week, for which he is reported to have been paid handsomely; more important, he received access to the facilities of the hospital for his patients.

When he was still a member of the PR, Dr. Santos had arranged to have a medical post with a clinic built in Capela Nova. The funds were provided by the state government, which also continued to supply medicines after the construction was completed. As the only physician in the community, Dr. Santos retained control over the health post and the medical supplies from the state after changing his political allegiance. Therefore, in 1965 he had access to the medical facilities and the pharmacy both of the health post in Capela Nova and of the hospital in Cidade Linda.

Dr. Santos, then, had been a member of the PR and had switched his political allegiance to support João Goulart and the PTB. To the members of the PR in Capela Nova, this action was taken to be treason. However, in changing his loyalty in the pursuit of his personal ambition, Dr. Santos had switched from the forces that supported Magalhães Pinto and the revolution to those that supported João Goulart, the man against whose policies the coup of 1964 was directed and who was overthrown and replaced. These facts might lead us to conclude that in the gubernatorial race of 1965, Dr. Santos and his followers in Capela Nova would be opposed by the Resende faction and its supporters of the coup and the military who would be supporting his PR opponents who had remained loyal to their party and to the candidates and programs it had supported by means of coalitions. Why, then, were Sebastião Cardoso, his son, Zinho, and his friends permitted to remain in jail, or to be put there in the first place by police controlled by Dr. Santos, the supporter of the administration the present government had ousted by force and now was opposing in an electoral showdown? The answer was simple and unrelated to any of the ideological issues thus far discussed. Dr. Santos controlled the majority of the votes in Capela Nova, which in total came to less than 3,000. The new regime, however, was sufficiently intent on being able to demonstrate popular support for itself that it chose to back him rather than its loyal local supporters, because its leadership was convinced that Dr. Santos could deliver the vote. Therefore, the Magalhães Pinto government turned a deaf ear on the pleas of the PR in Capela Nova to have the police changed. It also refused to respond to the repeated requests seeking the release of the jailed members of the group. Instead, it tacitly supported Santos in the hope that his votes would contribute to an electoral victory.

The local PR forces were in an untenable position. The only course of action left for them was to support the opposition candidate for governor and to realign themselves in the state political picture. However, this would have to be done from weakness, since the opposition candidate and his forces also knew that Dr. Santos controlled the vote in Capela Nova; and, knowing this, they also courted the doctor and certainly would do nothing to oppose him openly.

We must now inquire as to the basis of Dr. Santos' political strength, a strength that not only permitted him to survive the military takeover directed against the head of the party he had supported—in breaking with the members of the faction that now was in power—but also enabled him to end up with the endorsement and support of the new military regime untainted by his previous behavior.

The basis of the doctor's political strength was his medical practice. Illness is endemic in most of the poverty-stricken communities of the interior of Minas Gerais like Capela Nova.

Nutritional levels are low; sanitation is poor; and illness, ranging from infections and diseases that are minimally debilitating to those that render the patient totally helpless, is widespread. Just about everyone, at one time or another, is stricken by disease.[2]

In response to this ever-present situation, efforts at healing are widespread. Curing practices derived from several cultural traditions are to be found in use in varying frequency and intensity throughout the state and the nation. In the Zona da Mata of Minas Gerais, the pragmatic superiority of modern medicine is accepted, although doctors must compete openly with several forms of Afro-Brazilian curing traditions and European-derived forms of spiritual healing. Trained doctors, however, are few and in very short supply in comparison with the demand for their services. For example, in the nine municípios that comprised the region studied, trained, practicing physicians were to be found only in three. Thus, for the 83,500 people living in the 1,750 square kilometers of impoverished hills, there were a total of 16 doctors, 13 of whom lived and practiced in the large *muncípio* and regional center of Boa Vista. Two-thirds of the municípios were without doctors, a figure somewhat higher than the state average, where 400 of the 722 municípios were without a doctor. One hundred and five of the state's municípios were like Capela Nova in that they had but one doctor.

Dr. Santos had been practicing in Capela Nova since completing his medical training in the late 1940s. He had been born in the município, the son of a more than moderate sized landowner. After completing his primary education, he went off first to Boa Vista to secondary school, and then to attend the medical facility in Rio de Janeiro. He returned home just after graduation to start his practice in Capela Nova and has remained there for more than two decades as the only doctor in town.

As the son of a landowner, and a member of the traditional local elite, Dr. Santos has other material interests in the life of the município than just his medical practice. He has inherited land from his parents, for example, the amount of which he has increased with several purchases. Although he has some two dozen sharecroppers raising corn, beans, coffee, potatoes, and sugar cane and caring for his cattle, he performs most of the supervisory and management functions himself. He does this, he claims, because he enjoys it, and, as he tells it, because without direction the people will not produce. In addition, he must arrange for the sale of his share of the crops at harvest time and for the processing required to make them marketable. Also, he has a still *(alambique)* in which sugar cane juice is distilled into *cachaça,* a type of rum which is marketed and consumed locally and regionally. In brief, Dr. Santos is a man of varied economic interests, only one of which is the practice of medicine.

As the only doctor in the município, however, there is a great demand for his professional services. Long lines always await him whenever he has visiting hours at the health post clinic, and he is regularly called at all hours of the day and night to attend the sick. Often, for example, he is interrupted while supervising on the land, or while overseeing the processing of coffee, or in the making of cachaça, or while seeing to his official duties at the *prefeitura* by patients or their relatives.

The demands on Dr. Santos' time are great. He gives of himself, however, generously and without complaint, almost at times, as some of his loyal followers reported, in the image of a saint performing a spiritual calling. Moreover, Dr. Santos appears to make little distinction between rich and poor in the practice of his profession. Hence, although he may spend more time with his rich patients–most of them are old friends–the poor have come to believe that they will not be turned away, even if they do not have the price of a *consulta* (visit). And, as important, they also know that they will receive the medicines they need from the doctor gratis, from the health post pharmacy, or from some other source to which he has access. Since most of the people of Capela Nova are poor, it follows that the majority of Dr. Santos' patients are poor and, for the most part, unable to pay him a fee for his services. And since he regularly supplies them with medicines without compensation, it may be concluded that his medical practice is far from sound economically.

The doctor will admit this when asked, but continues to devote long hours to seeing as many patients as have need of him. He claims to see this as a service, a way of helping the underprivileged much in the tradition of Christian justice and charity. But, although not profiting from his medical practice, Dr. Santos is by no means disadvantaged economically. In fact, he is one of the wealthiest men in the community, if not the region. His income in the years since he began his practice in Capela Nova has come from more and more diverse sources. This income, and Dr. Santos' wealth, I submit, is not unrelated to the practice of his healing art. More specifically, it derives from the relationship between his medical practice and his political strength, in that his personal wealth is the result of the latter.

Over the years, Dr. Santos has come to know many of the people of Capela Nova and the surrounding countryside. As the son of a landowner, and as a proprietor in his own right, he is a member of the local elite. His wife is a member of the largest and most prestigious family in the community. Most of the local elite are his patients, some are his kinsmen, and others are his friends. Those who have come to form what may be thought of as his network or faction have learned that he is easily approachable and most often will give generously of his time and resources. For example, those in his group know that, should their dependent laborers be in need of his professional services, all that is needed is a note to him from them and the dependent will be treated, often ushered by the nurse at the health post to the front of the line, given injections and medicines, and sent home feeling better and more secure without having to pay for either the examination or the medicine.

The dependent laborer now is in the debt of his landowner-patron. He also is in the debt of his benefactor, Dr. Santos. Being poor, he has no way to repay the debt and the kindness of his benefactors. Loyalty to them and a willingness to serve if asked are all that he has to offer. Through the intermediacy of the landowning patrons in his faction, Dr. Santos can call in these debts periodically. The time at which this is done is the annual election of public officials.

Dr. Santos' friends know that he can be depended upon in times of illness—their own and those of their dependents. In addition, the doctor will supply them, especially those living in the hinterland, with drugs and instructions for their use. In this way, they can attend directly to the more common maladies. As important, however, they also know that the doctor and all his personal resources and contacts likewise are at their disposal; all they have to do is ask.

For example, when João Oliveira established the school on his *fazenda* for his daughter to teach the children of the poor laborers, it was Dr. Santos who arranged for it to be made a part of the state system. As a result, books, materials, and other supplies became available. Also, João's daughter came to hold civil service status, earned the salary of a primary school teacher employed by the state, and was entitled to all the retirement, medical, and other fringe benefits enjoyed by other civil servants.

When Pedro Letão was looking for capital with which to purchase hybrid seed corn to plant on his land, he approached the doctor. Instead of lending him the money at the then going rate of interest, which he otherwise would have done, the doctor introduced Pedro to the representative of a state agency who, at least as it appeared to Pedro, more on the basis of the doctor's word than on what was put on the application forms the doctor filled out for him, arranged the money at a rate of interest far below that of the local money market. Pedro had not known that the state government had established a low-interest loan program to help agriculturalists convert to hybrid seed. He just asked the doctor who, as Pedro and others have come to expect, "took care" of him. He now is further indebted to the doctor.

Milton Andrade regularly turns to the doctor for the cash he needs to pay the laborers who grow his sugar cane. Dr. Santos obliges, and later purchases Milton's sugar for his still. Andrade probably would not survive a year without some source of credit. The doctor provides it interest-free as a favor, but may be expected to turn a substantial profit on the eventual sale of the cachaça made from the sugar bought from people like Milton.

Alfredo Machado wished to buy a truck. Dr. Santos lent him the money which he now pays back out of incomes earned transporting merchandise such as Pedro Latão's corn harvest and the doctor's cachaça.

In these and in many other instances the doctor is asked to help his friends and neighbors. When he obliges, as he is known regularly to do, the latter are in his debt. Although he often may profit from the favors he does for his associates, this does not change the fact of their indebtedness. Always obliging, always generous—to his friends at least—always giving of himself, his resources, and contacts, the doctor, it may be said, goes through life accumulating debts. The cashing in of these debts are the basis of his political strength. In contrast with the *coroneis* of the Old Republic, whose position was based on force, power, and the ability to frighten and intimidate (Nunes Leal, 1948; Petterson, 1964; Vilaca and Albuquerque, 1965), the position of Dr. Santos and the politicians of 1946 to 1968 was based on generosity, constant giving, and the inability, or so it appeared to the outsider, to say no to the continuous requests of those who constituted their patronage network and voting bloc.

With each new act of generosity, the number of those indebted to the doctor, and the degree of their indebtedness, is increased. More important, once in receipt of his patronage his clients know that they can seek it again and again with no further demands made on them other than the continuing loyalty for which they already are committed. Since from their perspective they stand only to gain from "following the doctor," they do so gladly. In return for all his kindness and generosity, all the doctor usually asks is that his dependents follow his suggestions when going to cast their ballot on election day.

Without hesitation, they voted for Dr. Santos as *vice-prefeito* when he ran on the PR ticket. They also voted for him when he next ran for the top spot as a member of the PTB. Their loyalty was to him, and not to the party he represented. He was the same kind Dr. Santos who continued to help them in their times of greatest need. Similarly, they will vote for whoever he tells them to—no matter who it happens to be, where the candidate is from, and whatever his party.

From the perspective of his many dependents, the doctor's switching of party loyalty and support has broadened the range of his contacts and also increased the resources to which he has access. For example, when the health post was built during his term as vice-mayor, the *prefeitura* administered the state funds that went for its construction. Plínio Moreira, a kinsman and long-time associate and political ally of the PR group, was given the construction contract. Plínio had a small construction company. He turned a substantial profit on the job, for which he was indebted to those who had arranged for him to get the contract. But Plínio had been a loyal supporter for many years.

When Dr. Santos decided to change parties in 1962 and oppose the candidate the PR directory had selected to run for mayor—the man sitting in jail during the 1965 gubernatorial campaign—Plínio, along with many others, had to choose between loyalties. His support went to Dr. Santos, as was the case with most of those who had come to know the doctor. When, shortly after the election, funds were received from the federal government—then controlled by João Goulart and the PTB—to construct a new school, Plínio was awarded the contract. In the process of completing the job, Alfredo Machado was hired to haul materials, while most of the bricks and tiles were obtained from the kiln just built on the new parcel of land the doctor had recently purchased in partnership with João Oliveira.

During the construction Plínio hired laborers, many of whom turned out to be supporters of the doctor whose requests for jobs and money now were being satisfied by their benefactor. In all of this, needless to say, the debt owed by each to the doctor was increased. While profiting in no small way himself, the doctor's political position also was being strengthened. Along with each new project he was able to bring into the community also came resources and jobs which were distributed to loyal supporters. When the indebtedness incurred from this was added to that owed him for his services as a healer and for his personal generosity, it is not surprising that Dr. Nestor Santos controls the vote in Capela Nova.

The representatives of Magalhaes Pinto organizing the gubernatorial campaign for Roberto Resende were well aware of Dr. Santos' political strength in his home community. They also were aware of the strengths and weaknesses of the political leaders in each of the municípios of the state.

The election of 1965 was important to them. Given their participation in the coup of the previous year, an electoral success was especially important. To win they needed more votes than could be polled by their opponent, first Sebastião Paes de Almeida, who was disqualified by a military tribunal three weeks before the election, and then the elderly Israel Pinheiro, the eventual winner. To obtain those votes they needed the support of people like Dr. Santos and his equivalents in the other municípios of the state. That the doctor had supported and had been elected on the party ticket of the man whose administration the military coup had overthrown was not to be held against him. For that matter, the party affiliations of the people with whom he worked in the numerous local communities throughout the state made little difference to them. All that mattered was that, by enlisting the support of a large enough number of them, the election could be won.

In return for the promise of support from men like Dr. Santos, the Resende forces were more than willing to offer future programs that would be of benefit to the local leaders and their dependents. Roads, schools, electric power facilities, agricultural programs, and so on were the primary inducements. Also, there were specific promises of jobs both in the state bureaucracy and in the numerous mixed and even private companies in which the supporters of Dr. Resende were influential.

The name of the game was to get the votes. Dr. Santos controlled most of those in Capela Nova. Although at best they constituted only a fraction of the total needed for victory, when added to those of the other local leaders they could have meant the difference between victory and defeat. Therefore, the government forces were not about to antagonize him. Consequently, when his opponents asked the PR leadership that was part of the government's coalition to have the sheriff and the police changed in Capela Nova, an act that would be viewed as hostile by Dr. Santos, no action was taken. And when advised of their efforts, the doctor had "his" police arrest the son of his opponent for breaking a law that customarily is enforced only against the poor, and even then infrequently. The obvious intent was to embarrass and humiliate the PR faction, whose powerlessness was being publicly flaunted. When the father of the boy went to his aid, appealing to norms of elite unity, he, too, was jailed. This enabled the doctor's group to rub salt on the wounds of their now helpless opponents. The only course of action open to the PR leadership, which they reluctantly took, was to mobilize their remaining people in support of Israel, the opponent of their party's candidate for governor. Should he win their support, even at this late stage, he might get them back some of their lost prestige, and perhaps even a new sheriff and police contingent who could be turned on their tormentor and his followers.

In the nine municípios studied in the Zona da Mata of Minas Gerais there were 16 doctors, 13 of whom, as we have seen, resided and practiced in Boa Vista, the largest municipal center in the region. Capela Nova is only one of two smaller communities to have its own doctor. The residents of the remaining six municípios must travel to Capela Nova, Estrela, which has two doctors, or Boa Vista for medical services.

All 13 doctors in Boa Vista, and both in Estrela, participate in the politicoelectoral activities of their communities. Eleven of the doctors in Boa Vista were associated with the dominant PR faction there, while the remaining two had aligned themselves with the PSD opposition. Both doctors in Estrela were with the PR.

Like Dr. Santos in Capela Nova, all the doctors are engaged in other economic activities besides their medical practice. However, no matter how much time these other activities require, all spend long hours attending to patients, most of whom are unable to afford even a nominal fee. In addition, they provide—individually and collectively—large amounts of medications free to the numerous patients sent to them by friends and associates scattered throughout the nine municípios. Economically, their medical practices provide them with at best a moderate income. However, all are wealthy men, not necessarily from birth, whose primary incomes are derived from other sources, usually related to their political activities and contacts. But all spend most of their time seeing patients, developing the image of the saintly healer ministering to the needy poor.

Of the 15-member governing committee of the PR in Boa Vista in 1965, four, the largest single representation from any occupational group, were doctors. In previous years most of the physicians associated with the party had served on the governing committee, and several had contested for and won public office. One of the doctors was a former mayor and two others had served as vice mayor. Several other physicians also had served as councilmen *(vereadores)* on the *câmara municipal.*

Of the two doctors in Boa Vista associated with the PSD, both, either together or in rotation, had been on the party's governing committee. Neither, however, had as yet run for elective office; but both were relative newcomers to the community.

The second largest occupational category in local politics were lawyers. There were 12 attorneys in the nine municípios studied. Ten lived and practiced in Boa Vista, one was in Estrela, and the other was a colleague and associate of Dr. Santos in Capela Nova.

Lawyers in their own profession functioned much as did doctors in theirs. They spent endless hours seeing clients, most of whom were unable to pay them for their services. However, like the doctors, the lawyers in the region generally had other economic interests that made them the second wealthiest group, second only to the physicians.

To illustrate how lawyers functioned in the patronage system articulating the local community and the state and national level institutions, I shall turn to another case, that of my friend and colleague, António Vieira da Sousa. In his late forties, António had only recently come forth as a candidate for elective office. In 1965, he was a member of the state legislature, a *deputado estadual,* on the PR ticket and had been put in charge of organizing the campaign of Dr. Resende's running mate for vice-governor in the region where my research was being conducted.

António had recently retired from his post as professor of sociology at the University in Boa Vista where he had served on the faculty for 25 years. During that time he had visited the United States twice, once to earn a graduate degree at the University of Wisconsin, and once to teach in the author's department just prior to the time the research was conducted. He also had visited and conducted research in Israel. During the quarter of a century he spent teaching at the university he had conducted several research projects in the region, in the course of which he had met many people whose concerns, problems, and aspirations he noted. He also came to know many of his students, some of whom had come from influential families in the state, and many of whom in time came to hold positions of importance in the state's bureaucratic agencies. When he decided to run for the office he then held, he contacted them and was able to obtain their support and votes. Of considerably more importance to his political career, however, was the legal practice he had conducted during the years he had taught at the university.

The Zona da Mata today, as previously noted, is a poor area. Hence, one might get the impression that there is little of value to be contested in the courts. In a sense, this is true; but the list of daily conflicts and grievances that result in law suits is considerable. And lawyers are needed to process these cases even if the amounts are trivial and insignificant to anyone but the litigants.

Land is still the primary productive resource and is valued greatly in the community. Most law suits in the Zona da Mata, if not all of Brazil, stem from conflicts related to land. In each generation, for example, there is a reallocation of landed property as the result of inheritance. By Brazilian law, parental property is to be divided equally amongst all children. However, old people do not regularly divide their holdings during their lifetime. Consequently, when their parents die, the group of children—and their spouses—must decide who is to get which share. The result, as one might expect, more often than not, produces disagreement and conflict that may end with the siblings not speaking. This is often followed by one or another going to court, usually after hostilities are intensified and violence is committed to persons and property. Each of the parties will, then, need a lawyer.

Most of the estates contested today are small; in only a few of the larger ones will there be funds available to pay a reasonable fee to the lawyer. However, for the others, and for the numerous boundary disputes, commercial transactions, disputes over animals, personal affronts and offenses, and so on that often can be resolved only in court, there is great demand for legal services.

From the early hours of the morning on, large numbers of people, most of them poor, are to be seen waiting outside the offices of the several attorneys in Boa Vista. Through the day, the lines will increase as additional clients arrive from the outlying communities and municípios.

To the average resident of the Zona da Mata, the law and the courts represent an impersonal authority that is feared and certainly is not to be trusted; however, many issues of importance to the individual only can be resolved by bringing legal action. The poor citizen's representative in this impersonal sphere is his attorney. Hence, most clients tend to believe that the success or failure of their case rests on their lawyer's personal prestige, ability, and willingness to exert himself on their behalf. One after another, therefore, they come before Dr. António[3] or one of the other attorneys to present their problems. In more cases than not, although they may be in the right morally, at least as they tell the story, legally they have no recourse. Should a lawyer say this, however, he is taken to be saying that he is not interested in helping them. Therefore, when the average client finishes his story, he waits for the lawyer to tell him how he will go to court and how the case will be won. Should the lawyer then try to explain the legal situation, no response will be forthcoming. Then, after a painful pause, the client will repeat his story, often word for word, ending by imploring the lawer to *dar um jeito para mim* (do something to help me).

The practiced attorney soon learns that he must make some kind of a promise in order to satisfy the client, if for no other reason than to induce him to leave the office. If he is lucky something will happen before the case comes to court to resolve the conflict. Then he must convince the client that the actual outcome was the best that could have been hoped for anyway. In the meantime, the lawyer has visited with most of the parties involved in the litigation. Often he has been able to work out compromises or at least to reduce the intensity of the conflict. When successful at this informal negotiation, or lucky, his reputation will spread, since he has, in fact, helped his client. Others, then, will come to him with their problems, including, perhaps, some of those with whom he previously had dealings while representing their opponents. As his clientele grows, however, he must spend more and more of his time making promises and figuring out ways to resolve matters out of court. He spends long hours at this, often receiving little compensation for his efforts. When added to the time he must spend in court and in preparing cases and writing briefs, the successful lawyer is a very busy man. As was the case with physicians, it is not unusual to see lawyers working a 15 to 18-hour day; and also like doctors, their professional practice is far from lucrative. However, again like the doctors, the lawyers have other financial interests that rank them amongst the more affluent members of the community.

A legal practice in the northern Zona da Mata is not in itself lucrative, but wealthy lawyers spend long hours working on the affairs of their clients. António, for example, acknowledges this by saying that someone must help those who are in trouble. He goes on to say that he is pleased to be able to do it, even if it is at a personal sacrifice. His, too, is an attitude that strikes of Christian charity. He openly professes a desire to help the many who have no one else to turn to, whether or not they can pay for his time and skills. Consequently, he, too, is attributed the qualities of a saint by his followers. The many he has helped over the years have come to revere him and look to his leadership in many areas of their life. Amongst other things, they follow his suggestions as to whom they should cast their ballot for at election time.

Doctors and lawyers can and do work with each other politically. Each represents a means of satisfying different, but at times related, needs. For example, many of the situations that precipitate conflict, or intensify it, are exaggerated out of proportion as a result of the low frustration tolerance levels of the participants due to the combination of poor nutrition and endemic illness. The wise lawyer often will spot this while interacting with his clients and others involved in a conflict. He then might send them to see a doctor, not any doctor, but a trusted associate who will treat them with the care and attention they have come to expect from him. The combination of personal attention and medication then might reduce the anger and desire for vindication and lead the client to drop his suit. The lawyer, then, can use this to gain concessions from the other party that can be used as proof that he has, in truth, helped the client with his problem. The client, however, now is indebted to both the lawyer and the doctor for their help.

Likewise, a doctor, in the course of attending to a patient, may learn of other problems that complicate their physical illness. In turn, he may send the patient to a trusted attorney who will help with the other problems.

In Capela Nova, Dr. Santos works closely with Roberto Andrade de Araujo, the only lawyer in town. Roberto is a member of the governing committee of the doctor's party and has served as a member of the municipal council.

António no longer works in cooperation with any of the doctors in Boa Vista. Instead, since two of his brothers whom he had assisted through school are physicians, he uses them as his medical associates. Although both reside and practice in the state capital, they visit their hometown regularly and are familiar with local conditions there. Also, from them António has learned about the more prevalent diseases of the region. Today he can diagnose these and also can prescribe the medicines to be taken for their cure. From his brothers, and from other sources, he has obtained stores of drugs that he dispenses to his clients. This further charity, of course, enhances the personal reverence in which he is held by those who are the recipients of his generosity. Of course, when confronted with illnesses he is not able to handle, he always sends the sick person to one of his brothers, or has one of his associates send him to a doctor in Boa Vista.

As a member of the state legislature, António came to have access to resources that were of benefit to the residents of local municípios in his area. His status as professor at the university enabled him to project himself as an expert in the field of education. Hence, after just a short time in the state capital, he had become influential in the office of the Secretary of

Education. As a result, he came to have more than a small say as to where schools were to be built and who, at least in his area, would be appointed as teachers. This, of course, was in addition to the usual patronage enjoyed by all state deputies. Consequently, those who came to his office for help with their legal and personal problems, and for medicines and access to medical facilities, now also could ask for jobs, for promises of contracts, and for other spoils. As he successfully provided these, his stature rose, and the loyalty and size of his dependency network increased—and so did the bloc of votes he controlled and could negotiate.

António Vieira da Sousa operated in several municípios. Within each, he had key individuals who served as what might be thought of as his lieutenants or representatives. Chico Ladeira was one of these. Chico's parents had been poor sharecroppers who had moved to Paraízo when he was a small boy.[4]

Chico had worked with his father as a sharecropper. Shortly after starting out on his own, he saved enough money to open a small shop *(venda)* in a rural neighborhood. After struggling to survive for the first year, while earning scarcely enough to feed his family, his former *patrão,* who was a large landowner with extensive sugar cane fields both in Paraízo and a contiguous município, asked him if he wished to "supply his cane cutters." Chico admitted honestly that although he appreciated the opportunity, he had neither the capital nor the credit to stock the amount and variety of goods that would be necessary. The landowner replied that he was not interested in Chico's credit rating. What he was looking for, he maintained, was an honest man whom he could trust. He said that he had been watching Chico and believed him to be honest. The landowner then offered to stock the shop if Chico would run it honestly and fairly and treat the laborers justly.

Most of the laborers on the estate, like most workers in the Zona da Mata, often survived the year by obtaining credit against their earnings from the following year's harvest. They would go to the landowner for advances; when he approved, he then would send them, or at least some of them, to Chico with a note; the shopkeeper then would provide them with the items specified by the proprietor. As he began to prosper, Chico came to feel sorry for those to whom the landowner did not extend credit. If they appeared to him to be honest, he often would "carry them" until they were able to repay him. In time, the number of customers to patronize his shop grew, as did the size and variety of his inventory. Also, every merchant in Paraízo soon offered to supply him on credit. To his good fortune, most of those to whom he had extended credit repaid him. In time, he prospered, and from his profits he not only enlarged his premises and moved from the countryside to the center of a district, but also continued to carry more and more laborers in the neighborhood.

When the landowner died, and his children stopped giving advances to the laborers, Chico made sure that many families that otherwise might have starved had, at least, food. Over the years, the number of Chico's friends, and those indebted to and dependent upon him, grew. By 1965, for example, he could boast of having almost 100 *afilhados* (godchildren) and many more *compadres.*

Once, when Chico had taken ill, he met and became friendly with Tarcísio Soares who, at the time, ran a pharmacy in Paraízo. Tarcísio had apprenticed in a pharmacy as a boy and as was the custom, had learned both to prepare and to prescribe medicines. In small municípios where there are neither doctors nor formally trained pharmacists, people like Tarcísio still do much of the curing. Tarcísio, at the time, already was associated with Joaquim Andrade, who had been a boyhood friend of an ex-president of the republic born in the region. Through Andrade, Tarcísio had been put in contact with Dr. Alvaro Paes in Boa Vista. As Tarcísio jokes today, the doctor saved many of his mistakes over the years. That is, Tarcísio used to send the patients he was unable to treat to Dr. Paes. Also, through Andrade, Tarcísio became associated with Ernesto Machado and

António Vieira da Sousa, both attorneys to whom those who approached Tarcísio with legal problems were sent.

As Chico and Tarcísio exchanged confidences, and a friendship developed, Chico came to be a part of the *roda, panelinha* (Leeds, 1964), or politicoeconomic group that included Tarcísio, Joaquim Andrade, Dr. Paes, António, and others. His many friends, *afilhados* and *compadres,* customers, and dependents, were seen as potential voters by Tarcísio and the others. In return for directing and delivering those votes to the candidates designated, the members of the group arranged for Chico to have access to resources formerly unavailable to him. From Tarcísio, for example, he obtained medicines that he soon learned to dispense. At the time of the research he kept a syringe in his home and gave injections to his customers and other dependents; and if unable to help himself, he sent "his people" to Tarcísio in the *sede* (seat) of Paraízo, or directly to Dr. Paes in Boa Vista. Chico had a horse and a cart which he made available to transport his friends. And with a note signed by him, even the most humble laborer would be treated with respect, not kept waiting needlessly, given the medicines prescribed, and then not charged.

Chico and his people also were able to go to António or Sr. Machado for legal help. And with António in the state legislature, they were able to approach him for jobs, contracts for public works projects, and so on. For example, through António, Chico had been able to have the school started by his daughter on the fazenda he recently purchased made a part of the state system. As a result, she now had civil service status with all its benefits.

With the death of Joaquim Andrade a few years ago, and the defeat of Ernesto Machado, António has come to the forefront as the dominant force in the group. His recent election to the state legislature and the political contacts he has made have added fresh resources to those already controlled by the group; this has enhanced their ability to help dependents. Consequently, their network and the bloc of votes they can negotiate has increased.

In each of the nine municípios there were numerous counterparts of Chico Ladeira. Some were shopkeepers, others were landowners, merchants, or small scale industrialists. Each had some resources of value to the many poor of the community. Also, each had established a reputation for helping the poor and of giving generously of his time and assets. As a result, each had developed a following of loyal dependents indebted to them for their generosity and assistance.

Each of these local leaders came to be associated with others with access to what may be referred to as complementary, as opposed to duplicating, resources. That is, a shopkeeper associated with a merchant, and/or a pharmacist, and/or a landowner rather than with another shopkeeper in the same area. In this way, each was able to increase the variety as well as the total supply of goods and services that could be made available to his dependents—thereby increasing their indebtedness and loyalty.

Each group, which was a local faction of a more far-reaching patronage network, then became associated with someone like António or Dr. Santos, often but not necessarily a professional, an educated person with the sophistication and contacts with state and federal level political leaders. The equivalent of António or Dr. Santos then would broker the contacts and resources from the outside so that they would flow into the local community. In return for a promise to deliver the votes of the entire group, and their respective dependents, the state and federal level political leaders would provide jobs, influence, public works projects, and other resources unavailable at the local level. Over the years, a vicious circle was established. The more dependents whose votes could be mobilized by the members of the group, the greater the resources its local leaders could obtain by negotiation. And with the additional resources, the number and loyalty of their diverse dependents also was increased, thereby further enlarging the number of voters that could be delivered at the next election. In the process, the local leader and his associates gained access to the resources and stood to profit personally. In time, the initial single resource that may have enabled each member of the group to first satisfy the needs of his dependents, such as credit at the shop or medical services, came to be supplemented so that eventually each local leader could offer his people multiple benefits. As his personal benefits increased, however, he also was able to increase the size of his following by giving more, both of his now enlarged resource base and of his original skill or valued commodity. However, as he prospered, so did his followers in that they came to have access to more resources and advantages. In brief, everyone stood to gain from participating transactionally in a successful network.

Looked at from the local level, the system depended on the resources obtained from the outside. The Zona da Mata as we have seen had been settled as part of the expansion of coffee cultivation in the nineteenth century. The northern region, however, which was less well suited to the crop, did not develop until the early years of the present century. By the 1930s, the region already was on the decline as the bottom fell out on Brazilian coffee. A relatively dense population was left with little in the way of local resources. The mostly hilly terrain had been cut clean of its forest cover and had become the victim of erosion. The leached soils today produce little in the way of surpluses that can be sold in order to purchase commodities and services from the outside.

The plight of the poor majority of the residents of the northern Zona da Mata is not atypical for Brazil. The nation as a whole had experienced a decline in agriculture in the years since 1930. However, in the years following the administration of Getúlio Vargas, first as dictator and then as elected president, Brazil began to be transformed from a primarily agrarian nation to an industrialized one. The federal government, first in Vargas' hands, and then in the hands of his elected successors, had stimulated, mobilized the capital and expertise for, and even organized industry (Leff, 1968). In addition, it took the initiative in creating what elsewhere (Greenfield, 1972) I have referred to as an industrial-service-welfare complex that in the years following World War II came to be the primary source of wealth in the society.

The agencies that constituted the industrial-service-welfare complex had been organized through the initiative of the federal and state governments which retained responsibility for their direction and for the distribution of the goods and services produced. The new wealth-producing agencies were located, for the most part, in the state capitals and in the federal district, far from the numerous local communities like Capela Nova, Boa Vista, and Paraízo with their poor and needy populations. In theory, if not in fact, the members of the local communities, who constituted the citizenry of the nation, were to be the beneficiaries of the industrialization and development programs established, and planned in greater numbers for the future. The question was: how were the resources now becoming available to be distributed to the rapidly growing, widely scattered population of the nation?

The answer was to be found in resolving another logistical problem created by the dismantling of the dictatorship in 1945 and the establishment of an electoral system to fill the offices of government. According to the constitution adopted in 1946, all candidates for public office had to run on a party ticket. No limitations were imposed on the number of parties that could be organized. In time as many as 14 political parties contested offices as major forces in the various states, although only three, the *Partido Social Democrático* (PSD), the *União Democrático Nacional* (UDN) and the *Partido Trabalhista Brasileira* (PTB), were important on the national level. At the local level, however, there were many more than the 14 to achieve prominence at the state level.

The political parties, as numerous and diverse as they came to be, were the basic units of government in the society. Since all candidates had to run as members of a party, the one whose candidate received a majority of the votes, or a plurality where there were three or more candidates, won the office. Contests for executive offices created little or no problem. Many governorships, mayorships, and even presidencies came to be held by candidates and their parties who received less than a majority of the votes cast. The legislative branch created more of a problem. It was difficult, to say the least, for any one party to elect enough deputies to have a majority in any legislative chamber. However, a majority of the votes in the assembly was needed to enact laws. The solution was the formation of coalitions of parties, under the leadership of the party whose candidate had won the executive office. The members of the several parties in the coalition then passed laws, many of them related to the establishment of development programs and agencies of the industrial-service-welfare complex, to be administered by the executive office. The advantages of office were obvious.

The next question to be asked is: why should the voters at election time cast their ballot for the candidates of one party rather than those of another? That is, why should the newly enfranchised voters in places like Capela Nova, Boa Vista, Paraízo, or any of the other local communities in the nation vote for the PSD candidate for an office rather than the UDN or PTB candidate, or one standing for any of the minor parties to be organized for each election? None of the parties ever really came to stand for ideological positions or philosophies. Uniformly, they stood for the gaining of office.

The electorate, as we have seen, was scattered across the nation in local communities. The vote cast by them exceeded in total that cast in the major metropolitan centers. Therefore, as important as the large cities with their at-times educated and ideologically concerned electorate were in national and state contests, victory or defeat still was determined by the voters in the large number of relatively small, poor, dispersed local communities strung out across the countryside.

To the average poor voter in these local communities, there was little to choose, other things being equal, between one candidate and another. In fact, there was little on the face of it to motivate them to take the time to vote at all. The incentive was provided by the political parties who articulated the logistics of distributing the resources produced in the agencies of the industrial-service-welfare complex, to be controlled by the party to win, with the logistics of motivating voters to cast their ballots for their candidates.

The electorate, like their local communities, for the most part, were poor. The real wealth of the society now was being produced by the entities the government had been and was creating in increasing numbers, whose output had to be distributed. In brief, resources from the agencies to be controlled by the party to win election at the state and national levels were distributed to those who delivered the votes at the local level needed to gain office. After all, roads, schools, dams, factories, agricultural programs, and so on had to be located somewhere if the goal of growth and development was to be attained. Since most local areas were poor and had little, almost any one would do as a place to start what was projected as a long term process. Distributing resources to those in local communities who had helped elect the government hurt no one and did start the development process by helping some. In the short run, the voters were happy and so were those in office.

The voters were scattered across the land in local communities. The state and national elites who came to contest and hold office were located in the state and federal capitals. To succeed in the new system, that is, to gain electoral victory and office, the latter needed contacts at the local level. Local and regional leaders like Dr. Santos and António, in cooperation with Chico Ladeira and others like him, who formed an unequal but interdependent group organized around a local political party, provided those contacts. The result was that in return for votes that were insignificant in their own right, the group, its leaders, and dependents obtained access to resources that otherwise would have been unavailable to them. In the abstract, networks of exchanges were established in which formerly unrelated persons now were brought together in an interrelated series of transactions in which material resources flowed down and out from the state and federal levels and votes flowed up to elect those who then came to establish and to administer the programs and agencies producing and distributing the wealth of the society.

At the local level, the few with resources available could distribute them if they chose, earning in return gratitude, loyalty, and the indebtedness of the recipients. Then, if articulated with a state or national level network by an intermediary like Dr. Santos or António, the debts could be converted into votes that as a bloc could be negotiated for resources and other consideration. The shortcoming for the community was that only those articulated with the winning faction were given access to the needed and valued resources. In comparison with the remainder of the local population, they prospered. At times, even the most lowly dependent in a faction that was successful for several years running might obtain a job and, with it, minimal economic security. Those not in the winning faction received little if anything. Furthermore, they were even worse off at times since their pleas were denied by those in power and they often were harassed to induce them, along with others uncommitted, to become a part of the dominant group.

The brokers between the local community and the state and national level systems, through which the resources flowed downward, were the Dr. Santos and the Antónios who articulated the two levels that otherwise might have remained apart. That they prospered from the complex of exchanges goes without saying. However, as the system matured and the size of the electorate grew as did the number of those participating as collectors and brokers of votes, the competition came to be brutal. Newcomers, for example, would promise greater spoils in an effort to win away segments of networks assumed to be committed to their opponents. At times, even victory could not provide them with enough to pay off on their promises. However, since their chances of success were so slim, the excessive promises appeared to offer the only hope. This strategy, though, then drove other participants to compete to increase their promises or chance possible defections in the ranks. This was the tactic employed by Dr. Santos in what for him proved to be a winning strategy in Capela Nova. Others to try it, however, came out on the losing side as often as not.

In 1965, the opposition to Dr. Resende and the military in Minas Gerais, it appears, promised more to more local leaders than did the members of the government. Consequently, Israel Pihneiro, campaigning as candidate for only three weeks, bested the Resende forces in what came to be interpreted as a vote against the military regime. Thus, failing to obtain popular endorsement at the polls, the military retrenched. When its popularity was further challenged in succeeding years by protests and demonstrations, it then discarded the principle of the consent of the people as expressed in elections as the basis of its legitimacy. Instead, it adopted other justifications for its continuation in office such as stopping the inflation, advancing the pace of development and the economy, and stopping subversion. Rather than filling positions in government by elections that required the mobilization of votes, the military gradually then came to appoint those who today administer most of the agencies of the state and federal governments. Since the local leaders no longer have this role to perform, they have passed from the scene, and the Dr. Santos and Antónios, along with the other members of their factions, have gone off to other things. A new system appears to have been devised to distribute the resources of the industrial-service-welfare complex, the specific workings of which are just beginning to come to light. Patronage, based upon a series of asymmetrical exchanges, still appears to be central. However, the details of the individual transactions, and the way in which local communities are articulated with the productive agencies of the nation and the states at present, must await further research.

NOTES

1. The UDN, which stands for the *União Democrático Nacional* (National Democratic Union), came into being as a coalition of those opposed to Getúlio Vargas. Vargas' supporters established the PSD, or *Partido Social Democrático* (Social Democratic Party) just after the constitution of 1946 was implemented. Other supporters of Vargas created the PTB, or *Partido Trabalhista Brasileira* (Brazilian Labor Party), the third party of national importance. Not long after the coup, however, the political parties were reorganized to form ARENA and MDB, the party of the government and the opposition. The UDN leadership that had supported the coup, of course, became the core of the government party, while those who opposed the military regime and remained in politics became part of the opposition.

2. A recent article in the Portuguese journal *Seara Nova* (1973) summarizes some of the more startling statistics For example, it states that there were some six hundred thousand active cases of tuberculosis in Brazil as of 1972 and a total of 40 million persons infected with the disease. Every five minutes, according to Dr. Jose Silveira, superintendent of the Brazilian Institute for the Investigation of Tuberculosis, a new case is discovered, and every 40 minutes someone dies of the disease.

The article also quotes the president of a congressional committee on health as estimating that some eight million people suffer from Chagas disease and another six million from malaria.

With respect to health care, or the lack thereof, World Health Organization figures show one dentist for each 10,472 inhabitants, and one hospital for each 4,000 persons. In 1,360 of the 3,950 municípios in the nation, no medical assistance was available. Of the 722 municípios in the state of Minas Gerais, the *Jornal do Brasil* reported, 400 were without a doctor, and in another 105 there was only one physician to attend the population. In the state of Maranhao only 24 of the 122 municípios had doctors, an average of one doctor per 20,956 inhabitants.

Sewage and water facilities are unavailable to vast numbers, the article continues, and malnutrition and hunger are endemic. According to FAO reports, for example, while the average per capita daily protein consumption in the underdeveloped countries is between 90 and 100 grams, Brazilians scarcely average 65.

In summary, the article concludes, "the Brazilians are a sick people," and the country may be likened, as the title states, to an immense hospital without beds.

3. Doctor is used as an honorific term of address in this and other parts of Brazil. All holders of bachelor's degrees, for example, are referred to as doctor, and most respected persons, including older persons with and without formal education, also are called doctor. António, as a professor and a lawyer, was referred to locally as Dr. António.

4. Chico was not really a Ladeira. His father's name had been Pedro Melo. His mother's family were Ladeiras. They were more numerous in Paraízo and slightly more affluent than the few Melos. They also helped Chico and his parents, who associated more with them than with his father's kinsmen. As he grew up, Chico came to be called Ladeira, the name he has used since adulthood and is known by today.

REFERENCES

GREENFIELD, S. M. (1972) "Charwomen, cesspools, and road building: an examination of patronage, clientage, and political power in southeastern Minas Gerais," in A. Strickon and S. M. Greenfield (eds.) Structure and Process in Latin America: Patronage, Clientage and Power Systems. Albuquerque: Univ. of New Mexico Press.

LEEDS, A. (1964) "Brazilian careers and social structure: a case history and model." Amer. Anthropologist 66.

LEFF, N. A. (1968) Economic Policy Making and Development in Brazil (1947-1964). New York: John Wiley.

NUNES LEAL, V. (1948) Coronelismo, Enxada e Voto: O Municipio e o Regime Representativo no Brasil. Rio de Janeiro.

PETTERSON, P. (1964) "Institutionalized confusion," in M. C. Needler (ed.) Political Systems of Latin America. New York: Harcourt, Brace & World.

Seara Nova (1973) 1536. Brasil: Un Imenso Hospital sem Camas.

STEIN, S. J. (1957) Vassouras: A Brazilian Coffee County, 1830-1900. Cambridge, MA: Harvard Univ. Press.

VILACA, M. V. and R. C. DE ALBUQUERQUE (1965) Coronel, Coroneis. Rio de Janeiro: Tempo Brasileiro.

Sidney M. Greenfield is a Professor in the Departments of Anthropology and Sociology at the University of Wisconsin–Milwaukee. He is author of English Rustics in Black Skin: A Study of Modern Family Forms in a Pre-Industrial Society *and coeditor (with Arnold Strickon) of* Structure and Process in Latin America: Patronage, Clientage and Power Systems.

GERTRUDE MATYOKA YEAGER
Department of History
Tulane University
New Orleans, LA 70118

BARROS ARANA, VICUNA MACKENNA, AMUNATEGUI

The Historian as National Educator

During the latter part of the nineteenth century, three historians, Diego Barros Arana, Benjamin Vicuña Mackenna, and Miguel Luis Amunátegui, came to epitomize a new sophistication which historical scholarship had attained in Chile. Taken together, the three men represent an important departure from previous romantic liberal historiography in that they were able to link Chile's past to its present without recourse to polemical rhetoric. More significantly, perhaps, these three scholars believed that history could serve socially useful functions. Much of their effort, consequently, was directed to making Clio a vital force for national development.[1]

In Chile the development of historical scholarship was intertwined with the growth of national consciousness. Early Chilean romantics such as José Victorino Lastarria and Jacinto Chacón had identified with two aspects of French romanticism—its flamboyant prose style and its advocacy of the French liberal restoration. Liberal romanticists, among them Madame de Stael, François Guizot, and Auguste Trognon, displayed obvious propagandistic intent in their writings. Chacón and

Journal of Interamerican Studies and World Affairs, Vol. 19 No. 2, May 1977

Lastarria adopted this characteristic readily. But the French authors had also argued that revolutionary liberalism sprang from medieval Gallic legal and contractual traditions. In the idiom of Madame de Stael, "liberty is ancient, despotism is new." Chilean romantic practitioners broke with their French counterparts at this juncture. Whereas the French saw their revolution as having clear precedents and as being firmly rooted in history, Lastarria and Chacón rejected what they regarded as a thoroughly benighted colonial past under the Spanish. Chilean romantics, then, negated the past and argued that their new independent state should purge itself of colonial vestiges (Jobert, 1949; Cox, 1938; Zea, 1963; Woll, 1974). A significant contribution of Barros Arana, Amunátegui, and Vicuña Mackenna was that they were able to discard this ahistorical vision and effectively come to terms with their past.

Numerous students have examined the contributions of the three men in rendering history a rigorous academic discipline and in making the historian's craft a respected and esteemed career. A smaller circle of scholars has treated other aspects of their multifaceted lives, including their experiences as politicians, diplomats, journalists, and pedagogues. This essay, however, will be concerned with a neglected aspect of the three historians' lives, their vocations as national educators. In their attempt to serve contemporary society, the historians inevitably affected the nature of their discipline. But they also influenced the course of Chile's history by molding its values and by prescribing a general formula for its development. In a broader context, the emergence of this trio as national preceptors contributes to our understanding of the role of the intellectual in modern Latin American society.

A close identification of government with historical scholarship developed shortly after Chilean independence. In 1836 Diego Portales, the founder of institutional republicanism, commissioned the French scholar, Claudio Gay, to write a general history of Chile at government expense (Jobert, 1949: 207; Feliú Cruz, 1958b: 51-53, 1965: 54-55). Portales made less visible contributions to historical studies as well. A political realist, he believed that a republic could not long survive without a citizenry schooled in the tenets of civic virtue. Although Portales sensed that the majority of Chileans lacked the most basic ability to understand, let alone practice, self-government, he remained optimistic because of a conviction that man was perfectable and that civic habits could be instilled in the population. To realize this end Portales fashioned a double-edged sword with which to carve away the vestiges of apathy and political illiteracy. For the masses he created the symbols of nationhood–a pantheon of heroes, a national motto, and a flag to be displayed before the populace on patriotic holidays along with the inevitable military parades and martial music. The purpose of such civic pageantry was to foster a broadly based sense of loyalty to the *patria*. Courting the elite required a more sophisticated approach, for Portales sought to train its scions as future leaders. It was in this goal that the Chilean *estado docente,* or teaching state, achieved its principal successes.

Portales' most lasting and important contribution to the final linkage between history as a discipline and the teaching of responsible citizenship came about almost accidentally–through his reliance upon the wisdom of Andres Bello, a Venezuelan intellectual who had immigrated to Chile (Jackson, 1968; Hanish, 1965). Bello took a rigorous and disciplined approach to history, so that students trained in his exacting methods seemed well equipped to assume leadership posts. In addition, Bello, whose thoughts on government closely paralleled those of Portales, systematized the principles of *peluconismo.* Bello grafted this body of political dogma to a philosophy of social evolution and proceeded to inculcate the resulting synthesis in generations of public school students. The effectiveness of his codification insured the continuing influence of Portales' innately cautious principles for almost a century.

The study of history received additional official support in 1842 when the Manuel Bulnes administration initiated an historical competition as part of the annual celebration of the founding of the Universidad de Chile (Jobert, 1949; Feliú Cruz,

1958b). Scholars generally trace the origins of modern Chilean historical writing to this contest. The purposes and scope of the competition were stated in article twenty-eight of the university's organic law, and Bello himself fashioned working guidelines for the participants. Each year the premier paper on a significant episode of the national past was to be read at a public ceremony. To be eligible for this distinction, it was required that a *memoria* be a valuable contribution to historical knowledge, that it be supported by substantial documentation, and that it be narrated in a vigorous but impassionate style. The contest generated an interest in history, and Chileans credit it with establishing a school of national historiography and with stimulating young men to take up careers as historians.

Perhaps the major preoccupation of nineteenth-century Chilean intellectuals was to shape and define the doctrines of liberalism and conservatism so as to make them relevant to the contemporary situation. In Chile the liberal-conservative controversy took on a unique character because the Hispanic past was not at issue. Indiscriminate imprisonment of creole leaders, whether of royalist or patriot persuasion, during the Chilean *reconquista* had left a bitter memory of the Spanish period for most of the elite. Because of this consensus, the colonial past did not become a viable topic for debate. Rather, the important issues turned upon the nature of the conservatism and liberalism which had developed since the inception of the republic.

The central concern of liberals and conservatives in nineteenth-century Chile was governmental authoritarianism. At least until mid-century, conservatives—more accurately styled *pelucones* during this period—demanded and established a highly centralized political system with an extremely powerful presidency and a largely impotent legislature. Conversely, liberals, or *pipiolos*, demanded a participatory republicanism with powers distributed equally between executive and legislative branches.

After 1850 Chilean politics took on a new complexity. Prior to the decade 1850-1860, the goal of liberals had been the destruction of the Portalean system, specifically the omnipotent presidency. The liberals' desire for change was reflected in various *motines* and abortive *golpes de estado.* While they did not succeed in dismantling the Portalean system, the liberals did emerge from the factional turbulence of the Montt decade having gained a substantial victory. They now enjoyed the right to participate in the process of presidential selection. The resulting compromise administration, that of José Joaquín Pérez, served as the threshold of what is traditionally considered the Liberal Republic (1861-1891).

After 1861, the goals and tactics of liberals altered and the desire to destroy the system was replaced with a new zeal to reform it. But once in power and deprived of a traditional common denominator—hatred for the Portalean system—liberalism began to splinter. Smaller, more homogeneous parties formed, and with the political atmosphere in constant flux, the composition of the new parties changed with kaleidoscopic rapidity. Under the broader banner of liberalism now existed the most diverse assortment of groups. Some expressed relative satisfaction with the new status quo and advocated slow evolutionary change; others were rabid anticlericals. Others were moderate reformers, and yet others were true democrats. If the writings of major liberal intellectuals often seem contradictory, it is because they accurately reflect the internal diversity of Chilean liberalism.

In their search for an alternative to the Spanish legacy, Chilean conservatives seized upon Great Britain for their model. Conservatives, of course, revered Bernardo O'Higgins and noted that figure's English education and general advocacy of British patterns. The choice of Britain, moreover, seemed a logical one for conservatives who perceived broad similarities between that nation and their own. Chilean conservatives admired the British system of social classes, a system which provided for social change and upward mobility, but within a structure of traditional relationships. Chile, again, had begun to benefit from British trade and was receiving British immigrants whose industriousness and technical skills made the modernization of Chile seem an easy venture. Finally, conservatives were impressed with the apparent similarities between their own system of government and that of Great Britain. Peluconismo had created a quasi-monarchical state. The president could easily be considered a species of constitutional monarch, while the aristocracy, composed of landed wealth and new commercial entrepreneurs, formed the core of the government party. The system seemed rigid and authoritarian at first glance, but even its founder believed it had the capacity to mature into a thoroughly democratic state. The anglophile leanings of the pelucones were seconded by Bello, who buttressed his conservative teaching with strong infusions of British utilitarianism, respect for tradition, and faith in evolutionary progress (Collier, 1967).

While conservatives took their lead from the English, the reconstituted pipiolos looked to France for inspiration. Stimulated by a group of Argentine romantic liberals who had found political refuge in Chile, the youthful pipiolos began to criticize the nature of their society and the peluconismo which provided its intellectual basis. A young but serious generation of new leaders assigned themselves the task of ridding the nation of its slavish reverence for outmoded social and political forms. They saw the Portalean institutions as antiquated and oppressive and began to demand tradition-destroying change. In the debate which ensued, issues became oversimplified and, consequently, not amenable to compromise. Tradition and gradual change became identified with conservatism, while rapid change and present-mindedness became synonymous with pipiolo liberalism (Melfí, 1937; Ingenieros, 1951, Vol. II: 451-515; Santana, 1942).

Barros Arana, Vicuña Mackenna, and Amunátegui undertook to bridge the abyss which separated pipiolo from pelucón. Armed with abundant documentation, scientific detachment, and inductive logic, they substantially proved that liberalism and respect for tradition were not antagonistic, but compatible principles.

Andres Bello's presence in Chile had much to do with the influence and power which the educated man came to wield in

Chile. When he docked at Valparaíso in 1829, Bello found a backward country lacking all but the most rudimentary educational opportunities. Awed by Bello's towering reputation as an intellectual, and increasingly aware of their own poverty of education, Chileans quickly entrusted their program of instruction to him. Government tapped Bello's considerable resources and employed his services in an unprecedented manner, while for the people Bello became teacher quo teacher, for he taught in everything he did (Jackson, 1968; Hanish, 1965).

Chileans may have been especially receptive to education in that it provided a means to compensate for their traditional position of inferiority among South American states. Furthermore, if one is to believe the national mythology, Chileans were self-made frontiersmen whose attitudes more closely resembled those of the socially mobile European bourgeoisie than those of the old world nobility. After the arrival of Bello, education provided a new avenue of mobility for the young man of middle-level status. In countries with a more sophisticated social order, these bright young men might have championed the middle class: in Chile they came to identify with the national elite. A career as educator thus became a highly regarded vocation, both for members of the elite and for those who aspired to membership in its ranks.

Not only did circumstances in Chile make it possible for the historian to emerge as a national political instructor, but the historian himself assumed the role with eagerness. Historians became involved in making as well as in recording and teaching history. Bello was himself an active intellectual who employed his knowledge to help establish a new sociopolitical order in Latin America (Jackson, 1968; Hanish, 1965). In the late 1800s his example would be reinforced by the influence of August Comte, who envisioned a new society in which the *pensador* would replace the politician and assume responsibility for the direction of the state. The native intelligentsia in a developing country like Chile could not indulge in detached philosophy when the state required the benefit of their wisdom.

What is perhaps most important in understanding the pedagogic activities of Barros Arana, Vicuña Mackenna, and Amunátegui is that they never specifically envisioned themselves as polemicists. Rather, they have been traditionally identified with the Bello-Gay school of erudite historiography (Cox, 1938; Jobert, 1949; Feliú Cruz, 1958b, 1965). Their works are monuments to the professionalism of Chilean historical writing because they rest upon extensive documentation and attention to detail. A sharp distinction grew up in Chile between patently biased, politically motivated history and a more objective style of documentary scholarship. This rift no doubt derived from an especially sharp polemic between Bello and his antagonists Lastarria and Chacón concerning philosophies of history (Feliú Cruz, 1958b, 1965; Woll, 1974). Chacón defended those historians who wrote interpretive history with only slight regard for factual evidence. Indeed, he considered the use of facts to be an unhappy imitation of European historians and urged Chileans to emancipate themselves from this form of intellectual colonialism. Bello, on the other hand, urged that the historians' principal duties were to gather, evaluate, and present the evidence impartially.

In emphasizing the Bello influence and the flight from romanticism, students of Chilean historiography have consistently produced the same analysis of the great liberal historians. The typical historiographical essay presents a biographical sketch, reproduces the historian's lengthy bibliography, and dwells upon his methodical approach. Almost without exception the student assumed that the work of Amunátegui, Barros Arana, and Vicuña Mackenna was dispassionate and apolitical. This assumption obscures the true significance of the historians' contribution. Because the liberal historians did not undertake intuitive scholarship does not imply that they refrained from employing the muse to a political end. Indeed, much of their impact may be traced to their subtle use of history. While their works were being praised as "prolific and dispassionate chronicles . . . devoid of interpretation," they had in fact fashioned a past to legitimize the liberal position (Donoso, 1931).

Schooled in Bello's concepts and methods, yet sharing the aspirations of their liberal associates, the classical historians constructed a most curious past. Indeed, they seemingly accomplished the impossible—a synthesis of the principles of Bello, Portales, and revitalized mid-nineteenth-century liberalism. Through this bizarre blend they managed to preserve the continuum of progress which the pelucones had envisioned since 1833. By adopting evolution as the foundation of a new liberal interpretation of history, they not only salvaged the past, but the governmental institutions which Portales had created as well.[2] What separates nineteenth-century Chilean historians from other Latin American pensadores who wrote political history was their sophisticated professionalism. The greater the skill and training which the historian brought to his craft, the better equipped he was to leave his stamp on his society.

It is only through close examination of the principal works of Barros Arana, Vicuña Mackenna, and Amunátequi that their political intent becomes apparent. Often the historians conveyed messages clearly designed to alter the political status quo. Frequently, however, the motivation is not explicit and must be gleaned carefully from the pages of their works.

Of the three, the talent of Amunátegui bloomed first, perhaps because family poverty dictated a need for employment and recognition. Not only did his first major work, *La reconquista española,* published in 1849, establish Amunátegui as a promising young scholar, but it won him a two-hundred-peso prize.[3] The political merit of this initial work may have been slight, but it did contribute to the idea of Spanish bankruptcy, a favorite preoccupation of nineteenth-century liberal writers. Three years later Amunátegui penned another prize-winning memoria, *Los tres primeros años de la revolución en Chile* (Amunátegui, 1852, 1928a). This disquisition developed two themes—the evolution of republican institutions and the growth of political parties—which had reassumed importance in the 1850s. By narrating from abundant documents, Amunátegui demonstrated that the development of republican institutions occurred independent of Portales. Moreover, he emphasized, the parties which had formed during the *Patria Vieja* at the turn of the century had espoused a variety of views concerning independence and the nature of politics. This argument was presumably designed as a weapon to be used against the monolithic politics being advocated by the Montt administration. A review committee praised the work for having treated the political immaturity of early creole leaders in as detached a manner as it did the glorious events of the revolutionary period (Cox, 1938; Amunátegui, 1928a).

In 1853 Amunátegui presented a work which added another chapter to his study of the Chilean quest for liberty, *Una conspiración en 1780* (Amunátegui, 1853). The final work in which Amunátegui synthesized his thoughts on the nature of the independence movement appeared in 1870. In this three-volume study, *Los precursores de la independencia de Chile* (Amunátegui, 1870), the author presented a message which would not be wasted on his audience. According to *Los precursores,* Chileans were committed to the idea of emancipation in 1810, for the movement would not have succeeded without a backlog of broadly based support. Amunátegui also attempted to explain some of the inconsistencies and initial timidity of independence leaders. One reader believed that Amunátegui had written more than a book, that *Los precursores* was "a brisk wind which dissipated shadows from our [Latin American] history" (Amunátegui, 1928b). Another commentator remarked that the book, published during Amunátegui's tenure as Minister of the Interior, was as much an outline of his ministerial program as it was a literary masterpiece (Santa Cruz, 1928: 69).[4]

Although Amunátegui's message was a mild one, it did have an important impact upon the liberalism of his age. For the first time since national consolidation, liberals understood their role in the historical process. Prior liberals of Lastarria's persuasion had ignored history, a convenient way of closing their eyes to the seemingly destructive nature of pipiolismo. In the mid-nineteenth century the past belonged to the pelucones alone. Liberalism had caused *La anarguía,* while Portales and the pelucones assumed credit for the establishement of an orderly society. The value of Amunátegui's work lay in his explanation of the role of liberalism. Liberalism, under his pen, was not alien to Chile, but had sparked a desire for liberty in the early years of the century. Liberals, in Amunátegui's idiom, were not responsible for the many errors committed during the first days of national existence. Rather, such mistakes were the result of political ignorance, because Spain had denied the creoles participation in government.

The small but important body of historical literature which Amunátegui produced while creating a liberal historical tradition has been generally overshadowed by his masterpiece, *La dictadura de O'Higgins* (Amunátegui, 1914). In this volume the author studied the administration of Chile's first executive in order to castigate dictatorship as a form of government and to demonstrate its demoralizing effect upon public morality. Although subsequent generations of students have recognized the political content of this work, they have explained it as merely a quirk of Amunátegui's age, an example of the application of Voltairean theory to Chilean history (Feliú Cruz, 1949). For Chileans, the adjective "Voltairean" did not refer to the *philosope's* advocacy of Enlightened Despotism. Instead, it sprang from Chileans' admiration of Voltaire as father of the Enlightenment and as combator of all forms of traditional authority and irrational despotism. The romanticism of the era obviously affected Amunátegui, yet the message he conveyed in 1853 was addressed specifically to an immediate problem. Published in the middle of Montt's first term, the work impressed Chileans as a bold attack upon the practices of this "tyrant." According to Barros Arana, Amunátegui's tract threw Santiago into a state of agitation, for such a candid and brutal assault upon the president was not expected of the ordinarily mild-mannered scholar.[5] Amunátegui's message was concise and clear, and the parallels that he developed between the regime of

O'Higgins and that of Montt were readily perceived by his contemporaries. Nor did the historian content himself with this analysis by analogy; he moved on to provide a prescription for the problems of dictatorship and malfeasance. Rulers who abused public power and lost the people's trust, according to him, should resign or be removed from office forcibly. Amunátegui had presented a significant lesson for Chileans of his, as well as future generations. In its defense of the right to revolution, *La dictadura* provided Chileans with a formula, sanctioned by history, for removing presidents from office when their views and those of an incumbent diverged.

Despite a pompous and unexciting style, Amunátegui's works were well accepted and apparently read by those in influential circles (Cox, 1938; Amunátegui, 1928a, 1928b; Jobert, 1949). Succeeding generations of Chileans committed to memory his prescription for removing executives by forming a nonideological united front. One measure of his impact must be the fact that his suspicion of all authority and his support of the right to rebel were reflected consistently in the later works of Vicuña Mackenna and Barros Arana.

Benjamin Vicuña Mackenna shared his colleagues' dedication to documentation and investigation. Stylistically, however, he departed from their use of colorless, boorish prose, and his independence proved costly. A desire to create work of artistic merit earned him as many detractors as it did disciples. Vicuña Mackenna, too, announced forthrightly that the historian's role was that of a "priest of the past," and that his proper role was one of preserving public morality. Through a clever interlacing of data he turned history into a "living thing." Whereas contemporaries wrote for a limited audience of intellectuals, Vicuña Mackenna's vivid prose style enabled him to attract a much wider readership. The effect was to increase his influence upon the larger society, but it earned him a reputation as a "popular" historian, a strong pejorative among intellectuals of his generation (Feliú Cruz, 1949, 1958b; Cox, 1938; Encina 1949).

The history Vicuña Mackenna wrote reflected a vibrant and energetic personality. While Barros Arana, and to a greater extent Amunátegui, attacked Montt from the safety of a *tertulia,* Vicuña Mackenna openly participated in conspiracies and was consequently imprisoned and exiled. Throughout his voluminous writings, Vicuña Mackenna used the past to serve the liberal cause. He preferred to write biography because he felt that history's primary concern was to tell the story of man (Feliú Cruz, 1949). In telling history through the lives of individuals, writers created heroes and identified villains, and Vicuña Mackenna performed both tasks with consummate skill.

A major preoccupation among Chileans after independence involved the selection of a figure from among the revolutionary leaders worthy of a role as father of the nation. Of the many men who participated in the independence movement, none seemed to project the untarnished image needed to inspire patriotism in the masses. Vicuña Mackenna's attempts to resolve the question and to create an heroic tradition met with unprecedented criticism because he employed unorthodox methods and tied the past to the present with shocking boldness.

Vicuña Mackenna presented his most radical interpretation in his treatment of the Carrera family (Vicuña Mackenna, 1857). To most of his contemporaries, the Carreras' contribution to independence offered little that was worthy of admiration. Many Chileans had come to view the family as the major cause of Chile's ruin in 1814. Vicuña Mackenna turned to the Carreras in order to fill the need of the revitalized pipiolo movement for a hero and a respectable ancestory in the revolutionary tradition. On a more personal level, José Miguel Carrera's volatile and anarchistic personality undoubtedly appealed to the historian. The most feasible way to rehabilitate this figure was by emphasizing his service to independence, at the same time dismissing his selfishness as a lack of political sophistication typical of independence leaders. This interpretation was greeted with interest and not a little amazement. One irate reader stated that only an "apostle of anarchy" could find admirable qualities in the Carreras, and speculated that had Vicuña Mackenna been called to judge between Cain and Abel, he would have vindicated the rebel. The same observer believed that the type of patriotism which Vicuña Mackenna admired was destructive and involved a complete negation of authority (Irisarri, 1931).

To raise the position of Carrera on a scale of revolutionary leaders, Vicuña Mackenna found it necessary to adjust the role assigned O'Higgins. In *El ostracismo de general O'Higgins,* he presented that figure in a most controversial manner. Using a ploy of Bartólome Mitre, Vicuña Mackenna attempted to transform O'Higgins into Chile's first soldier. The assignment of this role was made after much deliberation, and because the historian believed that O'Higgins' military deeds had alone established his reputation. After a thorough examination of his subject, the historian concluded that O'Higgins was unacceptable as a political hero because his regime was lacking in the "two fundamental conditions of all legitimate government—morality and liberty" (Vicuña Mackenna, 1931, 1868b).

Taken together, Vicuña's two biographies present a coherent, provocative commentary on the independence period. The revolution created two potential heroes. Each, however, was a man replete with human failings. One was brash and rebellious; the other was sober and methodical. Carrera loved liberty too much, while O'Higgins, in the end, loved it too little. Carrera represented the spirit of liberty, while the O'Higgins depicted by Vicuña Mackenna epitomized only Chile's dedication to freedom from Spain. Both served independence and were, therefore, worthy of Chileans' respect.

Throughout his treatment of Carrera and O'Higgins, Vicuña conveyed his hatred of despotism. More than Amunátegui or Barros Arana, he was deeply affected by the romantic movement which swept Chile in the 1840s. His view of history oscillated between the romantic view that it served the present, and that of Bello, who held that it explained only the past. Vicuña Mackenna emphasized the necessity of liberty with such fervor that his readers often felt that he believed anarchy preferable to any form of authority. The people's right to revolution in the defense of freedom was a sacred right that should be used against all who would limit an individual's freedom. Chilean history was replete with examples of this war between liberty and tyranny, many of which the historian chronicled in the 882-page introduction to his multivolume history of the Montt decade (Vicuña Mackenna, 1868a). In this compendious introduction, Vicuña sought to demonstrate that the liberal assault on Montt was nothing more than the most recent manifestation of a hoary traditional struggle.

Amunátegui defended liberalism with documents, Vicuña Mackenna with moving words. What Amunátegui presented to the elite, Vicuña Mackenna wrote for the many. One was determined to persuade national leaders, the other to instruct the public in the rudiments of citizenship and politics. To these two historians' combination of research and forceful persuasion, Barros Arana added a framework of systematic logic.

At mid-century, while Amunátegui and Vicuña Mackenna occupied the center of Chile's intellectual stage, Barros Arana remained largely in the wings. His first work, the *Historia jeneral de la independencia de Chile,* was published in 1854 and was well received, as were a number of articles and essays which appeared in periodical and pamphlet form (Barros Arana, 1854). While Amunátegui published scholarly treatises and while Vicuña Mackenna wrote popular interpretive pieces, Barros Arana typically expressed himself in short pieces, most of which have since fallen into obscurity. Yet it was this quiet and methodical man, writing prodigiously and teaching classes of students throughout his life, who constructed and synthesized a liberal interpretation of Chilean history which would stand unchallenged for many years. After twenty-five years of compiling data and sorting documents, Barros Arana began writing his monumental *Historia jeneral de Chile* in 1884 (Barros Arana, 1884-1902). This sixteen-volume work, generally considered the most masterful accomplishment by a nineteenth-century Latin American historian, was completed in 1902.

If the description of Lastarria—that he was an eclectic because he lacked the ability to sustain a single thought—was correct, then the opposite was true of Barros Arana. With excruciating patience he constructed a work in which he developed a central theme through nine thousand pages of text. Writing later than either Amunátegui or Vicuña Mackenna, he synthesized their ideas concerning liberalism and wove them carefully into the national past (Matyoka, 1972).

Barros Arana, like his colleagues, identified with the pipiolos, as his journalistic and political careers suggest. But the scholar felt the need to maintain Chilean traditions as well and, rather than sacrifice the national heritage, he chose to fuse it with pipiolo dogma. In the *Historia jeneral* he viewed the colonial and independence eras through the prism of his own time. He found it convenient to stress the long development of republican government because once liberals possessed the institutions which Portales had erected, they no longer wished to destroy them. Barros Arana consequently traced the republican instincts of Chileans through four centuries, arguing that they were a part of the Spanish legacy, although they had at times been nearly extinguished because of the actions of despotic rulers. The historian concluded from his study that the frailty of republican institutions made perpetual vigilance and citizen armament necessities (Barros Arana, 1884-1902).

Barros Arana went on to trace the thread of incipient liberalism through independence and into the early republic. After separation from Spain, Chileans had experimented with various forms of government; a succession of constitutions were written and discarded, and a variety of administrations had existed for short periods.[6] In 1833 Chileans drafted a document of which Barros Arana approved because it promised the people liberty and a republic form of government.

Although the Spanish legacy contained a germ of liberty, it also included a large measure of despotism, and this Barros Arana did not ignore. In his depiction of the early colonial period, he argued the case for a black legend of Iberian oppression. With great detail he traced Chile's sufferings at the hands of royal officials (Barros Arana, 1884-1902, Vols. I-VII).

He believed that a tendency to despotism was inherent in all men and admitted that it had even infected national heroes.

In order to protect freedom, Barros Arana instructed Chileans to remain vigilant. He demonstrated the means by which creoles had safeguarded their rights during the colonial period, and the tone of his argument differed very little from that of the admonitions he leveled against Montt, Santa María, and Balmaceda.[7] For Barros Arana, violent means were eminently justifiable in the defense of freedom—a rationale which proved especially timely in that it was delivered on the eve of the Chilean revolution in 1891.

Nowhere did Barros Arana demonstrate his contemporary thinking more clearly than in his treatment of the Constitution of 1833. Once liberals had achieved some prominence in the affairs of the nation, they no longer regarded the document which Portales had dictated with disdain. In the late 1800s, liberalism concerned itself with modifying governmental institutions. Liberals came to conceive the constitution as an essentially democratic instrument, and argued that its only imperfection stemmed from the fact that men had misconstrued or perverted its essence. Barros Arana, then, was easily able to defend the constitution while remaining well within the confines of liberal thought.

Barros Arana manifested a Basque heritage and personal austerity in his depiction of national virtues. What he admired in men were essentially commonsense traits: pragmatism, realism, dedication, and purpose. Chileans, to him, were not a race of titans as Vicuña Mackenna had imagined them, but honest, yeoman-like workers (Barros Arana, 1884-1902). He saw evil as avarice, sloth, and lack of purpose—all components of the Spanish national character for him. Such deficit traits were epitomized by Carrera. Barros Arana demonstrated that Chileans were sensible people dedicated to self-government; they were self-reliant and capable of great accomplishments in the present as they had been in the past.

In the sections of the *Historia jeneral* which concerned education, Barros Arana revealed his pedagogic instincts and positivistic orientation. He made numerous references to the lack of education in Chile; ignorance, he believed, best explained the early failure of Chilean republicanism. He thought, too, that reforms could only succeed when a people had been educated to accept them. The nature of a republic presupposed an educated citizenry, or the populace would become the prey of unprincipled men. Education was the key to the construction of an orderly society. Those who ruled were to be trained to their task, while the masses were to be educated to protect their rights.

Barros Arana, Amunátegui, and Vicuña Mackenna demonstrated great flexibility and ingenuity in the pursuit of their goals as national educators. Through their lectures at the Instituto Nacional and the Universidad de Chile, Amunátegui and Barros Arana influenced young minds over a period of several decades. For students who were denied such direct contact, they wrote numerous textbooks (Amunátegui, 1856; Barros Arana, 1865). And because they proved to be extremely effective teachers, they developed large coteries of disciples, many of whom maintained contact with their former mentors as adults. While Amunátegui and Barros Arana devoted much of their lives to teaching, Vicuña Mackenna remained unimpressed by the opportunities which formal education offered for influencing his countrymen. Only free public education appealed to his crusader spirit, and in 1856 he formed the Sociedad de Instrucción Primaria, a private organization which supported government establishment of elementary schools throughout Chile (Fuentes and Cortés, 1965).

The accolades of former students testify to Barros Arana's and Amunátegui's effectiveness as teachers. An impoverished Amunátegui began giving classes at the Instituto Nacional in 1847 largely for economic reasons. Teaching was necessary to his early survival, but he continued to meet classes throughout his life. At the colegio he taught literature, but not history. In 1853 he was admitted to the university faculty. His students found him a firm but reasonable man (Amunátegui, 1928a; Santa Cruz, 1928). In the Bello tradition he took a personal interest in his students, who became colleagues and friends after leaving his classes. Since he conceived education as a continuing process, Amunátegui offered special classes for more advanced students in *literarios jóvenes.* Young men, usually from the upper divisions, would periodically meet at his home, where they discussed literature and developed writing talent in a salon setting (Amunátegui, 1928a). The historian first presided over such a tertulia in 1853, and it convened regularly for over thirty years. Because the mid-nineteenth century was an intensely political age, the group regularly turned to a discussion of politics and the affairs of the Chilean state.

Events in the 1850s reflected the tensions caused by the Montt administration, which had come to power during a period of intense unrest and rebellion. Students formed the core of the antipelucón movement, and, because they identified with resurrected liberalism, they devoured revolutionary pipiolo literature. Rather than object to their reading preferences, Amunátegui urged them on. The mentor allowed politics to enter his classroom and permitted students to write essays on issues of contemporary importance.

More significant than his classroom technique was the example which Amunátegui himself presented. He was a modest man who believed that Chileans should develop a spirit of political toleration, feeling as he did that more progress could be achieved through cooperation than through confrontation. Unlike many theorists, Amunátegui practiced his beliefs. In 1856 Chile was relatively quiet, and Montt was in a conciliatory mood. In an attempt to placate the liberals, he named Amunátegui to a government post, as a section chief in the Ministry of Public Instruction. The scholar found no contradiction in serving the Montt administration while opposing it politically. The literary salon which Amunátegui had established in 1853 continued to meet regularly. When he was suddenly ousted from his new office, however, the salon changed form considerably.

Lastarria baptized the new seminar "La Picantería," and it quickly became the liberal counterpart of the conservative's tertulias. La Picantería offered a forum for Montt's opponents to express their views. It never became identified with openly revolutionary activity as did other opposition tertulias, most notably Filarmónica (Santa Cruz, 1928). The political stature of Amunátegui and his tertulias increased during the subsequent government of José Joaquin Pérez (1861-1871), which the scholar served in the capacity of Sub-Secretary of Interior. Amunátegui was a principle architect of this compromise regime. As part of the preparation for a new era of political toleration, Pérez wished to engage as teachers only young men capable of developing the correct political attitudes in their charges. With Barros Arana, Amunátegui supplied lists of candidates for teaching posts in the national public schools. Not surprisingly, Amunátegui fastened upon this opportunity as a means to place his former students in key positions. The final political triumph for Amunátegui and his tertulia occurred in 1868 when Pérez named him Minister of Interior (Amunátegui, 1928a; Santa Cruz, 1928; Barros Arana, 1875 and 1888). Amunátegui, then, exerted considerable political influence, both through direct participation in the political system and by grooming a cadre of functionaries and educators.

Barros Arana, by contrast, wielded his power as professor less conspicuously. Like Amunátegui, he began teaching while still a young man. More involved in politics than Amunátegui, Barros Arana's hatred of Montt drove him into a European exile in 1858. This episode would prove to be of crucial importance, for in France he became aware not only of the inadequacies of Chilean education, but of positivism as well. In Paris Barros Arana hosted a salon and soon recognized the limited scope of his own education. Upon return to Chile, he set out to modernize that country's system (Barros Arana, 1873).

As a friend and colleague of Amunátegui and a supporter of Pérez, Barros Arana shared the political spoils made available to liberals in the sixties. In 1863 he became rector of the Instituto Nacional; only 33 years old, he set about implementing an ambitious program of reforms (Orrego Barros, 1958, 1943). Barros Arana was an educator by will, not by training. He believed that children should be taught to reason, and that the purpose of education was to discipline minds. As rector he was an innovator: he supervised classroom technique, relaxed discipline, increased library holdings, and formed a student literary society. Because he disapproved of much of the available curricular material, Barros Arana wrote a variety of textbooks on history, geography, and literature to be used in the public schools.

Politics helped Barros Arana secure the rectorship in 1863, but also caused his removal from the post a decade later. In the early 1870s the "educational question" became a focus of a heated political debate and Barros Arana's reforms attracted numerous traditionalist barbs. The controversy raged for two years and the historian resigned his post in 1873, but continued to teach (Barros Arana, 1873).

As professors at the Instituto Nacional, Amunátegui and Barros Arana instructed young men from Chile's best families over a period spanning more than thirty years. Since university training was not essential in that era, many students did not pursue their schooling beyond the secondary level. The two historians taught young Chileans at the most impressionable age, hence their impact must have been substantial.

Teaching, however, could occur in different settings. While Vicuña Mackenna refrained from using the lectern as a pulpit, he excelled as a teacher when the class was the entire nation and the textbook a newspaper. Of the three historians, Vicuña Mackenna best exploited the public press. His talent for irony and satire, when directed at an adversary or an injustice, proved a most effective weapon. He wrote for many different papers throughout his life, but the first, *La Asamblea Constituyente,* was his most famous. He established the paper in the 1850s for the purpose of driving Montt from the presidency. In this paper Vicuña called for revolution against the dictator and, as the banner suggested, the adoption of a new constitution. He believed that a flawed constitution was the source of Chile's outstanding problems and that the logical solution was to replace it with one better suited to the national situation. *La*

Asamblea had the tendency to oversimplify problems and offer lists of rather ill-defined goals. It came to a predictable end when Montt closed its offices (Feliú Cruz, 1949; Donoso, 1949; Silva Castro, 1958).

Bitter irony and stinging wit characterized not only the essays of Vicuña Mackenna, but those of his colleague Barros Arana as well. In 1857 he made his debut as a political writer and editor. The purpose of *El País,* his first paper, was to goad Montt to make cabinet changes and liberalize the executive. When Montt complied the periodical ceased publication. The change, however, proved a ruse, and in 1858 Barros Arana established another paper, *La Actualidad Política.* In his articles and editorials the historian developed several themes, most notably the idea that Montt had violated the laws of evolutionary progress. He also defended the right to revolt and rebuked elected officials who did the president's bidding. Unlike Vicuña, Barros Arana defended the Constitution of 1833 and called for all citizens to unite behind it to oppose the dictator (Matyoka, 1972).

After many years of abstention from political journalism, Barros Arana resumed his activity in the 1880s. Liberals established *La Libertad Electoral* to provide a forum for their assault on President Domingo Santa María (1881-1886), charging him with attempting to reinstitute the strong executive. One of the most popular columns in this organ was written by Barros Arana, although under a pseudonym. Continued outbursts of presidential rage, however, ultimately forced the author to identify himself (Matyoka, 1972).

Amunátegui refrained from the type of political commentary his friends produced. Rather than contribute to small, narrowly political papers which reached a small audience, he first wrote for *El Araucano,* which he edited in 1849. Adopting a milder tone than that of his counterparts, he tried to persuade his readers of the worthiness of his position. During the 1860s he established *El Independiente* in order to win support for the Pérez administration and to defend the coalition between liberals and conservatives. He also contributed articles to *La*

República and encouraged his students to follow suit. Several years later he founded another paper, also named *La República,* to defend the principle of academic freedom and his friend, Barros Arana, in the education question (Amunátegui, 1928a).

Perhaps the best podium available to those who wished to influence political development was provided by public office. All three historians sought and held elected offices and appointed posts during their careers. Vicuña Mackenna first engaged in politics as a revolutionary. Twice, during Montt's first term, in 1851, he participated in abortive attempts to oust the president. For his actions in the Uprising of Urriola, he was imprisoned and sentenced to death. He escaped, however, and immediately joined a group of rebels led by José Miguel Carrera in the so-called Revolution of La Serena. The rebellion was suppressed in 1852 and Vicuña Mackenna went into exile for six years. In 1858 he was again imprisoned for conspiracy and exiled. During the 1860s Vicuña participated in politics. Between 1864 and 1885 he served as a deputy and in 1875 when President Federico Errázuriz (1871-1876) declined to nominate an official candidate, Vicuña Mackenna himself sought the presidency. Some of his lasting contributions were made while serving in appointed posts. Errázuriz named him Intendant of Santiago, and in his energetic manner he undertook a major program of public improvements, including the creation of the Cierro Santa Lucía, the construction of the central market, and the beautification of the Alameda (Fuentes and Cortés, 1965).

Amunátegui's political career closely resembled that of Vicuña Mackenna. While the latter spent the 1850s in exile, however, the former served as an official in the Montt government, although he was already affiliated with the liberals. Throughout his adult life Amunátegui held numerous elected offices. Between 1864 and 1888 he held a seat in the *Cámara de Diputados.* He served in presidential cabinets regularly, and was elected to honorary posts such as an official of the Chamber of Deputies. In 1874 Amunátegui presented legislation that outlined major constitutional reforms and an explanation of the relation between church and state. A year later, like Vicuña Mackenna, he campaigned for the presidential nomination (Barros Arana, 1875).

Like Vicuña Mackenna, Barros Arana was punished for his first involvement in politics. In 1858 he was forced to leave Chile because the government disapproved of his political beliefs. When arrested he was charged with conspiracy, but later was released because the accusations could not be substantiated. The most important posts he held were appointive: rector of the Instituto Nacional and Minister Plenipotentiary to Argentina and Brazil in 1876. But both assignments ended unpleasantly. He became the target of criticism and a scapegoat in the educational question and was thoroughly chastized for his award of Patagonia to Argentina while serving as diplomat. Although elected office never interested him, Barros Arana served three terms as legislator in the lower house, from 1867 to 1873 and from 1885 to 1888. He ended his political career as he had begun it, fleeing presidential arrest orders in 1891 (Orrego Barros, 1958; Fuentes and Cortes, 1965).

Barros Arana, Vicuña Mackenna, and Amunátegui, through their scholarly, pedagogic, journalistic, and political endeavors, served to educate and convert their fellow citizens to the principles of liberalism. In their roles as national educators they sought to serve their age and to advance the tenets of liberalism. They employed the past to serve the present. They legitimized the neopipiolo movement by demonstrating its colonial ancestry and they created, by using history, a rationale which justified their methods, actions, and goals. Their careers demonstrate that historians could be effective national educators. As a result of their efforts history became politicized even though two of them denied they had used history to serve politics. Their efforts also made Chileans more intensely aware of the past. Unlike the romantic writers, the classical liberal historians did not seriously distort the past, and they supported their conclusions with exhaustive documentation that gave their writings an objective quality. Scientific detachment allowed them to do what other liberal writers could not; they created a credible liberal tradition for Chileans.

NOTES

1. A sample of the literature on this subject includes Arnade (1962), Barager (1959), Flaig (1974), Griffin (1957), Leff (1971), Mellon (1958), Mogollón (1957), Smith (1965), Sater (1972), and Woll (1974).

2. The use of an evolutionary scheme is characteristic of liberal historians. Such a development continuum stresses the worthiness of the institutions which survived.

3. The Amunátegui brothers, Miguel Luís and Gregorio Victor, coauthored most of the works credited to Miguel. Amunátegui (1928a) said the work was published in 1850, but Cox (1938) claimed it appeared in 1849.

4. For a contrary view see Encina (1949).

5. Barros Arana disapproved of Amunátegui's use of history to chastize Montt (Barros Arana, 1875).

6. Barros Arana devoted four volumes to the 1810-1820 period (1884-1902, Vols. XII-XVI).

7. For Barros Arana's complete bibliography see Chiappa (1907).

REFERENCES

AMUNATEGUI, M. L. (1928a) "Autobiografía." Revista Chilena de Historia y Geografía 56 (enero-marzo): 7-21.

––– (1928b) Carta, Bogotá, Septiembre 17-18 al Sor Miguel L. Amunátegui de M. Ancizar in "Epistolario." Revista Chilena de Historia y Geografía 56 (enero-marzo): 25-39.

––– (1914) "La dictadura de O'Higgins." Revista Chilena de Historia y Geografía 56 (enero-marzo): 25-39.

––– (1870) Los precursores de la independencia de Chile. 3 vols. Santiago de Chile.

––– (1856) Compendio de la historia política i eclesiástica de Chile. Santiago de Chile.

––– (1853) Una conspiración en 1780. Santiago de Chile: Imprenta del Progreso.

––– (1852) Los tres primeros años de la revolución. Santiago de Chile.

––– (1849) La reconquista española. Santiago de Chile: Imprenta de la Universidad de Chile.

ARNADE, C. (1962) "The historiography of colonial and modern Bolivia." Hispanic Amer. Historical Rev. 42 (August): 333-384.

BARAGER, J. (1959) "The historiography of the Río de la Plata area since 1830." Hispanic Amer. Historical Rev. 39 (November): 588-642.

BARROS ARANA, D. (1888) Don Miguel Luís Amunátegui. Santiago de Chile: Imprenta de A. Lahure.

––– (1884-1902) Historia jeneral de Chile. 16 vols. Santiago de Chile: Imprenta R. Jover.

––– (1875) Don Miguel Luís Amunátegui, candidato a la presidencia de la república. Santiago de Chile: Imprenta de "El Ferrocarril."

––– (1873) Mi destitución: apuntes para la historia del Instituto Nacional. Santiago de Chile: Imprenta de "El Ferrocarril."

——— (1865) Historia de America. Santiago de Chile.

——— (1861) Cuadro histórico de la administración Montt, escrito según sus propios documentos. Valparaíso: Imprenta y Librería del Mercurio de Santos Tornero.

——— (1854) Historia jeneral de la independencia de Chile. Santiago de Chile: Imprenta Chilena.

CHIAPPA, V. M. (1907) Bibliografía de Don Diego Barros Arana. Temuco: Imprenta Alemana.

COLLIER, S. (1967) Ideas and Politics of Chilean Independence. New York: Cambridge Univ. Press.

COX, I. J. (1938) "Some of Chile's historians as viewed by their fellow craftsmen." Proceedings of the First Convention of Inter-American Bibliography and History Association: 51-67.

DONOSO, A. (1916) Barros Arana y Mitre. Una amistad literaria. Santiago de Chile: Editorial Nascimento.

DONOSO, R. (1963) Diego Barros Arana. México, D. F.: Instituto Panamericano de Geografía e Historia.

——— (1949) "La sátira política en Chile." Historiografía Chilena. Santiago de Chile: Editorial Nascimento.

——— (1931) Barros Arana, educador, historiador y hombre público. Santiago de Chile: Imprenta Universitaria.

ENCINA, F. A. (1949) "Breve bosquejo de la literatura histórica chilena." Atenea 95 (septiembre-octubre): 27-68.

FLAIG, H. (1974) "The historian as pedagogue of the nation." History 59 (February): 18-32.

FELIU CRUZ, G. (1965) "Andrés Bello y la historiografía chilena." Mapocho IV: 3, 231-263.

——— (1958a) Barros Arana, historiador. 5 vols. Santiago de Chile: Ediciones de los Anales de la Universidad de Chile.

——— (1958b) Historiografía colonial de Chile. 2 vols. Santiago de Chile: Fondo Histórico y Bibliográfico José Toribio Medina.

——— (1949) "Interpretación de Vicuña Mackenna, un historiador del siglo XIX." Atenca 95 (septiembre-octubre): 144-181.

FUENTES, J. and L. CORTES (1965) Diccionario histórico de Chile. Santiago de Chile: Editorial Orbe.

GRIFFIN, C. (1957) "Francisco Encina and revisionism in Chilean history." Hispanic Amer. Historical Rev. 37 (February): 1-28.

HANISH, W. (1965) "Tres dimensiones del pensamiento de Bello: religión, filosofía, historia." Historia IV: 8-188.

INGENIEROS, J. (1951) La evolución de las ideas argentinas. 2 vols. Buenos Aires: El Ateneo.

IRISARRI, A. J. de (1931) "Carta a su hijo don Hermogenes." Revista Chilena de Historia y Geografía 70 (julio-diciembre): 178-197.

JACKSON, L. (1968) "Andrés Bello, Latin American humanist." Unpublished doctoral dissertation, Texas Christian University.

JOBERT, J. C. (1949) "Notas sobre la historiografía chilena." Atenea 95 (septiembre-octubre): 346-377.

LEFF, G. (1971) History and Social Theory. New York: Anchor.

MATYOKA, G. (1972) "Diego Barros Arana and the Historia Jeneral de Chile." Unpublished doctoral dissertation, Texas Christian University.

MELFI, D. (1937) "La generación de Lastarria." Atenea (marzo): 235-283.

MELLON, S. (1958) The Political Uses of History; a Study of Historians in the French Restoration. Stanford, CA: Stanford Univ. Press.

MOGOLLON, J. V. (1957) "Francisco Antonio Encina; su personalidad y sus ideas sobre la raza, la economía y la educación: escenario: Chile 1910." Atenea 129: 3-20.

ORREGO BARROS, C. (1958) Diego Barros Arana. Santiago de Chile: Universidad de Chile.

--- (1943) "Comte y su influencia sobre Barros Arana." Atenea 129 (octubre-diciembre): 45-59.

--- (1943) Barros Arana, rector del Instituto Nacional 1863-1873. Santiago de Chile: Prensas de la Universidad de Chile.

RUIZ URBINA, A. (1958) Barros Arana, educador. 2 vols. Santiago de Chile: Ediciónes de los Anales de la Universidad de Chile.

SANTA CRUZ, J. (1928) "Recuerdos de la Picantería." Revista Chilena de Historia y Geografía 56 (enero-marzo): 40-92.

SANTANA, F. (1942) "Hombres de 1842." Atenea (mayo): 291-325.

SATER, W. (1972) "The hero as a force of change in Chilean education." J. of Developing Areas 7 (October): 80-104.

SILVA CASTRO, R. (1958) Prensa y periodismo en Chile 1812-1956. Santiago de Chile: Ediciones de la Universidad de Chile.

SMITH, P. (1965) "The image of a dictator, Gabriel Garcia Morena." Hispanic Amer. Historical Rev. 45 (February): 1-24.

VICUNA MACKENNA, B. (1931) "Mi defensa ante el jurado de imprenta que tuvo lugar en Valparaíso el 24 de Junio de 1861." Revista Chilena de Historia y Geografía 70 (julio-diciembre): 31-136.

--- (1868a) La historia de los diez años de la administración de Montt. 6 vols. Santiago de Chile: Imprenta Chilena.

--- (1868b) Ostracismo del General don Bernardo O'Higgins. Santiago de Chile: Imprenta Chilena.

--- (1865) Los girondinos chilenos. Santiago de Chile.

--- (1857) El Ostracismo de los Carreras. Santiago de Chile: Imprenta del Ferrocarril.

WOLL, A. L. (1975) "For God or country: history textbooks and the secularization of Chilean society, 1840-1890." J. of Latin American Studies 7: 23-43.

--- (1974) "The philosophy of history in nineteenth century Chile: the Lastarria-Bello controversy." History and Theory: Studies in the Philosophy of History 13 (October): 273-290.

ZEA, L. (1963) The Latin American Mind (trans. J. H. Abbott and L. Dunham). Norman: Univ. of Oklahoma Press.

Gertrude Matyoka Yeager is an Assistant Professor in the Department of History at Tulane University. Since receiving her Ph.D. from Texas Christian University, her research has concentrated on Chilean intellectual history and the role of elites.

MITCHELL A. SELIGSON
Department of Political Science
University of Arizona
Tucson, AZ 85721

AGRARIAN POLICIES IN DEPENDENT SOCIETIES

Costa Rica

There is no area of investigation in the field of Latin American studies which has attracted more research in recent years than has the dependency theory. Countless words have been written and much academic "blood" has been spilled in the debate over the strengths and weaknesses of interpreting Latin American society, polity, economy, and culture within the framework of the dependency theory.[1] While there is still much heat generated by those who hold differing opinions on the dependency perspective, serious research is proceeding in a number of areas in an attempt to document the ways in which and the extent to which Latin American nations are dependent on forces beyond their control. This paper attempts to further

AUTHOR'S NOTE: The research on which this paper is based was conducted under grants from the Social Science Research Council's Foreign Area Fellowship Program (with funds from the Ford Foundation) and from the Danforth Foundation. An earlier version was presented at the 1975 Annual Meeting of the American Political Science Association, San Francisco, California. The author would like to thank James M. Malloy, Wanderlei Guiherme dos Santos, and Evelyn Stevens for their helpful suggestions on the earlier version. The revision was made possible with support provided by the Institute for Government Research of the University of Arizona.

Journal of Interamerican Studies and World Affairs, Vol. 19 No. 2, May 1977

that research by focusing on agrarian public policy in Costa Rica.

Research on public policy in Latin America is not a virgin field of inquiry. As early as 1963 Hirschman published his much quoted volume, *Journeys Toward Progress,* which focused on major policy areas. Two recent conferences, one organized by Guillermo O'Donnell and Oscar Oszlak in Buenos Aires on the subject of "Public Policy and its Impacts in Latin America," and another run by James Malloy and Carmelo Mesa-Lago in Mexico on "Social Security and Inequality in Latin America," attest to the continued interest. Perhaps the area in which the greatest volume of research has been conducted is public spending. Lending itself to easy quantification and relatively abundant data bases (characteristics whose value is not to be underestimated in the "data-poor" context of Latin America), research on public spending has focused on overall government expenditures (Ames and Goff, 1973) and on sectoral analysis (Wilkie, 1970; Coleman and Wanat, 1973; Daly Hayes, 1973; Baloyra, 1974). While most of these studies are longitudinal in design, they are limited by the unavailability of public expenditure data from the distant past. Thus, there is almost no work on public expenditures made before the present century. Research on the general field of public policy in long-term historical perspective is almost nonexistent.

While it is to be understood that an investigation of all areas of public policy in Latin American countries from colonial days to the present is beyond the ken of any one researcher, individual investigators can study particular areas. What will be attempted here is an examination of a single, although very important, sector in one country. I plan to outline the major policies formulated and implemented in the agrarian sector in Costa Rica from the colonial days up to the present. Because the time period under analysis is such a long one, the treatment will have to be limited to the major policies which helped determine the contours of Costa Rica's agrarian development.

While the nature of the subject requires a chronological approach, my central purpose is not to record the historical facts. Rather, in tracing the development of agrarian policies in Costa Rica, I hope to illustrate how Costa Rica's dependency on outside powers has had a significant impact on agrarian policy formulation and how those policies came, in turn, to shape the nature of Costa Rican social and economic life.

Agrarian Policy Under Spanish Control

Costa Rica was perhaps the poorest colony in the New World. The primary reason for its poverty was the near absence of gold and silver, metals which had served as a primary source of wealth in many other Spanish possessions. In the absence of these precious metals the colonists turned their attention to the production of cash crops for export in order to buoy up the depressed economy of the colony. However, this effort was not rewarded with success for a number of reasons.

By far the most significant reason for the failure of agricultural development in colonial Costa Rica was the severe shortage of Indian labor. While there is some debate as to the actual number of Indians in Costa Rica at the time of the conquest (Seligson, 1974: 309), it has been established that within several decades of the conquest epidemics had decimated their ranks (Macleod, 1973: 205-206). The acute shortage of Indians made it impossible for the colonists to establish the labor-intensive hacienda found elsewhere in the New World. From the perspective of the nineteenth and twentieth centuries, the failure to establish the hacienda can be viewed only as a blessing: Costa Rica did not have to cope with this institution, whose inefficient methods of production and labor repressive practices continue to be a major inhibitor of growth in the

TABLE 1
Production of Cacao in Colonial Costa Rica
(1678-1805)

Year	Number of Haciendas	New Trees	Old Trees	Total
1678	-	98,980	30,000	128,980
1682	55	59,600	18,900	78,500
1719	-	-	80,000	80,000
1737	89	99,290	137,000	237,138
1741	144	-	-	-
1751	142	-	-	-
1775	136	-	-	179,400
1778	-	26,556	163,349	189,905
1805	-	-	111,336	111,336

SOURCE: Vega Carballo (1972: 11).

agrarian sector of many Latin American countries. Nevertheless, from the perspective of the colonial era, the absence of the hacienda meant the absence of wealth.

With no gold and silver and an insufficent labor supply, ambitious Costa Ricans had no choice but to dedicate their attention to subsistence farming while they searched for an export crop which would require little attention and, therefore, little labor.

Cacao was hit upon as the ideal crop, and planting was begun in earnest in the Atlantic region in 1650 (Facio Brenes, 1972: 28). The area was chosen because, in addition to having the warm, humid climate necessary for growing cacao, it was close enough to the Atlantic ocean to make export an easy affair

(Lindo, 1970). In addition, the presence of the Urinama Indians guaranteed a minimal labor force (MacLeod, 1973: 333). The cultivation of cacao reached its peak in the eighteenth century.

The initial success of the crop was a direct result of what were perhaps the first agrarian policies established in the colony. In an effort to stimulate the production of cacao, the colonial government took several important steps. First, it abolished taxes on cacao production; second, it granted land to all those who initiated a plantation; and, third, it offered an additional prize of 30 *manzanas* of land (1 mz = .89 hectare) for each manzana of cacao trees brought into production (Lindo Bennet, 1970: 13). In addition, the government built a port in Matina and a mule path linking the capital of Cartago with the coast.

The cacao policies, while successful in stimulating the production of the bean, had an important unintended consequence: they created the colony's first major economic divisions. Up until the cacao boom nearly all Costa Ricans were poor. It is reported that even the governor of the colony was forced to till his own fields lest his family starve. The growth of the cacao industry was to change this situation substantially for the small number of families who ventured into this business. However, even at its height, cacao was being produced on no more than 139 plantations, and in many cases several plantations were owned by a single person (Stone, 1975: 61). Thus, a wealthy Greek immigrant to Costa Rica, Antonio de Acosta de Arévalo, owned 8,176 cacao trees, or an estimated 6 percent of the total number of trees (MacLeod, 1973: 337-339). The wealth that was earned through cacao production, therefore, was concentrated in a very few hands. We can estimate that fewer than 100 individuals of the 6,000 Spanish colonists living in Costa Rica in the eighteenth century profited from cacao production. Many of these people later became the central figures in the coffee boom of the nineteenth century and thereby retained their superior economic position. Costa Rica's first agrarian policies thus influenced the future economic and political development of the country.

Despite the efforts of the colonists to make cacao a success, the crop was completely abandoned in the early part of the nineteenth century, and Spanish colonial policy was the cause of the failure. The imposition of stiff taxes kept profit margins at a relatively low level. In addition to the taxes imposed directly by Spain, there were taxes levied by the local Audiencia of Guatemala, to which Costa Rica belonged. However, some profits were still being made due to the fact that a significant portion of the crop was smuggled out of the country and therefore evaded the taxes entirely. A more significant problem for the growers was that, since the plantations were located close to the sea, they were subject to constant pirate and Indian invasions. The fierce Zambos-Mosquitos Indians and the infamous pirate Henry Morgan invaded the area continually, killing the plantations' workers and making off with the crops. The responsibility for the defense of the plantation was in the hands of the Audiencia of Guatemala. Unfortunately, the audiencia was too far away and too little interested in distant Costa Rica's problems to make any serious effort to protect the plantations. For years Costa Rica had sought to leave the Audiencia of Guatemala in order to become part of the nearby Audiencia of Panama, from which the cacao producers hoped to obtain greater protection for their crops. Not only did the Crown not accede to this demand, but, as late as 1811, on the eve of the destruction of Spanish hegemony in the New World, the Audiencia of Guatemala prohibited Costa Rica from trading with Panama (Facio Brenes, 1972: 28-29). Because of high taxation and frequent losses of the crop to marauders, the Costa Rican cacao producers were unable to compete with the low prices of beans which were beginning to be produced in large quantities in Rivas, Nicaragua; consequently, the plantations were closed down (Vega Carballo, 1972: 15).

The net effect of Spanish colonial policy on Costa Rica was the prevention of the establishment of profitable and durable agrarian enterprises.[2] Thus, as long as the control of Costa Rica's public policy remained totally in foreign hands, there was little that the colony could do to develop a successful agrarian policy. With independence, however, Costa Rica was placed in control of its own agrarian policy.

The Early Independence Period: An "Independent" Agrarian Policy Stimulates Coffee Production

Costa Rica did not fight for its independence from Spain; in fact, the announcement in 1821 came as a surprise to most settlers of the colony (Monge Alfaro, 1966: 146-153). Even before official independence, however, Spain's grip on Central America had been loosening and the outlines of an independent agrarian policy were being formulated in Costa Rica. The policy was independent in the sense that it was made by Costa Ricans without overt interference from outside forces. The policy was not, however, free from the influence of those forces. In particular, the demands of the international capitalist system (what Wallerstein, 1974, has termed the "world-economy") were to be a heavy influence on the decision-making process.

The colonial era had kept Costa Rica in a state of dire poverty. The little country had neither the precious metals nor the native labor of the wealthier colonies of South America (Tinoco, 1945), and the restrictive policies of the mother country had prevented the development of a profitable export sector. As a consequence, there was a pent-up demand for imported goods, such as iron implements of all sorts, medicines, household goods, and so on. Costa Ricans needed to develop some means of generating a cash surplus so that they could import these items. Accomplishing this goal meant linking the economy to the international capitalist system through the export of some commodity.

Coffee, which has been introduced in Costa Rica in 1808, was not initially perceived as a crop with substantial profit potential. As of 1820 very few people cultivated the bean, but in 1821, a few months prior to independence, the local government took its first steps to promote coffee growing. In that year the Ayuntamiento de San José passed a decree that provided free state land to any individual who agreed to plant coffee on it. This resolution was followed by a similar one from the Ayuntamiento de Cartago a few months later. Real progress in the growth of coffee began in 1825 when Costa Rica's first chief-of-state, Juan Mora Fernández, decreed what was the first agrarian policy of the new republic: coffee was exempted from the payment of the *diezmos* tax. This exemption was followed in 1831 by a decree stating that anyone who cultivated coffee on state lands would automatically become the owner of those lands if he worked them for five years.

In the years that followed several more decrees were issued, each one granting new lands and encouraging the planting of coffee. As a result, coffee production soared. Exports, which stood at a mere 23,000 kilograms in 1832, increased 50 times this amount a decade later and nearly 400 times by the third quarter of the nineteenth century (see Table 2). As a consequence of the coffee boom, unheard of wealth began to pour into the little country.

In 1841 road construction began to be financed by a small tax levied on coffee exports. Roads were built from the *meseta* to the Pacific port of Puntarenas; to Sarapiquí to the north, and to Matina and Moin to the east. The ports of Puntarenas, Caldera, and Matina were also improved (Araya Pochet, 1971: 80-81; González Flores, 1933: 19). The prosperity produced by coffee was sufficient, even in those early years, to allow funds to be directed toward the creation of other, much needed infrastructure projects: the postal service was established, the

TABLE 2
Coffee Exports, 1832-1939
(in thousands of kilograms)

Year	Exports	Year	Exports	Year	Exports
1832	23	1874	10,780	1907	17,326
1833	45	1875	4,836	1908	8,978
1843	1,163	1876	11,176	1909	12,030
1844	2,300	1877	8,356	1910	14,397
1845	3,073	1878	11,587	1911	12,641
1846	3,821	1879	10,702	1912	12,238
1847	5,060	1880	7,934	1913	13,019
1848	6,900	1881	11,240	1914	17,717
1849	6,900	1882	7,408	1915	12,206
1850	6,440	1883	9,203	1916	16,844
1851	no data	1884	16,630	1917	12,267
1852	3,118	1885	9,150	1918	11,452
1853	3,680	1886	9,037	1919	13,963
1854	no data	1887	13,082	1920	13,998
1855	3,253	1888	10,318	1921	13,336
1856	3,818	1889	12,948	1922	18,617
1857	4,140	1890	15,395	1923	11,088
1858	2,776	1891	14,142	1924	18,211
1859	4,995	1892	10,798	1925	15,353
1860	4,138	1893	11,442	1926	18,249
1861	5,195	1894	10,777	1927	16,154
1862	4,964	1895	11,090	1928	18,842
1863	3,977	1896	11,716	1929	19,677
1864	5,179	1897	13,871	1930	25,537
1865	6,193	1898	19,486	1931	23,015
1866	8,344	1899	15,367	1932	18,499
1867	9,200	1900	16,101	1933	27,778
1868	9,384	1901	16,574	1934	19,063
1869	9,384	1902	13,749	1935	24,239
1870	11,558	1903	17,333	1936	21,326
1871	8,334	1904	12,578	1937	26,520
1872	11,592	1905	18,048	1938	24,981
1873	9,200	1906	13,774	1939	20,245

SOURCES: Dirección General de Estadística y Censos (1941: 14), Salas Marrero and Barahona Israel (1973: 533), Monge Alfaro (1966: 203), Vega Carballo (1972: 118).

city of Cartago (previously damaged by an earthquake) was rebuilt, the streets of San José and Cartago were paved, and in 1844 the University of Santo Tomás was opened (González Flores, 1933).

The cacao bean, which had been used as the medium of exchange in colonial days and which was, therefore, a symbol of the uncapitalized nature of the Costa Rican economy, began to disappear. In 1822 the first national currency, called "americana insurgente," made its appearance, and in 1823 the first silver and gold coins were ordered minted. The mint (la Casa de Moneda) was officially established in 1828 (Núñez, 1971: 123). With its newly found wealth, the republic was able to pay its debt to the ephemeral Central American Federation established in Guatemala in 1824 (Karnes, 1961). By 1826 the public treasury already had an income of 16,000 pesos; the total rose to 24,000 pesos in 1826, and to some 120,000 pesos in 1849. The major source of this steadily increasing wealth was the establishment of the first customs duty in 1839–a tax on the mountains of imported goods which filled the holds of the returning coffee ships (Araya Pochet, 1971: 81).

Other salubrious consequences of the "coffee miracle" were forthcoming. The ships which returned from the continent brought with them tools for agriculture and construction. These items made possible more efficient work in the fields and the construction of more healthful and comfortable homes. Damp adobe walls began to give way to brick and wood, and windows were installed to bring light and air into the once dark dwellings. Iron stoves replaced the smokey open-hearth arrangement of the past, and porcelain dinnerware replaced the wooden bowls of poverty. The steel hoe, plow, shovel, saw, machete, and ax brought about a revolution of efficiency, while the corn mill and rice winnower freed the housewife of hours of drudgery (González Flores, 1933: 20-21). The ships also brought new materials for more comfortable clothing, books to stimulate the mind, and medicines to cure the body. And with the cargo came immigrants (not a wave, but a ripple), seeking to take part in the newly found wealth. Doctors, lawyers, engineers, and educators–they all came in those golden days of the coffee boom (González Flores, 1933: 20-24).

It is quite clear that Costa Rica's initial contact with international capitalism was a happy one: much progress was made and standards of living were improved. One is forced to conclude that, at least in the Costa Rican case, the link with the outside market economy yielded definite benefits; those who argue that such links in and of themselves are always pernicious would not find their position substantiated by this data. However, such links did turn out to have their negative aspects, and, as time went on, these aspects became more and more explicit. They included the following.

FOREIGN CONTROL OF COFFEE FINANCING

In sharp contrast to other Latin American countries, where the major source of foreign exchange earnings traditionally has been in the hands of foreigners (e.g., copper in Chile, tin in Bolivia), Costa Rica has always kept its coffee production under firm domestic control. The elite of the colonial period, having accumulated some small amounts of capital through the profits of cacao production, became heavily committed to coffee. Extensive genealogical research has demonstrated the close links between the colonial elite and the major coffee growers of the nineteenth century. Indeed, many of the same families who originally settled Costa Rica in the sixteenth century and who later were dominant forces in cacao, were to become the largest growers and exporters of coffee (Stone, 1975).

While the production of coffee was locally controlled, the financing was not. The first exports of Costa Rican coffee, which went directly to London (the earlier exports had been first routed to Chile and exported as Chilean coffee), were carried on British ships and were sold to London import houses. These houses quickly recognized the high quality of the Costa Rican product and did not hesitate to finance the growing of future crops. Thus developed the tradition of London's being the exclusive financier of Costa Rican coffee.

Since the collateral for these loans was the coffee itself, there was very little risk involved in the transaction, and the interest on these short-term loans proved to be quite profitable for the London firms. Thus, on top of the already substantial profit margins they were earning, the importers made an additional sum by extending low risk loans to finance the crops. For Costa Rica this meant an additional loss of capital that would have otherwise been available for domestic development. The mentality of dependency was so deeply entrenched in Costa Rican financial circles, however, that the idea of domestic financing seemed ludicrous.[3]

DIMINISHING PRODUCTION OF FOOD CROPS

As coffee increased in importance, more and more land was turned over to its production. As a consequence, the food crops once grown on these lands were reduced and in some cases eliminated. Thus, while Costa Rica had been self-sufficient in the production of wheat during the colonial period, by 1845 most of the flour consumed by the country was being imported from Chile and late on from California (Meléndez, 1966: 37). Today no wheat at all is produced in Costa Rica, and a loaf of bread costs about 20 percent of an agricultural laborer's daily minimum wage. In a similar fashion other basic grains have been overtaken by coffee production, and continual shortages exist.

THE CONCENTRATION OF LAND

In colonial days land had been of little value and had not really been considered a commodity to be bought and sold. With the introduction of coffee, however, land became quite scarce, since coffee would grow well only in the cool highlands of the central valley, an area which comprises approximately 6 percent of the entire territory of the country. Land prices increased dramatically in the valley, and, as a result of the high prices, there was a strong incentive for the poor peasant to sell his land to the expanding coffee plantations. In fact, many peasants did sell (de Andrade, 1966), and at the same time laws were being passed granting larger and larger tracts to the coffee growers. While there are no records of the overall distribution of land in Costa Rica prior to the introduction of coffee, all indications are that the great majority of peasants had a plot of land to farm (Stone, 1975: 93). By 1864, however, the census (Costa Rica, 1868) reported that 49 percent of those employed in agriculture were employed as wage laborers, and by 1967 it was estimated (Dirección General de Estadística y Censos, 1968: 9) that this figure had risen to 73 percent. Thus, nearly three-fourths of Costa Rica's peasant population now consists of landless workers. In this respect Costa Rica is very similar to most other Latin American nations where landless laborers predominate (Feder, 1971: 84).

But what of the one quarter of the population that does own land? How is the land distributed? According to calculations based on the latest census (Dirección General de Estadística y Censos, 1974) Costa Rica ranks as the sixth most unequal of the 54 nations on which there are data (Hudson, 1973: 267). Costa Rica's Gini index of inequality in 1973 was 86.4 (100 is the theoretical maximum of this index). This figure ties with Colombia and Ecuador and is exceeded in Latin America only by Argentina and pre-1968 Peru. It is clear that the great majority of Costa Rican peasants do not own land, and that of those who do most own very little.

OUT-MIGRATION

As has been discussed, the coffee boom caused many peasants to sell their land in the central valley; the government, therefore, embarked upon a new agrarian policy designed to open up new lands to these peasants. Just as the homestead acts in the United States provided new lands for those without land in the East, so did the Leyes de Terrenos Baldíos and the Leyes de Cabezas de Familia serve Costa Rican peasants. The first of these laws was passed in 1840, when coffee was already beginning to take a solid grip on the economy. Several other laws followed between 1843 and 1859. As a result of these homestead acts, Costa Ricans began to move in substantial numbers to areas outside of the valley. Thus, while in colonial days nearly the entire population lived in the valley, by 1864 a little over 15 percent of the population lived outside of it. By 1892 this figure had risen to 20 percent, by 1927 to 25 percent, by 1936 to over 31 percent; today it stands at about half of the total population (Sandner, 1962).

As a result of this outward migration, Costa Rica succeeded in reaching its "manifest destiny." While in some ways the attainment of this destiny can be viewed as a positive consequence of the coffee boom, in other ways it had a more negative effect. For example, since the settlement was accomplished under the homestead acts, one would expect a relatively equal distribution of land to have resulted; however, an examination of the average Gini indices of land concentration of *cantones* (counties) in the valley and those outside of it reveals that the land in the newly settled areas was as unequally distributed as in the older areas. What can account for the unequal distribution of the nonvalley land? The answer lies in the public policies of the nineteenth and twentieth centuries.

The homestead acts were not the only land giveaways that the government decreed. (In fact, I suspect that the total amount of land given away under these programs was probably a great deal less than that which was given away under other laws, but as of 1975 there are no data available to prove this point.) These other programs were of two types. The first was a series of laws passed to pay off the country's debts to its domestic creditors. Thus, after the war against the North American adventurer William Walker in 1856-1857, the government of José María Montealegre passed a decree in 1860 amortizing its debt to the large coffee growers who had lent it money for the war effort. The decree provided that state land be given in exchange for the debt. Since the bulk of this land was outside of the valley and, therefore, not generally suitable for coffee growing, its value per hectare was quite low. Even those with small debts found themselves in possession of huge tracts of land. A similar plan was implemented in 1861 when the cost of a road-building project from the highlands to the Atlantic port of Limón was met by land grants to bond holders (Salazar Navarrete, 1962: 76-77).

The second type of land giveaway resulted from the squatter law (Ley de Ocupantes en Precario) which was passed in 1942. This law as designed to provide relief to land holders in the valley whose land had been squatted on. Under this law the government would purchase land squatted on and, in return, give the injured party land of equal value. Due to the high value of valley land and the low value of the land in other parts of the country, many large land owners used this law to exchange small pieces of territory in the valley for huge estates in the outlying areas. It has been reported that the *hacendados* of the valley even hired squatters to invade their property so that they could file a claim for the exchange lands (Clark, 1971: 32). As a result of this law, an enormous amount of land was given away to the already wealthy coffee growers. Many of the large estates that sprang up in the post-World War II era were built from land obtained through this law.

UNCONTROLLED ECONOMIC FLUCTUATION

Before the days of coffee, Costa Rica had only tenuous ties with the international economy and, consequently, its ups and downs had little impact on the country. However, once Costa Rica became linked—by foreign coffee exports—to the world economic system, her isolation was destroyed and downturns in the world economy began to affect Costa Rica severely. It has been said about Brazil that when New York sneezes, Brazil catches a cold. The same can be said about Costa Rica. Whenever the world economic situation became unstable—as it did in the European upheavals of 1848 and in the depressions of 1882, 1900, and 1929—Costa Rica's coffee-based economy suffered. For example, whereas in 1928-1929 Costa Rican coffee exports were valued at $9.8 million, in 1930-1931 they had dropped over 50 percent to $4.3 million (Dirección General de Estadística, 1941). Thus, while the coffee stimulating laws brought wealth to the country, they also subjected it to the vacillations of the world economy. In effect then, the independence which Costa Rica had won from Spain proved ephemeral, because it was soon replaced by an even stronger dependence on the world coffee market.

Public Policy and the Railroad

Since coffee is an export crop, it would have been ideal if it could have been grown along the Atlantic coast, thereby making the transportation costs to the port and shipping expenses to the European market as low as possible. As mentioned above, however, coffee is a highland crop and simply will not grow in the steaming coastal lowlands that were once used for cacao production. As the volume of coffee increased, the problem of shipping tons of beans from the highlands down to the coast became more and more acute. Moreover, since the route to the Atlantic coast was so hazardous, all the coffee was carted to the more distant Pacific coast and then shipped to Europe via a long trip around Cape Horn. It is reported that the sea voyage between the port of Puntarenas to England took between 130 and 140 days, and cost some five pounds sterling per *quintal.* While the trip from the Pacific port of Limón cut that down by almost three months and brought the price down to two pounds (Gonzáles Flores, 1933: 22-23; Nunley, 1960: 25), what was clearly needed was a safe route to the Atlantic; since this was the heyday of the iron horse, a railroad was the method of transportation chosen.

Constructing a rail system from the *meseta* to the Atlantic coast was no easy task, however. The jungle which separated the areas is one of the densest in the world, due to rainfall that exceeds 15 feet a year. In addition, since malaria, yellow fever, and dysentery were commonplace, it was an extremely unattractive area for laborers accustomed to the salubrious climate of the meseta. As a consequence, Costa Rica at first abandoned the idea of an Atlantic railroad and attempted to construct one to the Pacific coast, despite the higher maritime transportation costs. In 1854, Juan Rafael Mora Porras, president of Costa Rica at the time, decreed that Joaquín Jiménez had the exclusive right to use "carros de cuatro ruedas" on a route to the Pacific. That same year the Congress authorized the construction of a wooden or iron railroad to the port, and in 1857 the first nine miles were finished between Puntarenas and Barranca. This small stretch of track was the first railroad in Central America and also earned the distinction of being the first failure. It was not designed for the iron horse but for animal power; it was thus baptized the "Burrocar." But the poor burro was able to manage no more than two miles an hour with the car *empty.* Attention was focused once again on the Atlantic port (Garrido Guerrero, 1968: 4-5).

In 1871, the first railroad construction loan from the London firm of Bischoffshein and Goldschmidt was arranged. A complete lack of experience in matters of international finance on Costa Rica's part meant that this loan, and several that followed, were actually downright swindles. The first loan, for example, was for one million pounds sterling, but only 56 percent of the total actually reached Costa Rica. Bischoffshein and Goldschmidt retained 170,000 pounds as their commission for floating the bonds, even though there was no risk involved for them in the proposition (González Víquez, 1914; Soley Güell, 1946: 56). Since the net amount obtained by the loan was far too little to finance the construction of the massive project, a new loan for 2.4 million pounds was made through the Knowles-Foster-Erlanger Group of London, but this loan turned out to be even more fraudulent than the previous one, since only 900,000 pounds of the total actually ended up in Costa Rican hands. This time, however, the borrowers were not going to be pushed around (or so they thought), and they hired a law firm to sue the lenders. The case lasted six full years and, in the end, after paying 400,000 pounds in lawyers' fees, Costa Rica lost. Thus, the total gain on this 2.4 million pound loan was a trifling 500,000 pounds, or some $4.8 million. During the period 1870 to 1882 Costa Rica added $15 million to the project from her own budget. This sum was an enormous amount for the little country: it represented nearly half of her entire state income for this period (Soley Güell, 1946: 57). But railroad fever was high and she was ready to pay almost any price, a fact the "shylocks" in London seemed to be quite aware of.

With the loans secured, Costa Rica turned her attention to the question of the construction itself. The first rails were laid in 1872, but enormous difficulties in the construction process caused extended delays. In 1884 the government signed the now famous Soto-Keith contract. Under the terms of this agreement, Minor C. Keith, the railroad builder, refinanced the English debt and promised to finish the remaining 52 miles of the railroad's 142 miles within three years. In return, Keith was granted a 99-year lease on the railroad; 800,000 acres of state lands in any part of the country; and exemptions from import duty on all construction materials used to build and maintain the railroad bed, cars, and engines (Archivo Nacional, 1884). This contract later proved to be the mainstay of the banana monopoly. In 1886 Keith organized the Costa Rica Railway Co., Ltd., which took charge of completing the line and administering its operation (Zúñiga Huete, 1929: 77). The government of Costa Rica at first retained control of one-third of the shares of this company, but in 1889, when the government was unable to repay another English loan, it turned over its shares of the railway in return for Keith's personal repayment of the loan.

What consequences did the public policy decision to provide a rapid and inexpensive transportation system for coffee exports have on Costa Rica? First of all, it was anticipated that the railroad would yield substantial savings on the transportation costs of coffee. These savings, however, never materialized, because the government had lost the control of the railroad to the builders, and the rates that were being charged were a good deal higher than had been expected. Furthermore, whatever savings were achieved were absorbed by taxes imposed on coffee in order to pay off the construction costs. An ironic note was added to the entire sad story of the construction of the railroad with the opening of the Panama Canal in 1914; the long trip around the tip of South America was no longer necessary for coffee shipped from the Pacific Coast. Thus, the railroad was unnecessary once the canal was in operation.

The second consequence of the policy was the incursion of a high foreign debt. Until the beginning of the construction Costa Rica had a very favorable fiscal situation and no outstanding loans. Because of the construction of the railroad, however, the foreign debt had risen to nearly 3.5 million pounds by 1881 (Macune, 1963: 112).

A third and most important consequence of the policy was the development of the banana industry. In order to finance the construction of the railroad, its builders began to plant bananas along side of the already completed tracks. As a result, a business enterprise was formed in 1885 which eventually came to be known as the United Fruit Company. More will be said about this company in the next section of this article.

A fourth consequence of the railroad construction was the immigration of thousands of blacks to do the building. The government was forced to permit the immigration of shipload after shipload of Jamaicans in order to provide sufficient manpower to build the railroad. Today a small black minority remains in Costa Rica as a result of the migration of the last century.

The migration of blacks to Costa Rica would not in and of itself be significant if it were not tied closely to the rise of the labor union movement, the fifth consequence of the railroad. The plantations proved to be fertile territory not only for bananas but for labor union agitation as well. In the early 1930s, when Costa Rica was suffering under the dual pressure of the world depression and a ruinous disease in the banana plantations, the first massive strikes ever to hit the country broke out in the banana zones (Seligson, 1974: 138-163). Labor unions were given their real impetus from this strike and have gained in strength from the ones that have periodically followed it.

The Twentieth Century and the Beginning of Government Control

Public policy in the agrarian sector played an almost exclusively stimulating role in the first century of Costa Rican independence. It has been shown how government policy stimulated the production of coffee and, inadvertently, the production of bananas. In the twentieth century the government was to begin a slow but constant shift away from stimulation and toward regulation.

What were the reasons for this shift? The answer lies in the transformation of the society brought on by the coffee boom. Before coffee, Costa Rica was almost devoid of urban centers; most of the population was engaged in subsistence farming. But with the economic advances brought on by coffee, the population began to move into the cities and take up jobs in the service sector. Thus, there began to form a nascent middle class with its demands for paved streets and street lighting, hospitals, schools, sanitation, and—most important—jobs. Money had to be found to satisfy those demands, and, thus, attention was turned to coffee as the nation's primary source of income.

The expenditures of the central government were kept at a low level through most of the nineteenth century and were increased only to pay for the railroad. The only taxes placed on coffee during this period were nominal, amounting to only 25 *centimos* per quintal. The first radical departure from this "hands-off" policy occurred in 1893 when, due to a severe balance of payments crisis created by declining world coffee prices, the legislative assembly voted a tax of 6 shillings per quintal. The reasoning that was used to implement this tax is significant; article 4 of the law states that:

> Notwithstanding the desires of the Government to protect the agriculture of the country in order that it may reach its greatest development, in the present circumstances, although accidentally, it is necessary to ask of it the resources that the Nation needs. [Oficina del Café, 1954: 20]

Thus, for the first time, profits in the coffee industry were recognized as an acceptable target of state taxation to help bail out the nation in times of need. Of course, the coffee barons did not take kindly to such laws and did all they could in the ensuing decades to stop, or at least slow, the growth of taxes. But the economic realities of the day slowly overrode their opposition. Thus, due to international marketing problems caused by World War I, a new tax of $2.30 was imposed for each quintal of coffee exported, and in 1937 an 8 percent *ad valorum* tax took effect. And in 1939 the first land tax in Costa Rican history was enacted. Although the rate was low, it was a progressive tax, so that the larger and more valuable estates had to pay more. Since the largest land owners in the country were those in the coffee business, this tax directly affected them.

An even more direct intervention in the coffee industry occurred some six years earlier. At this time there was increasing suspicion on the part of the producers and government alike that the owners of the coffee processing plants (called *beneficios*) and export houses were failing to pay a fair price to the producers and the appropriate amount of taxes to the government; these suspicions resulted in the creation of a pricing board (Junta de Liquidacions de Café) which was in charge of setting the price that each *beneficio* was to pay to the producer. The board was to base its calculations on the quality of the coffee, with a maximum profit for the beneficio of 12 percent (Barrenechea Consuegra, 1956: 6). In that same year, 1933, the Instituto Nacional de Defensa del Café was established by the government as a quasi-public organization designed to promote the production and sale of Costa Rican coffee. The institute was abolished after the Revolution of 1948 and was replaced by the Oficina del Café, which is currently charged with the regulation of the coffee industry in all its aspects.

In the twentieth century, therefore, public policy toward coffee took a major shift from one of stimulation to regulation. What happened to the banana industry in this period? Did it, too, come under state control? The answer is an unequivocal no, which does not mean that efforts in that direction were not made, for indeed they were, but they were unsuccessful.

The fundamental reason why the banana industry did not fall under state control is that it operated as an enclave economy–i.e., the banana industry functioned as an independent economic island within the Costa Rican state. The taxes levied on it amounted to only a fraction of 1 percent of the retail price, compared to the 8 percent tax the coffee industry was paying (Seligson, 1974: 133). Furthermore, the United Fruit Company achieved enormous economies of operation by retaining the import tax exemption that had been granted to the original railroad building company from which it had grown.

As mentioned above, attempts were made to regulate the company. In 1930 a law was passed setting up a regulatory board to arbitrate conflicts between the local Costa Rican banana growers and the company; there is no record of this board's ever having been utilized, however. After the Revolution of 1948 a 15 percent tax on net profits was imposed on the company; this tax was later raised to 30 percent in 1954. To this day, however, the company has consistently reported losses on its Costa Rican operations and has not, it is alleged, paid any income taxes (Salas Marrero and Barahoma Israel, 1973: 564).

The banana industry, unlike the coffee industry, escaped attempts to regulate its affairs. Only in the 1960s, with the establishment of new companies in the area once farmed by the United Fruit Company but abandoned in the 1930s for better land along the Pacific coast, did the government attempt to take a firm hand in the regulation of this industry. This was most clearly evidenced within the past year when Costa Rica joined with other banana-producing countries in trying to impose a one dollar per box export tax. The governments of the banana-producing nations attempted to emulate the OPEC oil cartel, but found that the fruit companies were stronger than the governments. In the case of Honduras, for example, it has recently been revealed that the United Fruit Company was successful in bribing high government officials to prevent implementation of the new tax. Investigations in Costa Rica, begun in 1975, are looking into allegations that similar events occurred there.

Agrarian Reform Policy in the 1960s and 1970s

The last aspect of agrarian public policy which will be examined in this paper is that of agrarian reform. As described earlier in the discussion of the coffee industry, one of the consequences of the agrarian public policy in Costa Rica was the extreme concentration of land in the hands of a few which began to develop after the introduction of coffee. By the middle of the twentieth century the problem had become acute. The large number of landless and land-poor peasants was growing with each passing decade and, with the success of Castro's revolution in Cuba, Costa Rican law makers increasingly feared rural unrest. Signs of such unrest were evident when increasing numbers of peasants, unable to find land or work, resorted to squatting. It is estimated that over 11 percent of all rural families were squatters in the 1960s, with some 252,000 hectares of land being illegally occupied (ITCO, 1967).

In 1961 the agrarian reform agency, called the Instituto de Tierras y Colonización (ITCO), was created by law. During its first decade of operation, ITCO's efforts were not particularly successful, primarily because it lacked sufficient financing with which to carry out its programs. Thus, plans for an ambitious reform program were laid to rest as a result of capital scarcity.

ITCO's first efforts at reform were directed toward colonization schemes. These projects were designed to situate a substantial number of peasants on virgin lands owned by the state. It was felt that, in this way, landless peasants could be given their long sought after plot of land, while, at the same time, the expropriation of privately held land could be avoided. Thus, ITCO's initial efforts were in no way seen as a full scale land reform whereby the unworked and/or abandoned acres of the latifundios would be turned over to land-hungary peasants. Rather, such a politically sensitive redistribution was purposely avoided. Few objected to the granting of a plot of public land to an unemployed, landless peasant who wanted to work it. The objection would have arisen, however, if the plot that was to be given was privately owned, for that would have signified a direct attack on private property.

A total of 11 colonization projects—covering 35,412 hectares and benefiting 1,222 peasants—were initiated (ITCO, 1972). For the most part the colonies were unsuccessful, and, as a result of financial difficulties, further expansion of the program was halted in 1968. No new colonies have been opened since. The primary reason for the failure of these colonies is that they were located in such inaccessible areas that it was impossible for the peasants to obtain the needed seed and fertilizer and, more important, to transport their goods to market once the crop was harvested. ITCO had promised each colonist that he would be given the infrastructure support he needed to make a go of it, but the limited financial resources of the institute meant that the peasant received little more than a few pieces of tin roofing materials and some survival rations donated by international agencies such as CARE. The promised roads, trucks, agricultural extension facilities, credit, and medical services were painfully slow in coming. During the course of field research in 1973 the author had the opportunity to talk to several peasants who had abandoned these reform colonies. When asked why he had left, one peasant put it this way: "After carrying my sick child for 26 kilometers over the muddy dirt trail to the colony only to have him die shortly before we reached the county health station, my wife and I decided we had had enough. I would rather be poor and have a family than work ten years in the colony only to see my children die."

After abandoning the colonization program, ITCO spent the period of 1967 to 1969 concentrating on the solution of squatting conflicts that had emerged on lands owned by the state. In total, ITCO legalized the occupation by 3,264 families of 23,826 hectares of state land in the period 1962 to 1972. It also found a solution to squatting incidents on private lands, which involved 1,381 families and 30,603 hectares. Hence, ITCO has solved fewer than one-fourth of all the squatting conflicts that the institute estimated existed in the 1960s (ITCO, 1967). While there are no reliable estimates of the intensity of the problems in the 1970s, several ITCO officials readily admit that there were considerably more unsolved squatting incidents in the 1970s than there were in the 1960s (personal interviews). Thus, ITCO appears to be losing ground as each year more cases of squatting arise than are solved.

The last few years, however, have seen a rather dramatic shift in ITCO's program. In 1974 Daniel Oduber Quiros was elected to the presidency of the republic and declared his full support for a more active agrarian reform. The institute was given new sources of financing, and the size of its staff was greatly enlarged. By late 1976 ITCO had increased its number of projects from 11 to 38. These new projects included some which were of the more traditional parcel programs and others which involved communal ownership and work (*empresa comunitaria*). In addition to these projects, a massive land titling program was embarked upon, and new financial resources were pumped into the ailing colonies. Finally, a more aggressive attitude was taken on the issue of expropriation of private land, so that even the United Fruit Company is no longer immune; one project alone involved the expropriation of 18,678 hectares of United Fruit land, an area about half the size of all the original 11 colonies combined. However, ITCO may still be losing ground to the ever more serious land distribution problem.

While it is impossible to predict the long-term consequences of the present inequality of land distribution, there is reason to suspect that in the next decade considerable rural unrest will be manifested. Thus far, however, there are no strong peasant leagues which could serve to galvanize this discontent other than the communist-led banana workers unions. These unions, however, are mainly oriented toward achieving wage increases and improved working conditions, and not toward expropriating the banana company's lands. Thus, unless a strong peasant organization is developed, one can expect that rural unrest will continue to be expressed in the form of sporadic outbreaks of violence and squatting.

Summary and Conclusions

This paper has demonstrated that agrarian policy in Costa Rica has not been static; by sketching with broad strokes it has been possible to distinguish four major phases. Each new phase has been accompanied by a change in dependency relations.

The first of these phases occurred in the colonial period, during which time control of Costa Rica's agrarian policy was exercised totally by an outside force, namely Spain. The attempts of the local population to achieve economic advances were frustrated by Spain, and thus growth was quite limited and dependency was almost complete. The coming of independence was to radically alter this situation, bringing on the second phase of agrarian policy. Thus, the new republic embarked upon a highly successful policy to stimulate coffee production. The iron grip of dependence had been broken and the effects were rapidly felt; these, at least initially, were beneficial to domestic development. A new dependence was established, however, as coffee became the most important element in the Costa Rican economy. This dependence on a single export crop brought with it several consequences: (1) foreign control of coffee financing, (2) diminishing production of food crops, (3) concentration of land, (4) out-migration from the central areas to remote portions of the country, and (5) uncontrolled economic fluctuations.

The third phase of agrarian policy was initiated as a result of the need to establish a cheaper transportation route for coffee exports. A railroad was built to the Atlantic coast so as to avoid the long sea voyage around the tip of South America. With the railroad came the United Fruit Company's banana empire. Unfortunately for Costa Rican coffee interests, the monopolistic control exercised by the company over the railroad resulted in such high rail freight rates that they nearly counterweighted the savings gained by shipping from the Atlantic rather than the Pacific port. The rates were high because the Costa Rican government had given up its part ownership and control of the company in an effort to help repay the large foreign debt it had incurred in order to finance the railroad construction. Thus, the coffee industry, whose ownership and operation was under virtually total local control, placed itself in a position of dependence upon the foreign-owned railroad.

The establishment of the banana export industry meant that the monoculture export economy, previously dependent on coffee for almost all foreign exchange earnings, was now dependent on two crops. However, since neither commodity is a necessity, any economic downturns in the world economy would cause a sharp reduction in coffee and banana prices. As a consequence, the Great Depression hurt Costa Rica as severely as it did most Latin American nations. Furthermore, domestic attempts to have the banana company help underwrite the rapidly growing expenditures of the modernizing Costa Rican state were unsuccessful. Instead, the domestically owned coffee industry had to bear the burden.

The fourth and final phase of agrarian policy appears in the twentieth century and is—at least in part—a result of the previous two stages. Landless, unemployed peasants have been forced to turn to squatting as an alternative to destitution. Some peasants, of course, have moved to urban areas, but the limited industrial base in this small, economically dependent country means that few jobs are available in the cities. Most peasants, therefore, have remained in the countryside, under increasingly difficult economic circumstances. As a result, efforts have been made to establish a viable agrarian reform, thereby initiating the fourth and current phase of agrarian policy.

This paper has attempted to demonstrate the ways in which agrarian policies have influenced the development of Costa Rica. It is quite clear that much of the present social and economic structure of the country can be traced back to these policies. This finding alone may give new impetus to those interested in public policy in Latin America, a field which has too long sat on the back burner of the researcher's stove.

It has also been shown that Costa Rica's dependency relations have shifted over the years and, as a consequence, agrarian policies have changed. During the colonial period agrarian policy was determined exclusively from without, and consequently, agrarian production was stifled. Independence from Spain brought about an independent agricultural policy which was directed toward the stimulation of coffee production and export. While successful, that policy brought with it a number of unintended consequences detrimental to Costa Rica's development. Finally, in recent times, agrarian policy has begun to be directed toward rectifying some of the problems created by these earlier policies. Success to date, however, has not been notable, and it is, therefore, difficult to be optimistic about the future.

NOTES

1. The literature is already too vast to begin to cite it all here, but a good overview of the substance and the polemic of the debate on dependency can be obtained from the volume edited by Chilcote and Edelstein (1974), the special issue of the *Journal of Interamerican Studies* of February 1973 (Vol. 15, No. 1), and the new journal, *Latin American Perspectives.* A recent addition to the literature which focuses exclusively on Central America is Menjivar's (1974) volume.

2. Tobacco was also a promising crop in colonial Costa Rica. While it would take us too far afield to deal with it in detail in this paper, it can be said in summary that colonial policy toward tobacco had the same effect it had had on cacao. A state monopoly was imposed on the crop, and the lion's share of the profits was drained off and sent to the continent. As a result, tobacco was abandoned as a source of wealth in the colony (Fallas, 1972: 37).

3. The events of World War II were to prove that local bankers were operating under a delusion. Domestic financing was possible, but it required an economic crisis to prove it. By 1940 the London credit market had completely dried up and Costa Rican exporters were informed that England could no longer underwrite the crop. In response to this crisis the Costa Rican national banking system took over the financing of the crop in its entirety in 1942-1943. The fact that such a drastic change took place so quickly demonstrates that Costa Rica's previous reliance on foreign financing for its coffee was unnecessary. Thus, the entire first century of coffee exporting in Costa Rica was financed by foreign capitalists.

REFERENCES

AMES, B. and E. GOFF (1973) "A longitudinal approach to Latin American public expenditures." Paper presented at the American Political Science Association meeting, New Orleans.

DE ANDRADE, M. (1966) "Decadencia do compesinato costarriquenho." Revista Geografica (Brazil) 66 (Junho): 135-151.

Archivo National (1884) Seccion Histórica-Congreso. Cod. No. 17182.

ARAYA POCHET, C. (1971) "El desarrollo económico y social de Costa Rica a partir de 1821," in Oscar Aguilar Bulgarelli (ed.) El desarrollo nacional en 150 años de vida independiente. Cuidad Universitaria "Rodrigo Facio": Universidad de Costa Rica.

BALOYRA, E. A. (1974) "Oil policies and budgets in Venezuela, 1938-1968." Latin Amer. Research Rev. 9 (Summer): 28-72.

BARRENECHEA CONSUEGRA, F. (1956) "Una organización para empresarios del café." San José: Escuela Superior de Administración Pública de América Central.

BOOTH, J. A. and M. A. SELIGSON (1975) "Dimensions of political participation among Latin American peasants: an analysis of two Costa Rican samples." Paper presented to the annual meeting of the Southwestern Political Science Association, San Antonio, March.

CHILCOTE, R. H. and J. C. EDELSTEIN [eds.] (1974) Latin America: The Struggle with Dependency and Beyond. New York: John Wiley.

CLARK, D. S. (1971) Renting, Sharecropping and Other Indirect Land Tenure Forms in Costa Rica: A Legal and Economic Analysis. Cuidad Universitaria "Rodrigo Facio": University of Costa Rica School of Law Agrarian Project.

COLEMAN, K. M. and J. WANAT (1973) "Models of political influence on federal budgetary allocations to Mexican states." Paper presented to the annual meeting of the American Political Science Association, New Orleans.

Costa Rica (1868) Censo General de La República de Costa Rica (27 de Noviembre de 1864). San José. Imprenta Nacional.

DALY HAYES, M. (1973) "Ecological constraints and policy outputs in Brazil: an examination of federal spending patterns." Paper presented to the annual meeting of the American Political Science Association, New Orleans.

Dirección General de Estadística y Censos (1974) Censos Nacionales, 1973: Agropecuario. San José: Imprenta Nacional.

——— (1968) Encuesta de Hogares por Muestreo; Julio de 1966 a Junio de 1967. San José: Imprenta Nacional.

——— (1941) Boletín de Exportaciones de Café, Cosecha 1939-1940. San José: Imprenta Nacional.

FACIO BRENES, R. (1972) Obras de Rodrigo Facio, Tomo I. San José: Editorial Costa Rica. (originally published 1942)

FALLAS, M. A. (1972) La factoría de tabacos de Costa Rica. San José: Editorial Costa Rica.

FEDER, E. (1971) "Latifundia and agricultural labour in Latin America," in Teodor Shanin (ed.) Peasants and Peasant Societies. Middlesex, England: Penguin.

GARRIDO GUERRERO, J. I. (1968) El cultivo del banano en Costa Rica. San José: Litografía Lehmann.

GONZALEZ FLORES, L. F. (1933) "El desenvolvimineto histórico del desarrollo del café en Costa Rica y su influencia en la cultura nacional," as reprinted in Hector Rojas Solano, El Café en Costa Rica. San José: Oficina del Café, 1972. (Originally appearing in Jorge Carranza Solís, Monografía del cafe. San Jose, Tomo I.)

GONZALEZ VIQUEZ, C. (1914) Capítulos de un libro sobre historia financiera de Costa Rica. San José: Editorial Costa Rica.

HIRSCHMAN, A. O. (1963) Journeys Toward Progress. New York: Twentieth Century Fund.

HUDSON, M. C. (1973) World Handbook of Political and Social Indicators. New Haven, CT: Yale Univ. Press.

Instituto de Tierras y Colonizacíon (1972) "Boletín informativo sobre actividad realizada por el ITCO." San José: Fotolitografía nacional.

——— (1967) "Programa para la solucíon del problema de ocupantes en precario." San José.

KARNES, T. L. (1961) The Failure of Union: Central America 1824-1960. Chapel Hill: Univ. of North Carolina Press.

LINDO BENNET, E. (1970) "La actividad cacoatera en Costa Rica." Tésis de Grado, Cuidad Universitaria "Rodrigo Facio."

MACLEOD, M. J. (1973) Spanish Central America: A Socioeconomic History, 1520-1720. Berkeley: Univ. of California Press.

MACUNE, C. W., Jr. (1963) "The building of the Atlantic Railroad of Costa Rica, 1821-1891." M.A. thesis, George Washington University.

MELENDEZ, C. (1966) "Aspectos sobre la historia del cultivo del trigo en Costa Rica durante la epoca colonia." Anales (de la Academia de Geografía e Historia de Costa Rica): 25-49.

MENJIVAR, R.[ed.] (1974) La inversíon entranjera en centro américa. Cuidad Universitaria "Rodrigo Facio." Costa Rica: Editorial Universitaria Centroamericana.

MONGE ALFARO, C. (1966) Historia de Costa Rica. San José: Imprenta Trejos Hermanos.

NUNEZ M., F. M (1971) "La Moneda y la banca en ciento cinquenta años de independencia (síntesis)," in Oscar Aguilar Bulgarelli (ed.) El desarrollo nacional en 150 años de vida independiente. Ciudad Universitaria "Rodrigo Facio": Universidad de Costa Rica.

NUNLEY, R. E. (1960) The Distribution of Population in Costa Rica. Washington, D.C.: National Academy of Sciences.

Oficina del Café (1954) Recopilación de leyes relativas al café. San José: Imprenta Las Américas.

SALAS MARRERO, O. A. and R. BARAHONA ISRAEL (1973) Derecho agrario. Serie Ciencia Juridícas y Sociales, No. 22. Cuidad Universitaria "Rodrigo Facio": Publicaciones de la Universidad de Costa Rica.

SALAZAR NAVARETTE, J. M. (1962) Tierras y Colonización en Costa Rica. Serie Tesis de Grado y Ensayos, No. 15. Cuidad Universitaria: Publicaciones de la Universidad de Costa Rica.

SANDNER, G. (1962) La colonización agrícola de Costa Rica. Tomo I. San José: Instituto Geográfico.

SELIGSON, M. A. (1974) The Peasant and Agrarian Capitalism in Costa Rica. Ph.D. dissertation, University of Pittsburgh.

SOLEY GUELL, T. (1946) Historia económica y hacendaria de Costa Rica. San José: Editorial Universitaria.

STONE, S. (1975) La dinastía de los conquistadores: la crisis del poder en la Costa Rica contemporánea. San José: EDUCA.

TINOCO, L. D. (1945) "Panorama económica de Costa Rica a principios del siglo XVI." Revista de la Universidad de Costa Rica 1 (Septiembre): 46-56.

VEGA CARBALLO, J. L. (1972) "Bases para un periodización de la Evolución agraria centroamericana." San José: Programa Centroamericano de Desarrollo de las Ciencias Sociales.

WALLERSTEIN, I. (1974) The Modern World-System: Capitalist Agriculture and The Origins of the European World-Economy in the Sixteenth Century. New York: Academic Press.

WILKIE, J. W. (1970) The Mexican Revolution: Federal Expenditures and Social Change in Mexico Since 1910. Berkeley: Univ. of California Press.

ZUNIGA HUETE, A. (1929) "La cuestión ferroviaria y bananera del atlántico y el derecho positivo costarricense." Cooperativa bananera costarricense, trabajos y opiniones sobre las cuestiones agraria y ferrocarrileras en relación con los concesionarios extranjeros en Costa Rica. San José: Imprenta "La Tribuna."

Mitchell A. Seligson is an Assistant Professor in the Department of Political Science at the University of Arizona. He has spent several years in Costa Rica and is currently completing work on Costa Rican peasants. His publications have appeared in the Latin American Research Review, Social Forces, Journal of Common Market Studies, Revista de Ciencias Sociales, *and other journals.*

JOHN HOYT WILLIAMS
Department of History
Indiana State University
Terre Haute, IN 47809

FOREIGN TECNICOS AND THE MODERNIZATION OF PARAGUAY, 1840-1870

How on earth came you to Paraguay?
I considered that you were still in France inventing projectiles for the annihilation of the Russians, our mutual enemies. [Anonymous to William K. Whytehead, December 12, 1853. Archivo Nacional, Asuncion, Seccion nueva encuadernacion 707.]

In the Beginning

During the dictatorship of Dr. Francia, 1814-1840, few foreigners were permitted to enter Paraguay, and a small number of chiefly Brazilian merchants, restricted to the entrepôts of Ytapúa and Pilar, alone had an impact upon the nation and its development. The few foreigners who blundered into Paraguay uninvited were forced to remain.

With the death of *El Supremo,* however, the situation changed, and Paraguay's new leaders began to look outward,

AUTHOR'S NOTE: The author wishes to thank the National Endowment for the Humanities and the Indiana State University Research Committee for their generous support of his foreign research.

Journal of Interamerican Studies and World Affairs, Vol. 19 No. 2, May 1977

seeking recognition and commerce. Both of these goals were frustrated between 1840 and 1852 by the hostile attitude of the Argentine ruler, Juan Manuel de Rosas, who viewed Paraguay as an errant province belonging to the orbit of Buenos Aires. The issue hinged upon Buenos Aires' control of access to the La Plata River system, and for much of this period Rosas restricted Paraguayan use of the lower rivers, especially the broad Paraná.

When in 1842 British merchant W.R.B. Hughes sought permission from Argentine authorities to travel the Paraná to Asunción, he was flatly refused. Sir Robert Peel, of the Foreign Office, wrote of the affair that "It does not appear that the right of Bs Ayres to close the Paraná can be disputed" (Peel note on Hughes visit, February, 1843. British Museum [BM], Add. Mss. 40,525, Vol. 345, p. 86).

The British merchant community, however, was impelled by a somewhat exaggerated dream of Paraguay as a great potential market, a vision largely based upon an unrealistic estimate of the nation's population. As one merchant had written from Corrientes in 1827, "I suppose, was the trade open, about one Million and a half dollars worth chiefly of British Manufactures might be annually introduced" into Paraguay (Mr. Hope to Mr. Parish, Corrientes, March 17, 1827. Public Record Office [PRO]/ Foreign Office [FO] 239). Also, as the unruffled Thomas Carlyle (1843: 44) cynically noted, with "all South America raging and ravening like one huge dog kennel gone rabid," Paraguay was both peaceful and prosperous. While overstated, Carlyle's judgment was essentially correct, and carried great weight in Britain.

If that nation showed interest for reasons of commerce and out of a growing disenchantment with Buenos Aires, the leaders of Paraguay sought foreign contact for trade, recognition, and, above all, development. To achieve national development based upon Francia's legacy of unity, prosperity, and discipline, it would be necessary to reach out to the modern world for skills and hardware. To do this, the rivers must be opened.

Carlos Antonio López in 1842, while consul, initiated a long correspondence with British diplomats in Buenos Aires and, encouraged by their response, formally requested "explicit recognition of our Independence," sending the diplomats what he considered to be "the relevant documents" (López to British Minister at Buenos Aires, August 30, 1843. Archivo Nacional, Asunción [ANA], Seccion historia [SH]255-1-4/7). The documents were forwarded to the government in London for consideration, and López, aware of the growing tension between Britain and Rosas, which would lead to the former's military intervention against the latter, offered later "to contribute to the pacification of the Rio de la Plata," even if this meant the sending of Paraguayan troops to help oust Rosas (same to same, June 1, 1845. ANA, SH, 155-1-13). The British response was heartening. Diplomat W. E. Ouseley wrote that "It was extremely gratifying to the undersigned to receive from the Supreme Government of Paraguay so convincing a proof of the enlightened and liberal spirit directing its Councils." Britain, wrote Ouseley, agreed "entirely" with the Paraguayan goal of "seeking the liberation of that State from the political and commercial dependence enforced by Buenos Ayres." He further requested that López send accredited agents to Montevideo for talks, and noted that he had recommended to his government the immediate recognition of Paraguayan independence (Ouseley to López, Buenos Aires, September 23, 1845. ANA, SH 155-1-14). Ouseley himself went out on a limb by personally recognizing Paraguay's independence in a later missive, and in a still later communication he waxed enthusiastic about future close ties between the two nations, for "her population and resources equal those of all the Provinces over which the Gov^{t} of Buenos Ayres has exercised jurisdiction" (same to same, March 7, 1846. ANA, SH 255-1-50/51).

While years would pass before actual British recognition and chaos downriver would impede intercourse with the outside world, the door was beginning to open, and foreigners were starting to slip in to begin their share in the new Paraguayan Revolution: the technological.

In fact, by 1845, there were so many foreigners in Paraguay that it was necessary for López to publish a decree defining their status. All *extrangeros,* decreed the Citizen, were welcome at Ytapúa and Pilar, where they could "make their mercantile transactions in entire Liberty," but they would need government license to move about the country. The foreigners would pay only standard import-export duties, and would be allowed to privately exercise any religious belief. While the government reserved the right to expel anyone at any time, merchants were not to suffer even in the event of a break in relations between Paraguay and their own governments. Also conceded were safeguards for the property of foreigners who died in Paraguay, and "the most complete liberty in their traffic and in the exercise of their industry and art" (López decree, 1845. ANA, SH 272-9-1/3).

Well before the López decree formalized their position, foreigners were assuming a very important role in Paraguayan commerce and business. As Swedish scientist and wanderer Eberhard Munck wrote in 1843, "Foreigners are still looked upon by the government by a certain suspicion," yet this suspicion in no way acted to check their growing numbers (Morner, 1955: 13). The same year, in Asunción, of the 61 *tiendas,* or retail stores, 12 were owned by foreigners. Other outsiders were managing taverns, silver shops, and earning their livings as merchants, scribes, carpenters, ironmongers, and ship captains (List of employments, Cathedral District, Asunción, November 17, 1843. ANA, SH 259-10-1/13). A glance at the extant documentation also reveals that some were becoming citizens of the host country. In 1845 alone, despite the *trâmites,* at least 15 immigrants, mostly Spaniards and Argentines, became Paraguayans. This was not an exceptional year (Naturalizations, 1845-1854. ANA, SH 272-2-1/101).

In addition to entering Paraguay in record numbers, it is also clear that foreigners dominated the nation's river commerce in the 1840s. The vast majority of ship owners and captains, many of whom were resident in Asunción, were Italians, and despite interdiction by Rosas, scores of Italian boats were involved in the fluvial trade, 1840-1852 (Perez Acosta, 1948: 367-393). A brief look at the passport lists indicates the presence in Pilar of French, Genoese, Bolivian, and provincial Argentine merchants in 1847, despite the dangerous international climate along the river that year (Police Chief G. Mareque, Pilar, to López,

October 27, 1847. ANA, SH 281-23-1/26). Another Pilar report reveals a sizable resident community of foreign merchants in that small, squalid port. In 1849 there were men from Spain, Britain, Germany, France, Chile, Entre Rios, Corrientes, Italy, and Portugal. A later report from the same year notes passports given at Pilar to Swiss, Uruguayans, Colombians, correntinos, and Spaniards (Felix Barboza, Pilar, to López, August 7, 1849, and same to same, November 17, 1849. ANA, SH 278-5-4/5, 6).

Also appearing in this period were the first foreign experts and technicians; the first wave in a tide which would dramatically change Paraguay. In 1845 appeared a strange soldier of fortune, Hungarian Lieutenant Colonel Francisco Wisner de Morgenstern, a military engineer whose services were eagerly purchased by López for the training of his army. Not only was Wisner used as drillmaster and advisor, but at least twice he was given active command of major Paraguayan expeditions which intervened in neighboring Corrientes (López Instructions to Wisner, 1846. ANA, SH 286-14-1/11; and Governor Joaquín Madariaga, Corrientes, to López, July 24, 1847. ANA, SH 262-1-22). Wisner would remain in Paraguay and retain various important posts for more than 30 years. His influence upon the transformation of the Paraguayan army was profound—he acted as military advisor to López, designed the huge fortress complex of Humaitá, and wrote the "official" biography of Dr. Francia.

Other *técnicos,* especially medical men, arrived in the 1840s, often on their own initiative, to offer their services to the government or to pursue their scientific studies. In both ways they were elements in the sweeping changes affecting Paraguay. One of the earliest technicians to accept a legal contract to serve the López government was German *médico* Johann Frederick Meister, who signed up in Rio de Janeiro at the urging of Paraguayan diplomat Juan Andrés Gelli. Meister's contract stipulated that he would be "Chief Surgeon of the Army" for a period of two years, receiving 70 silver pesos monthly plus travel expenses and special food "corresponding to your class and rank—fresh meat, rice, flour, etc." His family's passage and lodging would also be paid by the government, and Meister would be permitted such private practice as his free time would allow (Meister contract, Rio de Janeiro, September 15, 1848. ANA, SH 284-3-1/2).

Eberhard Munck, who had arrived in Paraguay in 1843, did not formally serve the government until the outbreak of the Paraguayan War in 1864, but he was given permission in 1845 to practice medicine outside the capital, despite the fact that he was not a medical doctor (Munck to López, January 27, 1845. ANA, SH 272-30-8). In medicine, as in all technical fields, the shortage or utter absence of trained natives impelled the government to utilize what talent it could find at hand. This is all the more evident in a note from López to the Commander of San Ysidro concerning José Artigas, the Uruguayan hero who had been in exile in Paraguay for a quarter-century. The commander was to "tell him that I have decided on him for Instructor of the Army of the Republic," and "to ascertain whether the state of his age and health will permit him to accept the duties." Unfortunately, it is not known if Artigas accepted the proffered post (López to Commander at San Ysidro, March 21, 1845. ANA, SH 272-30-16).

The only reasonable index of the size of the foreign community in this epoch is a report on foreigners residing in the capital's Cathedral District in 1850. This barrio, merely one of four in the city, counted 166 *extrangeros,* including 35 Spaniards, 45 Italians, 19 French, 24 Brazilians, and lesser numbers of Swiss, Argentines, Germans, Portuguese, Bolivians, and British. Also surprising is the fact that only 61 are listed as merchants. There were also nine carpenters, seven sailors, six shopowners, five tinworkers, and others acting as medical doctors, shoemaker, baker, tailor, pharmacist, silverworker, and miller (List of foreign residents, May 1, 1850. ANA, SH 292-11-1/4).

The British Connection

Despite the steady trickle of foreigners entering Paraguay, it was not until the fall of Rosas in 1852 and the subsequent liberation of the rivers that López could embark on his program of enticing foreign experts to collaborate with and direct a coherent development of his inland nation. While Gelli in Rio had earlier contracted a few técnicos encountered on the spot, such as British engineer Henry Godwin and German mechanics Henry Graf and John George Bechman to work on the establishment of an iron industry (Pla, 1970: 345-346), it was not until Francisco Solano López was sent to Europe, 1853-1854, that major steps were taken.

In Britain, the young López made a series of contracts with J. and A. Blyth and Company of Limehouse, a major shipbuilding firm. Not only was construction begun of a modern steam warship, the Tacuarí, but the firm also agreed to act as general agent for the Paraguayan government in the purchase of strategic materials and recruitment of European technicians. Until 1864, Blyth and Company would have an enormous input into Paraguayan development. The British firm, one of the most advanced in Europe, hired hundreds of técnicos, purchased equipment and arms, and provided sophisticated apprentice training for dozens of Paraguayan youth chosen by the governments of the two López to be the first of the native technological elite.

To open its drive for experts, the Blyth Company permitted the contracting of its own Chief Consulting Engineer, young William K. Whytehead, one of the leading engineers of his age. Despite his youth, Whytehead awed the Paraguayan government with his reputation as a technical genius, and Carlos Antonio awarded him the title "Chief Engineer of the State" upon his arrival in Asunción in 1855. His salary that year was a princely £600 per annum, plus an amazing variety of fringe benefits and allowances (Pla, 1970: 351). He was to be the Master-Builder of the new Paraguay and would coordinate all major technical projects for the state. This projected leap forward was to focus on several basic endeavors: an iron foundry at Ibicuy, a modern arsenal in Asunción, a major shipyard also in the capital, a railroad, and a telegraph system. The engineer would be heavily engaged in each of these projects and more, paying special attention to the arsenal. With him, also contracted by Blyth, came at least 18 other British técnicos, for the most part machinists. Within the next four years at least 70 more would follow, and many more would appear unbidden in Asunción, seeking to exercise their professions in a skill-hungry land by then well known for its generally high contract wages (Pla, 1970: 352-353). Those contracted as general technicians were paid according to experience. Highly experienced, first class men were paid 80 pesos monthly, while less experienced, second class specialists drew 60 pesos, or £200 and £144 per annum respectively. Such wages were about double the going rate in London, and were rounded out with various fringe benefits, bonuses, and other encouragements. As Paraguay slid toward war, the salary scale climbed, for never did Paraguay need técnicos more, and during the war itself, wages were often double what had been offered earlier. This is one reason why so many técnicos chose to remain and take their chances with the Paraguay they had helped to arm (Pla, 1970: 353).

Whytehead immediately went to work on the problem-plagued foundry at Ibicuy, which Henry Godwin had failed to get established earlier. He ordered channeling of the Arroyo Mbuyapei for water-power, regularized the exploitation of crude iron at the small mines of Caapucú and San Miguel, and sent lists of needed equipment to López for transmittal to Blyth. Even given the carte blanche of the López, his band of British colleagues and plentiful (if unskilled)–often convict–labor, the engineer was forced to start his projects virtually from scratch, building the basic machines in situ: a brass furnace, a heavy crane, water wheels, lathes, a machine for making crucibles, ad infinitum.

Conquering these difficulties, the engineer wrote in 1856 that "Thus equipped, the Establishment . . . has answered to all the appeals made to it either for the army or navy." He sent iron samples to his homeland for analysis, and reported to Carlos Antonio of the "favorable opinions expressed by Scientific men in England" as to its qualities. He waxed ebullient that "there is reason to hope that when the mines of Paraguay are explored and worked on a suitable scale, she will be able to supply La Plata with the best quality of iron at a cheaper rate than is now paid for an inferior quality imported from Europe." Urging that Paraguay utilize its resources to begin a major shipbuilding industry, Whytehead proudly informed López that "A country which can transport cheaply is master both of the producer and consumer and shares the profit of both." In fact, noted the técnico, again with pride, the first steamship built in Paraguay (under British direction), the Yporá, was already in service, and "Her performance leaves nothing to be desired." Two other steamers of advanced design, built almost entirely from local materials, were in advanced stages of construction, and the euphoric report closed in praise of the "aptitude displayed by the young men who are being trained in the different mechanical arts" at the request of the government (Whytehead report, Ibicuy, 1856. ANA, SH 312-2-1/14).

Within a very short time, Whytehead and his colleagues, increasing in number as time passed, made notable progress. The Asunción shipyards, under the guidance of a dozen British experts using modern, recently purchased, or constructed machinery, began to hum. The British-built Tacuarí and the newly purchased Rio Blanco, were joined in 1856 by the Yporá and Salto de Guairá, in 1857 by El Correo, in 1858 by Rio Apa, and in 1859 by Rio Jejuí, all sizable, modern steamers designated for naval and commercial service (Perez Acosta, 1948: 315-317). Not only were these vessels constructed at Asunción, in a shipyard progressively more modern, but extensive repair and maintenance work were carried out on ships locally built or foreign-bought. On all Paraguayan steamers, foreign, mostly British, machinists served. Many, in fact, worked in the engine rooms of the flotilla for ten years or more, even taking part in the few naval battles of the war.

A British engineer, Thomas Norton Smith, with the title of "Ship Constructor in Service to the State," managed the shipyard under Whytehead's general supervision from 1855 to 1860, at a salary of £275 annually and, among other works, constructed a massive, modern wharf and drydock designed by his chief. Many Paraguayans, selected by the government, labored there as well as hundreds of common laborers (Pla, 1970: 359).

Under Whytehead's careful supervision, an arsenal was created in Asunción in 1856 to provide not only heavy caliber weapons but also to complement the shipyard by the production of large-scale metal naval gear. The Chief Engineer appointed Frederick Garton its first director, followed by his personal friend Alex Grant, who worked with a team of British and Paraguayans and Master Caster (*fundidor*) engineer William Richardson (later replaced by William Newton). Mechanical drafting at the arsenal was entrusted to compatriot Richard Marshall, who arrived in 1857, while architect Alonzo Taylor was asked to design a new, larger, and more modern physical plant. A foundry was built for the arsenal, moulding shops, metal workshops, drafting rooms, and metal-cutting circular saws were installed. By 1858, the arsenal was producing many cannons, mountains of balls, machine tools, propellers, and other naval equipment (Pla, 1970: 361-362).

The projected railroad, which was to link Villa Rica with the capital, was another major concern of the técnicos. Blyth sent reasonably modern locomotives and several loads of rails, and a team of North American experts led by civil engineers George Paddison and William Wheelwright began work in 1858. Soon joined by three well-known British contract engineers—George Thompson, Henry Valpy, and Percy Burrell—the team made outstanding progress in their difficult undertaking (Pla, 1970: 363-364). Thompson, who demonstrated unusual skill in designing and constructing fortifications, worked with the army during the war and, as a colonel, was given active command of a major section of the Paraguayan defense in 1868, eventually captured by Brazilian troops (Thompson, 1869).

Health care, especially for the army, was yet another project of the Corpulent Despot, and to this end he had recruited a number of British doctors to replace Meister, who had left Paraguay in 1852. Blyth handled most of the arrangements and in 1856 sent to Paraguay Dr. John Johnston and pharmacist

James Prickett, contracted at excellent salaries for an initial two years. Johnston died soon after his arrival (one of the first of many to expire in Paraguay), but was quickly replaced by the team of Drs. John Fox, George Barton, and William Stewart, who arrived the same year. Prickett stayed on until 1861. Barton, named chief of the *Sanidad Militar,* or medical corps, received £500 annually for his services, plus a house, a horse, servants, and living allowance. No doubt it was due to this good treatment that he renewed his contract two years later. The other doctors were remunerated at rates only slightly less. All salaries moved upward by 1863, and Dr. Stewart, only in his mid-thirties, would earn £800 per annum by the end of that year. The medical men established military clinics, treated the sick and injured, and formally trained a large corps of local paramedics (Pla, 1970: 365-366).

Other foreigners were contracted to work with the military, for the most part as advisors, as had Colonel Wisner years earlier. In addition to the many technicians serving in the navy, Europeans and North Americans acted as technical experts to both naval and terrestrial artillery, teaching skills acquired as professional soldiers in other lands. The Paraguayan military benefited greatly from this guidance, and their placement of artillery throughout the war was superb. As with other areas of contract service, however, not all worked out well with the military técnicos. Witness the case of one Claudius B. Piers.

Paradise Flawed

Mr. Piers, recruited by Blyth, was, upon arrival in Asunción, appalled by Paraguay, by Paraguayans, and by his treatment by both. After one year of service, he complained to the government about alleged mistreatment. A López official, José M. Tellez, was detailed to respond, and he minced no words, accusing Piers of having inflated his military credentials. Instead of having served as Captain of British Horse Artillery and Lieutenant Colonel of Osmani (Turkish) Cavalry on detached duty, wrote Tellez, an investigation revealed no Turkish service at all, and only junior rank in the British army. The official also informed the officer that he could not expect the title of "Chief of Engineers," as that title was reserved for men who actually *were* engineers, which Piers most decidedly was not. Reminding the foreigner that he was both "without any rank" at all and subject to Paraguayan military regulations, Tellez then insisted that Piers' salary was £600 annually, and not the £700 claimed. Piers would also be expected to pay his wife's travel expenses out of his pocket, as no provision for this appeared in the contract he signed in London, and, further, that he would receive no special food unless he chose to pay for it himself. Tellez chided the officer for being one of several foreigners who harbored absurd pretensions (Tellez to Piers, July 4, 1857. ANA, SH 255-1-91/95).

A deeply stung Piers angrily retorted, claiming that inaccuracies in his service record were due to poor translation by an English clerk unfamiliar with Spanish. He also asserted that, contrary to official Paraguayan views, he was not in the Paraguayan army, "for I have neither contracted nor do I intend to enter it—the fact of my duty being Military and not Civil Engineering in no way warranting such a conclusion." "I acknowledge no laws," continued Piers, "but those to which a British Subject residing in this Country, apply to me, and I do not hold myself accountable to the ordinances of the Army or Military Laws in general." Explaining in a condescending manner that "It is the duty of every English Gentlemen to vindicate his honor," he noted that he had requested Blyth to send a full and clear explanation "of what they consider I am entitled to under the said contract." According to the officer, this included higher pay, a full expense account, two servants, two horses, and he requested "that your Excellency will either give directions that I be supplied with fit and proper rations or an allowance in lieu of the same" (Piers to Francisco Solano López, July 23, 1857. ANA, SH 255-1-96/99).

The government responded, after a considerable delay, that in view of Piers' attitude and his escalating demands it might be wise to consider terms for canceling the contract, as had been done in several other cases. The López regime, however, was not prepared for the officer's cheerfully exhorbitant assent. Piers had indeed considered the matter, and to him it seemed the golden opportunity to gouge the Paraguayan government and escape the rustic nation at once. He wrote the authorities that he would be willing to retire from Paraguay if the government would honor its contractual obligations and pay £300 in travel expenses, £900 compensation for dissolution of the contract, and a further £100 in other, various allowances (Piers to anon., January 30, 1858. ANA, SH 255-1-102). To this, an irate government responded that "If there has been a breaking of the contract, it has been on your part," and due to this, no compensation was allowable. Piers was bluntly informed that if he abandoned Paraguay on the first available ship, the López government would pay his "simple passage" and half salary until his arrival in England. No doubt with severely ravaged pride, Piers did depart immediately (Pablo Gonzalez to Piers, February 23, 1858. ANA, SH 255-1-103/107).

Paraguayan authorities had a host of other headaches with their contract experts, some of which served inexpertly, if at all. In 1859, J. Blyth wrote Francisco Solano López, admitting that "We hear with surprise of the disappearance of the Assistant Surgeon Mr. Henry Wells, and we shall not of course make any payments to his order," without López' approval (Blyth to López, May 7, 1859. ANA, SH 255-1-112). It was also necessary to arrest técnicos from time to time for brawling and other visibly poor conduct. At root in most of these cases was the pronounced predilection of many foreign contract experts for the poorly made but extremely potent Paraguayan *aguardiente.* As George Masterman wrote in 1870, after his seven "eventful years" as a contract pharmacist, the liquor was dangerous, and "The English Mechanics in Asunción, with the usual recklessness and improvidence of their class, consumed it in enormous quantities, and the death of nearly half their number could be traced directly or indirectly to its abuse" (Masterman, 1870: 71).

Arrests continued to be common occurrences throughout the period under consideration. Also a problem, accentuated by cultural shock, ennui, and firewater, was laziness and absenteeism. Probably the record holder in these areas was machinist John Twiddell, who "has lost two hundred thirty-nine days in a period of twenty-six months, for no reason." Twiddell was fired on the spot, along with his friend and fellow malingerer Andrew Bryson, who just missed capturing the slacker's trophy by a few days (Venancio López to Mr. Whytehead, May 30, 1863. ANA, SH 334-13-36). Anger over sloth often resulted in the arrest of those accused, as in the case of foundry technicians Smith and Boothby, jailed in 1865 "for their obstinate failings, for not wanting to work" (same to same, April 6, 1865. ANA, SNE 707). It was rare, however, for a técnico to languish long in prison. Conditions in the *calabozo* were so medievally harsh that even the most slothful became charged with energy and a desire to return to work.

In general, despite the contretemps, the foreign experts worked out surprisingly well. The shipyard was finished and functioning smoothly by 1860, the arsenal and the Ibicuy foundry poured out an avalanche of cannon and shell, the railroad, despite some spectacular accidents, connected the capital with Pirayú and the huge army camp at Cerro León, and was pushing eastward, and many other major works were completed.

"Susceptible . . . To Teaching"

In addition to these undertakings staffed and directed largely by English-speaking technicians, one should note the telegraph system, directed by Whytehead but effected by a German team headed by contract engineer Robert Von Fischer Treuenfelt. That gentlemen, contracted specifically to create a telegraph network which would link Asunción with Humaitá and other military nerve centers, arrived in Paraguay in 1864, on the eve of war. Within three months Villeta and Paraguarí were connected to the capital, and in the following year, the line, part of which passed under the broad Tebicuari, reached strategic Humaitá (Perez Acosta, 1948: 290-293). As the war progressed, Treuenfelt extended the line all the way to Curupaití in the extreme southwest tip of the country. The German engineer also collaborated in the training of a corps of Paraguayan telegraphers, and, during the war, created a national paper industry at Luque. He was repaid in 1868 by being brutally tortured and shot on orders of the paranoid *Mariscal* López, one of many victims of the San Fernando "purge."

Besides the imposing proofs of modernity noted above, foreign experts also had much to do with a renaissance of Paraguayan culture and education. In addition to the several score Paraguayan youth sent to England for education in the "Mechanical Pursuits," many in the factories and workshops of Blyth, many individual foreigners were put on salary to expand modern education at home, as the major negative legacy of El Supremo had been an almost nonexistent cultural structure.

One of the most fruitful educational técnicos was Ildefonso Bermejo, a Spanish *littérateur* who arrived early in 1855. He had contracted to act almost as literary consultant to the López government, and he began his labors with some trepidation, after seeing a young German photographer, his fellow passenger on the trip upriver, thrown in jail because he could not adequately explain his "infernal machine" to Paraguayan authorities (Bermejo, 1973: 31-32).

Among his early assignments was to edit one of the first "newspapers" published in Paraguay, *El eco del Paraguay,* after which he edited, with the aid of President López, another, *El Semanario,* from 1857 to 1863, also training a small group of Paraguayan youth to take his place when he left the country. He also founded the first Paraguayan normal school in 1855, an ill-fated venture, which was soon closed due to lack of interest and support. Bermejo then created the *Aula de filosofía,* where advanced students were taught history, grammar, geography, literature, and modern languages. In this endeavor the Spaniard was more successful, as it lasted until his departure. According to a contract signed with the government in 1857, Bermejo earned 150 silver pesos monthly, or about £600 annually, an excellent salary even by the standards of engineering and medical técnicos of the day (Bermejo contract, June 1, 1857. ANA, SNE 2753; Bermejo, 1973: 11-13). He magnified his cultural impact by giving lectures, organizing social evenings and costume balls, and, in 1859, enticing a Spanish light opera company then in Buenos Aires to come upriver and present to Asunción's elite a piece of his own authorship (Bermejo, 1973: 13).

Bermejo, however, despite the challenge involved in his multifaceted cultural labors and his fine salary, was never content in Paraguay (few técnicos were), uncomfortable in such a rustic society. As he described it with mixed emotions, "Paraguayans are naturally docile and susceptible to all forms of teaching," but, "Accustombed to obey, they were submissive . . . that servile and fearful submission makes them fake and suspicious. Their laugh is usually forced." According to the savant, "The Dictator Francia, amoral atheist, converted the countryside into tribes of animals who did not understand what was moral and what was not" (Bermejo, 1973: 197, 199). In 1860, with some misgivings, he returned to the government a slave which they had put in his service, noting with disappointment that the slave, Cirilio, whom he had taught reading, writing, and carpentry, had become an "incorrigible drunk." The government, showing more faith in Bermejo's teaching than in the slave's drinking, employed him henceforth in the military carpentry shop (Bermejo to Mariano Gonzalez, December 12, 1860. ANA, SH 329-16-1). In 1863, with the Corpulent Despot in his grave and international tensions mounting, Bermejo returned to Spain.

Another leading educator contracted was Pedro Dupuis, who appeared in Asunción in 1854 and immediately opened a school of mathematics to prepare students chosen by the government for careers in engineering. Many of the 51 students who appear in his first official report, such as Natalicio Talavera, Juan Crisóstomo Centurion, and Candido Bareiro, would become important forces in cultural and political spheres in the near future. Dupuis noted in his report that he was generally pleased with his students, although most of the work was remedial in nature. The French pedagogue soon learned, as would Masterman later, that Paraguayans were unfamiliar with mathematics. As the latter once noted, describing his trip to the paymaster, he was shocked that "It is scarcely credible, but they were actually more than an hour trying to do the simple sum of dividing so many dollars and reals by twelve" (Masterman, 1870: 43).

As Dupuis struggled with his student's sums, he spotted one, José Dolores Valiente, who showed "an irregular conduct, not wishing to work—on the contrary, trying to distract his neighbors." Perhaps because the teacher wrote that "something useful to the Nation" should be found for Valiente, Carlos Antonio noted in the margins that "the denounced José Dolores Valiente will be sent to the Navy" (Dupuis school report, March 1, 1854. ANA, SH 311-8-9).

Dupuis continued his work for several years, and returned after the war to become director of the new Colegio Nacional, in 1875. His wife, Ana, taught piano at her private music school during both stays in Paraguay. Other *Franceses* were also involved in burgeoning Paraguayan education, mostly, as was the case of Ana Dupuis, active in the private sphere. Among these were Dorotea Duprat, who opened a private *escuela francesa* for girls on the eve of the war; a Monsieur DeCluny, who taught his native tongue in the 1860s; and Francisco Sauvegeod de Dupuis, who founded and directed a music school from 1853 until his death in 1861. The latter added to his income by accepting various part-time contracts with the state, as when he agreed to teach four infantry, one cavalry, and an artillery band to play martial music and acceded to direct a band "anytime that there are comedies at the National Theatre" (Dupuis contract, September 1, 1856. ANA, SNE 2748, and Perez Acosta, 1948: 529-530).

Nor were the French alone in their didactic efforts. Shortly before the outbreak of war, in 1864, Gustavo Mackenson, probably a German, came to Paraguay after years of teaching in Uruguay. In Asunción he set up a commercial and linguistic school, teaching five languages and basic financial skills. Mackenson supplemented his income by doing considerable in-home tutoring (Perez Acosta, 1948: 530-531). A European lithographer, Carlos Riviere, also taught engraving and other sophisticated specialities in Paraguay at government request. Riviere was contracted in 1856 to produce paper money for the government and to teach at least ten Paraguayan apprentices his trade. His pay was a percentage of the bills he printed, a substantial sum in local currency, but he was only allowed to work under "the vigilance of two Officers, without whom the Lithographer will not enter the workshop nor engage in any work" (Riviere contract, 1856. ANA, SNE 2748).

Another major area in which the foreigners worked and taught was that of architecture. Aside from numerous sumptuous private homes (most of which were property of the López family) planned and directed by foreign architects, a number of larger projects were undertaken, largely entrusted to either Alejandro Ravizza or Alonzo Taylor. The former, a professional Italian architect, arrived in Paraguay in 1854 with his brother and began a series of impressive private structures for the small elite. While his brother went into private commerce, the architect accepted the charge of "State Architect" and over the next decade designed and supervised the construction of the Oratory (today's Panteón de los Héroes), the National Theatre, the Club Nacional, and several city churches. He was still constructing and teaching lithography while the Allies were destroying and killing his graduates during the war (Perez Acosta, 1948: 51-53, 501).

Alonzo Taylor, a British engineer and draftsman who worked on the new arsenal plans and elsewhere, left his mark on Paraguayan architecture by designing and building the harmonious Government Palace, which has been used by every Paraguayan president since. It is perhaps the one outstanding building to be seen in Paraguay. Taylor was also responsible for most of the pleasant railroad stations near the capital, and his work was enhanced by the skills of two contracted sculptors, John Owen Moynihan and Andrés Antonini, whose delicate work softened many an angular line (Pla, 1970: 387).

Billiard Parlors and Yerba

The individual and highly skilled técnicos contracted far and wide represent only the most visible tip of the foreign iceberg which floated in Paraguayan waters under the two López. Engaged in the less spectacular but more ubiquitous routine tasks were literally hundreds of foreigners who were the middle class of the host country. In 1863, foreigners were heavily represented in the lists of business licenses granted by the government. Some 230 such licenses were given to foreigners, well over half of those granted to businesses in the capital. These were awarded to foreigners in the wholesale trade, taverns (10), silver shops, iron shops, hatmaking establishments, paint stores, shoe shops, construction materials, pharmacies (3), billiard parlors, and a large number of oficios related to the river trade. A similar report of the same year, which covers the entire republic, indicates that foreigners held 44 percent of all licenses granted that year (License list, Asunción, June 30, 1863. ANA, SH 334-28-2; Mariano Gonzalez report on licenses, April 13, 1863. ANA, SNE 1579).

During the same period, incomplete data pertaining to passports issued between February 1857 and June 1861 (38 of the 53 months) show that 516 of 836 or 62 percent of these were made out to foreigners. These are passports issued at Asunción and do not include those given elsewhere. Fully 112 of the passports were issued to Italians, 78 to Spaniards, 77 to Porteños, 57 to French, and 29 to British travelers. In all, 308 passports were for Europeans, and these included virtually every European nation, including Poland, Ireland, and Switzerland. Also, many nations of the Western Hemisphere were included, with several from the United States (Passport data, 1857-1861. ANA, SH 323-8-1/15, 326-6-1/30, 328-11-1/19).

In Asunción, in a short period of months, Italians Santiago Caniza, Geronimo Falcon, and José Vagliani opened a tavern, billiard parlor, and "Optical Cabinet which contains the best European Views, for public recreation," all in the Encarnación district of the capital (López approval of solicitudes, February,

March, and October 1853. ANA, SNE 1506). Also in the capital in the same epoch one could encounter a German watchmaker, a North American cigar maker, and an English printer, as well as many other resident specialists (Bermejo, 1973: 44, 58, 150).

Another brief perusal of the documents shows Luis Mysznowski purchasing tax yields in Limpio; Henrique Cramon, a French resident, asking permission to construct a sawmill in the Chaco; and Italian Lázaro Costa buying tobacco harvests in the Villa Rica area (Mysznowski solicitude, November 13, 1858. ANA, SNE 1567; Cramon solicitude, July 1, 1854. ANA, SH 312-4-1; Costa solicitude, January 15, 1855. ANA, SH 312-4-5). A surprising number of foreigners were to be found in the interior, though few actually lived there. Swedish naturalist Munck supported his studies by buying and selling livestock taxes in Misiones, Italian Miguel Angel Queirolo ran a yerba station in Caaguazú, paisano Juan Ferrares was a jeweler in Villa Rica, Agustín Piallo regularly purchased tobacco in Curuguatay, and John Pablo Lynch was doing the same in Villa Rica (Morner, 1955: 22; Solicitudes of Queirolo, Ferrares, Piallo, and Lynch, 1855. ANA, SH 314(B)-1-41, 54, 23, and 68).

The foreign impact on Paraguay through limited industrialization, training, education, and general economic activity helped strengthen the nation in a formal sense. The hundreds of heavy caliber guns mounted at Humaitá and elsewhere, the modern navy, railroad, telegraph, and munitions manufacturing establishments—all helped bring about the horrendous War of the Triple Alliance and their own destruction by providing the hardware with which Francisco Solano López could become Mariscal and self-appointed arbiter of the Rio de la Plata. The dizzying speed with which his nation was "modernized" and strengthened tempted López to flex his new muscle and seek an ever-expanding, activist role in international affairs.

Even as tension grew and war approached, the foreign technicians continued to sign up, and Blyth was kept busy purchasing rails, rifles, machinery, and other hard goods for its best customer. So good a customer indeed was the government of Paraguay that at one point Blyth allowed Francisco Solano to carry an impressive £50,612 in debts on the books, a huge sum for the era (J. Blyth to López, April 8, 1862. ANA, SH 255-1-174).

When López declared war on Brazil in late 1864 by confiscating one of her steamers in Asunción, he immediately turned to his técnicos, ordering Whytehead to send some machinists to outfit the ship for active military service (Venancio López to Whytehead, December 15, 1864. ANA, SNE 707). In the next several months, Whytehead ran the shipyard specialists ragged working on and arming ships seized from hostile nations or bought from neutral powers. While British and other foreign técnicos worked feverishly in the shipyards, arsenal, and at Ibicuy, only a few chose to leave, and the optimistic Mariscal, while increasing salaries, felt he could even refuse contract renewals to those he considered less than ardent workers (Venancio López to Whytehead, April 18, 1865. ANA, SNE 707).

Conditions, however, deteriorated for all in Paraguay, foreign workers were not accepted, as the war progressed, López' blunders cost the cream of the army, and the Allied blockade made itself felt. The absence of contact with their loved ones and friends in other lands, the increased hours of labor, and, occasionally, combat duty—all tended, as Josefina Pla notes, to accentuate (especially among the British) an already noted fondness for the strong spirit, as well as acute depression, listlessness, illness, and suicide. In the only major naval engagement of the war, the battle of Riachuelo in June 1865, the Paraguayan fleet, despite heroic efforts by a score or so of British machinists aboard, was ravaged, and at least two of the técnicos died of their wounds. Two others, John Watts and Cuthbert Westgarth, were decorated in a formal ceremony by López for exceptional bravery (Pla, 1971: 24-25).

After Riachuelo it became clear to most foreign técnicos that the war would be a long one and probably a disaster for Paraguay. What this resulted in psychologically cannot be known, but the work, at an increasingly frantic pace, continued. In July, for a combination of reasons unknown, Chief Engineer

Whytehead took his own life. He had been ill and very depressed, and he was neither the first nor the last to kill himself. An inventory of his effects showed a telescope, a portable pump, 258 books, three horses, a magnesium lamp, and 324 pesos in paper money, a poor estate for a man who had almost single-handed guided the modernization of Paraguay for a decade (Inventory, 1865. ANA, SH 255-1-188/194; Pla. 1971: 25).

Other technicians still manned what was left of the fleet and manufactured truly gigantic cannons at the arsenal and at Ibicuy, but the war came closer and closer; several deserted to the Allies or sought refuge in foreign legations or in the winding sheets of death.

In 1868, when Allied forces overran the defenses of the Ibicuy foundry, some 20 British specialists were evacuated at the last minute by order of the Mariscal and rushed to "safety." No doubt, at that point their conception of safety and that of the Mariscal differed markedly. Most were brought to similar jobs at the Asunción arsenal, and that plant expanded its output notably. There they were soon joined by machinists of the abandoned fleet, and, when the capital was threatened, both groups and loads of machinery were transferred to Caacupé, where the arsenal was reestablished. Despite the fact that many of the técnicos, especially those who had served the fleet, knew little of the job of casting and rifling cannons, they showed themselves remarkably adept at doing just that. Until the last days of the war they produced scores of very good quality cannons and mortars, although the pace and strain of events killed at least 15 of them at Caacupé (Pla, 1971: 36-37). When Brazilian troops finally captured the new arsenal in mid-1869 they were surprised to find there 22 recently produced cannon and some 900,000 projectiles (Pla, 1971: 39). Twenty-three British técnicos, a U.S. citizen, and men of other nationalities were captured there as well. The foreign medical men serving with the army also stayed at their posts. Those who did not pack their valises in 1865 remained at their labors for the duration of the war or their lives. Several came to the end of the latter in the midst of the former.

Several medical men, as well as scores of other foreigners, were arrested in the Mariscal's paranoid reaction to the supposed plot of 1868 against his rule and life. Doctors Rhynd and Fox and pharmacist Masterman, who had been arrested earlier, were rearrested—as were, according to the latter's estimate, 80 Italians, 20 French, all resident Bolivians, and a scattering of English speaking experts. Among these, John Watts, the machinist decorated by López for his heroism at Riachuelo, was executed, as were another British técnico and Swedish scientist Munck, to name but a few. A British merchant named Stark was sent to the wall, and German engineer Treuenfelt and Portuguese Consul and Vice-Consul were also executed. A German expert named Neuman was beaten to death, as were several other foreigners. Even some of the soldiers of fortune who had come unbidden to aid Paraguay during the war were shot by the unbalanced López (who also did away with a good part of his immediate family at this time). Such was the case of Major Manlove, an ex-officer of Confederate cavalry, who had appeared in 1866 with a scheme to create a privateer navy for Paraguay based in the Caribbean, and who had later served with the Paraguayan army (Morner, 1955: 5; Pla, 1971: 47-60).

Those who survived told tales of horror, of sadistic beatings, unusual tortures, interminable interrogations, threats, generally abominable treatment, and snap decisions of life or death by drum-head military tribunals. As haggard survivor Masterman wrote shortly after his ordeal: "The blind obedience of the rest to the orders of López, an obedience almost as unreasoning as that of an ox to his master, but which has been mistaken in Europe for devotion and patriotism," was the true tragedy of Paraguay (Masterman, 1870: x, 137, 149, 198-203, 259, 270).

When the war terminated, there was precious little evidence of the titanic work which had been done. Many public buildings and some fine private edifices still stood; the railroad, in need of major repairs, still functioned; and part of the shipyard could be seen by the curious. But gone were the técnicos and the hundreds of Paraguayans trained by them. The foreigners who came to Paraguay after 1870 would in large parts be parasites, buying the natural resources and alienating the public domain of the prostrate nation.

The Paraguayan experience with rapid modernization was a unique one. The government of Carlos Antonio López alone of South American regimes achieved a large measure of "industrialization" without inviting the massive amounts of foreign investment capital which was impatiently waiting in the wings, and, hence, Paraguay in the years 1840-1870 did not mortgage her financial future and escaped the pressures which were brought to bear on neighboring nations by small groups of European investors. Paraguay paid for what it needed from the more modern world with cash on the barrelhead and purchased only what it could pay for. Also, thinking of the future, Paraguay relied not on imported capital, but on imported skills. Again, paying as it went, Paraguay not only made use of selected foreign experts who represented fortunes spent in other countries on research and education, to construct a new Paraguay, but also to construct, through training, a new, technologically oriented Paraguayan to manage the future nation. Had it not been for the war, it might have been that way. There is no doubt that, in 1864, Francisco Solano López ruled a nation both unified, debt-free, and technologically advanced in relation to other countries of the continent.

It bears note that virtually all of the modernization and "industry" carried out in this period was military, or defensive in nature. This applies to the railroad, the arsenal, Ibicuy's foundry, the telegraph, the naval vessels, the military advisors, the army medical corps, and Humaitá and other fortresses. It would not then be an overstatement to say that Paraguay's leap into the mid-nineteenth century was on one foot only, an unbalanced development at best which left the average Paraguayan scratching in the soil with the same instruments and ideas used two centuries before. One cannot say that the progress noted above caused the war, but there is no doubt that it made the war possible. Even El Mariscal would not have dared do more than defend his immediate borders had not his military materiel encouraged him to redefine those borders and play the wider and infinitely more dangerous role of fulcrum in the regional balance of power.

REFERENCES

Archivo Nacional, Asunción [ANA] Sección historia [SH] Sección nueva encuadernación [SNE].

BERMEJO, I. (1973) Vida paraguaya en tiempos del viejo López. Buenos Aires: Editorial Universitaria de Buenos Aires.

British Museum [BM].

CARLYLE, T. (1843) Critical and Miscellaneous Essays. New York.

MASTERMAN, G. (1870) Seven Eventful Years in Paraguay. London.

MORNER, M. [ed.](1955) Algunas cartas del naturalista sueco Don Eberhard Munck af Rosenschold escritas durante su estadía en el Paraguay, 1843-1869. Stockholm: University of Stockholm.

PEREZ ACOSTA, J. (1948) Carlos Antonio López, "Obrero Máximo." Buenos Aires: Editorial Guaranía.

PLA, J. (1971) "Los británicos en el Paraguay." Revista de Historia de América 71: 21-60.

--- (1970) "Los británicos en el Paraguay." Revista de Historia de América 70: 340-371.

Public Record Office [PRO]. London: Foreign Office [FO].

THOMPSON, G. (1869) The War in Paraguay. London.

John Hoyt Williams is Associate Professor of History at Indiana State University, Terre Haute. He has written widely on Paraguayan history, including the recent monograph El Dr. Francia y la creación de la República del Paraguay *(Asunción, 1975), and is currently finishing another study,* The Rise and Fall of the Republic of Paraguay, 1800-1870.

REVIEW ESSAY

PANTALEON AND THE VISITORS

Chaplin, David, ed. PERUVIAN NATIONALISM: A CORPORATIST REVOLUTION. New Brunswick, New Jersey: Transaction Books, 1976.

Lowenthal, Abraham F., ed. THE PERUVIAN EXPERIMENT: CONTINUITY AND CHANGE UNDER MILITARY RULE. Princeton, New Jersey: Princeton University Press, 1975.

While I was reading these two significant collections of essays and, at the same time, listening to and reading the latest news from Peru, I was constantly thinking of a parable that Mario Vargas Llosa, a Peruvian writer with socialistic beliefs but who has chosen not to involve himself in direct political action, had written with all sorts of implications about the predicament of Latin American countries today, and with obvious allusions to the Peruvian experience. The story, written in the form of a factual chronicle, tells of what happens when the Peruvian army tries to solve a problem that affects the relations of its garrisons in the jungle area with the local population. The problem is the conflict that occurs and reactions produced among the population of Iquitos when army privates are enjoying their weekly leave.

To solve this problem, the army decides to create a "special service" under the direction of Pantaleon, an officer who has distinguished himself as an efficient and effective organizer of provisioning services in Lima. Pantaleon, with his characteristic zeal and devotion to the army, assumes his tasks rationally, selects his personnel with great care, operates on a reasonable budget, and even performs certain scientific observations suggested by heavy tomes and "do-it-yourself manuals." The service is a model of administration and, when put into operation, works with the expected efficiency, and the conflict disappears for a time. The army and Pantaleon are satisfied and happy with the results.

Unexpectedly, however, trouble and problems crop up from three sources. Some of the colonizers in the jungle have heard of the "service" and, wanting to take advantage of it, even resort to force. From across the border in Brazil, a lay "brother" comes spreading a kind of revivalist Catholic cult among the lower-class population of the jungle, even managing to affect some of the "visitors," and by rumor and gossip the moral indignation of the provincial city becomes exacerbated to the point of public scandal. There is also some evidence that the officers of the garrisons want to share the "services" with the privates.

Various tragic incidents take place and threaten to create chaos beyond the control of the local military and civil authorities. The problem is reported to Lima. Army headquarters is taken by surprise and hastily decides to discontinue the service, reassigning Pantaleon to a distant garrison in the Altiplano. The incident ends in tragicomic fashion for the army when Pantaleon, before leaving for his new assignment, decides to celebrate a funeral ceremony with military honors for one of his most devoted "visitors." To prevent further chaos, the army decides that the time has come to take "drastic measures"—a temporary suspension of warranties and curfew is declared in Iquitos, and the situation returns to normal. I will leave the readers to deduce the various morals of the story.

The two books under review attempt with considerable success to describe and explain the events and consequences that followed when the Peruvian army, after October 3, 1968, offered its services to solve the problems of the Peruvian state and society. They stop shortly before 1975, when the army decided to take "drastic measures" to restore order again, while continuing to provide the country with its services. Like many other "Peru watchers," the writers represented in these two volumes were surprised by the speed with which the new military government took control of Peru and proceeded to take a series of actions that differed considerably from those of previous military or civilian governments. Those actions placed Peru in the international spotlight immediately and provoked the most contradictory reactions from observers and foreign governments, showing a lack of information about the country even though a wave of interest had been aroused by the reaction of the previous Belaúnde government to the peasant invasions and guerrilla movements of the sixties. Most of the information on these events, however, was confined to professional journals and monographs circulated mainly among scholars. As the preparation and publication of these two books took time, they come to light somewhat tardily. Notwithstanding the fact that the recent turn of events in Peru seems to conform more to traditional expectations, these books are nonetheless valuable because they provide a necessary background for any new attempts to explain change in Peru.

The element of surprise is present in most of the articles not only because of the speed of changing events precipitated by the Peruvian government, but also by the scale of the changes in an essentially peaceful manner and some of the unexpected reactions of Peruvian society. This makes many of the contributors cautious and somewhat uncertain in their efforts to categorize the nature of the process. Beginning with the titles of the books, I find that they express this hesitancy. Chaplin, while labeling the phenomenon a revolution, precedes it with the adjective "corporatist" in his introductory article to point to the many traditional elements in the Peruvian situation, which in a previous version of the essay made him say that revolution was being delayed for Peru. Lowenthal calls it "The Peruvian Experiment" and uses the phrase "continuity and change," which sets the tone of the articles in the book. In his introductory article and throughout the text, he uses the phrase "ambiguous revolution" to express his opinion about the events, which reminds one of Hobsbawm's "peculiar revolution." Hence, the two books can be adequately viewed as useful exercises in the analysis of "continuity and change," giving these frequently used words a specific meaning with relation to the Peruvian situation. Viewed in this perspective, they tend to complement each other, the Chaplin volume giving more emphasis to background and continuity, while the Lowenthal volume devotes most of its space to change.

Those aspects of the Peruvian "revolution" which deal with the most drastic political and economic transformations introduced by the Revolutionary Government of the Armed Forces are analyzed in both volumes. While making a comparison between Peru and Chile during the processes of change, Strasma's essay in the Chaplin volume points out that there are some similarities in that both governments at the start followed an essentially peaceful road, Peru persevering in this path longer than Chile. The commonalities of the proclaimed programs in both countries include not only economic policies that can be identified with the continuation of growth and development, but also more profound transformations such as a redistribution of income, changes in the social structure, recovering control of national resources, incorporation of large sectors of the peasant and Indian population, increased participation and mobilization of the population, and the presentation of a more dignified image of the countries to the external world.

The Peruvian army, after taking power by the traditional coup, surprised everybody by declaring itself a revolutionary government and rapidly taking such steps as the expropriation of the International Petroleum Company, implementing a more forceful agrarian reform law, and enacting decrees giving the state greater control of mining, banking, and industry. At the same time, the Junta took measures to transform the unequal structure of the Peruvian society, taking not only antioligarchic measures but inviting the population to participate in the process of freeing themselves with the help of the revolutionary government. It was the military's intent not only to continue the promotion of growth and modernization, but to continue governing until a new type of society, "neigher capitalist nor communist," emerged in Peru. Implementing all these changes, the revolutionary government has prepared itself for the task and proceeded with speed, imagination, and resourcefulness to find civilian advisors. Once appointed, they introduced a series of organizational reforms and innovations that, while not totally successful, have modified completely the structure of Peruvian society. The most important of these transformations are: increased participation of the state in the management of the economy, reserving for it the control and exploitation of the most basic resources; a substantial transformation of the agrarian structure; a new approach to the process of industrialization and the participation of foreign investors; and a manifest intent of providing new incentives for the participation of "the masses" in the process. Although the speed with which they have proceeded has allowed them to succeed in general, many setbacks have forced them to take some backward steps. This was accomplished until 1975 without noticeable deviation from their original intent, without notable deterioration of the economic situation of the country, and with a surprisingly low display of repression on the part of the government.

The economic organizational innovations of the government are projected by Peter T. Knight in the Lowenthal volume against the traditional background of the country and the manifested ideological orientation of the government to produce a "fully participatory democracy." To accomplish this, the government redefined the Peruvian economy into four sectors defined as social, state, reformed private, and fully private, of which the social is the predominant, although in accord with their intent of being neither capitalist nor communist. Because the precedents in the history of the country for these organizations are few the revolutionary government appears daring and innovative in spite of the setbacks that started to appear as soon as they were confronted with reality. In this view, the most successful have been the Agrarian Production Cooperatives (CAP) and the Agricultural Societies of Social Interest (SAIS). Attempts to introduce labor communities in the industrial sector have found numerous obstacles in their way, due mainly to the resistance of investors and workers to the intrusion of government. In all cases, resistance has forced the government to intervene, limiting increase in participation and failing to increase jobs for new workers. In the industrial sector, it has also discouraged new investment from the private sector and induced the use of many ploys by private investors to limit the participation of the workers.

With reference to the new role of private and foreign investors, Shane Hunt, in the Lowenthal volume, reviews all earlier legislation and the previously slight participation of the Peruvian government in the regulation of private foreign investment, giving considerable credence to the picture of dependence held generally about "pre-Revolutionary" Peru. In contrast to this, the new rules of the game introduced by the revolutionary government (1) give the state control of all basic industries and natural resources and (2) channel all foreign investments through joint ventures or private companies, but subject to the revision and control of the state. The results of this policy have been that the great foreign investmens of the past have diminished considerably in importance, some have disappeared, and the economic functions of the state have grown enormously. All this enhanced the image of the Peruvian government with huge gains in the political area, but the economic outcome has not been equal to expectations, due to factors probably beyond the control of the revolutionary government or, for that matter, any government. Not only did implementation of the new rules require endless negotiations, revisions, and a formidable increase in a bureaucracy that absorbs resources, but the very political image that Peru projected tended to frighten most of the major foreign investors, who have either demanded more stringent guarantees or have withheld investment and credit to an extent that "perhaps never before or since has the meaning of external dependence seemed clearer in the context of the Peruvian Revolution" (p. 328).

Bold as these transformations appear in the general picture, they diminish in relief when seen in the context of the government's policy to achieve one of its most radical ambitions, the better redistribution of income and improved standard of living among the poorer classes. To explain this, Hunt, in the Chaplin volume, looks at the relationship between government expenditures, distribution, and growth, while

Richard Webb, "Government Policy and the Distribution of Income in Peru, 1963-73," looks at the effects of the different policies for this distribution. Both authors compare closely the performances of the Belaúnde regime and the Revolutionary Government of Velasco. The continuing existence of glaring inequalities in power and wealth, however, makes it difficult to dismiss this rationale, and Hunt finds in this pattern the reason why the government expenditures designed to affect distribution have not noticeably altered the existing inequalities although they have contributed slightly to growth. Thus, the power of the oligarchy has expressed itself preferably in the control of agrarian and manufacturing and, to a lesser extent, agricultural resources, while the expenditures of government in education, public health, transportation, agriculture, and public works have had an impact on the growth of the country, even though budget expenditures have been payments of transfer and not of investment.

Webb paints a slightly different picture. Comparing the results of distributive policies of the governments of Belaúnde and Velasco, he demonstrates that while the numerical results do not show much variation, there has been some redistributive change that has taken place predominantly among the urban sectors. The distributive impact on the rural population has been in the nature of "trickle down," which has benefited some tenant farmers but has left untouched a much larger group of poorer peasants.

Events analyzed in the preceding section depict some of the accomplishments of the revolutionary government in its attempt to gain control of the resources of the country and promote industrialization, while indicating the political and economic obstacles that prevent the full achievement of such goals. Turning now to the corollary goal of transforming the traditional social structure of Peru by creating a "humanistic participatory democracy," it becomes necessary not only to see what is being done by the government, but also to explore those features of the traditional social structure that limit conditions for reform or revolution. The task is difficult because, while there seems to be agreement as to the general configuration of the Peruvian society, the internal structure and the social organizations of this configuration have not been adequately explored. It is to the credit of contributors to these books that they are, up to a point, aware of the fragmentary and somewhat superficial past analyses of Peruvian society.

The three articles that deal more extensively with the background and features of the traditional Peruvian social and political structure are those of Chaplin on "The Revolutionary Challenge and Peruvian Militarism," of Julio Cotler on "The Mechanics of Internal Domination and Social Change in Peru," and Paul L. Doughty on "Social Policy and Urban Growth in Lima." Supplementary to these are essays on militarism, the Catholic Church, blue-collar workers and three on peasants.

In his very comprehensive introductory chapter, David Chaplin argues that "Peru's continuing failure to experience a violent mass revolution requires some explanation, in view of the persistent expectation since the early thirties that such a revolution was about to occur." As his major intent is to explain why such a revolution had not materialized, he analyzes those aspects of the social and political structure which he calls "counterrevolutionary factors." The first of his three basic factors, the historical role of APRA in insulating Peru's industrial proletariat from communist influence, is well taken, but his other two, Peru's diversified economy and geography, are briefly mentioned only in relation to stability and guerrilla warfare. Their role in determining perhaps the main characteristics of the Peruvian social and political structure are not dealt with by him or any of the other writers, with the possible exception of Doughty. Since pre-Columbian times the very difficult geography of Peru has been an extremely important factor in determining the interaction of the human economy and the dynamics of its population, making any attempt at integration of the society in an articulate fashion very difficult without the investment of great resources of power and organization.

Thus, when those resources were used for integration by the Incas, Spaniards, and Republican Peruvians, the results have produced a kind of "centralist" state that is today Peru—that is, relatively strong at the center, but almost always with an unsteady and weak control over the periphery that leaves the population of the different regions relatively autonomous as long as order is preserved and the demands of the center do not imperil the fragile and difficult adaptations that have taken centuries to develop. While in pre-Columbian times and prior to the arrival of the Spaniards "centralism" always developed from the highlands, it has since been displaced to the coast, creating the present pattern of dependence and domination that characterizes Peru today. However, geography is still dominant in that most of the country is divided into a discrete number of regions with independent traditions that make real the metaphors of the "living museum" of Anderson and the "archipelagos" of Murra and Matos Mar. Therefore, the "relatively peaceful history of Peru," I think, can be approached in terms of the interaction of centralism within the limitations of geography and population dynamics, which in turn produce constant localized conflicts while the country appears peaceful.

Since the other factors indicated by Chaplin do not all hinge on the geography and the economy and are dealt with extensively in other chapters, I pass now to the consideration of the "Mechanics of Internal Domination and Social Change in Peru" by Julio Cotler, who looks at the same factors from the perspective of structural dualism and internal colonialism and in terms of the theory of dependence. His intent is more ambitious than Chaplin's and his arguments are more complex in that even with repeated readings, I run the risk of mininterpreting his meanings. Consistent with his dependence orientation, Cotler sees the flowing of domination in a mechanical fashion from the center (the industrially developing coastal areas) to the periphery (the underdeveloped agrarian highland and jungle areas). While he gives some attention to the facts of internal variation and geography, the gist of his arguments gives more importance to the vertical flow of domination from the coast in a hierarchical and arborescent manner. They give the impression that hc is talking about a perfect pyramidal structure, with the power of the government, the oligarchy, and the military presiding alternately at the apex of the pyramid. However, I am of the opinion that present-day Peruvian political structure is more analogous to Kubler's interpretation of the colonial political structure of Peru as "the great contrast between Inca and Spanish colonial government . . . designated by the terms 'unique hierarchy'," referring to the absolute pyramid of Inca authority, as contrasted with "multiple hierarchy," describing the proliferation of practically independent systems of authority on the *encomiendas* (Kubler, 1946: 376).

As a framework or model that describes the general features of the recent Peruvian social and political system, Cotler's study has provided a frame of reference for most of the studies in these two books. Useful as it is, due to its tendency to look at events from the center to the periphery in terms of domination, the events and processes that occur in the different areas of the highlands are explained as a consequence of the domination effect in terms of specific strategies such as "privatization" in the case of the power of the landlords, or "segmentary incorporation" of the new groups which develop to challenge the power of the established groups. Those events appear, then, as situational solutions to specific cases in a historical sense, but not as a consequence of the structure of the system itself and of its limitations in terms of the exercise of power. What appears to Cotler to be a strategy may be a consequence of the limitation of the domination effect due to the structure of the administrative organizations of the state and the difficulties of communication imposed by the geographical environment, which seem to be at the source of all forms of privatization. The strategy appears not as a reaction to domination, but as a response to the vacuum of power imposed by distance and isolation. And privatization affects not only the landlord class but also the mestizo and Indian rural populations which take advantage of this vacuum of power to challenge the local powers, to gain minor advantages from patronage, or to isolate themselves when local conflicts tend to threaten them.

When major conflict threatens the peace of the society, there is a tendency to explain the outcome in terms of the "inconsistencies" and "contradictions" of the system, but such explanations fail to satisfy completely. The repetitive nature of many of those conflicts, events such as the permanent university crisis, peasant movements and rebellions, and many others that are usually suppressed but rarely solved, would seem to indicate that there are some historical or structural factors that require a better explanation. Utilization of the "multiple hierarchy" concept of Kubler might provide a more helpful explanation of these and others endemic conflicts in Peruvian society.

The suggestive articles of Chaplin and Cotler provide the background on which to project the events of change in conflict that have characterized the process of slow modernization and development of Peru in the last fifty or sixty years. The most important of these events have been the modernization of agriculture and industrialization of the coast, urban growth and the extension of the market system following the policy of road building of all Peruvian governments since the times of Present Augusto B. Leguia, massive population growth as a consequence of public health policies and gradual diminution of Spanish colonial conditions, and improvements in education and changes in the composition of the social stratification in spite of a rigid system of social mobility, to culminate with the events of the revolution of the Peruvian Army in 1968 and after. To say the least, all of these changes have disrupted the traditional picture of Peru that one might still have had during the forties. These disruptions have intensified the opposition of traditional groups and have produced new ones, especially as a response to population growth and increased traffic and communications, raising the level of conflict to almost unmanageable proportions.

Of all the events mentioned above, the most disruptive has been the gradual deterioration of the social conditions of the rural areas due to growth of population and the expansion of the market system, a situation that has produced, on the one hand, numerous movements and rebellions among the peasant population, and, on the other hand, the progressive and increasing migration of peasants, first to the sugar and cotton plantations of the coast and later to the cities of the coast, primarily Lima. This has produced a rural proletariat in the north and changed the traditional urban picture of Peru.

Events in rural areas to which the policies of agrarian reform of the Revolutionary Government responded are dealt with fragmentarily in the Chaplin volume by William F. Whyte, Giorgio Alberti, and Chaplin in terms of two polar situations: the events during the fifties in the Valley of Yanamarca in the Central Highlands, and the guerrilla movement of Hugo Blanco in the Valley of La Convención in southern Peru during the sixties.

In his essay on "Rural Peru: Peasants as Activists," Whyte uses the case of the Yanamarca Valley to show that the Peruvian peasants were not simply passive recipients of external change, but also could initiate change when exposed to migratory labor and education under favorable conditions. This is complemented by Alberti's essay, an analysis of the movement initiated by those peasants in Yanamarca to oppose the local *hacendado* and take possession of the land. On the basis of his good analysis of the situation, Alberti constructs a model that, with some modification, can be applied to other parts of the Central Highlands of Peru. In the effort to present their case clearly, the historical background and long tradition of the Central Highlands is simplified or ignored: e.g., constant land litigation and existence of a "communal" ideology that is probably of Spanish origin (Adams, 1959; Escobar, 1968). Movements such as those in Yanamarca have been happening since the time of Independence in the Central Highlands, and they are not always favorable to the poorer peasants of the area who, under pressures of subsistence, are forced to become migrant proletariats in the fringes of cities and rural areas.[1]

In "La Convención Valley and the 1962-1965 Guerrilla Uprising," David Chaplin makes a comprehensive and complete review of this "rather unusual" movement during the sixties. In his compact summary and discussion of ideological issues generated nationally and internationally among members of the left, he covers the efficacy and timeliness of guerrilla movements which produced these abortive efforts with the participation of urban and rural masses. The conflicts in La Convención province of Cuzco between the landowners and tenant farmers of peasant extraction became progressively more acute during the fifties. When the landlords attempted to recuperate the lands they had leased to the tenants, the latter organized peasant syndicates to resist the pressure of the landlords and received the help of the Communist Party in Cuzco. By this time the communists were already divided into two or more factions: one, the old guard of the party that did not believe in rural agitation, and second, the several factions of the New Left that appeared after the Castro revolution in Cuba, one of which, the Frente Izquierdista Revolucionario, was able to organize, under the direction of Hugo Blanco, a successful strike and armed takeover of some of the estates until defeated by the Peruvian police in 1963. Although the movement was a failure, it led to a more rapid, but still incomplete, application of the agrarian reform in the area during the governments of Pérez Godoy and Belaúnde. The failure of the movement for the revolutionaries of the left arose from the fact that while it was possible to organize the peasants for insurgence when they felt that their interests were threatened, they ceased to give support to the revolutionaries once they had secured their immediate gains. The uniqueness of the movement came from the fact that this was the first time that urban revolutionaries collaborated effectively with rural peasants. They failed, however, to bring about the revolution due to errors on the part of the revolutionaries operating in a very difficult geographical environment. A comparable revolutionary effort may be tried again, but the chances for success are slight due to the army's experience in counterinsurgency during the sixties, and even more because of the insulation from the left achieved by the revolutionary government.

These and other events in the rural highlands of Peru combined with the Peruvian economic crisis of the late sixties are said to have convinced the Peruvian army to assume the power of the state in 1968, this time not as a personalistic takeover by one powerful army leader, but as an institutional Revolutionary Government of the Armed Forces presided over by General Juan Velasco Alvarado. One of their more dramatic acts of revolution, after the takeover of the oilfields of the International Petroleum in the north, was the passing of a new Law of Agrarian Reform in 1969 and its immediate application for the transformation of the agrarian social structure of Peru. The new law introduced some drastic changes in the agrarian law passed by the government of President Belaúnde, which allowed the revolutionary government to proceed to the immediate expropriation of the sugar estates and refineries of the coast and many efficient cattle estates in the Central Highlands and the north. Expropriations in the more distant parts of the highlands were made at a slower pace and are yet far from complete, in spite of the fact that the government has set 1975 as the data when most of the transfer of the land to the workers of the land, that is, the rural proletarians of the coastal north and the peasants of the highlands, would take place. The many intricate political, economic, and administrative measures are explained in great detail by John Strasma ("Agrarian Reform") in Chaplin and by Colin Harding ("Land Reform and Social Conflict in Peru") in Lowenthal. They are very appropriately supplemented by the case studies of David S. Palmer and Kevin J. Middlebrook ("Corporatist Participation under Military Rule in Peru") in Chaplin and with Susan C. Bourque ("Transforming the Rural Sector: Government Policy and Peasant Response") in Lowenthal.

In brief, both Strasma and Harding deal with the revolutionary government's speed in applying the law in a forceful and imaginative way in the initial stages of the revolution, avoiding the development of conflicts. In spite of the complexity of the task, the legal aspects of the transfers were solved in such a manner that the sugar refineries continued to function and the productivity of the cattle and agricultural estates did not diminish the flow of goods to the food market of the coast. The expropriation of the estates was immediately followed by the granting of titles to the workers on the coast and to the peasants in the highlands, just as they were organized into cooperatives (CAP, Cooperativas Agrarias de Produccion) and societies (SAIS, Sociedad Agraria de Interes Social) to provide the technical and administrative support of the state that would maintain and increase the productivity of the land and avoid the fragmentation and chaos that a simple distribution of titles would have produced. From this picture of successful transformation carried out while the surprise and novelty qualities of the reforms were in operation, the revolutionary government enhanced considerably its prestige and arrived at a point of no turning back.

However, soon after the new organizations created by the government to secure the participation of the population were adopted, a series of crises and problems appeared in different parts of the country which treatened the reform process and produced impasses with the government or between groups. Although many of those conflicts could be attributed to traditional interests or conflict within the reform, many can be attributed to ambiguity between the ideological statements of the government and its frequency of intervention, together with the hopes and expectations of the populace to participate and secure certain advantages. Those aspects are well analyzed by David Scott Palmer and his two collaborators, Susan C Bourke and Kevin J. Middlebrook, when they study the government policies of reform and participation of the population as they are applied to the rural sector. The result of participation is that most of the decision tend to flow from the top down to the population, which is left with little power to influence the outcome and is frustrated in its expectations. So, when they cannot communicate their expectations or complaints through officials, the population takes recourse to "escape mechanisms" such as land invasions, strikes, marches, and violence to get the attention of the government elite.

While it could be argued up until 1971 that these conflicts emerged from the situational factors in these events, this interpretation cannot be defended after the revolutionary government made clear what it meant by "social participation" and formulated strategy for achieving this goal and the organism to implement its realization. In the National Development Plan, quoted by Palmer and Middlebrook, "social mobilization" is defined as "the process by which the emerging groups come to exercise a basic structural participation by gaining access to control of the society's key resources." "The responsibility of the state is 'to stimulate, channel, and consolidate' the participation of the people, arguing that '[our] people are relatively untrained and incapable of assuming fully and in the short run [their] responsibilities [under the present dynamics of change]'." This kind of statement is reminiscent of similar statements made by the army in the past.

The organism to carry out this policy is SINAMOS, defined as "The National System of Support for Social Mobilization," a vast organization of people trained to channel participation through persuasion in direct conversation with the population and in which, while formal organization is decentralized, all important decisions are made in a centralized and hierarchical manner. For Palmer and Middlebrook, "this tension between the ideological commitment to full citizen participation and the felt need to control each aspect of participation from the center is the major paradox in the revolutionary government's ideology of political participation" (p. 432, Chaplin). Therefore, irrespective of the ideological protests of the revolutionary government, the power of the state is strongly reinforced, and expectations of participation by the population in the important decisions continue to be extremely limited.

In summary, when one looks at the total policy carried out by the revolutionary government, it can be argued that reinforcement of the power of the state does not flow from the manifest goals given as a reason for the revolution, but from the tradition of military intervention with which we are familiar in the recent history of Peru, this time in an institutional form and with the intention of remaining in total control of power until their goals are achieved.

The nature of the movement and possible outcome are adequately summarized in Cotler's controversial essay, "The New Mode of Political Domination in Peru," which takes into account the novel and traditional elements of the process. Consistent with his theoretical orientation, Cotler sees the transformations effected by the revolutionary government, revolutionary as they are, not susceptible to producing the kind of revolution that would allow the participation of the Peruvian masses, but to introducing a "new mode" of domination: developing full capitalism with multinational corporations, thereby replacing traditional domination gained by control and structuring of popular participation. The main obstacle to achieving this goal comes from the fact that this attempt to order political relations in a corporative fashion (which Palmer and Middlebrook see as flowing from the Latin American "corporatist" tradition) has created conflict due to the limitations of participation imposed by the process and the frustration of expectations of redistribution, as well as the enormous variety of new situations created in the process itself. Cotler predicts that even with enormous control of the means of communication now commanded by the revolutionary government, the level of conflict will rise and force the adoption of "drastic measures" that will diminish the democracy of participation expressed i the ideology of the movement.

The nature of political events in Peru since 1974, when the governmen took over all independent newspapers in Lima, lends considerable validity to Cotler's assertions. Since that date, the government's policies have followed an unsteady course influenced by internal conflicts and the international economic picture. Given the magnitude of the task, the economic crises that followed forced successive monetary devaluation which in turn have precipitated riots in Lima, innumerable strike throughout the country, have made the revolutionary government mor concerned with the preservation of order, decelerating its revolutionar impetus and limiting further the democratic participation of the popula tion in the process.

—*Gabriel Escobar M.*
Department of Anthropology
Pennsylvania State University
University Park, PA 16802

NOTE

1. A more complete picture of events in the Central Highlands can be found in Giorgio Alberti y Rodrigo Sánchez, *Poder y Conflicto Social en la Sierra Central del Perú*, and Brian Roberts and Norman Long (eds.) *Peasant Cooperation and Underdevelopment in Central Peru* (University of Texas Press, Austin, forthcoming).

REFERENCES

ADAMS, R. N. (1959) "A community in the Andes: problems and progress in Muquiyauyo." Seattle: Univ. of Washington Press.

ESCOBAR M., G. (1968) "Sicaya: problems of cultural change in a community in the central highlands of Peru." Chicago: University Microfilm.

KUBLER, G. (1946) "The quechua in the colonial world," pp. 331-410, Vol. 2, in J. H. Steward (ed.) The Handbook of South American Indians. Washington, D.C.: Smithsonian Institution.

REVIEW ESSAY

AUTOBIOGRAPHY AND DECISION-MAKING IN MEXICAN POLITICS

Balboa, Práxedis. APUNTES DE MI VIDA. México: 1975.

Bremauntz, Alberto. SENTENTA ANOS DE MI VIDA. México: Ediciones Jurídicos Sociales, 1968.

Garrido, Luís. EL TIEMPO DE MI VIDA. México: Porrúa, 1974.

Rivera Silva, Manuel. PERSPECTIVAS DE UNA VIDA, BIOGRAFIA DE UNA GENERACION. México: Porrúa, 1974.

Silva Herzog, Jesús. UNA VIDA EN LA VIDA DE MEXICO. México: Siglo XXI, 1972.

Torres Bodet, Jaime. ANOS CONTRA EL TIEMPO. México: Porrúa, 1969.

---. LA TIERRA PROMETIDA. México: Porrúa, 1972.

---. EQUINOCCIO. México: Porrúa, 1974.

---. LA VICTORIA SIN ALAS. México: Porrúa, 1970.

Villaseñor, Eduardo. MEMORIAS-TESTIMONIO. México: Fondo de Cultura Económica, 1974.

Recently, the published memoirs of a number of retired public figures n Mexico have begun to appear, providing fascinating and insightful erspectives of Mexico's development since 1920. The seven authors have everal qualities in common: they were born in or close to the decade of 900-1910, all of them received university educations, and all have been rominent in public life since the 1930s.[1] On the whole, then, their memoirs view the myriad changes in Mexican culture from approximately 1910 until the 1960s from the point of view of seven men with middle- to high-level public careers but different personal and ideological viewpoints.

Most scholars have bemoaned the lack of numerous autobiographies by public men in Mexico which might give researchers a clearer perspective and more insight into the mysteries of the Mexican political system.[2] Although Mexican autobiographies have often tended to be apologies for controversial public careers, such as former Governor Braulio Maldonado's *Comentarios Políticos* (1960), they contain immensely useful interpretations of how personnel and policy decisions have been made in Mexico. Furthermore, as James W. Wilkie (1973: 9) recently noted, such works can contribute to the development of elitelore, which he describes as a "body of (a) self-perception; (b) self-organization of ideas about personal (as well as group) past; and (c) self-justification for actions through which a leader develops a meaningful life-history framework."

Historically, these works are all valuable because they contribute brief microhistory studies of the communities these men grew up in. Their recollections provide the same type of flavor of the times which the recently translated work of Luis González (1974), *Pueblo en vilo,* captures for the reader. Comparisons can be made among various regions and cities in Mexico as to the impact of certain events, such as the campaign or death of Francisco Madero, which, like González's microhistory of San José de Gracia, is discussed by Luis Garrido, who resided in Mexico City as a young man, by Alolfo Bremauntz, who was a student in Morelia, the capital of Michoacan, and by Jesus Silva Herzog, who was stirred as a young student when he first heard Madero speak the words "The People do not want bread, they want liberty" in a campaign speech in San Luis Potosi (p. 21). Others describe the cultural-social significance of the Revolution, suggesting that the educational and artistic works had a tremendous impact on their personal formation. Manuel Rivera Silva's work, which is subtitled "Biography of a Generation," is perhaps the best of these works in dealing with his own personal development from childhood through maturity, as a reflection of his generation. While it is more philosophical in tone and contributes little to our knowledge of Mexican politics, it contributes greatly to Mexican elitelore. Furthermore, it is the only work which covers the personal problems of adolescence and marriage in great detail. In fact, its emphasis is on youthful development rather than on the author's role or contributions to public life as a supreme court justice from 1958-1973. It is most useful as a picture of a middle-class, Mexico City youth growing up with the first post-Revolutionary generation of youths who have governed Mexico after the 1940s.

As each of these authors write about their activities as students, one can readily sense the importance of this experience on their future careers in public life, as well as the contribution of educational institutions in initiating successful public careers. All seven men were active in student intellectual and political activities. For example, Manuel Rivera Silva was a cofounder of *Barandal,* an intellectual publication of The National Preparatory School students; Jaime Torres Bodet was already distinguishing himself as a poet and writer among future literary figures as a member of the Ateneo de la Juventud in 1917 and in his later contributions to *Contemporaneos.* And Luis Garrido, who was student with Torres Bodet, was writing for student newspapers and was the cofounder of an intellectual society.[3] The other four writers were involved in student politics or a mixture of literary and political activities. Villaseñor and Bremauntz both were involved in the formation of the *San Nicolasito* group at the Colegio de San Nicolás in Morelia, while Silva Herzog participated in the campaign of a childhood friend for governor, and Balboa organized a student political group to support Calles in the 1923 campaign. All seven distinguished themselves in various activities before their public careers began, and this suggests why they were recruited into public life.

Friendships developed in secondary, preparatory, and university levels are often long-lasting and even critical in the careers of public men (Camp, 1974: 464). Such friendships become the basis for knowing the abilities of an individual and trusting him with an important public position, and they occur among students and between students and professors. Alberto Bremauntz, who attended one of the most notable regional universities, El Colegio de San Nicolás, describes Professor Jesús Romero Flores as his teacher, friend, and ideological comrade in arms (p. 51). They both became members of the influential political clique of Francisco J. Múgica, a cabinet member in the Cárdenas administration and precandidate for president of Mexico in 1939. Jesús Silva Herzog, a professor emeritus of the National University, describes how he selected his finest students to become collaborators in various positions he held throughout his lifetime (p. 86). He is responsible for initiating the careers of dozens of successful public men.

Once initiated into their public careers, the authors illustrate several salient points about the Mexican political process in their autobiographies. In reality, we have two general types of public careers among the seven authors: party-electoral and administrative-bureaucratic. Among the first category are Praxedis Balboa and Alfredo Bremauntz, both of whom were politically active for many years in their respective states of Tamaulipas and Michoacán, became identified with particular factions in those states, and held elective political offices. Their autobiographies are superb illustrations of the *camarillas* which are an integral part of the Mexican political process (Johnson, 1971). Bremauntz, on one hand, illustrates rather clearly how his association with a group has advanced his political career, with this identification later becoming a limiting factor as to advancement within the official party, and, on the other hand, Balboa presents a rather fascinating account of a young Mexican public figure who breaks with his powerful *camarilla* leader, Emilio Portes Gil, and how he suffers from but survives the intrigues of his former patron to wreck his political career. Balboa's book is a rather objective and revealing account of just how difficult, but possible, such a break is, and the techniques used by Portes Gil to prevent his appointment to important public posts (p. 174).[4]

The other authors are typical of a different category of career patterns followed by Mexicans in public life, the men who have emerged in top-ranked positions through years in the national bureaucracy. They too, illustrate the importance of political friendships established early in their careers. More important are the numerous examples from Villaseñor, Silva Herzog, and Torres Bodet, combined with illustrations from the careers of Balboa and Bremauntz, which provide some rather detailed examples of how persons are chosen for public office and by whom. Among the most persistent and nagging questions about the Mexican political system is how and by whom such decisions are made.

These autobiographies suggest three important qualities about personnel decision-making in Mexico. First, that persons holding middle and upper-level positions in the Mexican bureaucracy can be appointed by their immediate superior, the agency director, or the president of Mexico and that the pattern of personnel decision-making depends entirely upon the relationship between the president, the agency head, and the appointees. Second, long-term personal friendships are often responsible for a person being appointed or being brought to the attention of someone who has the power to make an appointment, but in most cases a person's ability and his appropriateness for the political environment are equally important. Third, administrative or political skills, rather than political friendships alone, appear to be most important for the careers of public men who repeat in high public office.

Who chooses high-level officials in Mexico? In a recent interview with a retired public official (June, 1975), the author was told that there are generally three patterns followed in the appointment of cabinet secretaries and their immediate subordinates: a person is a representative of an important political faction or a respected collaborator of a previous president, and does not have the personal confidence of the new president; the secretary is a personal friend of the president but is a compromise choice among several political groups who want their man in the post, and may not be particularly well qualified for the particular position; and last, the secretary is appointed because of his ability, and not because of political ties to the president or other groups. In the first case, if a president is unsure of his secretary, he may select the subsecretary himself, to watch over the activities of the secretary. In the second and third cases, the president may or may not select the subsecretary, but in most cases suggests someone for one of several top positions while giving the secretary complete freedom to select the others. Undoubtedly, as Daniel Cosío Villegas (1975) makes clear in his recent book on the presidential succession in Mexico, the president has the power to make these decisions, but, as numerous public officials have suggested to the author in interviews, he does not personally know enough capable persons to fill such posts.

For example, Jaime Torres Bodet was surprised to learn that President Manuel Avila Camacho appointed him Subsecretary of Foreign Relations in 1940. As he makes clear in *Equinoccio,* the president did not know him and he was appointed at the suggestion of the new Secretary of Foreign Relations, Ezequiel Padilla, a friend since 1921 (p. 241). This example also suggests that Padilla had the confidence of Avila Camacho in order to select his own collaborators. Another example at this same level, although even more extreme in the extent of decision-making power given to a cabinet secretary, is Jesús Silva Herzog's appointment as Subsecretary of Public Education by Narciso Bassols, Secretary under President Abelardo Rodríguez. "Eight days after I agreed to be subsecretary, I asked him if President Rodríguez knew about my appointment. Bassols told me: 'What a barbarity, I forgot.' He picked up the phone of the secret [government] system and spoke with the President requesting that he be permitted to designate Professor Silva Herzog, *oficial mayor* of the secretariat, subsecretary. A minute passed, he hung up the phone: 'It is arranged' " (p. 41).

To illustrate our point that appointments at various levels depend upon the relationship between the concerned parties, let us look at the foreign service, for which we have several examples from different autobiographies. In 1931, when Eduardo Villaseñor was director of the consular department, the Secretary of Foreign Relations called him and asked him to recommend the most efficient consul on the basis of his reports to Villaseñor. He recommended the Mexican consul to Japan, who he did not know personally. That person was Manuel Tello, who was appointed Secretary of the Mexican Delegation to the United Nations, and later rose to the office of Secretary of Foreign Relations (p. 81). Torres Bodet (1974: 248) indicates that during the first twelve months he served as Subsecretary of Foreign Relations, that ambassadors were selected by the secretary in consultation with the president. However, by 1942, after he had earned the respect of the president, he was asked to recommend someone to serve as minister to the USSR, which he did, and his recommendation was approved (p. 314).

Cabinet-level appointments vary with the relationship of the decision-makers. We can cite the appointment of Jaime Torres Bodet in mid-term (1943) to the secretaryship of Public Education. In this particular situation, Torres Bodet as well as his subsecretary were chosen personally by the president of Mexico, but Torres Bodet himself selected his other collaborators, including his oficial mayor. Later, when Torres Bodet was appointed Secretary of Foreign Relations, he prevailed in the selection of his subsecretary, but the president appointed his oficial mayor (Bodet, 1970: 17).

An example of the interplay of friendship, ability, and political environment in the selection of a person to an important post is revealed in *La Tierra Prometida* by Torres Bodet, when President Adolfo López Mateos asks him who should head the controversial Free Textbook Commission. When Torres Bodet suggested Martin Luis Guzmán, the president replied that he knew his abilties, admired him greatly, but thought him too pugnacious for the position and asked for another name. Torres Bodet argued for his first choice, and explained why he felt he was the best qualified person for the position (pp. 243-244). In this case the president finally agreed, but the example illustrates that the president, despite a close personal friendship and respect for Guzmán, considered other factors as well.

Of the seven authors, the most successful in public life, but the least political, is Torres Bodet. Beginning with his appointment as Secretary of Public Education, in 1943, it becomes apparent that he is reappointed continually to high offices by three presidents because of his intellectual and administrative abilities, not because he knew them well or because he represented a particular political group. Even Praxedis Balboa's arduous fight back to the top of public life as a subdirector of Premex is made possible by his knowledge and skills in that field, rather than any political friendships. It is also clear that had he not had powerful political enemies, or had more numerous political friends, he would have succeeded more quickly. As President Ruiz Cortines allegedly told Governor Braulio Maldonado, "Look Braulio, if you had not been popular nor were politically strong in your state, even though you are my friend, we wouldn't have designated you the candidate." Alberto Bremauntz also notes that despite his support of Francisco J. Múgica for president of Mexico in 1939-1940, Avila Camacho, his opponent and the successful candidate, reappointed him as a Justice of the Superior Court of the Federal District and Territories (p. 123).

Although the autobiographies reveal a considerable number of examples of how personnel decisions are made in Mexico, they also supply, to a lesser extent, some insights into who was responsible for various decisions, and, in particular, the relationships between decision makers. For example, in *Años Contra el Tiempo,* we see how president Avila Camacho used some of Torres Bodet's answers to important foreign policy questions verbatim (p. 64), how at certain periods in Mexican administrative history there has been coordination among various cabinet agencies (p. 200), or the role of subsecretaries and secretaries in budget making. In *Una Vida en la Vida de México,* we are given a rather clear picture of how deans and rectors are chosen, and the relationship between the president and the rector of the National University (pp. 243, 327). *Apuntes de mi Vida* is extremely informative on the politics of decision-making between the government and the unions (pp. 46ff.). In sum, these books offer many unknown facts to support various interpretations of the Mexican political process.

For example, several of these autobiographies illustrate, in part, the Purcells' explanation of why Mexican economic decision-making is arbitrary: "Security in the Mexican social system tends to derive from vertical, patron-client relationships rather than from horizontal ties of common interest or universally applied legal and individual rights" (Purcell, 1973: 38; Purcell and Purcell, 1975: 21). They also provide firsthand information on the subject of Peter Smith's (1974) work on mobility and continuity among political elites. Hopefully, public men will be encouraged to continue writing memoirs which increasingly will fill gaps in our understanding of contemporary Mexico.

–*Roderic A. Camp*
Department of Political Science
Central College
Pella, IA 50219

NOTES

1. Briefly, they have held the following important public offices: Praxedis Balboa, Federal Deputy from Tamaulipas, 1928-1930, 1930-1932, 1934-1936; Subdirector of Pemex, 1952-1963; Governor of Tamaulipas, 1963-1969. Alberto Bremauntz, Mayor of Morelia, 1929; Federal Deputy from Michoacán, 1932-1934; Justice of the Federal Tribunal of Justice of the Federal District and Federal Territories, 1935-1963. Luis Garrido, Director General of *Seguros de México,* S.A., 1939-1947; Rector of the National University, 1948-1952. Manuel Rivera Silva, Director General of Social Welfare, Secretariat of Labor, 1952-1958; Justice of the Supreme Court, 1958-1973. Jesús Silva Herzog, Minister to the Soviet Union, 1928-1930; Subsecretary of Public Education, 1933-1934; General Manager of Pemex, 1939-1940; Subsecretary of the Treasury, 1945-1946. Jaime Torres Bodet, Subsecretary of Foreign Relations, 1940-1943, Secretary of Foreign Relations, 1946-1948; Ambassador to France, 1953-1958; Secretary of Public Education, 1958-1964. Eduardo Villaseñor, Director General of the Agricultural Credit Bank, 1936-1938; Subsecretary of the Treasury, 1938-1940; Director General of the Bank of Mexico, 1940-1946.

2. An important contribution which complements recent written autobiographies is the work of James W. Wilkie and Enda Monzón de Wilkie (1969), in their oral interviews with prominent Mexicans.

3. Jaime Torres Bodet published five autobiographies before his death in 1974. In a letter to the author dated August 1, 1972, he suggested that the period dealing with his youth was covered in an earlier autobiographical work called *Tiempo de Arena* (1955), which is one of the essays in his selected works published by Fondo de Cultura Econónica (1961). We have reviewed only four of the later volumes, since the fifth volume, *El Desierto Internacional,* deals with his years as Secretary General of UNESCO, which is outside the general topic of this review.

4. Balboa's book is the first of two volumes, covering his life until 1952. His second volume, which is forthcoming, will deal with his career from 1952 through his years as Governor of Tamaulipas.

REFERENCES

CAMP, R. A. (1974) "Mexican governors since Cárdenas, education and career contacts." JIAS (November): 454-481.

COSIO VILLEGAS, D. (1975) La Sucesión presidencial. México: Joaquín Mortiz.

GONZALEZ, L. (1972) Pueblo en vilo. México, D.F.: El Colegio de México. English translation (1974). San José de Gracia, Mexican Village in Transition. Austin: Univ. of Texas Press.

JOHNSON, K. F. (1971) Mexican Democracy: A Critical View. Boston: Allyn & Bacon.

MALDONADO, B. (1960) Baja California: Comentarios Políticos. México: Costa Amic.

PURCELL, S. K. (1973) "Decision-making in an authoritarian regime: theoretical implications from a Mexican case study." World Politics (October): 28-54.

PURCELL, J.F.H. and S. K. PURCELL (1975) "Mexican business and public polity." (To appear in a book edited by James Malloy on authoritarianism and corporatism in Latin America, Pittsburgh University Press.)

SMITH, P. H. (1974) "Making it in Mexico: aspects of political mobility since 1946." Amer. Pol. Sci. Association.

WILKIE, J. W. (1973) Elitelore. Los Angeles, Latin American Center, UCLA.

--- and E. M. de WILKIE (1969) México Visto en el Siglo XX. México, D.F.: Instituto Mexicano de Investigaciones Económicas.

BOOKS RECEIVED

GENERAL AND REGIONAL LATIN AMERICA

Adams, Richard N. CULTURAL SURVEYS OF PANAMA-NICARAGUA-GUATEMALA-EL SALVADOR-HONDURAS. Detroit: Blaine Ethride Books, 1976 (reprint of 1957 edition, Pan American Sanitary Bureau, World Health Organization). 669 pp. $35.00.

Ambrosi, Luis Alberto Musso. URUGUAY-BRASIL Y SUS MEDALLAS. Montevideo: Instituto de Cultura Uruguayo-Brasileño, 1976. Indices, Bibliografía. 195 pp. (paper).

Hanson, Carl A. DISSERTATIONS ON IBERIAN AND LATIN AMERICAN HISTORY: AN INTERDISCIPLINARY BIBLIOGRAPHY OF DISSERTATIONS COMPLETED IN THE UNITED STATES, GREAT BRITAIN, CANADA, AND IRELAND, 1889-1969. Troy, NY: Whitston Publishing Co., Inc., 1976. Notes, addendum, author index. 400 pp. $20.00.

Lomnitz, Larissa A. de. COMO SOBREVIVEN LOS MARGINADOS. México, D.F.: Siglo veintiuno editores, S.A., 1975. Bibliografía. 229 pp. (paper).

Lyday, Leon F. and George W. Woodyard. A BIBLIOGRAPHY OF LATIN AMERICAN THEATER CRITICISM 1940-1974. Guides and Bibliographies Series 10. Austin: Institute of Latin American Studies, University of Texas Press, 1976. Bibliographies, index. xvii, 243 pp. $5.95 (paper).

Malloy, James M., ed. AUTHORITARIANISM AND CORPORATISM IN LATIN AMERICA. Pittsburgh: University of Pittsburgh Press, 1977. Bibliographical notes, selected bibliography, index. 549 pp. $19.95 (cloth), $5.95 (paper).

Naciones Unidas. ESTUDIO ECONOMICO DE AMERICA LATINA, 1974. México: Comisión Económica para América Latina, 1975. 375 pp. $12.00 paper.

Silvert, Kalman H. and Leonard Reissman. EDUCATION, CLASS AND NATION: THE EXPERIENCES OF CHILE AND VENEZUELA. New York: Elsevier Scientific Publishing Co., Inc., 1976. Appendix, notes, index. xvi, 242 pp. $12.95.

Zea, Leopoldo. FILOSOFIA Y CULTURA LATINOAMERICANAS. With SINTESIS INFORMATIVA. Caracas: Centro de Estudios Latinoamericanos "Rómulo Gallegos," Colección Repertorio Americano, 1976. 228 pp. and 30 pp. (paper).

COUNTRIES OF LATIN AMERICA

ARGENTINA

Archivo Histórico de la Provincia de Buenos Aires "Ricardo Levene." MENSAJES DE LOS GOBERNADORES DE LA PROVINCIA DE BUENOS AIRES 1822-1849, Volumenes 1 y 11. La Plata, Argentina: Provincia de Buenos Aires, Ministerio de Educación, 1976. Indice. Vol. I, 301 pp., Vol. II, 286 pp.

BRAZIL

IBGE (Fundação Instituto Brasileiro de Geografia e Estatística). SINOPSE ESTATISTICA DO BRASIL 1975 (Statistical Abstract of Brazil). Portuguese and English. Rio de Janeiro: Fundação Instituto Brasileiro de Geografia e Estatística, 1976. Paper.

REVISTA DE ANTROPOFAGIA. Introdução de Augusto de Campos. Reedição da Revista Literária Publicada em São Paulo 1ª e 2ª "Dentições" 1928-29. São Paulo: Editora Abril Ltda. e da Metal Leve S/A., 1975. 94 pp. + 16 pp. newspaper page copies.

CARIBBEAN REGION

Demas, William G. ESSAYS ON CARIBBEAN INTEGRATION AND DEVELOPMENT. With an introduction by Alister McIntyre. Jamaica: Institute of Social and Economic Research, University of the West Indies, 1976. References, index. ix 159 pp. J$6.50 paper.

Jainarain, Iserdeo. TRADE AND UNDERDEVELOPMENT: A STUDY OF THE SMALL CARIBBEAN COUNTRIES AND LARGE MULTINATIONAL CORPORATIONS. Guyana: Institute of Development Studies, University of Guyana 1976. List of tables, note on currency units, appendix, bibliography. xvi, 390 pp

Perez, Louis A., Jr. THE CUBAN REVOLUTIONARY WAR, 1953-1958: A BIBLIOGRAPHY. Metuchen, NJ: Scarecrow Press, 1976. ix, 225 pp. $9.00.

Quintero Rivera, Angel. WORKERS' STRUGGLE IN PUERTO RICO: A DOCUMENTARY HISTORY (translated by Cedric Belfrage). New York and London Monthly Review Press, 1976. Appendix, notes, bibliography. 236 pp. $11.95.

Souza, Raymond D. MAJOR CUBAN NOVELISTS: INNOVATION AND TRADITION. Columbia: University of Missouri Press, 1976. Bibliography. ix, 120 pp $10.00.

CENTRAL AMERICA

Looney, Robert E. THE ECONOMIC DEVELOPMENT OF PANAMA: THE IMPACT OF WORLD INFLATION ON AN OPEN ECONOMY. New York: Praeger Publishers, 1976. List of tables, appendix, bibliography, index. xiii, 248 pp.

CHILE

Cori, Osvaldo, ed. LAS CIENCIAS NATURALES EN CHILE: VISION CRITICA Y PERSPECTIVAS. No. 36. Santiago: Corporación de Promoción Universitaria, 1976. 183 pp. (paper).

von Wolff, Manfred Wilehlmy. DOCENCIA–INVESTIGACION–EXTENSION: SOBRE INTEGRACION ANDINA EN LA UNIVERSIDADES DEL AREA. No. 37. Seminario Andino 1975. Santiago: Corporación de Promoción Universitaria, 1976. 195 pp. (paper).

COLOMBIA

Cepeda Ulloa, Fernando and Claudia González de Lecaros. COMPORTAMIENTO DEL VOTO URBANO EN COLOMBIA: UNA APPROXIMACION. Bogotá: Universidad de los Andes, 1976. 61 pp. (paper).

Flora, Cornelia Butler. PENTECOSTALISM IN COLOMBIA: BAPTISM BY FIRE AND SPIRIT. Cranbury, NJ: Fairleigh Dickinson University Press, 1976. Tables, figures, appendices, bibliography, index. 288 pp. $13.50.

MEXICO

Carrasco, Pedro, Johanna Broda, et al. ESTRATIFICACION SOCIAL EN LA MESOAMERICA PREHISPANICA. México, D.F.: Centro de Investigaciones Superiores, Instituto Nacional de Antropología e Historia, SEPINAH, 1976. Notas, siglas, bibliografía, índice. 301 pp. (paper).

Carrasco P., Pedro and Jesus Monjaras-Ruiz. COLECCION DE DOCUMENTOS SOBRE COYOACAN. Volúmen Primero. México, D.F.: Instituto Nacional de Antropología e Historia (Centro de Investigaciones Superiores), 1976. No. 39, Colección Científica. Indice. 252 pp. (paper).

Caso, Alfonso. THIRTEEN MASTERPIECES OF MEXICAN ARCHAEOLOGY. Translated by Edith Mackie and Jorge R. Acosta. Detroit: Blaine Ethridge Books, 1976 (reprint of 1938 edition, Editoriales Cultura y Polis, Mexico). 131 pp. $11.00.

Chapman, Samuel. THE POSTAGE STAMPS OF MEXICO. (From the commencent in 1856, to the end of the provisional period in 1868.) Published under the auspices of the Collectors' Club, New York City as Handbook Number 4 (reprint of 1926 edition). Lawrence, MA: Quarterman Publications, Inc., 1976. Appendices. xxxi, 376 pp.

Cosío Villegas, Daniel. MEMORIAS. Mexico, D.F.: Joaquin Mortiz, 1976. Indice de nombres, índice. 320 pp. (paper).

Dennis, Philip Adams. CONFLICTOS POR TIERRAS EN EL VALLE DE OAXACA. Mexico, D.F.: Instituto Nacional Indigenista, Colección SEPTINI, Número 45, 1976. Notas, bibliografía. 239 pp.

Martínez Saldaña, Tomás y Leticia Gándara Mendoza. POLITICA Y SOCIEDAD EN MEXICO: EL CASO DE LOS ALTOS DE JALISCO. Presentación de Gustavo del Castillo V. México, D.F.: Centro de Investigaciones Superiores, Instituto Nacional de Antropología e Historia, SEPINAH, 1976. Bibliografía, índice. 289 pp. (paper).

Molina, Virginia. SAN BARTOLOME DE LOS LLANOS: UNA URBANIZACION FRENADA. México, D.F.: Centro de Investigaciones Superiores, Instituto Nacional de Antropología e Historia, SEPINAH, 1976. Appendices, bibliografía, índice. 239 pp. (paper).

Mols, Manfred and Hans Werner Tobler. MEXIKO: DIE INSTITUTIONALISIERTE REVOLUTION. Bohlau Verlag, 1976. Glossary. 235 pp.

Novela, Victoria. ARTESANIAS Y CAPITALISMO EN MEXICO. Mexico, D.F.: Centro de Investigaciones Superiores, Instituto Nacional de Antropología e Historia. Bibliografía, índice. 270 pp. (paper).

Ojeda, Mario. ALCANCES Y LIMITES DE LA POLITICA EXTERIOR DE MEXICO. México, D.F.: Colección Centro de Estudios Internacionales XVII, El Colegio de México, 1976. Bibliografía, índice de cuadros. 220 pp. (paper).

Ramírez, José Fernando. MEMORIA ACERCA DE LAS OBRAS E INUNDACIONES EN LA CIUDAD DE MEXICO. Introducción y notas de Teresa Rojas R. México, D.F.: Centro de Investigaciones Superiores, Instituto Nacional de Antropología e Historia, SEPINAH, 1976. Prólogo, notas, anexo, índice. 254 pp. (paper).

VENEZUELA

Martz, John D. and Enrique A. Baloyra. ELECTORAL MOBILIZATION AND PUBLIC OPINION: THE VENEZUELAN CAMPAIGN OF 1973. Chapel Hill: University of North Carolina Press, 1976. Abbreviations, notes, bibliography, index. xxvi, 339 pp. $17.95.

MONTALBAN, No. 5. Caracas; Universidad Católica Andrés Bello, 1976. Biblio-grafía. 1151 pp. (paper).

MISCELLANEOUS

COMMUNICATING THE SOCIOECONOMIC IMPACT OF MULTINATIONAL CORPORATIONS IN DEVELOPING COUNTRIES. New York: Council of th Americas, 1976. Appendices. 95 pp. $4.50 (paper).

Dorn, Georgette M., compiler. LATIN AMERICA, SPAIN, AND PORTUGAL: AN ANNOTATED BIBLIOGRAPHY OF PAPERBACK BOOKS. Washington, D.C. Library of Congress, Hispanic Foundation Bibliographical Series No. 14, 1976 (second revised edition). 323 pp. $3.00. (paper).

Unesco. MOVING TOWARDS CHANGE: SOME THOUGHTS ON THE NEW INTERNATIONAL ECONOMIC ORDER. Paris: Unesco, 1976. Appendix. 13 pp. $4.00. (paper).

University Center for International Studies, University of Pittsburgh. UNITED STATES POLITICAL SCIENCE DOCUMENTS. Pittsburgh: University Center fo International Studies, University of Pittsburgh, 1976. Part 1, Indexes: 798 pp Part 2, Document Descriptions. 555 pp. (paper).

Williams, Maurice J. DEVELOPMENT CO-OPERATION: EFFORTS AND POLICIE OF THE MEMBERS OF THE DEVELOPMENT ASSISTANCE COMMITTEE 1976 Review. Paris: OECD, 1976. Tables and charts, annex. 271 pp. (paper).

MIGRATION AND ADAPTATION:

Tzintzuntzan Peasants in Mexico City

by ROBERT V. KEMPER, *Anthropology, Southern Methodist University*

A new study presenting a description and analysis of rural migrants and their adaptation to life in a rapidly growing metropolitan setting, this volume deals with a microcosm of Mexican urbanization: emigration from the traditional peasant village of Tzintzuntzan, Michoacán to Mexico City. Professor Kemper reports on the background of the migrants as well as on their cultural and social adjustments to an urban environment. A model of rural-urban migration applicable to similar populations in other developing nations is also presented and will be of interest to anthropologists and urban specialists involved in a variety of disciplines.

CONTENTS

Preface
Part I. Rural Background
1. **The Modernization of Tzintzuntzan**
2. **Emigration from Tzintzuntzan**

Part II. The Urban Setting
3. **Mexico City as Destination**
4. **The Migrants: Population and Mobility**

Part III. Urban Adaptation
5. **Household and Family Organization**
6. **Economic Organization**
7. **Social Organization**

Part IV. Conclusion
8. **Migration and Adaptation**

Appendix: A Personal Perspective on the Fieldwork
References Cited

"Tzintzuntzan is especially well suited for a microcosmic study of the emigration process. On the one hand, since the bulk of the emigration is recent, we can deal with real people, and not simply with statistics. And these people are known, as are their families, their socioeconomic status, and their histories, to an extent not normally the case."

— *from Chapter 1*

Volume 43 Sage Library of Social Research **ISBN 0-8039-0687-0 cloth $11.00**
April 1977 **224 pages** **ISBN 0-8039-0688-9 paper $ 6.00**

SAGE PUBLICATIONS, INC.
275 South Beverly Drive
Beverly Hills, California 90212

SAGE PUBLICATIONS LTD
St George's House / 44 Hatton Garden
London EC1N 8ER

Vol. 19 No. 3
August 1977

OURNAL OF NTERAMERICAN TUDIES

nd ORLD AFFAIRS

A Publication of the Center for Advanced International Studies,
The University of Miami

SAGE PUBLICATIONS

Journal of INTERAMERICAN STUDIES and WORLD AFFAIRS

The editors and publisher wish to acknowledge with gratitude the assistance and encouragement of the Center for Advanced International Studies, University of Miami, in providing ancillary services and support for this journal.

Journal of
INTERAMERICAN
STUDIES
and WORLD AFFAIRS

Vol. 19
No. 3
August
1977

CONTENTS

Higher Education and the Politics of Development in Venezuela
ORLANDO ALBORNOZ 291

Conflict and Mediation in a Latin American University
LARISSA LOMNITZ 315

Government Expenditures and Political Change in Brazil, 1880-1899: Who Got What
RICHARD GRAHAM 339

Fertility Decline and Socioeconomic Change in Venezuela
BARRY EDMONSTON
FRANK Wm. OECHSLI 369

Costa Rica and the 1920-1921 Union Movement: A Reassessment
RICHARD V. SALISBURY 393

REVIEW ESSAYS

The Surrogate Americans
CLAUDIO VELIZ 419

Spatial Planning and Development in Latin America: The Critical Approach
FERNANDO KUSNETZOFF 429
Translation by MARJORY MATTINGLY URQUIDI

BOOKS RECEIVED 445

SAGE PUBLICATIONS / *Beverly Hills* *London*

POLICY: THE JOURNAL OF INTERAMERICAN STUDIES AND WORLD AFFAIRS reflects the interests of the scholarly community and interested public concerned with the social, economic, political, and cultural aspects of life in Latin America (including the Caribbean); particularly in those instances where the subject is of concern to more than one of the traditional disciplines. As these concerns change, so will the content of the journal.

ARTICLES which have special relevance for interrelationships between American nations and of those nations with the rest of the world will be given special consideration. An effort will be made to include occasional articles that state an unusual or even discordant position on a subject of broad interest to be supplemented by critical comments of authorities representing differing positions on the topic. The editors continue to welcome articles by scholars from all parts of the world.

MANUSCRIPTS should be submitted in duplicate to: Editor, JOURNAL OF INTERAMERICAN STUDIES AND WORLD AFFAIRS, Box 24-8134, University of Miami, Coral Gables, Florida 33124. Manuscripts should be typewritten, double-spaced, with footnotes, references, tables, and charts on separate pages, and should follow the current journal style. A brief biographical paragraph describing each author's current affiliation, research interests, and recent publications should accompany the manuscript.

CORRESPONDENCE regarding book reviews should be sent directly to: Book Review Editor, JOURNAL OF INTERAMERICAN STUDIES AND WORLD AFFAIRS, Box 24-8134, University of Miami, Coral Gables, Florida 33124.

JOURNAL OF INTERAMERICAN STUDIES AND WORLD AFFAIRS is published four times annually—in February, May, August, and November.

Subscriptions: Regular institutional rate $26.00. Individuals may subscribe at a one-year rate of $15.00. Add $1.00 per year for subscriptions outside the United States. Orders from U.K., Europe, the Middle East, and Africa should be sent to the London office (address below). Noninstitutional orders **must** be paid by personal check.

Second-class postage paid at Beverly Hills, California.

Inquiries: Address all correspondence and permissions requests to SAGE PUBLICATIONS, INC., 275 South Beverly Drive, Beverly Hills, California 90212. Inquiries and subscriptions from U.K., Europe, the Middle East, and Africa should be sent to SAGE PUBLICATIONS LTD, 28 Banner Street, London EC1Y 8QE, England. Other orders should be sent to the Beverly Hills office.

Advertising: Current rates and specifications may be obtained by writing to the Advertising Manager at the Beverly Hills office (address above).

This journal is abstracted in **Historical Abstracts, Human Resources Abstracts, Sage Urban Studies Abstracts,** and **International Political Science Abstracts.** It is indexed in **Public Affairs Information Service, Current Contents, Social Sciences Citation Index, Social Sciences Index,** and **ABC POL SCI.**

Back Issues: Information about availability and prices of back issues may be obtained from the publisher's order department (address above). Write to London office for sterling prices.

Claims for undelivered copies must be made no later than three months following month of publication. The publisher will supply missing copies when losses have been sustained in transit and where the reserve stock will permit.

Change of Address: Six weeks' advance notice must be given when notifying of change of address. Please send old address label along with the new address to insure proper identification. Please specify name of journal.

ORLANDO ALBORNOZ
Instituto Societas
Torres Andres Bello
Piso 15–Apartado 50.061
Caracas 105, Venezuela

HIGHER EDUCATION AND THE POLITICS OF DEVELOPMENT IN VENEZUELA

Since the end of World War II, nations have been characterized according to membership in various international power blocs, the Western World being used for capitalist countries and the Iron Curtain for socialist ones. Within these categories countries are also characterized according to level of economic (and sometimes political) development. The capitalist world recognizes two types of nations, the developed and the underdeveloped. In contrast, the socialist world presents a single development model characterized by centralized planning and homogeneous development.

Analyses of Latin American development produced two theories. One, worked out by the Economic Commission for Latin America (ECLA), explains underdevelopment in terms of failure to reach a certain minimum level, as measured by particular indicators that are a precondition for further progress toward that optimum level enjoyed by the developed countries. The other, the dependency theory, explains underdevelopment as a function of the relations between Latin America and the large multinational companies dominated by North American capitalist centers.

Journal of Interamerican Studies and World Affairs, Vol. 19 No. 3, August 1977

Within the framework of the ECLA theory of development, Venezuela is defined as an underdeveloped nation with unusual potential when compared with the rest of Latin America, thanks to the financial resources derived from her oil revenue. From the point of view of the dependency theory, however, Venezuela's situation is similar to that of all Latin American countries, i.e., characterized by dependence upon North America, to a greater or lesser extent, in the fields of economics, politics, science, technology, and culture. Precisely because Venezuela *has* greater financial resources than her neighbors, she is more involved with the international and North American markets, more vulnerable to outside influences, and displays an even greater dependency.

Dependence has been defined as a situation in which the economy of certain countries is conditioned by the development and expansion of another economy. An interdependent relationship between two or more economies, and between these and the world market, assumes the form of dependence when some of the countries (the dominant ones) can expand in accordance with their own wishes, whereas the other countries (the dependent ones) can act only as a reflection of that expansion, actions which may or may not be to their advantage. As a result, the dependent countries are at the mercy of the exploitative powers of the dominant countries, a situation which hinders the full release of the productive forces within the dependent society. In this sense we may say that the phenomenon of dependence produces a process of "denationalization," wherein planning in the national interest of the dependent country is discouraged, if not obstructed, in favor of the national interest of the dominant country. Venezuela fits this definition well, for it is highly dependent upon outside centers of domination which are not Latin American. This is also true of the rest of Latin America, which makes it unable to offer any countervailing force (Cardoso and Faletto, 1969; Cardoso, 1971; Ianni, 1970; Jaguaribe et al., 1969; Ribeiro, 1971; Frank, Cockroft and Johnson, 1970; Hinkelanmert, 1970; Garcia, 1969; Dos Santos, 1969).

Faced with this situation, Venezuela nationalized its basic resources, oil and iron, on the assumption that when the country had direct control of these two basic products, greater national growth would be fostered. In taking the decision to nationalize, Venezucla might well have been hearkening to Henry Kissinger, who, in March 1975 in Milwaukee, suggested that it was the countries of the Third World who were themselves responsible for solving their own problems, and who rejected the idea that the poverty and backwardness of the countries in this region were a consequence of the policies of the developed nations. He said, on that occasion: "Either societies create the conditions for saving and investment, for innovation and ingenuity, for enterprise and industry which ultimately lead to self-sustaining growth, or they do not. There is no magical short cut and no rhetorical substitute. And to claim otherwise suggests need for permanent dependence on others" (Time, 28 July, 1975).

Nationalization, however, could be only a partial panacea at best, for Venezuela suffers from another dependency of potential volatility: the dependency of its economy upon a single product, oil. Venezuela is a country with an enormous fiscal revenue which has increased remarkably, thanks to rises in the price of oil. This is borne out by a brief analysis of the national budget, the best indicator of an economy in which the state is the most powerful agent. Table 1 illustrates the variations in the national budget over the last decade, particularly the startling increase which occurred in 1974, and the decline, already of some relative importance, for the following year. Table 2 indicates the share that oil revenue has within the total income for the national budget and the degree to which this share has increased in recent years, from 66 percent of the total income in 1965 to 84 percent in 1975 (this last a slight drop-off from 1974).

One might conclude that this situation offers potential for great disequilibrium; the distortions brought about by the weighty budgets of the last few years present a false prosperity which may produce a severe crisis of readjustment in the near future.

TABLE 1
The National Budget 1965-1975, Real Income
(figures in millions of bolivars)

Year	Amount	Percentage Increase
1965	7.376	--
1966	7.961	7.92
1967	8.678	9.14
1968	9.159	5.54
1969	9.677	5.65
1970	10.252	5.95
1971	12.122	18.24
1972	12.546	3.49
1973	16.433	30.98
1974	42.833	260.65
1975	40.550	(-6.44)

SOURCE: Banco Central de Venezuela.

One might also conclude that Venezuela is a rich country, judging by the life style of the dominant members of its society who obtain a favorable share of the distribution of wealth generated by the exploitation of oil, but who really represent only an enclave of wealth in a country of poverty. At the present time Venezuela cannot boast of an industrial economy which might eventually replace the income derived from oil, and, what is even more alarming, its economic structure is not capable of feeding or providing essential services for its growing population.

Utilizing the enormous financial resources at its disposal, Venezuela has gone through a series of remarkable changes in the last 30 years so that it now possesses an infrastructure of industry, trade, and services which compares very favorably with other countries in the area. Nevertheless, this very infrastructure cannot be maintained indefinitely in the future. Once this extraordinary income has been disposed of, there is no alternative source of exportable wealth likely to produce a similar income. National industry is still small. Agricultura

TABLE 2
The Changing Place of Oil Revenues in Relation to Other Income in the National Budget
(figures in millions of bolivars)

Year		Amount	Percentage Increase	Percentage of Total Income
1965		4.826	--	66
1966		4.992	3.44	64
1967		5.717	14.52	66
1968		5.836	2.08	66
1969		5.483	(-6.44)	63
1970		5.774	5.30	60
1971		7.760	34.39	66
1972		7.966	2.65	65
1973		11.272	41.50	70
1974		36.813	326.59	86
1975	(est)	34.268	(-6.42)	84

SOURCE: Banco Central de Venezuela.

goods have to be imported, and trade is basically one of importation. The enormous fiscal resources have aided the development of a state bureaucracy. Individuals and groups have become wealthy, thanks to the management of public funds, but that does not mean that there is a bourgeoisie. The bourgeoisie, as a social class, is a productive class, and, instead, Venezuela has acquired a consumer state bureaucracy.

The extent of this recent wealth has also had an effect upon the population and demography of Venezuela. Its population is expanding at the rate of 3.7 percent a year, one of the highest rates in the world. Parts of this growth can be attributed to Venezuela's reputation for wealth, which has attracted immigrants from neighboring countries, those people described as "*indocumentada*" (without documents). According to various estimates, these migrants may comprise around one million of Venezuela's 12 million inhabitants. Up to the present, Venezuela's population exhibits certain characteristics which have not, in the short run, changed much: a high fertility, a predominantly youthful population, a rapid rise in internal population movements, accelerated urbanization, and a high concentration of population which has produced densely populated nuclear areas as opposed to vast "empty spaces" (Dos Santos, 1969: 180).

The most outstanding feature accompanying this growth is the distortion caused by the process of urbanization, so great, in fact, that a large proportion of the total population is amassed in and around the capital, Caracas. The concentration of population in Caracas is going to cause a disequilibrium which will have important consequences for the future of the country. From the sociological point of view it is easy to foresee some of these consequences, above all, that of the problem of "marginality." By that we mean the presence of vast sectors of the population who live around the great urban centers of the country in inadequate dwellings, and who are marginal to the general economic and social activity of those urban areas.

It is worth emphasizing the problem of marginality, because each day this process generates an uprooting of rural life and a corresponding concentration in the urban areas, processes one might reasonably assume to be irreversible. The marginal population derives from two different sources: the rural zones of Venezuela, and the invasion of other rural populations during the last half dozen years from neighboring countries, mainly Colombia, but also from Ecuador and Peru. It is appropriate to point out that this immigration from abroad does not consist solely of marginal population, but also includes a substantial number of professionals from these countries of the Cono Sur. They become assimilated into Venezuelan society, bringing with them their expertise, even when this is an expertise which Venezuela already possesses, and which is inappropriate. In quantitative terms, this immigration of professionals does not join the marginal sector, but the middle class.

Nearly a fourth of Venezuela's 12 million population is concentrated in metropolitan Caracas, where approximately one million of the inhabitants can be characterized as marginal. That this pattern of marginality is even more marked in other urban centers throughout the country is well illustrated by a recent study carried out for the Ministry of Public Works by Pedro Sosa Franco, an architect, and Beatriz Ornés de Albornoz, a sociologist. They found that for the 31 urban centers studied with a total population of 3,040,000, nearly half, or 1,481,000, could be classified as marginal. Table 3, which provides a city-by-city breakdown, was derived from this study.[1]

The members of these marginal groups, like those already referred to in the metropolitan area, are individuals who live in social conditions which vary from those merely comfortable to a majority within this group who lack the most elementary amenities. This marginal population, which includes a great proportion of unemployed and underemployed, is the consequence of a social system which has failed to solve the basic problems of this population. In all societies, at least in the capitalist world, portions of the population are marginal, but when the proportion reaches the levels cited for Venezuela, the situation is clearly explosive. It is evidence of unequal distribution of social wealth. It is obvious that if the greater part of the country's fiscal revenue is going to stop at the boundaries of small social sectors, with high levels of consumption, a style of life is generated which creates apathy and frustration at both extremes of society.

Faced with this situation, national plans give clear warning of the dangers which appear to threaten the already precarious situation of the country. The National Plan, worked out by the central planning body in Venezuela (CORDIPLAN), sets out the particular obstacles to national development and the kind of society whose construction they have in mind. The Fourth National Plan had the following to say:

> To achieve a democratic and participatory society where each person has available to him the conditions and opportunities for his personal liberation, it is essential that the education given should be suitably placed within the historical process of social development in order to accelerate this process. In this sense, education, as well as fulfilling its transcendental and universal functions, must contribute to the creation of a critical consciousness and to the spread of innovations, turning itself into a medium of personal and social development. The ultimate aim of all this is to prepare and consolidate the bases of a just social order. The knowledge and values

TABLE 3
Overall View of Studies in Marginal Areas

City	Number of Barrios	Stable Barrios	Unstable Barrios	Barrios Part. Unstable	Units of Arrangement	Number Interviews Unstable Barrios	Total Number Interviews	Total Population in City	Total Marginal Population in City
Barcelona	17	15	-	2	3	843	5,901	76,410	20,999
Pto. La Cruz	34	18	10	6	5	2,271	15,891	63,276	18,714
Guanta	7	-	3	4	1	126	882	9,017	5,213
Mérida	41	19	22	-	6	1,235	13,445	74,214	20,601
Barinas	27	17	10	-	6	1,977	13,839	56,329	28,540
Cd. Bolívar	30	20	5	5	8	6,080	42,560	103,728	49,657
El Palito-Moron	11	3	8	-	3	-	-	19,451	8,226
Pto. Cabello	31	10	21	-	5	1,252	8,764	73,380	19,987
Valencia	47	43	4	-	7	-	-	367,154	190,026
San Juan de los Morros	23	13	3	7	5	1,478	10,346	37,810	14,941
San Felipe y Cocorote	26	20	6	-	7	1,829	12,803	53,698	22,344
Maracay	47	40	7	-	6	1,904	13,328	255,134	173,000
Cabimas	55	46	2	7	6	2,156	15,092	192,120	116,496
San Fernando de Apure	11	4	2	5	4	895	6,262	38,960	14,256
Maracaibo	109	88	9	12	22	7,958	55,706	650,002	332,208
San Cristobal	56	51	2	3	6	1,376	8,256	152,239	72,513
Valera	27	4	19	4	2	1,324	9,268	74,353	38,500
Barquisimeto	56	31	5	20	5	2,558	17,906	334,333	143,885
Coro	25	12	4	9	3	-	-	68,701	39,403
Pto. Fijo	22	13	9	-	4	-	-	55,483	30,272
El Tigre	6	6	-	-	3	1,100	7,700	49,801	22,871
San Carlos	19	15	-	4	5	-	-	21,019	10,952
Yaritagua	19	19	-	-	3	-	-	21,363	8,545
Acarigua Araure	17	17	-	-	4	-	-	93,115	37,246
Aroa	6	3	-	3	-	-	-	5,418	2,167
Nirgua	11	6	-	5	4	-	-	21,003	8,401
Guanare	15	8	-	7	6	-	-	49,898	21,336
Chivacoa	11	11	-	-	2	-	-	23,270	9,308
TOTAL	806	552	151	103	141	36,362	257,949	3,039,679	1,480,607

SOURCE: Research Department, Urban Planning Division, Ministry of Public Works, Caracas (June 1975).

> transmitted by the educative process must also orientate themselves towards the attainment of socio-political development and prepare the population for the exercise of freedom.[2]

But, as well as putting forward the idea of a society which is "democratic and participatory," the same document speaks of

> The rigidity of the prevailing pattern of industrialization and the gradual broadening of the problem of economic and social marginality, present a critical situation whose solution proves extremely difficult within the framework of conventional schemes. In fact, the steady increase in investment, the growth in productivity, the search for external markets, agrarian reform and the expansion of various social services, among other measures, is undoubtedly leading to a greater development of the economy, but, nevertheless, in spite of the institution of these important measures, they will not be sufficient to overcome, in the short or even medium term, the problem of social marginality nor to break the vicious circle which hinders national development from within.[3]

How to cope with this increasing problem of a marginal population is, therefore, of the greatest moment to Venezuela's future development. Thus, the goal of education "turning itself into a medium of personal and social development" as a means of reversing the growth of social marginality also is a matter of basic concern.

Is this process taking place? In this context, let us examine the situation of higher education in Venezuela, the priority assigned to it in government planning and budgeting, and the role it plays in national development.

We will focus our attention on the program for higher education, since it is primarily this sector of the educational system which is responsible for providing the trained manpower required for national growth and development, and it is the acquiring of higher education which enables that sector of society which had previously been only marginal to enter into the mainstream of full social acceptance and reward.

First let us look at education as a whole in order to determine its relative importance in Venezuela's national development policies. Some indication of its priority status can be obtained by examining the distribution of the national budget and comparing the percentage allotted to education with that allocated to other sectors. The amount devoted to education in the budget for 1976 corresponds to 16.1 percent of the total sum of 33,167 million bolivars, which was the October 1975 estimate of the total national budget for the financial year of 1976.

Sector	*Percentage of Budget*
Internal Affairs	20.8
Finance	16.1
EDUCATION	16.1
Public Works	10.8
Health	6.5
Defense	5.57
Development	2.5
Communications	2.4
Justice	1.8
Foreign Affairs	1.1
Labor	1.1
Mines	0.7

In absolute terms, education is one of the sectors of public expenditure which has increased most:

Year	*Amount (millions of bolivars)*
1964	1,131,000
1968	1,706,000
1969	2,144,000
1970	2,485,000
1974	3,362,000
1976	5,346,000

These figures, however, do not tell us how these sums are allocated within the educational system, nor whom they benefit. The annual rate of growth in both preschool and higher education sectors is very high, even though the greatest proportion of the education budget is given to the primary sector, and

TABLE 4

Distribution by Numbers Enrolling at All Scholastic Levels

LEVEL	1969-70	%	1970-71	%	1974-75	%	Annual Rate
Preschool	43,186	1.9	46,879	2.0	78,333	2.7	12.6
Primary	1,656,270	74.7	1,749,157	73.8	2,066,889	70.7	4.5
Secondary	446,080	20.1	494,917	20.3	652,373	22.3	7.9
Higher	72,649	3.3	77,762	3.3	127,074	4.3	11.9
TOTAL	2,218,185	100	2,368,715	100	2,924,669	100	5.7

SOURCE: Ministry of Education, Planning Division, Social and Cultural Planning Department. CORDIPLAN.

the smallest proportion to preschool education. The proportion of the budget allocated to higher education is 34 percent, due mostly to the high cost of education at this level. This means that of the 5,000-million bolivar education budget for 1975, some 1,500-million bolivars were spent on higher education alone. Since the estimated 1976 education budget was forecast as 5,346-million bolivars, we can apply this percentage to arrive at a corresponding higher education expenditure for 1976. Given the mechanism by which no limit has been set on the

TABLE 5

Distribution of Student Enrollment at All Levels According to Type of Institution (private or public)

LEVEL	1969-70	1970-71	1971-72	1972-73	1973-74	1974-75
Preschool	43,186	46,879	52,200	59,624	67,971	78,333
Official	17,403	18,493	19,403	21,003	22,863	24,963
Private	25,783	28,386	32,797	38,621	45,108	53,370
Primary	1,656,270	1,749,157	1,830,460	1,913,217	1,991,338	2,057,889
Official	1,452,723	1,521,767	1,592,500	1,664,499	1,732,464	1,789,193
Private	203,547	227,390	237,960	248,718	258,874	268,696
Secondary	446,080	494,917	547,279	592,561	629,397	652,373
Official	360,020	372,535	410,382	448,307	478,929	497,453
Private	86,060	122,382	136,897	144,254	150,468	154,920
Higher	72,649	77,762	86,891	98,376	112,339	127,074
Official	64,200	67,517	75,432	85,380	97,465	110,223
Private	8,449	10,245	11,459	12,996	14,874	16,851
TOTAL	2,218,185	2,368,715	2,516,830	2,663,778	2,801,045	2,915,669
Official	1,894,346	1,980,312	2,097,717	2,219,189	2,331,721	2,421,832
Private	323,839	388,403	419,113	444,589	469,324	493,837

SOURCE: Ministry of Education, Planning Department, Social and Cultural Planning Department. CORDIPLAN.

growth of higher education, and given the costs of this type of education, it is reasonable to suppose that the proportion given to this subsector of the total national educational budget will increase even more over the next few years. Such a trend will continue to have an effect upon the nation's capacity to maintain a qualitative level acceptable at other levels of the educational system.

It is convenient to note here (because, as I shall later show, it is relevant to the quality of education) that the Venezuelan educational system can be divided financially into two subsectors: the public sector, to which the above figures refer, and the private sector. Tables 4 and 5 give the student enrollment by scholastic level (preprimary, primary, secondary, and higher), and Table 5 analyzes student enrollment both by scholastic level and by type of financing.

In quantitative terms, it is clear from Table 5 that public education takes up a much greater proportion of students than does the private school establishment. In qualitative terms, however, private education may have greater impact upon the developmental process, particularly in the area of higher education, for it is the institutions of higher education which train the future leaders of Venezuela, and it is both the quality and nature of the training which they provide that determine whether Venezuelan educational institutions can meet the country's human resource needs. Table 6 illustrates the explosive growth in student numbers in higher education over the past few years.

The numbers entering higher education are distributed among a series of educational institutions, of which the majority (about 70 percent) attend universities, while the remainder (30 percent) attend polytechnics, teacher training institutes, technical colleges, university colleges, and military schools. Out of the 70 percent who attend universities, only 8 percent go to private universities—a relatively small group, but one which represents a social significance disproportionate to its numbers.

At present there are 15 universities in Venezuela. Of these four are autonomous (i.e., publicly funded but self-governing in terms of curriculum and administration), six are classified as experimental (publicly funded but nonautonomous), and five are private (largely privately funded and administered). Apart from the universities, there are five teaching colleges, three polytechnics, six technical universities, seven university colleges, 11 private institutes for higher education, and four military schools.[4]

It is worth pointing out that of the total number of students in higher education, 50 percent are accounted for by the autonomous universities, 12 percent by the government's experimental universities (nonautonomous), and 8 percent by the private universities. The other 30 percent who do not attend universities are distributed among the various specialized institutions as follows:

Type of Institution	*Student Enrollment Percentage*
Polytechnic	4.25
Teacher training	11.93
Technical colleges	3.24
University colleges	8.95
Private institutes	.66
Military schools	.5

All these components, universities as well as the specialized institutions of higher education, come under the jurisdiction of the Ministry of Education. This body, in turn, contains a National Council for Universities, which has basic control of the universities, and a Division of Higher Education supervising, to a greater or lesser extent, the various specialized institutions of higher education mentioned above. Also linked with the Ministry of Education is a Planning Office for the University Sector (OPSU) and, since 1974, an Advisory Committee to the Higher Education Division. Up to now, all higher education has been subject to the Law of Education, although, since 1970, when the Law of the Universities was promulgated, it has governed the university sector. When the Advisory Committee to the Higher Education Division was created, it was charged with

TABLE 6
Enrollment in Higher Education

Year	Number Students Enrolling	Population Age 20 to 24	Percentage Population 20 to 24	Annual Growth Rate
1950	6,901	473,748	1.46	
1951	1,993			
1952	5,100			
1953	7,279			
1954	7,480			
1955	7,532			
1956	9,443			
1957	9,467			
1958	11,513			
1959	22,476			
1960	24,883			
1961	30,534	618,411	4.94	
1962	33,552			
1963	37,114			
1964	40,587			
1965	45,813			
1966	49,055			
1967	54,155			
1968	65,796			
1969	73,834			
1970	83,499			13.09
1971	104,739	957,611	10.94	25.44
1972	115,482	1,010,184		10.26
1973	159,269	1,062,757	14.99	37.92
1974 (est)	200,000	1,114,000	17.95	

SOURCES: *Statistical Bulletin* Nos. 1 and 2, OPSU, 1973 and 1975. Various differences may be noted in the data when one compares the *Statistical Bulletin* of the Ministry of Development, General Statistical Division of National Censuses.

drafting a proposed Law of Higher Education which would integrate into a single system the universities and other institutions of higher learning.

At present, and until such time as a new Law of Higher Education is implemented, no such integration exists. Each uni operates according to its own plan. Without going into the whole history of higher education, it is important to remember that, up until the mid-fifties, the entire system of higher education was paid for exclusively out of public funds and, in the case of the universities, consisted of universities only on the autonomous model. These four autonomous universities have followed the Napoleonic model of professional teaching universities and closely resemble each other. They follow the model of the oldest, the Central University of Venezuela in Caracas, and each is in charge of its own administration, free of state control although financed by the state.

Private universities started to operate in 1953 during the military government of Pérez Jímenez (1948-1959). The organization of the first experimental, or nonautonomous, governmental universities began in 1960. The University of Santa María is a private lay university which follows the traditional model of a professionalizing university, strictly a teaching institution without any interest in scientific research or in the widening of cultural horizons (all three functions being those of the true traditional university). On the other hand, Simón Bolívar is a governmental nonautonomous university where attendance is free. It is a model of an efficient modern university aimed at the training of engineers at the highest level possible.

The universities occasionally duplicate their forces, but do not concentrate them. Each university, especially the autonomous type, feels obliged to satisfy the popular demand for particular subjects, and their training units remain permanently open. Once facilities have been established to train professionals in a particular branch of study, they remain permanently, untouched by fluctuations in the supply and demand for a particular field of study.

Since the majority of students enrolled in higher education in Venezuela are enrolled in a university based on one of these models (70 percent), we are justified in regarding higher education in Venezuela as basically university education, hence the concentration of this study on that subsector. Further, since a majority of the university students are enrolled in the public, rather than the private, sector, what is at issue is whether the quality of public education justifies the enormous proportion of public funds devoted to it. In this regard, we cannot overlook the phenomenon which I will call the theory of social sectors. Just as underdevelopment can be explained as a function of the relations between dominant (rich) and dependent (poor) countries, or between strong and weak economies, so the level of development *within* a country can be explained as a function of the relations between the "private" (dominant, elite minority) sector of society and its "public" sector (the dependent or marginal majority).

This theory of social sectors is an attempt at an overall explanation of Venezuelan development by distinguishing between the public and private sectors in its society. Each of these sectors creates its own institutions to serve its own advantage, and each is characterized by a growth which is in inverse proportion to the numbers involved and to its social wealth. The public sector's population increases as its social wealth decreases, whereas the reverse is true of the private sector: its population decreases as its social wealth increases. If we wish to ascertain which group is best served by the state, we need only examine five basic social amenities (health, education, accommodation, transport, and leisure) to determine which sector benefits most from these services. In this sense the state does not represent society as a whole but, rather, favors the private sector at the expense of the public sector, attending the needs of the latter only insofar as necessary. The general planning and development for the future are in the hands of the private sector, so that, while both sectors share common interests, the private sector easily identifies its own self-interest with the national interest.

This is what happens in the case of the universities. The government universities (both autonomous and nonautonomous) have the task of providing the human resources for industry and administration at the level of modernization decreed by the private sector, usually a level most advantageous to the private sector. In Venezuela we have a situation in which the private-governmental universities (that is, the nonautono mous ones which are, by definition, most susceptible to private sector control) have been created primarily to fill the human resource needs determined by the private sector. At the same time, these universities are able to utilize whatever public sector resources are available within the ideological context of the current attitude toward development.

Thus, in terms of decision-making control, the private sector (the dominant minority) controls almost 50 percent of the total higher education establishment, since the private sector has jurisdiction not only over the purely private institutions, but also over those that come under government control. The private sector controls not only the minuscule 8 percent of private university students, their educational standards and curriculum, but also the 12 percent attending the government-subsidized nonautonomous universities, as well as the 30 percent attending the nonuniversity institutions of higher education. In terms of financing, though, this is almost all public sector money that finances higher education. With the exception, again, of the 8 percent of the students in private universities, all the rest of higher education is publicly supported, although control of how half these funds are spent, and whom they will benefit, is in the hands of private sector personnel.

The basis of our argument is that, due to private sector control over the quality of education as well as over admissions, the students in the private and government nonautonomous universities are qualitatively more important than the rest of the university population. It is this group who will assume administrative control of the wealth of the private sector one day; it is this group which will provide the human resources needed for the development of the private sector of Venezuelan society.[5] It is in these universities that the members of the elites, those just emerging as well as those already established, are to be found. It is the students in these universities who will assume general control over the attitudes and goals of Venezuela, for they receive the most competent training needed to assume the responsibility for ensuring the country's continued social modernization.

Because of the growing emphasis on educational quality by the private sector, higher standards of education are possible in the private-governmental (nonautonomous) universities than in the public (autonomous) ones. By the same token, due to the increasing social prestige of these institutions, their administrators are able to control the increase in demand for admission. This increased demand reflects the increasing awareness of both the private and public sectors that the private-governmental universities offer greater educational opportunities for those with aspirations for personal advancement. One can only conclude that the current university system has been conceived principally for the purpose of developing the private, rather than the public, sector of society.

By comparison, the public (i.e., autonomous) universities suffer from a relative stagnation, both of quality and of aspiration. They are confronted by a demographic explosion of demand, which they are unable to control on the one hand, and which contributes to the general lower educational quality on the other. At the same time, their very freedom from government control perpetuates a more traditional student curricula, which fails to reflect the needs of a developing industrial state.

In Venezuela, as with any other country with scarce human resources at the highest level, education is a great investment for the individual as well as for the state.

To the individual, possession of higher education is a matter of fundamental importance, since it confers membership in one social class or another. It is the instrument by which the dominant elite reinforces its position in terms of intellectual power rather than financial power. When considered as a professionalizing institution, the Venezuelan university provides a professional certificate that qualifies its graduates to undertake a profession in society. In general, the individual investment made by a student in studying for four years (the minimum time possible for acquiring a professional qualification) is highly economical when one considers the return of a professional salary as compared with nonprofessional ones. However, the social cachet conferred by the title of "doctor" can be seen by the performance of the labor market at the professional level, since in order to practice one's profession effectively, it is as important to belong to a defined pressure group (whether political party or group organized along class lines) as to be efficient or capable in one's specialty.

Venezuela's public universities have produced hundreds of professionals, but the majority are incapable of performing a task effectively, at least at a level which might raise the country's productivity. Their curricula and programs of study reflect an oral culture rather than an industrial one. The traditional Venezuelan university does not train its students in basic productive activities, nor is the scientific and technological research carried out of an innovative or developmental type. Instead, it recreates or adapts imported science and technology. From 1901 to 1970 some 48,199 students were granted professional credentials by Venezuelan universities, the majority of which were for careers providing services as opposed to careers associated with production activities. This is best illustrated by an analysis of career choices of the graduates of the Central University of Venezuela between 1901 and 1959 (Universidad Central en Venezuela, 1972: 23):

Major Field	*Percentage Degrees Granted*
Medicine	33.32
Law	20.09
Engineering	13.47
Dentistry	7.10
All other	17.20

Naturally, it is not held that the professionals in the various categories mentioned might not make a positive contribution to development, but the fact remains that, at present, Venezuela suffers from a remarkable lack of those qualified to deal with the exploitation of basic resources. If one assesses the situation of higher education in Venezuela, and if one does not take the Keynesian view that education is simply a question of consumption, one is led to recognize that higher education has thus far functioned more in social than in economic terms. This has given rise to a new and emergent social class, that of the professionals, but without education having recognized its essential role as a factor in national economic development.

This recognition has been especially lacking on the part of the public sector in Venezuelan society. Those individuals from the public sector (especially those in the public universities) who study for careers only marginal to the tasks essential to an industrial society are simply regarded as members of the university proletariat. They are individuals who, in the normal run of things, end up unemployed, or even outside the labor market, precisely because the possession of a university degree qualifies them for a type of work superfluous to the emerging industrial society.

The point is that Venezuelan universities ought to bc oriented toward tasks other than those they assume at present. Venezuela needs human resources in all its activities, but unquestionably needs to dedicate all its academic forces to create those human resources essential to basic activities of its economy. At the moment, an imbalance exists between the demands of the expanding economy for trained manpower to meet developmental needs and the ability and/or willingness of the higher education establishment to supply those needs. As a result, the country has had to resort to the importation of technical and professional manpower from abroad, or has had to create special scholarship programs like that of the Gran Marischal de Ayacucho to speed up the training of Venezuelans overseas. A list of the priorities established by this latter plan gives an idea of the fields where the greatest shortages exist: oil and petrochemicals, agriculture and livestock, metallurgy and steelworking, oceanography and fishing, aeronautics, naval industries, scientific research, or teaching at the postgraduate level in all these areas.

Up to now, Venezuela has not built up the basic human resources needed for development. This is but one more area where the country's dependent position is apparent. Furthermore, this dependency is only strengthened and perpetuated by schemes which rely on importation of skills and training from abroad. These solutions help to produce a double current of influence from outside the nation, weakening the already fragile contours of a country which does not have a strong sense of identity as a nation.

It is urgent that Venezuela define a profile from which a scientific-technological model might proceed, defined from within the country itself, and not simply in response to outside pressures exerted by capitalist consumption. The influence of capital consumption is such that the country expends an enormous proportion of its income buying a variety of nonessential products from other countries, as well as paying for activities which have a doubtful value in terms of development, such as entertainment of all types.

Education can be an essential factor in a developing society only when it forms part of a broader social plan, either direct (as in the case of socialist planning) or indirect (as in planning according to the market), which allocates the training that education provides to those activities crucial for the national development. For this to happen in Venezuela there would have to be a *national project* for higher education. Such a national system of education should be structured in such a way that the public sector, as well as the private sector, could contribute in a reasonable manner to the formulation of policies, even if this were possible only with the Venezuelan government acting as balancing agent.

As a matter of fact, there *are* sectors of opinion in the country which, for purposes of modernization, consider it appropriate that consideration be given to higher education as a mechanism of an industrial society, as a unit of production—of human resources production—for which it will be necessary to make a definite investment appropriate to the needs of the collectivity. To do this, the proposed Law of Higher Education has under consideration the creation of a body that could establish programs and other requirements for the training of human resources. The requirements would then be fulfilled by the different units in the higher education system. This would enable rational financing of higher education, together with general rationalization of the operations of each unit and of the system as a whole.

At the same time, there is no general accord on this matter. Other interest groups want to maintain the present decentralized system just described. There is a great Latin American faith in the principle of autonomy, in which universities are understood to be suprastate entities, entitled to all the financial support they deem necessary, but without any obligation to the source of that support, namely, the state. Consequently, at the present time, the drafts of the new Law of Higher Education presented thus far favor only a partial modification of the present situation.

Conclusion

It is apparent that there is an unnecessary and costly discrepancy between Venezuela's higher education program and the country's development policies. Venezuela is a small country, in terms of population density, and a new one. Although Venezuela obtained its political independence a century and a half ago, it is only into its first half-century of life as a unified nation. What is more, it is only since 1945 that it began to acquire the characteristics of a modern nation.

Basically, Venezuela is a country of resources which, though not scarce, are at least inflexible, and which have to be used for the national benefit. Thanks to an advantage which Venezuelans aptly call "the shit of the devil," the country benefits from the enormous financial revenues befalling an oil country. In order to create an economy with a firmer basis, to lay the foundation for future harmonious development enabling the whole society to attain a decent standard of life, human resources of every type must be cultivated and trained.

From now on, Venezuela is responsible for its own development as an industrialized society. Iron and oil can be nationalized, but the country must develop not only the technology to exploit them, but also the organizing capacity to do so effectively. This can be accomplished only through the development of the appropriate national human resources, and the conscientious determination to put into effect what belongs to the nation and to nationality.

NOTES

1. The study by Sosa and Ornes de Albornoz is entitled "Problemática de las áreas marginales en Venezuela, el caso de Caracas" (11 July 1975, Caracas). Also refer to another paper by the same authors, "Las implicaciones del crecimiento urbano en Venezuela, y el desarrollo de las áreas marginalles," presented to the organizational meeting of the Habitat Conference (held by the United Nations in May and June 1976) which took place in Caracas from 30 June to 4 July 1975. For further details of the social situation of Venezuela, refer to my book, *Sociedad venezolana* (Valencia, Estado Carabobo: Universidad de Carabobo, 1973). For an excellent reference work on Venezuela, see D. F. Maza Zavala and others, *Venezuela, crecimiento sin desarrollo* (Caracas: Universidad Central de Venezuela, 1974).
Venezuela, see D. F. Maza Zavala and others, *Venezuela, crecimiento sin desarrollo* (Caracas: Universidad Central de Venezuela, 1974).

2. The Fourth National Plan, p. 202.

3. The Fourth National Plan, p. 185.

4. A list of the universities by categories: *autonomous*—Central University of Venezuela, University of Carabobo, University of the Andes, and University of Zulia; *experimental*—University of the East, Simón Bolívar University, University of the Midwest, University of Táchira, Simón Rodríguez University, and Ezequiel Zamora University; *Private*—Andrés Bello Catholic University, Metropolitan University, University of the Avila, Santa María University, and Rafael Urdaneta University.

5. It is of interest to note that at present the universities with possibly the highest prestige and reputation in Venezuela are Simón Bolívar (a government university) and the Andrés Bello Catholic University (private). Furthermore, in Caracas' daily newspaper social pages, as they are called, one frequently reads that sons of leaders of the public sector, the politicians and other influential men, are graduates of the Catholic University and Simón Bolívar. This results from a long-standing tradition that members of the élite graduate from the Central University. On the contrary, each year this university, the largest in the country in quantitative terms, recruits a higher proportion of the population who do not form part of the dominant élite. They belong to the majority of the population absorbed into the public sector of society and wish to support themselves by providing services within the public sector.

REFERENCES

ALBORNOZ, O. (1972) El socialismo en Chile. Caracas: Tiempo Nuevo.

CARDOSO, F. H. (1971) Ideologías de la burguesía industrial en sociedades dependientes: Argentina y Brasil. México: Siglo XXI.

——— and E. FALETTO (1969) Dependencia y Desarrollo en América Latina. México: Siglo XXI.

DOS SANTOS, T. (1969) "La crisis de la teoría del desarrollo y las relaciones de dependencia en América Latina," in H. Jaguaribe, A. Ferrer, M. S. Wionczek, and T. Dos Santos, La dependencia político-económica de América Latina. México: Siglo XXI.

FRANK, A. E., J. D. COCKROFT, and D. L. JOHNSON (1970) Economía política del subdesarrollo. Buenos Aires: Ediciones Signos.

GARCIA, A. (1969) La estructura del atraso en América Latina. Buenos Aires: Pleamar.

HINKELANMERT, F. (1970) El subdesarrollo latinoamericano. Buenos Aires: Paidos.

IANNI, O. (1970) Imperialismo y cultura de la violencia en América Latina. México: Siglo XXI.

JAGUARIBE, H., A. FERRER, M. S. WIONCZEK and T. DOS SANTOS (1969) La dependencia político-económica de América Latina. México: Siglo XXI.

RIBEIRO, D. (1971) El dilema de América Latina. México: XXI.

Universidad Central de Venezuela (1972) La oferta de recursos humanos de nivel universitario en Venezuela. Caracas: Planning Division, Universidad Central de Venezuela.

Orlando Albornõz is Profesor Titular at the Universidad Central de Venezuela in Caracas. As a sociologist he has been working mainly on higher education in relation to politics and development. His most recent books are Poder y Liderazgo en la Escuela Primaria Venezolana *(1977),* Desarrollo Político en Venezuela *(1974), and* Ideología y Política en la Universidad Latinoamericana *(1972).*

LARISSA LOMNITZ
Applied Mathematics Institute
Universidad Nacional de Mexico
Apartado Postal stal 20-726
Mexico 20, D. F.

CONFLICT AND MEDIATION IN A LATIN AMERICAN UNIVERSITY

The evolution of national universities in Latin America is closely related to major political and social changes. The National Autonomous University of Mexico (UNAM) is no exception. As elsewhere in Latin America, we are witnessing in Mexico the transition from a preindustrial, agricultural society to an urbanized industrialized nation. The deep transformations are reflected in the transformation of the elitist universities of the turn of the century, strictly oriented toward the liberal professions, into a new type of university whose character remains as yet undefined (Trow, 1970).

The explicit objective of education in the old-style elitist universities was and remains the attainment of a professional diploma. This is not to diminish the important role played by these universities in the generation and diffusion of culture at the national level; the point is that the formative orientation of these universities was limited to the acquisition of information and professional skills. The general cultural education of the student was regarded as the job of the secondary school or the high school (Scott, 1968: 67).

Journal of Interamerican Studies and World Affairs, Vol. 19 No. 3, August 1977

As the middle class rose to prominence in many countries of Latin America, with the advent of industrialization, the elitist university ceased to interpret the aspirations of the leading strata of society. After 1920 the following basic changes in the situation of national universities became apparent: the avalanche of students toward the national university could not be contained; a need arose for more diversified professional careers, in accordance with the requirements of modern Latin American society; research institutes were organized everywhere within the national universities, on an equal with the old-style faculties. Some of these new institutes have been fulfilling important roles in national development (Soberón, 1974). The academic teaching jobs formerly in the hands of senior professionals teaching part-time courses for prestige have been elevated to a full-time career in its own right. On the other hand, as they grew in social and national importance, many large Latin American universities have become "ideological battlefields and centers of revolutionary critique" (López Cámara, 1974: 3).

In this paper I propose a dynamic model of the internal structure of the National Autonomous University of Mexico in terms of the relationship between the university and the national sociopolitical system at large. I submit that the functions of the National University are not limited to strictly academic roles such as teaching, research, and cultural extension, but must properly include certain important implicit functions: channeling social criticism, providing new options for social mobility, and building the ideological, moral, and political functions of the Mexican national ethos. Such a diversity of functions implies the possibility of conflict, particularly conflict between explicit and implicit functions, which may find its expression in strife between groups, and tendencies which uphold contradictory ideals concerning the character of the university. I propose to analyze the dynamics of the National University of Mexico as arising from the contradictions between implicit and explicit functions which the university is currently performing within the national system.

Origin of Conflict

Internal conflict in the university may be interpreted in terms of open or covert struggle between several more or less well-defined tendencies embodying different concepts or projects of what the university should be. These projects may be classified according to two main currents of thought: (a) the university should be a "a territory of study, critical reflection and discussion . . . an interpersonal community centered on truth as a fundamental value; and an organization for professional training which aims at the formation and specialization of the cadres of society" (Pérez Correa, 1974: 375); (b) the university should be "an expanse for revolutionary criticism; the first liberated territory in the revolutionary process; a springboard for political power" (Pérez Correa, 1974: 375).

Such a drastic conflict of goals must necessarily find its expression in a struggle between rival political forces. The various "projects" of the university (in Pérez Correa's terminology) are not only abstract ideals, they correspond to real functions currently being performed by the university. Indeed, they may be regarded as major components of "the duality between politics and academe, the internal tension between the objectives of the university, . . . [which] defines a specific form of rationality and certain political characteristics, certain conflicts, demanding a growing degree of attention from university authorities" (Pérez Correa, 1974: 375).

What, then, are the functions of the National Autonomous University of Mexico in relation to the national system? The explicit functions are easily defined, since they are spelled out in the *Ley Orgánica* (Fundamental Law) under which the university was reorganized in 1945. They are teaching, research, and the diffusion of culture. These functions are understood to include prominently the training of personnel for the liberal professions, as witnessed by the fact that an extremely high percentage of leaders in public and private administration, national politics, and the professions are alumni of the National University. The scientific research and extension functions have also increased to the point where the National University of Mexico is today the main cultural and scientific institution of the nation (Soberón, 1974).

Under "implicit" functions of the university we propose to describe all those functions which are not specified in the Fundamental Law or in the bylaws, but which are the result of external pressures or needs of the national system. These functions include particularly the following.

Social mobility. The university today is the main vehicle of upward social mobility for thousands of young people who aspire to middle class status, or who wish to rise in their position within the middle class (López Cámara, 1971). The university does this through the degrees it confers and, even more importantly, through the opportunity of social contact with professors and fellow students. Social networks established by students during their years at the university represent an extremely important socioeconomic resource to the alumnus (Smith, 1975: 379-413; Camp, 1976).

Furthermore, the university acts as a buffer, delaying and regulating the access to the middle class labor market. In this way the university controls the growth of the professional segment of the Mexican middle class (Pérez Correa, 1974).

Social and political critique. Within a political system which features few institutionalized outlets for dissent, the critical role of the university is of essential importance. This criticism is today predominantly from the left; however, this was not always the case (Rodríguez, 1958). At its most constructive, the critical function of the university represents a valuable mechanism for social change and an integrating force of the Mexican national consciousness. In the years immediately following the Mexican revolution, when the nation was close to dismemberment through political, cultural, ethnic, and religious strife, the National University became a conscious stronghold of the new national values, and the most notable exponents of Mexican culture militated in its ranks (Madrazo Garamendi, 1970). This tradition has been continued to the present day by an academic community of variegated extraction, from the social, regional, and political points of view.

Even destructive social criticism may be said to serve a positive function, if one thinks of the university as a safety-valve which released pent-up tensions in the national system (which might otherwise threaten its stability) in a relatively harmless fashion (Monsivais, 1973).

Battlefield. The National University of Mexico has often been used as a battlefield for political feuds, both figuratively and actually. There are plenty of opportunities for professional and amateur politicians among the student body to participate in political activity. One might think of partisan struggles within the National University as tournaments, such as used to take place during the Middle Ages, where knights in shining armor publicly clashed. Until recently, the National University campus was the ideal setting for these jousts because of its relative isolation and autonomy.

The battlefield provided by the university for skirmishes among different political camps (national as well as academic) is useful also as a training ground for future political leaders of all persuasions, particularly those belonging to the official line. An overwhelming proportion of political leaders at the top national level are National University graduates who earned their first political stripes within the university.

In conclusion, the internal dynamics of the university may be understood in terms of diverging and often conflicting functions assigned to the university, either explicitly or implicitly, by the national system. These functions have become identified as the positions of opposing interest groups, each of which proposes and defends a different project concerning what the university ought to be. To give one example, the National University of Mexico has now become the major center of scientific research in the country (Soberón, 1974). The need for creating a solid scientific and technological establishment in Mexico, in order to resist the pressures from foreign-generated technology, has been explicitly recognized (Conacyt, 1976). But the scientists and technicians at the university find the frequent disturbances, strikes, and other political interruptions on campus very hard to take. Thus, there arises a conflict between the university as a base for building up a national scientific and technological establishment and the need to permit the free expression of all kinds of internal political movements. Another rather obvious contradiction may be found in the fact that the National University has become a major sociopolitical force in its own right and a hotly disputed prize among external political forces. This development implies a serious risk that must be confronted if the university wishes to preserve its role as a melting pot of the national consciousness and a bulwark of sociopolitical criticism. If any one of these external forces were to succeed in controlling the university, this would immediately endanger its autonomy and undermine the special status which has heretofore protected the implicit functions of the university.

The Formal Structure

The National Autonomous University of Mexico, with its student body of 252,000 students, is one of the largest universities in the world. Its staff includes 18,000 professors and researchers, and 14,000 administrators. It awards degrees in 26 technical careers, 54 careers at the bachelor level, 63 postgraduate specialist degrees, 77 master's programs, and 37 doctor's programs. The 1975 budget of the university was on the order of 2.4 billion pesos (Soberón, 1974).

Since 1944 the National University has been administered internally by the following authorities: (1) a Board of Trustees *(Junta de Gobierno)* of 15 members, which appoints the president (rector) and the directors of all faculties and institutes, and (2) the University Council *(Consejo Universitario),* whose membership includes the president, all directors, and representatives of staff as well as students of the university. There are also representatives of the centers of university extension, of the administrative staff, and of the General Secretariat. The president (rector) is the official spokesman for the university and the chairman of the University Council. There is also a Managing Board *(Patronato)* which administers the university endowment and assets. All directors of schools, faculties, and institutes are selected by the Board of Trustees from a short list of candidates submitted by the president of the university. There are two coordinators (one for the sciences and one for the humanities) who are directly appointed by the president of the university and who chair the Technical Councils in these two areas. Finally, there are the authorities of the extension system, of the system of the Open University, the academic commissions, the College of Sciences and Humanities, and the new campuses which have sprung up around the city (Valadez, 1974).

The rapid growth of the university has increasingly tended to complicate this administrative structure. Each faculty, school, or institute has its heads of departments, internal councils, and various officials appointed by the director or by the staff and the students. The internal complexity has reached the point where the authorities as well as the academic and administrative officials spend most of their time attempting to conciliate conflicting interests between different levels in the hierarchy, or between the various academic and political interest groups. The system which has finally emerged is based on negotiation; i.e., a political system which aims for the balance of power and which seeks stability as a means of preserving the institutional values.

Life Careers

The term "life career" will be taken to designate a functional specialization in relation to the national system. Each student in the university undergoes a training process. It is not limited to the contents of the curriculum, but includes a number of activities and experiences that prepare him for a certain role within the national system. To use an analogy, the society of ancient Tenochtitlan featured certain well-defined life careers, such as priests, warriors, traders, artisans, and peasants. Similarly, in the National University of Mexico we should distinguish between formal academic careers, according to the explicit functions of the university, and careers which relate to the implicit functions of the university (such as politics). The university generates a wide variety of social roles reflecting the diversity of explicit and implicit functions entrusted to it by the national society; among others, there are specific life careers oriented toward civil service, business, the liberal professions, and the home.

Members of a given life career tend to defend their group interests, which may compete or conflict with those of other careers. Thus, the activities of political pressure groups may interfere with the academic quality through strikes and other disruptions. Conversely, the passive resistance of academically oriented students tends to inhibit political participation and to limit the objectives of politically oriented student groups. The present paper aims at providing an analysis of this type of conflict. I propose simplifying the analysis by considering four main life careers: the academics, the professionals, the politicians, and the fighting gangs.

Each of these life careers is represented by a social group with characteristic features, including an internal structure, a set of initiation rites, a set of norms and values, as well as characteristic mechanisms which govern the process of integration of their membership into a specific role in national life. All life careers coexist within the National University and may develop to a greater or lesser extent during a given historical period in the evolution of the university.

THE ACADEMICS

"Academics" are members of the university community who develop a preference for research and teaching as a way of life. They are concerned with the explicit functions of the university, and may eventually seek jobs on the academic staff of the

National University or other universities by the end of their period of formal training.

Notwithstanding the scarcity of economic means and the abundance of conflict at various levels, the National University of Mexico has been able to produce small groups of academically motivated students who are eventually incorporated into the staff. This is achieved by an unofficial semitutorial system which operates in a fairly efficient manner. Some of the better students, particularly those interested in scientific research, attract a professor's attention during the last stage of their careers. The professor personally directs their theses, helps them to obtain scholarships, and uses them as assistants. Most of the research personnel in the university, and many outstanding people as well, go through such informal apprenticeship periods under a staff member, who may eventually recommend them for an academic position (Lomnitz, 1976).

There are 946 (1975) full-time research professors in the National University. The channel for the selection and training of this research staff is provided by the research institutes, independently and complementarily with the training they receive in their respective faculties. The promising students are usually recruited during the two or three final semesters of their bachelor's training as research assistants in a research institute. Students who are interested in an academic career are thus encouraged to make a special effort in their performance, particularly with regard to their tutor; the result is often an enduring relationship of scientific and personal loyalty between the tutor and his assistant.

Once an assistant has been promoted to full staff member in an institute, he is brought face to face with the implications of an academic career in the National University. He becomes a part of the developing scientific and technological structure of the nation: small research groups are engaged in the task of creating the basis of a scientific tradition. This is a slow and difficult task. On the other hand, the prevailing power structure within the university (as in the country at large) places great rewards on administrative positions, since such positions are awarded as a form of recognition and represent practically the only available kind of promotion. Hence the well-known paradox, where advancement in the research profession requires abandoning one's research work.

Formerly all major administrative posts in the university, including that of university president, were held by professional people such as lawyers, physicians, and engineers. Within the past ten years, however, the research career has become established to the point where research scientists have gained access to many key administrative jobs in the university. As soon as a researcher is appointed head of department or director, he automatically joins the inner circle of authorities in charge of the administration of one of the largest of the world's universities. Among other responsibilities, he administers the budgetary and institutional support assigned to him by higher level authorities and distributes this support among his subordinate staff. This turns him into a mediator in charge of resolving conflicts of interest by means of the optimal transfer of material concessions and power in both directions. Every administrator represents his staff in his dealings with higher authorities, and vice versa. Thus, appointed authorities may be seen as articulations between the various levels of the power structure in the university; their role consists of absorbing administrative load from above and buffering aggression or unrest from below. Their performance guarantees the normal functioning of the system. Academics in administrative jobs are leaders, whose political abilities are often improvised according to the requirements of their new positions. Depending on performance, they may continue to rise in the hierarchy to positions which are increasingly demanding in terms of administrative and political ability. The job of these academic leaders has become more harassing because of the growth of the university itself and because of the large numbers of new pressure groups which are continuously being formed in the university. Such pressure groups often derive their power from their nuisance value in terms of the potential problems which they may cause to the university administration. Caso (see Pérez Correa, 1974:

379) points out that "university authorities have always played a twofold role as political authorities bidding for allegiance and support of groups, and technical authorities engaged in the solution of questions on the organization of research and teaching from a purely objective point of view."

THE PROFESSIONALS

The professionals represent a life career which is clearly oriented toward a role outside the university proper. For this reason they have probably suffered more directly from the prevailing conflicts between objectives and functions in the university. Demands for an effective reform in the professional careers of Latin American universities go back at least to the Córdoba Movement of 1918 (Scott, 1968). Unfortunately, much still remains to be done in this connection.

The Córdoba Manifesto took issue with a number of ills, such as absentee teachers, lack of responsibility in teaching performance, negligence in updating the curricula and the contents of the courses, and what was held to be a general lack of relevance of the curricula to the current needs of the society. Many of these grievances are still issues in several professional schools within the National University of Mexico. Many professors are practicing professional people who teach a few hours per week on the side, and who may therefore lack the necessary dedication or time to update their courses. The separation between teaching and research tends to produce a static curriculum which lags considerably behind the newer scientific and technical results in a given field (Lomnitz, 1972).

Yet many professors who teach by the hour are outstanding professional people whose practical experience is invaluable to the student. Such prominent practitioners of the liberal professions stimulate the ideals of their calling through personal example; furthermore, they quickly single out the more competent students in each class and provide personal opportunities for job training in public or private corporations, private firms or offices, and in the public administration (Lomnitz, 1976).

Such tutorial supervision represents a major complement to curricular teaching as well as a selective recruiting mechanism into the liberal professions. While it is true that the professional people are mainly oriented toward interests outside the university, such alumni continue to relate to their schools by means of occasional teaching as well as through their professional associations, many of which do carry considerable political weight. Thus, the political influence of professional groups in medicine, engineering, architecture, economics, and so on is felt in university politics as much as in national politics as a whole.

If any broad generalization holds for this professional group, it is that its general tendency is to support a university that reflects their technical and professional interests. This is true, with the possible exception of those professions that produce a large number of politicians (lawyers and economists, for instance). Most freshmen students register in the professional fields (about 10 percent; Coordinación de Planeación, 1975), and most of the teaching body is still made up of practicing professionals teaching by the hour. On the basis of sheer numbers, the professionals represent a life career of considerable influence and importance, which provides a counterweight to those currents of opinion which favor an increasing politicization of the National University. Yet the proportion of professionals who eventually become incorporated into the university academic staff as full-time professors or researchers is relatively small (1,386, plus 881 part-time in 1975). The professional faculties hold out the lure of social mobility and provide access to the middle class; the proportion of dropouts in these fields is low (Dirección General de Planeación, 1973). However, the professional faculties characteristically suffer from a problem which might be described as "implosion" (Galvis, G. y M.L., oral communication): many students take a long time to complete their degree requirements, and quite a few never hand in their professional thesis, which is a prerequisite of graduation. In theory, these subprofessional personnel retain student status, though in practice they saturate the labor market of the liberal professions at a lower level of qualification (*"pasantes"*). This accounts for the presence in Mexico of a broad undifferentiated mass of quasi-professionals competing for medium-level bureaucratic jobs in the public and private administrations, where their technical background may become a promotional asset. Incidentally, it has been found that those faculties which offer more restricted career opportunities also feature the highest degree of student unrest.

THE POLITICIANS

"Politicians" are those members of the academic community who have shown an active interest in political affairs from their student days. This interest is initially expressed in participation in student movements and other power conflicts. Broadly speaking, political participation may be either for or against the current political regime; more specifically, it may be identified with factions within official or academic politics. As a life career, the politicians tend to support a current of thought which holds that a major, if not the essential, function of the National University is to take a stand in matters of public affairs.

In the National University there are several characteristic styles of political activities. The most visible style is "activism," which may be found in student meetings, protest assemblies, or the distribution of leaflets. A less conspicuous, though not necessarily less effective, style of political action is "lobbying" through personal connections. Fitting these two styles into a pattern of class struggle is not as easy as might appear at first sight; they correspond to intraclass or intergenerational struggles within the middle class. The political leadership of both styles is frequently drawn from high school leaders; it seems that the tighter group interaction found in high schools favors the emergence of leaders at that level.

If some of the freshmen have had previous experience in political participation, others are attracted to it after entering the university. During the 1960s there was a great deal of political activity (comprising the entire political spectrum) in the high schools. Student elections and debating competitions were hotly disputed and represented a breeding ground for future student leaders. However, after the 1968 student movement, many leaders emerged from the political action committees *("comités de lucha")* in the university faculties. Nowadays leaders come from a variety of backgrounds: public or private high schools, the teacher's college, the action committees, and so on. Sometimes a full-fledged political group graduates from high school into the action committee of a given faculty. Ideologies and motivations are as varied as ever, ranging from nationalism or social idealism (of the socialist or Christian varieties) to the explicit ambition to make a career in politics.

As ingredients in the vast melting pot of the university student body, the politicians soon find themselves subjected to the pull of conflicting forces: the ebb and flow of national politics, the demands of academic life, and their own intellectual and emotional changes. There is a continuous process of backing away from old commitments and creating new allegiances. Eventually the "bases" of sporadic or potential activists or politically oriented students become differentiated from the mass of the politically passive student body. Such relatively small bases represent the proper field of action of the "politicians": all efforts of proselitisms or recruiting of activists are aimed at them. The life career of a politician is as demanding and time-consuming as that of an academic. In fact, at the higher echelons the two careers are mutually exclusive in the sense that there is rarely enough time to be an academic and a politician at the same time. Leaders of either life career are fully devoted to their calling.

The typical structure of a political group has a leader at the head, followed or surrounded by members of his immediate staff and supported by activists who gather and work with some regularity, but not full-time. Promotion within such groups depends on loyalty, dedication, and leadership. A political leader has a number of specific qualifications: in addition to his political talent (which ought to be evident), he must be well-informed. This is an essential prerequisite in a political system where information is restricted and decisions are often based on rumors. Access to relevant information represents a major political resource.

At the National University, political leaders must be able to maintain efficient personal contacts with members of the university administration: this enables them to play a role in any conflict between the students and the administration on matters such as registration, examination fees, changes in curricula, or complaints about a number of academic issues and problems. Eventually the leader may be recognized as a mediator or abitrator by both parties and, thus, acquires a personal niche in the university power structure. His dealings with the administration of faculties or schools increase his prestige and following among the students. From the point of view of the administration, a capable political leader controls student unrest, a fact which represents his basic power resource and his major drawing card. Moreover, within the broad political context of national and university politics, the leader plays an active role in the game of tactical alliances and strategic confrontations between rival groups. In a sense, these confrontations represent the most visible aspect of political life at the National University. Nevertheless, the essential qualities of a political leader are his talent and ability for perceiving and channeling the true fears and desires of the bases: this amounts to a task of interpreting and translating into words and actions the basic aspirations and the objective problems of the student body.

According to Smith (1975: 407), up to 70 percent of the top political leadership of Mexico is composed of alumni of the National University. Frequently the political "cliques" were actually assembled and consolidated within the university when their members were student activists. A strong indication of the persistence of this practice is illustrated by the fact that all ministers but one of the recently installed López Portillo cabinet are UNAM graduates, while several important functionaries of the preceding Echeverría administration have returned to positions in the university.

THE FIGHTING GANGS

At the National University of Mexico there are small groups of students organized according to the pattern of the youth gang, which represent a relatively small minority following a distinct and well-defined career. Perhaps the best example is found among the fighting students known as *"porros,"* who hire themselves out occasionally to pressure groups that provide the slogans and resources for their activities. These activities are essentially of a criminal nature. Between jobs in the employment of political groups, the gangs derive their occasional income from small-scale theft, robberies, and occasional street muggings. Their importance, however, lies not in petty crime bur rather in their role as shock troops in certain political battles within the university. Thus, they relate to a major implicit function of the university, and their notoriety at critical junctures of university history may rise out of all proportion to their real numbers.

The subject of the fighting gangs is too complex to be fully dealt with in this article. Since these student groups are related to certain implicit functions, they reflect the political styles which may be found in the university at a given time. Thus, after 1968 we find an increase in the utilization of left-wing populist slogans among fighting gangs. This fact contributes to the confusion and, hence, to the political inertia of the student body as a whole. Similar political symbols are shared by a wide range of students, from political activists of various denominations to common toughs. Originally the fighting gangs may have been utilized by the university administration itself; subsequently, they were awarded "contracts" by politicians outside the university. At present, one observes the rise of a new generation of politicians who have learned to combine shock tactics with modern-style political language. Finally, some student gangs are not particularly oriented toward political action; their main interest is in drugs or delinquency in general.

Until about 1970, the "porro" groups were formed mostly in the high schools, and their socioeconomic composition was derived mainly from the poorer strata (Guitian, 1975: 115-118). This is still largely true today. Gang members are juvenile rebels who have developed a system of values in which delinquency is identified with an attitude of defiance against bourgeois middle class values that they perceive to be shared by the rest of the student population. This attitude rests on an underlying "machismo" ideology. The "porro" is often turned into a culture hero, albeit grudgingly, by middle class high school students. The immediate rewards of high school gang membership are highly visible and include money, cars, girls, and a great deal of power over students and teaching staff alike.

A "porro" leader usually rises to prominence in confrontations which involve the use of force. He tends to be intelligent, well-informed, supple, and shrewd. His tasks include maintaining discipline and distributing the loot. Until recently, such gang leaders enjoyed total impunity from the law. Their connections with other gangs, student gangs as well as street gangs in slum neighborhoods, enable them to mobilize a considerable force at short notice. Leaders of "porro" groups may rise to become mediators in conflicts at the high school or university level, but their power is based largely on intimidation. The power of the leader is transferred to gang membership by means of individual "favors" which create obligations, to be recalled and converted into support at any time (especially when the leader needs the assistance of his men in a confrontation or in organizing a demonstration).

The eventual career of members of fighting gangs depends on their individual ability and their position in the group hierarchy. Some of them become policemen or low-level political henchmen; others become delinquents and eventually end up in jail, banishment, or death. There are cases of rehabilitation; yet, on the whole, the life career of a gang member is relatively rigid, presenting few alternatives from the time of his recruitment until his usefulness within the system ends.

SOME STRUCTURAL CONSIDERATION

What is the significance of the four life careers—academics, professionals, politicians, and fighting gangs? Their significance must be found in the implicit or explicit functions of the National University of Mexico, insofar as each life career is identified with one or the other of the concepts of the ideal university: either a community of scholars and a center for professional advancement, or a base for political action toward the transformation of society. Until now, the university administration has maintained the viewpoint that these two concepts and the strategies associated with them are not basically incompatible. It is true that the Fundamental Law of the university appears to favor the first tendency, but its major objective is felt to be conciliatory toward both ideas. Hence the system of mediation which currently prevails within the university, where formal and informal leaders join the process of give-and-take at many different levels. This process occurs between levels of the academic hierarchy as between fighting gangs and their sponsors, or between leaders of the various "life careers" in general. There is vertical intermediation between ranks in the power structure and interplay of alliances and exchange at horizontal levels.

The life careers resemble each other in their internal structure. Each life career emerges from the undifferentiated mass of politically and academically inert students as a group united by some community of interests. The immense majority of students at the National University are confused and habitually passive. Politically, the university must appear as a tangle of contradictions to anyone lacking the ability and information to distinguish between the symbols and those who wield them. A true "student movement" gets underway only on rare occasions. On the whole, since about 1929 the mobilizations of the student body tend to be motivated by causes and contingencies of a purely sporadic and circumstantial nature. These are issues which may be translated into short-term objectives of negotiation by the leaders. The concrete benefits of such movements yield diminishing returns from the leadership downward; this fact goes a long way toward explaining the skepticism and lack of politicization among the "silent majority" of the students.

The structure of a group is similar in all life careers: at the top there is always the leader, who generates loyalty and whose personality harmonizes with the nature of the life career. Immediately below the leader we find a small group of trusted assistants, first-level activists, followed by a second level, and so on. The social proximity to the leader is the basic factor for solidarity within the group, whether its purpose is experimental research, political action, or delinquency. Thus, the university may be described as a conglomerate built out of many pyramidal structures, some formally recognized and others informal, all of which compete for the resources of the system through alternate phases of confrontation and negotiation.

The formal authorities of the National University administration are members of the academic or professional life careers within the university; as such, they are commited to the tendency that seeks to fulfill the explicit functions of the university. Nevertheless, their implicit obligations include the task of safeguarding the political stability of the system. This implies frequent negotiations and compromises with the informal leaders. Political stability, a prerequisite for developing the conditions under which teaching, research, and cultural extension can prosper, eventually becomes another explicit function of the National University, an end in itself, and a cardinal principle of the system (Reyna, n.d.).

Now, just as a major objective of the university administration is the task of guaranteeing the stability of the system, the implied purpose of the informal leadership increasingly consists of furthering the social mobility of groups rising from the middle class. To this end, the major weapon of informal leaders consists of threatening the university administration with their potential for destabilizing the system by using their grasp of existing grievances and their capability for stirring up unrest. Since all unrest ultimately originates in real problems within the system, the activity of the informal leadership might be thought of as beneficial to the preservation of the system; unfortunately, the political bias which is always present in such confrontations also tends to complicate their reaching an equitable solution. Nevertheless, if the negotiations result in a compromise, both the formal and the informal objectives of the university will have been met once more. By the same token, the leadership on both sides of the issue will increase and consolidate its personal power within their respective groups.

The Outlook: Technological University or Political University?

The current opposition between "explicit" and "implicit" functions of the National University has important implications on the national level. Thus, the recent creation of administrative and academic staff unions in Mexican universities may be interpreted, to some extent, as a new outlet for the ambitions of informal leaders who wish to institutionalize their power by means of a structure which parallels the academic ladder. This is a challenge to the priest-like leadership of the academics, whose wielding of scholarly authority is perceived as arbitrary. Essentially, the strategy of the political leaders lies in accumulating objective grievances (whether academic, labor, or of a personal nature) and politicizing these grievances in terms of demands of the union. There has also been a certain amount of political penetration into the academic structures as such (staff assemblies of the institutes and faculties, academic committees, and so on).

The purpose of much of this activity is to effect a change in the present system of recruitment and promotion (currently favoring the "academics"), thus creating new options for the "politicians" to escalate the upper ranks of the university administration. Such changes are rationalized by means of calls for a greater "commitment" of science and higher education in general with national development and social change, and so on. The strongest opposition against these new orientations does not originate so much among the academics themselves as among the membership of the "professional" life careers; it is represented by powerful national associations of the liberal professions. Lately there has also been some increased participation of professionals in the university administration, and their relative influence has grown as compared to the "academical" career.

This development may also reflect an apparent generational change in Mexican politics. Recently there is much talk about a "new style of government," which seems to amount to the fact that the old-style pragmatic politicians (many of them former battle-hardened student leaders) are being replaced by a new kind of technocratic politician, including economists, political scientists, sociologists, and engineers. This new generation of politicians perceives the role of the National University in terms of teaching and professional formative efficiency rather than as a political battlefield and informal training ground for leaders. Old-style politicians were reluctant to intervene in the internal academic affairs of the National University, but this is no longer true for the younger public administrators, all of whom are acutely aware of the political importance of the university.

There is another obvious reason for the great interest in the university among political circles. In former times the academics and professionals were able to administer the university unchallenged, because of the relative lack of interference of politicians or professionals. To this date, all the main administrative positions in the university are held by professors and research professors, who have risen through the ranks step by step. Such administrators obviously believe in the ideals and values of the academic life careers, to which they belong. Lately, however, the size, influence, and budget of the National University have reached such a magnitude that control of the university represents a major political and economic prize. In fact, the budget of the National University exceeds that of several states of the Mexican Union. Furthermore, especially since 1968, the university has become, so to speak, the acknowledged barometer of the stability of the national system. Hence the tremendous political pressures which have lately turned the job of rector (or president) of the National University of Mexico into one of the most difficult and hazardous assignments in Mexican public life.

The future of the university depends on the outcome of the conflict between the concepts of the function of the university now struggling for control of the administration. Both the "technological" and "political" options have a great deal in common, since both imply definite restrictions to academic freedom and a certain amount of institutionalized repression. In the case of the technological university, such a repression would be directed against the implicit functions of the university: as the safety-valve of informal political activity is forcibly closed, any expression of nonconformity would become tantamount to subversion. Eventually political unrest would spread to other critical spots within the national system, and the university would become a factory turning out technicians according to government specifications.

The option of a political university is not very different or more attractive. Political orientation would be provided by the government, since the state cannot allow the establishment of an independent political base in open defiance of the central power within the Federal District. Such so-called "free territories" may exist only for a brief time, as was shown in the case of the Central University of Venezuela. Eventually the National University would function under an inquisitorial system, with complete loss of its autonomy and academic freedom and other consequences equally as serious as those discussed in the previous case.

The forfeiture of the present role of the National University as a school for national, political, and professional leaders seems likely with either of the two preceding options. It should be recalled that the present leadership of the National University in terms of scientific and technological development is far from firm: it could still be overtaken by other centers of higher education in Mexico. Should the National University relinquish its present role of scientific leadership, it would be taken over by private universities or possibly by some of the new federal or state universities. The Mexican state perceives the struggle against technological dependence as a major national goal that cannot be conditioned on the political ups and downs of any particular university.

In conclusion, it appears that the only practical option for the National University of Mexico is to persevere in its present policy of balance between explicit and implicit functions. Such a policy aims at the preservation of a dynamic equilibrium of opposing forces and tendencies. It may even be argued that this dynamic interplay of academic and political opposites represents the mainspring of the vitality of university life, and guarantees its creative and critical potentialities. Some would have us choose between science and conscience, but this is a false dilemma: both ideals have been successfully upheld in universities of the highest academic level. In a great university all functions are important, and all can be effectively protected by the university autonomy. A definitive victory of one tendency over the other would mean the loss of academic freedom, the dwindling of the National University into academic and political insignificance, and the abdication of the historical role of one of the most unusual and creative institutions in Mexico.

REFERENCES

CAMP, R. A. (1976) "Education and political recruitment in México: the Alemán generation." J. of Interamerican Studies 18 (August): 295-321.

CONACYT (1976) Plan Nacional de Ciencia y Tecnología. México.

Coordinación de Planeación (1975) Oral communication. UNAM, Mexico.

Dirección General de Planeación (1973) Oral communication. UNAM, México.

GUITIAN, C. C. (1975) "Las porras: estudio de caso de un grupo de presión universitario." Tesis profesional, México: Escuela de Ciencias Políticas y Sociales, UNAM.

LOMNITZ, L. (1976) "Antropología de la investigación científica en la UNAM," in L. Estrada y L. Canedo (eds.) La Ciencia en México. México: Fondo de Cultura Economica.

——— (1972) Estudio sobre el impacto del proyecto "Ciudad de la Investigación" en la comunidad universitaria in Coordinación de Ciencias y Coordinación de Humanidades. México: Documento de Trabajo C.I.1., UNAM.

——— and M. A. MORAN (1976) "Estudio a mexicanos graduados en el extranjero." Ciencia y Desarrollo 2 (Nov-Dic): 45-50.

LOPEZ CAMARA, F. (1974) "Hacia una concepción dialéctica de la autonomía universitaria." Deslinde 53.

——— (1971) El desafio de la clase media. Mexico: J. Mortiz.

MADRAZO GARAMENDI, M. (1970) "Los estudiantes en la transformación de la universidad." VII Conferencia Nacional de Facultades y Escuelas de Ingeniería, Hermosillo, Son. (Marzo). (mimeo)

MONSIVAIS, C. (1973) "Ghettos: todo el poder desde ayer." Excélsior, agosto 8.

PEREZ CORREA, F. (1974) "La universidad: contradicciones y perspectivas." Deslinde 53.

REYNA, J. L. (n.d.) "Control politico, estabilidad y desarrollo en México." El Colegio de México. (mimeo)

RODRIGUEZ, V. (1958) "National University of Mexico: rebirth and role of . . ." University Microfilms. University of Texas.

SCOTT, R. E. (1968) "Student political activism in Latin America." Daedalus (Winter).

SMITH, P. H. (1975) "La movilidad política en el México contemporáneo." Foro Internacional 15 (Enero-Marzo): 379-413.

SOBERON, G. (1974) "La Universidad Nacional Autónoma de México. Pasado, presente y futuro." Revista de la Universidad de México 28 (Julio).

TROW, M. (1970) "Reflections on the transition from mass to universal higher education." Daedalus 99.

VALADEZ, D. (1974) La Universidad Nacional Autónoma de México. México: UNAM.

Larissa Lomnitz, a Chilean scholar whose doctoral degree in anthropology is from Universidad Iberoamericana, México, is a Research Professor at the Applied Mathematics Institute of UNAM. She is the author of Cómo sobreviven los marginados, *being published in English this fall by Academic Press, and of many articles concerned with marginality and the function of the Latin American university within society.*

RICHARD GRAHAM
Department of History
University of Texas at Austin
Austin, TX 78712

GOVERNMENT EXPENDITURES AND POLITICAL CHANGE IN BRAZIL, 1880-1899

Who Got What

The establishment of a republican form of government in Brazil in 1889–to replace the Empire–has long been considered an important turning point in Brazilian history.[1] Historians once saw it as important in itself, for they thought of history as past-politics and were content to debate such issues as the relative importance of civilians and military officers within the republican movement. More recently, as scholars have turned their attention to social and economic aspects of the past, that event has been seen as a symptom of deeper change, a product of altering class relationships, a sign of shifting centers of economic power, or a reflection of the growth of new interest groups.

Much of the recent literature on the subject suggests either explicitly or implicitly that four major clusters of political actors were directly interested in the events of 1889. First, urban residents–from industrialists, engineers, doctors, and lawyers, to hoteliers, shopkeepers, bureaucrats, and clerical workers–were allegedly anxious for a more open social structure, for "progress," for industrialization. Next, some entrepre-

Journal of Interamerican Studies and World Affairs, Vol. 19 No. 3, August 1977

neurially minded coffee planters of São Paulo state are said to have wanted to open up frontier areas, bring in immigrants, and build railroads. These two segments of the population joined together to urge the "new" and condemn the "old." They complained, for instance, about the Empire's stuffy insistence on restricting the amount of currency in circulation and its continued reliance on traditional planter leadership from other areas. Both groups were supposedly impatient with the slow-footed manner in which the imperial government responded to new conditions and considered the Empire anachronistic and out of touch with the demands of a modern economy and society. They sought the satisfaction of their needs in a federated republic. The usual view today is that during the first five years of the Republic the urban groups were richly rewarded for their effort in creating it. By 1894, however, the *paulista* coffee planters displaced them from power, thus sowing the seeds of an urban discontent that was to surface on various occasions, culminating in the revolution of 1930. Taken together, the two groups' interest in the movement of 1889 has been seen as a first step toward a gradual bourgeois revolution.[2]

Military officers made up a third group, sometimes lumped together with the previous two in their advocacy of the "new." They were dissatisfied with their place in the imperial sun and the low position to which they had been relegated once their services in the Paraguayan War (1865-1870) were no longer needed. In November 1889, a number of officers directed the bloodless coup d'état which overthrew the Emperor, and they and their fellows soon occupied the key positions in the government. Their contempt for civilians was now extended to many erstwhile coconspirators, and the officers are said to have remained predominant in the government until 1894. Only then did the coffee-planting elite of São Paulo, by flexing the muscle of the state militia, gain a dominant position in the new regime, thus shoving aside both the military and the urban groups (Hahner, 1969: 34-72, 110-148; Schulz, 1973: 177-260; Dudley, 1975: 44-65).

The last of the four sectors of political society consists of all those who had benefited from the old system. They had filled the bureaucratic ranks and occupied the sinecures, they had allowed the government consistently to spend more than it received, they had rigged elections, and, worst of all, they had maintained a traditional society. The leaders of this element were the planters in the now-decadent Paraíba Valley and the sugar-mill owners of the Northeast, especially in Bahia and Pernambuco. With the initiation of the Republic they are thought to have lost political influence.

It is my contention in this article that these generalizations must be scrutinized with greater care and based on more solid data before they can be fully accepted. Evidence is here presented that suggests that in some respects, at least, the Empire did more for urban groups than did the Republic; that the change of regime resulted in greatest benefits for *paulista* coffee planters right from the first; that it was not the overthrow of the Empire but other, later events that allowed the military some momentary relative gains; and that in many ways the traditional elites maintained their position and continued to derive direct and impressive benefits from the state despite its altered constitution. So it is now my belief that urban groups, insofar as they differed from old and new planters, were weaker than I and others had previously argued, that the armed force of the military did not make up for this weakness even during the first five years of the Republic, and that the traditionally dominant landowners retained a good deal of power, despite superficial political changes. The coffee planters of western São Paulo, yes, were able to command what they wanted from the new system. In this point alone the accepted interpretations are correct, although these planters made these gains in 1889 rather than in 1894.

This argument is not so much about who desired or worked for a Republic (see Boehrer, 1966: 43-58), since those who plant often do not reap. But a study of the allocation of benefits within the Empire and the Republic can show which groups dominated politically and, at least indirectly, suggest which groups were in a position genuinely to push for change. It can also help us evaluate subsequent Brazilian events: if urban elements had been the chief beneficiaries of the events of 1889 it would make sense to view the army officers who overthrew the Empire as harbingers of a new era, precursors of the movements of 1930, 1937, or 1964; but if coffee planters were most successful even in 1889 (not to mention 1894), then the nature of the succeeding regime will be differently interpreted, the events of 1930 will be seen in an altered light, and the progressive, modernizing, pro-urban nature of military rule (at least in 1889) will be regarded more skeptically.

In this article I will suggest a first step toward measuring some of the relative gains and losses of the sectors described above and, especially, pinpoint areas of shifting emphasis in government activity that require further research. Indicators of benefits are various. Some groups would gain and others lose with the passage or repeal of laws, the filling of political and bureaucratic positions, the incidence of taxes, and the structure of the tariff. The Republic's federative system meant that politicians at the state level gained in power and the population of some states presumably received a larger return from their taxes. Yet it is not to these matters that I wish to direct attention here, but to another partial measure of benefits: the allocation of national expenditures.

An examination of the proportion of national expenditures directed toward various purposes is at least an initial rough test of the meaning of the overthrow of the Empire in 1889. If the military share of these expenditures went up, how far did it go, and when? Was there a simultaneous increase in expenditures for those categories that favored urban groups—industrial subsidies, educational institutions, urban services—or those that benefited coffee planters—an expanded transportation system, the fostering of immigration, or strengthened agricultural education? Alternatively, if the overthrow of the Empire was merely a changing of the guard within the same elite group, the division of the expenditure pie would presumably remain unchanged. The underlying assumption here is that the distribution of government expenditures will reflect to a point the interests of those sectors that have greatest influence upon it. Evidently, in order to study these changes one must examine the last years of the Empire as well as the first years of the Republic. I have chosen the period from 1880 to 1899.[3]

The sources for such a study are the balance sheets drawn up three to five years after the end of the fiscal year in question (Brazil, Contadoria Geral da Republica, 1883-1904).[4] The budget items remained relatively constant over the period, as well as the manner in which the tables were presented. Only the title page would indicate any alteration had occurred in 1889, probably because the upper echelons of the Treasury's bureaucracy remained unchanged. Since we have these final accounts, there is no need to consider—for our purposes—the difference between amount budgeted and amount spent. Only the latter is in question here.

A couple of preliminary points should be noted regarding these figures. It is the proportional division of government expenditure that is at issue here, not the absolute amount.[5] Given the often declining purchasing power of the milreis and an occasional alteration in the fiscal year, this is the most rewarding course to follow. Not only is comparability maintained, but it obviates the need to judge the validity of the specific currency figure presented.

Surprisingly, the creation of a *federal* republic and the allocation of certain tax revenues to the states and municipalities did not diminish the total size of the national budget which, rather, grew steadily. Possibly the growing revenue of the state of São Paulo would otherwise have been added to those of the central government, but only further research on provincial and state budgets (before and after 1889) will show how such a course would have affected the proportional distribution of expenditure.[6] But the minimal effect such division had on the overall structure of the budget is itself an important conclusion of this study.

Perhaps the most striking point about the proportional division of expenditures is that, while military spending did undergo a sharp upward fluctuation during the 20-year period being examined here, it was not in 1890 as one might have expected. As can be seen from the Appendix and in Figure 1, the military's share of the budget was somewhat cut in 1884 and 1885 and then stabilized at about 17 percent until 1889. These were the years of the "military question" in which officers verbally asserted their corporate rights and identity as distinct from those of planter-politicians. If they were provoked by imaginary slights, they also had "pocketbook" matters to complain about; perhaps these explain their irritability.[7] During the first two years after the Republican revolution, they reaped some fruits of their action by raising their share of the budget to 22 percent, but this was only slightly above what it had been in 1883. Furthermore, in 1892 their share began to decline, and perhaps it would have continued to do so had it not been for two major revolts which faced Brazil in 1893: one in Rio Grande do Sul which spread northward until its forces were turned back at the São Paulo state border in 1894, and the other, quelled that same year, among the naval officers of the squadron in the bay fronting Rio de Janeiro.[8] The budgetary result of all this was almost a doubling in the share of the budget going for military expenditures between 1892 and 1894. It began to decline again in 1895, and, despite the 1897 campaign against the mystical folk movement at Canudos in the backlands of Bahia, by 1898 their share receded to the level of 1883. The military, then, were not major beneficiaries of the 1889 coup.

Very little of what either the Empire or the Republic spent went to finance what we would today consider genuinely developmental needs. No group at that time saw the state as the mainspring of economic progress. Insofar as they did wish to use it to foster growth, that growth was seen in terms of greater international trade. Agriculture and industry—which we today would separate—were then considered as one category.

To give those historians who allege a developmental impetus to the political change of the period the largest possible base upon which to stand, I have cast a very wide net in my search for those expenditures that could possibly be seen as being of interest to the "new" sectors of society or conceivably aid in the transformation of Brazil under the leadership either of urban groups allegedly anxious to modernize their country or of entrepreneurial coffee planters from frontier regions.

The modernization of agriculture would in itself have been a major transformation for Brazil. Yet very little was actually

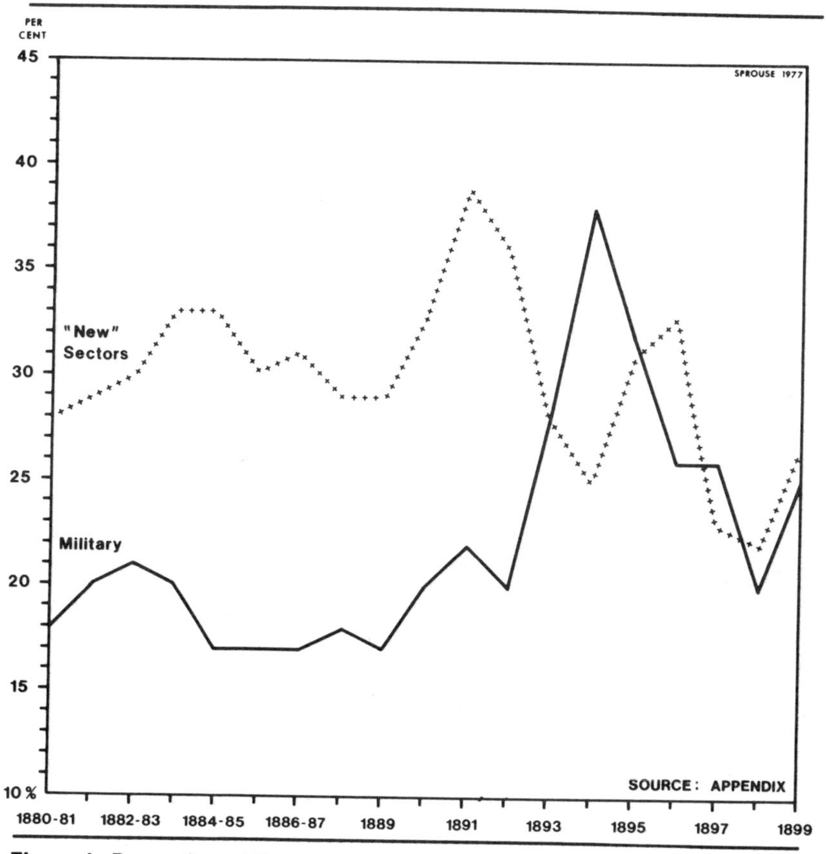

Figure 1: Proportion of Expenditure for the Military and for the "New" Sectors

spent at the national level for such a purpose. The imperial government had tried somewhat unsuccessfully to foster the establishment of central sugar factories to replace rudimentary *engenhos.* It guaranteed a return on investment therein, and, since the factories that were built were mostly financial failures, the government soon found itself paying out to the investors (Graham, 1968: 149-157; Eisenberg, 1974: 85-118). In 1885-1886, a year during which the government spent 0.54 percent of the total budget on agriculture and industry, central sugar factories accounted for 560 *contos* of the 827 *contos* listed under this rubric. Agricultural education that year cost only 85 *contos.* Contemporaries alleged that anyway the students in these schools came from wealthy families and upon graduation "did not wish to become plantation administrators," much preferring to move to Rio de Janeiro and "seek public employment" (Brazil, Congresso, 1888: VI, 397). A subsidy of 6 *contos* was paid to the Sociedade Auxiliadora da Industria Nacional, which concerned itself mainly with agricultural issues, since "industry" at that time meant any productive human activity and practically the only "national" industry was agriculture (Luz, 1961: 46). Nothing was even paid that year for subsidizing the publication of the *Flora brasiliensis* of the early nineteenth-century botanist Karl Friedrich Philipp von Martius, although this item was frequently considered by the Treasury, in both the Empire and the Republic, as an aid to agriculture. The costs of maintaining the Botanical Gardens were also often placed under this heading.

The iron factory at Ypanema in the state of São Paulo was a government enterprise with a potential for developmental impulse. It had been founded early in the nineteenth century at a time when the royal government wished to foster steel production, but it never prospered. In 1877 it had been taken out of the Ministry of War's control, and the following year a planter complained that it was not being used to make rails for the railroads then being built (Brazil, Congresso, 1883: 33; Congresso Agricola, 1878: 152). It did not succeed in diversifying its production, and in 1893 its budget was once again placed within that of the Ministry of War alongside the powder factory. In 1885-1886 its share had been 166 of the 827 *contos* spent for agriculture and industry, and during the last year for which it was separately listed (1892) it still accounted for only 201 out of 665 *contos.*

The Republic eventually closed the iron factory, weaseled out of its commitment to pay guaranteed interest on central sugar factories (quite wisely), and ceased to subsidize the Sociedade Auxiliadora da Industria Nacional. Only the Botanical Gardens continued to receive funds as an agricultural venture. Agricultural education was almost entirely eliminated from the federal budget. São Paulo state created a vigorous agricultural school in the early twentieth century, but the quality of agricultural education elsewhere probably worsened after 1889 (Winter, 1910: 226; Souza, 1915: 390). During the period 1880-1899 the federal government never spent as much as 1 percent on agriculture and industry, and under the Republic it lowered the proportion to 0.03 percent. If the military government of Floriano Peixoto (1891-1894) fostered industrial development, as has been alleged, it did so by means other than federal expenditure (cf. Sodré, 1964: 223; and see Appendix).

Railroad construction and operation were the most important directly developmental expenditures made by Brazilian governments. Since 1852 the government had guaranteed interest on the investment in certain railroads, and if a company earned more than the guarantee it would split the earnings with the government. This rarely occurred. Some lines were such consistent losers that the government bought them back from the stockholders rather than continue to pay interest. The Pedro II railway, which ran inland from Rio de Janeiro and was one of the most important in all Brazil, was government property almost from the first, as were some minor lines (see sources cited in Graham, 1968: 51-72). Some of the service on the public debt can be attributed to railroad building expenses, but most of these were charged directly to the annual budget.

The Appendix shows the proportion of the annual expenditures devoted to railroads during this 20-year period. It is notable that the declaration of the Republic did not bring any marked increase, despite the advantages of railroads for both landowners in new regions and urban residents. There was some small increase, to be sure, especially in the early Republic. The average annual proportion for the years 1880-1885 was 16.37 percent, and this went up to 17.05 percent during the next five years and then to 17.86 percent for the period 1891-1895, declining, however, in the remaining years to 15.21 percent. Not much change. Interestingly, new construction of railroads by five-year periods starting in 1881 was 3,532, 3,007, 3,030, and 2,349 kms. (Instituto Historico e Geographico Brasileiro, 1922: I, 736-737).

A further analysis of these expenditures on railroads shows that they were more or less evenly spread throughout Brazil.

After 1889 the coffee region, if anything, received less attention than others, probably because in the new coffee areas profits were high enough so that private investment was attracted to railroad enterprises and in the old coffee region the system had been completed. Of the railroads in the coffee area, only the old Pedro II railway, renamed Central railway, increased its expenditures. Otherwise, expenses, when they increased, did so on railways all the way from Ceará to Rio Grande do Sul, but not on interregional links. This fact may suggest the search for publicly supported sinecures and opportunities for the exercise of patronage, rather than the development of better or expanded service, a point I shall return to below.

Better communications are often considered an essential prerequisite for the modernizing state. During the Republic the expenditure on the post office and telegraph rose significantly (see Appendix), from an average annual figure of 2.79 percent to 4.36 percent of the total. It would be tempting to jump to the conclusion that this increase was due to a vigorous expansion program, but only further research will permit us to discard the possibility that it resulted primarily from an expanding list of civil servants hired for political reasons: the post office has long been famous as a source of public employment.

The population of the federal district of Rio de Janeiro increased by 43 percent in the ten-year period from 1890 to 1900 (Wileman, 1909: 35; Instituto Historico e Geographico Brasileiro, 1922: I, 247). In view of the alleged growth in the strength of urban interests and the widening of the electorate under the Republic to include all literate persons, one might have expected to find increasing expenditure on urban services. Certainly the demand for them was intense, and historians have viewed the failure of the Empire to satisfy their demands as one cause of its demise.[9] Under "urban services" in the Appendix, I have included public lighting, water supply, and the construction of sewers, all in the city of Rio de Janeiro; maintenance of public parks and squares there such as the Passeio Publico and the Jardim da Praça da Acclamação; the Rio de Janeiro corps of firemen; and the "construction of the new slaughterhouse in the capital." It is appalling to consider that on such limited purposes Brazil spent as much as 4 percent of its total national budget. More to our purpose, the figures in the Appendix demonstrate that there was relatively little change in the proportion spent for these services following the republican revolution, but such change as there was was downward. The average proportion spent during the Empire was 2.53 percent, whereas the Republic spent an annual average of 1.93 percent on these matters. Possibly this failure to keep up with increasing urban population has something to do with the virulent "jacobinism" or lower-middle-class rightist radicalism and xenophobia noticeable in Rio de Janeiro during the 1890s (Hahner, 1976: 125-154). At least it is clear they were aware of inadequate urban services, whether or not they understood any relationship to the division of the national budget.

By "public works" I mean port works, river dredging, and unspecified expenses, mostly carried on outside the capital, but by engineers and technicians who were presumably progress oriented. The "pork-barrel" mentality so familiar to North Americans does not seem to have been operative at this time in Brazil, probably because political support outside the capital did not depend on the possibility of mobilizing large numbers of voters but on the loyalty of a few landowners. The average proportion spent on this item declined from 4.36 percent before 1889 to 2.95 percent after that date. Whatever local interests won, it was not federally financed public works. Nor did the engineers find much employment here.

Perhaps no figure is more indicative of the sluggishness of Brazilian modernization than the amount spent on education, science, and cultural matters. During the Empire, primary education was the responsibility of the municipalities, where it remained, like them, forgotten. The only central government expenditures on elementary schooling was the inspection of private schools in the municipality of Rio de Janeiro. Secondary education was a provincial matter, except that a model preparatory school and a vocational school for draftsmen and mechanics—the only public ones in the capital—were maintained by the central government. Higher education was its only clear responsibility: it maintained two law schools, two medical schools, one engineering school, and one school of mines; also a normal school or teachers' college, a school of fine arts, and an institute of music. Small subsidies were granted two remote schools, one in Pará and one in Goiás. No change in these central government commitments was made by the Republic.[10] The Appendix brings together the expenditure on the above items as a proportion of total government spending. One may note that when Rui Barbosa—part of whose claim to fame rests upon his concern for educational reform in the 1880s—was minister of the Treasury (1890), no significant increase in educational expenditure was made, although he did keep it from falling even lower, as it did after 1892.

The maintenance of an adequate labor supply for the coffee plantations was probably the most often debated issue during the last years of the Empire. The slave system was in crisis for reasons that have been adequately discussed elsewhere (Conrad, 1972). Many planters believed that European immigrants could be imported in large numbers as a substitute for slave labor, and, indeed, several hundred thousand were brought in each year after 1885 (Hall, 1969). The provincial government of São Paulo had taken a direct financial role in fostering immigration, but after the declaration of the Republic, the bulk of the burden fell upon the central government. If the Republic did not increase expenditures for agriculture and industry, for transportation, or for urban services and other public works, it made up for this lack by financing immigration. In so doing it clearly favored the interests of coffee planters.

At first sight, expenditures on public health and social assistance would seem to be a matter of interest to the progressive, modernizing groups. Under this heading I have included the vaccination institute, epidemic relief, the health authorities in the ports, the Leprosarium, the beggars' asylum, and general expenditures on "public hygiene," "improvement in sanitary conditions," and "public assistance." But, during the period examined, the only significant alteration in the amount spent for these items occurred in 1889 (and the next three years) and was provoked by the drought of that year in the northeastern states. The degree to which local elites there benefited from the programs of public relief for droughts is now well known (Cuniff, 1970). These unusual expenditures were, therefore, more closely linked to the "old Brazil" than to the new and should be considered separately from the items we have been examining.

As can be seen from Figure 1, the proportional expenditures on the "new" sectors went up from an average of approximately 30 percent before 1889 to 39 percent in 1890 and 1891 and declined slightly in 1892. They then suffered a sharp decline (reaching a low of 26 percent in 1894), precisely at the time the military was vastly expanding its share of the revenue pie. Although this decline was reversed in 1895, it rarely reached the levels to which it had become accustomed during the last ten years of the empire, and never returned to the 1889-1892 level, at least not before the end of the century. Whether significant increases occurred in this category at the provincial–i.e., state–levels remains to be studied. Especially important will be to see whether the states other than São Paulo increased such expenditures.

What factors account for the increase on matters of interest to the "new" sectors in 1890-1892? A look at Figure 2 will show that this increase was principally the result of larger allocations for railroads and subsidies for immigration, especially the latter. This fact would suggest that at this time it was the planters of São Paulo (where most immigrants went) who were drawing principal benefits from the new regime. After the army quelled the threats to the Republic represented by the revolts of the squadron and in Rio Grande do Sul, it was once again (in 1895 and 1896) to railroads and to immigration that budgetary attention turned. Surprisingly, in 1897 and 1898, however, both these items were cut. During the revolts, the amount expended on communications (the post office) increased, and, although this item's share was diminished slightly in 1897, it was reestablished in 1898. Urban services and public works enjoyed their heyday during the 1880s, being squeezed in 1888 and again in 1890, gaining only slightly in 1892 at the very peak of the new euphoria. Subsequently it was kept to 2 or 3 percent of the budget.

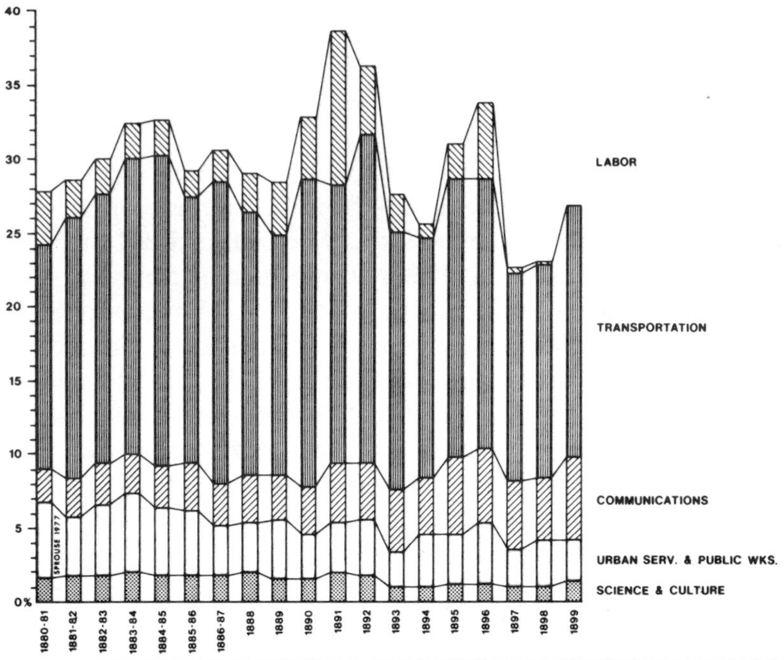

Figure 2: Changing Expenditure for The "New" Sectors.

SOURCE: Appendix.
NOTE: See the text for an explanation of each category. For reasons outline there I have omitted the items on public health and social services. As expenditures for agriculture and industry never accounted for as much as one percent of the total, I have also omitted these items from this figure.

One possible conclusion to be drawn from these figures is that the progressive urban segment did not exercise real influence at any time after 1889. The expenditure on immigrants was the major fluctuating item, and immigrants were mainly demanded by *paulista* planters. To be sure, immigrants eventually swarmed into the cities and worked in industry, but it was not an urban lobby that pushed for measures to attract them. And it could thus be said that what mattered were regional, not sectoral, clashes. If a study of state expenditures were to show, as seems likely, that only São Paulo state enjoyed larger revenues after 1889, this conclusion would be reinforced.

Despite the often nondevelopmental quality of many of these expenses, they are the only ones—with the possible exception of the service on the public debt—that could reasonably be attributed either to the interest of rising urban groups or to modernizing landowner-industrialists.

Servicing the public debt accounted for a fifth to two-fifths of public expenditure during the period surveyed here. On the whole, the average percentage used for this purpose by the Republic was less (27.73 percent) than that during the last years of the Empire (31.55 percent), although the highest figure (40.78 percent) was reached in 1898. Given the size of this item, it deserves closer scrutiny than can be done here.

There were several types of public debt. Since 1822, governments characteristically spent more than they received, and rare are the exceptions to this rule. As one statesman said, "The Empire is the deficit" (Brazil, Congresso, 1888: III, 83).[11] "Special credits" were sometimes authorized by the legislature and sometimes opened by the executive, exercising its constitutional powers. In either case, the government negotiated short-term renewable loans through the banks or major merchant houses. During the last ten years of the empire, currency was not issued to pay for deficits. When the floating debt reached such a level as to concern the Minister of Finance, and when the financial market was judged auspicious, he would consolidate these debts by a long-term loan financed by sale of government bonds. From time to time these loans would be further consolidated and absorbed into new loans. No systematic and clear-cut study has been made of the internal indebtedness of the Brazilian government, showing the destination of the money raised. The costs of war, especially the war with Paraguay, had occasioned major increases in both the internal and foreign debts, and large internal loans had to be raised to finance relief measures at the time of the major drought disaster in 1878-1880. Part of an internal loan raised in early 1889 was specifically earmarked for loans to planters, for drought relief, and for sanitation measures in Rio de Janeiro, but it is not known how much of it was actually used for these purposes (Cavalcanti, 1890: 32 ff.; Carreira, 1889: 618-619, 789-791; Figueiredo, 1899: 98).

Loans were also raised abroad, oftentimes to pay off old loans while increasing the total foreign debt.[12] Only three foreign loans in the nineteenth century had a specifically developmental purpose. In 1858 £1,526,500 was raised in London to pay for the costs of state acquisition of the Pedro II railway linking the city of Rio de Janeiro with the interior of the country. Two years later another £1,373,000 was borrowed to finance the Recife and São Francisco Railroad, the União e Industria stagecoach and toll-road company, and the Mucury immigration, colonization, and river-transport company. Finally, in 1871 a part of the foreign loan of £3,459,600 was used to pay for the extension of the Pedro II railway, the other part being used to consolidate the internal floating debt and complete payments on the short-term loans raised to finance the Paraguayan War. How much was actually used for which purpose is not yet known. In 1878 it was alleged that most foreign loans had been used for war expenses or to cover deficits with only "a very limited amount being spent on railways" (Congresso Agricola, 1878: 234; but cf. Wileman, 1896: 182). The government intended to use part of a loan of £6,297,300 raised in London in 1888 to soften the blow of abolishing slavery by lending to banks without interest, on condition they would make short-term low-interest loans to planters to help them pay their workers during the first few slave-free harvest seasons; some of this money was used instead, after 1889, to finance new industrial ventures, many of which were ill-starred. This initiative is probably the best evidence of a pro-industrial spirit after 1889 and deserves to be closely studied. Aside from these loans, all the other foreign indebtedness of the Empire was devoted directly or indirectly to meeting annual deficits. By 1889 the outstanding foreign debt alone amounted to £30,351,500, up from £16,553,800 in 1880 (Bouças, 1950: 91, 93, 109, 119, 131, 137).[13]

Upward fluctuations in debt service charges mainly reflect a decline in foreign exchange earnings without corresponding decline in local currency expenditures (Dantas, 1885). The lowering of the proportional cost of servicing the debt in the late 1880s and early 1890s (see Appendix) resulted from good coffee crops at good prices. The corresponding rise in the exchange rate lowered the milreis cost of servicing the debt and persuaded foreign lenders to consolidate previous loans at a lower interest rate. In the latter half of the 1890s coffee prices slumped badly, and even a large increase in the amount exported brought in fewer pounds sterling. The decreasing ability to import meant a declining government revenue from customs duties, the major tax source of public income. Expenditures were not cut correspondingly, and the government rolled up large deficits. An additional complexity was the expansion of the currency which began in 1889 (Villela and Suzigan, 1973: 66, 76, 108). Some of the debts incurred in the latter 1890s were the result of the complications for public finance produced by a volatile currency structure.[14]

It has been argued by Furtado (1963: 182-183, 191) that the declining exchange rate was encouraged by coffee producers to increase their share of export earnings at the expense of the rest of the population including urban groups. This argument has been countered by Buescu (1969: 373-393). Be that as it may, it is probably safe to say that the financial instability of the post-1889 years brought more suffering to members of the urban sector than to others. To be sure, a small group of bankers who knew what was happening probably profited from the government's indebtedness to them. But, on the whole, this financial instability, reflected in the high cost of servicing the public debt, may have been the result of a victory of coffee planters over urban interests. As in so many other areas of government expenditures, the city dwellers seem to have been on the losing side.

Some scholars have described the Brazilian government during this period as a "notarial state" characterized by a steadily expanding bureaucracy whose function was to absorb personnel set adrift by the declining economy of the traditional areas such as the Northeast and the Paraíba Valley (cf. Jaguaribe, 1973: 480, with Faoro, 1958: throughout; also see Luz, 1964: 13-27; and Chaffee, 1972: 116-123). An examination of this argument would take us too far, but it is obvious that what has been said heretofore about expenditures on the military, on the "new" sectors, and on the public debt, must be placed in the context of the other, regular, administrative expenditures.

The annual costs of operating the government ranged from a low of 10.41 percent (in 1894) to a high of 24.05 percent (in 1899) of the budget. As can be seen from the Appendix, the Republic did manage to reduce the proportion spent on this item during some of the years studied—when extraordinary expenditures were being incurred by the military or for servicing the debt—but ended the period by spending a greater share for ordinary administration than the Empire ever had. Curiously, there is no evidence that it was the creation of a federal system that had helped reduce these expenditures even temporarily.

An obvious saving to the Republic was the cost of maintaining the apparatus of royalty. After the declaration of the Republic most of these costs were eliminated and the salaries of the president, the vice-president, and the expenses of the presidential palace were substantially lower. The percentage of the total, however, had never been higher than 1.6 percent, so the overall effect was not very large. Furthermore, there was a slight increase in the average percentage spent on the legislature (to 1.5 percent), despite the elimination of the Council of State. Although by separating church and state the Republic was able to save taxpayers' money in expenditures for religion, this amount had also always been a neglible one (0.6 percent at the most).

The relative cost of two items, pensions and police, hardly varied. Each of these items remained in the 1.5 to 2 percent range throughout the period studied here, regardless of regime. A large portion of the pensions were paid to ex-military officers or their families.[15] The police forces and jails of the city of Rio de Janeiro, plus the costs of the island penitentiary of Fernando de Noronha, accounted for the bulk of police expenditures. In view of the population increases of the city, the average *carioca* received less police attention in 1900 than in 1890.[16] Insofar as the army may have helped control or prevent urban disorder, the increase in its budget may have compensated for this per capita decline in police expenditure. The possibility remains, however, that the riots occurring in Rio de Janeiro during the period were more disruptive because of lessening police control as well as of larger social changes.

The proportion of the budget spent on the judiciary went down rather sharply. The average percentage of the budget spent on justice went from 2.36 percent in the period before 1889 to 0.88 percent in the succeeding period. Perhaps the new regime set about the process of eliminating from their posts many tenured judges who owed their position to their political pull in the previous system, although no evidence to that effect has yet come to light. Of course, in a period of inflation a proportional decrease in these expenditures could have been compatible with a steady number of civil servants. No study has yet been made of the impact of federalism on the courts.

Variations in the cost of tax collecting in proportion to the total can best be seen in the Appendix. The decline in 1889 of more than a percentage point, occurring as it does for the year before the declaration of the Republic, suggests administrative changes having nothing to do with the new regime. The further decline of a percentage point in 1892, however, would appear to be related to initiatives of the new government. No research has yet been done on alterations in the tax-collecting mechanism. The rise in the proportion spent on this item in 1899 may reflect the effort, then in progress, to set the country's financial house in order.

The relatively steady proportion of central government expenditures on administrative matters reflects in part the worldwide and timeless ability of bureaucracies to justify themselves. At the same time, it also suggests that the declaration of the Republic did not undermine the ability of traditional elites to use the government for the purpose of patronage. A cursory examination of the correspondence of prominent politicians during both the Empire and the Republic suggests that the great bulk of their time was taken up with matters of patronage. The regional origins of those who filled public positions remains to be studied, but no contemporary evidence suggests a great sweeping away of occupants from the Northeast or from the Paraíba Valley. Furthermore, as I have noted, expenditures for railroads—including principally the cost of personnel—were centered in the Northeast. Helio Jaguaribe's suggestion that declining regions like the Paraíba supplied personnel for such agencies as the post office seems likely, since the areas experiencing rapid economic expansion were not beset by hordes of the unemployed and overtrained. If the political system is thought of—as it seems to have been at that time—principally as a source of employment for relatives and dependents, then it is clear that the declaration of the Republic brought no great tremor to the system.

One purpose of this article has been to draw attention to those areas requiring further research if the larger questions raised here are to be answered. First of all, it is clear that only a partial measure of benefit allocations has been attempted here. Other issues referred to at the beginning of this article, such as general legislation, tariffs, taxes, and currency, need to be studied as well. More particularly, provincial and state spending must be examined both before and after 1889, as well as alterations in municipal budgets. It will be especially important to discover how much state governments spent on agricultural development, agricultural education, immigration, transportation, urban services, and education, and whether these expenditures suffered significant alterations after the creation of a federal system. Were the foreign loans raised by the states used for developmental purposes? Also, what was the impact of federalism on the court system? Regarding federal expenditure itself, we need to know more precisely how railroad building was affected by the changing regime. The historian will also consider the effect of lessening police control in Rio de Janeiro on the frequency of urban disorder. To what extent were government-owned railways, the post office, and the telegraph system a refuge for the unemployed, and to what extent were they serving an expanding demand for developmental infrastructure? What were the changes in the tax-collecting mechanism that account for fluctuations in expenditures for this purpose? What use, specifically, was made of the funds raised through internal and foreign loans, and to what degree did these funds find developmental uses? Especially important will be more research on the government loans to industry in 1890 and 1891, as well as tariff legislation and other measures that may have been impelled by the strength of diverse interest groups. The attention of scholars must return to monetary issues and exchange-rate fluctuations, their causes, the motivation behind the decisions that affected them, and their short- and long-term effects. Was the rise in the public indebtedness indirectly the result of currency changes encouraged by coffee planters? These questions can be answered only by further research. Finally, it will be important to know what diverse groups wanted and whether they were satisfied with what they got.

Figure 3 summarizes the findings of this article. The military profited only reasonably in 1890 and 1891 from the declaration of the Republic, whereas the São Paulo coffee planters drew substantial and immediate benefits, especially through an increase in the subsidy for immigration. Insofar as an urban sector was important, it gained more, proportionately, from the expenditures of the Empire than from those of the Republic. The traditional government activities were not much affected during those years although the individuals occupying positions within it may have been newcomers. The major item to decline in this period was the cost of servicing the public debt, a decline that had begun before the declaration of the Republic. This decline may be attributed, on the one hand, to the able financial measures of the last two imperial ministries, and, on the other, to the booming coffee trade.

The outbreak of the revolt in Rio Grande do Sul and the rebellion of the squadron in Rio de Janeiro in 1893 radically altered these relationships. The military share of the budget vastly increased at the expense of both the traditional government tasks and the "new" sector. Some increase in the proportional cost of servicing the foreign debt also took place.

By 1896, however, the military share of the budget was once again in decline, traditional government expenses returned almost to their normal place, and expenses for immigration were rising. The astronomical increase in the cost of servicing the debt in 1897 and 1898 threw both the military and the "new" sectors into retreat, whereas traditional government expenditures suffered only a momentary setback in 1897. If, indeed, the increase in the cost of servicing the public debt

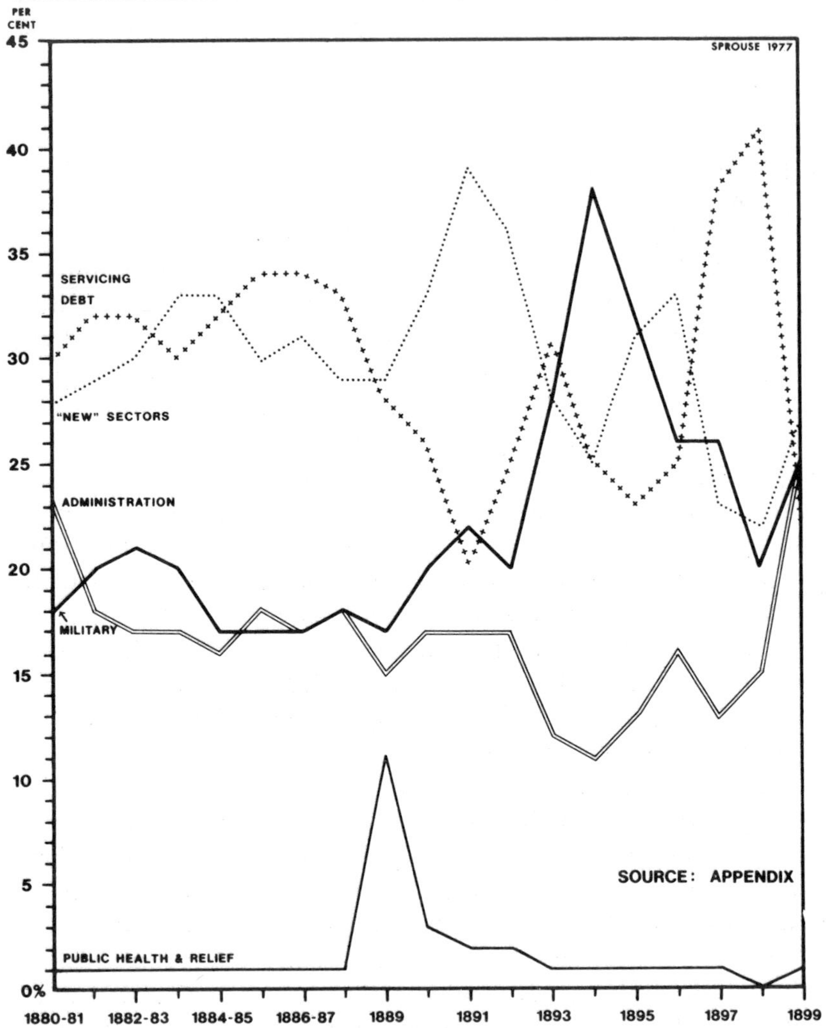

Figure 3: Proportion of Expenditure for Each Major Category

stemmed from changes in the exchange rate of benefit to coffee planters, then we could conclude that they were indubitably the chief beneficiaries of the republican revolution of 1889.[17]

As it is, we can at least maintain that new coffee planters were the first to benefit, that they shared only a reasonable amount of their lucre with the military officers, and that the urban groups benefited hardly at all. The bureaucratic sector was seriously hurt only by two crises: the revolts of 1893-1894 and the cost of servicing the debt in 1897. By 1899 it occupied a larger share than it ever had before during the period being studied. The military, contrary to what might have been expected, increased its share of the federal budget in really striking degree only in the face of civil war. The overall conclusion is not that surprising, however. The creation of the Republic did little to alter the sectoral allocation of budgetary expenditures, and, insofar as it did, that shift can be understood as much in terms of a regional one to São Paulo as an interest-group victory.

One other conclusion is inescapable: reality was more complex than some historians have made it seem. The events of 1889 did not represent a clear and permanent victory of one sector over another. The military gained from the events of that year, but not as much as one might have expected, and only regained a position they had enjoyed at the beginning of the 1880s. The urban groups were not as important, by this measure, as other historians and I have previously suggested. The coffee planters succeeded in getting national funds to subsidize immigration, but not in directing increased expenditures for railroads toward their area. The instauration of the Republic may have disturbed the traditional beneficiaries of the system but by no means replaced them. The direction of change was indecisive and its pace was halting.

Still more significant is the implication of these findings for our understanding of Brazilian political groups. Urban, agricultural, traditional, developmental, seigneurial, bourgeois, civilian, military—these are still useful, even indispensable, categories. But they are distorting in their effect if they are taken to mean groups that were fully distinct from one another. Interests overlapped. Coffee planters created banks while close family members ran urban merchant houses. Bureaucrats who were landowners and rural oligarchs who were entrepreneurs pepper the social history of the period. Where precisely can one draw the line between urban interests and those of agriculture? Even when distinct they were not necessarily in conflict. Were urbanites not also traditional in their world view and businessmen aristocratic in their consciousness? Individual actors had multiple conflicting roles. Even regional distinctions will not work in a society where great families located their landholdings and/or their daughters over the entire country. The observer must question the accepted categories and ask what happened when individuals were caught in contradictory situations. These blurring, shifting roles must be unraveled in the analysis of specific actions at specific times, where the jockeying back and forth can be precisely captured and the position of actors on one side or another not overstated. That will be both the challenge and the reward of historical study.

NOTES

1. While doing research on this article I received financial support from the John Simon Guggenheim Memorial Foundation, the National Endowment for the Humanities, and the University of Texas Research Institute. Helpful comments on a previous draft were generously made by Sandra Lauderdale, Robert Levine, Joseph Love, Peter Smith, and Steven Topik. Aldemir Maia Batissaco has been a tireless research assistant.

2. This now conventional view is conveniently summarized in the argument of Costa (1965: 183-187). Her dismissal of more traditional interpretations (pp. 169-192) is especially convincing in the light of the excellent historiographical review that preceded it (Costa, 1964: 63-120). Her interpretation of these events is basically the same as those I have presented (Graham, 1968: 39-40; 1969: 8-12), and in the present essay I express some doubts as to the complete validity of my own former interpretations. An influential exponent of the view that urban groups were dominant from 1889 to 1894 and would return to prominence in 1930 is Sodré (1964).

3. My purposes are less ambitious and very different from those of Wilkie (1970), and many of the criticisms of his work by Skidmore and Smith (1970: 71-85) are not applicable to the present modest undertaking. The categories I use are substantially different from those adopted by Cavalcanti (1890: 15 ff.), and his figures are not based on the same source.

4. In the present study I have done as the Treasury did and considered all government expenditures in one account. Thus, although the maintenance of lighthouses was partially paid for by a lighthouse tax on entering ships, I have not deducted this revenue from the expenses. Similarly, I have not deducted the income

of the post office from the cost of operating the mail system. More questionable, perhaps, is that I have not deducted the income of government-owned railroads from the expenditures on them (expenditures always outran the income). In effect, I have considered railroad fares and freight charges as a users' tax. The exception to this single-budget system occurs in 1898. In that year a major reorganization of the country's monetary system was carried out and the issues of certain banks were converted to government currency. The Treasury ran this operation through its books, but it was simply an accounting procedure and would completely distort the comparability of the data if considered as an additional "expenditure." I have, therefore, deducted this amount from that year's total. I have not made any attempt to separate capital expenditures from operating costs, since my purposes are to determine the direction of change in terms of interests served and not a study of the budget per se.

5. There is, of course, room for doubt as to whether the actors involved knew what was happening to them in proportion to other sectors. At those times when the pie was growing larger, recipients of declining proportions may have been gaining in absolute terms. These difficulties are compounded by the fact that the real value of the currency varied greatly and there were no tools then available for measuring the cost of living and judging one's own success vis-à-vis others. During the last two years of the Empire the overall size of the budget increased even when measured in pounds sterling; but during the Republic it returned to the earlier level, even though the local currency amount spiraled ever upwards. Despite all this, one measure of power surely is the possession of sufficient knowledge and ability to watch over one's interests, and it is clear that during this period some groups gained while others lost.

6. Robert Levine, Joseph Love, and John Wirth are currently engaged in a collaborative research project that includes data on post-1889 state expenditures in Pernambuco, São Paulo, and Minas Gerais.

7. Information on selected earlier years suggests that up to the time of the Paraguayan War the military normally accounted for 35 to 40 percent of the national expenditure; that during the war this figure rose to 50 and 60 percent; and that during the 1870s it was only gradually brought down to 25 or 30 percent. If these figures are correct, the 1880s were indeed a time of comparative penury for the military. See Lima and Klein (1970: 67) and Andrade (1971: 195). On the military question see Hahner (1969: 12-19), Schulz (1973: 140-165), and sources cited in each.

8. On these and other contextual matters see Hahner (1969: 59-72, 125-182). The data confirm the view that, in general, the navy did not share in the new-found prosperity of the armed forces. The naval revolt of 1893-1895 has been described as a protest against this declining share of military expenditures, and the figures in the Appendix demonstrate that, as many others have learned, there is no substitute for violence to provoke the redress of grievances: the navy's share of the budget jumped by more than 50 percent between 1894 and 1896.

9. See the evidence on urban demands for a better water supply and other sanitation measures in Costa (1965: 186, 188, and illustration facing 183) and Freyre (1970: 344-345).

10. Both imperial and republican regimes also helped finance scientific and cultural institutions such as the National Museum, the Astronomical Observatory, the National Analytic Laboratory, the Academy of Medicine, the Institute of History and

Geography, the National Library, and the public archive. Finally, they paid for a school for the blind, a school for the deaf and dumb, and a school for abandoned children. Considerable political "pull" was needed to get a child into any of these institutions; e.g., see Henrique Francisco de Avila to João Mauricio Wanderley, barão de Cotegipe, Rio, 3 May, 1886, AIHGB, Coleção Cotegipe, L. 7, D. 39.

11. For a defense of the Empire on this matter see Figueiredo (1891: 22-23).

12. See, for example, José Antonio Saraiva to Francisco Ignacio de Carvalho Moreira, barão do Penedo, Rio, 7 July 1885, AIHGB, L. 277, D. 11.

13. Despite these facts, it was often argued at the time that loans were being used to pay for economic development, see e.g., Brazil, Ministerio da Fazenda (1882: 13).

14. The abrupt decline in 1899 of the cost of servicing the public debt is the result of a "Funding Loan" negotiated in England in 1898 which included a temporary moratorium on the amortization of the foreign debt (Campos, 1909).

15. In 1882, for instance, the figures were the following:

Pensionistas	
Meio-soldos (payments to widows of army officers)	520:072$
Monte-pios (payments to widows of navy officers)	201:805
Tenças (payments to retired military officers)	3:309
Pensões (grants to wards of the state who had not been civil servants)	780:469
Aposentados (payments to civil servants)	
Ministerio do Imperio	186:368
Ministerio da Justiça	190:792
Ministerio . . . Estrangeiros	2:956
Ministerio da Marinha (civilians)	91:644
Ministerio da Guerra (civilians)	44:942
Ministerio da Agricultura	36:102
Ministerio da Fazenda	362:653
Empregados de Repartições Extinctas	25:862
Total	2.446:972$

Further information on the subject may be found in Ourem (1883).

16. The last Minister of the Empire (Interior) raised the number of Rio policemen to 1400 (Figueiredo, 1891: 93).

17. Any cut in time is artificial, and ending the study in 1899 was a decision arbitrarily made. A preliminary examination of the figures for the next three years–1900, 1901, and 1902–revealed the following average figures on proportional distribution of expenditures:

Sector	Percentage
Military	24
"New" sectors	25
Public Health & Assistance	1
Servicing the public debt	32
Administration	18
Total	100

Note that the proportion absorbed by administration was at the level characteristic of the Empire; that the military absorbed only 3 percent more than it had in 1882-1883; that the cost of servicing the debt remained relatively high in comparison with other items, but actually a bit lower than it had been in 1882-1883; and that the "new" sectors received a substantially smaller proportion of the whole than they had during the Empire. Also, the seeming shift in proportions in 1899 was merely a one-year aberration and did not indicate a change in directions.

REFERENCES

ANDRADE, L.A.G. de (1971) "Dez anos de orçamento imperial, 1867-1877." Revista Brasileira de Estudos Politicos 31 (May): 181-206.

BOEHRER, G.C.A. (1966) "The Brazilian Republican Revolution: old and new views." Luso-Brazilian Rev. 3 (Winter): 43-58.

BOUCAS, V. F. (1950) História da dívida externa. Rio de Janeiro: Edições Financeiras.

Brazil, Congresso (1888) Anais da Câmara dos Deputados. Rio de Janeiro: Imprensa Nacional.

--- (1883) Anais da Câmara dos Deputados. Rio de Janeiro: Imprensa Nacional.

Brazil, Congresso, Comissão Parlamentar de Inquerito (1883) Informações apresentadas pela Commissão Parlamentar de Inquerito ao corpo legislativo na terceira sessão da decima oitava legislatura. Rio de Janeiro: Typographia Nacional.

Brazil, Contadoria Geral da Republica (1883-1904) Balanços gerais da União . . . [1880-1899]. (Author and title vary.) Rio de Janeiro: Imprensa Nacional.

Brazil, Ministerio da Fazenda (1882) Relatorio. Rio de Janeiro: Imprensa Nacional.

BUESCU, M. (1969) "Café, cambio e inflação no Brasil (1850-1900)." Revista Verbum 26 (December): 373-393.

CAMPOS, B. de (1909) Funding Loan: o accordo do Brasil com os credores externos realisado pelo governo do dr. Prudente de Moraes em 15 de junho de 1898; documentos ineditos; varias apreciações. São Paulo: Duprat.

CARREIRA, L. de C. (1889) Historia financeira e orcamentaria do imperio do Brasil desde sua fundação. Rio de Janeiro: Imprensa Nacional.

CAVALCANTI A. (1890) Resenha financeira do ex-Imperio do Brazil em 1889. Rio de Janeiro: Imprensa Nacional.

CHAFFEE, W., Jr. (1972) "The Cartorial state: a study of the growth of the Brazilian middle class." Revista Interamericana Rev. 1:116-123.

Congresso Agricola (1878) Coleção de documentos. Rio de Janeiro: Typographia Nacional.

CONRAD, R. (1972) The Destruction of Brazilian Slavery, 1850-1888. Berkeley and Los Angeles: Univ. of California.

COSTA, E. V. da (1965) "A proclamação da República." Anais do Museu Paulista 19: 169-207.

——— (1964) "Sobre as origens da República." Anais do Museu Paulista 18: 63-120.

CUNIFF, R. L. (1970) "The great drought, 1877-1880." Ph.D. dissertation, University of Texas at Austin.

DANTAS, M. P. de S. (1885) "Breve noticia sobre o estado do Tesouro." Ms. in Arquivo do Instituto Histórico e Geográfico Brasileiro, L. 227, D. 16.

DUDLEY, W. S. (1975) "Institutional sources of officer discontent in the Brazilian Army, 1870-1889," Hispanic Amer. Hist. Rev. 55: 44-65.

EISENBERG, P. (1974) The Sugar Industry of Pernambuco. Modernization without Change, 1840-1910. Berkeley and Los Angeles: Univ. of California.

FAORO, R. (1958) Os donos do poder: formaçáo do patronato politico brasileiro. Porto Alegre: Editôra Globo.

FIGUEIREDO, A. C. de A., father (1899) "Finanças," in A década Republicana. Rio de Janeiro: Typographia do Brazil.

——— (1891) Advento da dictadura militar no Brasil. Paris: F. Pinchon.

——— (1876) As finanças da regeneração. Estudo politico oferecido aos mineiros. Rio de Janeiro: Typographia da "Reforma."

FREYRE, G. (1970) Order and Progress: Brazil from Monarchy to Republic [trans. R. W. Horton]. New York: Knopf.

FURTADO, C. (1963) The Economic Growth of Brazil: a Survey from Colonial to Modern Times [trans. R. W. de Aguiar and E. C. Drysdale]. Berkeley and Los Angeles: Univ. of California.

GRAHAM, R. (1969) A Century of Brazilian History since 1865: Issues and Problems. New York: Knopf.

——— (1968) Britain and the Onset of Modernization in Brazil, 1850-1914. Cambridge, England: Cambridge Univ. Press.

HAHNER, J. E. (1976) "Jacobinos versus Gallegos, Urban Radicals versus Portuguese Immigrants in Rio de Janeiro in the 1890s." J. of Interamerican Studies and World Affairs 18: 125-154.

——— (1969) Civilian-Military Relations in Brazil, 1889-1898. Columbia: Univ. of South Carolina.

HALL, M. (1969) "The origins of mass immigration in Brazil, 1871-1914." Ph.D. dissertation, Columbia University.

Instituto Historico e Geographico Brasileiro (1922) Diccionario historico, geographico, e ethnographico de Brasil (commemorativo do primeiro centenario da Independencia). 2 vols. Rio de Janeiro: Imprensa Nacional.

JAGUARIBE, H. (1973) Political Development: a General Theory and a Latin American Case Study. New York: Harper & Row.

LIMA, O. B. de, Jr., and L.M.G. Klein (1970) "Atôres políticos do Império." Dados 7: 62-88.

LUZ, N. V. (1964) "O papel das classes medias brasileiras no movimento republicano." Revista de Historia 28 (January-March): 13-27.

——— (1961) A luta pela industrialização do Brasil (1808-1930). São Paulo: Difusão Européia do Livro.

OUREM, barão de (1883) Notice sur les institutions de prévoyance au Bresil: Communication faite au Congrés Scientifique Universel des Institutions de Prévoyance. Pau: Imp. Garet.

SCHULZ, J. H. (1973) "The Brazilian Army and politics, 1850-1894." Ph.D. dissertation, Princeton University.

SKIDMORE, T. E. and P. H. SMITH (1970) "Notes on quantitative history: federal expenditure and social change in Mexico since 1910." Latin Amer. Research Rev. 5 (Spring): 71-85.

SODRE, N. W. (1964) História da burguesia brasileira. Rio: Civilização Brasileira.

SOUZA, T.O.M. de (1915) O estado de São Paulo: Physico, politico, economico e administrativo. São Paulo: Universal.

VILLELA, A. V. and W. SUZIGAN (1973) Política do governo e crescimento da economia brasileira, 1889-1945. Rio de Janeiro: Instituto de Planejamento Econômico e Social.

WILEMAN, J. P. (1909) The Brazilian Yearbook, 1909. (No place, no publisher.)

——— (1896) Brazilian Exchange: The Study of an Inconvertible Currency. Buenos Aires: Galli. (Reprinted New York: Greenwood, 1969.)

WILKIE, J. W. (1970) The Mexican Revolution: Federal Expenditure and Social Change since 1910. Berkeley and Los Angeles: Univ. of California.

WINTER, N. O. (1910) Brazil and Her People of To-Day: An Account of the Customs, Characteristics, Amusements, History and Advancement of the Brazilians, and the Development and Resources of Their Country. Boston: Page.

Richard Graham is a Professor of History at the University of Texas at Austin. He is the author of Britain and the Onset of Modernization in Brazil, 1850-1914 *and* Independence in Latin America, *as well as co-editor of* New Approaches to Latin American History. *He has contributed to various scholarly journals, edited the* Hispanic American Historical Review, *and now serves on the Board of Editors of the* American Historical Review.

APPENDIX

Allocation of Brazilian Government Expenditures by Category, 1880-1889 (in percentages)

	1880-81	1881-82	1882-83	1883-84	1884-85	1885-86	1886-87	1888	1889	1890	1891	1892	1893	1894	1895	1896	1897	1898	1899
Military	17.93	20.37	20.65	19.96	16.86	17.44	17.00	18.19	17.05	20.39	22.07	20.32	27.98	38.34	32.12	25.69	26.42	20.83	24.79
Army	(9.82)	(11.17)	(9.78)	(10.04)	(9.58)	(9.93)	(9.89)	(10.17)	(10.37)	(13.39)	(14.23)	(12.58)	(18.29)	(31.86)	(23.31)	(15.93)	(16.90)	(12.69)	(16.17)
Navy	(8.11)	(9.20)	(10.87)	(9.91)	(7.28)	(7.51)	(7.11)	(8.01)	(6.68)	(7.00)	(7.83)	(7.74)	(6.69)	(6.49)	(8.80)	(9.76)	(9.52)	(8.14)	(8.62)
Agriculture and Industry	0.21	0.21	0.26	0.40	0.83	0.54	0.35	0.32	0.43	0.21	0.28	0.20	0.07	0.07	0.10	0.09	0.04	0.03	0.04
Transportation	15.12	17.63	18.18	20.07	21.03	17.96	20.47	17.74	16.18	20.77	18.80	22.18	17.36	16.25	18.88	18.19	13.93	14.46	17.05
Railroads	(12.97)	(15.46)	(16.24)	(18.09)	(19.12)	(16.11)	(18.74)	(16.03)	(14.76)	(19.62)	(17.54)	(21.22)	(16.65)	(15.65)	(18.25)	(17.48)	(13.24)	(13.86)	(16.25)
Shipping[a]	(2.15)	(2.17)	(1.94)	(1.98)	(1.91)	(1.85)	(1.73)	(1.71)	(1.42)	(1.15)	(1.26)	(0.96)	(0.71)	(0.60)	(0.63)	(0.71)	(0.69)	(0.60)	(0.80)
Communications	2.29	2.50	2.78	2.57	2.81	3.17	2.85	3.19	2.93	3.23	3.95	3.75	4.14	3.84	5.14	5.00	4.52	4.32	5.68
Urban Services	3.98	2.49	3.20	1.87	2.65	2.64	2.07	2.14	1.71	1.52	2.46	2.27	1.30	1.56	2.03	1.99	2.04	1.85	2.28
Public Works	1.30	1.61	1.60	3.38	1.94	1.74	1.27	1.27	2.37	1.55	1.03	1.50	1.17	1.09	1.30	1.01	0.62	0.43	0.49
Education, Culture, and Science	1.67	1.74	1.76	1.94	1.81	1.81	1.87	2.00	1.69	1.51	2.06	1.72	1.12	1.02	1.21	1.18	1.07	1.04	1.34
Labor Supply	3.50	2.56	2.42	2.30	2.21	1.87	2.21	2.66	3.59	4.29	10.39	4.57	2.60	1.05	2.30	5.21	0.32	0.20	0.08
Abolition	(2.28)	(1.33)	(1.76)	(1.63)	(1.53)	(0.95)	(0.95)	(0.15)											
Immigration	(1.22)	(1.23)	(0.66)	(0.67)	(0.68)	(0.92)	(1.26)	(2.51)	(3.59)	(4.29)	(10.39)	(4.57)	(2.60)	(1.05)	(2.30)	(5.21)	(0.32)	(0.20)	(0.08)
Public Health and Relief	1.22	0.93	0.98	1.06	1.28	1.30	1.25	1.10	11.30	2.95	1.69	2.28	0.89	0.71	0.92	0.79	0.54	0.48	0.71
Servicing Public Debt	30.12	32.15	31.58	29.66	32.25	34.01	33.57	33.08	27.52	26.48	19.96	24.63	31.16	25.17	23.11	25.18	37.82	40.78	22.98
Administration	22.66	17.80	16.58	16.78	16.33	17.52	17.09	18.31	15.21	17.09	17.30	16.59	12.21	10.88	12.89	15.67	12.68	15.60	24.56
Tax Collecting	(5.46)	(5.55)	(5.28)	(5.26)	(5.00)	(5.27)	(5.34)	(5.71)	(4.59)	(4.70)	(4.83)	(3.62)	(3.19)	(3.09)	(3.20)	(3.25)	(3.48)	(3.44)	(5.04)
Other	(17.20)	(12.25)	(11.30)	(11.52)	(11.33)	(12.25)	(11.75)	(12.60)	(10.62)	(12.39)	(12.47)	(12.97)	(9.02)	(7.79)	(9.69)	(12.42)	(9.20)	(12.16)	(19.52)
TOTAL[b]	100.00	100.00	100.00	100.00	100.00	100.00	100.00	100.00	100.00	100.00	100.00	100.00	100.00	100.00	100.00	100.00	100.00	100.00	100.00

a. Includes subsidies paid to steamship companies engaged in international, coasting, and river transportation. There were also occasional small subsidies granted for the construction of ships.

b. Totals may not be 100.00 because of rounding.

SOURCE: Brazil, Contadoria Geral da Republica (1883-1904).

BARRY EDMONSTON
Department of Sociology
Cornell University
Ithaca, NY 14850

FRANK Wm. OECHSLI
School of Public Health
University of California, Berkeley
Berkeley, CA 94720

FERTILITY DECLINE AND SOCIOECONOMIC CHANGE IN VENEZUELA

Venezuela has experienced significant economic development during recent decades, although rapid population growth has partially offset economic gains. During the five-year period 1969-1973, the gross national product increased at an annual rate of 5.0 percent, which, coupled with population growth, yielded real per capita increases of 2.6 percent annually. Relatively smooth transition in the nationalization of the Venezuelan oil industry in 1976 presents a favorable assessment for the economy during the next decade. Yet while there has been notable progress in conventional economic indicators, there have been less rapid improvements in education, nutrition, and

AUTHORS' NOTE: The research on which this paper is based was carried out at the Food Research Institute, Stanford University, under Contract NICHD 70-2189 with the National Institutes of Health, Department of Health, Education, and Welfare as part of an investigation of "Socio-economic Factors in the Reduction of Natality in the Less Developed Areas." Updating and revision of the paper has been aided by the support of the Interdisciplinary Communications Program, Smithsonian Institution for studies of Latin American demography. The authors wish to thank Dudley Kirk for his useful comments and suggestions and Anne Hoddinott for her helpful assistance in the preparation of the final draft of this paper.

Journal of Interamerican Studies and World Affairs, Vol. 19 No. 3, August 1977

health. This paper examines past trends in Venezuelan population growth within the context of general social and economic development. Because of the importance of fertility in affecting population growth, particular attention is paid to fertility trends.

An earlier paper (Oechsli and Kirk, 1975) showed that (a) half of the Latin American and Caribbean countries have had recent declines in fertility; (b) there is a close relationship between levels of social and economic development and fertility levels; and (c) there seems to be a threshold level of socioeconomic development—below that threshold level natality decline has generally not occurred, but when the threshold is passed natality declines are usually rapid. In brief, the demographic transition, at least in its broad outline, is in process in Latin America and the Caribbean among countries with above average threshold levels of social and economic development.

On the basis of Venezuela's level of development during the 1960s, one would have predicted a lower level of fertility than was indicated by official vital statistics—a moderately high registered crude birth rate in the mid-40s per thousand prevailed throughout the 1960s. Since birth registration in Venezuela is complicated by substantial delayed registration, there is some ambiguity in the officially reported number of annual births. This paper examines recent registration and census data in Venezuela, taking particular advantage of data from the 1970 census of population. This examination documents recent fertility trends, the demographic aspects of fertility declines in the past decades, the relationship of socioeconomic change to fertility decline, and the implications of fertility trends for national population growth.

Venezuela has recently had the highest crude birth rate among Latin American nations that have achieved moderate levels of social and economic development. Table 1 ranks 25 countries of the region by decreasing level of socioeconomic development as of 1962. The index of development, shown in the second column of the table, is a composite based on levels of literacy, life expectancy at birth, proportion of the labor

TABLE 1
Development Index, Birth Rates, and Population for
25 Countries of Latin America and the Caribbean

Country	1975 Population (thousands)	Development Index ca. 1962	1960-65 Birth Rate	Latest Birth Rate	Year of Latest Report	Average Annual Birth Rate Decline
Argentina	25,383	1.53	22.5	22.7	1973	+.02
Uruguay	3,064	1.50	22.1	20.9	1973	-.02
Trinidad and Tobago	1,113	1.34	37.0	24.0	1975	-1.04
Barbados	245	1.23	29.5	19.5	1974	-.87
Puerto Rico	3,087	1.11	31.2	23.3	1973	
Guyana	791	.86	41.6	31.6	1971	-.75
Chile	10,253	.72	35.9	26.3	1972	-1.01
Cuba	9,225[a]	.70	28.1	22.3	1974	-.50
Venezuela	11,993	.53	41.8	37.0	1975	-.38
Costa Rica	1,968	.38	46.1	29.5	1974	-1.44
Jamaica	2,029	.33	39.9	29.8	1975	-.81
Panama	1.668	.28	41.2	31.7	1975	-.76
Mexico	60,145	-.17	44.0	41.9	1975	-.17
Colombia	23,542	-.19	45.1	40.6	1970-75[b]	-.45
Brazil	107,145	-.37	38.5	37.1	1970-75[b]	-.14
Peru	15,615	-.38	44.1	41.0	1970-75[b]	-.31
Paraguay	2,647	-.46	44.0	39.8	1970-75[b]	-.42
Ecuador	6,733	-.63	46.3	41.8	1970-75[b]	-.45
Dominican Republic	4,697	-.74	48.5	45.8	1970-75[b]	-.27
Nicaragua	2,155	-.87	46.7	48.3	1970-75[b]	+.16
El Salvador	4,007	-.88	48.7	40.1	1975	-.69
Bolivia	5,634[a]	-1.09	44.0	43.7	1970-75[b]	-.03
Guatemala	5,890	-1.19	44.8	43.1	1973	-.16
Honduras	3,037	-1.24	50.1	49.3	1970-75[b]	-.18
Haiti	4,584	-2.32	44.1	35.8	1970-75[b]	-.83

a. Estimated by extrapolating the rate of population growth for available post-1970 years.
b. The United Nations considers official birth registration less than 90 percent complete and therefore the rates are estimates prepared by the United Nations.
SOURCES: Development Index, Oechsli and Kirk (1975); 1960-1965 Birth Rate, United Nations (1971); Latest Birth Rate and 1975 Population, United Nations (1976).

force in agriculture, proportion of the population living in places of 20,000 and more, availability of hospital beds, newspapers, and telephones, enrollment in primary and secondary schools, and gross domestic production—ten variables in all (Oechsli and Kirk, 1975: 406).

Venezuela's birth rate decline notably lags behind the others when Venezuela's development is considered: all other nations with development indices greater than zero either have birth rates less than 30 per thousand or have had more rapid fertility declines. It seems reasonable to attribute this lag to Venezuela's unbalanced socioeconomic development and the dualistic struc-

TABLE 2
Levels of Social and Economic Development, Venezuela Circa 1962 in Comparison with other Latin American Countries

Indices of Socio-economic development	Absolute value	Relative value
Percent of population ages 15+ literate	66	-.39
Life expectancy at birth in years	57	-.15
Primary school enrollment percent of children in school	72	.68
Percent male labor force not in agriculture	62	.78
Percent population in places 20,000+	47	.67
Hospital beds per 1,000	3.3	-.09
Newspaper circulation per 1,000	78	.32
Telephones per 1,000	29	.55
Secondary school enrollment percent of children of appropriate age	30	0.70
Gross domestic product, dollars	$757	1.62
Composite	--	.53

Relative to a general Latin American average of 0.0
SOURCE: See Oechsli and Kirk (1975) for details.

ture of the Venezuelan economy. Even if fertility does decline among those who participate in the most modern part of the economy, the national impact will be diluted by the bulk of the population living in the traditional part, whose fertility may well remain high.

Table 2 gives an indication of the imbalance in Venezuelan development. In the last column, Venezuela's development in ten indices is shown relative to the Latin American-Caribbean experience. The indices are arranged to offer a general regional average of 0.0, and a maximum development level of about 1.5 for the several indices.

In 1962 Venezuela was notably advanced in the purely economic sense of gross domestic product per capita, with an index of 1.6. The country was also somewhat above average in indices of education, labor force structure, and urbanization, but notably lagging in literacy, life expectancy, and hospital beds, not even reaching the Latin American-Caribbean average in these indicators, in spite of great economic advantages. As will be noted later, life expectancy at birth in the early 1960s was probably nearer to 63 than the 57 years estimated by the United Nations and used in Table 2.

In this paper we examine available evidence on the time trend of fertility for Venezuela and its component states from the censuses of 1950, 1961, and 1971 and from vital statistics reports. Fertility changes are analyzed in order to ascertain the relationship between fertility and an index of development, literacy, across Venezuelan states. Finally, the trend of population growth and its likely future course are related to fertility levels as well as the possible impact of international migration.

Venezuelan Population Changes, 1940-1975

Although fertility levels are still high given the average level of social and economic development in Venezuela, important declines have occurred in the last decade. We investigate the magnitude of those changes in fertility by first estimating a time trend for the crude birth rate (the number of births in a given year per 1,000 midyear population). To anticipate a conclusion, it appears that Venezuela's birth registration has been late rather than incomplete since 1960. The assessment of Venezuela's vital rates is complicated, however, by large and shifting tides of migration; there were large net migration balances from 1945 through 1958 or 1959, which were followed by large net out-migration balances until 1970. Data since 1971 indicate a return to net in-migration for Venezuela, although the rates have fluctuated considerably for the past four or five years. Fortunately, data on the size of these migration balances are given in the *Anuario Estadístico* and *Boletín Mensual* for documented international migration.

TABLE 3

Registered Vital Rates, Venezuela, 1940-1975

Year	Birth	Death	Migration	Natural Increase	Total Increase
1940-44	35.7	16.4	-.5	19.3	18.7
1945-49	38.4	13.5	2.8	24.9	27.7
1950-54	43.9	10.4	6.1	33.5	39.6
1955	45.2	9.8	8.9	35.3	44.3
1956	44.4	9.5	6.5	34.9	41.4
1957	43.6	9.5	6.7	34.1	40.8
1958	43.0	8.7	1.5	34.3	35.8
1959	46.1	8.4	1.4	37.7	39.o
1960	46.o	7.5	-1.4	38.6	37.2
1961	45.3	7.3	-1.0	36.4	35.4
1962	43.4	7.0	-1.0	36.4	35.4
1963	43.5	7.2	-0.9	36.3	35.4
1964	42.3	7.2	1.3	35.0	36.4
1965	43.7	7.1	0.9	36.6	37.5
1966	41.9	6.9	-0.6	35.0	34.4
1967	43.9	6.7	-2.6	37.3	34.6
1968	40.1	6.7	-6.1	33.3	27.3
1969	40.0	6.8	-3.7	33.2	29.5
1970	38.3	6.7	-6.2	31.6	25.4
1971	38.3	6.3	2.5	32.0	32.5
1972	36.8	6.8	0.3	30.0	30.3
1973	35.9	6.8	0.9	29.1	30.0
1974	37.2	6.3	6.1	30.9	37.0
1975	37.0	6.2	0.9	30.8	31.7

SOURCE: Venezuela, *Anuario Estadistico de Venezuela,* various years for the registered numbers of births, deaths, and net international migration for the 1940-1971 period. Venezuela, *Boletin Mensual,* various issues for the 1972-1975 period. Population bases were computed assuming constant geometric intercensal increase of population.

Table 3 shows Venezuela's crude rates of birth, death, migration, natural increase, and total increase computed from numbers of births, deaths, and migration balance given in the *Anuario Estadístico* and *Boletín Mensual.* Intercensal population estimates assuming exponential intercensal population change provides the base for the calculation of population rates. Registered births and deaths include those vital events occurring in the particular calendar years that were not registered late. The immediate question concerns the accuracy of the officially reported data.

The simplest check involves seeing if the demographic accounts, as given in the registered reports of births, deaths, and migration balance, agree with the census counts. The increase in population from one census to the next, if registration is correct, should be accounted for by the number of births and deaths adjusted for migration. Between 1941 and 1950 only 1.059 million (or 83.6 percent) of the total intercensal increase of 1.267 million is accounted for by registered events. It seems likely that this shortfall can most probably be accounted for by underregistration of births and in-migrants or both.

Since 1950 the census accounts and the vital registration records are in better agreement, the population increase accounted for by the registration system being slightly greater than the increase reported in the census. Between 1950 and 1961, for example, registration accounts for an increase of 2.421 million as against the census increase of 2.377 million; these agree to within 2 percent. Between the 1961 and 1971 censuses, the registrations account for an increase of 2.998 million as against the increase of 2.924 million found in the census; these numbers agree to within 2.5 percent.

Close agreements in population change for the period since 1950 are encouraging, although by no means conclusive, evidence that the figures may be taken at face value. Since there is always a possibility of compensating error, even in balancing accounts, the data need to be examined for plausibility as well as consistency. The migration data seem plausible in that the direction of migration conforms to what is known about government policy; prior to 1958 the immigration of foreigners, particularly skilled foreigners, was encouraged; post-1958 reversed that policy in favor of greater reliance on and development of indigenous skills; and, in recent years, the Venezuelan government has once again relaxed restrictions on immigration of foreigners, particularly those in the skilled occupations.

International migration has been an important component of Venezuelan population growth since the 1940s, with especially large numbers of foreigners entering during 1947 to 1959 (Carrillo Batalla, 1967: 76-77; Chen, 1968: 18-19). By 1971, about 600,000 people, or 5.9 percent of the Venezuelan population, were born outside Venezuela. During the heavy immigration of the 1950s, slightly over two-thirds of the migrants were from Europe, the largest number being from Spain and Italy. The third heaviest immigration was from Venezuela's western neighbor, Colombia. It was during the period of large immigration that Venezuela achieved strong economic growth from the impact of unparalleled expansion of the petroleum industry (Salazar-Carrillo, 1976: 71-127); however, in 1960 Venezuela began a policy of restricted immigration. Documented immigration decreased under the policy of restrictions, only to increase again with the relaxation of official restriction on foreign immigration in recent years.

Demographic investigation of international migration to Venezuela is complicated by the existence of considerable illegal immigration, particularly from Colombia. Ramón Ignacio Velásquez, head of Venezuela's immigration bureau, estimates that there are 150,000 Colombians now residing legally in Venezuela, and at least 300,000 Colombians residing illegally in the country (New York Times, 1976). The estimate of 300,000 illegal Colombians agrees in general with evidence on the outmigration of Colombians during the 1964-1973 period, legally or illegally, to the United States and Venezuela (Potter and Ordoñez, 1976). Unlike the legal immigrants who often have professional education or skilled trades, the illegal immigrants are generally unskilled workers who find employment in marginal service activities or transient agricultural labor. Illegal immigration affects the demographic situation in two ways: (1) it tends to increase population growth without indication in the registered vital rates, and (2) it must be considered to be a significant factor in affecting future population growth, even though it is difficult to determine the quantitative influence of illegal immigration from Colombia. The conclusion of this paper considers the possible contribution of international migration to future Venezuelan population growth, given the past changes in legal and illegal migration balance.

Birth and death rates seem plausible since 1950 or so, the period when the census and registration figures balance. The death rate dropped below 10 per thousand in 1953 and has been below 10 ever since. Such a rate is not unusual in rapidly growing populations with dramatic mortality declines; in Venezuela's case, the age destribution resulting from high fertility is supplemented by age distortion from migration currents. Moreover, given the pattern of the age distribution, if deaths have been underreported by 10 percent, it would have been by no more than enough to account for one point on the crude death rate in recent years.

Venezuela's completeness of birth reporting in recent years has been listed as above the 90 percent criterion for acceptable reporting set by the United Nations. If the true birth rate for a population were 40 per thousand, then a 10 percent underreporting of births would yield an underreporting of the crude birth rate by four points. Acceptance of the UN criterion for Venezuelan birth registration suggests a maximum deviation of three or four points for recent years. What is even more important in assessing Venezuelan fertility trends is that recent downward trends in the birth rate must be real unless there has been a deterioration in birth reporting, a condition not very probable in light of (a) the good agreement between registration and census counts since 1950, and (b) government effort toward improvement in the vital registration system. In the next section, Venezuelan fertility trends are analyzed in greater detail.

Venezuelan Fertility Trends

There is evidence that the chief defect in Venezuela's birth registration is late reporting, and that the extent of late reporting has been consistent since 1957. Ninety-seven to 99 percent of births reported in any one year are births that have occurred within the preceding ten years (Venezuela, *Anuario Estadístico*, various years since 1957). Whether one looks at promptness of reporting of births occurring in a given year or at births reported in a given year, nearly 55 percent of births are currently reported in the year of occurrence, and 92-94 percent are reported within three years. Conversely, some 33 percent of the births are not reported in year of their occurrence, and some 6-8 percent of births are not reported within three years of occurrence. The extent of lateness has not varied significantly since 1957.

To confirm long-term fertility trends, it is worthwhile to estimate the course of Venezuelan fertility from census data. It is clear from the foregoing that births were grossly under-reported between the 1941 and 1950 censuses. The large and shifting tides of migration make the estimation of vital rates in Venezuela a complex enterprise.

While there is some disagreement between the leading practitioners of the art of milking the maximum usable facts from inadequate demographic data, we develop new estimates of the birth rate in order to provide a time series covering the 1940 to 1971 period. If it is true that birth registration is complete, though late, since 1960, then there is a firm basis for determining whether fertility levels are consistent with reported births for the latter end of the series. By standard application of demographic techniques derived from stable population theory, mortality assumptions can be employed to estimate fertility levels. It is then possible to compare estimated and reported fertility levels for recent years.

Age categories 0-4 and 5-9 represent the survivors of those cohorts born 0-4 and 5-9 years previous to a population census. Given a correct mortality level, births and population bases can be found with which to estimate the crude birth rate for the two five-year periods preceding the census. Details of this reverse survival procedure may be found in United Nations (1967).

The set of mortality rates depends on a specified set of life tables. Based on Arriaga's estimates (Arriaga, 1968) for the 1926-1961 period and the Venezuelan government's estimates (Venezuela, 1972a, 1972b) for 1970, the following historical trends in life expectancy at birth, by sex, are derived:

Year	*Female*	*Male*	*Both Sexes*
1970	68.2	64.7	66.4
1961	64.7	61.2	62.9
1950	54.0	51.2	52.6
1941	40.7	39.2	39.9
1936	34.5	33.3	33.9
1926	32.8	31.6	32.2

There appears to be general agreement in the temporal trends between Arriaga's estimates and the Venezuelan government's estimate for 1970. Furthermore, overall mortality trends seem plausible in terms of the pace and tempo of improvement. After rather slow improvement in mortality through the first half of the 1940s there was a quickening in the late 1940s and the 1950s, probably related to malaria control and public health programs dealing with infectious diseases. Since the 1960s, and with increased levels of life expectancy at birth, mortality has improved more slowly. Such movement in mortality is consistent with changes in public health programs, economic development, and educational improvement since the mid-1940s in Venezuela.

Reverse survival techniques are applied to the census age distributions for the Venezuelan censuses of 1950, 1961, and 1971. With appropriate mortality levels found by quadratic interpolation from the nearest three known values of life expectancy shown earlier, Coale-Demeny model "South" life tables (Coale and Demeny, 1966) are used. Recent work on the empirical applicability of model life tables suggests that model "South" is particularly suited to Latin American population with relatively higher infant mortality (Adlakha, 1972).

Table 4 displays the Venezuelan crude birth rate for 1940 to 1971 based on the age distribution of females and males. As a historical record of the birth rate, the trend for males is probably more reasonable, since age misstatement and underenumeration of males is generally lower than for females in Latin American censuses of population (United Nations, 1967: 50).

TABLE 4

Estimates of the Crude Birth Rate for Venezuela, 1940-1971 [a]

	Regional Model Life Table Model South	
Period	Males	Females
1966-71	39.5	38.8
1961-66	45.9	44.2
1956-61	50.0	45.1
1951-56	49.0	48.2
1945-50	46.1	44.1
1940-45	48.5	43.9

a. Assumes a mortality pattern corresponding to estimates of life expectancy at birth from Arriaga (1968) and Venezuela (1972b). Number of births in the five-year periods are derived by reverse survival of the 0-4 and 5-9 age categories in particular Venezuelan population censuses. See the text for details of the estimation procedure.

For the 1966-1971 period, a crude birth rate of 38 to 39 indicates a significant decline. Since this evidence corroborates vital statistics data on births, we conclude that measurable decreases have occurred in Venezuelan fertility during the 1966-1971 period.

These results for the historical trend in the crude birth rate are comparable to those of Collver (1965), although Collver's estimates terminate in 1960 and are two or three points lower than those estimated here. Comparison of Tables 3 and 4 suggests that the officially reported birth rates are considerably underreported until the late 1950s. Since about 1960, government reporting and the independent estimates of Collver and those presented in this paper are in close agreement. As a check on recent fertility trends, further work should assess the continued changes of Venezuelan fertility in terms of additional methods of estimating fertility (see Edmonston and Sapoznikow, 1976, for discussion of other methods). Changes in the degree of late reporting may contribute to future fluctuations in the annual crude birth rate without actual changes in the pattern of underlying fertility.

So far, we have discussed the crude birth rate. It is always possible for temporal trends in the crude birth rate to reflect changes in the population age structure rather than true under-

TABLE 5
Woman/Population Ratio, Crude Birth Rates, and General Fertility Rates, 1941, 1950, 1960, and 1971

Year	W/P Ratio[a]	Crude Birth Rate	General Fertility Rate[b]
		Absolute Numbers	
1941	26.9	48.5[c]	-[e]
1950	22.0	49.0[c]	193.1
1961	20.0	45.3[d]	207.0
1971	21.1	38.3[d]	166.4
		Percent Change	
1941-50	-18.2	1.0	-[e]
1950-61	-9.1	-7.6	+7.2
1961-71	+5.5	-15.5	-19.6

a. W/P Ratio is women aged 15-44 as a percent of the total population.
b. General fertility rate is number of births per thousand women aged 15-44.
c. Estimated from the age distribution of males by Model South regional life table.
d. From reported registered births.
e. Not known.
SOURCES: Venezuela (1947, 1955, 1964a, 1964b, 1972a, 1973).

lying changes in the forces of fertility. Table 5 presents several available indices which indicate that changes in Venezuela's crude birth rate are not merely the result of changes in the relative numbers of women of childbearing age. From 1941 to 1961 there was a decline in the proportion of women in the childbearing ages of 14 to 44 years (the W/P ratio). During this period the crude birth rate increased slightly in the 1940s, then decreased 7.6 percent from 1950 to 1961. It appears that the birth rate decline during the 1960s was largely the result of a decreased proportion of women in the childbearing years, since the general fertility rate (number of children per thousand women 15-44 years of age) increased 7.2 percent during this same period. In the 1960s, however, the general fertility rate fell 19.6 percent, greatly offsetting the 5.5 percent increase in the W/P ratio and yielding a 15.5 percent decline in the crude birth rate. Conclusions regarding fertility declines in the 1961-1971 decade are substantiated by examination of the changes in age-specific fertility rates. During the decade of the 1960s, there were significant declines in all age groups, but particularly for women less than 30 years of age. Differences in the general fertility rates in 1961 and 1971 can be expressed in terms of (a) shifts in the age structure, (b) changes in the age-specific fertility rates, and (c) interaction between the age and fertility rate changes (Kitagawa, 1964). If there had been only a shift in the age structure during 1961-1971, the 1971 general fertility rate would have been 206.3, a decline of only 0.7 from the 1961 rate of 207.0. But if the 1961 age structure prevailed while taking on the 1971 age-specific fertility rates, then the resultant general fertility rate would be 168.0. Thus, 1961-1971 changes only in the age-specific fertility rates would decrease the general fertility rate by 38.9 points or 96 percent of the total decline in the period. The interaction of age shifts and age-specific fertility rate changes accounts for only a 1.0 decline in the general fertility rate during 1961-1971. Declines in the age-specific fertility rates were therefore chiefly responsible for fertility changes in the 1960s in Venezuela.

In summary, there was a small increase in underlying fertility before 1961, but there has been a recent substantial decline in fertility. Fertility declines in the 1960s were the result of age-specific fertility rate decreases at all ages, but primarily among those 30 years of age and younger. Can we conclude that fertility declines have been a consequence of Venezuelan modernization? A look at regional variation in fertility provides part of the answer.

Regional Variations in Fertility, 1950-1971

The extent to which regional variations in the recent decline of Venezuelan fertility are related to regional variations in modernization are based on data from the 1950, 1961, and 1971 population censuses. Only one index of modernization is consistently available in the three censuses: the percentage of the population literate among those 10 or older. As a measure of fertility, we use the child/woman (C/W) ratio or the ratio of children aged 0-4 years per thousand women of the childbearing ages 15 to 44 years.

The C/W ratio is chosen in preference to any of the various indices deriving from the registration system because most children and women in the census are allocated to the same geographical region, while the registration system allocates a birth to the place of registration which might not be the mother's usual place of residence. This is troublesome in the case of Venezuela, since a high proportion of births in the provinces near the Federal District of Caracas—especially the state of Miranda—are delivered by physicians within the boundaries of the Federal District. As a result, the registered number of births in the Federal District are considerably greater than expected, while the reported number of births are artificially decreased in provinces close to the Federal District. The use of fertility indices based on the registration data seems inadvisable for regional analysis without specific correction for births occurring outside of the mother's habitual place of residence.

The child/woman ratio is a somewhat conservative index of fertility decline for our purposes. It is similar to the general fertility rate in structure, except that it incorporates only the births that survive to be enumerated in the census. In this section, two types of comparisons are made. First, the C/W ratio is compared over time to see if there is a decline that accompanies modernization. Second, C/W ratios are compared for Venezuelan states at a point in time to see if the more modern do have lower ratios. In either case, if there were no difference in the underlying fertility levels, we would expect lower C/W ratios in the less modern states because fewer of their children survive to be enumerated. Thus, when more modern populations have lower C/W ratios even in the face of the expected bias in the other direction, it may be confidently concluded that the effect is attributable to the lower fertility in the more modern state.

To clarify the preceding argument, consider the course of the C/W ratio in a hypothetical population undergoing a typical sequence of improved mortality followed by declining fertility. At first, with low levels of modernization one would expect high childhood mortality accompanied by possible underenumeration of children in the census; these effects would produce moderate C/W ratios. With development would come, first, improvements in child survival and perhaps better census enumeration, both yielding rises in the C/W ratio. Somewhat later, after some threshold level of development had been reached—about 70-80 percent for literacy (Oechsli and Kirk, 1975)—one would expect fertility to decline, slowly at first, but eventually at a pace rapid enough to more than overbalance continued improvement in childhood survival and to result in a reduction of the C/W ratio. Thus, in the absence of deterioration in survival changes, a decline in the C/W ratio will be an understatement of a change in general fertility.

A similar relationship is found in comparing cross-regional correlations of literacy and the C/W ratio over time. At an early stage, when none of the states had literacy at the threshold level, one would expect that childhood mortality would be the prime determinant of the C/W ratio; in these circumstances, one would expect a positive correlation between literacy and the C/W ratio—the higher the literacy, the better is childhood survival.

As development proceeds and some states exceed the literacy threshold, one would expect declining fertility to begin to influence the C/W ratio and the correlation between the ratio and literacy to shift toward an inverse relationship. Indeed, any substantial shift to such an inverse relationship can be taken as good evidence for fertility decline in the more literate regions, unless there is the implausible assumption that these regions are undergoing declining chances of childhood survival. Venezuelan experience is examined to see if this model applies.

Tables 6 and 7 show, respectively, C/W ratios and percentage of the population aged 10 and older that is literate for Venezuela and the states for the censuses of 1950, 1961, and 1971, as

TABLE 6
Child/Women Ratios and Intercensal Percent Change, Venezuela and States, 1950, 1961, and 1971

Region	Child/Woman Ratio			Intercensal Percent Change	
	1950	1961	1971	1950-61	1961-71
Venezuela	767	912	768	+20.0	-15.8
Northern Cordillera					
Federal District	603	666	587	+10.4	-16.2
Miranda	786	785	611	-0.1	-22.2
Aragua	756	909	766	+20.2	-15.7
Carabobo	729	901	749	+23.6	-16.9
Lake Maracaibo					
Zulia	806	925	704	+14.8	-23.9
Andes					
Tachira	825	1,028	857	+24.6	-16.6
Merida	755	948	837	+25.6	-11.7
Trujillo	739	933	850	+26.3	-8.9
Transitional					
Falcon	795	1,000	832	+25.8	-16.8
Lara	696	937	808	+34.6	-13.8
Yaracuy	787	1,064	938	+35.2	-11.8
Plains					
Apure	796	1,118	1,059	+40.5	-5.3
Barinas	781	1,163	1,026	+48.9	-11.8
Portuguesa	762	1,024	931	+34.4	-9.1
Cojedes	815	1,135	974	+39.3	-14.2
Guarico	803	1,080	915	+34.5	-15.3
Anzoategui	874	1,020	859	+16.7	-15.8
Miscellaneous					
Monagas	972	1,099	958	+13.1	-12.8
Sucre	892	1,069	979	+19.8	-8.4
Nueva Esparta	762	853	788	+11.9	-7.6
Bolivar	825	1,066	931	+29.2	-12.7

SOURCE: Venezuela (1955, 1964, 1972a).

well as the intercensal percentage changes for these indices. The Federal District of Caracas differs appreciably from the rest of the country; it has the lowest C/W ratio (below 700) and the highest literacy (over 80 percent) in each census. This is in accord with our thesis, of course, that low fertility accompanies modernization. But to avoid biasing the results, for most of the remainder of the analysis we exclude the Federal District from correlations and comparisons.

In Table 6, the C/W trend for the states of Venezuela agrees broadly with the national pattern: there is a rise for every state

TABLE 7

Percent Age 10+ Literate and Intercensal Percent Change, Venezuela and States, 1950, 1961, and 1971

Region	Percent 10+ Literate 1950	1961	1971	Percent Change 1950-61	1961-71
Venezuela	51	65	77	27	18
Northern Cordillera					
Federal District	82	88	91	7	4
Miranda	51	73	86	44	17
Aragua	56	71	83	27	16
Carabobo	56	70	82	26	18
Lake Maracaibo					
Zulia	62	1	81	15	14
Andes					
Tachira	49	60	73	22	22
Merida	36	48	65	31	37
Trujillo	34	46	61	38	32
Transitional					
Falcon	44	59	72	35	23
Lara	38	54	69	44	27
Yaracuy	34	49	64	44	31
Plains					
Apure	34	47	59	38	25
Barinas	33	46	60	50	40
Portuguesa	29	42	62	45	46
Cojedes	29	43	61	48	41
Guarica	38	52	64	37	23
Anzoategui	50	64	75	28	17
Miscellaneous					
Monagas	49	59	71	19	21
Sucre	41	53	65	32	22
Nueva Esparta	50	62	74	23	20
Bolivar	54	69	80	29	15

SOURCE: Venezuela (1955, 1964, 1972a).

(except Miranda) in the 1950-1961 period and a decline for every state for the 1961-1971 period, although the sizes of these changes were spread unevenly.

Data on literacy (see Table 7) provide a partial key to understanding some of these patterns. First, for every census there is a clear division between those with literacy better than the Venezuelan average and those with poorer literacy. Thus, in 1950 the states with better than average—51 percent or more—literacy were in the Northern Cordillera and Lake Maracaibo areas and, from the miscellaneous group, the state of Bolívar. Exactly the same states also exceeded the average Venezuelan literacy in 1961 and 1971 when the percentage literate had advanced to, respectively, 65 and 77 percent. Though literacy advanced in all Venezuela, the relative positions of the states in the literacy scale remained roughly the same.

Accepting the range of 70-80 percent literate as a threshold for fertility decline, none of the states had reached that range—exempting the Federal District—in 1950. Thus, we should not expect to see any clear evidence of fertility reductions, and, indeed, with the exception of Miranda, there were general, and in many cases relatively large, increases in the C/W ratios in the 1950s. Apparently the chief influence on the C/W ratios during the 1950s was rapidly improving childhood survival chances. Moreover, these mortality improvements were greatest among those states that were the least literate in 1950. These changes are likely the consequence of some real rises in fertility and marked declines in mortality, following the antimalaria campaigns in states with previous high malaria prevalence and public health programs reducing infectious diseases.

In 1950 there was a low positive association between literacy and the C/W ratio, as indicated by the rank difference correlation of +.16. The changes that had occurred in the 1950-1961 period left the child/woman ratio in 1961 above 900 for every state except the Federal District, Miranda, and Nueva Esparta (which throughout had a somewhat lower C/W ratio than appropriate for its literacy). However, the more literate states tended to be within the lower end of the 900-1100 range, and the net result was that the 1961 correlation between literacy and C/W ratio had shifted to —.55. Moreover, by 1961 four states in addition to the Federal District had literacy rates within the 70-80 percent threshold range.

All four of the states within the threshold literacy range in 1961 experienced fertility declines in the 1960s and achieved the lowest C/W ratios in the country. By 1971 the correlation between literacy and the C/W ratio had become —.79. And also, by 1971, six more states had literacy levels within the 70-80 percent range—Táchira, Falcón, Anzoátegui, Monagas, Nueva Esparta, and Bolívar—to form the likely candidates for fertility declines in the 1970s.

Although it appears that all the states of Venezuela participated to some degree in the fertility decline of the 1961-1971 period, the decline was greatest in those parts of the country that had moved the furthest in the direction of modernization, as measured by the single index of literacy. By 1971 there was a marked gradient in fertility, which was inversely related to literacy and with several states posed on the verge of future fertility declines.

Conclusions

Venezuelan natality appears to have declined in recent years as an accompaniment of socioeconomic development. Our estimates indicate a birth rate in the mid to high 40s per thousand existing until the early 1960s, followed by declines to below the level of 40 per thousand; these estimates are supported by the registered birth data, census age distributions, and the pattern of regional fertility variations. Declines in the Venezuelan birth rate have not been the result of changes in the age distribution of the population. Moderate decreases are evident for all age-specific fertility rates during the 1961-1971 period, although the strongest declines were for women less than 30 years of age.

Venezuela's fertility decline in the 1960s is consistent with the findings for other countries of Latin America and the Caribbean that had reached relatively high levels of social and economic development. Thus, rather than appearing as the lone demographic exception in the upper half of Table 1, Venezuela appears to be at the beginning of the fertility decline phase of the demographic transition. Venezuela's lag in this process is presumably the result of the dual nature of the economy, in which a very large part of the population remains in the traditional sphere despite high per capita national income. Future research needs to investigate the relationship of variation in developmental changes, as well as the mean levels of developmental indices. It is likely that considerable differences exist in fertility levels stemming from individual variation within a country, which is not detailed by studies using aggregate indices of development.

From both a spatial and temporal perspective, Venezuelan regional experience follows on a smaller scale the pattern of change in the rest of Latin America. The most developed Latin American nations and Venezuelan states were displaying the first suggestions of fertility decrease in 1960. By 1970 the more developed countries of Latin America and the most developed states of Venezuela were obviously in the midst of significant fertility declines.

With a 1976 population size of about 12.4 million, what are the implications of this study for future population growth in Venezuela? Since development programs for the 1976-1980 period aim to support improved and expanded programs in the areas of health, nutrition, and agriculture (Rodriguez, 1976), infant and maternal mortality will likely be further reduced in the next decades. Improvements in life expectancy will contribute to increased population growth by reducing slightly the death rate. Laudable progress in reducing mortality will, therefore, partially offset declines in fertility.

As shown in Table 3, legal immigration contributes an insignificant amount to annual population growth: the net average number of migrants for 1972-1975 was about 23.5 thousand, or only 0.2 percent annual growth. Unless there is a dramatic change in the attractiveness of Venezuela for foreigners with skilled trades, future population growth derived from legal immigration will be small. Moreover, the Venezuelan government may, as a matter of public policy, reduce legal immigration as was effectively accomplished in the early 1960s.

Illegal immigration contributes an unmeasured number of people to the annual growth of the Venezuelan population. If the estimated 300,000 Colombians illegally residing in Venezuela presently (New York Times, 1976) were to have entered

Venezuela at the rate of 30,000 per year during the past decade, this constitutes less than a .3 percent annual rate of illegal immigration. No change in government regulation of illegal immigration plus a continuation of present policies on legal immigration might anticipate a maximum of .5 percent annual growth from both sources of international immigration.

Venezuelan government estimates of future population growth range from projected sizes in the year 2001 of 22.5 million, if fertility falls to the replacement level between 1971 and 2001, to 30.0 million if no decreases in fertility occur (Venezuela, 1976). Under the assumption of moderate but not extreme fertility reductions to, say, an average of 3.5 children per family in the year 2001, Venezuela would grow by 2.8 percent annually to reach a population size of 24.9 million in 2001. A rate of .5 percent immigration would yield a population size of about 28.0 million in 2001 if added to the pattern of moderate fertility declines. Venezuelan population policy thus incorporates consideration of modest growth due to immigration as well as government measures relating to fertility changes. With substantive reductions in fertility during the past decade, likely prospects of further declines in selected states in the near future, and the chance to influence fertility changes by government programs (see Freedman and Berelson, 1976 for a discussion of the impact of programs in the area of family planning), Venezuela will likely be in the midst of significant fertility reductions for the next several decades. Since reduction in fertility will lower population growth and make more apparent the contribution made by immigration, government concern with population increase will necessarily be directed toward immigration as a policy issue.

REFERENCES

ADLAKHA, A. (1972) "Model life tables: an empirical test of their applicability to less developed countries." Demography 9 (November): 589-601.

ARRIAGA, E. E. (1968) New Life Tables for Latin American Populations in the Nineteenth and Twentieth Centuries. Berkeley: University of California Institute of International Studies.

CARRILLO BATALLA, T. E. (1967) Analisís Cuantitativo y Cualitativo de la Economía de la Población Venezolana. Caracas: Ediciones de Cuatricenenario de Caracas.

CHEN, C. (1968) Movimientos Migratorios en Venezuela. Caracas: Univ. Católica Andrés Bello Instituto de Investigaciones Económicas.

COALE, A. J. and P. DEMENY (1966) Regional Model Life Tables and Stable Populations. Princeton, NJ: Princeton Univ. Press.

COLLVER, A. O. (1965) Birth Rates in Latin America: New Estimates of Historical Trends and Fluctuations. Institute of International Studies Research Series No. 7. Berkeley: Univ. of California.

EDMONSTON, B. and J. SAPOZNIKOW (1976) "Measuring fertility in Latin America." Estadística: J. of the Interamerican Statistical Institute 30 (July): 68-78.

FREEDMAN, R. and B. BERELSON (1976) "The record of family planning programs." Studies in Family Planning 7 (January).

KITAGAWA, E. M. (1964) "Standardized comparisons in population research." Demography 1: 296-315.

New York Times (1976) "Illegal immigrants plaguing Venezuela." December 5: 22.

OECHSLI, F. W. and D. KIRK (1975) "Modernization and the demographic transition in Latin America and the Caribbean." Economic Development and Cultural Change 23 (April): 391-419.

POTTER, J. E. and M. ORDONEZ G. (1976) "The completeness of enumeration in the 1973 census of the population of Colombia." Population Index 42 (July): 377-403.

RODRIGUEZ, G. (1976) "Crucial to third world growth: the development of human resources." Documentación: Venezuela Now 2 (October 15). New York: Venezuelan Mission to the United States.

SALAZAR-CARRILLO, J. (1976) Oil in the Economic Development of Venezuela. New York: Praeger.

United Nations (1976) Population and Vital Statistics Report: Data Available as of 1 October 1976. Statistical Papers, Series A XXVIII, 4. New York: United Nations.

--- (1971) Estimates of Crude Birth Rates, Crude Death Rates, and Expectations of Life at Birth, Regions and Countries, 1950-65. ESA/P/WP/38. New York: United Nations (February 22). (mimeo)

--- (1967) Manual IV: Methods of Estimated Basic Demographic Measures from Incomplete Data. New York: United Nations.

Venezuela (1976) Proyección de la Población de Venezuela. Tomo I. Caracas: Dirección General de Estadística y Censos Nacionales.

--- (1973) Anuario Estadístico: 1971. Caracas: Dirección General de Estadística y Censos Nacionales.

--- (1972a) X Censo General de Población: 2 Noviembre 1971. Caracas: Dirección General de Estadística y Censos Nacionales.

--- (1972b) Anuario Estadístico: 1970. Caracas: Dirección General de Estadística y Censos Nacionales.

--- (1964a) IX Censo General de Población: 26 Febrero de 1961. Caracas: Dirrección General de Estadística y Censos Nacionales.

--- (1964b) Anuario Estadistico de Venezuela: 1957-1963. Caracas: Dirección General de Estadística y Censos Nacionales.

--- (1955) VIII Censo General de Población: 26 de Noviembre de 1950. Caracas: Dirección General de Estadística y Censos Nacionales.

--- (1947) VII Censo Nacional de Población levantado al 7 diciembre de 1941, Resumen General de la República. Tomo VII. Caracas: Direccion General de Estadística y Censos Nacionales.

Barry Edmonston is Assistant Professor in the Department of Sociology, Cornell University, and also serves in Cornell's International Population Program. His current research deals with Latin American population trends, nutritional and demographic interrelations, and aspects of U.S. population distribution.

Frank Wm. Oechsli is a research demographer in Child Health Development Studies of the School of Public Health at the University of California, Berkeley. His current work focuses on life table methodology and the consequences of birth order and child-spacing patterns.

RICHARD V. SALISBURY
Department of History
Western Kentucky University
Bowling Green, KY 42101

COSTA RICA AND THE 1920-1921 UNION MOVEMENT

A Reassessment

Carlos Pereyra (as quoted in Herrarte, 1955: 187) has written that "the entire history of Central America has been a struggle between union and separatism." While this may be somewhat overstated, it is undeniable that the unionist-separatist syndrome has provided a major theme for nineteenth- and twentieth-century isthmian interrelationships. Indeed, from the collapse of the original Central American Federation in 1838 to the recent failure of the Central American Common Market, isthmian leaders have made numerous attempts to achieve some form of Central American integration. At times the threat of a forceful imposition of union, posed by such men as Guatemala's Justo Rufino Barrios and Nicaragua's José Santos Zelaya, tended to discredit the unionist cause. Central American unionists, however, have been, if anything, resilient, and, despite temporary setbacks, the ideal of union has remained a constant in isthmian affairs.

Journal of Interamerican Studies and World Affairs, Vol. 19 No. 3, August 1977

Perhaps at no other time in Central American experience were conditions more propitious for the achievement of union than during the 1920-1921 period; yet in this instance, as on many other occasions, the dream of creating a lasting isthmian federation remained unfulfilled. One factor in the repeated failure of union has been the negative attitude of Costa Rica, an attitude which contributed substantially to the frustration of the 1920-1921 union crusade. Both Central American and North American scholars who have studied the Costa Rican role in the 1920-1921 union movement have generally emphasized Costa Rica's rejection of isthmian federation. Such factors as Costa Rica's longstanding isolationist tradition (Gutiérrez, 1956: 37; Karnes, 1961: 215-218; Mendieta, 1934a: 103-104), the North American presence in Nicaragua (Chapman, 1922: 617; Cox, 1927: 759), the lack of harmony between the Costa Rican executive and legislative branches of government (Herrarte, 1955: 265-266; Moreno, 1928: 341), and President Julio Acosta's alleged indifference regarding the unionist cause (Mendieta, 1934b: 308-309) all figure prominently in the various assessments of the 1920-1921 union campaign. While these points certainly have merit, they by no means represent an exhaustive approach to Costa Rica's involvement in the union drive. In their efforts to analyze the reasons for the failure of the 1920-1921 union movement, scholars have ignored the significant pro-union campaign mounted in Costa Rica by President Acosta and the relationship of this campaign to Acosta's quest for the recognition of Costa Rican rights in the Nicaraguan canal route. Both the rationale behind the executive's union policy and the course of the policy itself suggest that the long-held views of Costa Rican isolationism and international passivity are not entirely accurate. Indeed, Julio Acosta's varying responses to the union question reveal the president's elaboration of an aggressive, shrewdly calculated, and ultimately successful policy for his nation in the complicated world of Central American international politics. For these reasons the

Costa Rican role in the 1920-1921 union movement deserves some serious reconsideration.

The origins of this particular isthmian quest for union can be traced back to the late 1890s and the development of a more sophisticated approach to the problems of Central American integration. Under the dedicated leadership of Salvador Mendieta, an entire generation of young unionists categorically rejected the roughshod tactics of isthmian strongmen of the Barrios stripe and instead prepared the way for eventual union through the medium of a carefully directed and well-organized educational campaign. The *partido unionista centroamericano* became the multinational vehicle for the movement, a movement which gained increased popularity and respectability in direct proportion to the unflagging efforts of Mendieta and his young disciples. Realizing the dangers inherent in any precipitous action and believing that time was indeed on their side, the unionists accepted evolutionary programs for isthmian unification and pledged themselves to work within the institutional machinery elaborated at Central American international conferences held during the early 1900s.

By 1920 the unionists must have felt that their preparations over the past generation were finally ready to bear fruit. In April of that year the twenty-two-year dictatorship of Manuel Estrada Cabrera came to an end in Guatemala, with the major instrument in the dictator's relatively peaceful fall from power being the partido unionista centroamericano (Munro, 1964: 460-466). In May of the same year Julio Acosta assumed the presidency in Costa Rica. The new Costa Rican executive was an admitted unionist—the first Costa Rican leader since the 1850s who openly advocated the unionist cause. Thus, the presence of pro-union leaders in both Costa Rica and Guatemala—two countries that in the past had been unreceptive to the idea of union gave a definite impetus to the unionist campaign. This phenomenon, combined with the high level of unionist sentiment prevalent in El Salvador and Honduras, the Nicaraguan government's public declaration of support for union, and the highly symbolic and rapidly approaching centenary of Central American independence in September 1921, appeared to provide an extremely favorable augury for the reestablishment of a Central American federation.

Given the revival of union sentiment on the isthmus, various proposals began to circulate regarding the desirability of holding an isthmian international conference. The Central American governments, in an effort to expedite matters, decided to delegate the entire question of the conference time, site, and agenda to the Central American International Bureau—one of the pro-unionist organizations established earlier in the century. The bureau subsequently selected San José, Costa Rica, as the conference site and suggested December 1, 1920, as the opening date. The agenda proposed by the bureau called for the establishment of a Central American union as the primary order of business at the conference (La Tribuna, 1920a).

When the first session of the conference met on December 4, 1920, the delegates unanimously elected Costa Rican Foreign Minister Alejandro Alvarado Quirós to serve as chairman, and Alvarado in turn gave a welcoming speech in which he made an impassioned plea for Central America's National Reconstruction. In the second session of the conference, held on December 6, the delegates agreed to celebrate a treaty of union and appointed a special committee to draw up the pact and present it to the conference at the earliest possible date. Cleto González Víquez, the Costa Rican representative on the committee, greatly facilitated matters by presenting the committee with a draft treaty of union that he had prepared previously. Relying to a great extent on this draft, the committee, after five days of study and minor revision, presented the conference with a tentative pact of union (Costa Rica, Ministerio de Relaciones Exteriores, 1921: 17-26, hereinafter cited as CRMRE).

All but one of the provisions of the draft treaty were acceptable to the different delegations. The Nicaraguan representatives at the conference objected to the article that dealt with the status of international treaties under the proposed federation.

This article stated: "The treaties effective between the states of the Federation and foreign nations will be respected in agreement with the designs of international law" (CRMRE, 1921: 108). Such language apparently was not explicit enough to satisfy Nicaragua, for Ramón Castillo, one of the Nicaraguan delegates, made it quite clear that his government demanded

> an express and categorical declaration that the states of the Federation recognize the Bryan-Chamorro Treaty in all of its consequences and that no law, act, or sentence of the Federation would have any effect . . . against the Treaty. [CRMRE, 1921: 119]

Negotiated between the United States and Nicaragua in 1914 and eventually ratified in 1916, the Bryan-Chamorro Treaty gave the United States the right to construct a canal through Nicaragua as well as the right to build a naval base in the Gulf of Fonseca. Nicaragua also agreed to lease the Corn Islands in the Caribbean to the United States. The canal rights were granted to the North American government in perpetuity, while the right to construct a naval base and the leases to the Caribbean islands were granted for a renewable period of ninety-nine years. In return for these rights the United States agreed to pay Nicaragua three million dollars.

Costa Rica, El Salvador, and Honduras protested that the Bryan-Chamorro Treaty violated previously existing and mutually understood Central American treaty rights. The Costa Rican government insisted that Nicaragua had no right to grant canal concessions in the San Juan River without prior consultation with Costa Rica, for the river formed a common frontier between the two nations. El Salvador and Honduras protested that Nicaragua could not unilaterally alienate the Gulf of Fonseca, a body of water shared by all three nations. Both Costa Rica and El Salvador took their cases to the Central American Court of Justice. The court, in turn, decided in favor of the Costa Rican and Salvadorean claims and requested that Nicaragua rectify the situation. Nicaragua refused to take any action, however, thus preparing the way for the confrontation at San José.

Once Nicaragua had injected the issue of the Bryan-Chamorro Treaty into the deliberations of the conference, isthmian battle lines were quickly drawn. The Costa Rican delegation immediately objected to being forced to accept the treaty and suggested that a reservation be made calling for negotiations with the United States "in such terms that will not harm the interests of the Republics that are going to unite" (CRMRE, 1921: 120). After a long, acrimonious, and unproductive debate over these and other related issues, the Costa Rican delegation made another proposal that was conditionally accepted by the Nicaraguan delegates. This proposal provided that

> so long as the Federal government by means of diplomatic negotiations has not been able to obtain the modification, derogation, or substitution of the various effective treaties . . . each state will respect and continue complying with the treaties that link it with any foreign nations. [CRMRE, 1921: 121]

Nicaragua's tentative acceptance became outright rejection when Castillo received telegraphic instructions from Managua indicating that the only acceptable solution for Nicaragua would be a specific declaration of Nicaraguan rights as guaranteed under the terms of the Bryan-Chamorro Treaty (CRMRE, 1921: 124-125). Still hoping for a possible change in Nicaragua's attitude, the delegates continued their deliberations on the other less controversial aspects of the treaty, and had actually given full approval to all other portions of the draft treaty when Castillo again informed the conference that his government would not accept a treaty that did not contain the specific guarantees demanded by Nicaragua (CRMRE, 1921: 138). At this point Castillo decided to return to Managua to consult with his home government in an effort to break the conference deadlock (CRMRE, 1921: 140).

The next session of the conference met on January 3, 1921, with all of the delegates present except Castillo. The remaining

Nicaraguan delegate, Manuel Pasos Arana, proposed that the other Central American nations accept a special Nicaraguan reservation which would recognize the validity of the Bryan-Chamorro Treaty and allow Nicaragua to fulfill the obligations and consequences of the treaty (CRMRE, 1921: 40). Responding to this proposal, Costa Rica's Cleto González Víquez explained that everyone recognized and respected Nicaragua's obligations, but what Nicaragua did not seem to understand was that the rights of Costa Rica, El Salvador, and Honduras were also affected by the Bryan-Chamorro Treaty. Consequently, in conjunction with El Salvador and Honduras, the Costa Rican delegation introduced a second reservation which called for negotiations with the United States in order to guarantee the rights of these three states in relation to the Bryan-Chamorro Treaty (CRMRE, 1921: 40-43). Pasos, after receiving instructions from Managua, announced that this second reservation was entirely unacceptable to his government and that if the other states insisted upon its inclusion in the treaty, Nicaragua would not be able to sign the prospective Pact of Union (CRMRE, 1921: 48). González Víquez immediately criticized Nicaragua's refusal to accept the second reservation as being indicative of the Nicaraguan government's general lack of interest in joining the proposed union. Conference Chairman Alvarado followed his colleague by condemning Nicaragua's latest refusal as nothing more than another in a long series of obstacles placed by Nicaragua in the path of the union movement (CRMRE, 1921: 54).

The conference appeared to be on the verge of a complete collapse when Salvador Falla of the Guatemalan delegation managed to bring some life back to the discouraged delegates. Falla suggested a compromise that appeared to resolve the dilemma created by the Bryan-Chamorro Treaty. The essence of the Falla proposal was that the Nicaraguan reservation concerning the status of international treaties be allowed to stand, but that another reservation be added echoing the U.S. Senate reservation to the Bryan-Chamorro Treaty, a reservation which provided that nothing in the treaty was intended to affect any existing rights held by Costa Rica, El Salvador, and Honduras. Falla quite logically assumed that Nicaragua would not object to a general isthmian acceptance of the position taken by the United States, and for a time it appeared that the compromise would indeed restore a degree of harmony to the conference. Indeed, after a general discussion of the Falla proposal, the delegations unanimously voted to accept the compromise (CRMRE, 1921: 59-67). The euphoria produced by this rare showing of unanimity, however, was soon dissipated by the Nicaraguan government's refusal to ratify the acceptance given by its delegation. The Nicaraguan delegation was ordered to return to Managua immediately, and the remaining delegates were left to sign the Pact of Union alone (CRMRE, 1921: 75-76).[1]

Although Nicaragua's action had shattered isthmian unity, prospects for at least an attenuated form of Central American federation appeared to improve somewhat during the next several months, as the legislatures of El Salvador, Guatemala, and Honduras all ratified the Pact of Union. The Costa Rican Congress, however, dealt another blow to isthmian solidarity when it rejected the union treaty in June 1921. Deprived of the support of their two recalcitrant sister states, the three northern isthmian republics nonetheless maintained the truncated Federation in the hope that Costa Rica and Nicaragua would eventually change their stand. Even this hope, however, proved to be ephemeral, for, on December 5, 1921, a revolutionary movement overthrew the Carlos Herrera government in Guatemala. Although the Federation authorities technically had the capacity to redress the internal difficulties of Guatemala, the governments of El Salvador and Honduras, still maintaining de facto control over their armed forces and well aware of the North American aversion to isthmian internecine strife, were reluctant to initiate military action to restore the legitimate Herrera government to power. In February 1922, following Guatemala's formal withdrawal from the Federation, both El

Salvador and Honduras reassumed their formal sovereignty, thus bringing an official end to the Central American Federation of 1921.

There is little doubt that Nicaragua bears a major share of the responsibility for the failure of the Federation. By assuming such an intransigent position at the San José Conference, Nicaragua introduced the initial and, perhaps ultimately, fatal note of discord into the isthmian quest for union. Although Nicaraguan participation in the Federation would have by no means guaranteed its eventual success, Nicaragua's refusal to sign the Pact of Union severly crippled the isthmian venture from the very beginning. Coming in the wake of Nicaragua's defection, the Costa Rican refusal to take favorable action on the union treaty served to compound the frustration in the unionist ranks. A lasting and viable Federation that did not include Nicaragua appeared highly improbable; a lasting and viable Federation that included neither Costa Rica nor Nicaragua appeared virtually impossible. Although the December 5, 1921, Guatemalan coup d'état was the catalyst which hastened the demise of the union, the eventual outcome had indeed never been seriously in doubt. As the result of positions assumed by Nicaragua and Costa Rica, the Central American Federation, for all intents and purposes, died aborning.

While Nicaragua's rationale for sabotaging the San José Conference seems rather clear, Costa Rica's attitudes regarding the union question present the investigator with more questions than answers. For example: how sincere was the Acosta administration's advocacy of union? According to one biographer (Nuñez, 1968: 131-132), Julio Acosta was a "convinced and fervent unionist." Acosta's apparent devotion to the unionist cause came into dramatic focus on the eve of the San José Conference when the president publicly expressed his willingness to resign if such action would facilitate the "realization of such a great ideal" (El Diario de Costa Rica, 1920a). Another authority (Mendieta, 1934b: 308-309), however, in reviewing the 1920-1921 union movement, dismisses Acosta's unionism as "weak and indifferent." An analysis of President Acosta's professed unionism provides, therefore, an interesting point of departure for an evaluation of the seemingly ambivalent Costa Rican role in the 1920-1921 union movement.

His union rhetoric aside, Julio Acosta must be considered first and foremost as a fervent Costa Rican nationalist and only in a very marginal sense as a sincere adherent to the unionist cause. One of the primary goals of the Acosta government was to seek redress for Costa Rica's grievances with Nicaragua and the United States over the unsettled question of Costa Rican rights in the Nicaraguan canal route. If espousal of the unionist cause would achieve these ends, then Acosta was prepared to support Central American union. If the satisfaction of Costa Rica's claims could come through other agencies and/or avenues, then Julio Acosta was fully prepared to explore and exploit these possibilities at the expense of union.

Well before the inauguration of the San José Conference, President Acosta was deeply involved in efforts to secure Costa Rica's rights. In August 1920 Acosta sent Alberto Echandi on a special mission to the other Central American countries. Ostensibly Echandi was to give official thanks to each of the isthmian governments for its representation at President Acosta's inauguration. In Nicaragua, however, Echandi's mission went far beyond the routine exchange of diplomatic platitudes. In conversations with Humberto Pasos Díaz, the Nicaraguan undersecretary of state for foreign affairs, Echandi suggested that Costa Rica might exchange some of her San Juan River land for a strip of territory along Lake Nicaragua. Echandi reportedly claimed that it would be advantageous for Costa Rica and Nicaragua to maintain a joint fleet on the lake and that the time had come "when Central America should become closely united and run its affairs without outside interference" (Benjamin C. Jefferson, Managua, to Bainbridge Colby, September 20, 1920, Decimal File Number 717.18/19, U.S. State Department Papers, National Archives, Record Group 59.; hereinafter State Department Papers will be cited by decimal file numbers). Although

Echandi's initiative did not receive a favorable reception in Managua, the implications of his overtures were clear: Costa Rica was willing to negotiate directly with Nicaragua regarding Costa Rica's canal rights. By the same token, Costa Rica was favorably inclined toward a Central American union which would safeguard isthmian interests from North American interference.

Echandi's diplomatic failure was subsequently repeated on a larger scale at the San José Conference as Nicaragua categorically rejected any and all efforts on the part of Costa Rica and the other isthmian states to compromise her treaty obligations with the United States. The possibility that Nicaragua might provide a serious obstacle to the union effort had been given serious consideration in the Costa Rican press well before the conference began. Costa Rican journalist and pro-union spokesman Vicente Sáenz had long conducted a vigorous campaign against North American intervention in Nicaragua, the Bryan-Chamorro Treaty, and the Nicaraguan Conservative government.[2] When the announcement of the Central American conference was made, Saénz simply intensified his already considerable activities. Other newspapermen, although somewhat more restrained in their approach, also criticized Nicaragua's special relationship with the United States (El Diario de Costa Rica, 1920b; La Tribuna, 1920b). When the conference began and as Nicaragua's position gradually became known, the Costa Rican press became much more critical. Although the conference met in secret sessions, Sáenz managed to obtain accurate inside information concerning its deliberations. His denunciations of the Nicaraguan position in general and the Nicaraguan delegation in particular provoked a strong reaction in San José. The Costa Rican government felt constrained to apologize to the Nicaraguan delegation for the bitter attacks against Nicaragua in the local press (La Gaceta Oficial, 1920). The reaction on the part of the Nicaraguan delegates was somewhat stronger, for one of the junior members of the delegation had to be restrained from challenging Sáenz to a duel (John G. Martin, San José, to Colby, December 31, 1920, 813.00/1041).

The status of Nicaragua and its relation to the upcoming San José Conference also elicited some serious commentary on more official levels. Roberto Brenes Guidiño, the president of the Muncipality of San José, came out directly against any plan of union until "something was done to remedy the sad condition of our sister Republic, Nicaragua." According to Brenes, union at the present time would impose upon the other Central American nations "the chains of slavery which oppress our unfortunate neighbor" (Martin to Colby, November 10, 1920, 813.00/1022). Foreign Minister Alvarado, in a conversation with the North American chargé, declared that the demands of Costa Rica and El Salvador against Nicaragua could only be met by means of a strong and harmonious union (Martin to Colby, November 10, 1920, 813.00/1022). In yet another talk with the chargé, Alvarado suggested that the delegates at the conference might ask the United States to withdraw its marines from Nicaragua (Martin to Colby, November 23, 1920, 813.00/ 1024).[3]

Once the Nicaraguan delegation had made its demands at the conference regarding the Bryan-Chamorro Treaty, the Costa Rican government moved to uncover the inspiration behind Nicaragua's policy. Foreign Minister Alvarado ordered the Costa Rican minister in Washington, Octavio Beeche, to go directly to the Department of State and ask "if the attitude of Nicaragua . . . conforms with the feeling of the American government." According to Alvarado, Nicaragua's position placed an "unacceptable condition" in the midst of the conference that could "frustrate the union effort." Alvarado believed that the United States might be inclined to support the Nicaraguan position because "there might be financial interests or a personal judgment of American diplomacy very closely related with the leaders of Nicaragua" (Alejandro Alvarado Quirós, San José, to Octavio Beeche, December 22, 1920, Archivos Nacionales de Costa Rica, Sección Histórica, Cajas Diplomáticas.; hereinafter cited as ANCR).[4]

After having conferred with the undersecretary of state, Beeche reported that the Department of State denied sending any instructions to Nicaragua regarding the conference and that the Nicaraguan delegation, in the opinion of the undersecretary, was operating independently. Beeche emphasized that all of this information was unofficial, for the undersecretary had indicated that he was reluctant to give an official opinion when he was still unfamiliar with the text of the union treaty, thus making it impossible for him to make any official statement relative to the specific clauses demanded by Nicaragua (Beeche, Washington, to Alvarado, January 13, 1921, ANCR). Alvarado, upon receiving this information, noted that the news was "very opportune" in the light of Nicaragua's withdrawal from the conference (Alvarado to Beeche, January 24, 1921, ANCR).

Although frustrated at the San José Conference, Costa Rican leaders remained constant in their resolve to secure recognition for their nation's rights in the Nicaraguan canal route. The vehicle for the attainment of this goal continued to be isthmian federation; accordingly, congressional approval of the union treaty became a matter of crucial importance for the Acosta administration. During the early part of 1921 the ratification process had been brought to a successful conclusion in El Salvador, Guatemala, and Honduras (La Gaceta Oficial, 1921a). When Guatemala ratified the Pact of Union, the Central American Federation became a reality, and the new member states now eagerly waited for Costa Rica to join the Federation. The addition of Costa Rica to the new union was extremely important, for this traditionally separatist nation was a highly respected member of the isthmian community; thus, Costa Rican acceptance of union would bring prestige to the Federation and would also serve to influence Nicaragua to reconsider her isolationist position. Accordingly, when the Costa Rican Congress began to consider the union treaty, a considerable amount of attention was focused on Costa Rica and the congressional ratification debates.

Costa Rican constitutional procedures stipulated that the incorporation of Costa Rica into a union would have to be approved by a two-thirds majority in the Congress and then passed on for final resolution in a specially elected Constituent Assembly (La Gaceta Oficial, 1921b). Technically, the function of the Congress was not to approve or disapprove of union per se, but simply to indicate whether or not it "agreed" to pass the matter on to the Constituent Assembly. Actually, the Congress had no intention of serving as a mere rubber stamp, and the deputies decided to exercise what they considered to be their full prerogatives when the Pact of Union was placed before them. Thus, the signatures of the Costa Rican delegation on the Pact of Union simply cleared the way for a more formidable scrutiny by an extremely critical group.

On May 1, 1921, President Acosta appeared before the Congress and urged the deputies to approve the Pact of Union. After making a general appeal to the deputies' spirit of Central Americanism, Acosta specifically mentioned the "recent events" that demonstrated the desirability and necessity of union. Acosta was referring to Costa Rica's brief but nonetheless sharply contested border clash with Panama. Guatemala, Honduras, and El Salvador had all quickly responded to the situation by offering both moral and material support. According to Acosta, this display of solidarity demonstrated by the other Central American nations was an important reason why Costa Rica should look favorably upon the proposed union (La Gaceta Oficial, 1921c). Several days later Foreign Minister Alvarado sent the Pact of Union to the Congress with a brief message calling for its approval (La Gaceta Oficial, 1921d).

Following standard congressional procedure, the Pact of Union was given to the Foreign Relations Committee for study and evaluation. Once the committee had considered the treaty, an official report would be prepared containing specific recommendations for congressional action on the treaty. The five-man committee, however, was unable to reach a unanimous agreement on the treaty; therefore, two separate reports were eventually submitted to the Congress.

The majority report was brief and to the point. The three members referred to the "innumerable reasons" in favor of accepting the pact and, without going into too much detail, requested that the Congress approve the submission of the pact to the Constituent Assembly so that the people would have the opportunity to decide the matter for themselves. The majority deputies therefore proposed that the Congress decree August 1, 1921, as the date for elections to the Constituent Assembly and August 8, 1921, as the date for the Assembly's opening session (La Gaceta Oficial, 1921b).

The minority report, in sharp contrast with the majority report, was quite extensive. The representatives of the minority opinion began their report with a lengthy section extolling the advantages of union, then—in a supposedly dramatic gesture—the deputies drew a heavy black line across the page to symbolize "the barriers that reality often places in the way of high expectations." The deputies followed with a detailed account of why Costa Rica was not yet ready to join a Central American union. The committeemen suggested that the present position of Costa Rica was analogous to the position of Moses on Mt. Horeb. Like the Biblical patriarch, Costa Rica was able to see the Promised Land, but was unable to enter it. The deputies gave lack of popular support in Costa Rica and the general absence of preparedness for union in the other Central American nations as the major reasons why Costa Rica, for the present, should refrain from entering the Federation (La Gaceta Oficial, 1921e).

The minority deputies managed to resist the blandishments of both the pro-union press and President Acosta in their determination to maintain their negative position. The deputies warned against placing too much faith in the ability of the Costa Rican press to influence Costa Rican public opinion. The union press, according to the report, was simply the reflection of a small group of individuals and did not represent the national sentiment on the union issue. Alluding to a recent conference between themselves and President Acosta, the minority deputies stated that "even the accustomed eloquence" of the president was not enough to make them change their position. This conference was quite important, for the deputies that supported the minority position were individuals who had long been known for their close support of the Acosta program in Congress, thus making their present opposition to the union question even more significant. Even though the deputies did admit that the Pact of Union was a piece of "political wisdom," they insisted that such wisdom did not suit the Costa Rican Sancho in his dialogue with the Federation's Quixote. Anticipating that the Federation would undoubtedly leave the door open to Costa Rica for future membership, the deputies concluded their report by proposing that Congress should defer all consideration of the union question until the next session of the Costa Rican Congress in May 1922 (La Gaceta Oficial, 1921e).

On the surface it appeared that the minority deputies were not entirely hostile to the idea of union. After all, the concept of union was never really criticized, and the dissenting members of the committee seemed to be content to adopt a wait-and-see attitude regarding the Federation. If the Federation proved to be viable, then the deputies felt that Costa Rica could reconsider her stand during the next session of the national legislature. Ostensibly, this would appear to be a very moderate stand. Such a stand, however, is highly vulnerable, for the deputies did not have to specifically attack the question of union in order to avoid the responsibility of facing the issue directly. To attack union, was, of course, bad politics, for virtually everyone held the ideal of union in high esteem; therefore, the proper method of sidestepping the matter was to praise the general goal of union while suggesting that its immediate implementation be deferred. The proposal that the next session of Congress consider the question was quite convenient, for most anti-unionists were sure that the Federation would collapse before the next session of Congress met, thus allowing Costa Rica to avoid involvement in an undesirable situation.

The Costa Rican Congress considered the Pact of Union from June 6 to June 21, 1921. Because the first and possibly final test for the union treaty would be in the Congress, the ratification debates assumed a great deal of importance. This was especially true because several newspaper polls (El Diario de Costa Rica, 1921a; La Tribuna, 1921a) of the deputies indicated that the required two-thirds majority had not yet been obtained by the pro-union forces; thus, once the debates began in the Congress, the Acosta administration accelerated the pace of its already well-established union campaign.

The highwater mark of the administration's drive for union came on June 17, 1921, when Foreign Minister Alvarado addressed the Congress. Whereas many of the pro-union deputies had elaborated during the debates on the fraternal and spiritual benefits of union, Alvarado tended to emphasize more pragmatic considerations. The foreign minister's arguments in favor of union were based in part on a recently published newspaper report (The New York Times, 1921) which indicated that the U.S. government was not only sympathetic to the idea of union but would also encourage the Nicaraguan government to join the Federation. Acting on the assumption that this was an accurate reflection of North American policy, Alvarado presented the administration's case to the assembled deputies.[5] According to President Acosta's spokesman, the benefits of union would include the normalization of relationships between the other Central American states and Nicaragua as well as the reconciliation of outstanding differences between Central America and the United States. Once the Federation was fully established, Alvarado predicted that the new Federal authorities would take immediate steps to come to an understanding with the United States that would include the signing of a new treaty "covering broader and fairer bases . . . and defending the interests of these nations, especially those of Nicaragua" (La Gaceta Oficial, 1921f).

Alvarado's remarks prompted the North American chargé to sound out the foreign minister as to just what he meant regarding the United States and the Federation. Alvarado, in turn, replied that if the Federation materialized "it would promptly undertake to effect the revision of the Bryan-Chamorro Treaty." The Federation, according to Alvarado, would grant the United States similar privileges contained in the present treaty with Nicaragua, but new provisions would be added "recognizing and remunerating El Salvador, Honduras, and Costa Rica insofar as their rights are concerned" (Walter C. Thurston, San José, to Charles Evans Hughes, June 20, 1921, 813.00/1085). In essence, Alvarado was calling for a unified Central America that could deal with the United States from a position of greater strength and, thus, be able to renegotiate the Bryan-Chamorro Treaty to the advantage of the Central American states, Costa Rica included, which felt that their vital interests had been threatened by the treaty.

Unfortunately for Foreign Minister Alvarado and President Acosta, the Costa Rican Congress preferred to maintain the safe tradition of Costa Rican isolationism at the expense of seeking satisfaction for Costa Rica's aggrieved rights in the Nicaraguan canal route. On June 21, 1921, when the final vote was taken on the union question, the count revealed that nineteen deputies favored and twenty deputies opposed passing the union question on to the Constituent Assembly (El Diario de Costa Rica, 1921b). Far short of the two-thirds majority required for approval, the Costa Rican Congress had not even deigned to give a bare majority to the Pact of Union.

Why, then, had the Costa Rican Congress so categorically rejected Central American Federation? Although unionist support in Costa Rica had probably never been better mobilized, Costa Rica's basic isolationist tendency simply remained too strong for the unionist partisans to overcome. According to several congressional opponents of union, such a policy of isolation was even more incumbent on Costa Rica given the intervention of the United States in Central American affairs.

These deputies expressed their distrust of North American canal policy and suggested that Costa Rica would be better served by assuming a position of complete neutrality between the existing canal in Panama and the prospective waterway in Nicaragua (La Gaceta Oficial, 1921g). Although none of the opposition group attacked the principle of union, all insisted that the present was simply not the time for such an ambitious and idealistic undertaking. Instead, the congressional opposition looked to the future for the resolution of the question of Costa Rica's incorporation into an isthmian federation.

Although endowed with their share of forensic and intellectual prowess, members of the opposition group in Congress, in an effort to sustain their position, depended to a great extent on the ideas, influence, and prestige of an individual outside of Congress. Indeed, it was a widely accepted fact in Costa Rica that Ricardo Jiménez Oreamuno was the unquestioned *eminence grise* of the anti-union forces. As a skilled and highly respected international lawyer, a brilliant polemicist, and perhaps the most respected living Costa Rican, the former president (1910-1914) was to have a decided impact on the fate of the union question in Costa Rica. A long-time advocate of Costa Rican isolationism, Jiménez emphatically restated his views at the outset of the San José Conference. In a newspaper interview (El Diario de Costa Rica, 1920c), Jiménez mockingly compared Central American union with the association of five bankrupts in one single company and indicated that he saw no real advantage for Costa Rica in a federation that was, in his opinion, doomed to eventual destruction by the currents of isthmian separatism. Another problem that bothered Jiménez was the fear that in a union the racially homogenous and culturally advanced Costa Rican society would be diluted and brought down to a more unsatisfactory level by the surrounding cultures. The Bryan-Chamorro Treaty was also a major stumbling block, for the United States, according to Jiménez, would never allow the treaty to be changed in any way that would be prejudicial to its own national interests; thus, any Central

American efforts to change the treaty would encounter severe resistance in Washington.[6]

The only condition under which Jiménez felt that Costa Rica could ever successfully enter a Central American union was if the other isthmian states formed a federation which proved its viability over an extended period of time. Then and only then would don Ricardo consider that it was time for Costa Rica to "knock on the door" (El Diario de Costa Rica, 1920c). It was no coincidence that the position assumed by Jimenez became, with very little variation, the stand adopted by the anti-union forces in the Costa Rican Congress. Indeed, according to the authors of the minority report, Ricardo Jiménez was the only person who expressed "the real feeling of the Costa Rican people" regarding the union question (La Gaceta Oficial, 1921e). Thus, Costa Rican currents of isolationism had effectively countered Julio Acosta's push for isthmian integration. The question now at hand was whether or not President Acosta would allow this challenge to go unanswered.

In a communication to the Central American International Bureau, Foreign Minister Alvarado officially informed the Federation authorities of the defeat of the union treaty in the Costa Rican Congress. Alvarado also indicated, however, that it was his government's hope that the treaty could once again be submitted to the Congress after the December 1921 congressional elections (La Gaceta Oficial, 1921h). Costa Rican unionists were reassured by this implicit pledge of continued administration support as well as by pro-union articles appearing in the local press (El Diario de Costa Rica, 1921c). Accordingly, Costa Rican unionist organizations began to look to the December 4, 1921, congressional elections as the next major step in their campaign to bring Costa Rica into the Central American Federation.

As the elections approached, however, the Costa Rican unionists began to question the Acosta government's commitment to the unionist cause. A check of the congressional voting lists favored by the administration revealed the names of a significant number of individuals who were well-known opponents of union. Although the government carried eighteen out of the twenty-one contested congressional seats, the victory was far from a new and popular mandate for favorable congressional action on the union treaty. Indeed, the election of six out of seven of the administration-supported anti-union candidates suggested that the Acosta government had made a significant change in its isthmian policy (La Tribuna, 1921b). Had such a change, however, really been made?

Julio Acosta's lack of support for the unionist cause in December of 1921 was both a consistent as well as a logical element in his administration's isthmian policy. Costa Rican entrance into the Federation was simply one possible means of achieving Acosta's major policy objective: the clarification and satisfaction of Costa Rican claims in the Nicaraguan canal route. Denied any significant degree of congressional support for union in June of 1921 and becoming increasingly aware that Nicaragua's disinclination to join the Central American Federation seemed to represent long-term policy, Julio Acosta began to look elsewhere in an effort to fulfill his administration's international goals. Isthmian federation, however, was not a key factor in the eventual denouement of Acosta's isthmian policy.

It would be extremely difficult to find a more candid expression of the president's true isthmian posture than during the negotiations leading up to and including the 1922-1923 Washington Conference. The Central American nations were to meet in Washington on the invitation of the U.S. government in an effort to reinforce the bonds of isthmian peace and stability which had been stretched dangerously close to the breaking point following the collapse of the Central American Federation. During the preliminary negotiations for the conference, however, President Acosta made it abundantly clear that he was not interested in seeing the revival of the union question at the Washington Conference (Beeche, Washington, to Alvarado, February 15, 1922, ANCR; José Andrés Coronado, San José, to Beeche, April 24, 1922, ANCR; Roy T. Davis, San José, to

Hughes, August 9, 1922, 813.00/1201). Once the conference began, the Costa Rican delegation, acting under specific instructions from President Acosta, consistently and successfully opposed efforts to add the union issue to the conference agenda (Costa Rican Foreign Ministry to Beeche, December 8, 1922, ANCR). On the other hand, President Acosta also instructed his representatives at Washington to enter into direct negotiations with the United States in order to gain North American recognition of Costa Rica's rights in the canal route (Miguel Obregon, San José, to Beeche, November 27, 1922, ANCR). The Costa Ricans refused to sign either the Convention for the Establishment of an International Central American Tribunal or the Convention for the Establishment of International Commissions of Inquiry, two conventions designed to promote isthmian peace and stability and strongly supported by the U.S. government, unless the problem of Costa Rica's rights had been resolved (Rafael Oreamuno, Washington, to Julio Acosta, December 22, 1922, ANCR). After a considerable amount of intermittent dialogue, Costa Rican and North American diplomats signed a protocol which recognized the Costa Rican rights in the canal route. Accordingly, the Costa Rican delegation signed the aforementioned conventions, and the work of the conference continued without any further evidence of Costa Rican obstructionism (Oreamuno to Acosta, January 26, 1923, ANCR; Oreamuno to Obregon, February 1, 1923, ANCR).

When viewed in light of Costa Rica's experience at the San José and Washington conferences, the implications of President Acosta's policy are clear. The clarification and protection of Costa Rican rights in the Nicaraguan canal route were the administration's paramount isthmian policy objectives. With this in mind, Julio Acosta's initial flirtation with and ultimate rejection of Central American union as an instrument of Costa Rican policy can be more readily understood. The Echandi mission to Nicaragua marked President Acosta's initial effort at resolving the undetermined status of Costa Rica's canal rights.

The failure of this bilateral approach prompted the Costa Rican executive to seek satisfaction for Costa Rica's claims through the multilateral vehicle of Central American union. Indeed, this was the policy that Acosta pushed during the San José Conference and the ratification debates in the Costa Rican Congress. Unable to achieve Costa Rican objectives through the medium of Central American cooperative effort, Julio Acosta cast aside his unionist cloak and entered into direct negotiations with the U.S. government. Accordingly, any study of the Costa Rican role in the 1920-1921 union movement which fails to take into account the primacy of President Acosta's canal policy remains, at best, incomplete.

Those contemporary observers who hold an optimistic view regarding the future of isthmian integration would do well to consider the Costa Rican role in the 1920-1921 union movement. Never was Costa Rica so close to entrance into an isthmian union, yet never was Costa Rica's fundamental isolationist tendency more clearly defined than during the early 1920s. Despite the significant pro-union efforts of the Acosta administration, Costa Ricans continued to perceive their national interests in the light of isthmian separatism rather than isthmian federation. Given this expression of Costa Rican reality, Julio Acosta readily demonstrated that his longstanding commitment to union was definitely subordinate to the realization of purely national policy objectives. Although over fifty years have passed, what President Acosta ultimately recognized in a Costa Rican context apparently remains valid for the rest of the isthmus as well. Indeed, the centrifugal economic and political forces unleashed throughout the isthmus in the wake of the 1969 Honduran-Salvadorean conflict and the subsequent collapse of the Central American Common Market rather emphatically suggest the continued ascendancy of national over collective interests within the isthmian community.[7]

NOTES

1. Another factor in the Nicaraguan rejection of union was the apparent desire of the Conservative government to retain all the apparatus of political power in Nicaragua. Membership in the Federation would have meant a surrendering of governmental prerogatives to the federal authorities (Moreno, 1928: 471; La Prensa, 1920).

2. Sáenz was an extreme nationalist who exercised his considerable polemical talents in a long fight against foreign intervention in Central America. Through such Costa Rican newspapers as *La Información, La Prensa, La Opinión,* and *El Diario de Comercio*, Sáenz maintained his role as gadfly intermittently throughout the 1920s.

3. Martin believed that the U.S. government should anticipate this resolution by making an announcement that if union were formed, North American forces would be withdrawn from Nicaragua. He felt that if this were done, then discussion of the Bryan-Chamorro Treaty might be averted. The Department of State, however, indicated that even though Martin's arguments were valid, the possibility of revolutionary activity in Nicaragua precluded the evacuation of the marines. The department also indicated its reluctance to make any advance commitments, because "Central American Federation at this time is improbable" (Colby to Martin, Novemeber 26, 1920, 813.00/1024).

4. Actually, the United States did not really need to send specific instructions to the Nicaraguan government relative to the Bryan-Chamorro Treaty. Nicaraguan officials were already well aware of just what the U.S. government expected, and this unofficial empathy was sufficient to encourage Nicaragua to follow the proper course. Before the conference even began, the Nicaraguan government had supplied the American minister with a copy of the official instructions given to the Nicaraguan delegation. These instructions called for the Nicaraguan delegation to "set forth Nicaragua's close relations and obligations to the United States and not to sign any Central American union pact that would in any way conflict therewith" (Benjamin Jefferson, Managua, to Colby, November 26, 1920, 813.00/1025).

5. In his speech, Alvarado referred to a toast given by Secretary of State Charles Evans Hughes of June 2, 1921, at a banquet in honor of Maximo H. Zepeda, the Nicaraguan foreign minister who was about to depart for Europe. In the course of his remarks, Hughes made some general statements favorable to the union movement. Basing his information on the New York *Times* account of the Hughes toast, Alvarado interpreted the secretary of state's remarks as a North American carte blanche for union. He was so impressed with the *Times* article that he quoted it in toto in his own address to the Costa Rican Congress. The *Times* article reported that Hughes had declared that it would be a "happy result" if the Central American republics could be brought together in "closer cooperation." The *Times* went on to say, however, that these remarks would influence Nicaragua to reconsider her position and that the doubts concerning the Bryan-Chamorro Treaty could now be resolved. Alvarado made the assumption that the *Times* interpretation was the official expression of North American policy. He perhaps would not have made such an assumption if he had been in possession of Octavio Beeche's report on the Hughes toast. Beeche, who was present when Hughes spoke, observed (Beeche to Alvarado, June 7, 1921, ANCR) that the secretary of state's remarks had been delivered with

"no vigor or expression." Beeche commented in addition that Hughes simply stated the "very minimum expected for such an occasion." It seems reasonable to believe, therefore, that Beeche's report to Alvarado did not reach the foreign minister before he spoke to the Congress.

6. In a subsequent newspaper interview (La Tribuna, 1922), long after the 1920-1921 union movement had abated, Ricardo Jiménez made the statement that it was an "open secret" that the union treaty had been "directed against the United States." He went on to describe the motivation behind the San José Conference as being an effort "to become much stronger in order to confront the United States."

7. Several recent studies, one by a political scientist (Wynia, 1972) and one by an economist (Orantes, 1972), elaborate on the corrosive effects that the currents of isthmian economic and political nationalism have had on Central American regionalistic structures during the past decade.

REFERENCES

CHAPMAN, C. E. (1922) "The failure of Central American Union." Rev. of Reviews 66 (July-December): 613-617.

Costa Rica, Ministerio de Relaciones Exteriores [CRMRE] (1921) Conferencia de plenipotenciarios centroamericanos. San José: Imprenta Nacional.

COX, I. J. (1927) Nicaragua and the United States, 1909-1927. Boston: World Peace Foundation.

El Diario de Costa Rica (1921a) May 25; (1921b) June 22; (1921c) October 23, 26; (1920a) December 2; (1920b) October 21; (1920c) December 4.

GUTIERREZ, C. J. (1956) "Neutralidad e intervención." Revista de la Universidad de Costa Rica 14 (November): 2-60.

HERRARTE, A. (1955) La Unión de Centroamérica. Guatemala: Editorial del Ministerio de Educación Pública.

KARNES, T. L. (1961) The Failure of Union: Central America, 1924-1960. Chapel Hill: Univ. of North Carolina Press.

La Gaceta Oficial (1921a) February 6, 27, April 14; (1921b) May 20; (1921c) May 3; (1921d) May 5; (1921e) June 2; (1921f) June 28; (1921g) June 25; (1921h) November 13; (1920) December 24.

La Prensa (1920) December 17, 18.

La Tribuna (1922) June 9; (1921a) May 22; (1921b) December 6; (1920a) October 16; (1920b) December 2.

MENDIETA, S. (1934a) Alrededor del problema unionista de Centro-América. Barcelona: Tipografia Maucci.

--- (1934b) La enfermedad de Centro-América. Barcelona: Tipografia Maucci.

MORENO, L. (1928) Historia de las relaciones interesatuales de Centroamérica. Madrid: Compañia Ibero-americana.

MUNRO, D. G. (1964) Intervention and Dollar Diplomacy in the Caribbean, 1900-1921. Princeton, NJ: Princeton Univ. Press.

The New York Times (1921) June 3.

NUNEZ, F. M. (1968) "Vida, obra y pensamiento de Don Julio Acosta." Anales de la Academia de Geografia e Historia de Costa Rica: 108-134.

ORANTES, I. C. (1972) Regional Integration in Central America. London: D. C. Heath.

WYNIA, G. W. (1972) Politics and Planners. Madison: Univ. of Wisconsin Press.

Richard V. Salisbury is Associate Professor of History at Western Kentucky University, Bowling Green, Kentucky. His monograph Costa Rican Relations with Central America, 1900-1934 *appeared as No. 71 of the Special Studies Series published in 1975 by the Council on International Studies at the State University of New York at Buffalo. Recent articles have appeared in* Hispanic American Historical Review *and* Revista del Pensamiento Centroamericano.

REVIEW ESSAY

THE SURROGATE AMERICANS

Ogelsby, J.C.M. GRINGOS FROM THE FAR NORTH. Essays in the History of Canadian-Latin American Relations 1866-1968. Toronto: 1976.

Lyon, P. V. and T. Y. Ismael, eds. CANADA AND THE THIRD WORLD. Toronto: 1976.

One of the best books ever written about Australia is splendidly entitled *The Tyranny of Distance* (Blainey, 1966) and is, naturally, an explanation of the country's development as a function of remoteness. Indeed, the title is so good that it almost makes it unnecessary to read the book.

A comparison of the Australian with the Canadian experience could easily lead to the conclusion that great distance from the metropolitan centers need not be wholly unfortunate. This is especially true with respect to the early experiences of the former dominions in the field of foreign affairs. Very far from Europe and the United States, distant as well from the other major powers, Australia appears to have found her newly independent status—at least since its formal affirmation by the Statute of Westminster in 1931—easier to live with. When the demands of war and its aftermath thrust upon her the task of formulating a national foreign policy, she found this less difficult than Canada, possibly because of her relative isolation from any single and overwhelming influence. On the other hand, the difficulties encountered by Canada in the formulation of a truly independent external policy appear either to have originated in, or to have been exacerbated by, her uncomfortable proximity to the United States. Far from Europe and much too close to the North American colossus, the Canadian plight inevitably brings to mind that old witticism about Mexico: so very far from God and so near to the United States. Although distant from its cultural sources in France and England, Canadian society appears to be unwilling, or perhaps unable, to break entirely free from them. Quite the opposite, the most popular approximations to a definition of national aspirations would seem to be founded on an acceptance of the continued relevance of those sources, even to the extent of influencing some aspects of external policy—toward Francophone Africa, for example.

A sympathetic observer could well be forgiven for thinking that Canada has not found it altogether easy to formulate a truly national policy consistent with a generally accepted statement of national objectives. It is worth speculating whether Canada's enviable reputation outside North America, for fairness and impartiality, is not a consequence of an inability to impress a more decisive course to her foreign policy; but, then, who are we to say that to be impartial by default is not better than to be partisan by design? However, the enjoyment of an almost Scandinavian prestige as a dependable referee comes as an unexpected consequence after many years of pugnacious efforts to formulate a forthright and independent foreign policy. After all, it was during World War I—in 1915—that Sir Robert Borden made himself conspicuous by demanding that Canada should have a voice in the making of imperial decisions, partly in recognition of the fact that she was shouldering a considerable part of the military effort while smaller countries with less impressive contributions—Serbia and Montenegro, for example—were rightly consulted and generally treated as fully fledged independent and sovereign allies.

It was also the vast North American dominion that first put the Balfour Declaration of 1926 to good use by appointing its first diplomatic representatives abroad, to Washington, Tokyo, and Paris. Again, it was as early as 1923 that Canada took the momentous step of signing the otherwise forgettable Halibut Fisheries Agreement with the United States without prior or subsequent consultation with Westminster, thereby firmly driving the required nails into the coffin of direct imperial control.

These purposeful beginnings can well be regarded—a posteriori—as a portent of what followed during the ensuing four or five decades. It would not be difficult to compile a list of instances when Canadian initiatives opened the way to important developments in international affairs: her role in the dramatic change of Western policy with respect to China or her flexible position with respect to the Cuban blockade are worth mentioning. There seem to be no excuses for thinking of Canadian foreign policy as hesitant, diffident, or unimaginative. And yet, and yet, there persists the faint suspicion of an echo, a reverberation, an intimation of cultural loyalties as well as the persistent awareness of the practical implications of being the immediate neighbor to the most powerful country the world has ever known. Even those vigorous first steps would perhaps merit reexamination.

Canada's triumphant debut in the perilous stage of international politics was her courageous opposition to the renewal of the 1902 Anglo-Japanese Treaty. The treaty had served both Japan and Britain well during two decades of unprecedented international tension and conflict. Japan's victory over Russia in 1905 was one of its direct consequences, as well as Japan's entry on the side of the Western Allies in the First World War. However, the United States and China were opposed to its continuation—it had already been renewed once, in 1912—and when it came up for renewal for the second time, in 1921, these countries discovered an articulate and enthusiastic ally in Canada, who openly and firmly attacked the position defended by Britain, thereby gaining a reputation for independence and impartiality, and, most important, having the strong support of two Pacific powers, won the day and was justly able to claim credit for the abrogation of the treaty.

Canada could well have acted solely moved by an independent appreciation of what she considered her better interests in the Pacific, but it is also possible to speculate on the influence which the United States may have had on her resolute stand. The British lion was already showing signs of old age, and, for those who knew how good-tempered and toothless it really was, public defiance must have appeared a tempting course of action, especially if it merited the private approval of such a powerful neighbor.

On the other hand, during the same decade of the twenties, after playing a signal role in securing the Balfour Declaration which practically opened the door to constitutional autonomy, Canada renounced the right to alter her constitution unilaterally, precisely because of the need to safeguard the rights of the French Canadian minority against the remote possibility of abuses by the Anglo-Canadian majority. There is no need to expand on these themes to accept that Canadian foreign policy in the last few decades appears to have responded to at least two additional demands —additional, that is, to the normal bundle of contradictory claims made on any country's policies—first, those resulting from her proximity to the United States, and second, those arising from the cultural divisions characteristic of her society. The influence of the first of these demands is certainly apparent in Canada's relations with the countries of Latin America and with the so-called Third World as examined in two very good books published recently in Canada.

The history of Canadian-Latin American relations during the past hundred years is the main theme of a book by J.C.M. Ogelsby. The blurb describes it as a collection of essays, which it undoubtedly is, but these are so well arranged and cover such a large portion of what little there is to know about these relationships that one wonders why neither author nor publishers succumbed to the legitimate temptation of changing the essays into chapters and presenting the book to the public as a single study. Collected essays, after all, are seldom read, and it would be a pity if this entertaining and useful book were to suffer because of this.

Another reason why the casual reader may decline to purchase Ogelsby's fine book is its awful title. If Blainey's *Tyranny of Distance* is one of the best titles of recent times, then Ogelsby's *Gringos from the Far North* must be one of the least attractive. Let me add simply that the book is much better than its title. It is a scholarly and well-written work which, perhaps unwittingly, lends support to the suspicion that in Latin America Canadians have acted, or been used, or have been perceived either as surrogate Americans or as countervailing influences to that of the United States. This may explain why Canadians have stressed "trade, investment, and the uplifting of peoples by improving the standard of living," while Latin Americans "have stressed diplomatic exchanges and urged Canada's political involvement in the inter-American system" (Ogelsby, p. 287).

This difference in approach is apparent from the very earliest contacts in 1865, when an official Canadian mission was sent south in order to ascertain "in what manner the traffic of the Provinces with those countries could be extended and placed on a more advantageous footing" (Ogelsby, p. 11). Behind this was a rumor that the United States was considering abrogating the 1854 Reciprocity Treaty with the Canadian Provinces, and this sent the Canadians to Latin America in search for alternative markets for their lumber, fish, and grain, and other sources for tropical produce. The mission was a pleasant outing in the sun at a time when Canada was under snow. A conscientious report was written and shelved as the rumor about the threatened abrogation turned out to be baseless.

Other missions traveled south in the winters of 1930, 1940-1941, 1946, 1953, 1959, and 1968. None produced spectacular results, but, then, none had disastrous consequences, which should perhaps be noted. The most important of these missions, however, as well as the most noteworthy of Canadian initiatives with respect to Latin America, appear almost without exception to be responses to decisions—or indecisions—on the part of the United States. This is most clearly shown in the history of the establishment of diplomatic relations between Canada and the countries of Latin America.

As Ogelsby correctly points out, in the 1930s "Latin America was among the lesser of Canadian priorities," and when, in the late 1930s, it was thought appropriate to add to the small number of Canadian representations abroad, missions were established in Belgium and The Netherlands. It was at this time that Brazil took the initiative of suggesting that diplomatic missions be exchanged with Ottawa not, as Ogelsby disconcertingly suggests, because of the importunate persistence of the Secretary to the Brazilian Minister for Foreign Affairs who wanted the Ottawa post, but because Itamaraty has for almost a century been in the vanguard in many important aspects of Latin American international relations, including the establishment of diplomatic representation in Canada.

To be fair to Ogelsby, in this book he qualifies his statement by using the word "apparently," but in another essay, also published in 1976, in the volume edited by P. V. Lyon and T. Y. Ismael, he drops the qualification and boldly affirms that "Brazil was persistent . . . because of the ambitions of a secretary to the foreign minister who hoped to head the mission to Canada" (Ogelsby, in Lyon and Ismael, pp. 167-168). It is, of course, perfectly possible that the unnamed Secretary was keen to go to Ottawa, but this does not necessarily make him the Deus ex machina of Brazilian foreign policy.

At any rate, the persistence of Itamaraty encountered Canadian indifference even when it was supported by Argentine interest early in 1940. It was not until November of that year that Mackenzie King announced in the House of Commons his decision to establish missions in Brazil and Argentina. However, as Dr. Ogelsby notes, it took him another year to appoint the Canadian ministers.

This delay hides yet another aspect of the matter. Within a fortnight of Mackenzie King's announcement, Chile informed Canada that it wished to exchange diplomatic missions. Here, again, Ogelsby prefers an ad hominem explanation and attributes Chilean interest to the "personal ambition of the Chilean Consul General in Montreal, Luis Feliú [who had] a strong desire for a rise in diplomatic rank" (Ogelsby, p. 45). This, of course, cannot be ruled out, but one would suspect that all diplomats wish to rise in their profession, and this hardly constitutes an explanation of the policies their governments entrust to them.

At any rate, the addition of Chile—always the initiative clearly on the Latin American side of the court—to Brazil and Argentina was motive for further procrastination, motivated partly by the cost of establishing three separate missions, partly because of shortage of trained personnel.

The months went by, and it is not difficult to see that, with the war complicating things, Canada could have allowed the matter to rest there for an indefinite period had it not been for the decisive intervention of the United States. Cordell Hull, Sumner Welles, and Roosevelt himself informed the Canadian government, through different channels and at different levels, and these pressures were eventually brought together in a famous memorandum prepared by the Canadian Department of External Affairs, in which it was firmly stated that "the United States has virtually requested Canada to do it" (Ogelsby, p. 48). And that was that. The Canadian representatives were appointed, but then, with the classical earnestness of the loyal subordinate, Canada went too far.

Eager to fulfill its new hemispheric role, Mackenzie King—without consulting Washington—thought it a good idea to participate in the Rio de Janeiro meeting of foreign ministers planned for January 1942, and to join the Pan American Union as well. A cable was accordingly sent to Jean Desy, the Canadian Ambassador to Brazil, "authorizing him to tell the Brazilian authorities . . . that Canada would be prepared to accept an invitation to join the Pan American Union. The following day Desy received another cable, which said that 'technical obstacles' [had arisen] which would be difficult to overcome in time for [Canada] to participate in the proposed conference." The "technical obstacles" were the opposition of the U.S. government. The United States thought it inappropriate for Canada either to participate in the Rio Conference or to apply for membership in the Pan American Union, and that was where the matter rested.[1]

The influence which the United States has evidently exercised over the relations between Canada and the countries of Latin America is also apparent, though possibly in a less decisive way, in Canadian attitudes toward much of the so-called Third World. These relationships are examined in an excellent volume of essays, carefully edited and very well organized. It includes papers on Canadian relations with South Asia, Anglophone Africa, Francophone Africa, Latin America, the Caribbean, the Middle East, Southeast Asia, and generally with the development problems of that vaguely defined "Third World." Altogether this is the best possible introduction to a complex subject, and it unavoidably reflects, perhaps not as tellingly as Ogelsby's book, the pervasive influence of United States on Canadian policies and attitudes. An example will probably suffice in the light of recent U.S. experience with conditional aid programs.

Clyde Sanger, writing on "Canada and Development in the Third World," is convincingly critical of the simplistic efforts to control the use of contributions either by tying the funds to purchases in the donor country or, more crudely, by dictating the manner in which the funds are to be used by the recipient. He could have added the type of unsubtle blackmail that can be exercised by donor countries when making their aid conditional on this or that change of domestic political arrangements in the recipient country. Of course, the foremost exponent of this type of interference is the United States, before and after Carter became president. The very least one would expect of Canadian scholars familiar with the dismal record of their powerful neighbors in such matters is to refrain from falling into the same trap. Unfortunately, if Sanger's advice is representative of general Canadian opinion in this matter, the prospects are dark indeed.

For example, he criticizes the Canadian government for extending a thirty million dollar loan to Botswana to enable it to purchase power-generating equipment for the new copper mine at Selibe-Pikwe, "not apparently caring about the social problems that are undoubtedly being created because of the new mine" (Lyon and Ismael, p. 281). Presumably Sanger knows better than the sovereign government of Botswana and would—if asked—tell them what's what about social problems before those thirty million dollars are delivered, but would this not leave Sanger in the same invidious paternalistic, not to say downright arrogant, position of those donors he criticizes for imposing conditions on their grants?

Further on in his fascinating paper, Sanger drives the point home with even greater accuracy by complaining about a thirty-one million dollar loan to the sovereign government of Niger to build the *Route de l'Unité et l'Amitie,* a 265-mile road between Goure, in the eastern half of Niger, and the region to the west of Lake Chad. The government of Niger wants this road constructed precisely to facilitate the integration of their country and thereby to ease the arduous process of nation-building, but Sanger disagrees, thinking that the road is "an expensive bit of nonsense" and that it would have been wiser if the Canadian officials who agreed to this loan had prevailed on President Diori to be "less nationalistic and yield to considerations of regional development."

This makes strange reading in a book whose introduction has invited us to agree that the one "national interest that is clearly served by an enthusiastic, active involvement in the problems of the Third World [is] Canada's interest in maintaining national independence and national identity."[2] Why is this goal acceptable for Canada but not for Niger? One wonders whether Sanger would be prepared to suggest that Canada should yield more readily to considerations of regional development (vis-à-vis the United States, for instance), instead of worrying unduly about maintaining national identity and national independence.

Alas, the arrogance of the well-meaning United States appears to have traveled north to Canada, and, although we have already witnessed the inglorious failure of the great power to play the role of world's policeman, we may—sadly—be on the threshold of a period when eager Canadians, like Dr. Sanger and his friends, may drag their country onto the world stage, not as a second-string policeman, but perhaps as an equally doomed Sunday school teacher.

—*Claudio Veliz*

NOTES

1. When the U.S. minister in Ottawa learned about the cable, "he was very upset that the Canadian government had not discussed the matter with him." The Canadian minister in Washington was urged to call on Sumner Welles, who informed him that the position of the United States was based on interamerican agreements which made it absolutely impossible for any government to be represented at the forthcoming Rio conference. The United States, furthermore, feared that the United Kingdom might use Canadian membership to become involved itself in hemispheric affairs. So much for Canadian independence. Mackenzie King received the visit of the U.S. minister in Ottawa and, although "he appeared disappointed at the American position," loyally toed the line and asked the American minister to inform Roosevelt "that it was only the thought of possible cooperation in a matter which would be helpful in U.S.-South American relations . . . which has caused [him] to acquiesce in the suggestion put forward to have Canada [in the Rio conference]" (Ogelsby, pp. 52-53).

2. Lyon and Ismael, p. xiv. Precisely because this volume is such an accurate and useful reflection of Canadian attitudes, it is full of interesting contradictions. In the introduction, for example, we are told that it would "certainly be presumptuous [to] claim superiority for the values and methods characteristic of our industrial civilization and seek to impose them on others," and more, that "the key decisions [should

be] left to the peoples of the Third World." But this is qualified: "especially in those countries where the ruling elites enjoy a genuine measure of popular support." We are not told, however, who is going to be the judge of this. Further on, however, Mitchell Sharp is approvingly quoted as saying that he hoped that Canadian aid would give people "the sinews they need to rise and cast aside the cruel weight of unjust and unprincipled government," and, further still, that "successful revolt, like successful government, calls for effective infrastructure, the kind of thing aid programs are designed to provide." Perhaps it would be wise for recipients of Canadian generosity to buy this book and read with care.

REFERENCE

BLAINEY, G. (1966) The Tyranny of Distance. New York: St. Martin's.

Claudio Veliz is Professor of Sociology at La Trobe University, Bundoora, Victoria, Australia. Previously he was a senior research fellow at Chatham House and founder and first director of the Institute of International Studies of the University of Chile. He is author of Historia de la Marina Mercante de Chile *and editor of several well-known collections of essays concerned with the contemporary society and politics of Latin America.*

REVIEW ESSAY

SPATIAL PLANNING AND DEVELOPMENT IN LATIN AMERICA
The Critical Approach

Bedrack, Mosés. LA ESTRATEGIA DE DESARROLLO ESPACIAL EN CHILE (1970-1973). Buenos Aires: Ediciones SIAP-Planteos, 1974.

Borja, Jordi. MOVIMIENTOS SOCIALES URBANOS. Buenos Aires: Ediciones SIAP-Planteos, 1975.

Castells, Manuel (compilador). ESTRUCTURA DE CLASES Y POLITICA URBANA EN AMERICA LATINA. Buenos Aires: Ediciones SIAP, 1974.

Pastrana, Ernesto and M. Threlfall. PAN, TECHO Y PODER. Buenos Aires: Ediciones SIAP-Planteos, 1974.

Rodríguez, Alfredo et al. SEGREGACION RESIDENCIAL Y DESMOVILIZACION POLITICA. Buenos Aires: Ediciones SIAP-Planteos, 1973.

Rofman, Alejandro. DESIGUALDADES REGIONALES Y CONCENTRACION ECONOMICA. Buenos Aires: Ediciones SIAP-Planteos, 1974.

Schteingart, Martha (compilador). URBANIZACION Y DEPENDENCIA EN AMERICA LATINA. Buenos Aires: Ediciones SIAP, 1973.

Stöhr, Walter B. EL DESARROLLO REGIONAL EN AMERICA LATINA—EXPERIENCIAS Y PERSPECTIVAS. Buenos Aires: Ediciones SIAP, 1972.

I

Compared with the three years just past, 1977 apparently overflows with promising signs for the Western Hemisphere. A new administration in the most powerful nation of the system has started out with an ambitious foreign policy that proposes a program of cooperation to preserve peace and to promote prosperity the world over. A consensus of conclusions and recommendations concerning improvement of human settlements was reached by those attending Habitat, the spectacular conference organized by the United Nations in June 1976 in Vancouver. Finally, a very positive image of Latin America vis-à-vis the advanced industrial world was presented at the end of that year by ECLA (Economic Commission for Latin America). The foregoing are some of the more important elements among others indicating that, at the level of public opinion, there is increased confidence in the immediate future of the Hemisphere and, therefore, of Latin America.

At the same time, since there are still serious imbalances and problems within Latin America, as well as grave social injustices, there is a renewed interest in planning, both as an ideology justifying intervention to modify the social system and as an operative instrument to carry out such intervention. A country's state apparatus is basic to any planning action, for it is in economic policy that the strategy for development can be defined. In the 1960s, the practice of planning actually became less attractive because of the persistence and even worsening of the depressed situation of huge sectors of the Latin American population; nevertheless, due in part to the accelerated expansion of technical and bureaucratic teams engaged in planning implementation, the latter is still considered the sine qua non tool of development.

It should be added here that, although planning is conceived of as a presumably neutral technique to promote a development measured in terms of economic growth which, in turn, is supposed to help guarantee social stability, it has been advocated by governments of all types, including military and authoritarian governments that view planning as an instrument useful to and consistent with their ideas of efficient development within the prevailing status quo.[1]

The crisis of the so-called "optimistic equation"—more economic development equals more political democracy (O'Donnell, 1972)—largely dominates the works here under review, which have been published since 1970 by SIAP (Inter-American Planning Society). These writings try to explain the political function of planning as well as its principal agents in the state apparatus. SIAP was created in the 1950s as a private society of professional and academic people from both Americas interested in "comprehensive planning," and it has been a fairly accurate reflection of how the thought of Latin American planners has evolved from predominantly rationalist positions to attitudes more sensitive to specific political and historical values, as can be seen in SIAP's editorial policy.[2]

Thus, in recent years the texts of SIAP have tended to deal with three areas: (a) *urbanization* in Latin America, which is an attempt to go beyond the ecological-demographic aspects in the study of the high rate of urban growth in the region and its consequences, by understanding urbanization as a complex process that must be analyzed in order to interpret historically how it is influenced by Latin America's dependency relations with the central or dominant nations; (b) *urban-regional development*, in which studies of specific policies and programs for economic-spatial development are alternated with attempts at a theoretical interpretation of the socioeconomic inequalities within regions and national subspaces, necessarily involving a political-ideological framework for urban-regional development; and (c) *urban policy and demands*, a topic that stems directly from the two preceding and that explores state action at the urban level in either confronting or repressing the collective pressures of a population subject to substandard working and living conditions, especially as regards housing.

II

It has frequently been said that Latin America is a single unit not only because of its geography but also because of a culture derived from a common colonial heritage. This unit seems to be consolidated at present by the determinant intervention of capitalist practices that impose similar political and economic patterns on the region—with the notorious exception of Cuba. But this historical-cultural unity does not conceal the profound differences among the countries of Latin America, as is shown in their very different rhythms and levels of development. Nevertheless, it is clear that, without a global approach taking into account and explaining not only the historical genesis of the Latin American societies and their particular form of development, but also the conditions determining the behavior of their social sectors in terms of political alliances and conflicts, there is a risk of ending up with simple descriptive or partial typologies of the countries of the region.

The studies on urbanization and its "dependent" character edited by Schteingart (1973) furnish interesting and varied examples of the use of a historical-structural approach, especially those authored by Quijano, Castells, Singer, Kaplan, and Cardoso. They all trace the present international system of nations to an origin linked to the expansion of European commercial capitalism, which, as it progressed to its competitive and then its monopolistic stage, gradually integrated economies into the world market that, because of their varying levels of production, would play different but complementary roles in the areas of production and distribution. It is interesting that the Latin American nations, unlike other regions equally dependent on present-day capitalism, "created their dependency relations at birth," in the words of Quijano (Schteingart, 1973: 23). Therefore, it cannot be expected that these nations will simply repeat the processes that led to the expansion of the societies originating capitalism, which had those other still underdeveloped regions available for their "takeoff." Furthermore, the penetration of advanced forms of capitalist development produced and still produces in Latin America a coexistence of diverse and interdependent systems of production and modes of life, unlike the relatively ordered and successive stages that characterized European development. Urbanization, considered as a subprocess of the overall process of social change, which some authors identify in a limited fashion with "modernization," offers fertile ground for an analysis of the relations and effects of dependency in Latin America.

Although the above-mentioned authors generally agree on the interaction of the developed and underdeveloped nations in their analysis of *dependent urbanization*, they differ in the degree of importance they attribute to the external or metropolitan factors of domination. For example, Castells (Schteingart, 1973: 70-92) directly relates the social determination of urbanization to the stages in the formation of world capitalism; these stages generated characteristics in the transformation of Latin American space that became "a specific expression of the social contradictions produced by the form and pace of international domination." Singer (Schteingart, 1973: 93-102), without overlooking the negative effect of capital exports by the international monopolistic sector, rightly points to the intrinsic limitations of internal capitalism as determinants of underdevelopment in terms of insufficient capital accumulation, which would explain the weak development of productive forces and their resultant inability to give employment to the growing urban masses. Cardoso (Schteingart, 1973: 176-205) considers it essential to go beyond the domination of the Latin American economies by the external market to an understanding of the organization and behavior of the classes and segments of classes as the key to the historical stages of urbanization up to its present urban-industrial character, with emphasis on the technical bureaucratization and the marginalization of a sector of the dominated groups. Kaplan (Schteingart, 1973: 132-175) broadens his analysis to deal with the way in which factors that encourage urbanization are superimposed on and intermingled with changes in the power structure and increased state intervention, with this last element appearing as the only organized and institutionalized body for (p. 169) "preserving the bases of the system and achieving stability, minimal growth, and relative modernization for a dependent capitalism that seems to have passed directly from a fragile infancy–skipping youth and maturity–to a barely disguised senility." Quijano (Schteingart, 1973: 19-69) offers an interesting synthesis of how urbanization, social change, and dependency are interrelated, describing the multidimensional character of urbanization and its gestation and persistence in the framework of societies connected with the overall capitalist system. From this framework, Quijano goes on to define the concept of the "urbanization of society" and to analyze its *exclusionary character* in the sense of generating a "marginal" population, understood as a broad sector of the inhabitants inserted in an unstable and fragmentary way into the dominant trends of capitalist production.

The foregoing discussion makes it possible to outline a general approach to Latin American urbanization not confined to the classic ecological-demographic dimension that lends itself so well to the descriptive and comparative studies dear to academic circles. This approach centers on structural situations of dependency which, we repeat, *condition or limit* but do not mechanically determine the alternatives or options actually open to a given society. Such alternatives or options will be definitively established by the play of interests, alliances, and interrelations of social forces, as expressed politically by their insertion into and their control over not only the state mechanisms but also production and consumption activities. Urbanization as a process and the big cities as their spatial continent thus become functional in terms of the reproduction needs of dependent capitalism, in which the steadily increasing organic component of capital is in conflict with the also-increasing needs of the urban population, thereby presenting one more expression of the classic objective contradiction between the social character of production and the private character of its appropriation.

III

Small wonder that the gradual perception of the severe social and physical problems–unemployment, transportation, housing–in the principal cities, together with the secular backwardness of the rural economy in almost all the countries of Latin America, has opened the way since the 1950s to growing efforts by scholars and policy makers to develop a theoretical and instrumental framework that would permit the joint solution of urban-rural contradictions and of the points of greatest conflict in each polarity. So the time had arrived for regional planning; that is, the rational and scientific manipulation of the national subspaces, as is well described by Soja, cited in de Souza and Porter (1974: 19; emphasis added): "More specifically, spatial planning usually takes the form of intervention in the urbanization process through the selective concentration of development inputs in certain types of centers. This, it is presumed, will streamline the urban system and encourage a more efficient and rapid diffusion of development outward from core areas downward through the urban hierarchy. *If successful*, system-wide development will be accelerated, regional inequalities will be significantly reduced, and the distribution of employment opportunities will be brought in closer accord with the distribution of employment seekers."

Such a definition incorporates its own categories of the macroeconomy and of the modernization-diffusion approach, such as center-periphery models, dual societies, regional imbalances, and growth poles which, taken together, represent a strong effort to limit the development region to its economic-spatial determinants, thereby removing it from its principal historical determinants. Thus, the idea that economic development will reduce regional inequalities is directly derived from neoclassic economic thought, which assumes that production factors operating in conditions of perfect competition lead to equilibrium. This theory, applied to Latin America, is far removed from reality which, to the contrary, shows an increase in the economic and social inequalities within and between regions, despite growing state intervention intended to correct the situation.[3] In other words, economic forces cannot function autonomously in space without taking into account the essential factors that condition space—especially the production and power relations prevailing in the national society under study. The heavily concentrated way in which productive forces expand in Latin America and their spatial impact warrant the statement by Rofman (1974: 69) that "in an underdeveloped capitalist system, ecological-demographic equilibrium does not, by definition, exist."

Stöhr (1972) analyzes in detail the genesis of the development and urban-regional planning policies that have been tried out in Latin America, ranging from programs thought up for emergency situations to the complex medium- and long-term policies aimed at integrating national space in economic terms (for example, mobilization of natural resources in the peripheral areas or broadening the internal market to support industrial expansion), as well as in social and political terms (for example, incorporation of the peripheral areas into the decision-making process and reduction of the interregional disparities in living standards). Regional planning would be the most useful discipline-instrument for such objectives, since (Stöhr, 1972: 104) "regional planning, because of its intermediate state between national and local levels offers a special potential to interrelate the economic component (which depends mainly on national factors) with the component of 'participation' in development (which depends mainly on local factors)." Stöhr classifies possible processes of regional development into (a) internal (closed systems), (b) externally induced by decisions and capital originating in other areas of the national space, and (c) a diffusion of development outward from the urban system within the region, which is the process emphasized by most specialists. These processes would gradually lead to self-sustained growth, insofar as there is adequate interaction of the economic, social, and political determinants. Stöhr recognizes that such determinants are strongly conditioned in their actual scope and intensity, so that Myrdahl's "spread" and "backwash" effects arise among the regions, thereby reinforcing the spatial disparities that are meant to be corrected. The specific examples of the regional programs commented on by Stöhr show a generally striking dependence on the central or national level of decision-making, which is the Achilles heel of the most sophisticated theories of regional planning.

In fact, dependence on government decisions implies that in Latin American countries there is an unfounded confidence that the central political body will impartially try to harmonize and mediate among the many interests in order to deal equitably with all sectors of the population. To the contrary, if we observe the entrepreneurial capitalistic nature of the processes of industrialization and the resistance of the large landowners and agricultural entrepreneurs to moderate programs of agrarian reform in the various Latin American countries, we must conclude that state decisions are reached under strong pressures and control by the dominant sectors of these societies, whose political and economic interests are in constant conflict with the national majorities who are supposed to benefit. The works of Bedrack (1974) and Rofman (1974) make clear the actual distance between what is proposed and what is feasible in urban-regional planning in the present circumstances of Latin America.

Chile is one of the few Latin American countries in which the theoretical concepts of regional planning have had any possibility of being applied from the highest political level, beginning with the reformist Christian-Democrat administration of the preceding decade. Paradoxically, both this administration and the aborted "transition to socialism" that succeeded it in 1970 undertook a relatively similar regional policy—concentrated decentralization—based on diametrically opposed political philosophies and strategies. For the Frei theoreticians, decentralization was not only an appropriate tool for economic development, but also a means of stabilizing integration and social participation. For the UP (popular unity party), spatial decentralization involved a strategy to dismantle the earlier centralized and exclusionary economic structure in order to weaken the former dominant classes and open the way to new social actors.[4] Although both concepts are loaded with ideology, they typically underestimate the economic and class interests committed to perpetuating centralization,[5] and they are overconfident in the ability of the state to change that historical trend in the short space of a six-year administration. Bedrack (1974: 24-26; emphasis added) envisions the possibility of a new spatial structure in "*social control* of the location of production activities and in state use of the basic tools that promote and regulate the economic process . . . the spatial structure of the *new economy* includes . . . a process of decentralization and of urbanization that, based on a regionalization of the production sectors, will *vitalize* the country's rural space and, furthermore, will both foster and benefit from locating a *system of industrial centers* that form a territorial structure maximizing the potential for national development." The growing internal and external difficulties that the Allende government had to face in its three years of existence did not give it time to implement the above-described spatial strategy, which depended for its viability on political and economic assumptions having a high degree of voluntary choice.

The failures of the Chilean attempts to decentralize can be better understood in the light of the article by Rofman (1974), who makes a penetrating analysis of regional inequalities before going on to the case of Argentina.[6] He maintains that the regions or subspaces must be closely linked to the national system, which thus determines the fundamental behavior of the former while allowing for the specific characteristics of each region. For this purpose, Rofman (1974: 21) describes the inadequacies of the neoclassic and functionalist economic approaches which, by attributing some autonomy to the spatial dimension "shift emphasis from what should be the most important element in the discussion—

structure of the production apparatus, control of power, state intervention, etc.; in short, it is the linking together of all the instances of social formation that produces a given settlement pattern." As may be seen, Rofman deals with the same subject as Stöhr, but using a different language. Whereas the latter author largely assumes that the rationality of these regional strategies—with the support of modernizing government and with the mobilization of investments from certain centers of diffusion—must necessarily produce a more balanced and equitable development, Rofman analyzes the production levels, the social structure, and the political-institutional apparatus to show that historical centralizing trends maintain conditions of dependency and internal domination in Latin America. From this viewpoint, the region, like the city, virtually loses its personality. National development and, therefore, the basic conditions for spatial development, will then be determined by specifically how the surplus is appropriated and by the rate of accumulation necessary for expansion of productive forces.

The foregoing leads to the conclusion that there is little possibility of applying a real urban-regional policy in an unstable and dependent Latin America, except for certain modernizing strategies that, more often than not, paradoxically help perpetuate the characteristics of underdevelopment. As Singer (1975: 160) says so well in his article on the concentration of activity and capital in São Paulo:

> It is very clear that São Paulo is not going to stop growing, since it is the symbol and the epicenter of Brazilian capitalist development. The contrasts it exhibits only reveal the contradictions of a system which, in order to develop productive forces . . . is always raising new problems. *Criticism of urbanization, by not taking into account this basic characteristic of capitalism*, makes the mistake of trying to avoid these problems by limiting the system's dynamism, which is, after all, its only historical justification. A capitalism without contradiction and change is no more than a reactionary Utopia inspired by examination of isolated problems by those who refuse to analyze the essence of the system that gave them birth. [italics added; English translation from J. E. Hardoy, *Urbanization in Latin America*, Anchor Books, 1975]

IV

We have briefly reviewed some interpretations of accelerated urbanization and the regional planning strategies that have been tried, or at least formulated, to counteract the distortions produced by this process in the different spheres of life of most Latin American countries. Recognition by governments of the impracticability of the short-term policies for spatial decentralization, together with the heightened urgency of the physical and social problems in the principal cities—problems that are sometimes directly connected with political practice and that threaten maintenance of the status quo—partly explain why these governments are prone to execute immediate urban and housing policies, which can be understood as a response by the state to the contradictions generated in the city by capitalist development itself. It should be mentioned that when governments put such policies into practice, they also expect to strengthen their support by giving accumulated social pressures an outlet, even if only an apparent one. As has been mentioned earlier, these policies, despite the ambitious rhetoric of their programs, are invariably reduced to simply attacking some details of the more visible effects or expressions of those urban contradictions that provoke greater needs for the development of production and for reproduction of the labor force—needs that will have to be met with inadequate and scarce resources of equipment and infrastructure.

While governments insist on implementing their "ever more aggressive urban policies," according to Borja (1975: 14), which are supposedly capable of simultaneously serving not only capital accumulation requirements but also the living conditions of the urban population, it happens that the former engenders forms of defense and demands by social sectors that are manifested in different degrees of pressure or confrontation. The works under discussion edited by SIAP can be broken down between those that deal with the urban problem from above—that is, from "policies"—and those that study it from its base, understood as urban social movements. In both cases, the authors relate their viewpoints to the overall social behavior, emphasizing the political character of urban problems and the decisive role played by state mediation.

The special conditions of urban growth in Latin America with its high urbanization rates and steady trend to metropolization, in the face of the evident inability of the production sector to provide employment to a rapidly expanding labor force, has brought about an impressive manifestation in the pronounced deterioration in housing conditions. This topic, therefore, usually figures prominently in any discussion of the urban problem, as Pradilla Cobos (Castells, 1974: 40-41) points out in his analysis of the Colombian housing policy:

> In the bourgeois state, which refuses to recognize the relations of capitalist production as relations of the exploitation of wage labor by capital, housing is

> where the wretched conditions of the masses are expressed and, therefore, *where the forces capable of overthrowing bourgeois institutions are incubated. It is also . . . the location of the key to unleashing the expanded reproduction of neocolonial capitalism and to solving the problem of unemployment.* Doubly mistaken, we say, for if structural limitations . . . make expectations hypothetical in the second instance, the forces needed to subvert the bourgeois order are not incubated in the wretched conditions of the slum or tenement, *but in the factories and agricultural enterprises*—modern or outdated, hygienic or unhealthy, comfortable or uncomfortable . . .—where capital and labor are in direct opposition, where the appropriation of social production by the capitalist class begins and ends. Misery, poverty, hunger, and unemployment *are only the effects of these relations of exploitation and not their causes.* [emphasis added]

The works of Pradilla Cobos, Nuñez, Sánchez, and Schteingart and Broide assembled by Castells (1974) give an account of the recent housing policies of some of the relatively more developed countries in Latin America, like Colombia, Mexico, Venezuela, and Argentina, where there is evidence of the limitations and obstacles inherent in such policies. In particular, the fact that the urban masses *cannot pay for housing* explains the additional pressures exerted by the private sector on a state already overburdened with commitments and with no more housing programs that seriously propose to "absorb and deficit," while there are plenty of alternatives such as self-help projects and "informal housing." These alternatives are temporary solutions that have the effect of directly overexploiting and demobilizing the participating groups when they are carried out within the framework of a state dominated by the several segments of capital. The book by Rodríguez et al. (1973), provocatively entitled *De invasores a invadidos (From Invaders to Invaded)*, gives an excellent example of these effects in the Peruvian capital, where by skillful action various national and external private institutions successfully manipulated the Lima *barriadas*—settlements that began with the invasion of peripheral areas—thereby politically and ideologically neutralizing the inhabitants. A variation of this is found in Mexico, where the role of "benefactor" is played by the governing party.

Nonetheless, the Latin American region offers several cases of confrontation, such as land invasion and political unrest in the principal cities, growing out of dissatisfaction with basic housing and services. In itself, the dramatic increase in the number of "marginal" families in these cities, as a result of the centralizing and exclusionary development mentioned before, explains the concern with the potential for explosion that is inherent in a situation of urban scarcities and unstable incomes. The subject has become a real subspecialty for North American political scientists and sociologists,[7] reaching levels of sophistication about the relative passiveness or radicalization of these social sectors. Broadly speaking, after an initial tendency in the past decade to predict catastrophe, there came volumes of empirical works that for the most part disputed the hypothesis of conflict, on the basis of the "conservatism" of the recent rural migrant and the apathy and pragmatism of the inhabitants of the urban peripheral settlements. These analyses, which were generally focused on the psychological characteristics and individual behavior of the "marginal" inhabitant, have finally been succeeded by studies that seek in the social context, and especially in the overall political conditions, a better understanding of the role of such urban groups, as is well described by Handelman (1975: 50):

> Thus the relevant question is not whether shantytown dwellers are always latent revolutionaries or inherent conservatives, but rather, what are the most important socio-economic and political preconditions for the political mobilization or radicalization of Latin America's urban migrant population? That is to say, under what conditions are migrants likely to remain politically apathetic or conservative and under what circumstances are they likely to challenge the status quo?

These questions are addressed in the works of Castells (1974: 191-234), Pastrana and Threlfall (1974), and Borja (1975), even though they discuss not just recent migrants, but all urban inhabitants who lead an insecure and exploited existence. Most frequently cited is the case of Chile, because of the wealth of experience gathered under changing and dynamic political alternatives from the years preceding the government of Salvador Allende until the bloody military coup of 1973. In this case, a detailed study is made of how the successive reformist policies and structural changes are connected with the demands for housing and services through powerful mediation by the political parties. For purposes of this essay, it is important to establish the relationship between urban and social thematics and its logic, beginning with a situation of conflict within an urban contradiction that, in turn, reflects the general contradictions of the system. Borja (1975) uses a classification of urban conflicts as a basis for identifying the different actors: conflicts between dominant urban agents and the population; conflicts between capitalist agents and the state; and conflicts between capitalist agents competing for the same space. Of interest is the first type of conflict—where Borja furnishes a detailed typology of "popular" urban movements in terms of social homogeneity and territorial base—which he divides into three broad types: (a) protest movements, *based on one or several specific contradictions*, such as lack of housing in a low-income neighborhood; (b) democratic movements, based on a *program* expressing a series of demands that together reach a global level, like a comprehensive program of low-cost housing; and (c) movements in terms of duality of power, where "*the political objective is overwhelmingly determinant*" and sectoral conflicts unite, leading to an open power struggle in periods of social crisis. Each of these movements succeeds insofar as it reaches its objective—from satisfying a specific demand or getting a program approved by the authorities to the complex situation of duality of power, which includes rapid transformation of the urban structure[8] and changes in the living conditions of the popular sectors. In this last case, as was noted in the 1972-1973 Chilean experience, the exercise of some power by these sectors—power to take action and economic and ideological power; that is, "the ability to coerce other social sectors"—generated new contradictions not only with the previous sector or hegemonic class, but also among the state agencies now controlled by popular parties and urban organizations with a territorial base, as well as among the programs of popular consumption, improvement of housing, and so on, and other more properly political programs.

Most of the works edited by SIAP help make clear the real possibilities in Latin America for guiding over the next few years such complex processes as regional development, population movements, and policies to provide housing and urban services. Specifically, these works conclude that the principal determination of these processes, as summed up by Castells (1974: 12), "passes essentially through political mediation and, in particular, through mediation by the state apparatus." We have also observed that the Latin American state, in trying to establish a model of capitalist development, pays special attention to areas like housing, in order to mobilize the social sectors it needs around important demands of popular consumption, with which it hopes to distract these sectors from the fundamental contradictions of the relations of production. To return to our introduction, we believe that the next years will be crucial in the entire Latin American region for the pursuit or abandonment of such a pointless strategy in the face of a slow and erratic but inexorable rise in the consciousness of expanding sectors of the population that will force intellectuals and planners to make unequivocal statements, such as those we have just reviewed.

—*Fernando Kusnetzoff*

[Translation by Marjory Mattingly Urquidi]

NOTES

1. In this respect, it should be added that the present decade virtually marks the end of the democratic-representative ideological concept as a viable political mechanism for Latin America; ironically, its disappearance is justified by the argument that it is being rescued from the "internal enemy." The official spheres of the dominant power accept the fact pragmatically and propose a "pluralist" concept with new guidelines for development insofar as the latter is understood to reproduce the capitalism model, associated or dependent. In contrast, many North American scholars continue to analyze Latin American political behavior with parameters derived from the political sociology of their own countries, thereby forcing democratic analogies that do not actually operate, like the system of competitive parties or levels of local community participation (Cardoso, 1972: 13-36: Solari et al., 1976: 494-516).

2. The editorial program of SIAP is probably the most complete Spanish-language medium for circulating Latin American thought and experience in urban and regional planning. Since 1967 it has been publishing the *Revista Interamericana de Planificación (Inter-American Journal of Planning)* and has just issued number 40. Mention should also be made of the nineteen books it had edited by the end of 1976, eight of which we selected for this review. Furthermore, it has organized eleven international conferences on planning, heavily attended by delegates from both Latin America and the United States.

3. The program for the northeast of Brazil is made remarkable by the experience of the SUDENE, an ambitious program of regional investment, chiefly industrial, with strong political support since 1959. Various authors (Gilbert, 1974; Singer, 1975; Stöhr, 1972) agree that, in spite or, rather, because of the introduction of highly capital-intensive industries, regional disparities were increased, income redistribution was not achieved, a large part of the income generated was returned to the southeast of the country, and relative development was concentrated in the capital cities of the region.

4. The Christian Democratic Party followed very closely the guidelines recommended by a group of Ford Foundation experts (URDAPIC); criticism of hyperurbanization and of Santiago's excessive influence on national space led to proposal of a "strategy of deliberate urbanization" to spread modern values and attitudes with greater political and social participation by the medium-sized cities and the consequent attraction of investment. The UP kept much of the earlier strategy, but added to development poles and centers the thesis of "areas integrated into development," which included a detailed "system of populated centers" covering the national territory with successively smaller units. This system, superimposed on and integrated into a network of agricultural production units, would structure rural space in a way that showed elements of central planning, including the regional experiences of Cuba.

5. An interesting comparative analysis is found in Ramírez (1974), *Planning in a Social Vacuum*, where the author states that failure of decentralization policies is due mainly to the divorce between spatial plans and the social forces participating in the country's development.

6. This work is supplemented by another by Rofman and Romero (1974), which presents a theoretical framework of six dimensions: the international system, the

national system, the power relations between systems, systems of decision-making, the urban-regional systems, and the historical process in the evolution of systems.

7. To our earlier study (Kusnetzoff, 1975) should be added the excellent article by Handelman (1975) that completes the panorama of the American scholars with a critical approach emphasizing the global political dimensions. Handelman proposes a typology of relations between "marginal" urban sectors and the dominant political system with five alternatives: (a) paternalism without mobilization, in Brazil and Guatemala; (b) government-directed cooptation, in Peru and Mexico; (c) populism, in Colombia 1970; (d) reformist political organization, in Venezuela, Peru, prior to the present regime, and Chile under Frei; and (e) radical mobilization, in Chile 1968-1973.

8. Borja (1975: 41-42) is especially careful to differentiate his concept of urban structure from a physical or territorial image. Thus, urban structure "is the *specific form of social organization of the territory* considered as a unit that ensures centralization of production activities and of the means of collective consumption. It is the totality of mechanisms and institutions that ensures reproduction of the general conditions of production in a territorial unit. This production is, in principle, guaranteed, *subject to the dominant social logic*; for example, reproduction of the labor force at minimum cost. . . . Its function is to make certain that surplus value is obtained (and increased through socialization of the conditions of production and the private appropriation of urban land and properties) and that the social hierarchy and, therefore, the social division of labor are reproduced through the reproduction mechanisms of the labor force" (emphasis added). For societies of advanced capitalism, Harvey (1973) proposes an overall theory having specific points of contact with Borja's approach.

REFERENCES

CARDOSO, F. H. (1972) "Alternativas políticas en América Latina," pp. 13-36 in F. H. Cardoso, Estado y Sociedad en America Latina. Buenos Aires: Eds. Nueva Visión.

de SOUZA, A. R. and P. W. PORTER (1974) The Underdevelopment and Modernization of the Third World. Resource Paper No. 28. Washington, DC: Association of American Geographers.

GILBERT, A. (1974) Latin American Development. England: Penguin.

HANDELMAN, H. (1975) "The political mobilization of urban squatter settlements." Latin Amer. Research Rev. 11 (December): 35-72.

HARVEY, D. (1973) Social Justice and the City. Baltimore, MD: John Hopkins Univ. Press.

KUSNETZOFF, F. (1975) "Housing policies and housing politics." J. of Interamer. Studies 17, 3: 281-310.

O'DONNELL, G. A. (1972) Modernización y Autoritarismo. Buenos Aires: Paidós Editorial.

RAMIREZ, R. (1974) Planning in a Social Vacuum. London: University College Development Planning Unit.

ROFMAN, A. and L. A. ROMERO (1974) Sistema Socioeconómico y Estructura Regional en la Argentina. Buenos Aires: Amorrortu Editorial.

SINGER, P. (1975) Economia Politica de la Urbanización. México: Siglo Veintiuno Editores.

SOLARI, A. E., R. FRANCO, and J. JUTKOWITZ (1976) Teoría, Acción Social y Desarrollo en América Latina. México: Siglo Veintiuno Editores.

Fernando Kusnetzoff, after a year and a half in Tegucigalpa, Honduras, as Team Leader for the United Nations Development Programme advising on the country's housing policies and programs, recently returned to the Department of City and Regional Planning as a Visiting Professor at the University of California, Berkeley. He was Dean of the College of Architecture and Urban Planning at the University of Chile from 1968-1973.

BOOKS RECEIVED

GENERAL AND REGIONAL LATIN AMERICA

Atkins, G. Pope. LATIN AMERICA IN THE INTERNATIONAL POLITICAL SYSTEM. New York: Free Press, Macmillan Publishing Co., Ltd., 1977. Tables, bibliography, index. x, 448 pp. $11.95.

Burkholder, Mark A. and D. S. Chandler. FROM IMPOTENCE TO AUTHORITY: THE SPANISH CROWN AND THE AMERICAN AUDIENCIAS, 1687-1808. Columbia: University of Missouri Press, 1977. Appendices, figures. xi, 253 pp. $15.00.

Burns, E. Bradford. LATIN AMERICA: A CONCISE INTERPRETIVE HISTORY. Second edition. Englewood Cliffs, NJ: Prentice-Hall, Inc., 1977. Statistical tables, glossary, guide to paperback literature in English, index, list of maps. xi, 307 pp. $7.95 paper.

Cabieses Cubas, Hugo. COMUNIDAD LABORAL Y CAPITALISMO: ALCANCES Y LIMITES. Lima: DESCO, 1976. Presentación, conclusiones, anexo estadístico. 159 pp. Paper.

Espinosa, J. Manuel. INTER-AMERICAN BEGINNINGS OF U.S. CULTURAL DIPLOMACY, 1936-1948. Washington, DC: Bureau of Educational & Cultural Affairs, U.S. Department of State, 1976. Historical Studies No. 2. Map, terms and abbreviations, appendices, index. xvi, 365 pp.

Hanson, Carl A. DISSERTATIONS ON IBERIAN AND LATIN AMERICAN HISTORY. Troy, NY: Whitston Publishing Co., 1975. Notes, addendum, author index. v, 400 pp.

Morris, Richard, Josefina Zoraida Vásquez, and Elias Trabulse. LAS REVOLUCIONES DE INDEPENDENCIA EN MEXICO Y EN LOS ESTADOS UNIDOS, Volumenes I, II, III. México: SepSetentas, 1976. Index. Vol. I, 187 pp.; Vol. II, 166 pp.; Vol. III, 180 pp. Paper.

Needler, Martin C. AN INTRODUCTION TO LATIN AMERICAN POLITICS: THE STRUCTURE OF CONFLICT. Englewood Cliffs, NJ: Prentice-Hall, Inc., 1977. Selected bibliography, notes. ix, 358 pp. $11.95.

Organization of American States. INTER-AMERICAN YEARBOOK ON HUMAN RIGHTS, 1969-1970 (English and Spanish). Washington, DC: General Secretariat of Organization of American States, 1976. Bibliography and index. vii, 542 pp. $20.00.

Portes, Alejandro, and Harley L. Browning, eds. CURRENT PERSPECTIVES IN LATIN AMERICAN URBAN RESEARCH. Austin: Institute of Latin American Studies, University of Texas, 1977. xi, 179 pp. $9.95 cloth, $3.95 paper.

van Oss, Adriaan, comp. LATINOAMERICANISTAS EN EUROPA: REGISTRO BIO-BIBLIOGRAFIA DE 1976 (Spanish). Amsterdam: Centro de Estudios y Documentación Latinoamericanos, 1976. 100 pp. Paper.

Wooderidge, Hensley C. and Lawrence S. Thompson. PRINTING IN COLONIAL SPANISH AMERICA. Troy, N.Y.: Whitston Publishing Co., 1976. Illustrations, personal name index, short title index. vii, 172 pp.

BRAZIL

Basic Plan for Scientific and Technological Development. Brasilia: Secretaria de Planejamento, SEPLAN, 1976. 186 pp. Paper.

Biblioteca Academia Paulista de Letras. Vol. 1: Comentarios de Vicente de Azevedo. CARTAS DE ALVARES DE AZEVEDO. Vol. 2: Francisco de Assis Vieira Bueno. A CIDADE DE SAO PAULO. Vol. 3: Antonio de Oliverira. O URSO. Romance de Costumes Paulistas. São Paulo: 1976. Vol. 1, 253 pp.; Vol. 2, 66 pp.; Vol. 3, 216 pp. Paper.

BRAZILIAN INDEX (Portuguese and English). Brasilia: Secretaria de Planejamento, SEPLAN, 1976. 322 pp.

Haar, Jerry. THE POLITICS OF HIGHER EDUCATION IN BRAZIL. New York: Praeger Publishers, 1977. Praeger special studies in international politics and government. List of tables and charts, appendix, bibliography. xiv, 222 pp.

Ministério das Relações Exteriores. RELATORIO 1974. Brasilia: 1974. 279 pp. Paper.

Moran, Emilio F. AGRICULTURAL DEVELOPMENT IN THE TRANSAMAZON HIGHWAY. Latin American Studies Working Papers. Bloomington: Indiana University, 1976. Figures, tables, map, bibliography, appendices. xi, 136 pp. Paper.

Rodman, Selden. GENIUS IN THE BACKLANDS: POPULAR ARTISTS OF BRAZIL. Old Greenwich, CT: Devin-Adair Co., 1977. 160 pp. $10.00

CARIBBEAN REGION

Azicri, Max. THE GOVERNING STRATEGIES OF MASS MOBILIZATION: THE FOUNDATIONS OF CUBAN REVOLUTIONARY POLITICS. Latin American Monograph Series No. 2. Erie, PA: Mercyhurst College, Northwestern Pennsylvania Institute for Latin American Studies, 1977. 32 pp. Paper.

Perusse, Roland I. HISTORICAL DICTIONARY OF HAITI. Latin American Historical Dictionaries, No. 15. Metuchen, NJ: Scarecrow Press, Inc., 1977. 142 pp. $6.00.

CHILE

Loveman, Brian. STRUGGLE IN THE COUNTRYSIDE: POLITICS AND RURAL LABOR IN CHILE, 1919-1973. Studies in Development No. 10, International Development Research Center. Bloomington: Indiana University Press, 1976. List of figures, tables, maps, abbreviations, notes, bibliography, index. xxxvi, 439 pp. $12.50.

Varona, Albert J. FRANCISCO BILBAO: REVOLUCIONARIO DE AMERICA. Buenos Aires: Ediciones Excelsior, 1973. Introducción, apéndices, bibliografía. xxix, 457 pp. Paper.

COLOMBIA

Davis, Robert H. HISTORICAL DICTIONARY OF COLOMBIA. Latin American Historical Dictionaries No. 14. Metuchen, NJ: Scarecrow Press, Inc., 1977. 288 pp. $11.00.

MEXICO

Bernal, Ignacio. THE OLMEC WORLD. Translated from the Spanish by Doris Heyden and Fernando Horcasitas. Berkeley: University of California Press, 1977. Bibliography, plates, index, list of illustrations. 283 pp. $7.95 paper.

Jones, Grant D., ed. ANTHROPOLOGY AND HISTORY IN YUCATAN. Texas Pan American Series. Austin: University of Texas Press, 1977. Bibliography, index. xxiv, 344 pp. $16.95.

Raat, William D. EL POSITIVISMO DURANTE EL PORFIRIATO, 1876-1910. Versión castellana de Andrés Lira. México: SepSetentas, 1975. Bibliografía. 175 pp. Paper.

Rutherford, John. AN ANNOTATED BIBLIOGRAPHY OF THE NOVELS OF THE MEXICAN REVOLUTION OF 1910-1917 IN ENGLISH AND SPANISH. Troy, NY: Whitston Publishing Co., 1972. Footnotes, bibliography. 180 pp.

Ulloa, Berta. LA REVOLUCION INTERVENIDA: RELACIONES DIPLOMATICAS ENTRE MEXICO Y ESTADOS UNIDOS, 1910-1914. México: El Colegio de México, Centro de Estudios Históricos, Nueva Serie, 1976 (segunda edición corregida). Siglas de los archivos públicos utilizados, otras abreviaturas utilizadas, apéndices, índices analítico y de ilustraciones. xii, 451 pp. Paper.

UNAM (Universidad Nacional Autónoma de México). ANUARIO BIBLIOGRAFICO 1963. México: Instituto de Investigaciones Bibliográficas, UNAM, Biblioteca Nacional, 1976. Abreviaturas, apéndices, índice. xx, 735 pp. Paper.

Weinstein, Michael A. THE POLARITY OF MEXICAN THOUGHT: INSTRUMENTALISM AND FINALISM. University Park: Pennsylvania State University Press, 1977. Notes, index. xi, 128 pp. $11.95.

PARAGUAY

Arens, Richard, ed. GENOCIDE IN PARAGUAY. Epilog by Elie Wiesel. Philadelphia: Temple University Press, 1976. Illustrations, contributors, prefatory note, editor's afterword. xvii, 171 pp. $10.95.

PERU

ILDIS. LAS SOCIEDADES DE CAPITAL EN EL AREA ANDINA. Lima, Peru: Instituto Latinoamericano de Investigaciones Sociales (ILDIS), 1976. 466 pp. Paper.

Kerbusch, Ernst J., ed. CAMBIOS ESTRUCTURALES EN EL PERU, 1968-1975. Lima, Perú: Fundación Friedrich Ebert, Instituto Latinoamericano de Investigaciones Sociales, 1976. Spanish edition. Bibliografía selecta, índice. 199 pp. Paper.

VENEZUELA

Alborñoz, Orlando. PODER Y LIDERAZGO EN LA ESCUELA PRIMARIA VENEZOLANA. Caracas: Societas, 1977. Bibliografía, índices. 315 pp. Paper.

Arcila Farias, Eduardo. EL PENSAMIENTO ECONOMICO HISPANOAMERICANO EN BAQUIJANO Y CARRILLO. Caracas: Consejo Nacional de la Cultura Centro de Estudios Latinoamericanos "Rómulo Gallegos," 1976. 150 pp. Paper.

Erminy, Peran (texto) and Godofredo Romero (diseño y fotografias). PINTORES POPULARES DE CARACAS. Caracas: Concejo Municipal del Distrito Federal, 1976. 159 pp.

Mudarra, Miguel Angel. CIEN SEMBLANZAS DE CARAQUENOS NOTABLES. Caracas: Concejo Municipal del Distrito Federal, 1976. Spanish. Indices y bibliografía. 242 pp.

MISCELLANEOUS

Caltofen Segura, Rodolfo. JUANITA: PAGINAS DA GUERRA CIVIL DE ESPANHA. Lisboa: Editorial Aster, 1975. 151 pp. Paper.

Espinosa, J. Manuel. INTER-AMERICAN BEGINNINGS OF U.S. CULTURAL DIPLOMACY, 1936-1948. Cultural Relations Programs of the Department of State, Historical Studies No. 2. Washington, DC: Bureau of Educational and Cultural Affairs, U.S. Department of State, 1976. Map of American Republics in 1940s, terms and abbreviations, appendices, index. xvi, 365 pp.

Finsterbusch, Gail. MAN AND EARTH: THEIR CHANGING RELATIONSHIP. Indianapolis: Studies in Sociology, Bobbs-Merrill, 1977. References. 55 pp. Paper.

Inter-American Foundation. THEY KNOW HOW . . . AN EXPERIMENT IN DEVELOPMENT ASSISTANCE. Rosslyn, VA: Inter-American Foundation, 1977. xii, 159 pp. $2.50 paper.

Navarro, Vicente. MEDICINE UNDER CAPITALISM. New York: Neale Watson Academic Publications, Inc., 1977. 230 pp. $14.95 cloth, $5.95 paper.

Silvert, Kalman H. THE REASON FOR DEMOCRACY. New York: The Viking Press, 1977. Notes. 136 pp. $8.95.

Stacey, C. P. MACKENZIE KING AND THE ATLANTIC TRIANGLE. The 1976 Joanne Goodman Lectures delivered at the University of Western Ontario. Toronto: Macmillan of Canada/Maclean-Hunter Press, 1977. References. xvi, 74 pp. $7.95.

Thompson, Kenneth W., Barbara R. Fogel (Vol. 1) with Helen E. Danner (Vol. 2). HIGHER EDUCATION AND SOCIAL CHANGE: PROMISING EXPERIMENTS IN DEVELOPING COUNTRIES. Analysis of overall topic and case studies of institutions in Africa, Asia, and Latin America. Vol. 1: Reports; Vol. 2: Case Studies. New York: Praeger Publishers; Vol. 1, 1976; Vol. 2, 1977. List of tables, abbreviations, appendices, glossary, index. Vol. 1, 224 pp. $7.50 paper; Vol. 2, xxiii, 564 pp. $10.00 paper.

MIGRATION AND ADAPTATION
Tzintzuntzan Peasants in Mexico City

by ROBERT V. KEMPER, *Southern Methodist University*

A new study presenting a description and analysis of rural migrants and their adaptation to life in a rapidly growing metropolitan setting, this volume deals with a microcosm of Mexican urbanization: emigration from the traditional peasant village of Tzintzuntzan, Michocan to Mexico City. Professor Kemper reports on the background of the migrants as well as on their cultural and social adjustments to an urban environment. A model of rural-urban migration applicable to similar populations in other developing nations is also presented and will be of interest to anthropologists and urban specialists involved in a variety of disciplines.

CONTENTS

Introduction
PART I: THE RURAL BACKGROUND FOR CITYWARD MIGRATION
1. The Modernization of Tzintzuntzan
2. Emigration from Tzintzuntzan
PART II: THE URBAN DESTINATION
3. Mexico City and Mexican Development Since 1945
4. Tzintzuntzan in Mexico City: Population Characteristics
5. Geographical Mobility in the Metropolitan Area
6. Social Network and Urban Ecology
7. Family and Household Structure
8. Economic Organization
9. Cultural Transformations
PART III: A MODEL OF RURAL-URBAN MIGRATION AND URBANIZATION
10. Tzintzuntzenos and the Mexican Case
11. The Situation in Developing Countries
PART IV: SUMMARY AND CONCLUSIONS
Appendix: Fieldwork Strategies and Long Term Research Plans
Notes / References Cited / Index

"Tzintzuntzan is especially well suited for a microcosmic study of the emigration process. On the one hand, since the bulk of the emigration is recent, we can deal with real people, and not simply with statistics. And these people are known, as are their families, their socioeconomic status, and their histories, to an extent not normally the case." — from Chapter 1

Volume 43 Sage Library of Social Research
April 1977 224 pages
ISBN 0-8039-0687-0 hardcover $11.[illegible]
ISBN 0-8039-0688-9 softcover $ 6.[illegible]

Vol. 19 No. 4
November 1977

JOURNAL OF INTERAMERICAN STUDIES and WORLD AFFAIRS

A Publication of the Center for Advanced International Studies,
The University of Miami

SAGE PUBLICATIONS

Journal of INTERAMERICAN STUDIES
and WORLD AFFAIRS

The editors and publisher wish to acknowledge with gratitude the assistance and encouragement of the Center for Advanced International Studies, University of Miami, in providing ancillary services and support for this journal.

Journal of
INTERAMERICAN
STUDIES
and WORLD AFFAIRS

Vol. 19
No. 4
November
1977

CONTENTS

The Chilean Presidency in a Developmental Perspective
JORGE TAPIA-VIDELA 451

Policy-Making and the Quest for Consensus: Nationalizing Venezuelan Petroleum
JOHN D. MARTZ 483

On the Economic Cost to Panama of Negotiating a Peaceful Solution to the Panama Canal Question
ALFRED E. OSBORNE, Jr. 509

Policy Change in an Authoritarian Regime: Mexico Under Echeverría
MERILEE S. GRINDLE 523

Mexico: The Impact of the 1968 Student Protest on Echeverría's Reformism
YORAM SHAPIRA 557

INDEX 581

SAGE PUBLICATIONS / *Beverly Hills London*

POLICY: THE JOURNAL OF INTERAMERICAN STUDIES AND WORLD AFFAIRS reflects the interests of the scholarly community and interested public concerned with the social, economic, political, and cultural aspects of life in Latin America (including the Caribbean); particularly in those instances where the subject is of concern to more than one of the traditional disciplines. As these concerns change, so will the content of the journal.

ARTICLES which have special relevance for interrelationships between American nations and of those nations with the rest of the world will be given special consideration. An effort will be made to include occasional articles that state an unusual or even discordant position on a subject of broad interest to be supplemented by critical comments of authorities representing differing positions on the topic. The editors continue to welcome articles by scholars from all parts of the world.

MANUSCRIPTS should be submitted in duplicate to: Editor, JOURNAL OF INTERAMERICAN STUDIES AND WORLD AFFAIRS, Box 24-8134, University of Miami, Coral Gables, Florida 33124. Manuscripts should be typewritten, double-spaced, with footnotes, references, tables, and charts on separate pages, and should follow the current journal style. A brief biographical paragraph describing each author's current affiliation, research interests, and recent publications should accompany the manuscript.

CORRESPONDENCE regarding book reviews should be sent directly to: Book Review Editor, JOURNAL OF INTERAMERICAN STUDIES AND WORLD AFFAIRS, Box 24-8134, University of Miami, Coral Gables, Florida 33124.

JOURNAL OF INTERAMERICAN STUDIES AND WORLD AFFAIRS is published four times annually—in February, May, August, and November.

Subscriptions: Regular institutional rate $26.00. Individuals may subscribe at a one-year rate of $15.00. Add $1.00 per year for subscriptions outside the United States. Orders from U.K., Europe, the Middle East, and Africa should be sent to the London office (address below). Noninstitutional orders **must** be paid by personal check.

Second-class postage paid at Beverly Hills, California.

Inquiries: Address all correspondence and permissions requests to SAGE PUBLICATIONS, INC., 275 South Beverly Drive, Beverly Hills, California 90212. Inquiries and subscriptions from U.K., Europe, the Middle East, and Africa should be sent to SAGE PUBLICATIONS LTD, 28 Banner Street, London EC1Y 8QE, England. Other orders should be sent to the Beverly Hills office.

Advertising: Current rates and specifications may be obtained by writing to the Advertising Manager at the Beverly Hills office (address above).

This journal is abstracted or indexed in **Historical Abstracts, Human Resources Abstracts, Sage Urban Studies Abstracts, International Political Science Abstracts, Public Affairs Information Service, Current Contents, Social Sciences Citation Index, Social Sciences Index, ABC POL SCI** and **United States Political Science Documents.**

Back Issues: Information about availability and prices of back issues may be obtained from the publisher's order department (address above). Write to London office for sterling prices.

Claims for undelivered copies must be made no later than three months following month of publication. The publisher will supply missing copies when losses have been sustained in transit and where the reserve stock will permit.

Change of Address: Six weeks' advance notice must be given when notifying of change of address. Please send old address label along with the new address to insure proper identification. Please specify name of journal.

JORGE TAPIA-VIDELA
Department of Political Science
Wayne State University
Detroit, Michigan 48202

THE CHILEAN PRESIDENCY IN A DEVELOPMENTAL PERSPECTIVE

In contrast to other countries in Latin America, Chile emerged from the chaotic postindependence period with a strong state apparatus. Fashioned by the leadership of Diego Portales and institutionalized in the Constitution of 1833, the Chilean state became (and remains) the central focus for national development. Portales was able to marry the existing social and economic order, which was sharply hierarchical, to the institutional structures of a corporate state. In doing so, he shaped political conflict throughout Chilean history into a series of struggles for inclusion in the coalition in control of the state apparatus at any given time. Problems of violence and instability can be seen as the the natural by-products of these multiple attempts to define and redefine both the legitimate scope and orientation of the state and the composition of the dominant groups exercising power. Revolution and counter-revolution are the two polar extremes of a

AUTHOR'S NOTE: The author is very grateful to Charles J. Parrish for helpful comments on an earlier version of this article, originally presented at the American University's Presidential Conference (Washington, D.C., 1976). The author is responsible for all errors and omissions.

Journal of Interamerican Studies and World Affairs, Vol. 19 No. 4, November 1977

political continuum characterized by the continuous attempts to cope with the larger question of underdevelopment and the related problems represented by crises of integration, participation and distribution (Jobet, 1955; Pinto, 1962; Lechner, 1970).

An analysis of political and governmental institutions acquires an important dimension from this perspective; it is more than a mere formalistic examination of the often neglected institutions and structures through which political power has been exercised in Chile. These mechanisms could have had great importance in shaping the style of national policies. Allende's conception of the "peaceful transition to socialism" rested on the basic assumption that it was possible to transform a dependent, capitalist-based, liberal democracy into a socialist society through the use of the very institutions and structures which supported the old regime. Few will dispute the contention that such a notion played a key role as a major constraint on both governmental and opposition strategies and actions.

In order to highlight some of the major features of the Chilean presidency, one must analyze it within the context of the larger developments taking place at the societal level because the Chilean experience has clearly showed the intimate link existing between social, economic, and political institutions, structures, and processes (Edwards, 1959; Faletto et al., 1972). The first section includes a short, general discussion about both constitutionalism and the rule of law in the Chilean context. The clarification of some concepts may aid in correcting some misconceptions. These are deemed important for the understanding of the operation of Chilean constitutional mechanisms. The second section includes an overview of the general patterns of development characteristic of Chilean society. An effort will be made to illustrate the strong link between social and political developments, corresponding to changes at the institutional level. Special attention will be given to the functioning and transformation of political institutions in the specific context of changing political systems characterized either by conciliatory or confrontational styles of politics. As illustrated by the Chilean experience, the indiscriminant use of institutional and procedural mechanisms designed to cope with political conflict in a specific context is usually doomed to fail when applied to all contexts. The final section presents some brief and tentative conclusions regarding the Chilean presidency in an historical perspective.

The Constitutional Bases of the Political System

Few Latin American issues have been so misunderstood and misrepresented as those revolving around the notions of constitutionalism and rule of law. Traditionally, very little attention has been given to the particular patterns of historical development that have shaped the nature and characteristics of the notion of rule of law. In Chile, as was the case in other Latin American countries, initial efforts aimed at establishing a viable nation-state were doomed to failure.

The attempts to find formulas for the replacement of the colonial patrimonial state were unsuccessful in coping with a growing trend fostering centrifugal separatism, further stimulated by demands posed by competing strongly rooted groups making up the Latin American societies of the period. The natural reaction against the colonial past led many groups to accept the basic tenets of positivism and liberalism. As pointed out by Morse (1974: 60-61), positivism was looked upon as being the new inclusive doctrine and instrument of order needed to replace the scholastic roots. The effort, however, implied the attack on a sociocultural past within which Latin American traditions had been shaped.

The internal tensions were reflected in the processes of constitution-making. In the long run, however, it becomes evident that the basic tenets of pluralistic democracy did not have a cultural base for legitimacy in Latin America. Quite to the contrary, in actual practice even a modicum of stability and legitimacy at the national level was possible only when the dominant groups were able to establish institutional arrangements of a clearly monistic nature, as illustrated by the Chilean Constitution of 1833 (Encina, 1964). In a stricter sense, the corporate formula was only an indication of the return to the tradition whose roots were in the colonial past. It is within the context of the corporate tradition that one must grasp the nature and role played by the constitutions of Chile.

From this perspective, the constitution is often viewed as the basic theoretical outline of the common good and by extension the "juridical definition of the *summum bonum*" (Dealy, 1974: 82). The role of the state is defined in legal terms in order to assert the critical role it has been accorded by the community as being responsible for the general interest. Private interests are to be subordinated to those goals which are considered to be expressions of the ideals of the society. As a logical extension of this conception, the nature and role of both individual and group rights and of political representation are affected.

In the first place, the scope and strength of individual rights are seen as limited by the common good and, subsequently, by the will of those in positions of authority who are responsible for its care. Individual rights are to be defined and limited in order to prevent the possibility that they may impair the fulfillment of national goals—representing, by definition, the common good. In the same manner, the nature and activities of interest groups are affected in important ways; thus, it is unquestionable that interest group activity in the Chilean context has been characteristically corporate in nature (Sunkel, 1965). The traditional attempts to incorporate larger groups within the framework of a corporatist state have been characterized by a style which grants certain rights (analogous to the colonial *fueros*) to particular groups as they are coopted into a social order and value system based upon hierarchy and order. The role of the state as the arbiter of conflict between social classes and powerful interest groups has been noted in a number of studies of Chilean political development (Cusak, 1970; Menges, 1966; Zeitlin, 1966).

As far as representation is concerned, here too the corporate tradition evidences a particular conception and emphasis. The representative, once elected, is not supposed to represent either a concrete group and/or mandate. Rather, he is supposed to represent the common good as redefined in the notion of national interest. In the Chilean context, it has been argued that it was the responsibility of the major political parties to define this interest—a point critical to the operation of a system that became increasingly characterized by strong competitive parties with rigid ideological cleavages (López, 1968; Prothro and Chaparro, 1974). In fact, as will be explored later on, this is one major problem from which significant limitations to presidential powers were to be derived.

Chilean Political Development

In the early republican era, Chile suffered from political anarchy and predatory militarism. During this period, the major political tendencies (conservative and liberal) clashed around a wide variety of issues. Around 1830, however, the schism within the governing class culminated in the triumph of the conservatives over the liberals. The conservative victory inaugurated the "autocratic republic," firmly established under the de facto leadership of Portales. This gifted man saw the need to establish the bases of an efficient and stable state. In order to do so, he organized the Chilean state to reflect both the political will of the aristocracy as well as its basic conception about social order. Portales founded a tradition of "impersonal" civil administration and legitimized the aspirations of the aristocracy in the Constitution of 1833 (Encina, 1964; Lechner, 1970: 26-30).

Constitutional arrangements were to reflect the basic consensus prevalent in oligarchical groups for systemic stability. Political anarchy and administrative chaos were to be eliminated by resorting to highly authoritarian and hierarchical institutional arrangements. The executive naturally emerged as the most important governmental institution established by the constitution. Even though important residual powers were vested in congress (i.e., the power to approve or reject laws in certain areas, such as the annual budget and the size and location of the armed forces, and so on), in actual practice its relative power was small. Political conflict revolved primarily around the question of presidential power. Conflicts over these became so extreme that the opposition liberals went into open rebellion twice in the 1850s with bloody results. Conservative rule was weakened by these conflicts. This period also saw rapid social and economic transformations leading to a new, strong intellectual ferment (Campos, 1956: 251-266). The divergences among members of the Chilean oligarchy resulted in the development of the groups which later formalized themselves into political parties.

In the presidential election of 1871, the liberals captured the presidency. The era of the "liberal republic" (1871-1891) was a time of rapid constitutional change. The reforms, one by one, strengthened congress vis-à-vis the presidency. The attempts to curb presidential powers took place simultaneously with the active participation and consolidation of the political parties, the incorporation of the northern provinces through armed conquest in the War of the Pacific, the economic prosperity derived from the nitrate boom, the general expansion of the social and economic activities under the laissez-faire economic philosophy, and the beginning of the inflationary process in the currency problems faced by the Pinto administration (Campos, 1956: 305-372). During the liberal republic which the president continued to dominate, he nevertheless found it increasingly necessary to employ a system of shifting political alliances in order to maintain his dominance. Long before the election of Balmaceda in 1886, then, the tensions between congress and the executive reflected a profound conflict of leadership. New and powerful socioeconomic groups were espousing liberal ideas and were opposed to what was perceived as presidential tyranny. The "Portalian regime" was under serious criticism and beginning to decay (Encina, 1952). Events were to precipitate one of the most decisive institutional crises of of Chilean history. The attempts by Balmaceda to rebuild the foundations of the "Portalian State" (which included executive control of the electoral mechanism) and to foster strong, nationalistic economic policies oriented to the strengthening of industrial development of the country ran against the interests of both key national and international groups. Balmaceda was openly resisted in his attempts by a powerful set of actors: the traditional landed aristocracy, the powerful foreign-controlled companies interested in Chilean nitrate, and the emerging financial oligarchy. The issues were finally resolved with Balmaceda's defeat in the Civil War of 1891 (Ramírez, 1958). From 1891 until 1920, presidential authority almost disappeared; political parties multiplied rapidly, and the oligarchs in congress became the dominant power. The operation of the state, however, remained a central political question due to its independent base of economic power. The revenues from nitrates were to be distributed through the state's actions, leading to the emergence of a series of changes with long-lasting implications. Thus, for example, the expansion of both educational and bureaucratic activities were mainly responsible for the emergence of a state-dependent, service-oriented middle class. The growth and strength of this new middle class was yet another indication of what was to become characteristic of the Chilean experience of development: the weak link existent between political and economic development. Under the influence of the newly emerging groups, political development was taking place in the absence of traditional developments (prerequisites) in the economic infrastructure.

The so-called "parliamentary" regime (bue see Loewenstein, 1949: 455) placed congress at the center of political power. A crisis in political stability developed immediately. The degree of instability of this period is shown by the fact that while from 1831 to 1886, a 55 year period, the Chilean government had 31 cabinets, in the 33 year period of the parliamentary republic there were 121 different cabinets with a total of 530 ministers. The lack of coherence in congress encouraged the further multiplication of political parties and destroyed party discipline. The original four parties of the Liberal period expanded to seven shortly after the Civil War of 1891. Party coalitions for securing parliamentary majorities were "subject to such kaleidoscopic changes as to make lines of responsibility unclear if not inexistent" (Gil, 1966: 49). Financial waste, political corruption, and the use of the public bureaucracy for political patronage became the order of the day. With much justice has the parliamentary period been called the futile years. No major issues separated the political parties of the period, and the few doctrinal differences (with the exception of the impotent Worker's Socialist Party of Luis Emilio Recabarren) centered primarily around the Church-State question. Moreover, even in these matters, party discipline and doctrinaire zeal were rather weak, except in the cases of opposing conservatives and radicals. Failure to provide energetic leadership for solving increasing social and economic unrest accompanied the political awakening of the large working class. Allied with a middle class in ferment, the workers contributed heavily to the downfall of the system. Arturo Alessandri's presidential victory in 1920 marked the revolt of an electorate disenchanted with the "traditional oligarchy, administrative chaos, the scandals of parliamentary majorities created by briberies and frauds, and a government on the brink of bankruptcy" (Gil, 1966: 57). However, Alessandri's program, (i.e., abolition of the parliamentary system; presidential election by direct vote; state control of banks; social security programs and so forth), viewed as radical by many, created suspicion among those in control of congress. The deadlock between the executive and congress was not resolved until a series of events led to a military intervention in 1924. After a confusing period, Alessandri led the country to the adoption of the Constitution of 1925 that ended the parliamentary republic and restored the presidential regime (Frías, 1971: 419-430).

The Constitution of 1925 was designed to be the golden mean between the previous two extremes: the presumed stability of the authoritarian state of the 1830s and the instability of the parliamentary republic. Under the new constitution, the governmental system was to be based in principle on the classical concept of separation of powers. The seemingly predominant role played by the executive in most governmental processes led some observers to suggest that the resulting system resembled a legal autocracy or an "empirical Caesarism" (Bernaschina, 1957: 62). The notion somehow implied the idea that the "possibility of a deadlock between President and Congress was broken in the 1925 Constitution by giving the former the edge in political power" (Silvert, 1965: 91). As painfully demonstrated by the experiences of Frei and Allende, among others, this was often not the case in actual practice.

A partial explanation is to be found in the social and political impasses typical of most of the period under the 1925 constitution. In fact, the constitution itself provided the basis for a system whose major requirement was to secure broad societal consensus among competing socioeconomic and political groups. The counterbalanced set of powers invested in the executive and congress was, in the final analysis, to produce a rather paradoxical feature: the critical shift in the balance of governmental power was to take place in the congressional arena. The actual combination of political forces represented in congress was going to provide or deny the necessary and sufficient political support for policies aimed to introduce changes other than incremental ones. Almost as a question of constitutional definition, dramatic and rapid policy changes were made extremely difficult if not impossible.

The constitutional regime established in 1925 had some important features that reinforced the potential for conflict between the executive and congress. The separation of the dates of presidental and congressional elections, for example, required the president to win two elections before he could exercise power if he planned to introduce substantial reforms. He not only had to win office for himself, but his party (coalition) also had to win the separately held congressional elections that followed (sometimes by several years) his victory. If his party (coalition) lost, he had to deal with several parties in order to gain and/or retain a supporting bloc within congress. This necessity led the president into a pattern of shifting alliances with profound influence on programmatic (policy) orientation.

A second related constitutional feature of importance was the existence of a system of proportional representation (Parrish et al., 1970-1971). Its operation further reinforced the tendency towards party fragmentation and congressional instability. In the long run, all different administrations were to be affected by a pattern of unstable alliances leading eventually to a general watering-down of any cohesive program of government. Immobilism was in this way further reinforced with long-lasting consequences for the institutional stability of the system.

A third major constitutional feature was the power invested in congress to elect the president in those cases when all candidates fail to secure an absolute majority. In a practical sense, the president so elected was forced to accept some degree of dependency on parties in congress supporting his election. Such a dependency, in all cases, was a costly one—either affecting critical policy issues and/or the control of the public bureaucracy. In the election of Allende, for example, such support was secured in an atmosphere that threatened an open institutional collapse. In fact, the argument can be made that the congressional passage of the so-called "Constitutional Statute of Democratic Guarantees" (*Estatuto de garantías constitucionales),* exacted by the Christian Democrats as a prerequisite for electing Allende, was but another example of a well-established process that usually operated on a far less dramatic scale (Echeverría and Frei, 1974: Vol. I, 10-13 and 29-105).

The adoption of the new constitution was not to bring the long-awaited stability. After a series of conflicts with congress, Alessandri resigned and, in 1927, Colonel Ibañez emerged as the strong man of Chilean politics. His dictatorship eventually collapsed in 1931, inaugurating a period of social unrest and political instability. The following fifteen months witnessed a sharp economic depression, two general strikes, a naval revolt, and the failure of nine different governments, including an attempt to establish a short-lived "socialist republic" (Gil, 1966: 60-62).

The return to "normalcy" was marked by the reelection of Alessandri in 1932. Increasing tensions derived from unresolved socioeconomic problems were the basis for political polarization, again focused in conflict between congress and the executive. As Alessandri began to move toward "conservative" positions in an effort to secure political support from the traditional parties, he began to experience the fierce opposition of the forces of the left and the center—represented essentially by the Radical Party, the congressional party par excellence. Alessandri's failure to cope with the basic demands of the middle and lower groups of society led to the formation of a center-leftist coalition in the Popular Front, which challenged successfully the parties that had governed the country for more than a century. The Popular Front introduced some important changes in the Chilean political system by establishing a working relationship between the so-called "revolutionary parties" (Socialist and Communist) and the Radical Party, which represented the interests of both the bourgeois capitalists as well as the urban petit bourgeoisie and the large and small landholders of the frontier areas. The Popular Front combination, while espousing national policies of development, at the same time favored middle class groups over the lower class. Most of the reforms advanced by the coalition were primarily in the area of social welfare benefits, wage and salary guarantees, and price controls. The major beneficiaries of these programs in the end were middle class groups and not the working and lower class (Faletto et al., 1972: 108-116).

The need to cope with the long-lasting effects of the economic crisis of the 1930s further reinforced in the Chilean context the notion that the state was to be responsible for the larger questions of development. Industrialization and planned economic development were tied together. The experience, similar to those in Europe, was far from being a success. It introduced a set of significant long-run trends. The first one provided a rationale justifying the expansion of the state apparatus that, in fact, was marginally concerned with the production of goods, and/or services. The expanded bureaucracy was essentially used for three closely related purposes: political patronage as a prop for the regime in power, and as a channel for upward social mobility by the state-dependent middle sectors. The second important trend was related to constitutional questions, namely, the executive's role of bearing major responsibility for economic questions (planning and development). Since the early 1940s, all presidents stressed the need to limit severely congressional powers in the economic arena, while favoring a higher degree of centralization at the executive level. Even though in the long run progress was made along this line, it was not sufficient. Paradoxically, the developments taking place in the administrative sector were to prove self-defeating: the abuse in the establishment of independent or quasi-autonomous agencies in critical areas of economic responsibilities and activities was to deny executive control and leadership. In practice, the many attempts to establish a coordinated and comprehensive national planning mechanism were to prove futile. Critical sectoral and functional areas theoretically covered by such national plans were, in effect, under the direct control of decentralized agencies which, in most cases, were more responsive to their immediate clientele groups than to executive pressure. This constraint proved critical for those hoping to introduce radical, massive change into the system (i.e., Frie and Allende).

Politically, the Popular Front experience was designed to confirm political control in the hands of middle-class parties and to reinforce Chilean parliamentary democracy. It was also designed to sell the idea that political competition in a plural society might be carried out to mutual advantage through the electoral machinery—the essence of liberal democracy. It was hoped that the revolutionary parties would accept the idea that this was a proper and plausible road to the conquest of political power (Zeitlin, 1966: 234). The left's failure to widen its political base to include a growing organized working class and the decision to "ignore" the peasantry deprived it of the necessary destabilizing force and threatened the balance of the system. At the same time, this influenced the left to adopt a position of seeking compromise with competing social and political groups (Tapia-Videla and Quirós Varela, 1974: 15; Loveman, 1976).

The resulting social and political pluralism, in fact, recognized an implicit veto power in every politically articulate social group. Social deadlock and political immoblism were the natural products of the Chilean brand of pluralism. To a large extent, these phenomena are intimately linked to the lack of flexibility shown by the social structure. In practice, each social group, of some importance, including those on the political left, was characterized by the presence of subgroups deeply interested in the maintenance of the prevalent status quo in order to secure their relative positions of advantage vis-à-vis their peers. This was possible by their capacity to achieve a privileged position in the intricate game of pressure politics characteristic to the system (Parrish and Tapia-Videla, 1970: 455-476). The resulting social deadlock tended to accentuate the rigidities surrounding the lack of political will and capacity to overcome the deadlock from a political perspective. In this way, social deadlock led to political immobilism and to the reinforcement of the need for compromise. The dynamic equilibrium characteristic of Chilean sociopolitical development can be explained on the basis of those deadlocks—further reinforced by constraints stemming from an economic infrastructure subject to endemic periods of stagnation (Pinto, 1962; Zeitlin, 1966: 234-235).

The short-lived Popular Front coalition was followed by a series of coalition governments centered around the Radical Party. While emphasizing industrialization, they systematically ignored the agricultural question. With a small population in which income was unevenly distributed, markets were just too small to sustain the import-substitution industrialization approach taken during this period. By 1950 rapid urbanization coupled with sharply increasing overall population growth produced additional strain on the economy. The governmental revenue system was heavily dependent on the often rapid fluctuations of the world price of copper. Moreover, on the social plane and in spite of many changes, Chile was still sharply divided in class terms.

The increasingly difficult social and economic situations created the setting for a challenge to the traditional pluralistic political process. The dictator of the 1920s, Carlos Ibañez, won the presidency as an anti-politics candidate. He fought the campaign on the basis that politics as usual was the culprit in the national crisis Chile faced in 1952. Inflation was rampant and exacerbated by such radical measures as a guaranteed annual readjustment of the salaries of white collar government employees which was in advance of the rate of inflation. The political disintegration became such that in the 1953 congressional election there were fifty-three different political parties registered. The voters clearly were dismayed by the inability of the traditional political parties to solve national problems, and they turned to Ibañez hoping that he would somehow be able to cut the increasingly snarled Gordian knot that their politics had become. He quickly disappointed them. He did not overturn the traditional political institutions as many expected. Instead, he resorted to the same political style in dealing with congress that had been characteristic of the previous period. By the end of his administration his performance helped to push the voters to voting for the traditional political coalitions.

In 1956, however, a leftist coalition was formed which aimed at capturing the traditional political structures represented in the Ibañez victory. This group was made up of the Communist and Socialist parties and a group of smaller leftist parties and was called the Popular Action Front (FRAP), under the leadership of Dr. Salvador Allende. By 1958, the FRAP became a strong contender for the presidency. It precipitated profound changes in the ideological definition and understanding of Chilean society and alternative strategies to cope with the problem of power.

From 1958 to 1964, the conservative coalition of Jorge Alessandri was in control of the presidency. Alessandri won the election in a four-way race in which Salvador Allende ran a close second. Very few new policy orientations were introduced by Alessandri, but there was a strong emphasis on fiscal responsibility (in the early years) and an expansion of the economy in close cooperation with the United States Aid Program under the Alliance for Progress. While symbolically relying on government by experts, or technocrats, he designed policies that were typically timid and conservative. Little planning took place and those broader reforms which were proposed quickly foundered on congressional opposition by the left and the indifference of the parties in the government coalition.

In 1964, the political contest between Allende and Christian Democrat Eduardo Frei (and a third minor candidate) resulted in an overwhelming victory for the latter. The Frei administration must be viewed as a transition period between the old politics and the new. The purpose of the Frei government was to alter the traditional pattern of Chilean society through the introduction of a series of reforms. In the political arena, the central aim was to introduce new structures which would allow for mass participation in politics.

In order to accomplish this, it was thought necessary to launch a massive effort at social mobilization; this was known as the "popular promotion" program. Another aspect of the social mobilization effort was expansion of the number of schools and teachers as well as extensive curriculum innovations.

In the economic area, the Christian Democratic program aimed at achieving economic development through considerable structural reform. This involved a basic change in the agricultural sector, a coparticipation with the foreign owners of the copper mining industry, as well as the introduction of a more complete form of national planning.

The record of the Frei government is mixed in terms of its accomplishment of its aims. Its most clear success lies in the area of education. Not only were there extensive curriculum reforms achieved, but the expansion in the number of student places on all levels of the educational system was considerable. It should also be noted that this is the area of reform proposals in which there was the least controversy. Almost everyone was in favor of educational expansion.

In other areas, Frei experienced either long delays in getting his proposals adopted or complete frustration. While he got the coparticipation scheme for the copper industry accepted fairly soon, he had to wait almost three years to get his agrarian reform proposal adopted by congress. In the case of the popular promotion program, he had to abandon it altogether. Mounting economic problems severely affected attempts to control newly mobilized social groups under the aegis of the Christian Democratic Party. Once more, economic stagnation set limits on populist-oriented policies (Tapia-Videla and Quirós-Varela, 1974: 19-30).

In this we can see the transitional nature of the political system which manifested itself in the Frei government. In certain terms, the failures of the Christian Democrats were symptomatic of the failures of the system itself. If one posits two tendencies as basic in Chilean politics since 1952, this point becomes clearer. On the one hand, there is the pluralistic tendency—the base of the conciliatory system that prevents the rapid mobilization of political resources to initiate structural reform; on the other hand is a tendency which might be labeled confrontational. Since 1952, this was a part of Chile on a national level. It has been given impetus by the political reforms which have encouraged the incorporation of the previously excluded masses more and more into the voting process. The electorate has expanded from about 1,300,000 in 1958 to 3,200,000 in 1970. The process of social mobilization has been further exacerbated by the strong ideological overtones accompanying it and in turn has generated the basis of confrontational politics—skillfully manipulated by all the political parties competing in the electoral arena. In a parallel fashion, the attempts to articulate political actions through organizational mechanisms (i.e., party-controlled organizations such as labor unions, federations of professional associations, and the like) became a major and distinctive characteristic of the period. The efforts to control these organizations by the political parties reached extremes—ranging from open violence to ideological penetration.

Given these changes, the populist tendencies in the political parties became more and more pronounced in the same period. At the same time that grandiose promises were being made to a previously nonparticipant electorate, the capacities of the government to solve the mounting problems of the system continued to be limited. The result was that the crises of stagnation and stalemate increasingly affected the traditional political institutions, which themselves developed out of pluralistic origin. The congress is without question the one political institution most characteristic of this pluralistic tradition.

It has been suggested throughout recent history that the Chilean Congress was progressively weakened vis-à-vis the executive. It is argued that since the 1940s the executive had expanded power through formal constitutional reforms and day-to-day practice. The basic idea, even though correct in the formal sense, tended to ignore the critical fact that congress, even after the hotly debated constitutional reforms of 1970 were approved, retained sufficient powers to make effective government nearly impossible for any president attempting to ignore its will. In fact, many of the major accomplishments and shortcomings of the Christian-Democratic era were related to its decision to break with the tradition established with the adoption of the 1925 Constitution—that no political party was to be able to govern in the single-party tradition. Although party leaders were extremely skillful in playing the incremental strategy in congress, their lack of a sufficiently structured set of alliances prevented the advancement of major goals. As the Frei administration was coming under increasing pressures for coping with competing demands for social and economic transformations, the political opposition in congress was becoming harder to overcome. By 1967, however, the emergence of strong factionalism within the Christian Democratic Party signaled the end of the minimum internal consensus necessary to confront opposition in congress.

The congressional role was primarily to act as a veto on presidential initiatives. Through the continuous expansion of the electoral arena, congress became progressively more and more representative of a wide variety of interests and orientations present in Chilean society. The numerous congressional mechanisms available to exercise control over executive activities were used to the fullest and, in some cases, were beyond the spirit of the law—

i.e., the use of the *juicio político* (political trial or impeachment) to force ministerial resignations, even though the ministers were politically responsible to the president.

In the context of this article, however, the most critical congressional feature was the standing committee system, for it is at this level that most of the public policy-making process took place. In actual practice, most of the work done in congress was done in the committees. It was here that bills were accepted, rejected, rewritten and amended. Due to their critical importance, parties were quite zealous in guarding their representation on committees. Usually, party representation was proportional to congressional strength. The work atmosphere in the different committees, however, was generally nonpartisan in character. The need to secure some sort of consensus in the legislative discussion resulted in a sense of comradeship. This feeling was further reinforced by the usual low rate of congressional turnover from one congressional election to the next, and by the existence of alternative mechanisms of conflict resolution—i.e., the definition of the nature of the policy at hand to determine the degree to which the committee member had to bind his decisions by following political, party or technical considerations.[1]

In a way that very closely resembles the workings of different policy systems existent in other pluralist contexts, the standing committees become the natural point for bargaining activities. The relevant social, economic and political actors were able (or at least had the chance) to influence policy-making at that stage. The pluralist nature permeating the system is further illustrated by the fact that in the legislative process, no single actor was able to monopolize the shaping of a given bill. The relative position of power (influence) of each actor depended on both the type of policy under discussion and the specific stage of the policy-making process. The notion that the executive, and by extension the bureaucracy, was so powerful as to be able to minimize the impact of congressional actions is further dispelled. In a historical perspective, it is almost ironic that the Christian Democratic attempts to secure comprehensive development were to exacerbate further social tensions and political cleavages that set down the basis for the emergence of a confrontational style of politics.

In the area of constitutional norms regulating the exercise of political power, however, the Christian Democrats were going to be able to secure what others before had failed to achieve: a set of constitutional reforms in critical areas of the public policy-making process. For example, they were able to strengthen further the executive powers vis-à-vis congress. The executive was granted sole responsibility for initiating economic and financial legislation affecting important areas of public policy such as controls on wages and salaries for both the public and private sectors. Moreover, placing emphasis on the technical nature of some major societal problems, the Christian Democrats were able to secure the delegation of legislative powers from congress to the executive in wide areas of administrative, economic, and social issues. Thus, within the limits of congressional authorization, the executive was empowered to legislate by decree in traditionally sensitive questions—taxation policies, control on levels of public expenditure, conditions and terms of employment in the public sector, reorganization policies affecting both the organization and operation of national and local administrations, and the workings of the complex social security system (Constitution, Art. 43, and Frei et al., 1970: 89-107).

A third major change introduced by the new constitutional reforms was the elimination of the so-called "omnibus legislation." Traditionally, efforts by the executive to secure the passage of critical legislation (i.e., the periodic salary readjustment bills) were "exploited" by individual congressmen to the fullest. Realizing that the president would hardly exercise his veto powers lest he endanger his own legislative proposals, congressmen exercised their powers to introduce "observations" (amendments) to presidential initiatives. In most cases, "observations" were not related to the central issues dealt with in the original proposal. Attempts to secure legislation in favor of particular individuals or pressure groups led to a chaotic system of law that eventually led to major politico-administrative problems. Its elimination meant the loss of an important patronage mechanism for congress. In future dealings, congressmen were to emphasize their role as "administrative brokers"—critical for securing favorable (selective) rule application and adjudication from a wide variety of public agencies responsible for major socio-economic policies.

Another institutional breakthrough established by the new reforms was the creation of a Constitutional Tribunal. The new tribunal was considered essential to the running of a system based on the close collaboration of executive and congress. As we have seen so far, such working arrangements usually proved to be conflictive in nature. The lack of a final arbiter further increased tensions and problems. Institutional deadlock was resolved by the actions of the Constitutional Tribunal. As in other areas, the reforms were approved at a time when the systemic crisis was going to render them useless almost as a question of definition.

Finally, it must be noted that the traditional left in Chile had at the time a long-lasting tradition of support for parliamentary traditions and prerogatives. Since the notion of capturing the executive branch through the electoral mechanism was considered to be beyond the realm of possibility,[2] the left had accepted the idea that its primary loyalty was to the maintenance of congressional powers. From there, and while using legislative mechanisms to the fullest, the left was able to influence public policy-making in a somewhat effective way.

It should not be a surprise then to see that in the process of discussing these constitutional reforms we find the left to be the most consistent source of criticism and opposition. The very notion of curtailing some of the traditional parliamentary powers and traditions was sufficient to generate strong rejections from both socialists and communists (Frei et al., 1970: 138-146). It goes without saying that their position was radically changed the minute Allende won the election. In the long run, the same situattion was going to affect the Christian Democrats when they began to advance the idea of transforming, in practice, the presidential regime into a parliamentary one. In keeping with long-established political traditions, the former governing party was trying to maximize its political power from a new base: congress. The impending confrontation between democracy and totalitarism forecasted by the Christian Democrats added a sense of urgency to their efforts.

The basic constraints that were characteristic of the executive-legislative relations system were further strained with the election of Allende in 1970. Within the limits of this article it is not possible to deal with the Allende experience in an exhaustive way. An attempt will be made, however, to indicate some of the major transformations of the system and its implications for the relations between the major political institutions at the national level.

In contrast with the Popular Front experience, the Unidad Popular was a political coalition revolving around two major mass-based political parties deeply committed to transforming the prevailing system in a radical fashion. The revolutionary changes, however, were to be instituted in accord with constitutional and legal precepts. Some of the major issues emerging from such a commitment were to arise very soon in the process of securing these transformations. After all, the Unidad Popular was controlling only the executive branch, while congress and a vast variety of key politico-administrative, as well as social,institutions were still under the control of opposition parties (Valenzuela, 1972: 65-82).

Initially, the experience of Allende was in no way different from that of former presidents. His election by congress was politically costly, and as suggested before, the approval of the so-called Statute of Guarantees as a pre-requisite for political support can be considered the first indication that the relationship between executive and legislative was going to be permeated by basic distrust. To a large extent, however, both the statute and what it implied were a logical product of the transformations affecting the political system. Political and social polarization were increasingly leading the country to a confrontational style where the major features were political mobilization and ideological confrontation.

Certain features of the Allende government were shaped by the heavy weight of political tradition. In a fashion similar to the experience of other coalition governments in the past, when confronted with the question of how to arrange distribution of governmental responsibilities, the Unidad Popular ended up in system that reinforced traditional practices. The political quota system employed by the Unidad Popular for allocating offices and making policy not only destroyed any attempts to coordinate control of the huge national bureaucracy, but also made planning activities futile.[3] After an initial period in which the government was quite successful in securing both the reactivation of the economy and the expansion of its base of political support, it became clear that the populistic actions of the government were destined to be self-defeating. The lack of strategic clarity within the coalition further enhanced the tendency of various groups within it to engage in political actions aimed at immediate results. Violence and instability began to emerge as the framework within which executive-legislative relationships had to operate.

In order to avoid early legislative confrontations with the opposition in the congressional arena, the government sought legal justification for implementing reforms within the already existing powers of the executive branch, quite often employing rarely used legislation which had been passed during the days of the "socialist republic" in the early 1930s. While the nationalization of basic natural resources (e.g., copper) was sought through congressional action and its approval gained, the nationalization of the banking system was effected through the government's purchase of all privately held shares of bank stock. Allende made the decision to buy these shares in order to avoid a defeat at the hands of the opposition majority in congress. A similar situation developed regarding the definition of different areas of the economy ("social" or "state-owned," "mixed" and "private"). The opposition once again had expected to have a powerful role in blocking Allende's plans in relation to this matter. Again, Allende chose to avoid congress. He instead sought justification for his definition of these areas through executive interpretations of existing laws.

The problem of the definition of the areas of the economy, however, was to become the central issue of never-resolved political and constitutional problems. The opposition, reacting against the government's decision to bypass congress, approved a project of constitutional reform regulating the different areas. The project, in essence, ran against the basic conception advanced by the executive. Allende vetoed the project. The impasse emerged as the executive and congress pressed contrasting interpretations of constitutional norms regulating the process of "constitutional reform."

Constitutional norms regulating such a process were indeed ambiguous. Constitutional reforms follow the same congressional procedures as those applicable in adopting ordinary laws, with a few noted exceptions. Thus, for the adoption of an amendment by congress, it is demanded that an absolute majority be obtained on three separate occasions: once in each house and later in a joint session. The president cannot reject a constitutional reform properly approved in its totality. He can veto it in order to introduce modifications or corrections. In the event congress accepts the president's observations (by a majority vote), the reform is ready for promulgation. In the Allende conflict the critical problem, however, derived from the constitutional failure to indicate, unequivocally, the congressional vote required to override presidential vetoes. The government's position was that since a constitutional amendment must follow the regular procedures of a simple law (with the exceptions noted above), it was clear that a two-thirds vote to override was required from congress. The opposition's argument supported a contrary view: namely, that the constitution required only a majority vote of congress in order to override presidential vetoes. After all, the point was made, the executive was vested explicitly by the constitution with the exclusive power to call for a plebiscite on those occasions when disagreement with congress proves to be unsatisfactory. Congress, it was argued, could not possibly be asked to confront the executive under such handicaps—a two-thirds majority vote and eventually a victory in a plebiscite (Constitución, Arts. 108-109; Echeverria and Frei, 1974: Vol. 3, 55-63; Silva, 1970: 262: Garces, 1974: 284-286).

Beyond judicial questions of constitutional interpretation, both government and opposition were quite aware of the important implications to be derived from each basic position. Acceptance of the congressional thesis, for example, would have created a powerful mechanism favoring opposition plans to bloc governmental plans. Moreover, the government was fearful that the opposition could easily use this mechanism in order to transform the very nature of the balance of congressional and presidential powers. In fact, it was conceivable that an opposition-controlled congress could initiate a series of "constitutional reforms" which would neutralize presidential powers—establishing eventually a de jure parliamentary system. It must be kept in mind that few believed that a government besieged by mounting economic problems in the context of political polarization was in a position to hope for success in any plebiscite in a constitutional dispute with congress.

Constitutional ambiguities and potential implications transformed a legal problem into a major political issue. By the time the Constitutional Tribunal studied the problem, the crisis had entered the point of no return. The opposition defined the problem in terms of the survival of a democratic, pluralistic system, while the government stressed the need to accentuate the revolutionary character of the process by reasserting executive powers. The Constitutional Tribunal, claiming lack of appropriate jurisdiction, failed to resolve the issue: the deadlock was to prove beyond possible political solution!

Even a superficial examination of the record of the relations between the executive and congress during this period will show that each side used and abused every possible mechanism available for gaining tactical advantages: vetoes, constitutional accusations against ministers and related politico-administrative officials, mass mobilization efforts and displays, and so on. As the systemic crisis became extreme, the delicate balance between government and opposition was mediated by the Armed Forces.

The formal resolution of the national strike movement of October 1972 opened the door for the last electoral contest to be held in Chile. Attempts to use elections as a conflict-resolution mechanism was a longstanding tradition in Chilean politics. March 1973, however, is unique in that it was the first time that an electoral contest was legitimized by the active presence of the Armed Forces at the cabinet level. Furthermore, the importance (practical or symbolic) ascribed to the election by the different actors was to reflect the generalized sense of impending systemic crisis. For some sectors, the goal was to seek an overwhelming majority at the electoral polls to make possible the constitutional impeachment of Allende—the thesis of the so-called "white coup d'état." Failure to achieve such a goal would leave room for the last resort: military intervention. For other political actors, the elections were to be useful indicators for future orientations of the government's actions. A defeat at the polls should have been sufficient to impose profound limitations on both the manner and substance of government policy-making. For some official sectors, the elections were considered critical, for at a minimum the opposition had to be prevented from obtaining a two-thirds majority in congress. For most actors, however, it had already become clear that the crisis affecting the system was too profound to be resolved in a simple electoral contest. In actuality, the election was inconclusive in its results, serving only to provide some degree of legitimacy to major competing positions on critical issues and hence further reinforcing a pre-existing political deadlock.

The election, a traditional mechanism for the conciliation of political differences and conflict, proved to be an insufficient means for coping with the problems faced. Within the context, it made little difference who was acting in accordance with the constitution or the law, and the crisis deepened.

The experience of the Unidad Popular has become a cause célèbre from which different groups and individuals have extracted different conclusions and lessons. There is little final consensus as to the determinant causes of the rise and fall of Chilean democracy. In the context of this discussion, however, there are two major, interrelated factors worth emphasizing. The first stresses the structural foundations of the Chilean political system. As pointed out earlier, the particular pattern of political development characteristic of Chile (that made the experience of the Unidad Popular possible to begin with) had placed a high degree of legitimacy on institutions and processes, reinforcing both pluralism and incrementalism in the context of a conciliatory political system. Eventually, such a combination led to social immobilism and political deadlock, placing severe limitations on the nature and scope of reforms. The Unidad Popular in attempting to carry out a process leading to radical transformations was, in fact, ignoring and/or breaking the traditional "rules of the game." The precarious stability of the system collapsed as it proved impossible to negotiate between the competing models of development (neo-capitalist versus socialist) espousing schemes for power (social, political and economic) distribution clearly antagonistic in nature.

The second relevant factor concerns the social bases of the political coalitions supporting the competing models. Even though it is true that both coalitions (government and opposition) could have claimed a multiple class composition, in fact there were some important differences. The opposition bloc was able to muster a wide coalition of support across social classes (or groups) whose objective interests were intimately linked with the maintenance of the status quo. The opposition alliance of the traditional sectors, the modern industrial bourgeoise and foreign capital (especially American) was expanded by the increasing support of groups with a significant electoral impact—i.e., the petit bourgeoisie, the urban poor and the peasantry. The failure of the government to mobilize and institutionalize an expanded base of political support was to prove costly, especially since the attempts to transform the nature and orientations of the state threatened traditional interests. From this perspective, growing numbers of the middle-sectors became increasingly alienated from the reforms proposed, which were seen as threats to their status and sources of livelihood. For those whose way of life was intimately linked with their role as political mediators in the conciliatory tradition, accepting these reforms came to be seen as tantamount to suicide!

Conclusion

The foregoing is an attempt to describe the transformations affecting the Chilean presidency in a developmental perspective. In understanding the presidency and the relations between congress and the executive, we see clearly that the question of the role and the organization of the state has been a key issue.

The resolution of the conflict about the state has oscillated between authoritarian and pluralistic extremes. In all cases, however, a paramount feature has been the definition of the powers invested in the executive and congress.

Chilean history shows a remarkable capacity for state structures to adapt to basic socioeconomic changes and, in turn, to shape these changes. As has been described above, the relevant groups of the Chilean aristocracy, when confronted with anarchy and chaos in the early years of the Republic, were more than willing to reach a consensus about the need to set the foundations of a centralized authority at the national level. Presidential authority, in keeping with the colonial tradition, was powerful and inclusive. The groups composing the *Fronda*, to use the felicitous expression of Edwards (1959), were more than suspicious about the emergence and actions of a potentially autonomous state. Once the early crisis of integration was overcome, there developed almost as a natural phenomenon an increasingly strong antipresidential movement. Presidential powers were gradually reduced, transforming the system considerably. The emergence of the "Parliamentary Republic" should be understood as a consequence of the struggle over the allocation of state resources. The nitrate industry had produced greatly increased revenues during the 1880s, and unfettered presidential control of these resources was resented by a number of the most articulate groups. Their opposition centered in the congress.

The crisis affecting the nitrate industry in the 1920s, however, precipitated, ironically enough, a reverse trend. The appearance of a strong, radicalized labor movement, the rising appeal of Marxian ideas and the political influence already achieved by sectors of the middle class combined to precipitate a revision of the system. The new formula was embodied in the Constitution of 1925.

That constitution was designed in such a way that, while providing for the pluralist representation of various, competing groups, it prevented two things: power monopoly and rapid changes at the societal level. The delicate balance between the executive and congress was thought of as being effective *only* in the pluralist context. The imbalance that existed between economic development and political institutions caused recurring problems. In the context of progressive sociopolitical mobilization, the temptation of populism was difficult to resist. The consequences were social deadlock, political immobilism and a stagnant economy—under severe stress to support an otherwise sophisticated institutional arrangement.

In order to cope with the most visible shortcomings of the system, attempts were made periodically to alter the system in minor ways so as to foster a more balanced process of development. Frei's government, for example, emerged as the last attempt at neocapitalist development on a pluralistic basis. Frei's constitutional reforms were intended to provide a workable political institutional basis for such development. By the time the reforms were adopted, however, they proved ineffectual. Conciliation, the essence of the 1925 arrangement, had become a very scarce political resource. Confrontational politics became the prevalent style, and with the election of Allende, the very substance of the system itself. Such a major qualitative transformation further eroded the already weakened constitutional foundations of the system. In this context, the collapse of the institutional edifice of Chilean democracy seems to have been unavoidable. Debate around this central issue, however, cannot be considered closed, for the systemic breakdown has raised a series of questions whose answers are critical to our understanding of Chilean society.

NOTES

1. In general, committee members' discretion was high when policy issues were defined as primarily distributive, regulatory, or technical in nature. Discretion was low when policy issues were defined as being redistributive in character. Conversely, party leadership was usually high in redistributive policy issues; moderate in those defined as distributive and regulatory; and somewhat low in dealing with technical policy issues (Tapia-Videla and Quirós-Varela, 1974b).

2. This skepticism became widespread after the electoral defeat of 1964. In fact, communists and socialists followed opposing strategies. The Communist Party tried to secure a wide base of political support for a popular program. The progressive elements of the national bourgeoisie were central to this strategy—pluralist in content and orientation. The Socialist Party, on the contrary, rejected any strategy based on the idea of class collaboration. Moreover, and by 1967, the Socialist Party clearly maintained that "the revolutionary violence . . . is the only way to secure political and economic power" (Jobet, 1971: Vol. 1, 130). Differences in approaches to the central question of revolutionary strategy had a tremendous impact on both the establishment and operations of the Unidad Popular. In practice, these differences set the foundations for internal deadlock, preventing the leftist coalition from adopting a commonly agreed-upon program and strategy.

3. In keeping with a long-standing tradition in Chilean politics, the Unidad Popular decided to allocate governmental and administrative responsibilities in a way that would ensure an equitable distribution among the various parties and groups within the coalition. The mechanism, initially aimed at preventing political conflict, was in the long run self-defeating. The quota system reinforced tendencies for politico-administrative imperialism in each one of the coalition members. Since relative power within the coalition was determined by electoral strength, the natural response was to use patronage to the extreme. Political sectarianism—the quintessence of the quota system—profoundly affected both internal relations and those with the opposition. On the one hand, its operation gave credence to those who charged the existence of a totalitarian scheme in the government aimed at gaining absolute control of critical societal institutions and structures—denying the very essence of pluralism. On the other hand, internal divisions exacerbated by this sectarianism made impossible the establishment of a centralized mechanism for political direction of the so-called revolutionary process.

REFERENCES

BERNASCHINA, M. (1957) Elementos de Derecho Constitucional Chileno. Santiago: Editorial Jurídica de Chile.

CAMPOS, F. (1956) Historia Constitucional de Chile. Santiago: Editorial Jurídica de Chile.

CUSACK, D. F. (1970) "The politics of Chilean private enterprise under Christian democracy." Ph.D. dissertation, University of Denver.

DEALY, G. (1974) "The tradition of monistic democracy in Latin America," pp. 71-103 in H. J. Wiarda (ed.) Politics and Social Change in Latin America. Amherst: Univ. of Massachusetts Press.

ECHEVERRIA, A. and L. FREI [eds.] (1974) 1970-1973: La Lucha por la Juridicidad en Chile (3 Vols.). Santiago: Editorial del Pacífico S.A.

EDWARDS, A. (1959) La Fronda Aristocrática. Santiago: Editorial del Pacífico.

ENCINA, F. (1964) Portales (2 Vols.). Santiago: Editorial Nascimento S.A.

——— (1952) Balmaceda (2 Vols.). Santiago: Editorial Nascimento S.A.

FALETTO, E., E. RUIZ, and H. ZEMELMAN (1972) Genesis Historica del Proceso Politico Chileno. Santiago: Empresa Editora Nacional Quimantú.

FREI, E., G. LAGOS, and S. MOLINA (1970) La Reforma Constitucional de 1970. Santiago: Editorial Jurídica de Chile.

FRIAS, E. (1971) Manual de Historia de Chile. Santiago: Editorial Nascimento S.A.

GARCES, J. E. (1974) El Estado y los Problemas Tácticos en el Gobierno de Allende. Madrid: Siglo XXI de España Editores S.A.

GIL, E. G. (1966) The Political System of Chile. Boston: Houghton-Mifflin.

JOBET, J. C. (1955) Ensayo Crítico del Desarrollo Económico-Social de Chile. Santiago: Editorial Universitaria S.A.

LECHNER, N. (1970) La Democracia en Chile. Buenos Aires: Ediciones Signos S.R.L.

LOEWENSTEIN, K. (1949) "The presidency outside the United States: a study in comparative political institutions." J. of Politics (August): 447-496.

LOPEZ, R. (1968) El Sistema de Partidos en Chile: Un Caso de Pluralismo Extremo. Santiago: Insora.

LOVEMAN, B. (1976) Struggle in the Countryside: Politics and Rural Labor in Chile, 1919-1973. Bloomington: Indiana Univ. Press.

MENGES, C. (1966) "Public policy and organized business in Chile: a preliminary analysis." J. of International Affairs 20: 343-365.

MORSE, R. M. (1974) "The heritage of Latin America," pp. 25-69 in H. J. Wiarda (ed.) Politics and Social Change in Latin America. Amherst: Univ. of Massachusetts Press.

PARRISH, C. J. and I. TAPIA-VIDELA (1970) "Welfare policy and administration in Chile." J. of Compar. Administration 1 (February): 455-476.

——— A. VON LAZAR and J. I. TAPIA-VIDELA (1970-1971) "Electoral procedures and political parties in Chile." Studies in Compar. International Development 6 (Series 074): 255-267.

PINTO, A. (1962) Chile: Un Caso de Desarrollo Frustrado. Santiago: Editorial Universitaria S.A.

PROTHRO, J. and P. CHAPARRO (1974) "Public opinion and the movement of Chilean government to the Left, 1952-1972." J. of Politics 36: 2-43.

RAMIREZ, H. (1958) Balmaceda y la Contrarevolución de 1891. Santiago: Editorial Universitaria S.A.

SILVA, A (1970) "El Tribunal constitucional," pp. 199-247 in E. Frei et al. (eds.) La Reforma Constitucional de 1970. Santiago: Editorial Jurídica de Chile.

SILVERT, K. (1965) Chile: Today and Yesterday. New York: Holt, Rinehart & Winston.

SUNKEL, O. (1965) "Change and frustration in Chile," pp. 116-144 in C. Veliz (ed.) Obstacles to Change in Latin America. London: Oxford Univ. Press.

TAPIA-VIDELA, J. I. and L. QUIROS-VARELA (1974a) Cambio Político y la Eleccíon Parlamentaria de Marzo de 1973: Antecedentes de una Eleccíon Crítica-Límite. Serie Documentos de Trabajo, Instituto de Ciencia Política U.C. Santiago: Universidad Católica de Chile.

——— (1974b) El Subsistema Político de la Seguridad Social en Chile. Serie de Documentos de Trabajo, Instituto de Ciencia Política U.C. Santiago: Universidad Católica de Chile.

VALENZUELA, A. (1972) "Political constraints and the prospects for socialism in Chile," pp. 65-82 in D. A. Chalmers (ed.) Changing Latin America: New Interpretations of its Politics and Society. Proceedings of the Academy of Political Science, Columbia University.

ZEITLIN, M. (1966) "Los determinantes sociales de la democracia política en Chile." Revista Latinoamericana de Sociología 2: 223-235.

Jorge Tapia-Videla is Associate Professor of Political Science at Wayne State University. He has published a number of works in English and Spanish on Chilean politics and comparative administration and is presently conducting research on corporatism and technocracy in Latin America.

JOHN D. MARTZ
Department of Political Science
University of North Carolina, Chapel Hill
Chapel Hill, NC 27514

POLICY-MAKING AND THE QUEST FOR CONSENSUS

Nationalizing Venezuelan Petroleum

On 1 January 1976, President Carlos Andrés Pérez formally proclaimed the nationalization of Venezuela's massive petroleum industry. Standing upon the site of Zumaque Number 1, in 1914 the first commercially drilled well in the nation, he thus observed a historic benchmark in the evolution of the relationship between the foreign corporations and the Venezuelan state (Pérez, 1976a).[1] After six decades' concessional exploration and exploitation, an era had ended. From the outset it was apparent that the 1976 nationalization was moderate and nonradical. As will be seen, both compensation and association agreements with international oil interests were central elements in the action. The latter in particular had been the focus during months of acrimonious national debate, as symbolized by article 5 and the Ley de Nacionalización de la Industria Petrolera. Moreover, it was largely upon discussion of its implications that a determined effort to achieve nonpartisan agreement ultimately foundered and sank.

As the most vigorous and intensely competitive of Latin America's remaining democracies, Venezuela provides a vivid case study in policy-making and consensus-building. The transcendent importance of oil nationalization, therefore,

Journal of Interamerican Studies and World Affairs, Vol. 19 No. 4, November 1977

recommends its study as a means of probing the dynamics of Venezuelan decision-making. Our analysis will be structured about three dimensions: national values, policy objectives, and policy instruments. A unifying thread running throughout the entire fabric will be decisional structures and actors.

Three of the values which characterize the Venezuelan polity are especially germane to the nationalization case. By definition, they are accepted by elites and public alike. On a different plane, a set of policy goals and objectives provide substance to the broader configuration of values. Here too, a clear national consensus exists. With policy instrumentation, however—concrete means of realizing objectives—significant differences of opinion were manifested. Moreover, the interplay of structures and actors mitigated against a determined government effort to win nonpartisan national approval for its own definition of appropriate instruments. While the fundamental question of attaining full sovereignty over Venezuela's major natural resource was never at issue, the means of framing and implementing nationalization constitutes an imposing obstacle to unqualified acceptance and support.

Prelude to Nationalization: Values and Objectives

If value is understood as "an enduring belief that a specific mode of conduct or end-state of existence is personally or socially preferable to an opposite or converse mode of conduct or end-state of existence" (Rokeach, 1973: 5), a cluster of Venezuelan national values are relevant to nationalization. Two are directly applicable to nonrenewable natural resources: self-determination and a reduction of economic dependence; and maximization of income and the efficacy of resource utilization. The third pertains to accepted rules of the political game—unqualified commitment to a pluralistic system. Together they provide the basic framework within which nationalization took place.

National Values	Goals and Objectives	Instruments
(1) independence, self-determination, reduction of economic dependence	(a) increased governmental control over utilization of nonrenewable resources	(a) immediate reversion
	(b) minimization of economic surplus extracted from domestic system by foreign actors	(b) agreements of association
	(c) prevention of foreign ownership of all basic means of production	(c) new administrative structures
		(d) indemnification to concessionaires
		(e) protection of employee's rights
(2) maximization of income and efficacy of resource utilization	(a) maximization of prices of resources	
	(b) maximization of capital investment in domestic sector	
	(c) development of administrative infrastructure	
(3) pluralistic politics	(a) legitimization of democratic politics	
	(b) consultation and dialogue	

Figure 1: Dimensions of Venezuelan Policy-Making

Self-determination and a reduction of economic dependence contributed to an elaboration of policy goals and objectives (presented schematically in Figure 1) by 1975. First among these was a commitment to increased government control over the utilization of natural resources. As former president Rafael Caldera stated during congressional debate, the "historic movement leading to the establishment of total sovereignty through the handling of this natural resource has matured so that, without delays or vacillation, the step of reserving this economic activity to the hands of the Venezuelan State can now be taken" (Caldera, 1976: 18). A related objective was the prevention of non-Venezuelan ownership of basic means of production. In the words of petroleum authority Juan Pablo Pérez Alfonzo, nationalization would assure a more just and adequate participation by Venezuela, "at the same time doing greater justice to the foreign consumer. Greater participation, without affecting the consumer, will permit a further reduction of production, guaranteeing for a longer period of time these extraordinary resources which we are presently squandering" (SIC, 1976: 144).

Nationalization was also consistent with income maximization and efficacious resource utilization. In turn, another set of policy objectives had taken shape. These centered on the concomitant maximization of prices and of capital investment in the domestic sector, and the development of a responsive administrative infrastructure. Caldera alluded to these in noting that petroleum prices had been increased nine times during the final year of his presidency (1973). This assured Venezuela not excessive income, but only what was necessary "to move from underdevelopment to development, to resolve our fundamental problems and realize the basic plans for national transformation" (Caldera, 1976: 32). President Pérez well summarized these desiderata in his August 1975 speech to the nation.

> The petroleum is ours, and in our hands we hold the opportunity of demonstrating that we are capable of managing it, that we can trust ourselves to make it a tool for democratic development and social justice. . . . It also must be a symbol of Venezuelan independence, of national will, and an affirmation of our creative capacity as a people and a nation. Venezuelan petroleum is a meeting with our destiny [Resumen, 1975: 30].

Of equal importance was the acceptance of pluralistic politics as fundamental to national life. Much has been written of the post-1958 era (Martz and Myers, 1977; Blank, 1973; Levine, 1973); a team of Venezuelan scholars recently recapitulated an overview of the political system by citing the "ability and flexibility of the political elite in establishing, by means of a party system, cohesive bonds of political integration" (Njaim et al., 1975: 84). In a more lengthy and sophisticated study, Levine similarly regarded mass parties as the crucial vehicle for managing political change in Venezuela, "combining effective popular mobilization with a new, widely shared sense of political authority and identity for the society" (Levine, 1973: 255). Stressing elite efforts at accommodation in the interests of insitutional continuity, he presented persuasive evidence of policy goals related to pluralistic values: legitimization of the democratic system, and a continuous process of consultation and dialogue.

Venezuela moved toward nationalization, then, within the context of clearly defined national values articulated through a series of policy objectives. As events were to prove, the consensus on the latter was more evident than agreement over instruments designed to realize them. This resulted in considerable part from the complexity of the industry (Tugwell, 1975). Venezuela by the beginning of this decade was producing in excess of 3 million barrels per day (bpd); oil accounted for two-thirds of annual treasury income, and virtually all foreign currency.[2] Roughly half of its exports, some 1.1 million bpd, were being shipped to the United States in 1976. The four-fold price increase from 1973 to 1974 led to a financial bonanza requiring an array of innovative policies to protect a population of 12 million from a tidal wave of nearly $10 billion in additional annual income.[3] Under a long established system of concessions, most scheduled for expiration from 1983-1985, some 5.4 million acres of land had been exploited. Twenty-one companies participated in the industry: 18 were foreign-owned concession holders; one was foreign and operating strictly on a contractual basis; and two were Venezuelan—one the state-owned corporation (CVP), the other a private firm. The total work force numbered 24,000, fewer than 3% of whom were foreigners.

At this writing, proven oil reserves total some 14 billion barrels. In addition, Venezuela possesses the so-called Orinoco Tar Belt, with reserves estimated at 700 billion barrels (although some figures run even higher). The content is glutinous and includes heavy admixtures of metals and sulphur. Only the most advanced technology is capable of productive exploitation; debate over the possible desirability of postponing exploitation of the Tar Belt reserves entered into the 1975 controversy. The most immediate antecedents for nationalization had been adopted by the 1971 Hydrocarbons Reversion Law, which provided that over 80% of the territory covered by concessions would revert to state ownership upon expiration between 1983-1985.

The 1971 law had been the product of multi-party collaboration, including President Caldera's Social Christian COPEI and the dominant opposition force, Acción Democrática (AD). During the subsequent 1973 electoral campaign, petroleum was not a salient issue for the electorate (Martz and Baloyra, 1976). The typical attitude was reflected by the AD candidate Carlos Andrés Pérez, who refused to inject oil into the campaign: "*no voy a petrolizar las elecciones.*" His platform promised merely to pursue those studies necessary to advance the reversion date; the ultimate decision to nationalize would be based upon formation of a "national consensus" (Pérez, 1973). Pérez's major rival, Lorenzo Fernández of COPEI, also promised extensive consultation prior to acting. "The decision . . . cannot be the fruit of emotional impulses but rather the product of careful studies which will permit us to act in the most appropriate form and at the most opportune moment" (Fernández, 1973: 8).

Predictably, the parties on the left were more insistent upon immediate nationalization. The candidate of a coalition including the Partido Comunista de Venezuela (PCV), Jesús Angel Paz Galarraga, promised to place the industry under the aegis of the state oil corporation; no further service contracts or agreements would be granted (Nueva Fuerza, 1973). The more radical of the leftist nominees, José Vicente Rangel, similarly insisted upon prompt reversion. His words in an election-eve interview might easily have been those of Pérez: "I am an advocate of accelerating the process of reversion . . . the major weight of which would fall to the CVP, for this State organism participates in all stages of the petroleum enterprise in sovereign form" (El Nacional, 1973).

In December 1973 the AD and Pérez recorded a stunning victory, winning all but one of Venezuela's 20 states and sweeping the three federal territories. With a margin of more than 500,000 votes over Fernández, Pérez and his party won an outright majority in both chambers of congress. In his inaugural address on 12 March 1974 the new president made an unqualified commitment to political consensus.

> Today we see the necessity of advancing the process to fix once and for all a new nationalist and national petroleum policy. It will be the National Congress which says the final word, but not by exercise of a simple parliamentary majority; rather, by decision of the entire nation. . . .
>
> I will proceed to name a broad Commission, composed of persons representative of national life, who will advise the Government in the study of alternatives to be examined prior to submission to the consideration of this Sovereign Congress. In this fashion I hope to obtain effectively the cooperation of all Venezuelans in the search for that great national consensus that must be possible for transcendental decisions which we are to adopt [Pérez, 1974: 5].

Ten days later, Executive Decree Number 10 called for creation of a Comisión Presidencia de Reversión Petrolera. Ultimately, its choice of policy instruments would prove contrary to that of the government in important specifics. In the meantime, nationalization of the iron ore industry produced harbingers for the later takeover of oil.

In April 1974 the President pledged the "immediate" return to the state of iron ore concessions granted in 1960 to United States Steel and to Bethlehem Steel. Following congressional authorization to nationalize the industry by executive decree—procedurally different from the subsequent petroleum process—the government began negotiations with representatives of the two corporations on 3 June 1974. In early December Pérez formally proclaimed nationalization before congress. This action, he declared, opened very favorable perspectives for the more difficult and complex situation which will be presented by the extinction of petroleum concessions which will be produced by the sovereign decision of Venezuela in coming months. On 16 December Decree Number 580 stated that "for reasons of the national interest, the industry for exploitation of iron ore is reserved to the state. Consequently, effective 31 December 1974 the concessions to exploit this mineral are extinguished, and are granted to the National Executive" (República de Venezuela, 1975).

Provisions of the negotiations with the corporations provoked relatively little dissent. Compensation was set at $84,720,930 for Orinoco Mining (U.S. Steel) and $17,674,418 for Iron Mines (Bethlehem). Payment would take the form of ten-year promissory notes carrying 7% interest. In addition, a one-year contract called for company officials to continue work at the major installations, subject to Venezuelan authority. A smooth and uninterrupted transfer was to be assured through signature of a three-year contract for technical assistance.

Privately, government officials argued the necessity of such an agreement as a safeguard against economic reprisal which total and unqualified nationalization might have produced. Moreover, an immediate expulsion of the two multinationals might also have led to a subsequent decline in output and revenues. Yet another important element was psychological, for there was some fear of human and political failure in Venezuelan operation of the industry—a theme to reemerge during the oil debate. The government felt constrained to deradicalize the implementation of policy objectives, especially in its timetable for effective managerial takeover. Manual Pérez Guerrero, Minister of Statc for International Economic Affairs, put this succinctly before congress.

> The danger of nationalization is that the State which nationalizes can lose prestige before its own people, before international public opinion, if instead of continuing the activity nationalized at the same level of efficiency, there is deterioration. . . . A faulty nationalization in the field of iron would put in question similar actions which might be undertaken in even more important ones, and there must be no doubt, especially concerning forthcoming petroleum nationalization [SIC, 1975].

On the surface, lessons to be drawn from iron ore nationalization were two: the first concerned governmental decision-making processes, the second the substance of policy as pertaining to foreign participation. In devising the former, the administration was dealing with a sector of the economy inordinately less important than petroleum. Consequently, the level of partisan conflict was scarcely impassioned. Following a congressional grant of extraordinary powers, Pérez simply directed his associates to negotiate an agreement. The issue of a continuing foreign presence provoked greater dispute, however, and presaged the possibility of conflict over oil. The governmental commitment to a continuing supply of ore and byproducts for the two multinationals nourished the suspicion that control of the industry would still rest in the hands of foreign interests. Thus, the government's choice of policy instruments had constituted the basis for political conflict and partisan debate. The same could be expected in forthcoming petroleum discussions. It was out of the iron ore experience that the Pérez administration moved toward oil nationalization.

Governmental Definition of Policy Instruments

Initiative came from the 36-man presidential commission formed in May 1974, and its report was delivered on 23 December. The Ministry of Mines undertook a study of the recommendations and, in March of 1975, Carlos Andrés Pérez marked the first anniversary of his inauguration by submitting to congress the proposed Ley de Nacionalización de la Industria Petrolera. Five major policy instruments were defined: immediate nationalization (articles 1-4); agreements of association with private enterprise (article 5); new administrative structures (articles 6, 9-11); indemnification to concessionaires (articles 12-19); and protection of employees' rights (articles 23-24; República de Venezuela, Congreso Nacional, 1975).

The first four articles spelled out the sweeping extent of the reversion and the new duties of the state. Everything related to the industry was reserved to the state effective 31 December 1975.

The single provision to depart significantly from the Comisión recommendations was article 5, in which the government was to be authorized to sign agreements of association, subject to prior congressional approval and to the requirement of state control over majority interest in any resultant partnerships. The provision ignited a political conflagration, the fires of which would burn for months.

> In special cases and when it suits the public interest, the National Executive or the above state entities may, in the exercise of such activities, enter into agreements of association with private entities, but with participation such as will guarantee State control, and for a limited duration. Such agreements will require prior authorization of Congress meeting in joint session to fix conditions of the contract after having been duly informed by the National Executive as to all pertinent circumstances [Republica de Venezuela, 1975].

The critical operable phrase was "*enter into agreements of association with private entities.*"

This contrasted with the draft of article 5 as proposed by the Comisión de Reversión which, in seeking to reserve and protect all phases of the industry for the state, had agreed merely for the government to "*enter into necessary agreements*" for the fullest realization of its activities. The government version provoked an uproar of opposition in the corridors of congress and beyond. The president promptly counterattacked. Assuming personal responsibility for this "single modification" of the Comisión recommendations, he expressed hope that there be no loss of the perspective of consensus that had been present in the decision of Venezuelans to nationalize oil. The possibility could not be discarded that during the course of parliamentary deliberations substitute formulas might be found for various parts of the proposals.

The three remaining policy instruments were less controversial. New administrative structures envisaged the creation of a host of state agencies, although the most important—Petróleos Venezolanos (PETROVEN)—would be established by separate legislation. Article 9 outlined a new Comisión Supervisora de la Industria y el Comercio de los Hidrocarburos, which would represent the state in negotiations with the concessionaires until the date for reversion. Considerations pertinent to compensation were outlined in eight lengthy and technical articles. Fundamentally, compensation was to be based upon the state's estimate of book value, less some $400 million in workers' benefits. (Ultimately, negotiators were to agree on a total of $1.018 billion.) Lastly, the draft devoted two articles to the defense of workers' rights. Number 23 pledged that all corporation funds set aside for benefits and social welfare measures would accrue to the state, with existing programs continuing as before. Employees were assured in the following article that their status would not be altered. Venezuelan petroleum workers—the aristocracy of the nation's labor force—would in no way lose any rights as the result of reversion from multinational to state control.

With the announcement of its definition of policy instruments, the government was faced with the problem of regaining the consensus which had disintegrated upon the presentation of article 5. For critics, the decision to opt for agreements of association had made a mockery of the president's oft-reiterated promise of achieving broad nonpartisan support. There were those who had argued that the president erred in not having proclaimed immediate reversion by executive decree upon his inauguration. From the outset, however, Pérez had been committed to extended consideration, participation by all political and socioeconomic elements, and the winning of the fullest possible national awareness through consultation and dialogue. Thus it remained for him to undertake the effort at extending agreement over national values and objectives to the instrumental policies required for nationalization. The result was to be a fiercely vigorous debate which gave renewed testimony to the pluralism of Venezuelan politics.

Debate and Opposition: The Politics of Article 5

The principal objection from the opposition centered on the belief that such accords were inimical to the realization of at least two policy goals: government control over petroleum, and the prevention of foreign ownership or interference in basic means of production. Consequently, the dynamics of transnational corporations became a major focus for discussion. Among the sharpest critics was Juan Pablo Pérez Alfonzo. He had feared that Pérez's deliberate and measured rhythm would provide foreign interests with the opportunity to manipulate the situation and further delay true nationalization; the administration's course was viewed as producing insecurity and uncertainty rather than consensus. Clemenceau was quoted to the effect that "when one wants to do something, he does it; if not, he turns it over to a commission." Venezuelan delay was described as paralleling the gradual takeover of copper by Chile a few years earlier, thereby "giving the transnationals time to render more difficult the functioning of the eventually nationalized administration" (SIC, 1975).

COPEI, the leading opposition party, officially declared its hostility on 21 March. Article 5 was denounced for accepting possible agreements of associations, which it interpreted as suggesting mixed enterprises in which both "transnational oil companies and Venezuelan companies, organized or in the process of organization, are eager to participate." While not unfriendly to either foreign or domestic capital, the party regarded such provisions as weakening nationalization while "wounding the nationalist conscience of all Venezuelans in their traditional desire to take the nation's primary resource into their own hands."

The fullest expression of *copeyano* opposition came in August when former President Caldera addressed the senate. He recalled from personal experience that the petroleum corporations had never supported Venezuela in its aspirations for greater sovereignty and better treatment for the industry. Rather, it was his impression that "each time they have been able to obstruct [those aspirations] they have done so, and that far from being good colleagues or good partners . . . they have tried to erect obstacles, to create barriers in Venezuela's path" (Caldera, 1976: 68-69). To be sure, only irrational nationalism would deny the nation's need for foreign technicians; Venezuela would have to pay for technological assistance to assure the most productive operation of the industry. However, the distinction between mixed enterprises and technology was significant, and agreements of association were very different from technological transfer.

From the left, opposition was also vocal. On 20 March the Movimiento al Socialismo (MAS) announced its own objections which, while broader than those of COPEI, also concentrated on article 5. The government version, it charged, opened the "grave possibility" that, within the nationalization of the petroleum industry about to take place, large private capital, both foreign and Venezuelan, would have important participation in the property of the mixed companies which would reach enormous proportions. Inevitably, the benefits of petroleum would remain those of privileged groups, while the immense majority of the population would be barred from its share. MAS was joined by similar leftist criticisms from the Partido Comunista, Vanguardia Comunista, Movimiento de Izquierda Revolucionaria, and Movimiento Electoral del Pueblo.

The government was therefore accused of demonstrating an enduring subordination to oligarchical interests, for article 5 opened the door to foreign participation. This appeared especially true of refining and marketing, each of which yields substantial profits. Non-Venezuelan interests could thereby enjoy a continuing share of precisely the most lucrative aspects of the entire process. Similar dangers were seen as emanating from Tar Belt provisions. In addition to the spectre of massive profits for international interests, there was the added argument that the Tar Belt resources represented insurance for the future, and should not be drawn upon in the years immediately ahead.

The issues were clearly profound, technical complexities great, and political stakes high. If the opposition had a strong and persuasive case, the same was true of the administration. Certainly there was justifiable concern over the shortcomings of Venezuelan experience, especially with transportation, marketing and distribution. Given the historical verticality of international oil activities, there were strong grounds for retaining some involvement from abroad. Moreover, the government was by no means deaf to frequently expressed opinions that productivity, efficiency, and profits would all suffer during the early stages of nationalization. The President and Acción Democrática repeatedly added to these arguments the fact that approval of any joint ventures was dependent in any event upon congressional review and approval; that foreign participation was restricted to a minority role; and that in no case would it be permitted for more than fifteen years.

Outside the arena of party politics, the business community had quietly lined up behind the government. Recognizing the inevitability of nationalization, business leaders undertook private encouragement of legislation least inimical to their interests, including the official version of article 5. When the original version of the Comisión report had appeared, Fedecámaras[4] President Paúl Delfino had complained that denial of involvement by either national or international private enterprise constituted a major flaw. Such business opposition dwindled with announcement of the government draft in March. The studied silence of both Fedecámaras and the Asociación Pro-Venezuela, the latter a more progressive organization representing middle-level industrialists and businessmen, was widely interpreted as tacit approval.

The basic points at issue had been clearly drawn, then, with release of the government bill to congress. Proposed agreements of association and the possibility of mixed enterprises represented a policy instrument on which there was profound disagreement. Pérez hoped that consultation might bring about an understanding on all sides. Yet it appeared that compromise might not be feasible for there was little flexibility in what struck many observers as irreconcilable positions.

Political Realities and Instrumental Dissensus

The initial arena for discussion, of course, had been the Comisión Presidencial de Reversión Petrolera. Carlos Andrés Pérez had insisted upon the importance of its work. "All precautions will be adopted to avoid pressures and demagogic or disorderly attitudes on the national destiny. It is necessary to consult and to look for the agreement of all, so that everyone feels identification and solidarity with the measure" (El Nacional, 1974). The Comisión membership had included representatives of political parties, business interests, and trade unions. The final product was completed on schedule, appearing in the press on December 5, 1974.

While the government prepared its own draft during January and February of 1975, partisan forces began to shape their own positions in anticipation of congressional debate. COPEI had already indicated latent opposition, although initially undecided as to the particulars. Fighting to retain its position at the head of the opposition while determined to regain power in 1978, COPEI was therefore anxious to seize upon all available opportunities of criticizing the government for "anti-nationalist" actions.

Several currents of thought emerged in party discussions. The first saw the importance of national consensus on such a vital matter, contending that COPEI should contribute to the preparation of legislation. Other *copeyanos*, however, projected greater political advantage from relentless opposition to official proposals. They believed that the party's 1978 campaign could best be enhanced if COPEI presented itself as an unqualified critic of the *adeco* government and its policies. And yet another group, including Caldera's former Minister of Mines Hugo Pérez La Salvia, had been disappointed by the party's failure to have nationalized the industry itself in 1973. Resentment of an AD government doing so was profound.

In the meantime, Acción Democrática sought an agreement which would be to its own advantage. Both Carlos Andrés Pérez and his party recognized the historically fortuitous opportunity to adopt and take credit for oil nationalization. Extended discussions had preceded presentation of the draft bill, although the role of the party itself was secondary. Provision for mixed companies was championed by the highest AD leaders—ex-president Rómulo Betancourt, Gonzalo Barrios, and Pérez himself. Concerned with efficient management of the industry, maintenance of productivity, and basically confident of governmental ability to assure control over foreign involvement, they found the notion of associational agreements both rational and comfortable. Not all party figures shared the view; significantly, one of the ranking AD authorities on oil, Arturo Hernández Grisanti (something of a protege of Pérez Alfonzo), was among those preferring so-called "operative agreements." The party's Comité Ejecutivo Nacional eventually accepted the commitment to mixed companies, but only after addition of the provision for congressional approval.

The parties of the left experienced less uncertainty and internal debate. It was a simple matter to view article 5 in terms of *entreguismo*, or an abdication of Venezuelan sovereignty on behalf of international capitalism and transnational imperialism. Yet even here differences of opinions existed, most notably within the Movimiento al Socialismo. The *masista* attitude toward nationalization was not without pragmatic political considerations. Early in discussions the party had appeared willing to consider mixed enterprises for international aspects of the industry, while rejecting any involvement in domestic activities. In time this gave way to more unqualified criticism of foreign participation. Meanwhile the Movimiento Electoral del Pueblo (MEP) was intransigent in its opposition. At one point, party president Luis B. Prieto told the press that the MEP was "going into the streets to denounce this betrayal [of national interests]. We will not leave the scene of debate to Congress alone" (El Nacional, 1975).

In May the initiative for compromise was seized by the Unión Republicana Democrática (URD), once Venezuela's second strongest party but by 1975 a decaying organization with but one senator and five deputies. Working with the AD, the URD redrafted article 5 to exclude agreements of association with foreign state agencies for activities within Venezuela, while leaving open the possibility of such arrangements abroad. When the MAS and MEP promptly rejected the proposal, the URD turned to COPEI. However, although amenable to some form of operative contracts, the Social Christians refused to accept mixed enterprises. By 23 May these talks reached an impasse, the URD proposals fell by the wayside, and the AD renewed its own direct efforts. Despairing of securing agreement from the left, the government party sought common ground with COPEI. Its new draft of article 5 provided for the formation of associations with foreign governments or private entities; these would apply to international transportation, refineries outside Venezuela, and those on national territory where technological assistance was required. Among other things, aid in developing the Tar Belt would be permissible.

The last point in particular was objectionable to COPEI, and the new *adeco* draft was swiftly rejected. Other parties followed suit, including the URD, which preferred associational arrangements limited to foreign state agencies. Thus the lines of party dissensus were ever more sharply etched. The government persisted in moving basically from the traditional concessionary system to one of association allowing a continuing role for international economic interests; opposition to such agreements had hardened perceptibly. With reluctance, the AD exercised its majority in the Commission of Mines and Hydrocarbons to report out its recommendations on 2 June. At the same time, however, the administration had not yet exhausted its efforts to widen the base of support for its policy proposal. Neither had political maneuvering come to an end as full congressional debate opened on 5 June.

COPEI suggested that its approval of the bill might be conditioned by revising congressional approval of agreements from simple majority to a two-thirds margin (referred to euphemistically as a "qualified majority"). This would have given the

Social Christians virtual veto power over proposals introduced by the AD majority, and the latter promptly rejected the possibility as patently political. COPEI then pushed further its effort to dominate the drive for consensus by calling for a "Pacto Nacional." Its basis would be acceptance of agreements of association, accompanied by repudiation of mixed enterprises and of accords relating to the Tar Belt. Furthermore, within two years Congress would adopt a so-called "Law of Bases and Norms for Agreements of Association."

There were brief indications that portions of the *copeyano* proposal might be acceptable to the government. However, provisions concerning the Tar Belt were not. Had the administration been willing to postpone action on the Orinoco reserves, an agreement to which the non-Marxist parties could subscribe might have proved possible. As it was, however, the president was adamant. The government bill soon passed its first reading, and second approval was voted on 28 July. The 104 members of Acción Democrática were joined only by two CCN deputies, while the remaining 94 deputies voted no. The scene then shifted to the senate, where the penultimate act in the drama was staged.

The upper chamber met on 5 August. With consensus doomed and the passage of government legislation by the AD majority a foregone conclusion, it but remained for one final elaboration of conflicting views. Many senators spoke, but attention focused on three preeminent leaders—Rafael Caldera, Gonzalo Barrios, and Rómulo Betancourt. The first delivered the opening address, defending his own administration's oil policies as well as criticizing the Pérez position. He expressed concern over reversals suffered in 1974-1975, along the road to nationalization, and viewed controversy over article 5 as having spawned unrealistic "phantoms" of fear among the populace. Declaring that the wording of the controversial provision was eminently infelicitous, Caldera read it as saying that transnational corporations—rather than private Venezuelan interests or foreign governmental entities—would constitute the core of any agreements of association.

To be sure, Caldera fully recognized Venezuela's need for technology. He supported its purchase and importation, but without entering into mixed enterprises with transnationals. Furthermore, he objected to immediate development of the Orinoco Tar Belt. Quoting a friend to the effect that Venezuela should not permit conversion of the Tar Belt into a chastity belt, he advocated a stay in its exploitation, that it might ultimately lead to fertile maternity for its Venezuelan parents. In closing, he eloquently addressed the indispensable necessity for unity on nationalization and invoked Simón Bolívar in the cause of full and unqualified accord (Caldera, 1976).

The former president was immediately followed by Barrios, speaking for Acción Democrática. Reviewing the long *adeco* trajectory in the evolution of petroleum policy, including the founding of OPEC and passage of the 1971 Reversion Law, he decried the presence of partisan politics in matters of such importance. Stressing the government decision to stimulate national dialogue and legislative participation, he praised the lengthy debate as healthy for Venezuelan democracy. Barrios emphasized that mixed enterprises were but one of several forms of collaboration permitted by agreements of association. Future historians, he concluded, would not be primarily concerned with the president or party which executed nationalization; rather, history would ask who were those responsible for the industry redounding to the full benefit of the people of Venezuela.

The following day former President Bentancourt spoke, alluding frequently to the industry's history and interlacing his address with anecdotal material. He saw article 5 as admitting of but two possibilities: operational contracts by the holding company which would administer the industry, or agreements of association subject to congressional approval. The clear intention was that of permitting the executive proper flexibility. Agreements of association would not be the order of the day, but rather modest and limited arrangements whereby outside expertise would be made available, always under Venezuelan control.

> I conclude by expressing my absolute faith in the success of the takeover by the State, once the Law has been approved . . . All we Venezuelans, including those who in the exercise of their democratic rights now dissent from specific aspects of the Law about to

> be approved, will lend their efforts to administrative success for the country with its basic source of wealth.
>
> We are at the point of taking an historic and transcendental step but, as in all other opportunities which have been given to us in Venezuela, we men and women of this land must act with a high sense of responsibility [Betancourt, 1976: 28].

Following senate debate, steps toward passage led in turn to final approval by the Chamber of Deputies on 21 August. Eight days later, Carlos Andrés Pérez signed the bill and stepped before the cameras to address the nation.

Claiming unanimity of national opinion favoring nationalization, he characterized the law as neither contradicting nor weakening the principles and interests of the nation. While indicating that no joint ventures would be undertaken during his term of office, the president emphasized fulfillment of nationalization as promising to bring about a new economic order. The era during which the natural resources of poor countries were plundered by the wealthy had closed, and the Third World would no longer permit underpriced payment for their primary products. Finally, "we pledge once again our irrevocable purpose of showing that a just society is possible only through respect for human freedom. We are committed, beyond any possibility of retreat, to a grandiose work of taking the initial steps for the economic liberation of Venezuela, and I invite my countrymen to achieve the task that is ours. *Manos a la Obra*!" (Pérez, 1976b: 15).

Conclusions: Policy-Making and the Failure of Consensus

A review of events demonstrates that it was the governmental role which stood out. Initiative lay in the hands of the Pérez administration, with opposition forces playing an essentially reactive part. The president simultaneously pursued two objectives: the substantive policy instruments he identified as necessary for nationalization, and the securing of nonpartisan consensual support through consultation and dialogue. With the former, controversy over the future role of international enterprise proved intractable. There was little real middle ground for compromise, as either government or opposition would have had to yield up its position. Realistically, only an accord between the AD and COPEI might have been engineered, for the left ultimately could accept government policy only at the sacrifice of its principles. Had the government been willing to exclude the Tar Belt from its plans—that is, delay its exploitation indefinitely —a negotiated settlement might have resulted. But here again, it would have required a basic shift in viewpoint.

In procedural terms, there were flaws in the government's campaign to build consensus. Eschewing the possibility of decreeing nationalization immediately after his inauguration, Pérez had insisted upon consultation and dialogue as a means of maximizing the legitimacy of the action. Having exercised this option, it was incumbent upon the president to carry it through to conclusion. Ultimately he failed to do so, thus creating needless rancor and uncertainty. The first step, appointment of the Comisión Presidencial de Reversión Petrolera, was sound. The naming of the membership helped defuse opposition by effectively representing diverse interests and political forces. While the December 1974 report did not enjoy total unanimity, the disagreement at that juncture was not profound. Only with governmental rewriting of article 5 did serious dissensus emerge.

Whatever the substance of debate over agreements of association and mixed enterprises, the presidential promise that proposed legislation would be "the same or similar to that which today is delivered to us for consideration" by the Comisión de Reversión was not fulfilled. The government appeared to have reneged on its pledge, with Carlos Andrés Pérez having imposed his own will unilaterally. This reflected in part the flawed communication between administration and Comisión. The latter completed its work unaware of the extent to which its views differed from those of the administration on proposals outlined in article 5. Whether or not the divergences could have been resolved is unknown, but also in a sense irrelevant. The government bore a responsibility to communicate its preferences to the Comisión and failed to do so.

In perceiving accurately a national consensus on the values and policy objectives related to nationalization, the administration apparently assumed its extension to policy instruments as well. The Pérez view basically held that government control over any and all agreements of association could be maintained, while reaping the benefits of foreign expertise and technology. COPEI and other centrist forces were highly skeptical at best, while for the left, non-Venezuelan participation was by definition inimical to national interests. Several questions remain unanswered. Should the government have undertaken the quest for consensus when there was profound disagreement on important points? Were the months of angry debate damaging to nationalization, or was such airing of differing opinions beneficial? Did it result in a consensus among the people (as the AD claimed), or did it engender further fragmentation of public opinion and loss of self-confidence over the means and capacity to operate the petroleum industry? From the broadest perspective these are among the crucial issues and cannot presently be answered definitively.

Preliminary observations arc not inappropriate, however. The debate undoubtedly contributed to a legitimization of nationalization, yet simultaneously projected the image of a government reversing its commitment to accept without qualification the recommendations of the Comisión de Reversión. There appears substance to Rafael Caldera's concern that the heat and acrimony nourished a sense of public uncertainty and doubt. If the detailed issues aired by article 5 were important, they can scarcely have provided notable enlightenment for the average Venezuelan. Thus the events leading to the ultimate failure of consensus appear at least incrementally dysfunctional to the government. It might be argued in retrospect that nationalization through presidential decree shortly after Pérez's inauguration would have been preferable. By not doing so, the government permitted the debate to assume a more partisan tone than the protagonists might have preferred, leaving the administration an even heavier burden of proof as it initiated nationalization in 1976.

Such judgments remain speculative in the absence of that insight provided only by retrospective reflection. It yet remains to be asked, however, what lessons may be derived. At least five can be posited: (1) the government may count upon broad systemic consensus over national values and the policy objectives which serve it; (2) the potential area of conflict centers on the instrumentation of a given policy; (3) disagreement over instrumentation emphasizes other differences which may be either pragmatic or ideological; (4) the commitment to political pluralism does not assure consensus on policy instrumentation; (5) important policy instruments may be defined and adopted without the support of a nonpartisan national consensus.

On the first, we described at the outset the accord which existed, cutting across public opinion and political forces from one end of the spectrum to the other. The government relied upon this reality throughout the debate, and continues to do so today. As this case illustrates, the realm for controversy concerns the definition of specific policy instruments. As the third proposition suggests, disagreement may take at least two different forms—pragmatic or normative. The first related to issues of political advantage, with partisanship and sectarianism writ large. The second focused more on content and substance as perceived from specific ideological perspectives. Realistically, the lack of accord will be produced by a blend of both the pragmatic and the normative. With nationalization, an awareness of political opportunism as related to 1978 elections was combined with such varying ideological viewpoints as Marxism (MAS, MIR, MEP), Christian Democracy (COPEI), Social Democracy (AD), and capitalist developmentalism (Fedecámaras).

The sheer presence of pluralist politics by no means guaranteed agreement on those mechanisms selected to realize basic objectives. The majority role enjoyed by Acción Democrática in congress was imposed upon the interests and views of the minority. The party had won elections decisively, and acted upon its mandate accordingly. This action contradicted neither pluralistic national values nor the concomitant goal of open democratic exchange, consultation and dialogue. It simply did not carry over to policy instrumentation. Certainly it could have done so, but in this case was prevented by differing attitudes toward article 5. Consequently, the formulation, articulation, and adoption of policy instruments on this occasion took place in the absence of nonpartisan accord. Neither extended public discussion nor carefully structured administrative mechanisms were adequate to build and sustain unqualified consensus.

The record of Venezuelan management of the industry is now in the making. The initial experience in enacting the terms of nationalization was instructive. National consensus was valuable, but the costs of seeking it were large. The benefits of national dialogue must be measured in the light of speed, efficiency, and the potential for dissensus and disunity. Certainly the effort to structure and guide debate in the formulation of public policy will inevitably suffer in the absence of complete information and constant communication. Yet Venezuela's pluralist politics clearly did not tie the hands of a regime intent upon nationalization and gives the lie to the argument that only an authoritarian system may successfully undertake such action. In devising its policy, the Venezuelans produced a form of nationalization which appeared managerially feasible and immune to the likelihood of provoking a systemic breakdown. Its nonradical quality doubtless contributed to the capacity for enacting such a policy. In its broadest terms, the nationalization of Venezuelan petroleum presents, then, a suggestive case study of policy making in one of the few open political systems remaining on a predominantly authoritarian continent.

NOTES

1. The flag-raising over Zumaque was followed later in the morning by a presidential address at Cabimas, both of which the author attended.

2. While production has been reduced by the Pérez administration, the share of export earnings and foreign currency resulting from petroleum has risen as a consequence of price increases. The only income from exports not provided by petroleum is the approximate $100 million annually from iron ore.

3. The government created the Fondo de Inversiones de Venezuela (FIV) as an entity to control, direct, and invest (both internationally and domestically) the massive funds earned through petroleum.

4. The Federation of Chambers of Commerce and Industry, Fedecámaras is a rough equivalent to the national Chamber of Commerce in the United States.

REFERENCES

BETANCOURT, R. (1976) Dueño de su petróleo. Caracas: Ediciones Centauro.

BLANK, D. E. (1973) Politics in Venezuela. Boston: Little, Brown.

CALDERA, R. (1976) La Nacionalizacion del Petróleo. Caracas: Ediciones Nueva Política.

El Nacional (1975) "El MEP y Petróleo." March 18: D-1.

——— (1974) "Nacionalización del Petróleo." March 23: A-1.

——— (1973) "Rangel y los Resultados Electorales." December 10: D-1.

FERNANDEZ, L. (1973) Directrices para una Acción de Gobierno. Caracas.

LEVINE, D. H. (1973) Conflict and Political Change in Venezuela. Princeton, NJ: Princeton Univ. Press.

MARTZ, J. D. and E. A. BALOYRA (1976) Electoral Mobilization and Public Opinion; The Venezuelan Campaign of 1973. Chapel Hill: Univ. of North Carolina Press.

MARTZ, J. D. and D. J. MYERS [eds.] (1977) The Venezuelan Democratic Experience. New York: Praeger.

NJAIM, H., R. COMBELLAS, E. JOSKO DE GUERON, and A. STAMBOULI (1975) El Sistema Político Venezolano. Caracas: Editorial Arte.

Nueva Fuerza (1973) Programa de Gobierno. Caracas.

PEREZ, C. A. (1976a) Salutación del Presidente de la República a la Nacion Venezolana con motivo de 1 de enero de 1976. Caracas: Imprenta Nacional.

——— (1976b) Mensaje de Nacionalización a la República. Caracas: Imprenta Nacional.

——— (1974) Mensaje del Presidente. Caracas: Imprenta Nacional.

——— (1973) Acción de Gobierno. Caracas.

Republica de Venezuela, Congreso Nacional (1975) Proyecto de ley de nacionalización. Caracas: Imprenta Nacional.

Republica de Venezuela, Gaceta Oficial. Decreto Numero 580. Caracas: Imprenta Nacional.

Resumen (1975) "Perspectivas sobre la Nacionalizacón Petrólera." Caracas (August-September).

ROKEACH, M (1973) The Nature of Human Values. New York: Free Press.

SIC (1976) "Nuevo enfoque de la Situación Humana y el Petróleo." Vol. 49 (March): 99-104, 137-144.

TUGWELL, F. (1975) The Politics of Oil in Venezuela. Stanford, CA: Stanford Univ. Press.

John D. Martz is Professor of Political Science at the University of North Carolina, Chapel Hill. The editor of the Latin American Research Review, *he is coauthor (with Enrique A. Baloyra) of the recently published* Electoral Mobilization and Public Opinion: The Venezuelan Campaign of 1973 *and coeditor (with David J. Myers) of* Venezuela: The Democratic Experience. *He spent the summer of 1977 in Ecuador under a grant from the Social Science Research Council.*

ALFRED E. OSBORNE, Jr.
Graduate School of Management
University of California
Los Angeles, CA 90024

ON THE ECONOMIC COST TO PANAMA OF NEGOTIATING A PEACEFUL SOLUTION TO THE PANAMA CANAL QUESTION

Negotiating a treaty between two sovereign nations is no simple matter. Even when there is consensus that a new accord is long overdue, a solution acceptable to both governments and their most vocal constituencies is most elusive and often difficult to conclude within a reasonable period of time. This is especially true when there is strong popular opinion aroused on both sides. Discussions usually drag on, and while diplomats publicly agree that "progress is being made," there are significant political and economic benefits unrealized by either or both countries involved in the negotiation proceedings (Lopez Guevara, 1976).

The present treaty negotiations between the Republic of Panama and the United States of America is a case in point. That Panamanian public opinion is aroused on the Canal issue is indicated by the 1964 Canal Zone border incidents in which twenty-one Panamanians and three Americans died and by subsequent demonstrations. U.S. public attitudes are presented as evidence

---

AUTHOR'S NOTE: This article is based on a paper entitled "Estimates of the Economic Benefits Foregone by Panama with U.S. Control Over the Panama Canal," recently read at the 6th annual meeting of the Latin American Studies Association in Atlanta, March 24-28, 1976. Helpful comments were provided by members of the Panel on U.S. Response to Nationalization in Latin America and John L. Martin. The financial support provided by a Regent's Faculty Fellowship at UCLA is gratefully acknowledged. The usual disclaimer, however, applies.

Journal of Interamerican Studies and World Affairs, Vol. 19 No. 4, November 1977

by congressional votes intended to end current negotiations. The issue has surfaced importantly in the recent U.S. presidential elections. Since the 1964 riots, the Panamanian government has earnestly sought to terminate the 1903 Hay-Bunau-Varilla Treaty so favorable to the United States (U.S. Department of State, 1974).[1] And although there have been important U.S. concessions to treaty revisions in 1936 and 1955, it has taken some 62 years since the Canal first opened to persuade the U.S. government that a modern, more equal partnership is long overdue. On February 7, 1974, Secretary of State of the United States Henry Kissinger and Panamanian Minister of Foreign Affairs Juan Antonio Tack issued a joint statement of principles.[2] These negotiating principles herald the possibility of a new day in U.S.-Latin American relations and signal the eventuality of the dominant control by Panama over her territory. Perhaps more important, however, is the possibility of a more reasonable economic return to Panama for the use of the Canal and the advantages of its unique location for world shipping. All Latin American republics show a deep concern for the issue of sovereignty in the outcome of these talks. The image of the United States as a "colonialist" power in the Western Hemisphere lingers and the eventual outcome of these negotiations is seen as a test of future U.S. intentions towards its neighbors.

However, more than ten long, frustrating years have elapsed since the present discussions began. These years have been a difficult experience for Panamanians as lack of tangible progress has seriously hindered the development aspirations of their nation to control its major resource—the interoceanic waterway across the isthmus (Burns, 1974).[3] The drawn out negotiations might have been concluded earlier if Panama had accepted various proposals under consideration. The fact that a new treaty with greater benefits for Panama has not yet been concluded, and may not be for several years, means that Panama has suffered an opportunity loss while the negotiations have continued.

The issues involved in the negotiations are complex. Involved are not only nationalist sentiments but also issues of sovereignty, national defense, international responsibility, and economic impact. This paper analyzes the nature of the economic benefits accruing to Panama under the terms of the current treaty, the inequitable nature of Panama's direct compensation compared to Canal revenues, and the opportunity cost to Panama resulting from protracted negotiations.

Given no property rights, Panama has been forced in the past to accept reluctantly any residual relationship defined by the United States. As a result of Panama's inability to set rates and obtain revenue sharing arrangements—indeed, being prohibited from any control over the territory leased to the United States—a substantial subsidy to world shipping interests has resulted, along with lower prices to the consumers in countries of cargo destination. While this is not the place for a definitive study of the many complex issues involved in the subject of pricing, cargo, alternative routes, and other questions directly related to Canal traffic, the economic issues fundamental to Panama in treaty negotiations are clear. These are simply to obtain maximum possible revenues from the Canal Company in direct payments and through Panamanian factor services in the operation of the enterprise. Our focus, therefore, is on the benefits unrealized over the 1965 to 1974 treaty negotiation period under draft treaty terms and our assumption that, at least, Panama should be a "more equal partner" regarding its share of the actual commercial cargo revenues which the Canal earns. Given estimates of the potential for increased tolls, we calculate similar unrealized benefits from shares of potential revenues for actual tonnage. The last section of this paper concludes with an evaluation of the cost of prolonged treaty negotiations with a small country for whom opportunity costs are a significant percentage of gross national product.

Panama Canal Revenues and Current Economic Benefits to Panama

Over the 1965 to 1974 treaty negotiation period there was modest growth in traffic through the Panama Canal. In 1965, 11,834 commercial ocean-going vessels crossed the canal paying toll revenues of $66.44 million. By 1974, the traffic had increased

TABLE 1
Percentage Rates of Growth for Selected Treaty Negotiation Subperiods

VARIABLE	SUBPERIOD 1970-74	1967-74	1965-74
Commercial Ocean Traffic			
Transits			
Total Increase	2.7 %	13.0 %	18.8 %
Average Annual Rate	0.54	1.6	1.9
Freight			
Total Increase	20.1	60.0	80.2
Average Annual Rate	4.12	7.5	8.0
Revenues			
Total Increase	26.2	55.5	82.0
Average Annual Rate	5.2	7.5	8.2
Non-Toll Revenues			
Total Increase	27.8	51.4	75.0
Average Annual Rate	5.56	6.4	7.5

SOURCE: Panama Canal Company, Annual Reports, 1965-1974.

18.8% to 14,033 vessels per year. Although transit growth for the decade was at the average annual rate of 1.9% in the 1970 to 1974 period, transits grew at one-third that pace at an average annual rate of .54%. This slow and decelerating growth in transits was accompanied by significant increases in toll revenue. Freight through the Canal increased by 80% during the decade ending in 1974.

The percentage growth rates during selected subperiods shown in Table 1 illustrate these trends. The virtual absence of recent growth in traffic accompanied by substantial increases in freight, suggest that larger vessels carrying more cargo (containerization) were responsible for the almost doubling of income between 1965 and 1974. While the most rapid growth occurred in nontoll, income-generating activities such as repairs to vessels in transit and Canal Company services to employees, the freight revenue is the basis for Canal income. Over the 1965 to 1974

TABLE 2
Aggregate Transit, Revenue, and Cargo Totals over Various Negotiation Subperiods

No. of years	Sub-period	Number of Transits	Toll Revenue (millions of $)	Long Tons of Cargo (millions)	Non-Toll Revenue (millions of $)	Total Revenue (millions of $)
5	1970-74	69,318	521.22	606.42	416.6	937.82
8	1967-74	108,075	769.32	890.53	617.0	1,386.32
10	1965-74	131,834	903.85	1,048.80	729.9	1,633.75

SOURCE: Panama Canal Company, Annual Reports, 1965-1974.

period of negotiations, revenue of $903.85 million was collected on 1,049 million tons of cargo. As shown in Table 3, revenue per transit increased during 1970-1974 in proportion to the increase in cargo per transit.

The Republic of Panama also benefited from this growth in interoceanic commerce. There are six sources of direct economic benefit to Panama from Canal operations principally based on the three treaties which govern U.S.-Panamanian relations. One, Panamanians benefit from the annuity paid by the United States for use of the Panama Canal Zone. This amount, slightly less than $2 million per annum since 1955, was $250,000 until 1936 when it was increased to $430,000 (ECLA, 1972).[4] This recent increase, however, is *not* paid out of Panama Canal revenues. The U.S. Congress has consistently shown a preference for keeping the treaty relationship separate from the Canal operation to subsidize world shipping interests—assuming, in doing so, that final

TABLE 3
Selected Operating Averages over Treaty Negotiation Period

Years	Tons/Transit	Tolls/Transit	Tolls/Ton
1970-74	8,748	7,519	.859
1967-74	8,240	7,118	.864
1965-74	7,955	6,856	.862

SOURCE: Panama Canal Company, Annual Reports, 1965-1974.

TABLE 4

Total Direct Economic Benefits to the Republic of Panama from the Panama Canal and Canal Zone for Various Subperiods

CATEGORY	1965–1974 Millions of Dollars[a]	%[b]	1967–1974 Millions of Dollars[a]	%[b]	1970–1974 Millions of Dollars[a]	%[b]
Total Foreign Exchange	$1,951.2	14.8[c]	$1,368.3	14.7	$ 927.6	13.8
Wages and Salaries	740.0	37.9	630.4	46.0	344.4	37.0
Retirement Benefits	71.2	3.6	63.4	4.6	47.3	5.1
Goods and Services (Official U.S. Agencies)	233.8	11.9	202.8	14.8	139.0	14.9
Private Sector Spending	209.7	10.7	175.2	12.8	114.6	12.4
Persons Resident in the Canal Zone	317.0	16.2	280.8	20.5	190.4	20.5
Annuity	19.5	1.0	15.7	1.1	10.0	1.1
Total Gross Domestic Product	10,699.7		9,320.8		6,713.3	

SOURCES: ECLA (1972), Panama Canal Company (1970-1974), U.S. House of Representatives (1974), United Nations National Account Data in U.S. House of Representatives (1975).

a. Dollars may not add to total due to rounding.

b. May not add to 100.0 due to rounding; proportion of Total Foreign Exchange.

c. As a % of the Total Gross Domestic Product.

prices to U.S. consumers will be kept down. However, recent rising costs and a change in accounting procedures has offered sufficient justification to raise tolls. The first toll increase since the canal opened, a 20% increase, was put into effect July 8, 1974, coincident with operating losses in fiscal 1973 and 1974 due largely to heavy depreciation expenses not previously claimed.[5]

A second source of economic benefits to Panama are the wages and salaries (including retirement and disability payments) paid to Panamanian employees in the Canal Zone. This item, primarily a result of the 1955 treaty, is the main source of income flow to the Republic.

Thirdly, U.S. government agencies in the Canal Zone purchase goods and services in Panama, and private organizations in the Canal Zone are another source of income to the Republic. Contractor purchases of Panamanian goods and services for projects in the Canal Zone provide a fifth source of revenue flow. Finally, there are the expenditures made in Panama by residents of the

Canal Zone. The aggregate dollar amounts paid to the Republic from these six sources are shown in Table 4 for the various negotiation subperiods.

Over the 1965 to 1974 period the Canal Zone provided nearly two billion dollars to the Republic of Panama. Over 40% of this amount was in the form of wages, salaries and retirement benefits to Panamanians. Another 16% ($317 million) is attributable to purchases by persons residing in the Canal Zone. Foods and services purchased by official and private agencies account for 22% ($443 million) of total foreign exchange. Finally, the annuity Panama receives for the use of her territory contributed $19.5 million (1%) over the period.

Total direct and indirect foreign revenue received by Panama from the Canal Zone is 14.8% of the total gross domestic product of $10.7 billion over the period. While these are important sources of direct economic benefits to Panama, it is the annuity that stands out. Annuity income of $19.5 million is only slightly over 1% of Panama Canal Company revenue of $1.63 billion. It is only slightly over 2% of toll revenue, and this has appeared to Panamanian officials a paltry return for use of her territory.[6]

We note that although there have been two important treaty revisions since the original agreement, at no time has the U.S. relinquished any control over the determination of rates or the manner in which Panama would benefit from the Canal operation. The Panamanian annuity was not proportionate to the growth in traffic, or revenues, demonstrating absence of a genuine partnership or sharing arrangement. This lack of proportionality amounts to the Panamanian economy subsidizing users of the Canal and consumers in countries of cargo destinations. But the size of the subsidy is much larger than that suggested by actual revenues lost. Canal tolls per ton of cargo are low. Independent consultants have estimated that an increase in tolls of 50% would cause no overall diversion of Canal traffic (U.S. House of Representatives, 1974). As tolls have been raised only once in 62 years of Canal operation (this occurred in 1974), and all other shipping costs have steadily increased almost threefold, a 150% increase is considered a reasonable upper bound.[7]

While ex post facto rules are easy to develop, there are some arrangements which deserve attention. Some which seem reasonable have been proposed by both U.S. and Panamanian negotiators in recent years. Discussion pursuant to the Kissinger-Tack Statement of Principles is not generally available, although agreement on the economic benefits will no doubt involve a more equitable profit sharing rule in spite of American insistence of a low toll, break-even policy.

Opportunity Loss To Panama Under Alternative Agreements

In this section, we consider the potential benefits not realized by Panama under a treaty proposal that arose during the negotiations of the 1960s. Also, given an alternative more equal sharing rule, we offer one additional estimate of the implicit Panamanian loss of foreign exchange.

In Table 5, assuming that tolls could have remained the same and could have been increased by 50% or 100% with no overall impact on tonnage, we compare the $0.17 per ton proposal to the present annuity (U.S. House of Representatives, 1974).[8] This proposal, developed between 1964 and 1967 by negotiators of both countries, was rejected by Panama in 1970. The proposal called for payment to Panama of $0.17 per ton for the first year to be increased by $0.01 per ton per year to a maximum of $0.22 per ton (Atlantic Pacific Interoceanic Canal Study Commission, 1970). At average canal tolls, this represents an effective share in revenues of 20% in the first year rising to 25% at the end of five years. The data indicate sizable unrealized benefits since 1965, 1967, or 1970.[9] The dollar value of foreign exchange, unrealized since 1967 when Panama could accept the offer, is calculated at $171.6 million. The indecision in 1967 to 1970 by both governments can be seen as costing Panama $57.3 million. In 1970, when General Torrijos became head of the government, Panama could have agreed to the draft treaty but choose not to. This decision to try to negotiate better conditions has cost the Panamanian government income of $114.3 million. Under this $0.17 per ton

TABLE 5
Unrealized Foreign Exchange Under 17 Cents Per Ton Arrangement for Various Periods (in millions of dollars)

ARRANGEMENT	1965-74	1967-74	1970-74
Annuity	$ 19.5	$ 15.7	$ 10.0
Current Tolls[a]			
Share	224.1	187.3	124.3
Ratio[b]	11.5	11.9	12.4
Foreign Exchange Unrealized	204.6	171.6	114.3
50% Increase in Tolls[c]			
Share	336.1	281.0	186.5
Foreign Exchange Unrealized	316.6	265.3	176.5
150% Increase in Tolls[c]			
Share	560.2	473.3	390.8
Foreign Exchange Unrealized	550.7	457.6	380.8

SOURCE: Panama Canal Company, Annual Reports, 1965-1974.
a. Account is also taken of the 1974 toll increase of 19.7% which adds at $.22 per ton .043 dollars to Panama's unrealized income. All calculations are based on tonnage for the various years within subperiods.
b. Ratio of Share of Annuity.
c. Assumes inelastic demand in aggregate, i.e., total tonnage on canal routes unchanged, as estimated by Panama Canal Company consultants.

proposal, the Panamanian share could have been at least ten times the annuity actually received. Our estimate for unrealized foreign exchange since 1967 is at least as large as the aggregate Canal Zone private sector spending for goods and services in Panama.

Again considering the 1967 to 1974 period, if we assume toll increases of 50% and 150% possible, foreign exchange receipts would have increased by $265.3 million or $457.6 million, respectively. The negotiation costs, of course, remain the same; only the magnitude of foreign exchange unrealized increases. These magnitudes are clearly nontrivial. $265.3 million is 19% of all foreign exchange income originating in the Canal Zone and 3% of total Panamanian Gross Domestic Product over the period. It could have been the second most important source of Canal Zone income to Panama—right behind wages and salaries paid Panamanians working in the Canal Zone. Thus, Panama's inability to set competitive tolls has increased the size of foreign

TABLE 6
Unrealized Foreign Exchange under "Equal Partner" Arrangement for Various Periods
(in millions of dollars)

ARRANGEMENT	1965–74	1967–74	1970–74
Annuity	$ 19.5	$ 15.7	$ 10.0
Current Tolls[a]			
50% Share	451.9	384.7	260.0
Ratio[b]	23.2	24.5	26.1
Foreign Exchange Unrealized	432.4	369.0	250.6
50% Increase in Tolls[c]			
Share	677.85	577.05	390.9
Foreign Exchange Unrealized	658.35	561.35	380.9
150% Increase in Tolls[c]			
Share	1,129.75	961.75	651.6
Foreign Exchange Unrealized	1,110.25	946.05	641.5

SOURCE: Panama Canal Company, Annual Reports, 1965-1974.
a. Account is also taken of the 1974 toll increase of 19.7%. All calculations are based on tonnage for the various years within subperiods.
b. Ratio of Share to Annuity.
c. Assumes inelastic demand in aggregate, i.e., total tonnage on canal routes unchanged as estimated by Panama Canal Company consultants.

exchange foregone to amounts 16.2 or 28.2 times the annuity actually paid.

In a sense, there are large opportunity costs to extended treaty negotiations as demonstrated by the calculations set out in Table 5. However, if the delay incurred is to achieve a more equal partnership, then this transaction cost must be taken into account when pursuing other assumed attractive potential arrangements. If alternative strategies are likely to lead to benefits of the magnitude shown in Table 6, then Panama is clearly better off to have rejected the earlier proposal. If Panama were a 50% equal partner, under existing toll arrangements an additional $369.0 million in income would have flowed into Panama during the 1967 to 1974 period. This amount is 115% *more* than the $171.6 million in foreign exchange unrealized under the $0.17 per ton arrangement. At the higher tolls, unrealized income is as large as the Gross Domestic Product of the republic, again illustrating the magnitude of benefit lost as a result of the lack of full Panamanian participation in the Canal.

Comparing Table 6 with Table 5, some insight regarding Panamanian aspirations from treaty negotiation is possible. It would make economic sense to reject $171.6 million in 1967 if three years later $250.6 million (instead of $114.3 million) were to be realized. Which is larger in real terms would, of course, depend upon the rate of discount chosen, although time preferences (in the economic sense) do not seem to be an important consideration in negotiations such as these.

Conclusion

Although the future course of treaty negotiations is uncertain, particularly now that there has been a change in the presidency of the United States, the present situation cannot continue indefinitely. A more equitable and reasonable arrangement is required to avert any potential violence or damage to the Canal and to avoid any further erosion in U.S.-Latin American relations. In a political and diplomatic sense, the lack of a timely agreement could prove costly to the United States.

The "equal partner" assumption, although short of nationalization and complete Panamanian ownership, more accurately reflects the essence of the present negotiations.[10] For a small country, negotiation costs of the magnitude discussed pose a significant burden on economic development objectives. The multiplier effects of foreign exchange influence the direction of economic growth. As the unrealized benefits over the years 1967 to 1974 would be in direct payments to the Panamanian treasury, actual "free" foreign exchange of $172 million consists of the basic subsidy to the rest of the world. Had a reasonable price increase of 50% been in effect and Panama accepted the proposed treaty in 1967, income to the republic would have increased by $226 million. As an equal partner, Panama could have earned another $561 million in foreign exchange. Unfortunately, waiting for a better deal is costly. As there are no clear signals to suggest that a resolution is near, Panama will continue to pay an economic opportunity cost it can ill afford.

NOTES

1. The original treaty granted the U.S. rights over the Canal Zone "in perpetuity" as if it were sovereign. For $10 million and an annuity of $250,000 the United States retained all "rights, power, and authority" to "construct, maintain, operate and protect" this ten-mile wide piece of territory.

2. There are eight principles which bind the governments of the United States and Panama in current negotiations. Principle 5 which suggests that "Panama shall have a just and equitable share of the benefits derived from . . . the canal" is the most relevant in this context. I will, however, make available to the interested reader a copy of these principles on request.

3. Recent political developments in the United States further frustrate Panamanians. Mr. Reagan, as a candidate for the presidency of the United States, tried to utilize the Panama Canal negotiations to further his personal ambitions by terming U.S. policy a "giveaway." See Robert Keatley, "The Big Flap Over the Canal," Wall Street Journal, April 29, 1976.

4. The 1936 agreements restored the real value of the annuity to Panama by increasing the nominal amount of $430,000. Token economic concessions were made regarding the supply of goods and services as well as the elimination of outdated U.S. interference rights in Panama. The 1955 treaty resulted in an increase of $1.5 million and the start of significant factor benefits to a special group of Panamanians living and working in the Zone. Payments are currently over $2 million per annum as the dollar has been devalued slightly.

5. Less important in previous years of "perpetual" rule, but not a matter of policy is the recapturing of *all* U.S. investment in the Canal.

6. Since all other sources of Panamanian income would have to be paid regardless of arrangement, the annuity becomes a crucial issue in negotiations.

7. Although the recent toll increase is partially based on depreciation expenses, the Panama Canal Company has been lobbying for another toll increase presumably to offset increased operating costs and some trade diversion, although revenues have continued to increase. As to the 150% toll increase, it is presented more to provide a basis for inferences regarding the size of any uncapitalized money income subsidy implicit in a low toll policy. We do not believe other routes and time costs are that uncompetitive in the long run.

8. In general, if demand is inelastic, as may be the case in the short run, overall revenues should rise. Over the long run, demand is certainly more elastic as substitute routes become more attractive. Although we do not consider these issues directly, our examination of reports of Panama Canal studies suggest that the inelastic demand assumption is reasonable. See the report performed by Dr. Leo Cole, entitled "Economic Ramifications of Future Panama Canal Control and Use," for the Congressional Research Service as requested by Congressman John McFall for the House Appropriations Committee dated April 3, 1975 (in U.S. House of Representatives, 1974: 66-79).

9. These years are important over the negotiation period. In 1970, the draft treaty was finally rejected by the Panamanian National Assembly after negotiators finished their three year effort in 1967. The magnitudes indicated would, of course, be large if compounded at some opportunity cost of capital.

10. Negotiations will probably be in two steps. The U.S. and Panama will be "partners" over some fixed period of time. At the end of this period, full control will be returned to Panama perhaps with residual military rights going to the United States.

REFERENCES

Atlantic Pacific Interoceanic Canal Study Commission (1970) Interoceanic Canal Studies. Washington, D.C.

BLANCO, B. (1971) "El Canal de Panama en la Economia Norte-americana." Anales de Ciencias Humanas 1 (December): 17-28.

BUNKER, E. (1975) "The Panama Canal negotiations: popular myths and political realities." Department of State Bull. 73 (December): 881-885.

——— (1974) "Panama and the United States: a design for partnership." Department of State Bull. (April): 453-457.

BURNS, E. (1974) "Panama's struggle for independence." Current History 26 (January): 19-22, 38.

Economic Commission for Latin America [Mexico Office] (1972) The Economy of Panama and the Canal Zone (2 Vols.) Mexico: Cepal/Mex/72/28/rev. 1.

LOPEZ GUEVARA, C. (1976) "Negotiating for a peaceful solution of the Panama Canal question." Presented to the Sixth Annual Meeting of the Latin American Studies Association, Atlanta.

U.S. Department of State (1974) "Developments in U.S. relations with Panama 1903 to the present: a chronology." Department of State Bull. 70 (April): 430-435.

U.S. House of Representatives, Committee on Appropriations, 88th Congress, 1st Session (1973) Public Work Appropriations for 1964. Washington, D.C.: Government Printing Office.

U.S. House of Representatives, Committee on Appropriations, 93rd Congress, 2nd Session (1974) Department of Transportation and Related Agencies Appropriations for 1975, Part 4. Washington, D.C.: Government Printing Office.

U.S. House of Representatives, Committee on Appropriations, 94th Congress, 1st Session (1975) Department of Transportation and Related Agencies Appropriations for 1976, Part 4. Washington, D.C.: Government Printing Office.

U.N. Statistical Office (1975) Yearbook of National Accounts Statistics, 1973, Vol. 2. New York: United Nations.

Alfred E. Osborne, Jr., is an Assistant Professor of Management at UCLA. A native of Panama, Osborne has lectured extensively on the Panama Canal question and is currently studying the economics of the Canal for the economy of Panama. He has authored several monographs and articles in scholarly journals and has traveled widely in Latin America.

MERILEE S. GRINDLE
Department of Political Science
Wellesley College
Wellesley, MA 02181

POLICY CHANGE IN AN AUTHORITARIAN REGIME
Mexico Under Echeverría

The six-year presidency or *sexenio* of Luís Echeverría Alvarez was initiated in December of 1970. Six years later, significant changes had taken place in the public policies espoused by the Mexican regime.[1] Most importantly, perhaps, the federal government shifted its public investment priorities away from an overriding preoccupation with industrial development toward greater concern for agricultural development. From 1971 to 1976, Echeverría's administration allocated more money to the agricultural sector than any sexenio since that of Miguel Alemán (1946 to 1952). The change occurred gradually, federal public investment in agriculture growing from 14.5% of the total in 1971 to 20% budgeted for 1975 and 1976. Increased attention to agriculture was achieved primarily through proportional reductions in investments for industrial and infrastructure development. Along with a revision in sectoral allocations went a change in policy concerning both the anticipated outcome and the target

AUTHOR'S NOTE: Field work for this article was made possible by a fellowship granted by the Social Science Research Council and the American Council of Learned Societies.

Journal of Interamerican Studies and World Affairs, Vol. 19 No. 4, November 1977

TABLE 1
Average Public Sector Investment Percentages
by Presidential Period, 1925-1974

Years	President	No. of Years in Aver-age	Indus-try	Commu-nica-tions/ Trans-port.	Agri-culture For-estry	Social Welfare
1925-28	Calles	4	----*	79.1%	15.1%	5.8%
1929	Portes Gil	1	----	73.5	10.2	16.3
1930-32	Ortiz Rubio	3	----	76.6	11.5	11.9
1933-34	Rodríguez	1	----	75.9	11.0	13.1
1935-40	Cárdenas	6	5.1%	66.3	18.1	9.6
1941-46	Avila Camacho	6	10.6	59.1	16.9	11.6
1947-52	Alemán	6	22.0	43.0	20.1	13.6
1953-58	Ruiz Cortínez	6	32.4	37.2	14.9	13.8
1959-64	López Mateos	6	34.6	29.9	9.8	22.4
1965-70	Díaz Ordaz	6	40.3	22.4	10.5	24.7
1971-74	Echeverría	4	35.5	24.1	15.4	25.0

*Zero or less than .5%.
SOURCE: Wilkie (1974); Banco de México, various issues.

population for agricultural investment. Large-scale commercial agriculture producing crops for an export market was given second place to production of food to meet domestic needs. This focused attention on Mexico's peasant population, much of which is oriented to subsistence farming and which has been largely ignored by official policy since the 1940s.

Changes in public policy such as this Mexican example provide a useful means for investigating the dynamics of governmental decision making. Albert Hirschman (1963: ch. 4) has suggested a number of provocative hypotheses about how policy change comes about and how decision makers can attempt to manage the introduction of reform-oriented development strategies. His three case studies, however endemic the condition, deal with situations of violence or crisis which bring development problems to the attention of decision makers and impel them to seek new plans and programs in response to important national problems (see also Collier, 1976). In contrast, policies introduced under noncrisis conditions, such as the rural development strategy that emerged under Echeverría, may be more valid indicators of both influences and constraints on the policy process and they may, therefore, provide insight into the more normal, day to day functioning of the political system itself.

This case study of the formulation of a rural development policy analyzes conditions surrounding changes in development strategy in an authoritarian regime under noncrisis, business as usual conditions. The choice of rural development under Echeverría is particularly appropriate because it involved a major shift in overall national policy. The strategy that was developed during his administration was the result of a conscious attempt on the part of the governing elite to reorient the trajectory of Mexican development. As such, it provides an example of the "contriving of reform" by political and administrative officials. In addition, the example of policy change under Echeverría is suggestive because Mexico has come to be regarded as a stable authoritarian regime (see Hansen, 1971; Purcell, 1973; Reyna, 1976; Stevens, 1974). In authoritarian regimes, the factors that influence decision makers and the style of the decisional system itself are considered to differ from nonauthoritarian systems (see Linz, 1970; Malloy, 1977; O'Donnell, 1973). The label seems to be appropriate to the policy process in Mexico. There is, for example, a characteristic pattern in which the president is the key figure in initiating interest in a policy area and mobilizing bureaucratic support for it. Moreover, there is a noticeable lack of public demand or open debate about policy content during the planning phase. In general, policy making in Mexico is an intrabureaucratic process which is clearly demarcated by the sexennial change of administrations. This pattern of decision-making is similar to the authoritarian model developed by Linz and others.

The following study is based on field research conducted in Mexico in 1974 and 1975 (see Grindle, 1977). At that time, 97 government officials and other informants, most of whom were employees of Mexico's agricultural marketing agency, were interviewed about their perceptions of the problems of agriculture, their roles in the planning process, and their knowledge about the overall development of the policy.[2] In the following pages, the effect of the sexenio on the behavior of government officials is briefly described. Then, the reasons why President Echeverría and his advisors became concerned with rural development will be discussed. The response of the bureaucratic apparatus to his policy interests and the management of opposition will also be considered. In the final portion of the article, the case study is evaluated in terms of what it reveals about policy change and stability in Mexico's dominant party authoritarian regime.

Rural Development: The Emergence of A Policy

Important shifts in public policy in Mexico generally coincide with changes of administration. Even though all presidents are elected from the dominant party, the PRI, each president, upon assuming office, sets objectives and policies for his administration which may differ from those of his predecessor. Thus, a change of government policy was clear between the Díaz Ordaz administration (1964 to 1970) and that of Echeverría (1970 to 1976), and between Echeverría and his successor, López Portillo (1976 to 1982). The Díaz Ordaz period, for example, was noted for its conservative, private sector oriented policies and its use of repression as a response to attempts to expand participation in the political system. Under Echeverría, on the other hand, more redistributive policies were stressed, the rural sector became a more important target for government programs, and the president attempted to secure the support of students and intellectuals (see Purcell, 1976). Under López Portillo, a return to more conservative and probusiness policies is evident (see, for statements of policy, Banco de México, 1976: 346, 384-385; Latin America Political Report, 1976: 381, 1977: 42; Latin America Special Report on Mexico, 1977).

With remarkable consistency, the large bureaucratic apparatus accepts and pursues the policy preferences of each new administration. Its responsiveness is in part a reflection of the extensive turnover of personnel that accompanies the new president into office. At the beginning of each sexenio, ministries and agencies are taken over by completely different administrators at both middle and high levels; virtually all those with decision-making authority are newly appointed, and while many have served in the government previously, they are generally newcomers to their current posts. Many of the officials, especially at high levels, are directly appointed by the president because of their past services on his behalf.[3] The control of the president over the career trajectories of his subordinates is particularly important in explaining their sensitivity to his priorities. As summarized by one high level official, it provides him with a very effective tool.

> The president's power to gain compliance with his policies from the various agencies of the government resides in the very instruments available to him through the political system. That is, they comply because of the possibility of upward political mobility within the system or because of fear of falling in political disfavor.

This resource of the president, should he choose to exert it in favor of a particular policy option, gives him a considerable capacity to counteract the constituent, professional, and bureaucratic groups which may attempt to influence individual agencies in favor of policies that diverge from his.[4] In addition, generally at the ministry or agency level, the top official—the minister or director—has enormous influence over recruitment and careers within the organization.

Thus, it is not surprising that when an administration takes office in Mexico, bureaucratic corridors hum with activity as newly appointed officials set about analyzing the policies, budgets, and programs of the agencies they have been selected to head (see Saldaña Harlow, 1974: 13-15). In fact, the entire first year of each administration is largely given over to planning and assessment. Much of the analysis, and the reorganizations and policy reformulations which follow it, indicate a need to stamp government agencies with the perspectives of the new administration. In addition, it provides officials with an opportunity to test new theories and to develop new solutions to economic and social problems. When it became clear that Echeverría was concerned with the problems of rural Mexico, for example, his subordinates were quick to acquire an interest in rural development, to explore explanations for the failure of this sector to grow in relation to other sectors of the economy, and then to define programs for their agencies in accordance with the new policy priority.

Official Interest in the Rural Sector

When President Echeverría assumed command of the vast bureaucratic and political apparatus which is the Mexican government, he had already expressed considerable concern about rates of agricultural production in the country. He had also indicated his feeling that conditions of life in rural areas were a threat to the country's future economic development and political stability. His presidential campaign had been marked by repeated statements about the role of the rural sector in Mexico's future (see Banco de México, 1971: 6; New York Times, November 17, 1969: 11). He emphasized that private and public investment was needed for the country to raise its agricultural productivity, especially in basic food crops. In addition, he spoke in favor of government programs that would be aimed at alleviating some of the great inequities in the distribution of income in

TABLE 2
Average Annual Growth Rates,
Mexico, 1940-1970

	1940-50	1950-60	1960-70	1965-70
Gross Domestic Product	6.7%	5.8%	7.1%	7.1%
Population	2.8	3.1	3.5	3.5
Per Capita Product	3.9	2.7	3.6	3.6
Agricultural Production	8.2	4.3	3.6	2.2
Manufacturing Production	8.1	7.3	8.9	9.0

SOURCE: 1940-1960, Hansen (1971: 42); Banco Nacional de Comercio Exterior (1971: 35).

the country. In his inaugural address, the president proclaimed his intent "to make the more fortunate groups and regions contribute to the development of the less fortunate" (Banco de México, 1971: 8; see also Banco Nacional de Comercio Exterior, 1970). Greater attention to rural areas, he claimed, would be an indispensable part of his administration's goals of increasing employment opportunities, productivity levels, and the size of the internal consumer market. His desire to ameliorate problems in the agricultural sector, he pointed out often, did not include a major emphasis on land distribution; the "first phase" of the agrarian reform of the Revolution of 1910 was really over, he proclaimed.

A number of factors are important in explaining Echeverría's interest in the agricultural sector. He was aware, as were others in the government, that agriculture was the most undynamic sector of the economy. In official policy statements of the new administration, it was stressed that the primary sector had failed to expand adequately (Banco Nacional de Comercio Exterior, 1971). Industrial sector growth, it was pointed out, rose by 8.1% per year in the three decades after 1940, while the comparable figure in agriculture was 5.4%. Of greater concern, growth rates in industry were accelerating, while those in agricul-

TABLE 3
Industrial Origin of Gross Domestic Product,
Mexico, 1960-1973
(constant 1960 prices)

	1960	1970	1973*
Agriculture, forestry, fishing, hunting	15.9%	11.5%	10.6%
Mining and quarrying	1.5	1.0	0.9
Petroleum and basic petrochemicals	3.4	4.2	4.2
Manufacturing	19.2	22.4	23.1
Construction	4.1	4.6	5.0
Electricity, gas and water	1.0	1.9	2.0
Transportation, storage and communication	3.3	3.1	3.5
Wholesale and retail trade	31.2	32.7	31.7
Public administration and defense	4.9	5.7	6.2
Other services	15.5	12.9	12.8
	100.0%	100.0%	100.0%
Gross Domestic Product	150.2	300.8	354.2

*Estimated
SOURCE: The Economist Intelligence Unit, *Annual Summary* (various years).

ture were declining. Between 1940 and 1950, annual growth rates in the primary sector had been 8.2%; by the 1960s, the rate was 3.6%, barely keeping pace with the country's population growth, and it declined especially rapidly in the late 1960s (Banco Nacional de Comercio Exterior, 1971: 35: Gollás and García Rocha, 1976: 419-424). This compared unfavorably with a rate of 8.9% during the decade of the 1960s in the industrial sector. Agricultural activities declined from contributing 16% of the gross domestic product in 1960 to providing only 11.5% in 1970 (Economist Intelligence Unit, various years).

As a result of declining agricultural productivity, the 1960s were also witness to the increase in Mexico's dependence on imports of food for domestic consumption. Table 4 indicates that

TABLE 4
Net Exports of Basic Agricultural Commodities,
Mexico, 1965-1971 (tons)

	Corn	Wheat	Beans	Rice	Milk
1965	1,469,377	751,369	17,960	(-15,703)	(-17,132)
1966	932,902	51,494	111,968	(-12,667)	(-18,975)
1967	1,374,006	233,633	61,660	(-36)	(-26,186)
1968	895,770	(-225)	77,621	14,603	(-34,256)
1969	779,861	247,310	53,118	(-4,945)	(-41,542)
1970	(-760,758)	29,810	2,469	(-16,388)	(-48,979)
1971	285,429	(-167,496)	(-499)	(-881)	(-51,944)

NOTE: Negative figures denote net imports.
SOURCE: 1965-1970, computed from Banco Nacional de Comercio Exterior, *Anuario Estadístico*; 1971, calculated from Secretaría de Industria y Comercio, *Anuario Estadístico del Comercio Exterior* (1971).

between 1965 and 1971 the country became a net importer of basic foodstuffs. Particularly upsetting to officials was the need in 1970 to import corn, a staple of the Mexican diet, for the first time since the 1960s. Informants repeatedly stressed the government's conviction that Mexico, with a large portion of its population engaged in agriculture, should be self-sufficient in basic foodstuffs (see also Banco de México, 1976: 114). This was important to Mexican policy makers in 1970 because figures indicated that the country was becoming increasingly dependent on the United States, where most of its imports originated, and was confronting higher and higher trade imbalances in the world market, in spite of the steady strides it had made toward economic development.

Echeverría was also sensitive to the problems of rural areas because of the potential for political unrest engendered by inequities in the distribution of wealth in the country. Rhetorically committed since the Revolution to the political and economic improvement of the underclasses, the Mexican regime has

TABLE 5
Foreign Trade Balance,
Mexico, 1964-1973
(millions of dollars)

Year	Exports	Imports	Balance of Trade	Exports as Percentage of Imports
1964	1,023.9	1,475.9	-457.0	69.4%
1965	1,113.9	1,559.6	-445.7	70.8
1966	1,185.6	1,608.6	-423.0	73.7
1967	1,103.8	1,745.8	-642.0	63.2
1968	1,180.7	1,960.1	-779.4	60.2
1969	1,285.0	2,078.0	-693.0	66.6
1970	1,372.9	2,460.8	-1,087.9	57.0
1971	1,474.5	2,407.3	-932.8	61.2
1972	1,813.7	2,936.8	-1,124.5	61.7
1973	2,452.0	4,145.8	-1,693.8	59.1
1974	2,850.0	6,057.0	-3,207.0	47.1
1975	2,859.0	6,580.0	-3,720.0	43.4

SOURCE: Economist Intelligence Unit, *Annual Summary* (various issues).

actually pursued policies that have encouraged the concentration of wealth in middle and upper income groups (see Hansen, 1971: 72-77; Navarrete, 1970; Prieto Vazquez, 1969; Tello, 1971). In

TABLE 6
Economically Active Population* by Sectors, Mexico

	1940	1950	1960	1970
Agriculture	65.4%	58.3%	54.2%	39.5%
Industry	12.7	16.0	19.0	23.0
Services	21.9	25.7	26.8	37.5

*Twelve years of age and older.
SOURCE: Mexico, *IX Censo de Población* (1970).

TABLE 7
Average Monthly Income Distribution*,
Mexico, 1970

Monthly Earnings	Agriculture	Industry	Services
Less than 500 pesos ($40)	77.2%	17.5%	30.0%
500-999 pesos ($40-$80)	16.8	44.7	29.7
1000-1499 pesos ($80-$120)	2.5	17.6	17.8
1500-2499 pesos ($120-$200)	1.5	10.9	11.9
2500 pesos and more ($200)	2.0	9.3	10.6
	100.0%	100.0%	100.0%

*Economically Active Population, twelve years or older.
SOURCE: Calculated from Mexico, *IX Censo de Población* (1970).

rural areas, where 42.3% of the population lived in 1970, the extent of the poverty and inequity was especially apparent. In spite of a long term decline in the number of Mexicans employed in agriculture, in 1970 close to 40% of the economically active were engaged in such pursuits—more than five million people. Over three fourths of these workers earned less than $40 a month, a figure which stood in great contrast to comparable proportions in the industrial and service sectors (see Tables 6 and 7).

Respondents indicated that Echeverría was particularly aware of the political problems that might result from the increasing gaps in income distribution in the country and the need to do something to curtail Mexico's high rate of rural to urban migration. During the Díaz Ordaz administration, Echeverría had served as Minister of the Interior and was aware, as the general public frequently was not, of the extent of rural unrest, guerrilla movements, and land invasions, and the threat these posed to the tranquility of the political regime. One informant stressed the president's perspective in the following manner.

> The President, when he was Minister of the Interior, must have seen a great many things which made him realize that the lid was not on so tight and that the apparent peace, especially in the

> rural areas, was not so deep as many believed. He seemed to realize that the very stability of the country depended on some redistribution of welfare and resources.

In addition, in accordance with a precedent set by Lázaro Cárdenas in the presidential campaign of 1933 to 1934, candidate Echeverría visited numerous rural communities where he was confronted with the dismal facts of poverty, ill health, illiteracy, and insecurity that are conditions of life to Mexico's peasants (see Turner, 1973: 153-154).

The president's evident concern for agricultural productivity and greater economic equity was sufficient encouragement for the officials he had just appointed to begin to study and evaluate these problems; his control over the career futures of individuals and the fortunes of public agencies made it advantageous for high level officials to respond to his policy interests. But while the president's concern indicated where policy makers in relevant agencies and ministries should focus their attention, it offered no ready solutions to the problem of the stagnation of the agricultural sector. In 1971 and 1972, however, policy making officials were influenced in their search for answers by a critique of the country's overall strategy for development and the explanation it provided for the underdevelopment of agriculture.

The Critique of "Developmentalism"

The Echeverría administration did not "discover" the unhealthy state of Mexico's economic affairs in late 1970. The problems of economic development faced by the country had become apparent to some economists during the late 1960s and had been studied by some government officials at that time. During the final years of the Díaz Ordaz administration (1964 to 1970), concerned officials from various agencies of the government discussed them in specially formed committees. Through their meetings, a number of individuals who would later become high level advisors to Echeverría became aware of critiques of Mexico's economic development that were being produced and discussed among intellectuals at that time. They were especially influenced by the work of Leopoldo Solís, who became a top level planner in the Ministry of the Presidency in the new administration (see, for example, Solís, 1971). Echeverría's future Minister of Finance and top officials in the Ministry of Agrarian Reform, along with the closest aides of these administrators were others who had been exposed to such ideas.[5]

As a result of their study and their experience in government, many of these officials accepted the idea that current economic problems were a result of the "developmentalist" policy pursued by administrations since the 1940s. "Developmentalism" referred to a strategy of industrialization based on import substitution (ISI) followed by the Mexican and other Latin American regimes. Pursuit of ISI policies had a strong relationship to agricultural problems, the critique pointed out, because it entailed the promotion of export-oriented agriculture to earn foreign exchange necessary to promote greater industrial development. This evaluation of "developmentalism" drew attention to the exploitation of agriculture, to the inequities in the distribution of wealth, and to the economic dependency which were a result of the import substituting policies (see, for recent examples, Gollás and García Rocha, 1976; Ibarra, 1973; and for another perspective, Hirschman, 1971; Pellicer de Brody, 1974; Wionczek, 1973). This, the critics claimed, was hardly a path to true development and could only entail greater balance of payments deficits and a constricted internal market (see Reyes Osorio and Eckstein, 1971).

Government officials also increased their understanding of the role of the agricultural sector in Mexico's economic development by studying the work of a number of scholars at the Centro de Investigaciones Agrarias.[6] These analysts stated clearly that the rural population and the country's economy were harmed by policies that encouraged only the production of crops for export. Commercial agriculture, through the use of modern technology, was developing in some sections of the country while other areas, involved in the production of crops for domestic consumption, were subjected to deprivation and increasing stagnation (see Centro de Investigaciones Agrarias, 1974; Reyes Osorio and Eckstein, 1971). In accordance with the priorities of ISI, public resources in previous administrations had been concentrated in zones that promised high returns on export crops such as coffee, sugar, cotton, wheat, fruit, and vegetables (see Barkin, 1970; Carlos, 1974; Gollás and García Rocha, 1976: 416-417). Regions which were not relevant to the development of large scale commercial agriculture for export markets were largely forgotten when public funds were allocated. In these disadvantaged regions, unemployment and underemployment were thought to be the source of the high rate of rural to urban migration that was causing grave concern among government officials (see Reyes Osorio and Eckstein, 1971).

Prior to 1971, however, there was little high level attention given to these studies and analyses. For example, one official recalled about the study groups of middle level administrators that met in the late 1960s, "I suspect the President did not even know they existed." But with the inauguration of the Echeverría administration in late 1970, rural development and the need to emphasize the agricultural sector in economic development were ideas that came into their own and acquired high level support. The change in the government's policies that occurred after 1970 can be considered a result of political interest in a problem for which a technical evaluation existed, as described by one informant.

> I think the present government was almost forced, because of economic conditions, to take new postures toward agriculture. Above all it was the fact of having to import corn—corn is religion, it's culture, it's economics, it's life, it's art in Mexico—which really brought things to the attention of the President and others. Simultaneously there was also a technical analysis which pointed up the problems of agriculture at the time; but technical dictates were not what *caused* the policy; circumstances did that. Before

that, no one really paid any attention to the *técnicos* and their proposals.

Thus, as a consequence of the research and study into the impact of previous policies, it was becoming accepted by a number of government officials that stimulating the agricultural sector would be the key to further economic development in the country. In addition, however, policy makers were also becoming convinced that growth in agricultural production and rural development were not synonymous terms. One informant expressed their doubts in the following terms.

> There is a tendency to identify development with indicators of productivity and therefore to think that development is occurring when actually it isn't. Increased production does not mean development when it occurs at the expense of an ever increasing marginalization of certain sectors of the population and an increasing rate of disequilibrium [in the economy].

Acceptance of the "Structural Barriers" Model of Subsistence Agriculture

Therefore, when government officials responsible for rural areas began to think how increased resources for the agricultural sector should be planned and allocated, they were led to focus on the subsistence sector and its role in national development. In a number of agencies, such as CONASUPO (the agricultural marketing agency), the Ministry of Water Resources, the Ministry of the Presidency, and the Ministry of Agrarian Reform, technical planning departments centered their studies on peasant agriculture. It was this subsistence sector that was responsible for producing the major part of crops such as corn, beans, and rice for domestic consumption and increased investment directed toward it would be important in increasing production of them and in expanding the size of the consumer market by providing peasants with larger incomes. The question that had to be addressed was how increased investment in this sector should be organized and allocated.

There was evidence to suggest that the peasant sector was actually becoming increasingly oriented to subsistence agriculture. This seemed to be a consequence of government policies that maintained food prices at an artificially low level in order to stimulate urban and industrial growth (see Fernández y Fernández and Acosta, 1961; Banco de México, 1975).[7] Because of a steadily rising cost of living, peasants earned less and less from their agricultural labors when they exchanged market crops for the goods and services they needed to survive—health care, medicines, food, transportation, clothes, farm implements, credit, and the like. Instead, it seemed that increasing numbers of peasants were planting crops only for their own consumption and then expending their remaining energy working in nearby urban areas. Alternatively, many peasants were abandoning agriculture altogether and seeking work in the labor markets of Mexico City, Guadalajara, Monterrey, and the United States.[8]

The solution to this problem of the disincentives for market oriented production among peasants was not to direct more money, education, and technology toward the subsistence sector, officials believed. Many became convinced that there were structural barriers to the development of peasant agriculture that could not be alleviated by direct infusions of money and modern farming methods. They believed instead that the peasants were regularly exploited when they became involved in dealings in the national economy because of their lack of economic and political resources. Thus, for instance, although a particular peasant might produce a surplus, he would not be able to invest it in increased productivity because the surplus he might generate would end up in the hands of middlemen—storeowners, truckers, economic bosses, crop buyers, large landowners, and other intermediaries—who could take advantage of the peasant's weak bargaining position (see Instituto de Investigaciones Sociales, 1975). According to this analysis developed by Mexican policy makers, the structure of rural economic relationships was, therefore, the main factor keeping the peasant from becoming a modern commercial farmer, not his traditional culture or his level of technology.

This perspective on the dynamics of agricultural development in the subsistence sector was a significant departure from the prevailing explanations on which previous policies had been based. By defining agricultural development solely in terms of increased production, the Mexican government had long sought to stimulate production through a variety of programs directed at large, efficient production units. For example, in the period after 1940, much government money was devoted to the construction of sizeable infrastructure programs like transportation networks and major irrigation facilities; credit was extended to those who could provide impressive collateral and prove their efficiency; the adoption of highly developed technology was encouraged; export crops were emphasized; a number of large river basin projects were funded; and regions with high output potential received priority (see Barkin, 1970; Carlos, 1974; Centro de Investigaciones Agrarias, 1974; Ibarra, 1973). The results of these policies, however, had not "trickled down" to the subsistence sector. They did not benefit traditional agriculture, many government officials thought, because they did not alter the impact of market forces and middlemen on the subsistence sector.

Policy makers in several government agencies under Echeverría proposed a different solution to this problem. The peasant must be allowed and encouraged to improve his bargaining position in the national economy and to invest in expanding production of domestically consumed crops. In 1971 and 1972, officials argued that the national government should pursue a vigorous policy of intervention in the rural sector to break the hold of intermediaries on the peasant economy and to encourage the subsistence sector to grow more food. This implied that attention to the subsistence sector would have to proceed on a variety of fronts at the same time—offering credit, improved marketing facilities, high support prices, production inputs, education, health and welfare services, consumer aid, small scale irrigation works, local roads, transportation facilities, and so on —all concerted in an effort to break the hold of economic intermediaries on the peasant economy. In order for this approach to agricultural and rural development to have any future, however, policy makers who were committed to a new perspective on Mexico's development were aware that it was imperative that the president be as committed to it as they were. He must, therefore, be encouraged to throw his impressive power behind an initiative for greater sectoral planning.

Response to the New Policy

The means used to convince the president of a new approach to rural development relied heavily on personal and individual contacts with Echeverría by ministry and agency heads and their top level planners. Committed policy makers in CONASUPO, the Ministry of the Presidency, the Water Resources Ministry, and the Finance Ministry used the analysis of traditional and commercial agricultural sectors as a basis for designing comprehensive programs for their organizations and then presented these proposals to the president in formal and informal meetings. Generally, they emphasized the need to channel more resources to subsistence agriculture and to coordinate government investments more fully through effective sectoral planning. According to informants, the Minister of the Presidency, a close friend and influential advisor to Echeverría, was often present at the more formal presentations and added his support to the new approaches proposed. At the same time, the Ministry of Finance was developing measures for the disbursement of funds to government agencies which would encourage greater coordination and cooperation among them. Policy makers attempting to influence the president were successful in establishing an image of socially concerned technocrats, one to which Echeverría was sensitive, and this also helped them to carry the day with him.

Through their efforts, he became committed to supporting a new approach to agricultural development.

As a result of his conversion, Echeverría established the Agricultural Sector Planning Committee (COCOSA) in February of 1973. Its chairman was to be the Minister of the Presidency, and its membership would consist of eighteen government agencies with major operational responsibilities in the rural sector. Important among these were the Ministry of Agriculture (SAG), the Ministry of Agrarian Reform (SRA), the Ministry of Water Resources (SRH), CONASUPO (the marketing agency), and the Ministries of the Presidency and Finance.[9] But enthusiasm to collaborate in the COCOSA effort was not unanimously forthcoming from all of these organizations. Informants involved in this planning indicated that each of the government agencies arrived at independent evaluations of the advisability of cooperating with the initiative. Especially for the top level administrators, career aspirations and the aquisition of resources were centrally important factors in calculating the rationale of supporting efforts at sectoral planning.

The Ministry of Agriculture, SAG, was among the most reluctant of the government agencies to cooperate willingly. With a multitude of different programs and a fragmented organizational structure, SAG was considered by many government officials to be unable to carry out its responsibilities in rural areas effectively, especially where the subsistence sector was concerned. Its operational problems were in part responsible for the decrease in SAG's proportion of the agricultural budget that it received each year. Ministry officials themselves seemed aware that cooperating with COCOSA would make the agency more vulnerable to attack from other government organizations by making its performance record more public and open to scrutiny. They sensed that this might easily result in further budgetary reductions. Moreover, the Minister of Agriculture was not one of the serious contenders for the presidency in 1976, and, therefore, he had less need than other officials to curry favor with the president who would choose his own successor in the fall of

1975. Even if he had such aspirations, there was little to be gained from enabling "outsiders" to have a closer look at SAG's performance and in integrating its responsibilities with the programs and timetables of other agencies.

The resistance to planning was also a result of the ministry's perceptions of the problems of agricultural development, the training of its leadership, and its role in encouraging and supporting the development of modern commercial agriculture. SAG officials were convinced that productivity in agriculture would result from greater infusions of technology and they argued for an extension of previous development policies that had been effective in the commercial sector. Moreover, bolstering the old development policy would not require that there be a greater amount of planning and cooperation among government agencies; instead, the best results would be gained from pursuing tasks as they had been in the past and giving SAG the central role in agricultural policy making, rather than including agencies like the Ministries of the Presidency and Finance. As expressed by one high level official, SAG was of the opinion that "other agencies were attempting to invade its territory." The reluctance of this Ministry to cooperate in COCOSA persisted throughout the sexenio.

Another ministry, Agrarian Reform (SRA), was less reluctant than SAG to work through COCOSA. This agency, whose responsibilities included administering and supporting Mexico's many *ejido* communities and managing land distribution programs, was aware that increased resources for the subsistence sector would probably mean increases in its own budget. Thus, even though agency officials might be somewhat concerned that a history of bureaucratic inefficiencies and even corruption in dealing with peasant clientele groups would come under greater scrutiny, its leadership still expected to benefit from cooperation with the Coordinating Committee (see Banco de México, 1973: 74). In addition, the minister was rumored to be a serious presidential aspirant and was eager to demonstrate his loyalty and responsiveness to Echeverría.

TABLE 8
Initial Support of Agricultural Sector Planning—1973

	Ministry or Agency					
	SAG	SRH	SRA	Presidency	Finance	CONASUPO
Sectoral planning perceived to mean:						
Opportunity to acquire more resources or decisional responsibility over their allocation;	No	Yes	Yes	Yes	Yes	Yes
Opportunity to demonstrate effective agency performance;	No	Yes	No	Yes	Yes	Yes
Confirmation of agency 'ideology';	No	Yes	Yes	Yes	Yes	Yes
Career opportunities for agency leadership.	No	Yes	Yes	Yes	Yes	Yes
Supported initiative	No	Yes	Yes	Yes	Yes	Yes

Even more committed to greater coordination in the agricultural sector was the Ministry of Water Resources, SRH. Widely known as an efficient technical agency, SRH received a considerable portion of the agricultural budget and could expect to receive more if the entire sector were to acquire greater resources (see Greenberg, 1971). Top level officials in SRH and their middle level technical staffs were also of the opinion that it was necessary to channel government resources to the subsistence sector to raise productivity and to solve the problem of rural backwardness. Friendship between the Minister, the President, and the Minister of the Presidency also encouraged SRH to cooperate with COCOSA. SRH, therefore, became a strong proponent of agricultural sector planning.

Additionally championing the new rural development strategy of the government, including sectoral planning, was the agricultural marketing agency, CONASUPO. Increased price supports as well as the opportunity to offer a variety of auxiliary services through its networks of rural warehouses and retail stores would be among the benefits deriving from the new policy for this organization. Indeed, of all government agencies, CONASUPO was ideally situated to increase its resources and power within the bureaucracy when the new policy was established. From the beginning of the sexenio, the director of CONASUPO had been in the forefront of the efforts to influence the president, especially with regard to subsistence agriculture, and he was well aware that his own political future would improve along with the power and impact of the agency (see Grindle, 1977).[10]

The Ministries of Finance and the Presidency were also strongly in favor of the agricultural development strategy and the sectoral coordination it implied. Finance, for example, was concerned with ensuring that government investments were made rationally and with a view to their long term returns. Moreover, the minister was aware of his own stake in performing his job ably. As expressed by one informant,

> Some ministries are evaluated on the basis of efficiency. Finance is one of them and the Minister knows it—other ministries like SAG are not evaluated on that basis. Performance on the basis of efficiency is a stimulant to integrated planning: he's going to be evaluated on what use was made of the resources he was given.

The presidency, as Mexico's central planning agency, was influenced by much the same logic, especially so as the minister had presidential expectations himself and was eager to influence Echeverría in his choice of successor.

The president's support of a new strategy of agricultural and rural development, reflected in increased budget allocations, and the backing of many key government agencies, was sufficient to encourage officials to move ahead in pursuit of the new policy goals. They were little concerned with having to deal with opposition from groups or individuals inside or outside the government. This is of interest because the new strategy did envision a marked change in the beneficiaries of government programs in

TABLE 9

Federal Public Investment by Objective, 1970-1974
(billions of pesos)

Year	Total	Percentage Increase	Agriculture		Industry		Social Welfare		Transportation/ Communication		Administration and Defense	
			Pesos	%	Pesos	%	Pesos	%	Pesos	%	Pesos	%
1970	29.2	---	3.9	13.4%	11.1	38.0%	7.7	27.1%	5.8	19.9%	.5	1.6%
1971	22.6	-22.8%	3.3	14.5	9.3	41.3	5.1	22.5	4.6	20.3	.3	1.4
1972	34.7	53.8	4.9	14.3	11.4	33.1	9.2	26.5	7.9	22.7	1.2	3.4
1973	49.8	43.6	7.0	14.2	16.2	32.5	13.1	26.2	12.7	25.4	1.6	1.7
1974*	66.4	---	11.5	17.3	21.2	31.9	14.8	22.3	17.4	26.3	1.4	2.2

*1974 reflect amounts authorized for spending. Generally, authorized funds in Mexico are 5% to 10% higher than amounts actually spent. See Wilkie (1967).
SOURCE: Banco de Mexico (various issues).

the rural areas and this might have been expected to engender the opposition of those who stood to loose by it. Several characteristics of the policy making process minimized such reactions, however.[11] For one thing, budgetary allocations to agricultural agencies were increased, and thus their proportional "take" of government investments, without decreasing the absolute amounts directed to other public sector efforts. As indicated in Table 9, those sectors of the budget with no direct input into agriculture did not suffer declines in the amount of funds they received, except in the case of administration and defense. While percentages may have dropped, absolute funding increased enough to offset even the effects of growing inflation in the early 1970s. This budgetary manipulation, along with the president's evident commitment to the policy, helped inhibit bureaucratic opposition to the policy.

Nongovernmental opposition was also muted and the activities of Echeverría were important in creating this situation. During his campaign for the presidency, he had indicated that the problems of agricultural productivity and inequity in rural areas could not be solved through additional distribution of land. When referring to the end of the "first phase" of the Agrarian Reform, Echeverría was reassuring large landed interests, especially commercially oriented farmers, that they had nothing to fear from his administration (but see Latin America Political Report, 1972: 237-238). While late in his administration, Echeverría did encourage peasant political activities such as land invasions, there seemed to have been little serious high level discussion of the land distribution issue, even though some middle level officials privately admitted that this should be a key element in any policy (see Economist Intelligence Unit 4, 1976: 4-7). Clearly, the officials interviewed did not consider redistribution to be a viable alternative, given the strength and vocalness of the commercial agricultural sector. When complaints were voiced that peasants simply had too little land to produce at levels beyond subsistence, the official response, at least rhetorically, was to promote collectivization (for a discussion, see Stavenhagen, 1975). Moreover, price supports and other services which benefited commercial agriculture were maintained by the government and support from industrial and banking concerns was solicited through arguments that the expansion of the internal consumer market resulting from the rural development strategy would stimulate the country's industrial capacity (Stavenhagen, 1975).

Because there was little apparent opposition to the reorientation of the government's agricultural development policy, the president and his advisors did not need to solicit or mobilize the support of the new target group, Mexico's peasantry. During interviews, few of the policy makers ever referred to demands from the peasant population for increased attention to their needs. Instead, the initiative for the policy change was always attributed to the president and his close advisors. As a result of this high level direction and management of potential conflict, by early 1973, various government agencies had planned and programmed a number of services and policy instruments in response to new definition of rural development. For the final three and a half years of the sexenio, the problems that remained to be dealt with were those of implementing the programs and delivering the services when and where they were needed.

Public Policy and Regime Stability

What caused policy makers in Mexico to single out rural development as an important goal of the Echeverría administration? As has been demonstrated, the formulation of a new national development strategy evolved in a series of steps from 1970 to 1973. First of all, the president indicated his awareness that problems of productivity and equity existed in the agricultural sector of the country. His concern served as a stimulus for high level officials to look for an explanation of these conditions. Their search led them to a critical analysis of Mexico's past development strategy and to accept the idea that the level of agricultural development would vitally affect Mexico's future economic and political viability. They also accepted a model which explained the underdevelopment of subsistence agriculture to be a result of structural barriers to increased productivity in that sector.

Subsequently, they attempted to convince the president of the wisdom of increasing investments in subsistence agriculture. In turn, the president set about popularizing this idea in the bureaucratic apparatus and mobilizing support for it. Economic and political conditions, as well as the availability of a technical analysis of them, therefore, can be said to have influenced the choice of the policy areas and the solutions which were proposed. These sources of policy change are similar to those singled out by Hirschman (1963) in his case studies of Colombia (land use and land tenure), Chile (inflation), and Brazil (regional development). In addition, however, of vital importance to any explanation of the Mexican case is the centrality of the role of the president in initiating and supporting the policy change.

The planning process proceeded largely unmarked by public debate or official announcements (Benveniste, 1970, 12-13; Purcell, 1975). As is generally the case in Mexico, neither the legislature nor officials of the PRI, even at high levels, were directly involved or consulted in the formulation of the policy. The only group outside the bureaucracy and the top political leadership that can be identified as having any role whatever in policy making was a number of scholars who presented a theoretical explanation for rural backwardness and underdevelopment that government officials found persuasive. Furthermore, the president was instrumental in ameliorating the potential for opposition to the policy. Thus, the competition among parties and interests that is a frequent characteristic of policy making in other Latin American countries was conspicuously muted in Mexico in the case of rural development (see Cleaves, 1974; Daland, 1967; Kaufman, 1972; Levy, 1973).

The lack of a more public process of debate and deliberation means that policy change in Mexico is frequently dependent on access to president and his high level advisors and on the quality of personal relationships established with them. Bureaucratic officials, sensitive to the capacity of the president to further or ruin their careers, are, therefore, likely to be sensitive to presidential interests in specific policy areas. The competition surrounding the selection of the next president by the incumbent provides him with a valuable means to elicit response from many of his high level officials. Of course, it is often the case that the president's power is constrained by the size and complexity of the bureaucracy and by competition, factionalism, and varying interests within it. Nevertheless, ultimately he is in a strong position to elicit responsiveness from his subordinates and has a variety of resources, including his control over appointments and dismissals and his influence over budgetary allocations, to pursue his interests.

The president's preeminence has other consequences for the policy process. Given his power, for instance, it is evident that initiatives for policy change will be taken seriously by government officials only if they emanate or receive support from the top of the governmental hierarchy. As was seen in the case of the rural development strategy, technical analyses are only influential guides to the formulation of policy if they are accepted and championed by decision makers at the highest levels. During the Díaz Ordaz administration, concern about the adverse consequences of Mexico's development strategy did not achieve presidential recognition, even though a number of middle level officials and many intellectuals were involved in studying them. Only with the accession of Echeverría and his own team of subordinates did such questioning become "official." Once recognized, however, the widespread acceptance in the bureaucracy of such analyses helps lend a technocratic image to the policy process in Mexico.

In addition, however, it was seen in the case of the rural development policy that there is little provision within the policy process for ensuring that adequate or correct information reaches top level officials. The information and analyses which attract the attention and support of the president are channeled to him by officials and aides who are his personal appointees and who are personally loyal to him. In general, public groups neither initiate demands nor consult, advise, nor directly influence the bureaucrats as they suggest plans for the development of the country. Instead, pressure and demand-making tend to be focused on the implementation stage of policy process where a variety of lower level political and economic elites seek to influence the allocation of public resources.[12] Demands made at this level are generally invisible to high level policy makers and are not, therefore, integrated into or made relevant to the formulation process. This provides a considerable potential for policies to go awry at the implementation stage (see Grindle, forthcoming).

As we have seen, however, this relatively closed policy-making system does not necessarily mean that the process itself is rigid and unresponsive to changing conditions. Importantly, the sexenio turnover in Mexico provides an opportunity to inject new direction into public policies and serves as a boundary on the hegemony of any given set of individuals over the planning process. Thus, the authoritarian model which has emerged in Mexico does permit government officials considerable scope in redirecting public policies in response to a changing political and economic environment. It can further be suggested that the capacity to accept changes in the content of public policy has been an important ingredient in Mexico's long term system stability (see Hansen, 1976). As is evident in the evolution of rural development policy, when and if the president and his advisors decide that the time has come for reform and innovation, and as long as these changes fall within the limits acceptable to the "Revolutionary Coalition," the governmental system does respond to their direction (Hansen, 1971, chaps. 5 and 6).

However, the critical factor in bringing about such changes is the sensitivity and astuteness of the president and his advisors as they evaluate both political and economic conditions and judge the direction of policy which would ameliorate those situations they consider to be most threatening to the regime. Therefore, while the system, through the sexenio change, provides an opportunity for the governmental apparatus to be responsive to new ideas and interests, the system itself does not ensure the quality or the responsiveness of the policy which is chosen. Ultimately, the Mexican policy-making process is dependent for six years on the judgments of a very small group of individuals. If these individuals, and particularly the president, isolate themselves or refuse to deal with problems which may lead to unrest, as Díaz Ordaz did increasingly during his administration, or if they misinterpret the extent of change which is possible within the system, as Echeverría seems to have done at the end of his term, then palliatives of public policy cannot be suggested or instrumented with any hope of success. Only the initiation of a new sexenio will provide this opportunity.

The end of the sexenio of Luís Echeverría also brought an end to his capacity to direct the policies he initiated. In the choice of his Finance Minister, José López Portillo, as his successor, Echeverría attempted to ensure a continuation of his own policy preferences into the next sexenio. Nevertheless, the loss of his exalted position meant that his capacity to elicit response from the governmental apparatus also deserted him. And López Portillo, in seeking alternative policies to those of his predecessor, can be relatively assured that his own appointed officials will follow his lead enthusiastically.

NOTES

1. Statements of the policy objectives of the Echeverría administration are found in Banco Nacional de Comercio Exterior (1971); Banco de México (1973, 1975). Budgetary data provide the best indication of administration policy goals; public statements by government officials in Mexico are often rhetorical evocations of the "revolutionary" nature of the regime. Echeverría, for example, was frequently considered radical in his public statements but the actual policies pursued by his administration were generally moderate (see Latin American Political Report, 1976: 463-464, 466; Reynolds, 1976).

2. Officials of the Ministry of Agriculture, the Ministry of the Presidency, the Ministry of Finance, the Ministry of Agrarian Reform, CONASUPO, the Ministry of Water Resources, and the agricultural banks were interviewed at high and middle levels,

in addition to nongovernmental informants. A more lengthy description of the policy formulation and implementation process as it concerned CONASUPO is found in Grindle (1977).

3. Other public officials are selected because of links to powerful groups whose interests are thought to require representation for political reasons. Those who are likely to have the greatest influence on the president, however, are those whose personal loyalty to him is unquestioned.

4. In the United States, in contrast, cabinet officials may respond to presidential leadership as only one among a number of strong pressures upon them (see Fenno, 1959: ch. 6).

5. The Ministry of Agrarian Reform was created in 1975 from the Department of Agrarian Reform and Colonization. For simplicity, it will be referred to throughout this article as the Ministry of Agrarian Reform, even when referring to periods before it was elevated to ministerial rank.

6. The Centro was engaged in a massive study of Mexican agriculture at the time (see Centro de Investigaciones Agrarias, 1974). Influential works included those of Flores (1961); Reyes Osorio and Eckstein (1971); Palerm (1968); Stavenhagen, Paz Sánchez, Cárdenas, and Bonilla (1968). For conditions of Latin American agriculture in general, see Barraclough and Collarte (1973); and Feder (1971).

7. As an example of government policies which discriminated against the production of domestic crops, throughout the Díaz Ordaz administration guarantee prices for staple agricultural products such as corn remained frozen at 1964 levels, while the price of living increased about 30%.

8. This migration of rural inhabitants caused a serious problem for the government, suggested one informant, because in the urban areas, the peasant "becomes a market consumer of those goods which he formerly produced for himself outside the market. . . . Thus, the government is suddenly faced with an acute scarcity of food products, especially staple items like corn and beans."

9. The agricultural credit banks were also important actors in the policy reorientation. However, due to a reorganization of the three banks into one agency which was proceeding while the research was being conducted, it proved impossible to gather sufficient or reliable data on the activities or perceptions of the individual banks.

10. Due to CONASUPO's active promotion of sectoral planning, its representatives to COCOSA were charged with drafting the first statement of overall agricultural policy which would be used as a basis for discussion and to guide the efforts of the other agencies.

11. Purcell (1975) describes the management of opposition to a policy of profit sharing and demonstrates the skill of Mexican presidents and administrators in dealing with potential conflict.

12. The lack of organized demands by low income groups for changes in the content of government policy conforms to a wider pattern of political paternalism in Mexico. Generally, government programs are designed by bureaucrats and then bestowed upon the lower classes; most demand-making from this part of the population takes the form of individualized applications for resource allocation at the implementation phase (Cornelius, 1974). The environment in which the policy is implemented is, therefore, very distinct from the one in which it is formulated. The question of policy implementation has not been discussed in this study, even though this is perhaps the most critical aspect of the policy process. There is some evidence that the rural development policy,

reflected in a variety of programs designed by individual ministries and agencies, is actually being put into operation by lower level officials and is having an effect on agricultural productivity (Banco Nacional de Comercio Exterior, 1975). In 1976, it was stated that "the recovery in agricultural output has reached the point where Mexico seems about to regain its earlier self-sufficiency in basic food products, except maize" (Economist Intelligence Unit 4, 1976: 13).

REFERENCES

Banco de México (various years) Review of the Economic Situation of Mexico.

Banco Nacional de Comercio Exterior (1975) "Reflections on Agricultural Development Policy." Comercio Exterior 21 (March).

——— (1971) La Política económica del neuvo gobierno. Mexico.

——— (1970) "Aspectos económicos del discurso de toma de posesión del Presidente de Mexico." Comercio Exterior 20 (December).

BARKIN, D. (1970) "Agricultural development in Mexico: a case study of income concentration." Social Research 37 (Summer).

BARRACLOUGH, S. and J. C. COLLARTE (1973) Agrarian Structure in Latin America. Lexington, MA: D. C. Heath, Lexington Books.

BENVENISTE, G. (1970) Bureaucracy and National Planning: A Sociological Case Study in Mexico. New York: Praeger.

BRANDENBURG, F. (1964) The Making of Modern Mexico. Englewood Cliffs, NJ: Prentice-Hall.

CAMP, R. A. (1974) "Mexican governors since Cardenas: education and career contacts." J. of Interam. Studies 16 (November).

CARLOS, M. L. (1974) Politics and Development in Rural Mexico: A Study of Socioeconomic Modernization. New York: Praeger.

Centro de Investigaciones Agrarias (1974) Estructura agraria y desarrollo agrícola en México. Mexico: Fondo de Cultura Económica.

CLEAVES, P. S. (1974) Bureaucratic Politics and Administration in Chile. Berkeley: Univ. of California Press.

COLLIER, D. (1976) Squatters and Oligarchs: Authoritarian Rule and Policy Change in Peru. Baltimore, MD: Johns Hopkins Univ. Press.

CORNELIUS, W. A. (1974) "Urbanization and political demand making: political participation among the migrant poor in Latin America cities." Amer. Pol. Sci. Rev. 68 (September).

DALAND, R. T. (1967) Brazilian Planning: Development Politics and Administration. Chapel Hill: Univ. of North Carolina Press.

Economist Intelligence Unit (various years).

FAGEN, R. R., and W. S. TUOHY (1972) Politics and Privilege in a Mexican City. Stanford, CA: Stanford Univ. Press.

FEDER, E. (1971) The Rape of the Peasantry. New York: Anchor.

FENNO, Jr., R. F. (1959) The President's Cabinet. Cambridge, MA: Harvard Univ. Press.

FERNANDEZ Y FERNANDEZ, R and R. ACOSTA (1961) Poliítica agrícola. Mexico: Fondo de Cultura Económica.

FLORES, E. (1961) Tratado de economía agrícola. Mexico: Fondo de Cultura Económica.

GOLLAS, M. and A. GARCIA ROCHA (1976) "El desarrollo económico reciente de México," in J. Wilkie, M. Meyer, and E. Monzon de Wilkie (eds.) Contemporary Mexico. Berkeley: Univ. of California Press.

GRINDLE, M. (forthcoming) Politics and Policy Implementation in the Third World.

——— (1977) Bureaucrats, Politicians, and Peasants in Mexico: A Case Study in Public Policy. Berkeley: Univ. of California Press.

HANSEN, R. (1971) The Politics of Mexican Development. Baltimore, MD: Johns Hopkins Univ. Press.

——— (1976) "PRI politics in the 1970s: crisis or continuity?" in J. Wilkie, M. Meyer, and E. Monzon de Wilkie (eds.) Contemporary Mexico. Berkeley: Univ. of California Press.

HIRSCHMAN, A. O. (1971) Essays on Development and Latin America. New Haven: Yale Univ. Press.

——— (1963) Journeys Toward Progress: Studies of Economic Policy-Making in Latin America. New York: The Twentieth Century Fund.

IBARRA, D. (1973) "Mercados, desarrollo y política económica: Perspectivas de la economía de México," in L. Solís (ed.) La economía mexicana: Política y desarrollo. México, D. F.: Fondo de Cultura Económica.

Instituto de Investigaciones Sociales (1975) Caciquismo y poder político en el México rural. México: Siglo XXI.

KAUFMAN, R. R. (1972) The Politics of Land Reform in Chile, 1950-1970. Cambridge, MA: Harvard Univ. Press.

Latin America Political Report (various years).

Latin America Special Report (1977) Mexico.

LEVY, Jr., F. D. (1973) "Economic planning in Venezuela," in C. E. Thurber and L. S. Graham (eds.) Development Administration in Latin America. Durham, N.C.: Duke Univ. Press.

LINZ, J. (1970) "An authoritarian regime: Spain," in E. Allardt and S. Rokkan (eds.) Mass Politics. New York: Free Press.

MALLOY, J. (1977) Authoritarianism and Corporatism in Latin America. Pittsburgh, Penn.: Univ. of Pittsburgh Press.

NAVARRETE, I. M. (1970) "La distribución del ingreso en México," in El perfil de Mexico en 1980. Mexico: Siglo XXI.

O'DONNEL, G. A. (1973) Modernization and Bureaucratic-Authoritarianism: Studies in South American Politics. Berkeley, Calif.: Institute of International Studies, University of California (Politics of Modernization Series, No. 9).

PARLERM, A. (1968) Observaciones sobre la planificación regional. Washington, DC: Union Panamericana.

PELLICER DE BRODY, O. (1974) Mexico in the 1970s and Its Relations with the United States: The Changing Political Realities. Stanford, CA: Stanford Univ. Press.

PRIETO VAZQUEZ (1969) "La distribución del ingreso en México." Comercio exterior 19 (Mexico).

PURCELL, S. (1973) "Decision making in an authoritarian regime: theoretical implications from a Mexican case study." World Politics 25 (April).

——— (1975) The Mexican Profit Sharing Decision: Politics in an Authoritarian Regime. Berkeley, CA: Univ. of California Press.

——— (1976) "The future of the Mexican political system," in J. L. Reyna and R. S. Weinert (eds.), Authoritarianism in Mexico. New York: Ishi.

REYES OSORIO, S. and S. ECKSTEIN (1971) "El desarrollo polarizado de la agricultura mexicana," in Miguel Wionczek et al, Crecimiento o desarrollo económico? México: SepSetentas.

REYNA, J.L. (1976) Control político, establidad y desarrollo en México. México: El Colegio de México, Cuadernos del Centro de Estudios Sociológicos, no. 3.

REYNOLDS, C. W. (1976) "Mexico and Brazil: models for leadership in Latin America?" in J. Wilkie, M. Meyer, and E. Monzon de Wilkie (eds.) Contemporary Mexico. Berkeley: Univ. of California Press.

SALDANA HARLOW, A. (1974) Observaciones sobre prácticas administrativas en México. Toluca, Mexico: Instituto de Administración Pública del Estado de México.

SMITH, P. (1976) "Continuity and turnover within the Mexican political elite, 1900-1971," in J. Wilkie, M. Meyer, and E. Monzon de Wilkie (eds.) Contemporary Mexico. Berkeley: Univ. of California Press.

SOLIS, L. (1971) La realidad económica mexicana: Retrovisión y perspectivas. Mexico: Siglo XXI.

STAVENHAGEN, R. (1975) "Collective agriculture and capitalism in Mexico: a way out or a dead end?" Latin American Perspectives 2 (Summer).

——— F. PAZ SANCHEZ, C. CARDENAS, A. BONILLA (1968) Neolatifundismo y explotación de Emiliano Zapata a Anderson Clayton & Co. Mexico: Nuestro Tiempo.

STEVENS, E. P. (1974) Protest and Response in Mexico. Cambridge, MA: MIT Press.

TELLO, C. (1971) "Un intento de análisis de la distribución personal del ingreso," in M. Wionczek (ed.) Disyuntivas Sociales. Mexico: SepSetentas.

TUOHY, W. (1973) "Centralism and political elite behavior in Mexico," in C. E. Thurber and L. S. Graham (eds.) Development Administration in Latin America. Durham, NC: Duke Univ. Press.

TURNER, F. C. (1973) "Mexican politics: the direction of development," in W. P. Glade and S. R. Ross (eds.) Críticas constructivas del sistema político mexicano: Critiques of the Mexican Political System. Austin: Univ. of Texas Press.

WILKIE, J. W. (1974) "Recentralization: the budgetary dilemma in the economic development of Mexico, Bolivia, and Costa Rica," in D. J. Geithman (ed.) Fiscal Policy for Industrialization and Development in Latin America. Gainesville: Univ. of Florida Press.

——— (1967) The Mexican Revolution: Federal Expenditure and Social Change Since 1910. Berkeley: Univ. of California Press.

WIONCZEK, M. S. (1973) "El desarrollo económico y el sistema político mexicano," in W. P. Glade and S. R. Ross (eds.) Críticas constructivas del sistema político mexicano: Critiques of the Mexican Political System. Austin: Univ. of Texas Press.

Merilee S. Grindle is Assistant Professor of Political Science at Wellesley College. She is the author of Bureaucrats, Politicians, and Peasants in Mexico: A Case Study in Public Policy, *and is currently engaged in research on policy making related to agriculture and agrarian reform in Colombia.*

YORAM SHAPIRA
Department of Spanish and Latin American Studies
Hebrew University
Jerusalem, Israel

MEXICO
The Impact of the 1968 Student Protest on Echeverría's Reformism

A great many of the political initiatives of Mexico's President Echeverría were responses to stimuli generated directly by the university community's behavior during the 1968 student government crisis. Prior to this 1968 confrontation, student activism had a marginal "nuisance effect"; since then, however, it has risen to political prominence in Mexico.

The following discussion focuses on establishing a casual relationship between student protest and Echeverría's reformism. It will begin with a possible framework for the student protest movement within the national political context in terms of structural-functional concepts. To that part pertains also the section dealing with protagonists' tactics in the confrontation—i.e., principal student measures to organize, communicate demands and mobilize support, and the government countermeasures aimed at discrediting the students' protest and reducing the effectiveness of their dissent. Issues concerning the link between the 1968 events and the reform policies of the Echeverría administration will be noted. Some of the salient features of this reformism and the President's tactics of assuring future policy continuity are portrayed.

Journal of Interamerican Studies and World Affairs, Vol. 19 No. 4, November 1977

It should be emphasized from the outset that the dissident university community of 1968, both in the systemic function it fulfilled as well as in the responses it triggered from the regime, represents a sui generis phenomenon that cannot be lumped together with "similar" protest movements that preceded it chronologically. Evelyn P. Stevens (1975: 371) stresses the similarity between Mexico's railroad workers' strike of 1958 to 1959, the doctors' strikes of 1964 to 1965, and the 1968 student protest. She maintains that "After the initial outbreak of protest, each of the three movements rapidly broadened its claims, proceeding in a series of precipitous leaps from the recital of particular grievances to proposals for broad programmatic changes." Furthermore, after examining elite response in these three cases, she infers also a similar pattern in the way the elite reacted and the tactics it used in dealing with the recurring manifestations of protest.

The proposition advanced by Stevens as to the comparability of these various kinds of articulated protest bears questioning. Although the process of "issue broadening" was indeed present in all three cases, the substance of the protest in the third is distinctive. The demands of the railroad workers and the doctors were confined and related to sectorial, professional, and economic interests of the groups involved. The students, rapidly developing a sense of community, but lacking similar professional-economic interests, developed a protest that embraced a much wider range of political, social, and economic issues.

From this follows another important difference, namely, that the activities of the top student coordinating organ during 1968, the National Strike Committee—the CNH—more closely fits the functional definition of interest aggregation than the interest articulation performed by the doctors' and workers movements. Thus, while the latter two elements acted as interest groups, the university community of 1968 approached a status of a transient political party. These differences also account for the dissimilarity of the elite response to the various challenges. The reaction following 1968 was not reminiscent of government responses to the 1958 to 1959 and 1964 to 1965 cases. The repression employed to quell the student dissent was qualitatively different from previous exercises. More important yet in the longer run, the process of system adaptiveness that has characterized government policies since 1971 was absent in the other instances.

The argument here is that while the striking workers and doctors precipitated confrontations that might be described as crises of control (in that they developed noncaptive interest group activity), the 1968 movement created a crisis of legitimacy. Hence, a substantial part of the immediate elite response to the 1968 challenge took the shape of a counter antistudent delegitimation campaign that was not experienced by the other dissident nonstudent groups.

Student Protests of 1966 and 1968

Severe student disturbances occurred in Mexico's capital in 1966 but they were clearly distinct from those of 1968 in scope, style, and substance. The 1966 student strike, or the "Chávez Affair," is still subject to controversial interpretations. The widely held view is that the students were manipulated by the Díaz Ordaz government in order to get rid of a political foe, Dr. Ignacio Chávez, the prestigious former rector of the National University (UNAM; Segovia, 1970: 297-336). Even if one considers the 1966 grievances as an authentic student protest movement, it was basically a "university reform movement" with an intrauniversity focus whose national significance was incomparably less, and whose challenge to the authorities was negligible when considering the alarming proportions of the 1968 movement. Yet, the 1966 UNAM crisis contained direct repercussions for the 1968 conflict. The former event might be viewed as the initial mobilizational experience for student activists and segments of the student body. Luis González de Alba (1971: 22), a central student activist and member of the CNH in 1968, considers the 1966 UNAM strike a landmark heralding an era in which the "left" within the National University was gathering force, striving for greater politicization of the student body. This is further reiterated by Carlos Monsiváis (1971: 246): "In 1966, the rector of the UNAM, Dr. Ignacio Chávez, was forced to renounce. . . . The interests [involved] in the conflict could not prevent a positive feat—out of the political confusion began the ferment of a new university left." Retrospectively, it also demonstrated that a university crisis, manipulated by forces external to the University community to serve political objectives, may boomerang by triggering an intensive process of student politicization. This process gathered momentum due to environmental stimuli and erupted eventually as an autonomous (i.e., noncontrolled externally) generalized protest. The 1968 student protest was not a university reform movement, and university problems as such—aside from the major political issue of university autonomy—did not rank high on the agenda. The student crisis of 1968 was unprecedented in modern Mexican history in that it evolved into general social protest articulated by the student body, which challenged, in manner and intensity previously unknown, the very legitimacy of the country's power elite and the political, economic and social structures it controls.

The Protest Movement: The Structural-Functional Angle

The 1968 student protest found expression in two separate and fundamentally different sets of demands that were formed simultaneously. The first constituted the "facade" or the formal list of student grievances, while the other contained the more substantive issues. The official "six points" manifesto was already formulated in early August, 1968 amid spiraling student disturbances and hard-handed police and army countermeasures. Although much before the violent climax of the student-government confrontation—the October 2nd bloodshed at the *Plaza de Tres Culturas* in the *Tlatelolco* section of Mexico City—the central theme of the "six points" list was an attack against the personal, legal, and institutional symbols of government physical repression.[1]

Uncommonly daring as they were in the context of Mexican politics, the "six points" still had basically a defensive and short-range character. A possible explanation for this relative moderation is that they were adopted by the students' National Strike Committee, thus representing the minimum consensus on which the diverse constituent activist groups were able to agree at that time. Furthermore, the phrasing of the "official" demands allowed a considerable number of university professors and intellectuals, who had ties with the "establishment," to at least publicly endorse this less belligerent aspect of student protest. The more aggressive, critical and longer range dimension of the 1968 student movement as an agent of sociopolitical protest was communicated via diverse media, often in a spontaneous or uncoordinated manner. The ample documentary evidence gathered by sympathetic "chroniclers" and interpreters of the movement, such as Ramón Ramírez (1969) and Elena Poniatowska (1971), reveal unequivocally the principal targets of the student attacks.[2]

Much of the movement's criticism contained demands for democratizing Mexican politics and making the political system more responsive and participatory. It also called for the correction of social and economic injustices and for a more equitable distribution of opportunities and national income. The students' criticism was extensive: the lower social strata are alienated by a bourgeois elite that uses "revolutionary" rhetoric to manipulate public opinion; governmental control is exercised through a system of nonautonomous interest groups aided by loyal press and strengthened by a deficiency of real inter-party rivalry; there is a lack of syndicalist autonomy among the urban workers, as well as in the *campesino* rural sector, both being manipulated and controlled via *Partido Revolucionario Institucional* (PRI) affiliated unions; though the government claims to represent the working masses, its development policies and tax structure benefit "big business" and discriminate against wage earners; political power is in the hands of a small group that obstructs attempts to weaken its monopoly; and the nonavailability of unbiased information, and systematic frustration of efforts to organize independent political organizations—accompanied by occasional electoral frauds—prevent development of effective participation, and foment apathy and "marginalism" in politics (Manifiesto a la Nacron "2 de Octubre," cited by Ramírez, 1969: 503-507).

It is evident that the Mexican 1968 student protest touched all the major political institutions of the country and their inadequacies. One crucial explanation to the emergence of the student body in the role of interest aggregator, albeit self-appointed, for the socially, economically, and politically alienated can be seen in its critique of the regime.

Since 1929, Mexico has been ruled by an authoritarian monopolistic governing party, the PRI and its earlier versions (PNR and PRM). The three additional satellite official "opposition" parties, the PAN, PPS, and PARM, give the regime the aura of a legitimate democracy by creating what critical Mexicans term "simulated plurality" (Martínez de la Vega, 1971: 26-27). But a viable, free and competitive multi-party system is still lacking. None of the official opposition parties represents a stand that is significantly more radical than the PRI's periodically vacillating position between right and center. Nor do they constitute a challenge of any real consequence to the ruling party. The major interest groups, particularly those representing lower-class interests—like the Confederation of Mexican Workers (CTM) and the National Peasants' Confederation (CNC)—are integral parts of the government party. Ironically, these "privileges" have placed them in a captive position. Many of the CTM's affiliated workers' syndicates are *Sindicatos Charros,* the Mexican term for unions run by a "sold out" leadership. The Demetrio Vallejo case and the ruthless treatment this union leader received because of his nonconformist attitudes from the Adolfo López Mateos administration until Echeverría's rise to power is a salient example of how little syndicalist autonomy the regime had been prepared to tolerate. To complete the picture one can add a subservient Congress and a largely mercenary Press.[3] The Congress is composed of the same four establishment parties with the PRI holding an overwhelming majority with no real opposition, and is overshadowed by the unchallenged supremacy of the executive.

In a context where channels for the transmission of demands and representation of interests are effectively controlled by the elite and where virtually all the classical political structures for interest articulation and aggregation (i.e., working-class interest groups, political parties, Congress and the Press) are essentially captive, coopted and lacking in autonomy, the function of interest aggregation was assumed by a noncaptive, sociopolitical group. Within the Mexican political context of the second half of the 1960s, the only significant group that could serve, even temporarily, as an alternate structure operating in lieu of the clogged ones, was the university community.[4]

Student Tactics and Government Countermeasures—Or How to Discredit Legitimate Dissent

The students' effort to carry on an effective protest was based on various measures undertaken to organize, mobilize support, and communicate demands with maximum impact. The movement's crucial test was its ability to break through the communications barrier and mobilize nonstudent popular support. On its part, the government acted to frustrate these attempts and to keep the movement isolated from those social strata that might otherwise lend support or unite with the students. Government reaction was harsh, and it held the upper hand, demonstrating its control over most of the country's mass organizations, interest representation structures, the Congress and the bulk of the national press. The students, under the direction of the CNH, employed diverse tactics to get their message through to the public. The most spectacular were the massive protest marches, like those held in Mexico City in August, 1968. At the same time as the students were acting in the open and in large numbers, they operated in small groups to enlist support, politicize, and build sympathy with the lower classes. This much riskier and semi-clandestine task was carried out by the "political brigades" working in lower class neighborhoods, at times even utilizing rides on popular bus lines or convening "lightning meetings" for "blitz" propaganda operations. Student attempts to mobilize support from laborers at work sites were frustrated by swift government action, and many arrests were made. Compared to their work among industrial laborers and urban dwellers, student activism among *campesinos* was meager (see, for example, Poniatowska, 1971: 44-46).

The students, who sought any possible public forum in order to express their views, tried unsuccessfully to force the government into an open, preferably televised, dialogue. Their failure to mobilize large scale lower class support was reflected in the pro-government declarations issued by the country's major worker and peasant organizations (the CTM and CNC). Even the center figure of the Mexican left, the late ex-President Lázaro Cárdenas (El Día: October 6, 1968), maintained a pro-establishment stance by condemning manifestations of student violence. The coopted "opposition" party of Vicente Lombardo Toledano, the PPS, demonstrated its loyalty even more diligently by issuing an enthusiastic statement against the "antinational provocation." In the few statements released by the PAN, criticism of the government was relatively mild, expressing a half-hearted and qualified understanding of the students, while real issues were avoided. The lack of clearcut commitment, if not timidity, was reflected in vague wording, and in the censuring of both government repression and abuses of power and corrupt student leaders and organizations (Ramírez, 1969, Vol. I: 116-117, Vol. II: 100-101, 178-181). Views critical of the government were rarely heard from central political figures. Positions held by prominent *Priistas* such as the maverick Carlos Madrazo, ex-governor of Tabasco and former president of the PRI, and of the liberal minded and former senate leader, Manuel Moreno Sánchez were exceptional and isolated. It would be erroneous to conclude that there was no widespread sympathy for the students within the general public. However, expressions of support from non-student elements were, on the whole, either spontaneous or represented marginal groups and organizations.

The noncompromising and repressive measures that were characteristic of the government's immediate response to the student challenge were accompanied by an intensive campaign aimed at discrediting the student movement with the public. Creating hostile public opinion would serve as an attitudinal support for the security forces' intimidation and punitive actions. In this task, the government was actively aided by the media which increased the movement's alienation by manipulating public opinion. Using mass media and its loyal mass organizations, the government skillfully activated popular appeals and sentiments for presenting the student protest as illegitimate.

In his address of September 1st, 1968, President Díaz Ordaz appealed for "Law and Order." The speech delivered by General Alfonso Corona del Rosal, Regent of the Federal District, to Mexico City transport and cleaning workers also invoked the appeal to "Law and Order" and is a masterpiece in controlling mass psychology (El Día: August 9, 1968). In other instances "antiintellectual" tones underlay attacks against the students. They were accused of striving for undeserved prerogatives reminiscent of the colonial *"fueros"* and of placing themselves above the law and the common citizen in their demands for university autonomy. Accusations of immorality also figured in the antistudent campaign. However, most powerful was the tactic of appealing to deeply rooted nationalistic and xenophobic sentiments by depicting the students as unpatriotic and even a danger to the "national security."[5] A variety of "conspiracy theories," placing the blame upon diverse "subversive" elements, either foreign or local, or some combination of both, also flourished that year. A case in point is an article by Raúl Prieto (El Día: August 7, 1968) where an elaborate explanation of the crisis is offered. He alleged that the everpresent Yankee twins, the FBI and the CIA, collaborated with Mexican reactionary elements in order to bring about a break of diplomatic relations between Mexico and Cuba by "exposing" the role of Cuban "agents" in the student movement. Quite naturally, the "rightist conspiracy" had its counterpart in the form of an alleged leftist plot (López Portillo, 1968). The government tried to give credence to such rumors by detaining five "prominent members" of the Mexican Communist Party (PCM) for investigation of their role in the student disturbances. The authorities also declared that they had proof that the PCM and their student front organization, the CNED, had sent "shock units" to provoke disorder and to aggravate student-police clashes (Press Bulletin, Procuraduría General de la Republica: 28 July 1968. Quoted in Revista 1968: 5).

Elite Response: From Repression to System Adaptiveness

The question of "system adaptiveness," or the regime's ability to accommodate new demands effectively, has been a crucial test for the political system. Two stages may be discerned in the government response to the students' challenge. The first stage, repression, extended from the crisis in 1968 to the end of the Díaz Ordaz administration. Several underlying factors determined the government's reponse during that stage. One was the character of the vastly expanded and noncustomary demands contained in the university community's protest which were much too intensive and far-reaching to allow short range accommodation. At the same time, student dissent was seen as a major threat to the elite's legitimacy. The president of the Republic, a traditionally revered figure and archpillar of political authority, had been a target for ruthless and offensive student attacks. The "revolutionary" character of the regime, which is its principal legitimizing "ideology" as heir to the Mexican revolution, had been mocked. Further aggravating the confrontation was the preparations then underway for a top priority event: the Olympic Games scheduled for late 1968. This put the government's credibility and Mexico's national prestige at stake. These perceived dangers triggered the harsh governmental reaction based primarily on tactics of physical repression, the counter delegitimizing campaign, and the effort to isolate the students from nonuniversity publics.

The second stage emerged with the new administration of President Luis Echeverría. In this phase there were clear indications of new policy trends, namely, an attempt to lower the repressive profile of the regime and improve its adaptiveness. The new policy was motivated by personal as well as by the incumbent elite's survival considerations. PRI showing in the 1970 presidential elections was alarming indeed. With 34% of the eligible voters abstaining, 25% of the ballots cast annulled, and another 20%

given to other parties (Pereyra, 1974: 59), rethinking of future government policies was imperative. As for President Echeverría, there is little doubt that he wished to rid himself of the "stigma of Tlatelolco" which had haunted him since his role as Secretary of *Gobernación* in 1968, and that he had been trying to build up a new progressive-liberal image. This converged with the more general tendency of his administration to try and accommodate the widespread discontent which had intensified since 1968, and whose most aggressive and visible manifestation has been the rise of the urban guerrillas in Mexico. The new guerrilla challenge, sustained in some cases by extremists among students and even young university lecturers,[6] culminated with the kidnapping from August 28 to September 8, 1974 of the president's father-in-law, José Guadalupe Zuno. The FRAP, a guerrilla group that claimed responsibility for the kidnapping, called its operation "Operación Tlatelolco, 2 de Octubre de 1968," a suggestive reminder. The surge of guerrilla activism was met, in most cases, with strong-handed government response.[7]

Of greater significance is a wide range of policy measures undertaken to tackle major functional characteristics of the regime, such as its extractive, distributive, and responsive capabilities. Many of these measures clearly relate to the 1968 socio-political critique, or to the roles played by the university community in the national political process. Within the realm of domestic affairs, the effort was directed on several fronts:

(1) measures taken to democratize the Mexican system either in its political aspects, or through redistributive policies employing fiscal and welfare mechanisms;

(2) a number of additional steps representing overtures to the university and intellectual communities, reflected in a series of appointments which included several of unmistakable cooptative nature, alongside relentless strides to create an atmosphere of improved liaison and interaction with these groups;

(3) another, and crucial, area is the development of a multifaceted strategy to deal with the phenomenon of an increasingly politicized and dissent-prone university community. This strategy has

> combined diverse tactics focusing mostly on the UNAM as the backbone and catalyst of any nationally significant and politically threatening student movement. These policies coupled conciliatory moves—highlighted by Echeverría's daring visit to the UNAM campus in March 1975, his first since 1968—with academic structural and personnel changes. These latter also included the replacement of rectors at the UNAM, considerably prior to his 1975 visit, and the launching of a vigorous reform and development scheme for higher education. A prime target of this scheme has been the reduction of the UNAM's weight within the national academic conglomerate.

The first signals ushering in the new liberalized political atmosphere were the general amnesty of imprisoned leaders of the 1968 movement ordered by Echeverría early in 1971. There was a declaration of intent by the president to renew the dialogue with the left; and the new slogan of *Apertura Democratica* (Democratic Opening) was launched. The government became more permissive and open to criticism. This permissiveness continues to be enjoyed by selected elements of the press which grew more daring and critical after 1971. Still, freedom of criticism was only selectively applied, as demonstrated by the closing down of the pro-guerrilla weekly *Porque?* (September, 1974) and the firing of *Excelsior*'s editor and senior staff members (July, 1976). Considerably greater leeway has been allowed the nonviolent, non-establishment left, and major figures among critical non-*Priista* leftists have been permitted public expression.

Although some prominent activists of the 1968 movement were eventually coopted by the government,[8] others made good use of the relaxed political controls to organize new leftist parties, appealing successfully for support from some workers and peasants. Of the two most important such groupings, the first made its debut as early as November, 1971, under the leadership of Heberto Castillo and Demetrio Vallejo. This group held its first national convention in August, 1974, where the Mexican Workers Party (PMT) was founded. In 1973, a splinter group broke away from the Castillo-Vallejo camp to form the Socialist Workers Party (PST). Both groups had been unsuccessful in their efforts to obtain legal registration which would qualify them for the 1976 presidential elections. Important personnel changes with general political significance have taken place. Prominent among these were the ousters of the Attorney General Lic. Julio Sánchez Vargas, and the Federal District's Regent Alfonso Martínez Domínguez. Although the act was linked to an intra-elite power struggle, both were removed from office after the scandalous *Halcones* incident of June 10, 1971, when armed hoodlums, with the alleged backing of certain conservative PRI quarters, attacked demonstrating leftist students.[9] This time, Echeverría's image-building drive and prostudent public opinion combined to produce a decision that would have been completely unlikely in 1968; the dismissal of politically powerful figures occupying central government positions in order to appease the public wrath. Futhermore, the ascendance in February 1972 of Lic. Jesus Reyes Heroles, a publicist and once teacher at UNAM and Lic. Enrique González Pedrero, ex-director of the faculty of political and social sciences of the UNAM, as new president and secretary general of the PRI's National Executive Committee (CEN) respectively, infused new blood into the party's leadership and were indicative of the government's intention to improve communication with intellectuals, and give greater credibility and respectability to the PRI.

The PRI national caucus convened twice (March of 1971 and 1972) to approve a new Declaration of Principles and an Action Program, as well as modifications of Party Statutes. Although these changes were officially heralded as a "reorganization of the ruling party" (Mexican Newsletter, 1972: 7), such an appraisal has not been universally shared. In his first treatise of the Echeverría administration, the historian D. Cosío Villegas (1973: 90-92) evaluated these changes as reflecting the president's thinking rather than viable intraparty deliberations. He maintained that their spirit was essentially conservative, and that the measure introducing secret voting for representatives in sectional, municipal, and district party committees, was accompanied by very few other innovations and thus fell far short of expectations.

Some foreign "Mexico watchers" put it even more bluntly, arguing that the party was "as unrepresentative as ever" and that the practice of "finger appointments" (*Dedazo*) was still very much in force (Riding, 1973).

A major target of the democratization efforts of the Echeverría administration had been the entrenched leadership of Mexico's captive unionism, or the *Liderazgo charro.* This confrontation produced one of the most outstanding political phenomenon characterizing the Echeverría *sexenio* (the six year presidential term)—the rise to political power of the workers' syndicates, which had been organized through the CTM. The unintentional outcome demonstrates not only the tenuous power base from which Echeverría had been operating, but also that some old postulates concerning the power and omnipotence of a Mexican president should be seriously challenged. As in the case of the fiscal reforms, the president has been unable to override resistance of major interest groups, who managed to force him to reconsider tactics and modify policies.

At the beginning of the sexenio, it had become obvious that the government's labor policy was aimed at purging the CTM of its old guard leaders. There was a very noticeable intensification in press attacks against the *Sindicatos charros* affiliated with the CTM. These attacks, directed mainly at the center figure of the charro leadership, the CTM's Secretary General Fidel Velázquez, were given official encouragement.[10] Velázquez had been serving as Secretary General of the CTM uninterruptedly since 1941. Under his control the Worker's Confederation became a docile organization fulfilling most valuable "system maintenance" and legitimation functions for the elite. The unions' "cleanup" and renovation, envisaged by the government as an important manifestation of the *Apertura* policy, encountered stiff and militant opposition on the part of the veteran *cetemista* cadres. Thus, the years 1972 through early 1974 witnessed strained relations between the government and this group, except for an occasional tactical lull.

The policy of government encouragement of independent unions in an effort to undermine the Velázquez group never gained sufficient momentum to topple the everlasting Fidel. In this power struggle, Fidel Velázquez developed such labor appeals (including a forty-hour work week; demands for significant salary hikes; demand for introduction of national unemployment insurance), and pressure tactics (threats of a general strike were employed on various occasions as well as the convening of mass solidarity demonstrations like the one held in Cuernavaca on October 8, 1972), which rallied massive worker support and converted the CTM into an effective pressure group. He not only asserted a new degree of CTM autonomy and power and rebuilt his own image as the workingman's champion, but also managed to outmaneuver his opponents in the syndicates and in government. That he finally gained the upper hand becomes evident when, in April 1974, the CTM's National Congress reelected Fidel Velázquez to his seventh consecutive term as Secretary General. At that stage, deescalation of the president-secretary general conflict was almost inevitable. Futhermore, the movement towards convergence of interests was accelerated with the advent of 1975, when the crucial process of selecting the PRI candidate for the 1976 presidential elections was set in motion. In the impending process of intraparty struggle for the succession, the president could not write off the support of a political force such as the CTM. At stake for Echeverría was the very fate of his fledgling reformist politics. The CTM was equally interested in staving off any sinister attempt, engineered by rightist forces, to advance a conservative candidate that would reverse the course of the "revolution." Hence, the stage for reconciling differences was set.

Of the economic redistributive measures referred to above, salient have been the establishment of *INFONAVIT* (National Workers Housing Fund Institute) and the initiation of several consecutive fiscal reforms. *INFONAVIT,* created by Article 136 of the New Reformed Federal Labor Law, is financed by a special levy imposed on businesses in all sectors who are required to pay the Institute 5% of their ordinary workers' salaries. In its first year of operation (1973 to 1974) the program was designed to build 100,000 low-cost housing units, constituting then 28.5% of the 350,000 units required annually (Journal of Commerce: June 7, 1973). Also social security payments by companies were increased significantly under the Echeverría administration (Riding, 1973b).

The three experiments at fiscal reforms conducted by the government in the 1971 to 1975 period demonstrate the political constraints of an aggressive redistributive economic policy. The 1971 Fiscal Reform Bill was aimed at increasing tax rates for the upper brackets (up to a maximum of 42% in place of the previous 32%, as well as raising rates on fixed incomes from bonds and securities. Its implementation was moderated considerably, however, because of pressures exerted by the private industrial-commercial community, and the high income groups remained only marginally affected. In early 1973, government attempts at reforming the fiscal system to expand its income base once more encountered private sector resistance that caused modification of some important proposed measures (Análisis Político, 1974: 3, 38, September 30).

Continuing inflation and increasing external debt prompted the government to embark upon its third fiscal reform, which went into effect in 1975.[11] But the power of the private sector to effectively oppose and modify governmental decisions has reduced significantly the redistributive character of the new legislation. Such opposition explained the administration's unwillingness or inability to seriously challenge the business community, as well as its choice of tactics. The recent fiscal reform affects middle-income groups by imposing a heavier taxation on the consumption of luxury items and further raises the income tax ceiling from the previous 42% to 50% (Excelsior: September 20, 1974). The middle class, being the socioeconomic sector with comparatively weak and diffuse formal organization, could not muster enough influence to do much about it.[12]

Although the government avoided direct taxation on the private business sector—and despite critical comments that the president's solution to the problem of just income distribution was to merely call for a rise in productivity (Cosío Villegas, 1973: 92)—Echeverría's fiscal policy does represent a departure from previous patterns. During the past administrations, taxation policies affected mostly workers and wage earners who cannot manipulate tax evasion. Under Echeverría, the tax base was expanded to include higher income levels. The new tax reform, therefore, was welcomed by the worker and peasant sectors as well as by the business community, while the middle class raised a loud, but ineffective protest (Análisis Político, 3, 43: November 4, 1974 and 44, November 11, 1974).

Rapprochement measures taken to placate the "intellectual community" and other government critics had various manifestations. These can be seen in granting the *Premio Nacional* to Daniel Cosío Villegas and expanding the *Colegio Nacional* to include "younger" figures such as Carlos Fuentes, as well as inviting several intellectuals and "independent" press personalities into the presidential entourage on official trips abroad.

Some of the diplomatic appointments made by the president went beyond the customary policy of the appointment of noncareer diplomats to ambassadorial posts. In early 1975, Echeverría nominated Carlos Fuentes, one of the initial supporters of the dissident Castillo-Vallejo group in 1971, as ambassador to Paris, and UNAM's Victor Flores Olea to represent Mexico in Moscow. Olea's critical analysis of the 1968 crisis was circulated nationally because of its publication in *SIEMPRE* of March 15, 1972.

Echeverría devoted considerable time to cultivating contacts with intellectuals, students and teachers—through *audiencias* and receptions in his office or at the *Los Pinos* official residence. Cosío Villegas (1974: 119-120) observed that the greatest number of visits (excluding diplomats and foreign personalities) have been made by this group.

As indicated above, Education Minister Victor Bravo Ahuja pursued a policy of trimming the power of UNAM by decentralizing its educational resources. The vastly expanded demand for higher education has been partially accommodated through a series of newly promoted institutions, largely independent of UNAM. Thus, in 1973, the Minister of Education founded its own system of *Colegios de Bachilleres,* and in 1974, a rival major university, the *Universidad Autónoma Metropolitana* (UAM) was established in the Capital. The UNAM itself created new interdisciplinary preparatory colleges—*Colegios de Ciencias y Humanidades,* dispersed in five campuses throughout the Federal District. Furthermore, existing private universities, such as the Catholic *Ibero-Americana,* have expanded significantly since 1968, offering additional options to circumvent the UNAM (Latin America, 1974: 250, 252).

Reformer Without Allies?

As has been suggested, the university community, which, in 1968, assumed an interest aggregation function by acting as a transient semipolitical party, had an undeniable impact on a wide range of policy measures initiated by the Echeverría administration. That there had been such an impact—the full extent of which is still controversial [13]—was due in no small measure to the availability of his reformist leadership.

At the same time, the dynamics of Echeverría's domestic policies reveal that his reform program met with serious difficulties: he was operating during much of his sexenio with few allies. Support for the president was forthcoming from the effectively controlled *campesino* sector (CNC), the anti-Velázquez segments of the trade unions, and the progressive "press cliques" such as *Siempre, El Dia,* and, to a certain extent, *Excelsior.* These were fortified by patronage appointments to higher echelon party, federal and state government positions, as well as by entry—following the July 1973 Congressional elections—of many new and younger personalities serving as PRI deputies in the national legislature. However, relations with important sectors remained strained and even antagonistic. Friction developed with private business on such issues as the government deflationary policy and the cutbacks in public spending which produced the economic slowdown of 1971; government support of trade union demands for large wage increases; the rising pace of inflation; increase of terrorism and kidnapping acts committed by urban guerrillas against business magnates; and even Echeverriá's pro-Allende foreign policy.

The private sector's opposition was spearheaded on several occasions by powerful Monterrey industrialists and business interests (e.g., the one-day business strike of June 1974 organized by Monterrey's Chamber of Commerce). The hard core of the "Monterrey Group"—operating from the highly industrialized and large capital of the northern state of Nuevo León—has been the Garza Sada family. The head of the family, prominent industrialist Eugenio Garza Sada, was assassinated in September, 1973 at the age of 82. The fact that the president found it politically expedient to travel to Monterrey to pay his last respects was another evidence of the power wielded by this group. Echeverría's presence at the funeral did not deter the family representative from launching a harsh attack against the Federal government in his eulogy. His accusations were seconded by the presidents of the national confederations representing private industrial and commercial interests—the CONCAMIN and CONCANACO (García, 1973; Garibay, 1973).

Furthermore, until 1974, relations with the old guard syndicalist leadership were belligerent. Fiscal policies have irritated the middle sectors, and the hostile reception of his 1975 visit to the UNAM showed that the president did not achieve full "rehabilitation" at least with the most politicized and dominant of Mexico's universities.

Echeverría was also at odds with the conservative wing of his party, a situation which erupted in a confrontation between the president and his arch rival, Alfonso Martínez Domínguez. At first it was precipitated by the *Halcones* affair of 1971 and ended with the ouster of A. Martínez Domínguez from his government post. But it was only after an attempt to bring him back to power through the governorship of the state of Nuevo León had been successfully blocked (in December of 1972) that the demise of Martínez Domínguez was a fait accompli.

Similar cases of intraelite struggles were extended to other gubernatorial nominations (Sonora, Veracruz, Michoacan, and Hidalgo). Yet, on two additional occasions, governors of important states who identified with strong local conservative interests, were forced out of office after becoming entangled in severe conflicts with their respective state universities. These were the cases of Governor Eduardo Elizondo of Nuevo León (July 1971) and of G. Bautista O'Farril of Puebla (May 1973).

The President's efforts to constantly maneuver and readjust policies were also reflected by the unprecedented pace of ministerial changes which occurred during his administration. In fact, all the *secretarios* heading the key economic ministries, incuding those of Finance *(Hacienda),* Industry and Commerce, Natural Resources (*Patrimonio Nacional*), Labor, and Agriculture, were replaced.

These cumulating events seem to support the proposition that the president's base of support had been narrow, a factor limiting the scope of his reformism. This state of affairs also explains why in a context of relative scarcity of supportive publics, the confidence of the intellectual and university communities became all the more important. Within this front, the UNAM remained a problematic "island" requiring special treatment and a policy aimed at its political neutralization. UNAM continued to serve as a stage for political conflicts, primarily during 1972 to 1973 with the paralyzing strikes of the *Normalistas,* and the UNAM's employee syndicates, the SITUNAM and STEUNAM, which resulted in a change of Rectors.

Whether or not, as critics suggest, Echeverría's political initiatives constituted modest and essentially "stylish" changes rather than structural reforms, the president worked for reformist continuation beyond the period of his own term in office by influencing the choice of a successor. Here the president masterminded a strategy that has already introduced a substantive change in the most crucial, and until recently, also the most guarded, of Mexican political processes—namely, the presidential succession process. The president commissioned Minister of Water Resources, L. Rovirosa Wade, to announce publicly (on April 11, 1975) the names of all PRI presidential aspirants *(pre candidatos*). This early move was widely regarded as putting an end to the long established tradition of *Tapadismo,* i.e., the secrecy shrouding the presidential candidates' selection process debated in innermost elite circles (Madrazzo, 1975). Publicly naming the precandidates served two fundamental, though seemingly contradictory purposes: control over the process as well as democratization of sorts. The control effect was achieved by limiting the competition to a small number of approved precandidates, by increasing predictability and preventing last minute surprise. The precandidates were also expected to make their political views known to the public, as has been spelled out by then Foreign Minister E. Rabasa (Madrazzo, 1975). At the same time this innovation could be legitimately presented as an impressive feat of the president's *Apertura* policy. Exposing the process and the contenders to public scrutiny through the media signifies a partial democratization of hitherto nondemocratic practice at the crux of the system.

But the ability to influence decisively the eventual "party decision" concerning a candidate did not provide a foolproof guarantee for *continuismo,* as witnessed by the case of Echeverría's own transformation from a "conservative" Minister of the Interior to a "liberal" president. To safeguard further policy continuity and reduce "system uncertainty," Echeverría initiated a move aimed at contractually tying his successor to his own political course. In April of 1975, the PRI's president announced the drafting of a party document entitled "a basic plan of government" for the years 1976 to 1982 with the purpose of consolidating and advancing the work of the Echeverría administration. The publication of this plan was to precede the announcement of the party's nominee for the 1976 elections (El Día: April 25, 1975).

This move was not entirely without precedent in Mexican political history. Although presidents have traditionally enjoyed wide degree of discretion in formulating policies and determining the course of events for their respective sexenio, on two different occasions in the past (1934 and 1940), six year plans were drafted to influence the orientation of an entering chief executive. Mexican observers suggest that there is a similarity in all three cases, i.e., all have occurred in periods characterized by acute divisions and conflicts within the ruling party, and where the choice of a presidential candidate would have far reaching implications in reorienting the political system. In all cases the party plan aimed at assuming some degree of continuity. However, on both previous occasions the plans failed to achieve the aim set by their authors and the newly elected president either ignored it completely (Avila Camacho), or manipulated it at will (Cárdenas).[14]

NOTES

1. For the detailed six-point list, see author's article "Student-Government Confrontation: Interpreting the Mexican Crisis of 1968," in *Scripta Hierosolymitana,* (Jerusalem, Publications of the Hebrew University, Vol. XXVI, 1974: 122).

2. In addition to the two major attempts at documenting the 1968 events and collecting the various expressions of dissent related to the student movement (mentioned above), see also Carrı́on et al. (1969), Lenkersdorf (1969), Goodsell (1969), and The United States Committee for Justice to Latin American Political Prisoners (n.d.).

3. Nevertheless, even in 1968 there were some exceptions to the rule. Two weeklies have taken a more independent and critical stance. These are the sensational *Porque*? (its editor, Mario Menendez Rodrı́guez was flown to Cuba in late 1971 as part of an exchange for the rector of Guerrero's State University kidnapped by guerrillas) and *Siempre,* the spokesman of the noncommunist left.

4. The emergent student movement of 1968 demonstrated its automomy from the outset by dissociating itself from captive student organizations, primarily from the pro-government FNET (*Federacı́on Nacional de Estudiantes Técnicos*) which became a target for harsh accusations of "treason". See Revista de la Universidad de México, (1968: 8, 10, 17).

5. For allusions to unspecified "foreign infiltration" of the movement, see Letter of Lázaro Cárdenas in *El Día,* (October 6, 1968). On the "non-Méxican character of student politics," see Blanco Moheno, (1969: 236-238).

6. For a first hand account of the role of students and young university lecturers in the guerrilla movement, see the confessions of two teachers of the Universidad Autónoma de Nuevo Leon who were detained and interrogated by the police, *Tribuna de Monterrey* (Monterrey Daily; January 19, 1972; Segunda Seccion: 3-4). Press references to the students' prominent role in the new guerrilla activities are numerous. See also Castillo (1971) Alvarado (1972), and *Excelsior* (February 22, 1972: 4A, Column 5).

7. These responses ranged from the arresting of militants to the ousting of five Soviet diplomats after discovering that a group of Mexican students had used the Soviet Union as a transfer station for receiving guerrilla training in North Korea. To these measures one might add the still obscure car accident in which the leading guerrilla figure, Genaro Vázquez Rojas, was killed. In late 1974, the Defence Ministry confirmed the death of the other *guerrillero* of national reknown, Lucio Cabañas, who—according to official ver-

sion—was shot during a skirmish with the army in the troublesome state of Guerrero, where he had been operating since 1967 (Siempre, December 11, 1974: 5).

8. The case of former CNH member, Socrates Amado Campos Lemus, who since October 2, 1968 had spent two years and 9 months in prison, is significant. Later he became an outspoken supporter of Echeverría and was nominated as coordinator for the Plan Huicot. See: "Al quemadura Dios lo ayuda," *Siempre* (May 24, 1974).

9. On alleged links between the *Halcones* and Mexico City Mayor (Regent) Alfonso Martínez Domínguez, see New York Times (June 14, 1971).

10. Worth mentioning in this connection is the interesting statement in Reyes Heroles' inaugural address: "queremos hombres libres en los sindicatos . . ." (We want free people in the unions). See Mexico City weekly magazine *Tiempo* (28 de Febrero, LX, 1556: 11).

11. For presentation of the latest fiscal reform by then Finance Minister J. Lopez Portillo before the Chamber of Deputies, see Siempre, (November 13, 1974: 57-59).

12. The indequacy of the PRI controlled CNOP in channelling middle class demands and grievances is a point repeatedly made by López Cámara (1971).

13. For some critical views of the degree of Echeverria's reformism see: Pereyra (1974: 52-65) "Cambio o no cambio en el sistema politico y 10 de Junio, Hipotesis Sobre el Silencio," *Excelsior* (June 14, 1972); and Cosio Villegas (1974).

14. "Plan Basico de Gobierno 1976-1982," in *Analisis Politico* (IMEP 4, 17, April 28, 1975).

REFERENCES

ALVARADO, J. (1972) "El ejemplo de los mayores." Siempre 971 (February 2). Análisis Politico (1974) Instituto Mexicano de Estudios Politicos.

BLANCO MOHENO, R. (1969) Tlatelolco, Historia de una Infamia. México D.F.: Editorial Diana.

CARRION, J., S. ARGUEDAS, D. CAZES, and F. CARMONA (1969) Tres Culturas En Agonía. México, D.F.: Editorial Nuestro Tiemp.

CASTILLO, H. (1971) Siempre 955 (October 13).

COSIO VILLEGAS, D. (1974) El Estilo Personal de Gobernar. México: Cuardernos de Joaquin Mortíz. (Tercera Edición)

——— (1973) El Sistema Político Mexicano. México: Cuadernos de Joaquín Mortiz. Tercera Edición)

GARCIA, C. J. (1973) "La derecha exige otra matanza." Porque? 275 (October 4).

GARIBAY, R. (1973) "Duelo y Dolo de un abogado patronal." Excelsior (September 20): 6-A

GONZALEZ DE ALBA, L.N. (1971) Los Días y los años. México D.F.: Ediciones Era. (Sexta Edición)

GOODSELL, J. N. (1969) "Mexico: why the students rioted." Current History LVI, 329 (January 1969): 31-53.

Latin America (1974) "Mexico: stifled students." VIII, 32 (London: August 16).

LENKERSDORF, K. (1969) "The philosophy of the 1968 Mexican student movement." Specialia 1, Latin American Institute, Southern Illinois University: 34-42.

LOPEZ CAMARA, F. (1971) E. Desafío de la Clase Media. México: Cuadernos de Joaquin Mortíz.

LOPZ PORTILLO, A. G. (1968) El Universal (August 3).

MADRAZZO, J. (1975) "Agita a la política Mexicana la fractura del tradicional metodo del tapadismo." La Opinion (Buenos Aires: April 17).

Manifiesto a la Nación "2 de Octubre" (1968) Consejo Nacional de Huelga (C.N.H.) El Día (December 5).

MARTINEZ DE LA VEGA, F. (1971) "Mas rivales comodos para EL PRI?" Siempre (November 24).

Mexican Newsletter (1972) 18 (August 31).

MONSIVAIS, C. (1971) Días De Guardar. México D.F.: Ediciones Era. (Cuarta Edición)

PEREYRA, C. (1974) "México: Los límites del reformismo." Cuardernos Políticos 1 (Septiembre), Mexico D.F.: 52-65.

PONIATOWSKA, E. (1971) La Noche de Tlatelolco. México D.F.: Biblioteca Era.

PRIETO, R. (1968) "Contra Díaz Ordaz y contra Cuba." El Día (August 7).

RAMIREZ, R. (1969) El Movimiento Estudiantil de México, Julio-Diciembre de 1968. Volumes I and II, Mexico D.F.: Ediciones Era.

Revista de la Universidad de México (1968) XXIII, 1 (Septiembre).

RIDING, A. (1973a) Miami Herald (June 3).

——— (1973b) "Unemployment woes rise in Mexico." Miami Herald (May 6).

SEGOVIA, R. (1970) "The strike and its aftermath: A narrative and perspective," and Mexican politics and the university crisis," pp. 306-321 in R. R. Fagen and W. A. Cornelius, Jr. (eds.) Political Power in Latin America, Seven Confrontations. Englewood Cliffs, NJ: Prentice-Hall.

STEVENS, E. P. (1975) "Protest movement in an authoritarian regime." Comparative Politics 7, 3 (April): 361-382.

United States Committee for Justice to Latin American Political Prisoners (n.d.) Mexico 1968: The Students Speak. New York.

Yoram Shapira is the acting head of the Department of Spanish and Latin American Studies, the Hebrew University, Jerusalem, Israel. He is the author of articles in scholarly journals, including the Latin American Research Review, Inter-American Economic Affairs, *and* Foro Internacional, *and a contributor of articles to various books, including* Israel and the Third World. *He has coauthored a forthcoming book,* Israel-Latin American Relations.

JOURNAL OF
INTER-AMERICAN
STUDIES and
WORLD AFFAIRS

INDEX

to

JOURNAL OF INTERAMERICAN STUDIES AND WORLD AFFAIRS

VOLUME 19

Number 1 (February 1977) pp. 1-136
Number 2 (May 1977) pp. 137-288
Number 3 (August 1977) pp. 289-448
Number 4 (November 1977) pp. 449-584

SAGE PUBLICATIONS, INC.
275 South Beverly Drive
Beverly Hills, California 90212

SAGE PUBLICATIONS LTD
St George's House / 44 Hatton Garden
London EC1N 8ER

INDEX

to

JOURNAL OF INTERAMERICAN STUDIES

AND WORLD AFFAIRS

VOLUME 19

Number 1 (February 1977) pp. 1-136
Number 2 (May 1977) pp. 137-288
Number 3 (August 1977) pp. 289-448
Number 4 (November 1977) pp. 449-584

Authors:

ALBORNOZ, ORLANDO, "Higher Education and the Politics of Development in Venezuela," 291.

CAMP, RODERIC A., "Autobiography and Decision-Making in Mexican Politics" (Review Essay) 275.

EDMONSTON, BARRY and FRANK Wm. OECHSLI, "Fertility Decline and Socio-economic Change in Venezuela," 369.

ESCOBAR M., GABRIEL, "Pantaleon and the Visitors" (Review Essay) 259.

FERGUSON, YALE H., "Through Glasses Darkly: An Assessment of Various Theoretical Approaches to Interamerican Relations," 3.

GAUHAN, TIMOTHY O'DEA, "Housing and the Urban Poor: The Case of Bogotá, Colombia," 99.

GRAHAM, RICHARD, "Government Expenditures and Political Change in Brazil, 1880-1899: Who Got What," 339.

GREENFIELD, SIDNEY M., "Patronage, Politics, and the Articulation of Local Community and National Society in Pre-1968 Brazil," 139.

GRINDLE, MERILEE S., "Policy Change in an Authoritarian Regime: Mexico Under Echeverría," 523.

KUSNETZOFF, FERNANDO, "Spatial Planning and Development in Latin America: The Critical Approach" (Review Essay) 429.

LeBLANC, LAWRENCE J., "Economic, Social, and Cultural Rights and Interamerican System," 61.

LOMNITZ, LARISSA, "Conflict and Mediation in a Latin American University," 315.

MALLOY, JAMES M., "Social Security Policy and the Working Class in Twentieth-Century Brazil," 35.

MARTZ, JOHN D., "Policy-Making and the Quest for consensus: Nationalizing Venezuelan Petroleum," 483.

OECHSLI, FRANK Wm., see Edmonston, B.

OSBORNE, ALFRED E., Jr., "On the Economic Cost to Panama of Negotiating a Peaceful Solution to the Panama Canal Question," 509.
RAAT, WILLIAM DIRK, "The Antipositivist Movement in Prerevolutionary Mexico, 1892-1911," 83.
SALISBURY, RICHARD V., "Costa Rica and the 1920-1921 Union Movement: A Reassessment," 393.
SELIGSON, MITCHELL A., "Agrarian Policies in Dependent Societies: Costa Rica," 201.
SHAPIRA, YORAM, "Mexico: The Impact of the 1968 Student Protest on Echeverría's Reformism," 557.
STEVENS, EVELYN P., "The Mexican Presidential Succession" (Comment) 125.
TAPIA-VIDELA, JORGE, "The Chilean Presidency in a Developmental Perspective," 451.
VELIZ, CLAUDIO, "The Surrogate Americans" (Review Essay) 419.
WILLIAMS, JOHN HOYT, "Foreign Técnicos and the Modernization of Paraguay, 1840-1870," 233.
YEAGER, GERTRUDE MATYOKA, "Barros Arana, Vicuña Mackenna, Amunátegui: The Historian as National Educator," 173.

Articles:

"Agrarian Policies in Dependent Societies: Costa Rica," Seligson, 201.
"The Antipositivist Movement in Prerevolutionary Mexico, 1892-1911," Raat, 83.
"Barros Arana, Vicuña Mackenna, Amunátegui: The Historian as National Educator," Yeager, 173.
"The Chilean Presidency in a Developmental Perspective," Tapia-Videla, 451.
"Conflict and Mediation in a Latin American University," Lomnitz, 315.
"Costa Rica and the 1920-1921 Union Movement: A Reassessment," Salisbury, 393.
"Economic, Social, and Cultural Rights and the Interamerican System," LeBlanc, 61.
"Fertility Decline and Socioeconomic Change in Venezuela," Edmonston and Oechsli, 369.
"Foreign Técnicos and the Modernization of Paraguay, 1840-1870," Williams, 233.
"Government Expenditures and Political Change in Brazil, 1880-1899: Who Got What," Graham, 339.
"Higher Education and the Politics of Development in Venezuela," Albornoz, 291.
"Housing and the Urban Poor: The Case of Bogotá, Colombia," Gauhan, 99.
"Mexico: The Impact of the 1968 Student Protest on Echeverría's Reformism," Shapira, 557.
"On the Economic Cost to Panama of Negotiating a Peaceful Solution to the Panama Canal Question," Osborne, 509.
"Patronage, Politics, and the Articulation of Local Community and National Society in Pre-1968 Brazil," Greenfield, 139.
"Policy Change in an Authoritarian Regime: Mexico Under Echeverría," Grindle, 523.
"Policy-Making and the Quest for Consensus: Nationalizing Venezuelan Petroleum," Martz, 483.
"Social Security Policy and the Working Class in Twentieth-Century Brazil," Malloy, 35.
"Through Glasses Darkly: An Assessment of Various Theoretical Approaches to Interamerican Relations," Ferguson, 3.

Review Essays:

"Autobiography and Decision-Making in Mexican Politics," Camp, 275.
"Pantaleon and the Visitors," Escobar M., 259.
"Spatial Planning and Development in Latin America: The Critical Approach," Kusnetzoff, 429.
"The Surrogate Americans," Veliz, 419.

Comments:

"The Mexican Presidential Succession," Stevens, 125.

Books Received:

127, 285, 445.

Advertising Supplement:

Journal of Interamerican Studies and World Affairs

This supplement has been prepared especially for our readers to bring them information and announcements of professional interest. By placing advertisements in the pages of this journal, our advertisers have indicated a desire to communicate with our readers. We hope our readers will acknowledge their indirect support of the journal and its purposes by mentioning the journal in correspondence with advertisers.